The Teaching of Reading

The Teaching of Reading

Sixth Edition

Martha Dallmann
Professor Emeritus of Education, Ohio Wesleyan University
Professor Emeritus of Elementary Education, St. Cloud State University

Roger L. Rouch
Professor of Elementary Education, St. Cloud State University

Lynette Y.C. Char
Professor of Elementary Education, St. Cloud State University

John J. DeBoer

HOLT, RINEHART AND WINSTON
New York Chicago San Francisco Philadelphia Montreal Toronto London Sydney
Tokyo Mexico City Rio de Janeiro Madrid

Cover: HRW Photo by Russell Dian.

Library of Congress Cataloging in Publication Data
Main entry under title:

The Teaching of reading.

  Bibliography: p.
  Includes index.
  1. Reading (Elementary) 2. Mainstreaming
in education. 3. Educational equation.
I. Dallmann, Martha.
LB1573.T38 1982   372.4′1   81–20010
ISBN 0–03–059884–2   AACR2

CBS COLLEGE PUBLISHING
Holt, Rinehart and Winston
The Dryden Press
Saunders College Publishing

Preface to the Sixth Edition

Since the publication of the fifth edition of *The Teaching of Reading*, national and world events have continued to reinforce the fact, sometimes with menacing certitude, that we are living in a pluralistic society. That we must deal with pluralism both on a nationwide scope and in global perspective, even in peacetime, so as to make pluralism an asset, not a threat, has been made unequivocally clear. Because achievement of this goal is by no means exclusively a political matter but to a pronounced extent also an education problem, schools need to be cognizant of it and make a constructive contribution toward its solution. Teachers of reading are in a pivotal position to render service in this respect. It is for this reason that the first chapter of the book is rightly entitled "The Teaching of Reading in a Pluralistic Society."

Another matter of deep nationwide concern, with which this edition deals, is that of providing equal educational opportunity for all. While the professed objective of education has long been equality of opportunity, it has been forcibly brought to the foreground of teachers' thinking by the enactment during the mid-seventies of important federal laws. Probably of greatest impact on schools, of these legislative acts, has been the Education for All Handicapped Children Act (P.L. 94–142), passed in 1975. Impetus for serious attention to it has been the provision that federal funds are to be withheld from schools not complying with the regulations. Because of the importance that teachers—reading teachers included—know what the legal provisions are and how to implement them, we are including in this edition a chapter entitled "Organizational Patterns, Including 'Mainstreaming,' for Accommodating the Uniqueness of the Learner."

Additional significant changes that have been made in this edition include, among others, the emphasis in Chapter 2, "Language Development and Reading," on the development of language in worldwide perspective and on language diversity in the United States. Chapter 14, "Socioeconomic Factors Influencing Success in Reading," of the fifth edition no longer appears as a chapter, but pertinent points on that topic are now included as part of Chapter 13, "Recognizing the Uniqueness of the Learner." The chapter on "Children's Interests in Reading" shows rather extensive revision, and the chapter on "Word Recognition" reflects significant changes.

Aspects of teaching reading related to methodology that are among our foremost concerns in this book include (1) the relationship of reading to other facets of the language arts, (2) the relative merit of various approaches to the teaching of reading, (3) means of honoring the uniqueness of the individual, (4) strategies for cultivating children's interests in and through reading, and (5) development of reading skills. Broader societal concerns, in addition to those related to the pluralistic nature of society, with which we deal, are (1) the importance of giving serious attention to the education of the gifted, (2) the right of equal opportunity for an education in the least restrictive environment for the emotionally, intellectually, and/or physically handicapped, and (3) the plight of children growing up in poverty.

The authors use the pronouns *he, his,* and *him* when referring to a teacher or student of either sex in order to avoid the repeated use of cumbersome expressions such as *he or she, his or her, him or her.* This usage is for ease of reading only, because our language has not given us a graceful way of designating humans without sex reference with singular pronouns.

The authors acknowledge with gratitude the assistance of all those who have been cited in prefaces to earlier editions of this book. They are grateful to the writers, editors, and publishers who have permitted them to quote material, and to the individuals, schools, school districts, and publishing companies that have made photographs available.

The authors wish to express their indebtedness to John J. DeBoer with special gratitude. He served as senior author of earlier editions until his death in 1969. The breadth of his concern with educational problems helped set the tone for subsequent editions of *The Teaching of Reading.*

—L.Y.C.C.
—M.D.
—R.L.R.

Contents

Part III The Reading Program in Action

Part I

Perspective in Reading

The Teaching of Reading in a Pluralistic Society

The teaching of reading continues to constitute one of the greatest challenges to the teachers in the United States. It is a continuing challenge because there is, and always will be, a need for increased effort to enable all individuals, to the extent of their capabilities, to attain the benefits, for themselves and for others, that are available through reading. We should neither be discouraged by failures of the past nor complacent about achievements that have been demonstrated, but we should continually renew our efforts to more nearly attain our highest goals.

The Values of Reading

The challenge in the teaching of reading rests to a large extent on the significance of the values, such as those listed later in this chapter, to which effective reading can contribute.

It has been suggested that new media will increasingly usurp the place of reading. The contention deserves our consideration. While we must recognize many of the benefits that can be derived from mass media, we should also be aware of the associated shortcomings and attending dangers. The American public is bombarded with information through mass communication, technological means of almost instantaneous transmission of sight and sound. This abundance of informational stimuli threatens to reduce the exercise of thought. Emotions are often aroused and attitudes shaped with bits and pieces of kaleidoscopic perceptions. The public is easily led to think that externally controlled mood-modifying information is a sufficient basis for intellectual decision making. However, it is not necessarily the quantity of information gathered that makes a vital differ-ence but the quality of thoughtful reflection which may ensue.

In spite of the availability of mass media, reading is becoming increasingly important. Greater complexities of living are compounded by the rapidity of change characterizing every sphere of our lives. There often seems hardly time for reflection before there is apparent necessity of moving on to something else, at work and during leisure, at home and in school. Reading encourages reflection, which is essential for maintaining perspective, even more so during rapidly changing times. The printed page reaches millions still untouched by electronics, and even for those who can take advantage of the newer devices, reading can still help satisfy needs which the more recent media cannot fully meet. Thus the role of the reading teacher is more strategic, as he guides boys and girls in applying techniques of critical evaluation, which are emphasized in reading instruction, to what is seen and heard on the radio and television and acquired through other mass media.

Values to the Individual

The knowledge explosion in our technological society places the burden of an increased need for higher levels of literacy on the schools. The individual who cannot read effectively is likely to lose more opportunities in many occupational areas. Even for those who take advantage of other media of communication, these media are insufficient as the sole means for maintaining economic proficiency.

Important, too, are the values that can accrue to the individual beyond those connected with competency in the vocational and the professional spheres. Reading for purposes beyond functional demands gives a person access to resources in print that can entertain or refresh the spirit. Reading allows the individual to view different value systems, which can help him in selecting those experiences which truly enrich life.

Reading affects the entire personality. The world of people and events encountered on the printed page may shape a reader's attitude toward his fellows, toward his school, and toward life in general. It may heighten his appreciation of the physical world around him and give him an increased interest in aesthetic and spiritual values. The teacher shares a great responsibility for insuring success and confidence for the beginning reader by understanding his needs and assisting him in the selection of appropriate reading materials. Also, he bears responsibility for providing expert guidance in interpreting what is read. Growth in character can result, in part, from reading about the lives of the truly great, about the needs of the world, about social wrongs, or about the intangibles that give meaning to life. Care needs to be taken by the teacher that desired feelings are translated into action. For example, the person who merely reads sympathetically about people in distress but evidences no change in his behavior pattern toward the unfortunate may miss the mark.

Values to Society

The importance of a literate people to a democratic society has long been recognized. People who cannot read critically may be easily manipulated by the unprincipled who may solicit their time, attention, or votes. Nor can they, as a rule, contribute to their country through intelligent participation in various other worthwhile and significant activities.

In the individual's role as citizen of the world, beyond the confines of his own country, he is likely to be handicapped if he does not have competency and interest in reading. As on the national plane, so on the world scene, he is in danger of being unduly influenced by others through mass media. If he is unable to weigh data presented to him or sought by him as evidence on an issue, he is often unable to understand ethnocentric biases as evidenced, for example, in the erroneous belief in the inferiority or superiority of his own cultural group. Through the spoken word he is usually exposed to the message but once, while the written record makes it possible, in many instances, for him to ponder what confronts him, as he reads it over again and again until he has comprehended it with desired discernment.

Through reading the individual can profit from studying the history of the world. Reading can still, better than other known time machines, recreate events of the past. Reading makes possible man's capacity for "time binding," the ability to perceive himself and the fluid universe around him in the historic process.

In order for the citizen of today to participate intelligently in the society in which he lives—on the local, national, and international scene—he must understand the great forces that in one or two generations have changed the face of the earth. Along with this understanding must come a keener realization of the dangers of modern war, made infinitely more destructive by the "knowledge explosion" of the last few decades. One of the highest common goals to be sought by all people is learning peaceful means of sharing the earth's resources in order for life to survive on this planet. National solutions do not suffice to solve global problems such as those of food, depletion of energy supplies, and environmental pollution.

As part of a solution to problems of survival, the attainment of world-wide literacy continues to be a challenge. Although the ability to read cannot be claimed as the only means to achieve world peace, reading can better equip an individual to cope with the enlarged realities with which he must deal. To the extent that it allows him to gain improved understanding within a complex matrix of events, a gigantic step forward is made. If reading can kindle self-understanding and acceptance of human diversity and destiny in a troubled world, it can be a major force toward the accomplishment of the dream of a happier world for boys and girls, for men and women everywhere.

Problems Inherent in our National and Global Society

Two of the problems cutting across the various levels—as they refer to the individual, the nation, and the world at large—which must be given serious attention by the teacher of reading as well as by other teachers, deal with the ethnically diverse population of our nation and with the interdependence of nations. It is to these problems that we shall next address ourselves.

In the United States, where universal public education for a sizeable population has been achieved to an extent not as yet enjoyed by most other countries, the teaching profession is being challenged to provide for all its citizens *equal* opportunity to benefit from free public education. Although the United States is composed of a culturally pluralistic society, recognition and acceptance of this invaluable national asset have not been fully realized. Nor has adequate attention been paid as to how the teaching of reading can contribute to a change in this state of affairs.

The Need for Building Unity in a Culturally Pluralistic Society

In spite of the continuing and increasing diversity of the population of the United States in terms of ethnic heritage, there persists in education and society an attitude which denies full appreciation of minority cultural contributions. As the educational system continued to provide for individual differences, inequities in educational distribution became more apparent. The civil rights movement in the 1950's and 60's attested to the resilience and persistence of ethnic identities. The compensatory education programs of the 1960's, so it is claimed by critics, bear testimony to the failure of the project to recognize the importance of ethnicity in the formulation of programs, insofar as they vainly attempted to enculturate minority ethnic groups into the Anglo-Saxon heritage.

Today the according of equal human rights in educational programs is considered basic to the provision for individual differences. In part this point of view has developed from necessity as destructive forces have been unleashed in society when inequities have not been rectified. Protests and riots at home and terrorist activities abroad demand attention.

Urgency in Understanding the Interdependence of Nations in Global Perspective

In the light of the interdependence of nations, it is of significance to note that almost half the men, women, and children in the world cannot read.

Barker and Escarpit[1] point out:

[1]Ronald Barker and Robert Escarpit, eds., *The Book Hunger* (Paris: UNESCO, 1973), p. 197.

Almost certainly, even in the most highly developed countries, a fairly large proportion of those who are able to read never read books, or rarely do so. Paradoxically, this proportion is probably larger in the developed countries, where schooling for all has made learning to read an obligation, than in countries where progress in development is in fact measured in terms of the literacy rate and those who can read are very highly motivated to do so.

The state of world affairs is such that an awesome responsibility accrues to those who can exercise the privileges of reading. The fate of people less fortunate lies in part in the hands of those who have access to a fund of information and who act upon this knowledge to the full credit of the human race. This consideration needs emphasis in our schools.

Complex and interrelated events in the world call for a much broadened education to understand the impact of global interdependence. But recent studies present evidence of an alarming ignorance among Americans regarding world affairs. And more than knowledge is needed in order for students in our schools to be prepared to help contribute to the solution of the grave problems urgently facing our times.

Meeting the Challenge

The challenge to the teachers of reading is, indeed, almost overwhelming, but it is one from which there is no escape if the individual, the nation, and the world are to receive the benefits that can accrue through adequate teaching of reading. Recognition of what some efforts have accomplished in the past and are accomplishing now can serve to indicate what, hopefully, can be done in the future.

Efforts of the Teaching Profession

The teaching profession has responded to the challenge by constant intensive efforts to discover ways of improving reading instruction. For example, the National Society for the Study of Education has devoted many of its scholarly yearbooks to the subject.

Conferences on reading and the other language arts are sponsored annually by colleges and universities, some of which regularly publish their proceedings. One such is the Western College Reading Association. Its *Proceedings* contains articles of interest to secondary-school, college, and adult-education teachers in developmental and remedial reading. It also contains articles on English as a second language. Numerous organizations—notably the National Council of Teachers of English, the National Conference on Research in English, the American Educational Research Association, the International Reading Association, and the College Reading Association—devote much or all of their attention to factors which might improve the teaching of reading.

The International Reading Association (IRA) publishes *The Reading Teacher*, the *Journal of Reading*, and the *Reading Research Quarterly. The Reading Teacher* deals primarily with reading in the elementary school, while the *Journal of Reading* is oriented to secondary-school, college, and adult reading. The College Reading Association publishes quarterly the *Reading World*, which includes articles of interest to elementary-school, secondary-school, and college teachers of reading.

The National Council of Teachers of English, founded in 1911, has always concerned itself with the teaching of reading. Two of its magazines, *Language Arts* (formerly *Elementary English*) and the *English Journal*, frequently carry articles related to reading.

Agencies other than professional teachers' organizations contribute to our knowledge of the teaching of reading. Independent periodicals, such as *Education*, the *Journal of Educational Research*, and the *Elementary School Journal*, are but a few examples.

Legal Provisions for Equal Educational Opportunity

Concerning the issues of equal opportunity for all, we can point out that there have been significant changes in the past century in the interpretation of what constitutes equal educational opportunity. Zettel and Abeson[2] summarize these changes thus:

1. In the early years, states were to provide a common school and uniform curriculum, but it was the individual's responsibility to take advantage of it.
2. In the 19th century, the "separate but equal" concept operated with educational facilities established for certain children.
3. In the 1960's the "separate but equal" concept was discarded for its obvious inequities; differential input for equal results was attempted, but faltered because the concept of educational equality was seen as practically unobtainable.
4. Currently, attempts to equalize educational opportunity are being translated

by providing individuals with equal access to differing resources for differing objectives.

Zettel and Abeson[3] also point out that throughout the twentieth century, the courts have profoundly affected the interpretation of educationally related issues by rendering decisions establishing:

1. The right to an appropriate education
2. Access to a "free" public education
3. Due process of law
4. The right to be educated in the least restrictive environment
5. The right to nondiscriminatory testing and evaluation procedures.

The decisions concerning equal educational opportunities can profoundly affect the teaching of reading, through all too often teachers have not known how to apply the interpretations most felicitously to that area. Means of making application of them in the teaching of reading are pointed out in parts of Chapter 13 and Chapter 14.

Other Means of Endorsement by the Government

Traditionally the responsibility for education has rested almost exclusively within the various states. However, the federal goverment has increasingly been playing a major role in educational projects. It has been spending millions upon millions of dollars on various special projects in the area of teaching reading. These undertakings are tangible evidence of the recognition of the continuing need for improvement in reading instruction. To be sure, not all money invested in such government projects has been judiciously used, if we are to give credence to many reports. Neverthe-

[2]National Society for the Study of Education, *The Courts and Education.* Seventy-seventh Yearbook of the National Society for the Study of Education, Part I, edited by Clifford Hooker (Chicago: The University of Chicago Press, 1978), "The right to a Free Appropriate Education" by Jeffrey J. Zettel and Alan Abeson. pp. 188–216

[3]Ibid., pp. 192–216.

less, even in cases where a large outlay of money by the government or other agencies has reportedly not resulted in the anticipated improvement in reading, these ventures document attempts to look for better ways to effect gains in reading achievement.

Promise of the Future

A great multitude of teachers, spurred on by successes of the past and yet painfully aware of the shortcomings of the reading efforts, are striving earnestly to accept the challenge confronting the teacher of reading. They are not satisfied with attaining what has been defined by various individuals and groups as functional literacy. Their goal is far beyond that, for they are dedicated not only to helping everyone to read up to his capacity, but also to become committed to reading materials that are worthwhile, both during childhood and throughout the rest of life. As increasingly attention is being paid to the need for building unity in our culturally pluralistic society and for encouraging greater understanding of the interdependence of man and greater literacy among people throughout the world, we look forward to a growing interest in goals for reading instruction that go beyond the direct needs of the individual.

The purpose of this book is to help the teacher meet the challenges ahead in the teaching of reading. It is for this purpose that, in the pages that follow, the book: (a) describes the reading process within the background of the language arts continuum; (b) presents information on ways in which children learn to read; (c) reports on procedures effective in cultivating steady growth in reading; (d) gives suggestions for stimulating boys and girls to a lifetime habit of worthwhile reading; and (e) presents an overview of considerations dealing with the "reading program in action."

For Further Study

Allen, James E., Jr., "The Right to Read: Education's New National Priority," *The First R: Readings on Teaching Reading,* Sam Leaton Sebesta and Carl J. Wallen, eds. (Chicago: Science Research Associates, Inc., 1972). pp. 7–13.

Bracken, Dorothy Kendall, and Eve Malmquist, eds. *Improving Reading Ability Around the World.* Proceedings of the Third IRA World Congress on Reading, Sydney, Australia, 1970 (Newark, Del.: International Reading Association, 1971).

Grant, Carl A., *Multicultural Education: Commitments, Issues, and Applications* (Washington, D.C.: Association for Supervision and Curriculum Development, 1977).

Karlin, Robert, ed., *Perspectives on Elementary Reading: Principles and Strategies of Teaching* (New York: Harcourt Brace Jovanovich, Inc., 1973). Ch. 1, "Emerging Concepts in the Teaching of Reading," pp. 3–10.

Staiger, Ralph C., *Roads to Reading.* A UNESCO publication (Newark, Del.: International Reading Association, distributor of English edition, 1979).

William, Robert L., *Cross-Cultural Education: Teaching Toward a Planetary Perspective* (Washington, D.C.: National Education Association, 1977).

Questions and Comments for Thought and Discussion

1. What arguments have you read or heard that attempt to indicate that reading is less important now than formerly? How could you respond to these arguments?

2. What do you think the statement "An illiterate society is an easily controlled society" means?

3. You may be interested in reading the book *Need Johnny Read?* by Frederick Goldman and Linda Burnett (Dayton, Ohio: Pflaum, 1971). If you read the book you may wish to report to your class about your reaction to the claims made.

4. To gain perspective on the status of literacy in the United States, you may wish to investigate the percentage of literacy prevailing in other nations and compare your findings with those in the United States. Speculate and analyze the reasons for the differences between countries and attempt to substantiate your argument.

5. That there is a relationship between learning to read and personality has frequently been noted. Teachers and writers have often pointed out that defects in personality are at times a cause of problems in learning to read. Not as often has it been mentioned that failure to learn to read can be not only the result but also the cause of development of undesirable personality traits. What observations have you made that support the claim that there can be a reciprocal relationship between the ability to read and personality traits?

6. Many countries adopt more than one national language (for example, Canada and India) in order to accommodate the cosmopolitan needs of their respective societies. You may wish to investigate instructional practices in one of these countries to gain an understanding of problems associated with achieving literacy.

7. The Laubach Literacy campaigns using the "each one teach one" motto have made excellent contributions in different parts of the world. You may wish to study about this effort as a noninstitutionalized example of teaching reading.

Language Development and Reading

Since reading is a facet of the language arts, in this chapter we will examine language development, emphasizing the points concerning the development of language that warrant attention when planning and putting into operation a reading program for the elementary school.

The Interrelatedness of the Language Arts

The four facets of the language arts—listening, speaking, reading, writing—are complementary in nature. In order to fully understand the process of teaching reading the teacher must be aware of these mutually reinforcing aspects. Frequently school programs have jeopardized a more successful learning of all phases of the language arts by overemphasizing one aspect in isolation. When a child is taught to read and write, for example, his tactile and auditory experiences should be augmented in meaningful situations. Growth in reading is best produced not from a program consisting chiefly of isolated drills in learning reading skills, but from a rich, diversified, and stimulating cirriculum that recognizes the many kinds of experiences with language the child may bring with him to school.

Linguists—persons who have specialized in studying the science of language—have contributed to the growing awareness on the part of teachers of the interrelatedness of oral and written communication. One of the points upon which linguists seem to agree—and there are many points of disagreement among them—is what they refer to as the "primacy of speech" over written communication. They stress the fact that speaking precedes writing in the development of the child and of the race. Educa-

tors interested in the application of their tenets to the curriculum of the school point out the importance of building on the child's skill in oral communication when teaching reading.

Language Development of the Child

Language development begins in earliest infancy. Universally, infants exhibit prelinguistic behaviors, when there is much experimentation with their vocalizing apparatus in cooing, crying, and murmuring. Although the sounds are made with minimal language consciousness or control, they are extremely important in later development, resembling, as they do, vowel and consonant sounds. Generally, between the ages of six months and a year, the baby enters the babbling stage in which he exercises some limited control over the sounds he produces. He converts them from the vocal noises made by all normal babies to those particular components of the speech of the community in which he lives. When he is about a year old, he makes one-word utterances.

Molyneaux[1] identifies the stages in vocalizing through which a child typically passes by the time he is one or one-and-a-half years of age as: (a) the crying period; (b) the vocal play period; (c) the sound-imitation period; and (d) the language-acquisition period. She points out that during the crying period, the child's earliest oral responses to his environment or to internal stimuli are at first undifferentiated, but later show some variation, so that a mother

[1]Dorothy Molyneaux, "Childhood Language Development," *Language Development: The Key to Learning* by Morris Val Jones, ed. (Springfield, Ill.: Charles C. Thomas, 1972), ch. 2.

can often distinguish between the various responses her infant makes.

Piaget[2] provides further insight into the language development of the child in his description of the child's intellectual development as beginning with the sensorimotor stage when evidence of intelligence rests with actions, movements, and perceptions without the use of language. He points out that the progression continues through language acquisition involving increasingly more abstract mental operations in which words are manipulated to express the thought processes which may not have objects as referents.

The child's language development continues so that by the time he enters the elementary school his knowledge of language is vast. After approximately six years of listening to speech and five years of expressing himself in words, he has gone far toward mastering the basic structural pattern of his language, in declarative, interrogative, imperative, and exclamatory sentences. Never in all the later years of his life will he even dimly approximate the stupendous growth in power of oral communication that he has made in his first five or six years. In subsequent years he will but refine his already acquired skill in oral communication. As the child continues to improve his command of the language, as in earlier stages, he shows a steady development rather than sudden spurts.

The sequence in the development of language is essentially the same for all normal children. However, the details of language development as they affect the step-by-step procedures of oral and written communication in the elementary school have not been established. The timing in the appearance of various phases in the developmental sequence shows marked variation from one individual to another. Various factors affecting language ability, discussed in the next section of this chapter, help determine the timing. Owing in part to widely varying amounts of exposure to language stimuli or to differences in the language through which stimulation is received, children, upon entrance to school, should be helped in developing greater facility in the language arts by means of a curriculum that recognizes their individual needs. There is a need to interrelate the teaching of the language arts so that instruction in its respective phases is not fragmented. The language experience approach is one such attempt (see p. 18 of this chapter and further discussion in Chapter 4, "An Overview of Reading Instruction," p. 42). Other school programs concerned with meeting the differences among learners are also discussed in Chapters 4 and 14.

The tireless care that parents provide in introducing the fortunate infant to the spoken word gives rise to one of the distinguishing characteristics of humans; this is language. But just as the response to and interaction with others encourage language exchange, so, conversely, will the lack of abundant speech cause children to be deprived of the opportunity to develop into fully comprehending human beings until other factors may compensate for this deprivation.

By hearing and gradually comprehending the speech of those around them, children learn to understand vocabulary before they speak. Although the usual source of speech stimulation for the young child is the mother, communicative interactions with other adults and with siblings can stimulate verbal growth. Indeed, the role of impersonal sources, such as television and radio, also serves as a significant factor in the child's acquisition of words. All these

[2]Hans G. Furth, *Piaget for Teachers* (Englewood Cliffs, N.J.: Prentice-Hall, 1970).

environmental factors have a bearing on the extent of language growth.

The Effect of Language Development on Reading

The interrelationship between reading and the other language arts is so close and significant that learning to read is greatly affected by the other facets of the language arts. Let us note the following factors closely related to language development, or a part of it, that influence and/or are influenced by reading: (1) the self-concept, (2) oral language facility, (3) concept development in relation to vocabulary growth, and (4) language as an instrument of thought.

The Self-concept

As an extension of self-expression, language ability shows a marked bearing on the development of a healthy self-concept. If the teacher wishes to help the students to acquire and/or maintain a desirable self-image, he should not only recognize the unique speech patterns of his students, but he should also show acceptance of the individuals who communicate through their learned speech patterns acquired prior to school entry. It is the role of the teacher to show acceptance of a child's speech and at the same time to assist him in extending the range of his language abilities, in order to effect better and wider communication. Fostering of this range of communication for appropriate circumstances is the foundation not only for attaining success in reading but also for increasing sophistication in thought processes. Well-developed thought processes which are the result of or are concomitant with elaborative speech patterns

enable the individual to experience a fuller range of expression and a greater potential for acceptance by his peers and by adults.

Since a large part of a child's waking hours is spent in school, experiencing success in academic and social activities in this setting should provide means to further enhance a growing sense of worthiness. Much of schoolwork entails reading, the success in which is reliant to a considerable extent upon language development. Therefore it is crucial that the interrelationship of these factors be dealt with by the teacher with extreme sensitivity. It is not logical to attempt to strengthen a child's self-concept by censoring his language expression where its linguistic patterns may differ and then to expect a transfer of success to reading. It is logical for the teacher to build bridges between the level of sophistication in the status of a child's language development and the expectation that the teacher may have for its further expansion. The success the teacher experiences in the teaching of reading may be determined to a marked extent by his attitude of acceptance towards the child's oral language characteristics and his ability to foster growth beyond its present level. (See also "Attitude of the Teacher," p. 36.)

Oral Language Facility

Beginning reading instruction presumably introduces the child to words in print with which he has familiarity in aural-oral language. The greater his speech fluency or facility with oral language, the more opportunity there will be for congruence in meeting words in print which when successfully decoded will bear meaning for him. Since there is little or no utility in pronouncing words which are meaningless in context, the importance of oral language experiences to expand the child's speaking and reading vocabulary as a result of having heard "new words" in meaningful context is further underlined. The interrelationship between these factors in a reading program suitable for a given individual is not limited to the beginning stages of learning to read but continues as long as desirable growth in reading takes place.

Concept Development in Relation to Vocabulary Growth

Under normal circumstances an individual's reading vocabulary eventually exceeds his listening, speaking, and writing vocabularies. This phenomenon is, in part, the result of natural exposure—that is, usually those to whom we listen and speak daily do not exhibit as wide a repertoire of vocabulary words as we would have access to in print. The printed word is the result of more deliberation than is usual in informal language exchanges. Therefore, although beginning reading materials may be limited to the recording of speech which is familiar, later stages of reading include exposure to materials which provide means for further vocabulary growth as new words are introduced and frequently explained by the context.

Concept development constitutes one illustration of how growth in language ability is inextricably related to reading. Thinking takes place as vocabulary is developed and concepts are formed through firsthand or vicarious experiences which enable an individual to attach meaning to words he sees or hears. Let us consider, as an illustration, the word *silo*. The city-dwelling child acquires meaning for this word as he hears about a silo, sees a silo or a picture of one, and/or reads about one. On the basis of this background of experiences he forms a concept of what a silo is. He learns to differentiate between silos and other farm buildings. Similarly, a child living in the country learns what an escalator is if he is provided with sufficient experience to enable him to differentiate between an escalator and an elevator. If a concept is not fully developed, if as a basis for thinking the learner has insufficient background, or if he fails to utilize all needed factors in that background, he may attach erroneous associations to a word. For example, if a child who lives in an apartment, a duplex, a cottage, or a bi-level house does not have experiences with homes other than his own, he may form an incorrect concept of the word *home*. The influence of culture on meanings is obvious in the case where the word *home* means an igloo to one child and a many-story apartment house to another.

Higher thought processes are required as a child forms concepts by: (a) seeing similarities among situations where there are also differences—as, for example, in the case of the word *home*, and (b) then formulating a generalization from his observations. The larger and more abstract the concept is, the greater the need for wide and repeated experiences to gain insights and for involvement of the higher thought processes. For instance, it would be easier for the child to conceptualize meanings attached to the word *book* than to the word *religion*.

In the development of concepts the teacher needs, first of all, to help supply the child with adequate background. He should also provide guidance, if needed, in inductive and deductive reasoning. The learner employs inductive learning as he notes details of similar objects or situations which he perceives and then forms generalizations on the basis of his observations. He uses deductive thinking as he makes application of his generalizations. Let us refer again to the development of a concept of the word *silo.* In inductive learning the teacher may need not only to provide the child with various illustrations and descriptions of silos but also help him in noting what silos have in common, thereby assisting him in making a generalization as to what a silo is and thus guiding him in developing a correct concept. In deductive learning the teacher may find it necessary to help the child in determining which of several structures are silos and which are not. The development of concepts often requires considerable time on the part of the learner. Yet teachers may become impatient with a child's inability to form concepts quickly. An appreciation of the complex nature of speech as an expression of meaning and a facet requiring thought when exercising it will indicate the importance of time in the development of many concepts.

The teacher's task in the development of concepts is to recognize the factors that influence language acquisition and then to use the experiences which the boys and girls have with language, in an atmosphere that allows the children to express their varying competencies. In so doing the teacher need not sacrifice the richness in the linguistic background of the boys and girls. Instead, he can build on their language base by arranging for sufficient time to provide adequate background and enriching experiences for all learners.

Language as an Instrument of Thought

With the realization that reading should be viewed as a thinking process, the teacher of reading should be aware of the total language system of the learner as one involving thinking.

Language is essentially a vehicle for transmitting meaning. Through listening

Interest in reading begins at home. (Roger Rouch)

and reading an individual can acquire meaning expressed by others; through speaking and writing he can convey meaning to others. Though meaning is transmitted by words, meanings do not lie in words themselves, but in the interpretation given to them by people. Consequently, they may differ from one individual to another. For example, the word *range* may mean something quite different to a child brought up on an iron range of Minnesota than it does to one who has lived on a cattle ranch on the wide plains of the West. The word *elevator* may not have the same connotation for a city boy or girl living in an apartment house as it does for the child of a farmer who takes his wheat to a grain elevator. Thus the meaning of a word is often affected by the background of the listener or reader, as well as by the speaker or writer.

Since the transmission of meaning frequently is made through words and since in that transmission a selective process of possible meanings takes place, both in choosing the words to convey meaning and in interpreting those used by others, it is apparent that thinking is often a concomitant of both oral and written communication. With this point in mind we will not teach reading merely as a set of mechanical operations but as a skill in which the higher thought processes need to be in operation if comprehension beyond the level of the literal is to be stimulated. To be sure, there is great variation in the depth of thinking required to comprehend various messages. "The sun is shining" will for most elementary-school children require less of the higher thought processes·than the statement, "The height of the tides along Cook Inlet exceeds that of tides anywhere else along the Pacific Coast."

The continuum of language development from rudimentary to complex is related to the refinement of thinking abilities, the full range of which is an awesome testimony of human potentialities. It is this freeing of the mind to exercise its highest limits toward self-development and in service to humanity that a dedicated teacher sees as he honors his professional commitment to assist individuals in improving their competencies.

The Role of the School

That the school has a strategic role in the language development of a child is universally recognized. How it can effectively perform this role in relation to reading is the purpose of this entire book. In the remainder of this chapter only a few of the basic tenets bearing on that general problem are briefly discussed.

Reinforcing the Interrelatedness of the Language Arts

Other things being equal, children who come to school with a well-developed speaking and listening vocabulary have an initial advantage in reading, both in learning to recognize words and in understanding what they read. As the teacher introduces the child to language in print, he relates the child's speech system to written language by using words and voice modulations familiar to the learner. The teacher tries to give the child confidence in his ability to express himself orally, and then, in turn, to comprehend what he sees in writing.

The child whose growing vocabulary matches the experiences for which he uses words as labels can become a truly advantaged reader. Let us consider, for example, a group of children who visit a fire station and see the engines, ladders, fire extinguishers, and other equipment. If they do not hear the words that identify the objects they see, they may not be adequately prepared for later reading about firemen and fire fighting. In many instances it will be necessary to introduce them to the verbal symbols in association with the observation of the objects and the processes. Discussion and explanation of terms should, therefore, accompany the direct experiences the shool provides. If an experience is to be of substantial aid in reading, it frequently needs to be accompanied by an adequate fund of experience with language.

In the same way that a well-developed speaking and listening vocabulary serves as an advantage for the beginning reader, the lack of it can be a distinct disadvantage. The disadvantage may stem either from paucity of stimulating language experiences or from possession of a speaking and listening vocabulary that does not coincide with the language used in the materials of instruction and/or that used by the teacher. The children from culturally different backgrounds, unless the teacher accommodates these differences, are thus faced with a stupendous task.

Lack of command of oral language continues to affect the success of a child. In many reading textbooks, even beyond the beginning stages of learning to read, an increasingly larger proportion of words whose meaning the child does not know are introduced in order to enlarge the vocabulary of those who read them. Nor is the degree of excellence of the vocabulary of the child the only factor in his oral language that affects reading. His familiarity through speech with the syntax or sentence structure of the language he is learning to read also serves to determine his ability to comprehend what he sees in writing. We recognize that a good command of the oral language is one of the greatest assets a child who is learning to read can possess. However, we do not concur with those who assert that writing is merely recorded speech. It is more than that. The writer serves as thinker, writer, and editor of his own writing. Furthermore, there is usually more opportunity for clarity, conciseness, appropriateness, and organization in writing than in speaking.

What is known as the language-experience approach to reading instruction (see Chapter 4, "An Overview of Reading Instruction." p. 41) constitutes one of the methods of teaching reading that emphasizes the complementary nature of the language arts. Although this approach can be used, to some extent, throughout the elementary school, it is much more prevalent in beginning reading instruction than in later stages. Typically, when this technique is used in beginning reading, the children discuss an experience they have had, and with the teacher's help they plan the content of a "story" or report, which the teacher records on the chalkboard or on a large sheet of paper. The boys and girls receive practice in learning to read their own language through use of the written material they have dictated to the teacher. For example, after the children have had a party, they could discuss it, decide what they want to have recorded about it, and after the teacher has written the report, learn to "read" it in part or in entirety.

Implications and Issues

In this section we will discuss some issues not yet resolved with implications for education affecting language development and more specifically reading.

Acceptance of Dialect Speech

While there may be recognition of linguistic diversity, there is widespread hesitance in full acceptance of this reality. However, with regard to dialects, or variant speech forms within the same language, there is growing awareness of the fact that nonacceptance of dialects (or valuing only one's own dialect) may be related to denial of cultural contexts existing in a pluralistic society. If speech patterns are culture-bound, the development of self-esteem may be greatly promoted through the acceptance of diverse linguistic behaviors as a prerequisite to and as a means toward teaching alternative language patterns for the purpose of appropriate communication. (The reader is referred to p. 358 for a discussion of dialect speech.)

Fostering Election to Bilingualism

Another issue with implications for teaching reading is the treatment of second languages (see p. 360). Usually it is assumed that reference is being made to the teaching of English as a second language to non-English speaking students or those whose mother tongue is other than English. However, it is defensible to ask whether it is not educationally sound to foster election to bilingualism among English-speaking students as well in a future-oriented society. Educational offerings of foreign languages in elementary schools have wavered in the past partly due to federal funding during periods of perceived national urgency and partly in response to needs of certain student populations in some regions of the United States. Increasingly, parents have sought resolution in the courts for the provision of the different language needs of their children.

Support of Multicultural Education

Some professional organizations and associations have defined policies with regard to multicultural education. Different models for implementing change exist. In fact some exemplary programs have been evaluated and discussed in the literature, but most schools have yet to come to grips with the value of orientation of teachers, the majority of whom have received little or no training in the rationale for support of multicultural education and its implementation. Too, some educators and some lay citizens fear the erosion of national unity as a possible result of this emphasis in education. Whether greater unity would exist with its denial is a consideration deserving serious attention, especially with international ramifications in a changing world.

For Further Study

Alexander, J. Estill, ed., *Teaching Reading* (Boston: Little, Brown and Company, 1979), Ch. 1, "Processing Print," by Brenda Kolker.

Burns, Paul C., and Betty D. Roe, *Teaching Reading in Today's Elementary Schools,* 2d ed. (Skokie, Ill.: Rand McNally & Company, 1980), Ch. 4, "Comprehension."

Douglass, Malcolm P., ed., *Reading in Education—A Broader View* (Columbus, Ohio: Charles E. Merrill Publishing Co., 1973), Part II, "Reading and Early Language Learning," containing articles by Joan T. Kunz, James L. Hymes, Jr., Ronald Macaulay, Margaret E. Smart, John Downing, Lois Fair Wilson, and R. Van Allen.

Goodman, Kenneth S.; E. Brooks Smith; and Robert Meredith, *Language and Thinking in the Elementary School* (New York: Holt, Rinehart and Winston, 1970).

Harris, Larry A., and Carl B. Smith, *Reading Instruction: Diagnostic Teaching in the Classroom,* 3d ed. (New York: Holt, Rinehart and Winston, 1980), Ch. 3, "Language and Reading."

Lapp, Diane, and James Flood, *Teaching Reading to Every Child* (New York: The Macmillan Company, 1978), Ch. 13, "Understanding Bilinqual Speakers."

Ransom, Grayce, *Preparing to Teach Reading* (Boston: Little, Brown and Company, 1978), Ch. 2, "The Sociocultural Environment," and Ch. 14, "Linguistically Different Children."

Smith, Richard J., and Dale D. Johnson, *Teaching Children to Read* (Menlo Park, Calif.: Addison-Wesley Publishing Company, Ind., 1980), Ch. 12, "Meeting the Needs of the Linguistically Diverse."

Smith, Frank, *Comprehension and Learning: A Conceptual Framework for Teachers* (New York: Holt, Rinehart and Winston, 1975), Ch. 3, "Two Faces of Language."

Questions and Comments for Thought and Discussion

1. Emphasis is placed by linguists and by others on the "primacy of speech" over written communication. What implications for the teacher of reading can this concept have? What problems can arise if the teacher does not recognize the fact that writing is more than recorded speech?

2. How many languages can you list as representative of ethnic groups in the culturally pluralistic society of the United States?

3. Some educators believe that reading can be learned as naturally and developmentally as the acquisition of the mother tongue. Reflect on this allegation and speculate as to reasons why learning to read usually requires instruction although a child learns to speak before school entry.

4. The needs of some culturally different children are met by teachers prepared for bilingual instruction. You may wish to investigate the policies of different states with regard to this matter and examine certification policies for bilingual teachers.

5. Do you know of any instances in which a teacher has responded to a child's deviation from "standard English" so as to give him the impression that his language is inferior? If so, how might the teacher have responded in an acceptable manner? Can you give instances when a teacher gave the impression in such an instance that he considered the child's speech different from, but not inferior to, "standard English"?

6. There is a growing body of literature on the relationship between self-concept development and reading. You may wish to research the literature to insure that your practices will not counteract success in beginning reading.

The Nature of Reading

The question "What is reading?" has been given much thought by experts. It is a practical question, too, for the classroom teacher of reading. His understanding of what reading is is of vital significance as he determines his objectives and procedures and his means of evaluating reading instruction. Without a working assumption—though not necessarily articulated—of what constitutes reading and consequently what the teaching of reading should encompass, the teacher is likely to be without a reliable guide in determining what he wishes to accomplish through reading instruction, what materials he should use for the attainment of his goals, what procedures he should follow, and how he can best appraise the success of his reading program. Without such a guideline he can easily succumb to the use of questionable procedures and materials of doubtful worth.

Definitions of Reading

Many definitions and explanations of reading have been proposed, some complementary to one another, others contradictory. Because of the complexity of the reading process and because of the incompleteness of existing knowledge as to the nature of the reading act, it is not strange that they are numerous and diversified. The list of quotations which follows is representative of both the striking similarities and the marked differences among points of view.

> Reading means getting meaning from certain combinations of letters. Teach the child what each letter stands for and he can read.[1]

[1]Rudolph Flesch, *Why Johnny Can't Read and What You Can Do about It* (New York: Harper & Row, 1955), pp. 2–3.

The process of learning to read in one's native language is the process of transfer from the auditory signs for language signals, which the child has already learned, to the new visual signs for the same signals.[2]

Reading is not a simple mechanical skill; nor is it a narrow scholastic tool. Properly cultivated, it is essentially a thoughtful process. . . . It should be developed as a complex organization of patterns of higher mental processes.[3]

Reading thus is the process of giving the significance intended by the writer to the graphic symbols by relating them to one's own fund of experience.[4]

Reading is an act of communication in which information is transferred from a transmitter to a receiver. . . .[5]

Certainly reading is more than sounding letters, calling words, or responding to print. It is the communication through language between an author and a reader—the sum total of the interaction which culminates in a child's relating printed word forms to ideas expressed by the author.[6]

Reading is interacting with language that has been coded into print.[7]

Reading is a verbal process interrelated with thinking and with all other communication abilities—listening, speaking, and

[2]Charles C. Fries, *Linguistics and Reading* (New York: Holt, Rinehart and Winston, 1963), p. 120.

[3]Arthur I. Gates, "Character and Purposes of the Yearbook," *Reading in the Elementary School.* Forty-Eighth Yearbook of the National Society for the Study of Education, Part II, Nelson B. Henry, ed. (Chicago: University of Chicago Press, 1949), p. 3.

[4]Emerald V. Dechant, *Improving the Teaching of Reading,* 2d ed. (Englewood Cliffs, N.J.: Prentice-Hall, 1970).

[5]Frank Smith, *Understanding Reading: A Linguistic Analysis of Reading and Learning to Read* (New York: Holt, Rinehart and Winston, 1971), p. 12.

[6]Robert M. Wilson and Maryanne Halle, *Reading and the Elementary School Child* (New York: Van Nostrand Reinhold, 1972), p. 8.

[7]Arthur W. Heilman, *Principles and Practices of Teaching Reading* (Columbus, Ohio: Charles E. Merrill Publishing Company, 1977), p. 5.

writing. Specifically, reading is the process of reconstructing from the printed patterns on the page the ideas and information intended by the author.[8]

Reading is responding. The response may be at the surface level of "calling" the word. It may be the somewhat deeper level of understanding the explicit meaning of sentence, paragraph or passage. . . . It may involve going beyond the facts to the discovery of new and personal meanings.[9]

. . . reading has been described as social interaction between the author of the book and the student.[10]

Reading involves the identification and recognition of printed or written symbols which serve as stimuli for the recall of meanings built up through past experience, and further the construction of new meanings through the reader's manipulation of relevant concepts already in his possession.[11]

When even experts disagree on what is the most acceptable definition of reading, we can hardly expect the classroom teacher to come up with a final best answer. However, we do recognize the necessity of the teacher coming to grips with the question and of being knowledgeable about some of the various interpretations of what reading is. Familiarity with a variety of points of view as to what constitutes reading can be of value in preventing the acceptance of too narrow and/or too broad and/or an inaccurate perception of what constitutes reading. Through reading and discussion with others the teacher can then be enabled to come to a working conclusion, temporary though it may be.

The premise on which this book is based is that reading is more than knowing what each letter of the alphabet "stands for," a definition suggested by the first of these quotations. They endorse the point of view that reading involves more than word recognition; that comprehension is an essential of reading; that without comprehension no reading takes place; that in reading the reader reacts to what is recorded in writing; that his reaction is determined to a considerable extent by his past experience, both firsthand and vicarious; that what the reader brings to the page is at times as significant to reading as what is actually written on it; that reading instruction should be given both to assist an individual in the acquisition of reading skills and concurrently to help him acquire the reading habit of value to him as an individual and as a member of society. Thus the emphasis in this book is placed on "reading as a process involving meaningful reaction to printed symbols."[12] Points of similarity between this concept of reading and that expressed by some of the other writers quoted are readily perceived.

The Reading Process

What happens in reading? Often the reader is looking at an object in the form of a book, magazine, billboard, or road sign. Most commonly the object consists of paper, usually white. On the paper appear certain marks, made, as a rule, by the application of dark-colored ink. That is all—just ink marks on white paper. And yet

[8]Daniel Hittleman, *Developmental Reading: A Psycholinguistic Perspective* (Chicago: Rand McNally, 1978), p. 5.

[9]David Russell, "Personal Values in Reading," *The Reading Teacher,* vol. 15. (December 1961), pp. 172–178.

[10]Robert C. Ziller, "The Social Psychology of Reading," *The Reading Teacher,* vol. 17 (May 1964), p. 587.

[11]Miles A. Tinker and Constance M. McCullough, *Teaching Elementary Reading,* 4th ed. (Englewood Cliffs, N.J.: Prentice-Hall, 1975), p. 9.

[12]Paul A. Witty; Alma Moore Freeland, and Edith H. Brotberg, *The Teaching of Reading: A Developmental Process* (Boston: Heath, 1966), p. 8.

looking at those marks may cause the reader to turn pale, as in the case of a letter containing bad news, or to laugh, smile, cry, or hold his breath in suspense. A laboratory test would reveal that a reader's pulse rate may at times rise sharply when he looks at those curious marks on paper. How can the sight of those marks bring about such mental and physical experiences?

There is no *meaning* on the page, only ink. The meaning is in the reader's mind. Each mark is a signal that arouses some image or concept that is already in the mind of the reader. The order in which these images and concepts are evoked, the context in which they are called forth, and the relations among these concepts and images as revealed by the arrangement of the marks make it possible for the reader to gain new meanings. But the process depends on what the reader brings to the printed page, his purpose for reading, his ability to recognize the words, the concepts he has formed, to mention only a few.

Association of Sounds and Interpretation of Meaning

An adequate background of experience in the exchange of oral language is important as the child begins to deal with the written form of that same language. It is, in part, the child's understanding that print corresponds to the aural/oral language he has experienced that makes it possible for him to benefit from reading instruction. Then, in approaching written or printed material the child typically converts the visual shapes of letters and words into their corresponding sounds. At the beginning he probably utters the sounds aloud. The sounds then evoke in his mind the images and meanings they represent. As he gains proficiency, he depends less and less on the

sound "bridge" between visual stimulus and meaning, although a faint awareness of speech sounds is probably always present in reading. If the sound images continue to be prominent in the child's reading, he will develop habits of vocalization and possibly lip movement. Both speed and comprehension may then suffer. The connection between visual stimulus and meaning must become as direct as possible as soon as possible.

The Complexity of Reading

Reading is a complex process, so intricate that in spite of many scholarly efforts it has defied total analysis. However, recognition of some of the known specific skills that the efficient reader needs to possess, is important in the teaching of reading. For example, it is of value to break down general comprehension into specific skills that constitute it. It is necessary to inquire how well the child is able to grasp the general meaning of a passage; how well he can differentiate between fact and opinion; how well he can follow directions; how well he can interpret maps, graphs, and tables; how well he can organize what he reads and classify ideas; how well he can visualize what he reads; and how well he can locate information.

A single reading skill, although a very important one, well illustrates the complexity of reading. Any teacher who undertakes to cultivate, for example, children's critical discrimination in reading finds that he is dealing with a whole cluster of abilities that often need special attention. Among these are classifying ideas, distinguishing between fact and fancy, establishing cause and effect relationships, making generalizations, interpreting idiomatic and figurative language, making inferences, recognizing emotional reactions and motives, judging relevancy, and drawing general conclusions.

Recognizing that reading is a complex of many specific abilities should not, however, keep the teacher from an awareness of the holistic nature of reading. While special attention may often need to be directed to specific skills, as a rule, the procedure to be emphasized is not practice on isolated skills but acquisition of the skills concurrently in the totality of the reading act as far as the learner can profit from it.

Aspects of Reading

Some of the aspects of reading which deserve both specific attention in isolated learning situations and, at other times, more balanced attention in a more normal reading situation are word recognition, comprehension, and reflection.

Word Recognition

The conception which for several centuries prevailed in many schools in the United States is that reading is a relatively mechanical skill. According to this interpretation, the degree of excellence in reading is determined, to a large extent, by the ability to recognize and pronounce words. The dominance of oral reading to check this performance was a practice that met the objective of mastering a mechanical skill, but neglected to encompass the definition of reading as a "meaningful reaction to printed symbols," with the accompanying emphasis on comprehension.

The point of view that reading is chiefly skill in recognizing words continues to enjoy support in respectable and influential quarters. Today the favorite expression of adherents to this view of reading is *decod-*

ing the printed page—that is, recognizing the oral equivalent of the written symbol. They frequently stress that language is, at base, spoken communication and that writing or print is merely a graphic representation of speech. The process is considered one of discovering the correspondence between the *grapheme* (the written or printed symbol) and the *phoneme* (the speech sound). In other words, as seen by those who stress reading as decoding, the basic task of the teacher during the initial stage of learning to read is to teach the child the sound or sounds of each letter of the alphabet and the combinations of some, such as the *st*. It would not, however, be correct to infer that all advocates of decoding are opposed to emphasis on comprehension in later stages of learning to read. Many emphatically assert that after the code of letter and sound equivalence has been mastered, attention should be paid to comprehension skills.

Comprehension

The vast majority of teachers do not endorse the claim that the individual who can recognize words can read. To them comprehension is an absolute necessity in reading. Even in beginning reading, the practice of equating the pronunciation of words in context with reading is faulty. To expect the child to understand what he pronounces reinforces the fact that reading is for the purpose of deriving meaning. While many might argue the point that reading at all stages of development must necessarily be much more than proficiency of word recognition, they do admit that somehow or other, sooner or later, the effective reader needs to have learned the code used in written communication so that he can translate the written symbols into sound or meaningful language sequences. Thus, they, too, view word recognition and comprehension as major aspects of reading.

The critical fusion of word recognition and comprehension into meaningful interpretation of print by the teacher deserves continued attention and stimulation by the teacher. A chief means for clarifying and stimulating ideas is the discussion method in which the teacher uses effective questioning techniques (see p. 176). The manner in which the teacher deals with responses by accepting, extending, elaborating, and refining them should allow for necessary time in which pupils can adjust their perceptions to approximate the meanings intended by the authors. Because this method is different from paper-and-pencil exercises, which exclude discussion and interaction, unless the teacher values the activity for the important purposes it serves, proportionate emphasis between word recognition and comprehension activities may be distorted. Furthermore, the teacher should convey an interest in the pupils' responses as a means for developing in them reactions to something read or discussed.

Reflection

Many educators have pointed out that word recognition and comprehension do not comprise the total of the reading act. Gray,[13] for example, also includes *reaction* and *fusion*. By *reaction* he refers to the reaction of the reader to what he has read. This aspect of reading may be thought of as critical reading. By *fusion* he refers to assimilation of ideas gained through reading with the reader's former experiences. Like

many other specialists in the field of reading who have been interested in determining the components of reading, Gray emphasizes the fact that the four aspects he identifies—word recognition, comprehension, reaction, and fusion—have bearing one on the other and, frequently, when efficient reading is taking place, are not dealt with by the reader as separate components.

Helen M. Robinson[14] agrees with the four aspects that Gray has designated, and she adds a fifth one—rates. David M. Russell[15] designates *utilization* of what is read as the aspect of reading that usually appears as the final step in reading. In fact, he claims that unless most reading is used for a purpose, the act of reading has, in a sense, not been completed. According to Russell, reading serves a purpose when, for example, an individual follows directions he has read, when, through reading, he obtains information of value in solving a problem confronting him or when he receives enjoyment from what he is reading.

Not all writers concur with either Gray, Robinson, or Russell in their designations of the aspects of reading. There are other classifications of the components of reading.[16] Regardless of which of the three here mentioned is accepted, it is evident that reading involves reflection. Let us, therefore, consider what reflection in reading means.

During the process of reading, when de-

---

[13]William S. Gray, "The Major Aspects of Reading" *Sequential Development of Reading Abilities*. Helen M. Robinson, ed., Supplementary Educational Monographs, 90 (Chicago: University of Chicago Press, 1960), pp. 8–24.

[14]Helen M. Robinson, "The Major Aspects of Reading," *Individualizing Reading Instruction: A Reader*, Larry A. Harris and Carl B. Smith, eds. (New York: Holt, Rinehart and Winston, 1972), pp. 10–12. Reprinted from *Seventy Years of Progress*, Supplementary Educational Monographs, 96 (Chicago: University of Chicago Press, 1966).

[15]David M. Russell, *Children Learn To Read* (Boston: Ginn, 1961), pp. 110–112.

[16]Robinson, pp. 7–9.

fined as gaining meaning from the printed page, it is necessary to be able to hold ideas as they occur and to conceptualize meaningful interpretation through reflection. This process involves the act of comparing the written stimuli with the reader's experiences, either vicarious or real. In other words, although the printed symbols present visual stimuli in a sequential manner, the "mind's eye" sees more than the words. Much of this activity of the "mind," which cannot be overtly observed, does not take place unless there is mastery or near-mastery of most of the words used. When comprehension is taking place as the result of reflection, a reaction occurs in the reader. This reaction may consist of concurrence of thought, comparison of thought, disagreement with the idea, association, or noncomprehension, as might be the case if the vocabulary is unfamiliar to the child.

Some light may be thrown on the concept of reflection when considering an example by Parker.[17] As an illustration of the type of mental images possible for sighted people to construct, he refers to "the blind attempting to conceive of the world in visual terms." He asks how the blind could possibly have a sense of perspective lacking spatial relativity. In regard to reading, through a consideration of the role of reflection, evidence is presented that reading is not simply a process of receiving sequential visual stimuli in the form of print. As was indicated earlier in this section, a chief value of reading lies in the ideas presented in print upon which the mind can reflect. Reflection makes possible the production of ideas beyond the consumption of them.

Teachers can encourage reflection by giving children time to think rather than requiring quick "right" answers.

Closely related to reading as a form of reflection is an additional dimension in reading which may relate to the reader's identification with the author in such a close relationship as to have the effect of having a dialogue with the writer, a mental "conversation" in a way. The writer who is able to offer a book in which the reader identifies with the author's point of view may be the one who writes because he *must*, not merely to sell a book. Higgins[18] describes this relationship between writer and reader engagingly as he states: "Books which reach the inner child are those in which an author—from the depths of his own uniqueness—communicates with the essence of childhood."

Elements Important to Growth in Reading

To gain further insight into the nature of reading, let us consider elements important to growth in all the aspects of reading. Some of these factors, which are discussed in this chapter are: (1) physical health, (2) mental health, (3) intelligence, (4) maturity, (5) background of experience, (6) attitude of the learner, and (7) attitude of the teacher. As we consider these points we need to be aware of the interrelationships among them. The work of biobehavioral scientists is making us increasingly conscious of the effect of the neurological and physiological equipment of an individual upon his behavior, academic and other.

[17]Harley Parker, "The Beholder's Share and the Problem of Literacy," *Media and Symbols: The Forms of Expression, Communication, and Education.* Ch. 4. Seventy-Third Yearbook of the National Society for the Study of Education, Part I, David R. Olson, ed. (Chicago: University of Chicago Press, 1974), pp. 81–98.

[18]James E. Higgins, *Beyond Words, Mystical Fancy in Children's Literature* (New York: Teachers College Press, Columbia University, 1970), p. 3.

They have an important message from which the teacher of reading can profit.

Fortunately, nearly all children come to school already possessing most of these elements in some degree. A minority of children learn to read in spite of the lack of some of these elements. Blind, deaf, and sick children can learn to read. But to the extent that children are lacking in the elements named, they will be handicapped in the process of learning to read.

The teacher and the school do not bear exclusive responsibility for providing all the necessary conditions. Other agencies, especially the family, bear major responsibility for some of them. The school, however, is inevitably involved, in one degree or another, in helping to create all of the conditions that contribute to growth in reading.

When we specify those factors in child development that are basic to success in reading, we are not suggesting a hierarchy of educational values. Physical and mental health, for example, are ends in themselves. They do not become important merely because they contribute to good reading, as though reading were the supreme purpose of the school. But since this book is concerned with methods of teaching reading, it must necessarily take the broad developmental context of reading into account.

Physical Health

We know that a reasonable measure of physical health is essential to all school learning. Physical discomfort, languor, a low energy level, and similar symptoms of health problems may often interfere with normal progress in reading. Nervous tension and even ordinary physical fatigue can reduce enjoyment and interest in reading, with a consequent decline in efficiency. Vitamin deficiencies and endocrine distur-

bances have been associated with poor reading. Frequent absence from school resulting from illness necessarily retards progress in reading and may produce attitudes of aversion or indifference toward reading.

We must let the clinician determine whether a case of extreme reading retardation may be attributed to physical causes. For our part as teachers we must do all we can in the classroom to promote the physical well being of our pupils. Free and inexpensive school lunches help to provide needed nutrition. (In one school, a pupil who was considered lazy proved to be just hungry.) We can help to provide a healthful physical environment in school—good light, proper humidity and temperature, appropriate seating. We can arrange for periods of rest and exercise.

In addition to attention to the general well-being of pupils, both the sight and hearing of those about to learn to read should be checked and attention paid to these factors throughout the school life of the child whenever there is reason to suspect a problem.

Sight

It has been estimated that about one-fourth to one-half of elementary-school children are in need of visual correction. One of the first questions the reading clinician asks about the nonreader is: "Does this child have satisfactory eyesight?" The child who must strain his eyes to read is not likely to enjoy the process and will usually try to avoid reading. All teachers should be alerted to signs of visual difficulties among their pupils.

It must not be assumed, however, that poor vision is generally the chief cause of poor reading. Cases of nearsightedness, farsightedness, astigmatism, muscular imbalance, and lack of fusion are found among both good and poor readers. Nevertheless, in good readers, as well as in poor readers, such conditions, unless dealt with, tend to result in fatigue and consequent loss in reading ability. Quite probably nearly all readers—slow, normal, and superior—who have visual defects would improve in reading ability if their defects were corrected.

Visual handicaps among children may be of many kinds. While the classroom teacher should not undertake to make a diagnosis of the difficulty in any individual case, he should be aware of the common types of visual deficiencies in order that he may know when a child should be referred to a specialist. In addition to the more usual phenomena of nearsightedness, farsightedness, and astigmatism, the eye specialist often encounters cases of monocular vision. In normal vision both eyes receive the image of an object, and the two images are fused in the process of perception. This kind of seeing is called binocular vision. Some individuals, however, ignore or suppress the image received by one eye and consequently "see" with only one eye. In some cases the individual alternates between one eye and the other; in other cases he alternates between monocular and binocular vision.

Since most reading involves near-point vision, it is important for the teacher to recognize the difference between far-point and near-point vision. A child whose vision tests normal when looking at a distant object but who has great difficulty in seeing an object singly and clearly at a distance of fourteen inches or less is in need of attention. Preschool children tend to be farsighted. For this reason, teachers in the first and second grades should place heavy reliance on the chalkboard and on large charts for group instruction. Children who have visual difficulties should be seated near the chalkboard. Long periods of near-point reading should be avoided.

Hearing

A child who suffers from hearing loss is at a distinct disadvantage. He will, for example, have difficulty in benefiting from the teacher's oral explanations. Especially if the child is taught by predominantly oral-phonic methods, auditory acuity is important in the process of learning to read. The child with hearing loss will have inadequate or inaccurate auditory images of the words he reads and consequently may encounter difficulty in word recognition.

As in the case of visual defects, hearing loss may be no more common among poor readers than among good readers. Nevertheless, all readers who have deficient hearing ability would probably be aided in reading performance if they received appropriate attention from parents, teachers, and/or physicians.

Estimates vary as to the number of children who have significant hearing defects. One of the most conservative estimates places the percentage of children with considerable hearing loss at $1\frac{1}{2}$ to $3\frac{1}{2}$ percent of all children. Other findings suggest as much as 30 percent for girls and 50 percent for boys. Whatever the precise figures may be, we are safe in concluding that careful attention should be given to the hearing ability of all pupils.

Speech

Since a child learns to recognize words more easily and reads with greater under standing those which he already uses in speaking, normal speech development is an advantage in early reading instruction. The child with a large speaking vocabulary is also one who not only reveals a wider background of experience but also an environment in which he has had the advantage of elaborative language reactions.

In the case of the child with a speech handicap, the teacher of reading needs to recognize the difficulty and to teach accordingly. For example, he needs to realize that a child with a speech impediment may not be able to produce correctly certain sounds during phonic instruction even though this fact does not necessarily undermine his understanding of the instruction when reading silently for comprehension.

Articulatory speech errors comprise a large percentage of the problems in speech correction. Some of these difficulties are transitory. Others, which persist, may require referral to a speech therapist for specialized attention in addition to the adaptation of instruction by the classroom teacher. When, for instance, a child substitutes sounds such as /w/ for /r/, the defective speech sounds transfer to and alter the intent of instruction in phonics. Therefore it is essential that every teacher be sensitive to the needs of individual pupils and to provide opportunities for informal speech development. Similarly, no matter whether the problems are observed in connection with distortions, substitutions, phrasing, pitch, or more serious results of speech impairment, often some means must be afforded to create exercises to sensitize the child's ear in the establishment of the required correction. It is faulty teaching that presumes that all errors in pronunciation reflect a diagnosed reading error. Since the cause of the problem may not be visual, it may stem from one related to speech development.

Mental Health

Among the basic developmental needs of children that affect growth in reading is a feeling of security, of being accepted and

loved, and of being adequate to the tasks they are expected to carry out. The importance of an adequate self-concept to growth in learning of various types has been established by research at all levels of learning.[19]

Everyone performs better in any activity if he has self-confidence, a feeling of successful performance, and a strong desire to achieve. One cannot learn up to capacity, in reading or in anything else, if he is distracted by anxieties, frustrations, and the sense of failure. For this and other reasons, effort is made in modern schools to build wholesome attitudes in children, to give them a sense of belonging and a feeling of being accepted and respected, and to provide many success experiences. Good reading is best carried on in a classroom atmosphere that is warm, friendly, and relaxed.

To assure success for every child in the process of learning to read, the teacher must know the child's capabilities. Expecting either too high or too low an achievement from him will mitigate against a feeling of accomplishment. For the same reason the teacher needs to ascertain the level of reading ability for each boy and girl, and then, in the light of his knowledge, adapt the reading program to the capacity of the learner. It will, in the case of many boys and girls, be necessary to point out to them signs of growth, such as an ability to identify new words, to comprehend better what they read, to read more advanced materials. Though praise needs to be deserved to be effective, the capable teacher, intent on finding the good in every situation, will usually not strive in vain to find reasons for sincere praise.

A success experience need not necessarily be in a reading activity in order to result

[19]Arthur W. Combs, Donald L Avila, and William W. Purkey, *Helping Relationships* (Boston: Allyn and Bacon, 1971), p. 151.

in growth in reading. Any experience that builds the child's feeling of general adequacy may help to increase his zest in attacking difficult reading situations and to remove the distractions and anxieties that result from the fear of failure in school.

Increasingly, teachers are realizing the significance of the relation between social and emotional factors and beginning reading. They recognize that the child accustomed to the give-and-take of a social group, especially of his peers, will be likely to adjust more quickly to the school situation and consequently will be likely to be ready to read sooner than the child who has lacked contacts with other boys and girls. Also, since reading is taught primarily in group situations, the child who does not feel at ease with others is less likely to be able to attend to the reading. Teachers also realize that such a child is less likely to enjoy what he reads when reading in a group, unlike the child who feels comfortable with his agemates.

Maladjusted home situations or poor family relationships have been shown to be contributing causes in many cases of reading disability. As one writer put it, "Children bring their families to school." They come with all the attitudes and predispositions that were formed in the home and neighborhood during those influential first years of life. Children who are overprotected or the victims of parents who are overly ambitious for their children, or boys and girls who are unwanted or neglected or insecure because of conflict between parents or because of the loss of one or both of them are often handicapped in their efforts to learn. On the other hand, children who come from stable home situations, who are accepted and loved by their parents clearly approach the reading task with great advantage.

When home conditions are unfavorable to the child, it is the responsibility of the school to take these conditions into account and to compensate for them as much as possible. Some children of normal or superior intelligence fail to learn to read because of emotional difficulty, severe anxiety, or insecurity that develops at the time they are first faced with the reading task. The cause may be the arrival of a new baby, parental hostility, or a feeling of anxiety on the part of the parents concerning the child's reading progress—an anxiety that is easily communicated to the child. Worries of this kind interfere with the concentration so necessary in making the fine discriminations involved in reading. To expect a child with severe emotional blocks to make improvement in reading ability comparable to his intelligences is an expectation that is likely to be unfounded. Such blockage frequently interferes with both the desire to read and the ability to concentrate on actions related to or forming a part of the reading act. Moreover, children with serious emotional problems often have difficulties with other aspects of language communication such as articulation and listening comprehension which, in turn, may contribute to retardation in reading.

The relationship between emotional and social immaturity and poor reading may be reciprocal. Often, to be sure, lack of various characteristics of the maturing emotional and social life can have a detrimental effect on reading, but the fact must not be overlooked that frequently inability to read well is a cause of personality maladjustment. The child who cannot read, no matter how normal he was in his emotional reactions when he entered school, is likely to develop undesirable traits if he cannot enter into the reading activities that form a large part of the typical elementary-school day. Aggression, withdrawal, irritability, and other forms of unsocial or antisocial behavior are often the visible manifestations of a personality thwarted because it cannot engage in activities satisfying to others in the classroom. An understanding teacher will consider resourceful means to support the child's faltering ego in order to channel his energies to more positive outcomes.

Intelligence

It is known that a fairly close relation exists between intelligence and the ability to read. This relation, however, may be ascribed, in part, to the fact that intelligence tests and reading tests set many tasks that are similar. The fact that the correlation between performance on intelligence tests and reading tests usually tends to be very high may mean merely that a large part of an intelligence test calls for abilities closely related to the ability to read. Moreover, it must be remembered that cultural background and present environment are likely to affect performance on both reading and intelligence tests.

How a teacher defines intelligence is likely to make a difference in the relation he finds between intelligence and reading. It may also affect the results he will achieve with the boys and girls he is teaching. If we define intelligence as the rate at which an individual is able to learn, we may assume that the rate of his growth in reading is affected by his intelligence. If intelligence is thought of as an inherited ability, the role of the school and the teacher is to provide an environment that will help the child function up to his ability. But there is reason to believe that in the early years of a child's life, environment may have a considerable effect not only on learning but also on what is commonly considered as intelligence.

The intelligence of the learner may have a less noticeable effect on progress in the early stage or stages of learning to read than later. The child who has been fairly successful in his initial development in reading may meet a barrier in later stages when the tasks to be performed require increased exercise of the higher thought processes. On the other hand, we also recognize the fact that there are many children slow in acquiring the initial adaptations in learning to read, who, for various reasons, both known and unknown, have a spurt in learning to read that brings their accomplishment considerably above earlier expectations based on previous progress in reading.

Maturity

One of the aspects of maturity for reading is the degree of physical growth and development, which, with most young children, is indicated primarily by age—though there is notable variation in the accuracy of number of years of living as an index of physical maturity. The extent to which age should be taken into consideration in planning the reading program for the learner is a matter of dispute. Undoubtedly physical growth alone cannot serve as a reliable determiner of when, for example, reading instruction should begin. Due consideration needs to be given to many other characteristics of the learner discussed in this section of the chapter. Thus, the emphasis to be placed on physical maturity will vary greatly from individual to individual.

While physical maturity is primarily and usually a characteristic not influenced greatly by environmental factors over which the school has much control, there are aspects of maturity, amenable, as a rule, to educational influences, that should figure prominently in reading instruction. For example, maturity as a condition for success in beginning reading is determined, in part, by the ability of the child to demonstrate persistence at a task and to exhibit attending behavior. His social and emotional development also greatly influence his skill both in working alone and with others in the classroom. His ability to profit from directions or suggestions from his teacher also reveals the extent to which he is oriented to school learning. Furthermore, the degree of an individual's mental maturity is revealed in part by his power to form correct concepts.

Background of Experience

If it is true that success in reading depends, in part, on what the reader brings to the printed page, much significance must be attached to the body of direct and indirect experiences he has accumulated in advance of the reading. The child's prior stock of impressions will determine in large measure how much meaning he will derive from the visual symbols before him. These impressions will include both the things that have happened to him directly and the symbolic experiences he has had with reading, listening, viewing motion pictures and television, and the like.

A simple example illustrating the point that written symbols acquire meaning for the reader because of his previous experiences is that of a reader who encounters what to him is a new word, the word *hogan*. The writer states that a hogan is a nonrectangular house used by the Navaho Indians as a dwelling. He may go on to give further details—the materials of which these houses are built, the presence or absence of windows and doors, and similar information. The reader has had previous experience with the letters of which the word is composed and he is able to pronounce it, but he has never before encountered the word *hogan*, nor has he ever seen

a hogan. How can this curious visual symbol have meaning for him?

Hogan acquires meaning for the reader because he has had direct experience with other words and ideas in the sentence. These words arouse images in his mind because he has encountered in personal experience the ideas and images they represent. He knows what a rectangle is and he has had experience with houses. Encountering the concepts of *house* and *rectangle* in a specific relation to each other, the reader is enabled to create a new image in his mind—an image approximating a hogan—which he has never seen. Thus, through the combination and recombination of familiar words, images, and concepts, the reader builds new meanings, which in turn provide the basis for further understandings.

It becomes apparent that the fundamental elements in reading comprehension derive from direct experience. References to such concepts as anger, love, hate, reconciliation, warmth, pain, light, and dark can have meaning for the reader only in the degree to which he has in one way or another had experience with them. Not only does direct experience facilitate the acquisition of meaning from the printed page but it also creates the conditions for that keen interest in reading that is so essential to reading growth. For example, a person who has visited the headquarters of the United Nations will read with redoubled insight and pleasure a story about a visit to the same place; a boy who is assembling a stamp collection will read a book about stamp issues with an intensity of interest that would most likely not exist in a boy who does not pursue this hobby. Thus, the reading of recent history also takes on significance and life as the reader recognizes in historical scenes the flesh and blood realities he knows from his own past. The depth and range of his comprehension will depend in part on the richness of that past.

Basic to all the reading experience through which children learn is the direct contact with things, people, and events. It is incorrect to argue that the concepts usually encountered in reading material are common to the experience of most or all children and that the instructor's primary task is to teach the recognition of the printed symbol. Such an argument overlooks the wide diversity of the environments of children in the country or in the city, in mining or industrial towns, in slums or wealthy suburbs, in cattle country or fishing villages. For example, consider the difference in the understanding that a country boy, especially one from the West, and a city boy might bring to a passage dealing with the branding of cattle, in which words such as *range, corral, gelding* are used!

Consideration of the bearing of an individual's background on his ability to read with comprehension forces one to be cognizant of the handicaps that a child from an impoverished environment experiences in the process of learning to read. If no adaptation in instruction is made to compensate for the language experiences he lacks upon entrance to school, the achievement outcomes are likely to be adversely affected.

Attitude of the Learner

The desire to read is the motivating force that leads to reading. It may be the desire to have needed information or to spend a pleasant leisure hour. Some boys and girls in the initial stage of learning to read will want to learn because they wish to identify with adult activities. Others will be eager to learn to read because it has been held up to them at home as a rewarding experience, possibly indirectly through the reading of

interesting stories to them. Most 5- and 6-year olds are highly motivated to learn to read. It is the school experience of some boys and girls that makes them dislike reading.

Whether the readers are in the beginning or later stages of reading development, the desire to read arises from a sense of need. The child who honestly exclaims, "I hate reading" should not be required to do a great deal of reading. Instead, he should be helped to see the values that can be accrued through reading—not chiefly long-time goals, but primarily those attainable at the time or in the near future. For example, the teacher might select stories of particular interest to the pupil to read to him in order to foster his valuation of reading through providing a joyful experience. Thus the sense of need can be cultivated by creating the necessary conditions.

The emphasis in reading guidance should be placed not upon arbitrary teacher-direction, but upon the awakening of pupil desire, the release of pupil energy, and the development of pupil self-direction. The teacher's aim is to guide, to lead—not to coerce; but the pupil must supply the voluntary effort if real learning is to take place.

Especially in the initial stages of reading, the factor of good motivation is of prime importance. Motivation is not a mere mechanical preliminary to the reading itself but is the result of the teacher's providing or helping the pupil discover clear goals. If the child's first experiences with reading are purposeful, he will be started on the road to meaningful reading. We cannot start him with a set of skills, mechanically acquired without reference to meaning, and then expect him later to put them to effective use in meaningful reading.

The principle of reading with a purpose, of *active* reading, has clear implications for reading assignments. We must not send children to the printed page without adequate preparation for the reading. A good assignment, as a rule, includes a discussion that will orient the pupil to the material he will encounter. It helps him to formulate questions to be answered and to visualize clearly the uses to which the information is to be put. It gives him some notion of the nature of the material to be read and the manner in which the material is to be approached. It helps him to anticipate some of the key words and perhaps the pronunciation of unfamiliar proper names. Frequently the best assignments are self-assignments. Such assignments arise out of problems, discussions, and activities that call for further information. The search may be initiated by the individual himself, by a committee, or by the class as a whole.

The reading connected with a unit of instruction may involve various purposes. Reading may be done as preliminary exploration or browsing in a variety of books for the purpose of general orientation to the subject of the unit. This would be a period of "sampling," a get-acquainted period to indicate the nature of the area to be studied. It may be done as differentiated research where each pupil pursues some special aspect of the main topic.

The number and types of purposes for which individuals read are almost unlimited. Children and young adults have many things that they want and need to know. They want to know what the good radio and television programs and movies are and what makes them good; how to apply for a position and how to behave in an interview; what makes wars and how they might be prevented; how they can be more popular among their friends; what they can believe in the newspapers; how they can get along better at home; where they can get the truth about the trouble spots around the world. They want to know about labor, prices, employment, and new scientific advances. They want to know what they must do to be safe when riding a bicycle, driving a car, or repairing a light switch. They want to know what attitudes they should assume toward sex, courtship and marriage, ethics, and religion.

The task of the school is to assist the reader in carrying out his purposes. If he is frustrated by obstacles too numerous and too great in the form of vocabulary burden or complexity of thought, he will soon give up his purposes to seek to achieve them by means other than reading. Too many young readers have abandoned the spontaneous search for meaning in books because they did not receive appropriate guidance or were not given adequate time to pursue their interests.

Closely related to purpose in reading is interest. Children are most likely to read with comprehension those materials that deal with topics of interest to them. In fact, it has been found that some pupils are able to read stories at a level of reading difficulty far beyond their normal abilities if the subject is one in which they are vitally interested. Thus, a boy who follows professional baseball closely may successfully read a sports story in a newspaper even though it is several years beyond him in reading difficulty.

Children's interests are at least in part the result of the experience they have had. They are closely related to the activities of play and work which constitute their daily living. Many of these interests are common to all boys and girls. Others are common only to boys or only to girls. Some are related to the earlier, others to the later, ages. Still others arise out of individual experience and are affected by the special aptitude or background of the individual. Since interests are learned, rather than inherited, it is possible to extend both their range and their quality. Any activity that will open new fields of exploration to children can help to expand a pupil's reading interests and his mastery of the printed page. Reading should, therefore, be taught in the setting of a wide variety of purposeful enterprises designed to expand the child's range of interests. Radio, television, films, field trips, class projects, group discussion involving the exchange of experiences—all these are methods by which the ground may be prepared for ever more zestful and meaningful reading.

Attitude of the Teacher

The teacher and the school do not bear exclusive responsibility for providing all the conditions necessary for favorable development in reading. Other agencies, especially the family, bear major responsibility for some of them. The school, however, is inevitably involved in one degree or another, in helping to create many of the conditions that contribute to growth in reading. How the school can do so is the theme of this book. Here we draw attention only to the difference that the attitude of the teacher can make.

The most important determinant of the effectiveness of a reading program is the teacher. Materials of instruction, the budget for reading, the reading curriculum of the school, the amount of time devoted to reading instruction, the administrative and supervisory staff, working conditions in general—all these, though important, are secondary to the importance of the teacher. A teacher of reading can be effective, though necessarily hindered, in spite of lack of materials, in spite of a highly limited budget, in spite of an inadequately de-

veloped reading curriculum, in spite of lack of constructive administrative and supervisory assistance, in spite of undesirable working conditions in general. On the contrary, no teaching materials, no budgetary provisions, no administrative or supervisory staff, no working conditions in general, however desirable, can make up for a poor teacher.

How successful a teacher is, is determined to a considerable extent by his knowledge of effective ways of teaching reading and his skill in teaching accordingly. The necessity of a firm foundation in the teaching of reading, emphasized throughout this book and especially in Part II, must not be underestimated. But a fact that is often overlooked or minimized is that the attitude of the teacher toward the learner and toward reading is also of prime importance.

What then are some of the distinguishing attitudes and actions of the teacher that are vital to successful teaching of reading? We list but a few, which are enlarged upon in other parts of the book.

1. *The teacher likes children, not just children as a group, but every child in every group, regardless of any undesirable traits an individual may possess.* His attitude is and his manner shows, when a situation warrants it, "I do not like this thing you do, but I care about you."[15] We are not, however, referring to a weak sentimentality. Rather, what is needed is an abiding and intelligent interest in the best welfare of each child. Unless the learner is able to sense this interest, he is unable to derive full benefit from it.

[15]Paraphrased from a poem of which the author is unknown to the writers of this book.

2. *The teacher is willing to expend the necessary effort in helping each child.* Helping each learner read up to the best of his ability, to be sure, is an aim to be desired but not a goal to be achieved in entirety. Only a diligent teacher can even approximate it.

3. *The teacher is familiar with the major tenets of the field of child growth and development and puts them into practice.* Sufficient familiarity does not have to result from intensive study of that area. Common sense, coupled with observation and limited study, can go far in convincing the teacher of the importance of such traits as kindness and patience. No research is needed to convince the teacher of the value of humor when associating with and helping boys and girls or of the importance of listening to them with understanding and paying due attention to the feelings and desires of each learner.

4. *The teacher shows respect for each individual.* A person who does not have the respect of others is not likely to have much self-respect. The difference self-respect can make in learning to perform in reading and in other areas has already been suggested (see p. 30). Fortunately respect by the teacher shown to the learner is likely also to generate respect of the latter for the former.

5. *The teacher conveys to the learner the belief that an individual has the right to make mistakes.* Overemphasis on the need of perfection can be most discouraging to the learner.

6. *The teacher's practice of the reading habit is important in exhibiting the belief that wide reading enables people to have ideas worthy of thought upon which to base action and from which to draw information.* Sharing with his

pupils ideas from his reading emphasizes the value of reading.

Educational Principles in Harmony with the Concepts of the Nature of Reading

The teacher's definition of reading, his understanding of the reading process, his knowledge of the factors that affect the process, along with his philosophy of education are factors that should determine the principles that govern his teaching of reading and reflect his deep belief in the life of ideas, namely getting ideas and generating them for the betterment of the conduct of living.

Below are listed some of the guidelines for teaching reading to which the writers subscribe. These and others are discussed and, in many instances, illustrated in succeeding chapters of this book.

1. Whether or not a teacher's view of reading is broad enough and in harmony with the best thought in the area of reading can determine to a considerable extent the effectiveness of his program.

2. Reading is a developmental process.

3. An orderly plan of organization of the reading program, yet one that allows for variations in plans as determined by students' needs, is conducive to effectiveness.

4. No one method of reading instruction has been established as the best.

5. What constitutes desirability in methods of instruction varies from one learner to another.

6. The teacher should help each child de-

velop or maintain self-respect and self-esteem.

7. The teacher's aim should be to help each child develop in reading ability to the extent of his capabilities.

8. Participation by the learner in the establishment of goals is an important educational activity.

9. In an effective reading program emphasis is placed not only upon the development of the skills of reading but also upon the student's desire to read worthwhile materials "on his own."

10. Use of a variety of instructional materials is likely to be more productive of results than use of but a few.

11. Careful diagnosis of the needs of each learner is essential to an effective reading program.

12. Frequent evaluations by students and teachers of the extent to which goals are being achieved can serve as incentive to the learner and as a guideline for the teacher.

13. No one can force an individual to learn to read; all the teacher can do is to provide the opportunity to learn.

Acquisition and Use of Reading skills

The omission thus far of much attention to the specific skills involved in the act of reading itself has been intentional. We believe that because so much of formal reading instruction has stressed the mechanical skills of word recognition and comprehension, a heavy emphasis on the background factors in reading growth is necessary. Nevertheless, no consideration

of the development of reading competence would be complete without careful attention to the matter of specific reading skills. Most of the chapters in Part II, "Cultivating Growth in Reading," discuss these in detail.

Some children acquire the necessary skills without formal instruction. Given the various conditions described earlier in this chapter and an environment that is in every respect conducive to reading growth, they learn from the beginning to get meaning from the printed page and almost unconsciously develop the habits of word recognition and comprehension of sentences and longer units. For such children the analytical reading drills can be more harmful than helpful.

Most children, however, can be materially aided by specific instruction in reading skills. They can make more rapid improvement if they can be shown how to recognize letters and phonic elements; how to discover familiar structural elements in the longer unfamiliar words; how to use context clues; how to note details; how to find the main idea of a longer passage; how to compare, evaluate, and visualize the author's intended message; how to locate and utilize needed information; how to follow printed directions; how to adapt rates of reading both to the nature of the material read and to the purpose of the reader. These skills can be learned through guided practice. In no case must there be neglect of either the factor of interest or the factor of skill in reading. Fortunately the two can go hand in hand since skill development is affected favorably by motivation. The child who recognizes the need for acquiring skill is more likely to attain his goal than the one who lacks purpose for learning it.

For Further Study

Heilman, Arthur W., *Principles and Practices of Teaching Reading*, 4th ed. (Columbus, Ohio: Charles E. Merrill Publishing Company, 1977), Ch. 1, "Principles of Teaching Reading."

Hittleman, Daniel R., *Developmental Reading, A Psycholinguistic Perspective* (Chicago: Rand McNally College Publishing Company, 1978), Ch. 3, "Understanding the Thinking and Reading Processes."

Kennedy, Eddie C., *Methods in Teaching Developmental Reading* (Itasca, Ill.: F. E. Peacock, 1974), Ch. 1, "Understanding the Reading Process."

Lamb, Pose, and Richard Arnold, eds., *Reading Foundations and Instructional Strategies* (Belmont, Cal.: Wadsworth Publishing Company, Inc., 1976), Ch. 1, "Reading Definitions, Models, and Beliefs," by Pose Lamb.

National Society for the Study of Education, *Innovations and Change in Reading Instruction*. The Sixty-seventh Yearbook of the National Society for the Study of Education, Part II, edited by Helen M. Robinson (Chicago: University of Chicago Press, 1968), Ch.

1, "What Is Reading? Some Current Concepts," by Theodore Clymer.

Ransom, Grayce A., *Preparing to Teach Reading* (Boston: Little, Brown and Co., 1978), Ch. 1, "Reading as Multi-faceted Communication."

Singer, Harry, and Robert B. Ruddell, eds., *Theoretical Models and Processes of Reading*, 2d ed. (Newark, Del.: International Reading Association, 1976).

Smith, Frank, *Understanding Reading: A Psycholinguistic Analysis of Reading and Learning to Read* (New York: Holt, Rinehart and Winston, 1971).

Tinker, Miles A., and Constance M. McCullough, *Teaching Elementary Reading*, 4th ed. (Englewood Cliff, N.J.: Prentice-Hall, Inc., 1975), pp. 3–9.

U.S. Office of Education, *Do Teachers Make a Difference?* (Washington, D.C.: Office of Education, 1970).

Zintz, Miles V., *The Reading Process*, 3d ed. (Dubuque, Iowa: Wm. C. Brown Co. Publishers 1980), Ch. 1, "What Is Reading?"

Questions and Comments for Thought and Discussion

1. It may be helpful for you to decide on a definition of reading to which you can at the present time subscribe. As you continue the study of how to teach reading, you may want to modify your definition. In fact, it is strongly recommended that you think of the one you now accept as subject to possible change as you gain more insight into the teaching of reading.

2. What are some of the implications for classroom practice that you see in the light of your tentative definition of reading? (See number 1 above.)

3. You may decide to interview children of different ages to see what they think reading is and compare your findings with a definition you may have accepted. (See number 1 above.)

4. It is often helpful to parents to understand what you as a reading teacher are attempting to achieve in the teaching of reading. You may

wish to prepare a dialogue as though it were intended for a parent-teacher conference in which you explain what reading is, in order to help parents understand your practices.

5. The background experiences of boys and girls entering school have become increasingly more varied due to exposure to television and early childhood educational opportunities. How can a teacher survey these differences in order better to accommodate the disparate needs of his pupils?

6. Many children associate reading with drills and workbook exercises to learn phonic elements. How can a teacher help build associations more directly bearing on the interests of children?

7. Have you noted any evidence to support the claim that has been made that how well a child is able to learn may be influenced by his teacher's expectations of him? You may be interested in reading *Pygmalion in the Classroom: Teacher Expectations* by Robert Rosenthal and Lenore Jackobson (New York: Holt, Rinehart and Winston, 1968) for a consideration of that point.

An Overview of Reading Instruction

Now that we have given consideration to the nature of reading, let us note the ways in which reading is frequently taught in the elementary school. With such a background of understanding we can then proceed to a more detailed study of how growth in reading can be cultivated—the subject of Part II of this book.

Contrary to the claims of some advocates of particular procedures and materials for reading instruction, no one system has been unequivocally established as the most propitious. It is doubtful that research will ever be able to give an unqualified endorsement to any approach or method of teaching reading as the best, either to one that is now in use or to one that may be employed at any future time.

In order to present the reader of this book with a general overview of ways in which reading is being taught, this chapter describes the three most commonly followed organizational plans, namely: (a) the language-experience approach; (b) the basal reader program; and (c) the individualized reading program. Since in teaching reading most teachers do not strictly adhere to any of these, we also identify a fourth one, namely the "eclectic approach," which is a combination of two or all three of the aforementioned major plans for teaching reading. Later chapters take up methods that can be used in connection with one or more of these approaches such as, for example, programed reading (see p. 392).

The Language-Experience Approach

In the language-experience approach to beginning reading instruction the child's own language and his environment form the nucleus of the reading material. The claim is that since the child comes to school with a wealth of language experiences, these should be utilized in the teaching of reading.

In some schools the language-experience approach is the plan of instruction upon which all or almost all reading is based in the kindergarten and during the first months of the elementary school. However, teaching according to this plan is not and should not necessarily be limited to the beginning stages of reading instruction. It can be used to advantage with older boys and girls, such as those with limited command of the English language and with slow learners. It can also be used effectively in content areas such as the social studies or science for recalling and summarizing the major points of a learning experience.

Language-experience activities may form only part of the total instructional program during any one stage of reading instruction. They are often used in conjunction with a basal reader or an individualized reading program.

Description of the Approach

Typically in the language-experience teaching procedure, a written record is planned cooperatively by the pupils and the teacher. With beginners it is usually recorded by the teacher, seldom by the learners. Since the record is often kept on a chart, it is frequently referred to as a language-experience or an experience chart, even when it is written on a smaller piece of paper or on the chalkboard. A record of an experience that the class might have had when finding leaves on a walk they took, might read as follows:

Leaves
We went on a walk.
We found some pretty leaves.
Some were red.
Some were brown.
We found yellow leaves.

Sometimes experience charts are based, not on experiences that the boys and girls have had, but on some they are planning. The wording of the following sentences for a chart is similar to that which a class might develop, with the assistance of the teacher, during the early months of the elementary school.

Our Party
We will have a party.
We will have our party on Monday.
We will have cookies.
We will drink milk.
We will play games.
We like parties.

There is argument among advocates of the experience-chart approach as to the extent to which the exact, unedited wording suggested by the children should be recorded. Some claim that the language in which children couched their suggestions for the chart should be retained without any alterations made through questioning or comments by the teacher. Others hold that there should be considerable guidance from the teacher in the formulation of the wording. Still others take a position between these two extremes. An argument advanced for use of the exact language of the boys and girls is that if changed through teacher assistance, the experience chart is no longer an expression of the child's language and thus loses one of its chief reasons for being used. In opposition to this claim is the argument that through help from the teacher—given, for example, by questions such as "What did we do next?"—the children can learn to improve their own language expression. On the other hand, some would argue even against correction by the teacher of ungrammatical expressions in the children's contributions. Others who might object to the inclusion of such expressions would favor the recording of sentence fragments, rather than complete sentences, that the pupils may have

suggested. In spite of these controversies among users of the language-experience approach, there seems to be general agreement that much assistance by the teacher in the wording can unfortunately make a chart chiefly a production by the teacher, not by the boys and girls.

Sometimes the record of an experience or of a planned experience is first written on the chalkboard and then copied, if greater permanency is desired, onto a large sheet of paper. At other times the record may be made directly on paper, without first having been written on the chalkboard. Paper about 24 x 36 or 18 x 24 inches might be used. Records can, however, be made on smaller sheets, as they often are when they are designed chiefly for individual, rather than group, purposes. If a chart is to be preserved for a considerable length of time, it may be desirable to write it on tagboard, while one that is to be used for only a short time may well be kept on less expensive paper, such as newsprint. Some experience records are kept in large notebooks, possibly made of butcher paper, maybe 18×24 inches in size. The records filed in a notebook often are on one theme, such as "Our Pets" or "Our Schoolroom" or "Our School."

Purposes Served by the Approach

The language-experience approach can serve a variety of purposes. Important among these, is that it provides the opportunity for continuing experiences in harmony with the language development trends of children, with due attention to individual differences among them. Also if this procedure is used, the interrelatedness of the language arts can be concretely expressed, as participants listen to comments by others, state their own opinions, note the role of writing, and develop one or more reading skills. An example of a reading skill which boys and girls may be helped to acquire through this approach is the left-to-right and top-to-bottom orientation in reading, as they observe the teacher write or more pointedly, as the teacher specifically draws attention to aspects of the directional sequence in writing and reading. Another reading skill which can be developed through work on a language-experience chart is learning to recognize words in written form, through development of a sight vocabulary, through use of phonetic analysis, and through attention to structural analysis. Learnings can also be acquired that form the basis for later development of dictionary skills. How each of these skills can be developed is indicated later in this discussion.

Teaching Procedures

There is, of course, no one way in which the language-experience approach can or should be used. There are many legitimate

The language-experience approach can foster writing. (Roger Rouch)

variations from the one described here. The teacher may wish to alter the suggested plan through omissions, substitutions, or other alterations, as he considers factors such as the subject of the language-experience report, the length of time to be devoted to work on it, and the needs and interests of boys and girls. Adaptation is also necessary when it is the work of one pupil, aided by the teacher, rather than of a group.

The steps below give the reader a general idea of means of using the language experience approach.

1. *After the boys and girls have participated in an interesting and significant experience, they discuss it.*
2. *If motivation for making a chart is not provided during the discussion, a pupil or the teacher suggests it thereafter.* The purpose may, for example, be that visitors coming into the room can read it or have it read to them, in order to find out what the class has done. Or the boys and girls may make a chart so that they can go to another room to read it to the children. It is not important whether the idea originates with a child or the teacher. What matters is that the children—at least, the majority of them—accept it as one providing sufficient purpose.
3. *The pupils, with the help of the teacher, plan the title, the general content, and the exact sentences as the teacher does the writing on the chalkboard or on a large sheet of paper posted so all can see it.* The teacher should proceed according to the overruling principle that too much teacher-direction in content to be included, in words to be used, in structure of sentences can defeat the purpose for making a language-experience chart. In fact,

some authorities on the use of this approach recommend a very low minimum deviation from the children's spontaneous suggestions. However, the teacher can guide the class in planning the chart by doing the following:

   a. Take care that many, preferably all, of the boys and girls take part in the planning.

   b. By questioning, help the pupils suggest significant items.

   c. Be of assistance in helping to formulate sentences.

   d. Help decide on the sequence.

   e. Guide the work so that the vocabulary used in the chart is fairly simple.

   f. Give the pupils help in vocabulary building by asking for more colorful or more descriptive words to be substituted for some suggested.

   g. After the first draft is written, assist the children in revising the sentences so that a more unified composition will result.

4. *First the teacher alone, then the pupils together with the teacher, and finally, if possible, the boys and girls alone read the report.*

5. *The group practices on identification of sentences.* The teacher may, for example, instruct the boys and girls to find various sentences that the teacher reads out of their natural order. After locating a sentence a pupil can read it orally.

6. *The boys and girls learn to recognize a few of the words that are new to their reading vocabulary.* As the teacher names one of the selected words, a pupil may point to it on the chart and then name it. The teacher may also wish to write the words to be given special attention in a list on the chalkboard so that the pupils can find the same words in the story or so that they can learn to identify them in the listing. Later these words may be written on cards to provide further practice and to serve as a word bank for the boys and girls, to which they can refer when necessary.

7. *The class review the words in the chart that they have previously learned.* They may, for example, name them as the teacher points to them or find them as the teacher names the words.

8. *One or more pupils read the chart alone.*

9. *The pupils receive further practice on the chart, as well as, at times, additional work on the development of vocabulary and of other skills important in reading.* In addition to the end activities already suggested, such as reading the chart to visitors or to pupils in other rooms, the teacher may wish to make a copy of the content of the chart for each child. On a separate sheet he may leave space near each word of the chart that can be illustrated, so that the pupil can draw a picture that goes with the word. For example, to illustrate the word *leaves,* the pupil may draw a picture of leaves. This activity can help the boys and girls recall the word more easily. The children can then make all these papers into a booklet and draw an appropriate picture on the cover. After a child has learned to "read" the chart, he may be given permission to take his booklet home to "read" to his parents.

How word recognition can be developed through acquisition of a sight-word vocabulary has been illustrated in the preceding itemization. Rudiments of phonic analysis can be developed when the teacher may ask, for example, as the boys and girls are working on the wording for the chart on "leaves" (see p. 42), with what sound the word *leaves* begins. Then he may tell them that the letter that stands for that sound is the letter *l*. Thereupon the pupils might name other words beginning with the same sound, as the teacher then writes them on the chalkboard and a child underlines the letter *l*.

The foundation for use of structural analysis in the development of facility in word recognition can be laid as the teacher draws attention to words with similar prefixes or suffixes. For example, if the word *walking* were used in an experience chart, the teacher could write the words *walk* and *walking* on the chalkboard and have the class tell through the addition of which letters *walk* is changed to *walking*. The teacher might then record additional root words which they were already able to recognize visually, writing them, with suffixes, on the chalkboard in a manner such as this:

talk	talking
play	playing
sing	singing

Similarly the basic instruction in the use of prefixes in unlocking new words could be taught. Care, however, needs to be taken to avoid spending so much time on word-recognition skills that the interest in the chart is jeopardized.

Making word banks, based in part, at least, on words studied on experience charts, can be another fruitful activity for development not only of reading, but also of writing, skills. Word banks can constitute a class project. As some words on an experience chart are being studied, they can be written by the teacher on slips of paper, possibly about two inches by four inches. These words can then be arranged alphabetically according to the beginning letters of the words and filed in a box similar to a file for recipes. From time to time the class can review reading these words. Word games can be played with the cards or the

boys and girls can classify them as to categories such as these: color words, doing words *(walks, playing)*, words about eating *(drink, cookies)*. When the pupils are writing, they can refer to the word bank for assistance in spelling. Added to the words from experience charts could be others that the class had learned or is learning to read, as, for example, names of objects in the room *(table, chair)* or names of the days of the week or of the months of the year. The children could also make individual word banks, with each child having his own bank of words he has learned or of words he is wanting to learn. They could arrange these words alphabetically if they are recorded on cards.

Evaluation

There is disagreement concerning the use of the language-experience approach to reading instruction. The controversy centers chiefly around the question, "To what extent should it be used in the early stages of reading instruction?"

Some of the arguments advanced in favor of extensive use of the language-experience approach during the initial learning-to-read process are:

1. The valuable and/or interesting experiences that boys and girls have can be made more meaningful to them at times if language-experience charts are based on them.
2. Reading about their own experiences is more interesting to boys and girls than using reading-readiness books found on the market.
3. The relation between reading and the other facets of the language arts is made evident to the boys and girls.
4. The vocabulary of the language-experience stories is more meaningful to the boys and girls and is less stilted than that used in basal readers.

Among the arguments advanced against much use of the language-experience approach during beginning reading is that the words that appear in the reports are not as carefully selected as those that are found in published reading-readiness books and in the more advanced readers for beginners. Writers of textbooks in reading for the primary grades have spent much time and energy in attempts to secure suitable vocabulary. An effort is made by many writers of basal readers to use words that pupils will meet frequently in other reading, to introduce only a few new words in each selection, and to give systematic review of words learned, by providing for repetition in the reading, at spaced intervals, both in the book in which the word is first used and in later books in the series.

Another argument offered against extensive use of the language-experience approach during the prereading or early reading stages is that boys and girls do not receive practice in the process of thought getting, which is needed for independent reading later on. Language-experience charts provide practice in reading what one already knows. Furthermore, criticism is often directed at the fact that frequently there is memorization of what is written on the chart, not reading in the true sense of the word.

In refutation of the arguments proposed by those favoring much use of the experience charts some opponents of that practice also claim:

1. The valuable and/or interesting experiences that boys and girls have will enrich their background of information and understanding without their necessarily planning a chart about their experiences.
2. Reading one's own report is not as interesting, in some cases, as reading

some of the published prereading materials.
3. The relation between reading and the other language arts can be made evident to the boys and girls without using language-experience charts.
4. The pupils are able, through effective teaching, to recognize the value of the reading vocabulary they acquire when reading well-graded and well-written reading-readiness books.

No one formula can be given for the amount of emphasis that should be placed on the use of language-experience charts. There may well be, in many classes, some boys and girls who will need few, if any, reading experiences with charts or with published reading-readiness materials before they begin regular book reading. The proportion of charts and reading-readiness books that should be used varies with factors such as the books available and the needs and interests of the pupils.

A main objective of experience charts can be not only growth in reading, but also development in one or more of the other facets of communication. For example, a second-grade class might make a series of charts on interesting experiences they have had—not to increase their ability to read but to help them remember important details or to obtain valuable practice in written communication. Or, with the assistance of the teacher, boys and girls could make individual experience charts, in which they tell their classmates about events that are important in their lives.

The Basal Reader Program

Since reading is a complex skill, many teachers favor a program of reading instruction that is highly controlled, both as to vocabulary and as to other phases of skill development. Such a program is the one popularly known as the basal reader program. In it one or more series of reading textbooks serve as the core of the reading program. It is the program followed in part or in entirety in the majority of the schools in the United States.

Description of Basal Reader Series

The authors and publishers of basal reader series set out to devise materials that can serve as the center around which systematic reading instruction can be organized. They attempt to present a psychologically sound sequence for the development of needed reading skills.

Materials Included in Basal Reader Series

A basal reader series is frequently designed for use from the readiness-for-reading stage through grade six, but many series also include the junior high school in their range. In most series each book is labeled in some manner to indicate its position within the series. Commonly the placement is shown either through designation of the name of the level or by either numerical or alphabetical labeling. While it is hoped by the publishers that the levels are indicated without promoting undue notice on the part of students, the majority of students probably figure out the code that is used. The table on this page illustrates all three of these methods of labeling.

Various types of materials to accompany the basal readers are included in the series. Many, especially for the lower levels, have consumable books that are sometimes referred to as "activity books," but are more commonly called workbooks. In these the boys and girls record their responses to questions asked or directions given in the pupils' and/or the teacher's books. The questions and directions reinforce the

Name Designation		Level	Level
R	(readiness)	1	A
PP	(first preprimer)	2	B
PP	(second preprimer)	3	C
PP	(third preprimer)	4	D
P	(primer)	5	E
1	(book 1)	6	F
2^1	(book 2; first book)	7	G
2^2	(book 2; second book)	8	H
3^1	(book 3; first book)	9	I
3^2	(book 3; second book)	10	J
4	(book 4)	11	K
5	(book 5)	12	L
6	(book 6)	13	M

learning acquired through study of the basal readers of the series. Many series also provide supplementary story books for additional practice on vocabulary presented in the readers or on phonic elements being studied. Some include picture cards to be used in the development of concepts with which the reading material deals or word cards with words found in the beginning books of the series. Suggestions for the teacher, if not included with the content of the pupils' books in a teacher's edition, are often bound separately in paperback form.

Although most basal readers are alike in that they are essentially based on learning a hierarchy of reading skills, there are major differences among them. Some of these variations are in: (a) vocabulary, as to choice of words, number of "new words" per page, repetition of "new words," and basis of selection; (b) illustrations, as to type, frequency of use, and purpose; (c) content; (d) style of writing; (e) supplementary materials; and (f) type of approach to skill development.

Controls in Basal Readers

Most basal reader series contain several controls, one of the most important of which is that of vocabulary. The words to be selected are often determined in part by earlier studies of words lists compiled to show frequency of use of words on various reading levels. The type and number of new words presented per page is regulated, as well as the repetition of words on the pages on which they first occur and on later pages.

In materials for boys and girls advanced beyond the beginning stages, the control of the vocabulary continues though it becomes decreasingly rigid. While in materials for the beginning stages of learning to read the aim of most writers is to select only words that are already in the learner's speaking and listening vocabulary, one of the objectives in vocabulary development with older boys and girls is to increase, through reading, not only their reading vocabulary but also their speaking, listening, and writing vocabularies. Partly in order to achieve this objective, there are included in readers beyond those for beginners a limited number of words whose meaning presumably has not previously been known to the learner.

One very important characteristic of most basal readers, which is usually not apparent merely upon examination of the pupils' books, but is emphasized in guidelines for the teacher, is the strict control of the hierarchy of reading skills being developed (in addition to vocabulary development, to which we have already referred). Authors and publishers strive to include all needed basic reading skills, with a range from the simpler to the more complex.

Another control exercised in many basal readers is that of the length of the sentence, along with other factors contributing to the complexity of a sentence. Thus, readability of sentences is given attention. The content of readers is also structured in the attempt to provide material that is on the level of understanding of the pupil, that is interesting to him, and that, as far as the total program is concerned, provides variety. Of late, many writers of textbooks have been careful to include stories with multiracial characters and multicultural settings and have recognized in their choice of content the background of boys and girls who are economically deprived. The authors of the readers thus are cognizant of the challenge given as criticism of many basal readers of the past for the lower grades, that they deal almost exclusively with Caucasian, middle-income suburban families. Consideration is also being given to equal representation of the sexes. Special attention is paid to the selection of suitable print for the age level for which a book is intended and to the appropriateness of the illustrations in terms of interest and/or informational value.

Teaching Procedures

Basal readers are used by teachers and pupils in a great variety of ways even when they form the core of the reading program. Some teachers limit their reading instruction solely or chiefly to the use of basal readers; others make considerable use of other reading materials. Some follow one type or set of procedures while others employ quite different ones.

Teachers' manuals or guidebooks provide the teacher with many suggestions for using the basal readers. While there are many variations in the suggestions given and in the ways in which teachers proceed in using the basal readers, often these three parts are followed or recommended for a typical lesson: (a) preparation for the reading; (b) directed reading; and (c) follow-up activities.

Preparation for Reading

During the initial step in teaching a lesson from a basal reader attention is often given to the following points:

1. Interesting the learner in reading the selection
2. Development of concepts important to the understanding of the selection
3. Study of "new words"—new to the pupils' reading and/or meaning vocabulary
4. Establishment of a purpose for reading.

Directed Reading

The sequence and procedure listed below is at times followed in this step:

1. Silent reading—Typically in lower grades the material is broken up into parts for silent reading, with an increase in length of the parts with more advanced learners. Beginning readers may be asked to read silently only one sentence at a time, as for example, when the teacher might say, "Read the next sentence to find out what Bobby's mother wanted for her birthday." By the time the pupils are reading in a sixth-grade book, and even before, the selection for directed reading for the day's study may be divided into only two or three parts, or the entire selection may be assigned for uninterrupted reading.
2. Discussion or question-and-answer procedure—Following each part read silently there may be discussion of content or questions may be asked, to check or increase comprehension or extend vocabulary.
3. Identification of purpose for reading subsequent parts of the selection if it is broken up into parts for the silent reading.
4. Oral reading—Sometimes the pupils are asked to read certain parts to answer questions or to prove a point. Reading may be done by parts, especially in the lower grades, with different pupils assigned the words of the various characters, providing direct quotations are used. Oral reading may also take place

as a follow-up activity, as, for example, when the boys and girls decide to give a play.

Follow-up Activities

As a rule, follow-up activities, either skill-development activities or enrichment activities, may consist of procedures for helping the pupil learn better to recognize words in written form, to increase his power to comprehend what he reads, to locate information, or to read at appropriate rates. Frequently workbooks are used during this phase of the activity.

Enrichment activities may include: (a) introduction to related projects in art or music; (b) reference to books on the topic of the day's selection; (c) reading of one or more poems that deal with the subject; (d) making plans for a dramatic production. Participation in enrichment activities may take place on the day of the lesson and/or on later days. Such activities afford an excellent opportunity to integrate the various facets of the language arts.

Evaluation

Among the alleged strengths of the basal reader program, stressed by persons favoring it as the core of reading instruction, are the following:

1. The basal reader program provides an organizational plan in which skills, including among others those related to vocabulary, are presented in a carefully controlled sequence, with no important ones omitted and with provisions for an appropriate amount of practice. The contention is that the classroom teacher, in many instances, has neither the time nor the knowledge of reading instruction to teach the needed skills effectively without the guidance given in a sound basal reader program.

2. The teachers' manuals or guides give helpful and varied aids to effective teaching.
3. By means of the basal readers as a core program inexperienced as well as experienced teachers can teach with success.
4. The basal reader series have a variety of interesting, worthwhile content, progressively more difficult and suited to the child who is provided with the books on his level of reading performance.

Counter arguments include:

1. Teachers with much knowledge about the teaching of reading can devise an outline of reading skills to be taught to their pupils or they can make use of some such listings available in print.
2. Though there are many useful suggestions in teachers' manuals, they do not constitute the only source of helpful ideas as to teaching procedures. Magazine articles, books on the teaching of reading, ideas from other teachers, creative thoughts on the part of the teacher can all serve as rich sources.
3. Although it is undeniably true that an inexperienced teacher, not highly skilled in the art of teaching reading, may find it very difficult to teach reading effectively without the guidance provided in a basal reader series, there are teachers who teach reading effectively without basal readers.
4. The basal reader, interesting and worthwhile though its content may be, is not the only source of such material, to wit, the wealth of excellent books for boys and girls. There are many ways in which the teacher can help the child select wisely material on his reading level in sources other than basal readers.

The following is a list of other criticisms often made of basal readers; possible responses to them are listed in parentheses.

1. Strict adherence to the teacher's manual may lead to class procedures that are boring for children and/or inhibit the creativity of the teacher. (Response: The teacher should not follow without deviation the suggestions in a teacher's manual but should select those that are of value to the boys and girls he is teaching. He should also feel free to include desirable activities not proposed in the manual. If learning to read from a basal reader series is boring, the fault may rest not in the series but in the teacher.)
2. Some boys and girls may already possess or not be ready for the skills recommended for development in connection with a given selection. (Response: If a pupil is already master of a skill recommended for development or reinforcement in the teacher's guidebook for a given lesson, he should not be required to have instruction on it. Similarly, if he is not ready for the acquisition of a certain skill, instruction in the use of it should be postponed for him.)
3. Some children are stimulated more to read if they can select their own reading material. (Response: Even if a basal reader series is used as the core of the reading program, boys and girls can and should be given many opportunities to select their own reading materials, in their independent reading.)
4. Differences in learning styles of boys and girls are usually not honored when basal readers are used. (Response: Intelligent use of basal readers does not prohibit the teacher from honoring the differences among boys and girls, as he adapts instruction accordingly.)

5. Strict vocabulary control in the beginning books of a series makes the language stilted and the ideas presented uninteresting and/or uninformative. *(Response:* The beginning reader, who has a limited vocabulary, is over-burdened if he is introduced to many new words in rapid succession.*)*

6. Workbooks accompanying the readers are boring and often do not fit the needs of the boys and girls. *(Response:* Wise use of workbooks can make this criticism invalid.*)*

7. The stories in many basal readers lack literary merit. *(Response:* Publishers are including more literary materials in readers for middle grades than were included, as a rule, during several decades preceding the '60s. However, to do so on a major scale on the lower levels admittedly is difficult, if not well-nigh impossible. With the highly limited reading vocabulary of the beginner most materials of literary merit are beyond his power of reading. An answer given to this dilemma is that, to make up for lack of such materials in the readers, the teacher should read or tell stories of value to the boys and girls.*)*

8. Much of the material in beginning readers deals with middle-class, Caucasian families and thus does not provide sufficient, if any, reference to the life style of a large number of the boys and girls who are using the books as basal readers. *(Response:* Publishers during the past few decades have tried to correct this shortcoming, but in many series the introduction of material dealing with multi-racial or low-income living situations has not been typical of those that many ethnically different or socio-economically deprived children meet. However, the basal readers could be supplemented in this respect by material in the field of literature for boys and girls, which affords wide resources for all children to gain acquaintance with other cultures and ethnic groups. Such books contain stories about children who share heritages that are different and more diverse than those included in basal readers and thus they provide for more intensive follow-up of readings in many areas.*)*

Since basal reader series differ greatly, care needs to be taken in their selection. A series should be chosen to meet the needs of the school making the adoption. These are among points about a series that may advisedly be studied before a selection is made: (1) the number of books in a series, (2) the authorship, (3) the date of publication or of the last revision, (4) supplementary materials available in the series, (5) the nature of the skill-development program, (6) the teachers' manual or guide, (7) recognition in selection of content of multi-racial and multi-ethnic cultures and of varying socio-economic levels, (8) attention to extent to which content does not stereotype gender roles, (9) the interest and worth of the content, (10) the format, and, of course, (11) the cost.

"Development of Comprehension Skills through Reading Lessons" (see p. 202) provides further discussion of the basal reader program. (See also Chapter 15, p. 413.)

The Individualized Reading Program

The wide range in reading ability and in other traits of the boys and girls in the same classroom make attention to individual differences mandatory. Teachers using the language-experience approach, if they are to attain maximum results, will find many opportunities to adapt their teaching procedures to the interests and needs of individuals. The effective teacher using a basal reader series as the core of his program will also need to plan his work so that variations among the boys and girls are considered.

That it is important to plan any program of reading instruction with due attention to the persons being taught is not a matter of argument in discussing any system of individualized reading. The point of dispute hinges on whether the core of the program should be individualized reading. It is such a program that we are here considering. Essentially it is one worked out by Jeannette Veatch.[1] The words *Individualized Reading* are hereafter in this book written with initial capital letters to indicate when a reading program has been organized chiefly on an individualized basis.

Description of the Program

Common elements that underlie Individualized Reading as practiced in numerous schools and school systems are: (1) the use within a classroom of many books diversified as to subject of the books, interest, and reading level; (2) major emphasis on self-selection of reading materials by the child, (3) individual conferences between the teacher and the child, (4) a good record-keeping system, and (5) pupil reporting on books. In general, the skills of reading are taught in connection with problems the child actually encounters while reading. However, Individualized Reading requires no rigid formula and the procedures differ greatly from teacher to teacher.

[1]Jeannette Veatch, *How To Teach Reading with Children's Books* (New York: Teachers College, 1964); *Individualizing Your Reading* (New York: Putnam, 1959); *Reading in the Elementary School* (New York: Ronald, 1966).

Though the procedure is varied and supplemented in numerous ways according to the needs of the learner and the creativity and philosophy of the teacher, typically an Individualized Reading program can be described as follows. In a classroom well equipped with books on a large variety of subjects and on different levels of difficulty, most of the boys and girls during the reading period will read books of their choice independently, while the teacher, confers with one pupil at a time. During the conference the teacher may listen to the child read orally and ask questions about his silent reading in order to determine the child's level of achievement, his strengths, and his weaknesses. The teacher provides help as needed and may guide, but not control, the child's future reading. Most of the reading is in general books, although the child may choose to read selections in basal readers, depending, in part, on their availability in the classroom or elsewhere. At times, flexible groups will be organized temporarily, in order to work on a common problem—often a skill-development problem. At other times, also, two or more pupils may work together to plan a presentation that they will give for the entire class—possibly a play based on a book they have enjoyed or a choral reading program of some poems they like. In some Individualized Reading programs pupils may be encouraged to keep a record of books read. They might also keep a written account of some of the acquired learnings, such as additions to vocabulary or generalizations related to reading skills, which they have learned to apply in other areas or to difficulties encountered. The teacher, too, keeps a record, making notations on each child's strengths and weaknesses, on progress made, and on "next steps" in needed help. Preferably he makes most of these notes during or immediately after individual conferences or small-group meetings. Careful record keeping by the teacher is an essential of an effective Individualized Reading program.

Evaluation

Many teachers seriously doubt the young child's ability to select reading material best suited to his needs. Another point of criticism of the plan, as voiced by some of its critics, is the necessarily limited length and/or the infrequency of the individual conferences a teacher can hold with each child. In a classroom of 25 pupils, it is doubtful whether a teacher could have more than one or two five-or-six minute conferences with each child during the course of a week. Therefore, to some critics it seems impossible for the teacher to accomplish effectively the multiplicity of tasks that are commonly designated for the conference period. Many also fear that skill development will not be effectively promoted in the Individualized Reading program. Furthermore, a teacher, who has many responsibilities in addition to teaching reading, cannot spend as much time in preparation for Individualized Reading as is necessary, without neglecting other areas of study. Critics of the plan as described here usually favor Individualized Reading as a supplement or a complement to a basal reader program, rather than as the core program of reading instruction. They assert that the advantages claimed for Individualized Reading can be achieved when two programs—a basal reader program and elements of an Individualized Reading program—are used jointly.

What are the alleged advantages as set forth by the proponents of Individualized Reading? Foremost among them is the claim that the method is instrumental in developing in more children a love for reading and habits of extensive independent reading. They state that it contributes to a happy, carefree climate in the classroom, builds self-confidence in children, and removes insidious distinctions between "slow" and "fast" readers.

At the present time we turn in vain to research to settle the argument for and against Individualized Reading. Studies that have been made do not reveal dramatic gains or significant losses in the pupils' performance under Individualized Reading as measured by standardized reading tests. It can be argued that, with teachers of comparable ability and creativity and with equally suitable instructional materials, there is no proven superiority of Individualized Reading over basal reader programs that stress the sequential development of reading skills.

In any case, the inexperienced teacher not trained in the techniques of Individualized Reading and lacking the advantage of a sympathetic, able supervisor is well advised not to plunge into the program. It is best to study the plan first, examine carefully books, articles, and manuals on the subject, and then to make tentative beginnings. Of supreme importance, also, is a wide knowledge of books for children. The young teacher who has not had a sound course in literature for children should probably spend at least a year in reading books for children and consulting the numerous guides, commentaries, and lists now available concerning children's books before launching an Individualized Reading program.

The Eclectic Approach

Now as in the past, many teachers are not committed to using any one program—the language-experience, the basal-reader, or the Individualized Reading approach. Some may prefer to use primarily the Individualized Reading approach with one or a few of the boys and girls in a room, while others may choose to use a combination of two or all three of these approaches in planning their own program of reading instruction. For best results, such combinations vary from one teaching-learning situation to another, because of differences between teachers and learners, and because of other factors. To help aid them in the selection of the elements of the various approaches, teachers can rely in part on the diagnosis of the reading ability of their pupils (see Chapter 12, "Classroom Diagnosis of Reading Ability," p. 337). They can also evaluate their own strengths and weaknesses as teachers, based in part on their philosophy of education, as they seek to establish an effective program of reading instruction (see Chapter 15, "Implementation of the Reading Program on a Schoolwide Basis," p. 406).

Here are listed a few of the ways in which a teacher basing his reading program primarily on the language-experience approach can make use of some of the salient features emphasized in a basal-reader program.

1. Pay careful attention to development of the child's skill in recognizing recorded words. The teacher can observe a sequential program in word recognition as he emphasizes needed skills in connection with words used in a language-experience chart, as well as in connection with other words that have some element in common.
2. Incorporate in the program the development of reading skills in addition to those connected with vocabulary development. The teacher may use as check a list of skills, such as finding the main idea or locating information in a dictionary, that are identified in the guidebooks of some basal readers or other

lists available in print. Or after considerable study he may compile his own list.
3. Use basal readers as a supplement even though the program is based primarily on a language-experience approach.

The teacher who uses chiefly a language-experience approach can also incorporate in his teaching many of the major characteristics of Individualized Reading. With careful attention to the needs of individuals, he can, for example, guide the children in the selection of topics for language-arts charts on their level of achievement and interest. Similarly, as he encourages participation in work on a chart, he can have in mind the needs of each child. Furthermore, he can encourage the boys and girls to choose some of their reading materials supplementary to the material produced in connection with a language-experience approach. Ideally suited to attention to individual differences are those times when the teacher assists one pupil alone in the construction of his own chart.

In the list above it is indicated that the hierarchy of reading skills deemed important for each pupil to acquire, those emphasized in many basal-reader programs, can also be developed in a language-experience program. The emphasis placed on these skills in basal readers can be reinforced through reading done concurrently in a language-experience approach. Thus when basal readers form the core of the reading program, factors characteristic of the language-experience approach can be used to complement or supplement the former.

In an Individualized Reading program of the type described in preceding pages (see p. 52), basal readers are at times used by at least some of the boys and girls. However, in such a program they are not required reading but are available to them on the same basis as other reading materials—as they choose materials they wish to read. Furthermore, during individual conferences, so characteristic a feature of Individualized Reading, the teacher can strive to determine which reading skills each individual needs to develop. Thereupon he can provide needed help through individual or small-group instruction. As need and interest are evident in the Individualized Reading program, language-experience charts can be used to advantage.

Long before the program of Individualized Reading described in this chapter attracted national attention, teachers have used individualized reading techniques along with the language experience and the basal reader approach, allowing the child at times to *seek* reading material, *choose* that which interests him, and *work at his own rate* with what he has chosen. Many have made use of individual conferences and have kept records to indicate the quantity and quality of materials read, the specific skills worked on, and the development of interests as they unfold. Teachers desirous of fitting instruction to the individual are continuing, in many classrooms, to proceed thus in an eclectic program regardless of their major approach to reading instruction.

In Part II, "Cultivating Growth in Reading," the reader is advised to consider how each of the skills discussed in those chapters can fit in advantageously in whatever major approach to reading is in operation in a classroom. He is also requested to note how the suggestions given in Part III, "The Reading Program in Action," may, in many cases, apply to all of these chief ways of teaching reading. As he studies the remaining chapters of this book, it is hoped that one of the abilities he will acquire is skill in recognizing how an effective program can be constructed, with a wise combination of important aspects of the approaches that are described in this chapter.

For Further Study

Auckerman, Robert C., *Approaches to Beginning Reading* (New York: Wiley, 1971).

Bush, Clifford, L., and Mildred H. Huebner, *Strategies for Reading in the Elementary School*, 2d ed. (New York: Macmillan, 1979), Ch. 10, "Reading Programs: Structure."

Gans, Roma, *Guiding Children's Reading Through Experiences*, 2d ed. (New York: Teachers College Press, 1979).

Hall, Maryanne, *Teaching Reading as a Language Experience*, 2d ed. (Columbus, Ohio: Charles E. Merrill, 1976).

Heilman, Arthur W., *Principles and Practices of Teaching Reading*, 4th ed. (Columbus, Ohio: Charles E. Merrill, 1977), pp. 306–322.

Lamb, Pose, and Richard Arnold, eds. *Teaching Reading: Foundations and Strategies*, 2d ed. (Belmont, Cal.: Wadsworth Publishing Company, 1980), Ch. 9, "Preparing the Child," by Lloyd Ollila.

Smith, Richard J., and Dale D. Johnson, *Teaching Children to Read* (Menlo Park, Calif.: Addison-Wesley, 1976), Ch. 5, "Selecting Reading Materials and Approaches," and Ch. 6, "Using the Language-Experience Approach."

Veatch, Jeannette, *Reading in the Elementary School*, 2d ed. (New York: Wiley, 1978).

Veatch, Jeannette; Florence Sawicki; Geraldine Elliott; Eleanor Barnette; and Janis Blakely, *Key Words to Reading: The Language-Experience Approach Begins* (Columbus, Ohio: Charles E. Merrill, 1973).

Weitzman, Lenore J., and Diane Rizzo, *Biased Textbooks: A Research Perspective* (Washington, D. C.: The National Foundation for the Improvement of Education, 1974).

Wilson, Robert M., and Maryanne Hall, *Reading and the Elementary School Child* (New York: Van Nostrand, 1972), Ch. 4, "Basic Approaches to Reading Instruction."

Questions and Comments for Thought and Discussion

1. Use of basal readers for reading instruction is the most prevalent approach in the United States. Speculate on the reasons for this occurrence and project the extent of its continuance. Consider what means a faculty could devise for curriculum development in which alternative approaches might be adopted without sacrifice to student progress.

2. If learning to read has as its purpose the acquiring of reading as a habit, what prevents teachers from releasing children to the existing literature more often for recreatory reasons during the school day? What effects might this practice have upon the development of reading as a lifelong interest and upon the development of interests through reading?

3. It may be possible for you to visit some elementary schools that use some of the different approaches to reading instruction discussed in this chapter. In making preparation for your visit it might be wise to examine appropriate reading materials so that your observation of the teaching method would be more meaningful.

4. The text and the illustrations of some basal readers have been found racist, sexist, and classist in their biased treatment of these differences in society. As you examine both content and illustration of some series, what is your reaction to this criticism?

5. Critics of basal readers claim that the techniques used for vocabulary reinforcement (controlled vocabulary) result in syntax that bears little resemblance to natural language usage. You may wish to examine the proportion of offerings in basal readers which are taken from literature for children to counteract the effect of stilted language of some stories. Is there recourse to a balanced rendering as to numbers and kinds of stories? If not, what can a teacher do to provide for balance?

6. If you were to have in your classroom children from countries other than the United States, how might the language-experience approach be used to build common vocabulary for both teacher and pupils through capitalizing on the learner's experiences?

7. In your classroom observations have you seen teachers using the basal reader, the language-experience, the Individualized Reading, or an eclectic approach? If so, what points of implementation of the program seemed particularly noteworthy to you, either because of their desirability or undesirability?

Part II

Cultivating Growth in Reading

5A

Readiness for Reading

Readiness for a task implies that an individual is ready to perform or learn to perform the task. Among other factors, it requires that he has previously acquired skills necessary for learning the task with comparative ease. For example, to be ready to learn how to take notes on a talk, one must have learned how to write, even though excellence in writing is not a requirement. Before a child is ready to look up words in a dictionary, he needs to have familiarity with alphabetical order. However, possession of that skill is not enough to assure readiness for using a dictionary. General maturational level, desire to learn to use a dictionary (coupled with purpose for doing so), power of sustained attention equal to the task—these and other factors may play a significant part in determining whether a child is ready to begin learning to use a dictionary.

Readiness, as applied to reading, is a broad term that can be used appropriately at every level of reading instruction. Thus, developing reading readiness may refer to the help given in preparing an individual for initial reading instruction, as well as to that which is given to prepare him for the next step, whatever it may be, in the instructional sequence.

While recognizing that readiness should be a matter of concern throughout the various stages of reading instruction, in this and in the following chapter, however, we are dealing only with those readiness factors that precede, at least in part, reading instruction. Attention to readiness for later stages of learning to read is given at various places in later chapters in terms of suggested or implied sequences.

When should reading instruction begin? Currently that is one of the crucial, unsettled questions in the field of teaching reading. In the earlier part of the century there were staunch advocates favoring postponement of reading instruction beyond the first grade. In fact, until fairly recently, many persons in the forefront of educational thinking proposed that systematic instruction in that grade should be preceded by a so-called reading readiness period. Often this period extended over a month or six weeks or more for all boys and girls. Frequently, it was even longer for some pupils. It was not unusual for one or more first-grade children in a room to spend the entire year in "getting ready to read." Now, however, educators are seriously questioning the need for a period of reading readiness for many boys and girls in the first grade.

An assumption upon which kindergarten programs had been planned ever since the rise of the kindergarten movement is now the subject of marked, at times bitter, disagreement. The argument centers around the role of the kindergarten in teaching reading, as well as its proper place in helping the child to become ready to learn to read.

A more radical position is highlighted as the controversy revolves around the question of whether reading instruction should begin in prekindergarten days.[1,2] Of the people favoring prekindergarten instruction in reading some, like Glenn Doman,[3] believe that it should start in the home. Others are of the opinion that provisions for an early beginning in reading should be made through publicly supported agencies.

[1]Dolores Durkin, *Children Who Read Early* (New York: Teachers College, 1966).
[2]Joseph E. Brzeinski, "Beginning Reading in Denver," *The Reading Teacher*, vol. 18 (October 1964), pp. 16–21.
[3]Glenn Doman, *How To Teach Your Baby To Read* (New York: Random House, 1964).

Bases for the Controversy about the Time To Begin Reading Instruction

One reason for the divergent views concerning the optimum time to begin reading instruction is that some teachers, when discussing the point, may be referring to somewhat formal teaching of reading and others to more informal instruction. There is also lack of unanimity in differentiating between *readiness for reading* and *reading*. For example, some teachers consider learning the letters of the alphabet and the sounds represented by them as part of reading readiness. Others refer to this process as reading. Work with experience charts—records of the experiences of the children—is thought of by some as reading, by others as reading-readiness procedure. However, even if all problems in semantics were removed, there would remain marked differences of opinion as to the best time to begin reading instruction. Furthermore, there is no rigid line of demarcation between reading-readiness and reading activities.

Another factor that complicates discussion of the question as to when reading instruction should begin is that teachers differ in the extent to which they will continue into the learning-to-read period some of the types of work begun during the period of reading readiness. One teacher might, for example, at first during the learning-to-read period continue to help boys and girls differentiate between the appearance of letters and words—visual discrimination—a practice he may have emphasized during the reading-readiness period. Another teacher, utilizing a similar procedure before beginning reading instruction, might discontinue it after the children begin to read.

Arguments Advanced for Earlier Instruction

Keeping in mind the difference in interpretation of what constitutes reading readiness, let us examine the arguments advanced favoring earlier instruction in reading.

The Reading-Readiness Period in First Grade

Opponents of the practice of having a reading-readiness period as customary procedure in the beginning weeks or months of the first grade point out that first-grade children of today differ greatly from boys and girls of a few decades ago in their readiness for reading as far as factors amenable to environmental stimulation are concerned. These persons state that the average six-year-old has traveled more extensively, has viewed television programs more frequently, has been in closer contact with people who have seen more of the world, has had more out-of-the-home experiences than children of the preceding generation. Since much of the usual readiness program of the past has consisted of efforts to broaden the pupils' backgrounds, it is claimed that a major purpose of postponement of reading at the beginning of the first grade has already been met by today's entrants to first grade. Furthermore, those favoring elimination of a reading-readiness period at the beginning of the first grade for the average child point out that a greatly increased number of boys and girls now attend kindergarten and that kindergartens avowedly have had as an objective, concomitant with the major aims of the kindergarten, to help boys and girls through ongoing activities to get ready to read and many even provide reading instruction. Moreover, many persons opposed to a reading-readiness period for all or almost all beginning first-grade pupils claim that the somewhat formalized instruction that boys and girls have often been receiving in the form of reading-readiness exercises—such as discriminating between sounds, between letters, and between words, as well as many other activities of reading-readiness workbooks—may be either below the learning level of the child or somewhat irrelevant to the task of learning to read.

The argument as usually advanced against a reading-readiness period in first grade is not against such a period for any one child or group of children in that grade. It is in opposition to a requirement that all or almost all children go through such a stage after they enter first grade. The claim is that only a minority of first-grade entrants are not ready to begin to read. That a sizable number has previously started to read is also pointed out to support the argument against a reading-readiness period for all. The broader experiences many pre-first-grade children have is given as further argument.

The Role of the Kindergarten in Learning To Read

In the not very distant past it was rather universally conceded that reading instruction had no place in the kindergarten. It was also generally agreed that the activities in the kindergarten that were included, in part at least, to help the child become ready to read should be limited to activities such as helping the child develop emotionally and socially, assisting him in expanding his experiences, and guiding his language development. Efforts to assist him in becoming ready for reading through a systematic program for the development of reading readiness were generally looked upon with disfavor. Learning the names of the letters of the alphabet and the sounds

they commonly represent was considered inappropriate at the kindergarten level. All these assumptions have been vigorously attacked by educators who support the position that the the kindergarten should play a significant role in preparing the child for beginning reading.

It has been claimed that teaching reading to five-year-olds may affect the left side of the brain unfavorably.[4] It may be that further studies to support or contradict this allegation will be forthcoming.

In spite of the existing controversy about the role of reading or prereading instruction in the kindergarten, today the kindergarten in which attention is not given to reading instruction for some boys and girls, as well as to activities closely related to book reading, is probably the exception. The primary concern no longer is: "Should reading be taught in the kindergarten?" Rather, the points of study and debate now focus on these questions:

1. To whom should reading be taught in the kindergarten?
2. What reading should be taught?
3. How should reading be taught?

Evidence Cited

Many books and articles argue for an earlier start in reading by citing evidence that reading has been learned by young children, both on the kindergarten and prekindergarten level.

Studies on the Prekindergarten Level

Two studies to which reference is often made in arguing for the effectiveness of reading instruction during the prekindergarten period are a study by Dolores Dur-

[4]Raymond Hook, "Dangers of Early Emphasis on Reading." *Intellect*, Mar. 1978, p. 352.

kin[5] and the Denver study.[6] A brief report on these studies follows.

A Study by Dolores Durkin Durkin carried on a longitudinal study with forty-nine children in California who learned to read outside of school. The boys and girls in her study initially learned to read at ages varying from three to five. When the children entered first grade the average reading achievement of those who learned at three years of age was 2.6 in terms of grade placement, while that of those who began to read at five was 1.7.[7]

Durkin reports the results of her longitudinal studies, which had been a target of her attention for ten years, in her book *Children Who Read Early*, a definitive work in the area.[8] One of the points that stands out in the research by Durkin is that the children were commonly described by parents, and later by teachers, as persistent, perfectionistic, and competitive children. A majority of them had, their parents and teachers agreed, extraordinary memories and possessed high ability to concentrate. In addition, they were described as curious, conscientious, serious-minded, persistent, and self-reliant. In all instances there were parents who took the time to answer children's questions; and there were older siblings who were both willing and able to teach interested brothers and sisters to read.

The Denver Study Another concern related to early reading instruction was one of the phases of the teaching of reading investigated by the public schools of Denver under a grant by the Carnegie Corporation. The grant enabled the school system to review and extend its parental instruction program. Much was accomplished in parent education through a series of lessons in the form of television programs and a parents' manual. Brzeinski[9] reports:

> Tests administered to parents showed that they could learn the pilot beginning reading process and use it to help their four- and five-year-olds to read. Also encouraging was the discovery that mothers and fathers who spent a reasonable amount of time [as little as five minutes a day of planned, regular help] preparing their children for reading were quite successful.

Studies on the Kindergarten Level

Arguments for initiating reading instruction in kindergarten include references to experimental studies in which kindergarten children have been taught to read. A phase of the Denver studies,[10,11] with the aid of a grant from the Cooperative Research Branch of the U.S. Office of Education, was designed to ascertain the effectiveness of reading instruction in the kindergarten. Four thousand boys and girls were tested at the end of the kindergarten, as well as at the end of the first, second, and third years in the elementary school.

[5]Durkin

[6]Brzeinski

[7]Dolores Durkin, "Some Unanswered Questions about Five-Year-Olds and Reading," *Changing Concepts of Reading Instruction*, vol. VI, proceedings of the Annual Convention (Newark, Del.: International Reading Association, 1961), pp. 167–170.

[8]Durkin, *Children Who Read Early*.

[9]Joseph E. Brzeinski, "Early Introduction to Reading— The Kindergarten," *New Directions in Reading*, Ralph Staiger and David A. Sohn, eds. (New York: Bantam, 1967), p. 28.

[10]Joseph E. Brzeinski, "Reading in the Kindergarten," *Teaching Young Children To Read*, Warren G. Cutts, ed., bulletin 1964, no. 19 (Washington, D.C.: U.S. Department of Health, Education and Welfare, 1964).

[11]Brzeinski, "Early Introduction to Reading," pp. 25–32.

The children who were in the experimental group showed superiority in size of reading vocabulary, in comprehension, and in rates of reading over those in the control group at each of these intervals. Brzeinski, when reporting on the study, also claimed that children who learn to read early enjoy it, and consequently will be more likely to read extensively than other children as a group.

Comments on Arguments for Earlier Instruction

Although an increasing amount of research deals with the question of an early start in reading and a sizable number of experimenters have concluded that on the basis of their work an early start in reading seems desirable, the evidence has not been conclusive. More longitudinal studies will need to be completed before many educators are willing to take anything as a final answer. Evidence undoubtedly shows that children—at least some children—can learn to read earlier than most boys and girls now do. Whether or not it is desirable for many of them to start learning to read at an early age has not been established.

In the Kindergarten

Opponents of reading instruction in the kindergarten argue that because a child of kindergarten age can learn to read is not sufficient reason to conclude that he should be taught reading at that period of his life. James L. Hymes, Jr., for example, sounds this warning: "Everyone loses if we produce early readers but in the process weaken humans. Everyone loses if we produce early readers but in the process kill the joy of reading."[12]

Questions such as these, in addition to those listed on page 64, must be considered in connection with teaching reading in the kindergarten.

1. Does teaching reading require time that should be spent on other types of activities?
2. Are methods used in teaching reading to the beginner in violation of the principles that should govern learning at that stage of the development of the child?
3. Are the children who learn to read in the kindergarten superior in their reading achievement to others by the time they leave the elementary school? (In answering this question care must be taken that children who learned to read early are compared with children equated for intelligence, home conditions, and other factors that may have contributed to making the pupils who learn to read early a selected group, even though it has been claimed that high intelligence is not an attribute of early readers as a group.)
4. Is there danger that the child who learns to read early may in later years lose, if he has already acquired, a love for reading?

In Preschool Days

As a group first-grade teachers have been quite vocal in their opposition to teaching reading at home to the preschool child. One argument frequently advanced by teachers is that many parents are not trained to teach reading. However, it would seem doubtful that a child who wants to learn to read before he enters school would be harmed much, if at all, through lack of professional training in the field of reading by his tutor, the parent. Undoubtedly, if preschool reading instruction is proved to be desirable, then it may well be the province of the school or some other agency to provide parents with information on the

---

[12]James L. Hymes, Jr., "Early Reading Is Very Risky Business," *Grade Teacher*, 82 (March 1965), p. 88.

subject. Some literature is already on the market advising parents as to how to teach their children to read or how to prepare them for reading. The book *Preparing Your Child for Reading* supplemented assistance given to parents of kindergarten children in the Denver experiment who listened to a sixteen-lesson television series on the subject. Whether one agrees or disagrees with the methods recommended in any one publication, it cannot be denied that many books could be published to help parents. Furthermore, the schools could sponsor workshops, provide lecture series, give demonstrations, and circulate bulletins designed to assist parents in guiding their children in learning to read. One point that should be emphasized in a program of parent education is that no preschool child should be forced to learn to read.

Another contention of many first-grade teachers is that parents should not help boys and girls of preschool age with reading because a parent may use a different method of teaching reading than the one that will be employed in the school. The child may, the argument continues, encounter greater difficulties in reading at school than he would be likely to meet if he had not had parental guidance. However, it seems difficult to imagine that a child taught at home by, let us say, a whole-word method would be handicapped if later at school he were taught by a phonic method, or vice-versa.

Still another reason why many first-grade teachers object to teaching the child to read before he comes to school is that they claim the child will then become bored if he is placed in a reading group of children without previous reading experiences. That argument is a poor one for the school to offer. A drastic change needs to be made in a lockstep program that requires a child who can read when he enters school to be treated as if he had no knowledge of read-

ing. If there are others in the room who can read, he can be placed in a group with them. If he is the only one who can read, he can be given individualized instruction.

Even though in the preceding paragraphs an attempt has been made to refute the common arguments teachers propose against preschool learning to read, there are serious questions to be raised about preschool reading. Because many preschool children *can* be taught to read, it does not necessarily follow that they *should* be taught to read. "What is to be gained by an early start?" needs to be investigated. More than parental pride in the achievement of a child at an early age must be the underlying purpose. Whether or not the child who learns to read in preschool days is spending time on learning to read that should advisedly be used for other activities is a point to be considered seriously. What effect learning to read at an early age may have on his reading later on, in terms of both reading skills and attitudes toward reading, should also be studied carefully, not only in connection with reading in the kindergarten but also in relation to reading at home on the part of the prekindergarten child.

It needs to be borne in mind that, whether or not research supports earlier teaching of reading, societal mores are such that increasing numbers of children whose parents are working are exposed to a variety of informal settings in which more extended learnings are acquired than in some homes. A growing number of children are exposed to early childhood education opportunities, such as day-care centers or other organized preschool experiences.

The extensive research literature on reading readiness now available proves, if nothing else, that the problem related to the time for beginning reading instruction, like all questions associated with human learning in general, is complex and that there is need for further investigation. We must remember, however, when interpreting the research now available and that to be done in the future that we are not dealing with objects on an assembly line but with human beings. The principal object is not to achieve efficiency in putting out a better product, in this case a child who makes better scores on standardized tests. The fullest development, well-being, and happiness of the child is the ultimate end, and reading is but a means to that end.

Factors Related to Success in Reading

When all arguments have been exhausted as to when reading instruction should begin, in the final analysis the decision needs to be made not for boys and girls collectively but for each child individually. Furthermore, in assessing a child's readiness for reading, the teacher should be concerned not chiefly with whether the child is ready to read but for what type of learning-to-read or readiness program he is ready. The teacher should then endeavor to plan the instructional program so that the child is given help in growing toward achievement of the maximum maturity in reading of which he is capable, regardless of where on that continuum he may be at any time of assessment.

Age and Sex

Due to some of the changes that typically occur as the young child advances in years, chronological age is a factor in readiness for reading. These changes in the physical, emotional, and intellectual characteristics of the child have bearing on the extent to which he is ready to read.

Since most boys and girls who have not been reading prior to their arrival in the first grade are usually given their initial reading instruction not long after the beginning of the school year, the entrance age to a first grade set by a school system determines to a considerable extent the age at which the great majority of children will begin the learning-to-read process. In most schools the ruling is that a child must be six years of age by a designated date after the opening of the school year. One problem is that it has not been established that six years or any other specific age is the optimum age for beginning reading instruction. Another problem arises from the fact that, with current rules about age for school entrance, in a given classroom the age of entrants may vary as much as a year minus a day. Obviously the child who became six one day later than the specified date would, when entering first grade, be a year minus one day older than the one whose birthday fell on the set date.

Another point that must be taken into account when considering the age of a child in terms of readiness for initial reading instruction is that studies and observation seem to indicate that the average girl in the first grade is more able to cope with many of the scholastic requirements as they now typically exist in schools—learning to read, included—than the average boy of the same age.

Though age should be given attention as a reading readiness factor, it would seem that too much, rather than too little, emphasis has been placed on it. Many considerations are more important than a specific age in their bearing on readiness for beginning reading instruction. Nor should broad sweeping generalizations be made regarding the influence of sex upon reading readiness. Here as in many other situations the differences within a sex are much greater than those between the sexes.

Attitude toward Reading

Of great significance in assessing a child's readiness for reading is his attitude toward learning to read.

Typically on the first day of school the first-grade teacher finds that there is marked variation in the attitudes that the boys and girls have toward learning to read. It is not unlikely that there will be one or more who are already reading material of the difficulty of books for beginners and who are eager to read more and more books. There may be some who are looking forward to school because they want to learn to read. Fathers, mothers, sisters, or brothers may have been reading fascinating stories to them. So they come to school, wanting to learn to read in order to be independent of others for their stories. They may have discovered, too, that a great deal of information is found in books. They may insist on being taught to read without delay.

But not all children in the room will be eager to learn to read. There may be some who have enjoyed hearing others read or tell stories to them who do not look forward to learning to read. They may prefer not to learn to read, because they feel it is more fun to have others read to them than to read by themselves. There may also be a child who enters school with fear and trepidation because he has heard disconcerting tales about what happens at school. Or there may be a child who is disturbed at the thought that now he can no longer spend most of the day playing. He may be in no mood to become interested in what is done at school.

In the average first grade, then, the children's attitudes toward learning to read may range from disinclination to indifference to anticipation. There are many other respects, however, in which first-grade children reveal great differences. They differ in

mental, physical, social, emotional, and other educational or psychological factors of great importance in beginning reading.

Mental Maturity

For several decades much emphasis was placed on a study by Washburne and Morphett[13], on the basis of which the investigators concluded that it was desirable to postpone beginning reading instruction until the child had reached a mental age of six years, six months.[14] The recommendation was put into practice in many schools. Its validity is now categorically denied by many who believe that mental age should not be the only deciding factor in determining when reading instruction should begin. They point out that the needed mental age for effective beginning reading should be determined to a large extent by the type of reading program that a school offers. They contend that if it is adapted to the needs of the boys and girls with varying mental ages, there is no reason why there should be delay in learning to read until a child has reached a mental age of six-and-a-half years. They can point out that boys and girls with a lower mental age have successfully learned to read.

Standardized Tests of Mental Maturity

One method of obtaining information on mental maturity is through the use of dependable mental tests. However, it should be remembered that even the best mental

---

[13]Mabel Morphett and Carleton Washburne, "When Should Children Begin To Read?", *Elementary School Journal*, vol. 31 (March 1931), pp. 496–503.

[14]Carleton Washburne, "Individualized Plan of Instruction in Winnetka," *Adjusting Reading Programs to Individuals*, William S. Gray, ed., Supplementary Education Monographs, no. 52 (October 1941), pp. 90–95.

test provides an imperfect measure of native ability or intelligence. A child who has had many rich and intellectually stimulating experiences will do better on an intelligence test than a child of equal innate ability who has been brought up in a very limiting environment.

One of the best-known individual tests of mental ability is the *Terman Revision of the Stanford-Binet Intelligence Scale*, available in two forms, published by Houghton Mifflin Company. Since this test involves some knowledge of language, it may not fully reflect the real abilities of children with language problems or of those for whom English is a second language.

Another frequently used individual intelligence test is the *Wechsler-Bellevue Intelligence Scales*, published by the Psychological Corporation. In it, as in the *Terman Revision of the Stanford-Binet Intelligence Scale*, the factor of language is involved. Both the *Stanford-Binet* and the *Wechsler-Bellevue Intelligence Scales* require special training for their administration and interpretation.

An intelligence test that can be given and interpreted by the classroom teacher is the *Peabody Picture Vocabulary Test*, published by the American Guidance Service, Circle Pines, Minnesota. However, the information obtainable through use of this test is much more limited than that which can be derived from the *Stanford-Binet* and the *Wechsler-Bellevue Intelligence Scales*.

Also on the market are individual nonlanguage psychological tests designed to reduce the invalidity of test results that might, with language psychological tests, be due to lack of proficiency in the use of the English language on the part of the person being tested. An example is the *Arthur Performance Scale*, published by C. H. Stoelting and Company. It can be used effectively with children from non-English-speaking homes as well as with those with other language divergences from standard English. The use of the *Arthur Performance Scale*, however, is not restricted to children with difficulties with the English language.

A much-used group test is the *Pintner-Cunningham Primary Test*, Form A, Form B, and Form C, published by Harcourt Brace Jovanovich. The subtests, which together are devised to examine general mental ability, give an indication of the nature of the abilities tested. They are: Test 1, Common Observation; Test 2, Aesthetic Differences; Test 3, Associated Objects; Test 4, Discrimination of Size; Test 5, Picture Parts (in which the pupil is tested in ability to find among several pictures one like a designated picture); Test 6, Picture Completion (in which the pupil is asked to indicate which of a number of parts is needed to finish an incomplete picture); Test 7, Dot Drawing (in which the pupil is asked to connect dots so that a picture like a given one will be drawn). Although all seven tests are composed entirely of pictures, an understanding of language is required for taking the test, since all the directions are given verbally.

The California Test of Mental Maturity, Pre-Primary Battery, published by McGraw-Hill, New York, is available in long and short forms. Certain of the subtests require a minimum use of language, while other sections reveal how adequately the child understands relations expressed in words. Since a pupil's score in nonlanguage tests may be higher or lower than in language tests, it is of great value to obtain test scores on the types of mental ability tested both by language and by nonlanguage tests. *The California Test of Mental Maturity, Pre-Primary Battery* is concerned with these mental factors: memory, spatial relations, logical reasoning, numerical reasoning, and verbal concepts.

The Pintner Non-Language Primary

Mental Test, published by Teachers College Press, Columbia University, New York, can also be used with children with language handicaps.

Other widely used group intelligence tests are the *Kuhlmann-Anderson Intelligence Test, Grade IA,* published by the Educational Test Bureau, Minneapolis, Minnesota, and the *Detroit Beginning First Grade Intelligence Test,* distributed by Harcourt Brace Jovanovich.

A criticism launched against mental tests that may be especially valid in the case of younger boys and girls is that the tests are not culture-fair. The literature suggests that more children of minority groups have frequently been placed as needing attention for mental retardation when, in fact, performance in tests is frequently lower not because of lower mental ability but because of lack of motivation to excel in test situations or bias in construction of tests causing them to be culture-bound. Parental rights for nondiscriminative testing for their children and subsequent placement are increasingly being insisted upon.

Subjective Data on Mental Maturity

Intelligence tests are not the only means by which the teacher can gain insight into the child's intelligence. Long before psychological tests were available there were rough methods of estimating a person's intelligence. Although mental tests are probably more reliable indexes of intelligence than many more informal methods, the latter should also be used. If no mental test has been given, the observant teacher may compare the child's reactions with those usually expected of children his age. By consulting books on child growth and development the teacher can find out what types of behavior are characteristic of children at various age levels. Information about an individual child's customary be-

havior can also be obtained from others who know him well, especially his parents. The teacher should also realize that environmental deprivations may make the child seem less intelligent than he is.

Physical Fitness

The teacher of the beginning reader should always consult such data as may be available in the office of the school nurse. Information that can be obtained through conferences with parents is also often helpful. Through observation of the child the teacher can frequently get clues to the child's physical well-being which may alert him to the need for referral to the nurse or doctor. Symptoms of illness or handicap may be discussed with the parents, who may be encouraged to consult a physician, dentist, or eye specialist. Rather easily observable factors such as sleepiness, listlessness, irritability, and languor often are signs of difficulties that may seriously interfere with learning to read.

Unfortunately, during the critical period of getting ready to read and of beginning reading, children are often absent from school because of illness. Not much can be done by the teacher to prevent such illness, except to provide frequent rest periods and frequent periods of physical activity, to check room temperature and ventilation, and to suggest that a child be sent home at the first sign of a cold or other illness. Since interruptions in school attendance are to be expected, the teacher should plan his work accordingly. When a child returns after an absence of several days, the teacher should try to make him feel that he still belongs, has his own seat, and follows the familiar routine. He should be greeted with pleasure by teacher and class, and instructional sequence which may have been introduced during his absence should be presented to him.

Vision

Since probably no phase of the physical well-being of the child affects reading as much as eyesight, the vision of a child who is about to learn to read should be checked as carefully as possible.

The screening test for vision that is most commonly used in schools is the Snellen Letter chart. The Snellen Symbol-E chart, which is an adaptation of the letter chart, is used in some schools with nonreaders. On the letter chart are seven rows of the letters printed in various sizes, decreasing from the top row to the bottom. While the examinee is being tested, he stands twenty feet from the chart and reads as far down the Snellen Letter chart as his vision permits. On the Snellen Symbol E chart the pupil indicates by the fingers of one hand the positions, like **E, ᴍ, Ǝ, ɯ**, in which the letter *E* occurs on that chart. The Snellen charts test vision only at the far point, at a distance of twenty feet. Since they do not check vision at reading distance, the near point, there is frequently little relationship between a child's performance on these charts and ability to read at the near point. Two of the instruments on the market that screen for visual defects affecting academic success are *The Keystone Visual Survey Telebinocular* (Keystone View Division/Mast Development Company) and *The Master Orthorator Visual Efficiency Test* (Bausch and Lomb Optical Company, Rochester, New York). Both measure such visual functions as binocular vision and fineness of discrimination at both far and near points, skills definitely related to the ability to learn to read. Both also test depth perception and color blindness.

Before choosing any test for checking visual efficiency teachers are advised to study carefully the literature furnished by the publishers of the tests to note what they purport to test and how the tests operate.

Vision screening should be part of the school reading program. (Keystone View Division/Mast Development Company)

In no case should the teacher or school nurse use vision tests to try to *diagnose* eye defects. The tests should be used in the schools merely as screening tests. If the results of the testing indicate that there is a possibility of a difficulty in vision, a referral for diagnosis and possible remediation should be made to a competent specialist in the field of vision.

Even without tests some symptoms of visual difficulties, such as inflamed eyelids, rubbing the eyes, confusing similar letters such as the *c* and the *e*, squinting, scowling, and frowning can be detected. The distance from the eye at which a child holds his books may also be a sign of trouble. Complaints of headaches after reading are frequently significant in discovering vision problems.

Hearing

Because of the negative relationship that can exist between marked hearing impairment and learning to read, in many schools an effort is made to secure accurate information about children's auditory acuity and then to adapt the instructional program to these findings. In some of these schools the health service checks hearing by means of an audiometer. Some audiometers are made for group, others for individual, testing.

In many schools teachers do not have access to audiometers. They should, therefore, be particularly alert to observable signs of hearing loss, which frequently goes undetected and which can seriously interfere not only with reading progress but with learning in general. Inattention, monotonous or unnatural pitch, lack of clear and distinct speech, frequent requests for repetition of questions, turning one ear to a speaker, mouth breathing, complaints of ringing in the ear, head tilting, confusion of words with similar sounds, and rubbing of the ear are among the indications of possible defects of hearing.

A test popularly known as the "watch-tick" test can be used to obtain a rough check of the hearing of a child. The teacher, with a watch with a fairly loud tick in the palm of his hand, stands behind or to one side of the examinee. The child covers one ear with his hand. The watch is held about three feet from the child and moved closer until the child indicates that he hears its tick. Both ears are tested in this way. By comparing one child's responses with those of others, the teacher determines which children should be examined by a nurse or doctor. Whisper tests and low-voice tests may also offer clues as to whether hearing difficulty should be suspected.

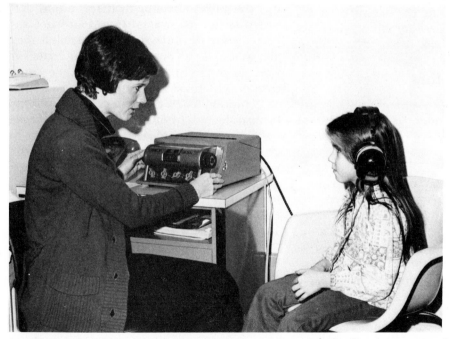

A school nurse checks a child's hearing with an audiometer. (St. Cloud, Minnesota, Public Schools)

Social and Emotional Development

The social maturity of a child can be determined in part by observing his "at-home-ness" in group situations. It is of special importance to note his ability to cooperate with others in a group. Emotional maturity can roughly be gauged by the child's reaction to conditions that to him are unpleasant, his willingness to consider the rights of others, and his ability to sacrifice immediate pleasures for future gains.

Language Development

In Chapter 2 is discussed the bearing of language development on reading. It is of great importance that the teacher consider the factors to which reference is made in that chapter, as he assesses the type of reading or prereading activities for which the child is ready. In Chapter 13 are given suggestions for helping the beginner in the learning-to-read process for whom so-called standard English is not the first language.

Educational Factors

Schools are trying to assess a child's readiness for reading through reading-readiness tests and/or a variety of nonstandardized procedures.

Reading-Readiness Tests

Reading-readiness tests are designed as a means of predicting readiness for beginning reading instruction. Makers of some such tests claim that the tests consist of items related to reading that can give insight, not only as to whether a child is ready at that time to begin reading but also, in case he does not measure as ready, how much longer it is likely to take him to be ready. Following a description of reading-readiness tests, we will note criticisms of them.

Many reading-readiness tests claim to appraise the child's background of information, either in subtests so labeled or in subtests by some other designation, in which other points are also tested. The breadth of a pupil's information which reflects, the authors of such tests hope, the richness of his experience, is supposedly tested by asking the child questions like, "How many cents are there in a dime?"

Many reading-readiness tests aim to measure the ability to discriminate between objects, between words, and between letters. A common method for evaluating the ability to discriminate among objects is to present a series of four or five pictures in a row, all but one of which is like the first one. The series may consist of pictures of five houses all alike except one in which no chimney is shown. The child is asked to cross out the one that is unlike the first one. Similar exercises are devised for testing the pupil's ability to discriminate between letters or words. Pupils are not expected to read the words or letters; all they are to do is to recognize which letter or word is different from others in the same row, or which are alike.

Comprehension of the meaning of words is also tested in many reading-readiness tests. In some tests the pupil is asked to give words that mean the opposite of the words named by the examiner. If, for example the teacher says *summer*, the pupil is to answer *winter*; if the teacher says *up*, the pupil is to say *down*.

One widely used readiness test is the *Gates-McGinitie Reading Tests: Readiness Skills*, published by Teachers College Press, Columbia University. It tests: (a) listening comprehension; (b) auditory discrimination; (c) visual discrimination; (d) following directions; (e) letter recognition; (f) visual-motor coordination; (g) auditory blending; and (h) word recognition.

The Metropolitan Readiness Tests,

rabbit begins. Another variation is to ask the pupils which pairs of words that the teacher names, such as the following, begin with the same sound: *mother, man; cat, came; bark, pie.*

2. Testing Knowledge of Letters According to John C. Manning:[14] "There is ample evidence to indicate that letter knowledge is indeed predictive of reading success." If it is predictive, we may well ask ourselves which particular aspects of letter knowledge contribute most meaningfully to that prognosis. The classic study by Donald Durrell and others[15] identifies several levels of letter knowledge of which the teacher should be aware, as he tries to determine the child's level on the continuum of being prepared for beginning reading instruction. Following is an adaptation of those listed by Alice Nicholson,[16] a member of Durrell's research force.

Ability to directly match letters (upper and lower case)

Ability to recognize letters shown (upper and lower case)

Ability to identify letters named (upper and lower case)

Ability to name the letters (upper and lower case)

Ability to relate upper to lower case letters

Ability to write letters

Samuels,[17] when summarizing his own and Ohnmacht's[18] studies, points out that they found no positive effect of knowledge of letter names on reading, but that he, as well as other investigators, have found training in letter sounds has a beneficial effect on learning to read.

Arthur Heilman, considered by many an outstanding authority on the question of phonics in reading instruction, states:

> Research on first grade reading instruction leaves little room for doubt that pupils exposed to systematic instruction in letter-sound relationships score higher on "reading achievement" at the end of grade one than do pupils who receive little or no such instruction.[19]

Undoubtedly in some programs of reading instruction—especially those with a synthetic approach to phonics (see p. 115)—letter knowledge acquired on prereading or reading levels would have a greater bearing on reading than it would in others.

3. Using an informal reading-readiness checklist The teacher may wish to devise a checklist[20] similar to the following:

[14]John C. Manning, "Early Letter Emphasis Approaches in First Grade Reading Programs," *Perspectives in Reading,* no. 5 (Newark, Del.: International Reading Association, 1965), p. 122.

[15]Donald D. Durrell, Alice Nicholson, Arthur W. Olson, Sylvia Gavel, and Eleanor Linehan, "Success in First Grade Reading," Boston University, *Journal of Education,* vol. 51, no. 3 (February 1958), entire issue.

[16]Durrell et al., p. 7.

[17]S. Jay Samuels, "Models of Word Recognition," *Theoretical Models and Processes,* Harry Singer and Robert B. Ruddell, eds. (Newark, Del.: International Reading Association, 1971), pp. 24–37.

[18]D. C. Ohnmacht, "The Effects of Letter Knowledge on Achievement in Reading in the First Grade," paper presented at the American Educational Research Association in Language Arts (February 1969).

[19]Arthur W. Heilman, "Research Findings Concerning Phonics in Beginning Reading," *A Decade of Innovation: Approaches to Beginning Reading,* Elaine C. Vilscek, ed. (Newark, Del.: International Reading Association, 1971), Proceedings of the Twelfth Annual Convention of the International Reading Association, vol. 12, Part 3, pp. 100–107.

[20]An unpublished list by Roger Rouch.

	Satisfactory	**Unsatisfactory**

Interest in Reading
1. Listens attentively to stories read
2. Is interested in picture books
3. Seeks out books to take home

Oral Language
1. Has command of a large number of words
2. Can communicate effectively
3. Speaks distinctly

Auditory Discrimination
1. Can hear rhyming words
2. Distinguishes differences in sounds represented by letters

Visual Discrimination
1. Can see differences in unlike letters
2. Can see differences in unlike word patterns

Listening
1. Recalls stories heard
2. Can follow simple directions
3. Can recall a sequence of events

Left-to-right Orientation
1. Scans a series of pictures from left to right
2. Recognizes the left-to-right sequences of letters within words

Letter Knowledge
1. Can identify letters named
2. Can name letters shown
3. Can relate upper- to lower-case letters
4. Begins to associate sounds with letters

Social and Emotional Factors
1. Can work in groups
2. Displays self-control
3. Works independently
4. Attends to task

4. Following other suggestions for making appraisals Through careful observation of a child the teacher can gain considerable information as to where on the continuum of learning to read he should have him start. The teacher can talk with the child to discover what his main interests are. A rough measure of his attitude toward reading can be gained by observing how often he looks at books on the reading tables, whether he asks for stories to be read to him, and whether he is interested in finding out what the written word says. Whether he has acquired the top-to-bottom and left-to-right sequence can be determined in part by observing him as he looks at pictures and as he "reads" captions and other labels. An index of his vocabulary can be gained by listening to him talk and by gauging roughly how well he understands what he hears.

Thus there are various ways in which the teacher can gain, during the opening weeks of school, insight that will be of value to him in relation to the probable success of a child in beginning reading. She can give both mental and reading-readiness tests; she can observe the child in various situations; she can converse with the child; she can have conferences with parents; she can examine school records that may be available. Some factors that she should consider are intelligence, hearing, vision, visual and auditory discrimination, experience background, vocabulary, emotional and social maturity, ability to remember, ability to follow directions, power to think critically, and interest in reading. On the basis of her judgment, as she weighs all the data that she has collected, the teacher will decide for what prereading or reading activities the individual child is ready.

Guidelines for the Prereading Period

What are guidelines that the teacher should observe when planning a program for the prereading period?

The teacher should recognize that there is probably no one optimum time for any given child to begin to learn to read. We can think of readiness for reading as extending over a continuum on which no point is the most propitious. The "best time" will be determined to a large extent by methods and materials used. Therefore, it is quite understandable that children who vary in their readiness for reading could be started at the same time on the adventure of learning to read, providing attention is paid to individual differences as the reading program is being designed for each of them.

Reading-readiness activities should be an integral part of the total program. By means of many of the activities that the

children carry on in any good first-year program many of the goals of the prereading period can be attained. For example, characteristic activities, such as storytelling, the examination of picture books, music and art activities, and excursions, can contribute greatly to the development of readiness for reading.

Direct help in the form of practice activities should be provided for some boys and girls. Although many of the activities of a good first-year program, even when not designed specifically to prepare children for reading, are instrumental in fostering reading-readiness, some boys and girls seem to require additional practice on certain skills which are essential to beginning reading. For example, practice periods set up to help children gain proficiency in discriminating between word forms are valuable when not enough meaningful repetition can be provided by incidental means. Such practice should not, however, replace abundant incidental instruction, which can be afforded, for example, when the children look for a name on a chart listing those who have special responsibilities for the week. The teacher may at that time say: "No, that word is not *Mark* (as the teacher points to *Mike* and then to *Mark*), although it begins like *Mark*. It is *Mike*. Find Christine's name. Is it longer or shorter than Carol's?"

The activities of the prereading period should provide background for initial reading tasks. Unfortunately, the usual reading textbooks, written for the child population as a whole, do not take account of the many variations in the social, cultural, and geographical backgrounds of all children. The characters and situations portrayed in any reading textbooks are usually drawn from the environments of fairly typical middle-class homes and communities. Happily, in recent years authors and publishers have been working to overcome this shortcoming. Moreover, many of the better television programs have had an equalizing effect on the background information that many boys and girls have. The city child who watches television may have a better understanding of the farm and the farm child of the city than was formerly the case. Nevertheless, this knowledge as obtained through television is often superficial. Furthermore, to the country child the incidents portrayed in a reader may be quite dull in comparison with the killing of a rattlesnake or the rounding up of cattle escaping through a break in the fence. Nor can it be taken for granted that the city child will understand references to a farm. He may not ever have seen a cow, and the illustration in the book may give him a misleading impression of her size.

Preparing the children for the basal reader series can therefore be a formidable task. Storytelling, discussion, and the use of various audio-visual aids may prepare the child for the situations encountered in readers. A rich "experience" program in the prereading period will provide the foundation on which the initial reading skills may be built.

Even in schools where no basal reader series is used and the program is individualized as the teacher attempts to help every child read material on his level, problems similar to those mentioned in relation to the textbook program persist. In such an individualized reading program it is still necessary to provide appropriate experiences in preparation for reading. Experiences such as field trips, discussions, and word study can help assure greater effectiveness for an individualized reading program, as well as for one based in part on textbooks.

The length of the reading-readiness program period, if one is needed, should vary. Some of the boys and girls will prob-ably be reading when they enter first grade. Others, though not reading, may know the alphabet and the sounds commonly associated with the letters or combinations of letters. Reading-readiness activities for these children can often prove to be worse than a waste of time unless preparation can help reduce possible lacks that might persist, even though in most respects the child is ready to read or is already reading.

A child should be taught to read as soon as he is ready. If he is ready before he starts school he should be permitted, even encouraged, to learn to read. The experience of reading, for the child who can read with success and pleasure, enriches his life and contributes to his general development. On the other hand, it is an error to assert that it is an established fact that a child who starts to read late has lost one or more years of his life and that he will continue to be one or more years behind in his capacity to read. First, there are many experiences besides reading that a young child can have to enrich his life. Second, although evidence has been presented indicating that an early reader may be able to maintain his superiority, there is also evidence to show that some children who do not receive reading instruction until the second year of school outstrip their counterparts who learned to read in the first grade, even before the end of the elementary-school period.

During the prereading period special care needs to be taken that the boys and girls enjoy the activities in which they are engaged. Boredom can easily result in a distaste for learning to read and for reading in the years to come. Overemphasis on drills and lack of variety in procedure are to be avoided.

A large variety of appropriate materials should be made available during the prereading period. Since one important objective of the prereading period is to develop and maintain an interest in reading, the children should have access to a large number of attractive books. Some of these may be placed on a library table, of height appropriate for the first-year child, while others may be arranged on low bookcases. Included should be books to which the pupils have been introduced as the teacher showed them or talked about them or read from them to the class. The display should not, however, be limited to books with which the pupils are familiar. There should also be some that are new to the children, so that through them interest in exploring books can be developed. To help the boys and girls realize that books are valuable not only for the stories but also for the information they contain, the book collection should include both stories and informational material.

Books that boys and girls have made can also stimulate interest in reading. Large books that other children have made in preceding years may be placed on the library table. For example, if the first grade the year before made a big picture book telling about a visit to a farm as a class project, the children can see how it is possible to share information with others by means of the book. Such a book is especially help-ful if there are captions or simple story material accompanying the pictures. The new class, too, might bring pictures on a subject like "Our School" or "Our Pets" and mount them to form a big book. Under each picture the teacher might write a sentence or two suggested by the children. It is easy to interest children in reading a book they have helped to make.

Displays on bulletin boards can be of much value. A bulletin board on which are mounted leaves, with captions telling the kind, may help extend the experiences of some of the children. It can also give them further proof that learning to read is worthwhile, since the words below the leaves give significant information. Pictures of the means of transportation that some of the boys and girls have used, like a bicycle, truck, automobile, and airplane, can serve similar purposes.

Many publishing companies that sell textbooks for elementary-school reading also have reading-readiness booklets that can serve a helpful purpose for some children. Some of the booklets provide specific preparation for a certain series of readers, while others can be used profitably by some boys and girls regardless of the reading books that will be used later.

5B

Developing Readiness for Reading

Fostering Emotional and Social Maturity

Developing Educational Readiness
Enriching the Child's Background of Experience
Going on Field Trips
Examining Objects
Looking at Pictures
Observing or Participating in Demonstrations and Experiments
Listening to Stories
Engaging in Other Activities
Stimulating Growth in Language Abilities
Developing Speech
Developing Listening
Developing the Speaking and the Understanding Vocabulary
Developing the Reading Vocabulary
Learning to Write
Learning the Letters of the Alphabet and Their Sounds
Developing Auditory and Visual Discrimination
Auditory Discrimination
Visual Discrimination
Improving in Ability to Remember
Stimulating Growth in Critical and Creative Thinking
Orienting to the Left-to-Right and Top-to-Bottom Sequence
Developing and Maintaining Interest in Reading
Illustrations of Work Involving a Language-Experience Approach

In Chapter 5A, "Readiness for Reading," the theory basic to a sound pre-reading program is discussed in some detail. Many of the points presented are applicable regardless of whether we are considering a preschool program or one in operation in a first grade. Since this book deals with the teaching of reading in the elementary school, we will note how the principles discussed in the preceding chapter can be applied to the development of reading readiness in the first grade. Nevertheless, many of the ideas presented can, with or without slight modification, be adapted to kindergarten and even some prekindergarten programs.

Fostering Emotional and Social Maturity

As the teacher adjusts his procedure to the emotional and social maturity of his pupils and strives to help them reach higher levels, he will keep certain principles in mind:

1. An atmosphere of calm, courtesy, industry, and happiness should prevail in the room.
2. Respect should be shown for the personality of each person.
3. Restrictions should serve a purpose and be relatively few in number.
4. Directions and suggestions should generally be positive rather than negative.
5. Praise is usually more effective than blame, but praise must be deserved to be of value.
6. Every individual needs security, approval, success, and means of self-expression.
7. The help and cooperation of parents should be secured whenever possible.
8. The teacher should not necessarily postpone reading instruction until a child is well adjusted socially and emotionally. Success in reading can contribute greatly to a feeling of security.

The teacher will encounter numerous problems of emotional and social maturity which directly affect a child's readiness for reading. Some children are shy, others overaggressive; some are overprotected; others are overassertive or lacking in self-control or in concern for others. What can the teacher do for them?

Often the shy child is the immature child. Insecurity may result from many causes. One of the common characteristics of the shy child is his fear of not being accepted by his peer group. If he has had little previous experience with participation in group activity, he may need gradual and patient introduction to group enterprises of many types. Certainly he should be made to feel, by every possible means, that he is liked. He should be brought into contact with other children who are friendly to him. He should receive praise for successful efforts at social adjustment. He should be encouraged to contribute constructively to the work of the group and thus secure the approval of his peers.

In the case of the child who cries easily or loses his temper on slight provocation, careful attention should be given to his general physical well being. Has he been getting enough rest and wholesome food? Does he show signs of illness? Where the crying may have become a habit, the teacher should be ready to supply suitable distractions and try to avoid situations that may give rise to crying. The positive approach is usually the more effective. Thus, when a child exhibits self-control in a situation, the teacher, instead of ignoring such desirable behavior, may say: "I noticed that Phyllis did not become angry when George broke her clay bowl. She helped George pick up the pieces and said she would make another bowl."

Although the overassertive child may be the most troublesome, he usually presents a less serious problem than the shy and retiring one. Tactful discussions with the group as a whole about respecting the rights of others may be helpful, and it may be necessary to provide experiences in which the child cannot get what he wants through aggressive behavior. Most of the children who manifest such behavior are merely seeking to gain recognition which they cannot get by more constructive methods. They should be given frequent opportunities to obtain such recognition by means that are socially approved.

The teacher will also encounter the overprotected child and the overly self-centered one. Wherever possible, he should seek the cooperation of the oversolicitous parents. The overprotected child, while feeling secure in the affection of the teacher, should be encouraged to assume ever-increasing independence in making and carrying out decisions. The teacher should insist on his doing for himself the things he can learn to do without adult assistance and should praise him when he succeeds. The child who often insists on having his own way should be taught to "take turns" in group activities. He can be made to understand that no one is able to have his own way at all times and that thoughtfulness for others creates pleasant relationships. In extreme cases it may be necessary to isolate the child temporarily from the group, if only for the sake of the other children. Such disciplinary measures should, however, be regarded as exceptional.

The following is a list of ways in which the teacher can help boys and girls develop emotional and social maturity important in the initial "learning-to-read" period.

1. Providing the shy child with opportunities to become increasingly involved in activities well graded for him
2. Helping the overaggressive child take a rightful place in the social scene of the classroom
3. Using praise when deserved but resorting to criticism sparingly
4. Adapting the curriculum to the needs of each child so that he is likely to have a maximum of success and a minimum of frustrations
5. Giving responsibilities to all pupils
6. Helping boys and girls in self-evaluation
7. Helping boys and girls become more self-reliant
8. Avoiding much competition with others
9. Placing a child in a group in which he is likely to be happy
10. Encouraging a child to express his own opinions and helping him to express them in acceptable ways

Developing Educational Readiness

As the teacher pays attention to the emotional and social development of boys and girls, he can at the same time help them grow in other characteristics that have a marked bearing on success in beginning reading. How this can be done through attention to the experience background, auditory and visual discrimination, and other factors is explained in the remaining pages of this chapter.

Enriching the Child's Background of Experience

One way in which boys and girls can be helped to become more ready for beginning reading instruction is through the extension of their experience background. However, experience is important, not merely because children must get ready for reading but because appropriate, wholesome, and varied experiences are an important part of each person's life, at any age. Even for the many children in the primary school who have already enjoyed a wide variety of experiences with places, persons, things, processes, and events, new and interesting school experiences are desirable. The school should provide all children with an interesting environment in which to grow up.

Experienced teachers are familiar with wide variety in the range and types of backgrounds found among school children. They know it is necessary to study the children carefully in order to meet the multifarious individual needs. In some cases it will be possible to distinguish between different groups in the first-grade class. Thus, for example, those children who have not attended kindergarten may be selected for an exploratory trip through the school building. If an individual child has never had a pet, the teacher may talk with him about animals, show him pictures of pets, or better still, arrange for the class to acquire one.

Socioeconomic level will often affect the nature of the child's previous experiences, but not necessarily their extent. Children from middle-class homes have often traveled considerably, some even to distant countries. They are likely to have more toys and books at home; and have more opportunity for gardening, experimentation with pencils, crayons, and paper and construction materials than lower-class children. On the other hand, the child from the ghetto knows a world that is quite unfamiliar to his more fortunate classmate. He may have developed, through the necessities of his life, a greater maturity and independence and often even a tragic sophistication about the ways of the adult world.

The ideal school environment for preparing boys and girls for reading, then, is one in which many things are going on. A primary class may be building a large model airplane, operating a store, viewing a film, making a terrarium, or caring for a pet. The child's background of experience can be extended by going on field trips, examining objects, looking at pictures, observing or participating in demonstrations and experiments, and listening to stories.

Going on Field Trips

The eagerness of most first-grade children to learn more about the part of the world near them should be fully utilized. There are many places in or near school that boys and girls enjoy seeing. Trips through the school, examination of playground equipment, walks to gather leaves or stones, trips to look at trees and birds—all can be made real learning experiences, contributing not only to reading but also helping the child find out more about the world in which he lives. But such trips must be carefully planned if the maximum value is to be obtained. Part of the planning should usually involve preparing the pupils for the trip so that they will know better what to look for. For example, before the boys and girls go on a walk to gather leaves, some pictures of pretty leaves may be shown and brief comments made. The purpose of the children in going on the walk, possibly to see how many different kinds of leaves each child can find, should be one that is wholeheartedly accepted by the group. During the trip itself help should also be given frequently in the form of suggestions or questions or directions. At this time the teacher may ask the pupils to notice if many leaves have fallen, and whether more green leaves are on the trees than on the ground. After the trip it is important to have a follow-up, when the pupils may engage in one or more activities such as showing their leaves, expressing rhythmically how the leaves fall, mounting them, drawing pictures suggested by their walk, making up a poem about leaves, or planning the sentences for a chart telling about their trip.

Examining Objects

By means of objects displayed in the room or otherwise brought to the attention of the boys and girls, the pupil's fund of information can be greatly extended. Discussion of material on a science table can be stimulated. The children can be encouraged to bring to school objects in which they are interested, such as stones or model airplanes or toy boats, and to explain them to the other children. Thus, through wise direction many significant facts can be learned as the children show a new doll, an interesting-looking shell, or a book that was recently received as a birthday present.

Looking at Pictures

Pictures serve as an important means of broadening the experience background of children. If motion-picture equipment is available, the teacher can select films that will fit the needs and interests of his group. Slides and filmstrips, too, can be used to make concrete the things that might otherwise be rather meaningless abstractions. Mounted pictures, postcards, and snapshots, brought either by the pupils or the teacher, can be a source of pleasure and of learning. Exhibiting them attractively will encourage children to study them and can also serve as a means of teaching them how to display pictures effectively. If the children share the responsibility of arranging the materials in an orderly fashion, they can develop skill in mounting pictures and arranging attractive displays.

Observing or Participating in Demonstrations and Experiments

Demonstrations and experiments are of special interest to many children, and they can be the source of much information. Many experiences in science lend themselves well to use with young children; these include finding out what happens to plants when they have and when they do not have sunlight, discovering what effect salt has on ice, noticing how steam becomes water, and discovering that air is necessary for a candle to burn. Often the teacher can let the pupils take part in experiments.

Listening to Stories

Storytelling at all ages can open vistas to the child. Although children should share in the storytelling since self-expression for the child telling a story is important, the welfare of the listener should also be considered. Consequently, the quality of the story and the method of telling it should be matters of concern not only for the sake of the storyteller but also for that of the listener.

Engaging in Other Activities

The teacher has at his disposal many other means of preparing boys and girls for beginning reading through extending their experiences. He can do this by providing records and/or cassettes to which the children can listen, by encouraging creative expression through music and art, by interesting the children in putting on plays or puppet shows, and by making provisions for discussions and conversation that is interesting, elevating, and informative.

Stimulating Growth in Language Abilities

Since there is close relation between reading and other language abilities, much can be done to help the pupil develop in all of the communication skills. Both during the preceding period and after the child has begun reading in books, his development in language can be stimulated in a variety of ways, so that he will become more ready for reading or will become a more efficient reader. The teacher can effect growth in reading skill or in abilities related to reading by wisely guiding activities that deal with speech, listening, and writing.

One period of the school day that can contribute richly to the development of language efficiency is the "sharing period." In a large number of primary grades a short period, popularly called "show and tell" time, is set aside daily so that pupils will have an opportunity to "share" some of their experiences with others in their group. They do so by telling their classmates and the teacher experiences of interest to them. During this period many teachers like an informal seating arrangement, often in circular or semicircular formation.

Typically, during the sharing period one pupil at a time, either while seated or standing at a place where others can see him, tells in a sentence or more something that he thinks will interest others. At times he has something to show to the class as he makes his explanation. A child showing a stone that he found on his way to school may say, "I found a pretty stone." With or without questioning by the teacher or the rest of the group he may add, "I found it on the way to school. I am going to keep it." Typical of other types of information given by pupils are:

> We have a new baby, It is a baby sister.
> Mother is taking me to the store tonight. I will buy a doll.
> I fell yesterday. This is where I hurt my leg. A dog chased me.

In conducting a sharing period these are points many teachers may find profitable to observe.

1. Good English should be encouraged but not to the point of undue inhibition of spontaneity in talking.
2. Participation should be well distributed. Although frequently not every

child can have a "turn" during every sharing time, no one should be slighted day after day and nobody should monopolize the time.

3. Opportunities to increase the pupil's vocabulary should be utilized. For example, if after a pupil has used a word that the teacher thinks is unfamiliar to some, the teacher can make the term clearer through comments or questions.

4. Sharing time should be a happy time.

5. The sharing period should not be a long period, probably not more than about twenty minutes.

6. A good time for a sharing period is the beginning of the day when the pupils are eager to tell what has happened since they were last with the teacher and their classmates.

Increasingly, the interrelation between reading and writing is being stressed. One of the gains possible from the use of the experience approach (see Chapter 4, "An Overview of Reading Instruction," p. 42, and the description given later in this chapter, p. 102) is that it highlights that relation.

Developing Speech

A chief objective of first-grade language arts programs, before and after reading instruction has begun, is to help the pupil express himself well orally. Skill in speech plays a significant part in learning to read. The child embarrassed by ridicule because of baby talk is not likely to want to participate freely in group discussions based on reading activities. The boy or girl unable to talk in short, simple sentences may be unable to anticipate the meaning of a sentence, even of the type found in beginning reading books. In these and other ways skill in reading and in speech often go hand in hand.

The following points should serve as guidelines in the selection of procedures for the development of speech.

1. Lack of a feeling of emotional or social security may frequently be related to faulty enunciation as well as other poor speech habits.

2. Most speech improvement comes about through informal classroom activities.

3. Provision should be made for a large number of enriching experiences that give opportunity for improved oral expression.

4. Attention should be given to various phases of speech, such as proper enunciaton and pronunciation, adequate speaking vocabulary, and interest in speaking with or to others with an understanding of courtesies and proprieties in speaking.

5. Pupils who need help in speech should be given opportunity for special practice.

6. In oral expression both content and form should be emphasized.

7. Relatively little effort should be made to correct speech defects that are due to the transition from temporary to permanent teeth.
8. The physical features of the room and the activities carried on by the class should be made so interesting that the children will have vital topics for discussion and conversation.
9. The atmosphere of the classroom should encourage children to converse freely at appropriate times.
10. The teacher's own speech should be a suitable model for the boys and girls.
11. The teacher should not talk too much.

The following are some ways in which the teacher can help pupils to improve the pattern of their expression.

1. Providing many opportunities for free discussion during various activities, such as planning a project or making the schedule for the day
2. Encouraging the pupils to tell stories that they have heard or experienced or made up
3. Asking pupils to explain pictures they have drawn
4. Placing on the bulletin board pictures the pupils can interpret orally to others
5. Providing opportunities for boys and girls to ask riddles that the class will try to answer
6. Retelling a story
7. Setting aside time for dramatizing some of the stories read or told by the teacher to the group
8. Helping the boys and girls put on simple puppet shows
9. Providing opportunities for dramatic play—for example, playing house
10. Helping the children do choral reading or otherwise saying poems in unison
11. Making provisions for many opportunities for singing
12. Talking individually to the boys and girls when they come to school in the morning, when they play during the noon hour, when they leave in the afternoon, or when they engage in activities during periods set aside for individual or committee work
13. Setting up some exercises to furnish practice on the correct pronunciation of words frequently mispronounced. For example, the pupils might play a game in which some of the children try to reach the top of a diagram of a ladder drawn on the chalkboard, on rungs of which are words—such as *running, yellow, was*—often mispronounced by the children.

Developing Listening

One aspect of the language arts that has not been emphasized sufficiently in many schools is listening. Frequently it has been taken for granted. Because of its close relation to reading and to many other significant activities both in and out of school, increased attention should be given to this ability.

In trying to help children develop better habits of listening, the teacher should utilize regular classroom activities whenever possible. The following are ways in which children can be assisted in becoming better listeners.

1. As the teacher tells or reads stories to the boys and girls, he stops occasionally to ask questions that test their attentiveness—for example, "Why did Bobby want to get some apples for his mother?"
2. After the teacher has told or read part of a story to the class, he says: "When I have finished the story, see if you can tell what happened to the snowman."
3. Before the teacher reads a story to the class, the pupils are told that after the reading they will be asked to arrange in order pictures that illustrate the action of the story.
4. The pupils are encouraged to listen carefully to stories so that they can tell them to others.
5. As the teacher taps a pencil on a table or claps his hands several times, the children, with eyes closed, give the number of taps or sounds they hear.
6. As the children listen to recordings of sounds characteristic of the home, the street, the farm, they identify the sounds.
7. The boys and girls identify sounds they hear while they are in their schoolroom, such as cars passing by, children walking in the hall.
8. The pupils play games in which children, who are blindfolded, try to identify sounds such as the tapping of a pencil on a desk, the crushing of paper, writing on the chalkboard.
9. The children go on a "listening walk" with the teacher, on which they try to discover as many sounds as they can while on the walk. Later a composite list of the sounds heard might be made.
10. The pupils draw up standards for good listening, such as looking at the person talking, not talking while someone else talks, and not playing with anything while someone is talking.
11. Evaluations of how well the pupils are listening, according to standards such as those mentioned in item 10, are made by the class.
12. Listening is encouraged by means of dramatization of stories or incidents.

Developing the Speaking and the Understanding Vocabulary

Since the vocabulary of beginning books and the sentence structure used in these books are necessarily below the understanding and speaking level of many of the children, it is important to extend their knowledge and use of words through listening and talking. Although much of the work on vocabulary development may be carried on by incidental instruction, it should nevertheless be carefully planned. Direct practice may sometimes be needed, but care should be taken that it is meaningful to the boys and girls.

Growth in children's understanding and speaking vocabulary can be fostered in many ways, such as:

1. Providing opportunity to engage in work on significant areas of study, such as community workers. "New words" should be introduced as the need for them arises.
2. Reading or telling stories that include some unfamiliar words. The meaning of the words should be made clear.
3. Asking pupils to dramatize words such as *walked, ran, crept, raced.*
4. Drawing attention to pupils' use of "new" or especially descriptive words.
5. Having children draw pictures illustrating such "new words" as *funnel, burrow, tractor.*
6. When showing motion pictures, slides, or filmstrips, drawing attention to the use of words that might advisedly be added to the children's vocabulary.
7. Bringing interesting objects to the room. If a rock exhibit is set up, for example, children may enlarge their vocabulary by learning terms such as *marble, granite, sandstone.*
8. Taking children on excursions and helping them become familiar with terms that give more meaning to their trip, such as *cash register, sales, customer.*
9. Introducing songs and poems that contain new words.

In helping children to add words to their understanding and speaking vocabulary the teacher may at times follow these steps:

1. Introduce the word in a meaningful situation.
2. Draw attention to the new word by giving its meaning, asking someone in the group who knows the word to give the meaning, or questioning the others so that they can tell what the word means.
3. Let some of the children use the word in a sentence.
4. Make certain that the pupils pronounce the word correctly.
5. Use the word in later conversation or discussion.
6. Encourage the pupils to use the word.

Developing the Reading Vocabulary

Even during the prereading program the teacher can help pupils acquire a reading vocabulary that will assist them greatly when they begin reading in a book. As in the case of the speaking and the understanding vocabulary, the words on which help is given in the development of a reading vocabulary should be those of which a meaningful application can be made. With this point in mind, the teacher may wish to label shelves where articles such as scissors, paste, and crayons are kept. Attaching the children's names to their lockers and desks can also be of value. But merely labeling articles is not enough, for looking at a word, without the intent to remember it, frequently does not result in learning on the part of the child. For this reason, attention should be called to the labels and the children should be given an opportunity for associating the words with objects. At times the pupils may be asked to match the appropriate cards with the labels, or they may read cards containing the words without comparing them with the cards used as labels. Labeling objects such as a table, a desk, or a chair is of little value unless a real purpose is served thereby. It may be profitable, for example, to place words on a table to show what is to be exhibited on it.

Picture-word cards—cards on which the picture and the name of the item pictured are given, such as *mother, father, sister, brother, cat, dog, school,* and *home*—can be displayed and used in practice exercises for pupils who seem to need such repetition. On the back of the card may be written the word that goes with the picture, so that pupils may practice recognizing words without looking at the illustrations. Sets of small cards such as these, possibly two inches by three inches, can be used by the pupils individually. Similarly, both large cards for group use and small cards for individual practice can be made, with the names of the primary and the secondary colors corresponding to the color illustrated on the reverse side.

There are many other means of adding words to the children's reading vocabulary. The teacher may put on the chalkboard or on large sheets of paper directions often used in the classroom, such as "Please get your coats" or "Please form a circle." Instead of giving the directions orally, the teacher can sometimes point to them. Plans for the day may also be written on the board daily before school: "We will take a walk" or "We will hear a good story today." A chart with the names of the children in the room can be used in a game in which one child points to a name while another says it.

Learning To Write

The simple writing experiences of children during the prereading period can be of help in later reading instruction. Often their writing during this stage is confined to the writing of their names or the copying of sentences from the chalkboard or from sheets of paper. Brief invitations to parents or short sentences to accompany illustrations they have made may be copied. Since many children enjoy reading what they have written, they should have the opportunity to read to others in the room or to their parents the captions under their pictures or the notes they write.

Learning the Letters of the Alphabet and Their Sounds

While some teachers do not believe that part of the reading-readiness period should be devoted to learning the letters of the alphabet and the sounds commonly associated with them, others place early emphasis on letter sounds and names. Many suggestions for teaching the letters and sounds with which they are associated are given in workbooks and teachers' manuals of series of readers that emphasize early learning of the "code" (the letter-sound or the grapheme-phoneme relation) on which the English language is based. A few suggested procedures are indicated below.

1. The boys and girls are given cards on each of which is written a letter of the alphabet. As the teacher names a letter, the pupils hold up the card on which it is written.
2. As the teacher or a pupil points to a letter of the alphabet written on the chalkboard, a pupil gives the name of the letter.
3. The children write a letter of the alphabet with which the name of the word representing an illustrated object begins. For example, the pupils write the letter *b* as the beginning letter of the word for a picture of a boy.

Developing Auditory and Visual Discrimination

Among the prerequisites for successful reading are the ability to differentiate between sounds of words and of letters and the ability to see the differences between written words and between letters. Since improvement in making such discriminations can be brought about through training, suggestions for their development are given here.

Auditory Discrimination

In helping children to discriminate between sounds they hear, teachers should remember that:

1. *There is a great variation among first-grade children in powers of auditory discrimination.* The difference is not necessarily due to degrees of auditory acuity. Two children, for example, may plainly hear the words *walk* and *walked,* but only one may be able to note the difference in the sound.
2. *Instruction in auditory discrimination should take individual differences into account.* Many children will have developed the needed skill in auditory discrimination before they first come to school. For them the exercises in discrimination would be a waste of time. On the other hand, the child who cannot tell whether *dog* and *cat* begin with the same sound or with different sounds needs help in learning to discriminate between sounds that are quite unlike.
3. *Instruction in auditory discrimination should be an integral part of regular classroom activities.* As children take part in the usual classroom activities, such as playing with their toys or pets, their attention can be drawn to the differences in sounds. When, for example, a child fails to distinguish between *car* and *cars,* the teacher may try to help

him detect the difference. At times there is no value in providing separate exercises in noting which pairs of words are alike and which different, as in the case of pairs such as *car* and *cars* and of *car* and *car.*

4. *Growth in power to distinguish between sounds should continue even after reading instruction has begun.* With the child who is unable to make rather careful discriminations between sounds of letters and between sounds of words that are somewhat similar, it must not be assumed that all efforts to develop this ability need to be completed before initial instruction in learning to read is given. As in the case of many other objectives related to reading that can be attained only in part during the prereading period, many methods for securing continuous growth in the ability to distinguish between sounds should be utilized in later stages of learning to read.

Some of the ways in which auditory discrimination can be developed during the prereading period consist of having the pupils do the following:

1. Giving orally words beginning with same sound with which another word begins. The teacher may write on the board the words named by the pupils, even though the pupils cannot read them.
2. Standing if their first names begin with the same sound as the name of one pupil whose name has been given by the teacher. For example, all boys and girls whose names begin with the same sound as Peter's might be asked to stand.
3. Telling whether a sound that the teacher specifies is found at the beginning, near the middle, or at the end of each of a group of words named by the teacher.
4. Naming the word in a list given by the teacher—such as *mother, man, many, few, market*—that does not begin with the same sound as the others.
5. Naming the word in a list—such as *at, talk, fit, get*—that does not end with the same sound as the others.
6. Telling which pairs of words—such as *rat, sat* or *bat, sit*—are rhyming words.
7. Telling which word in a list does not rhyme—as in *cat, bat, sat, sit.*
8. Naming rhyming words.
9. Making up rhymes.
10. Playing the game, "I spy." In this game, pupils guess what object a child refers to in a statement such as "I spy something that begins with the same sound as *Mary*" or "I spy something that ends with the same sound as *took.*"
11. Naming the objects in a picture that begin with the same sound as a word that is named by the teacher.
12. Supplying the last word for a two-line jingle of which the teacher gives all but the last word. The pupils could name the words that rhyme with the last word of the first line.

Visual Discrimination

In planning procedures for the development of visual discrimination during the prereading period, certain general observations should be kept in mind. (a) Some beginning first-grade pupils do not have enough skill in visual discrimination to undertake the reading task with ease. (b) Instruction should be adapted to individual differences. (c) So far as possible, skill in visual discrimination should be furthered in connection with meaningful classroom activities. (d) Not all deficiencies in visual discrimination need to be removed before reading instruction is begun. As the child learns to read, opportunities for making finer discriminations will present themselves.

Boys and girls can systematically be taught to discriminate visually between letter likenesses and letter differences. Directions for two exercises to promote visual discrimination between letters follow.

1. *Matching letters.* Prepare two sets of 3 x 5 cards on which upper-case or lower-case letters have been written, one of the twenty-six letters of the alphabet on each of the cards in a set. Limit the number of cards to be used with beginners, possibly to as small a number as four or five. So that it is easy to differentiate the cards of one set from those of the other, a different color ink can be used in writing the letters. To make the exercise self-checking, the two cards with identical letters can be placed on each other and a notch cut through both cards so that when the same letters are matched, the notches are in corresponding position.

2. *Testing visual memory of letters.* Purchase a slate or a magic slate on which you can write letters and erase or remove them at will. Use the sets of cards on which you have written upper-case or lower-case letters (see Exercise 1 above). Show the children a card and then remove it from sight or turn it over. Next write several letters on the slate, among which is the one shown earlier. Ask a child to point to or circle the letter you showed him.

Additional suggestions for methods of stimulating growth in the ability to make visual discriminations during the prereading period or later are:

1. Asking the pupils to find the word in a written series—such as *big, boy, big, big, big*—which is unlike the other words.

2. Asking the boys and girls to select words in a series which have the same ending as a key word as in:
   talking   talked   walking   walks   talks   singing.

3. After the pupils have dictated to the teacher a record of some experience they have had, such as taking care of a pet, asking one child to draw a line under all words in the story that begin with the same letter as a word indicated by the teacher.

4. Listing two parallel columns of words in which the same words are

used but in a different order. The pupils may draw lines connecting like words in the two columns.

5. Asking the pupils to cross out a given word, such as *dog*, each time it occurs in a group of sentences in which the word is used several times.
6. Having the children find on a chart all the names of pupils in the room that begin with a specified letter.

Improving in Ability To Remember

The ability to remember plays an important role in reading. One cause of inadequate retention in reading is found in poor habits of attentiveness. A child who does not pay careful attention to what is going on cannot be expected to remember. The teacher can attack this problem by assisting boys and girls to become more attentive. Some ways in which children can be helped to attend better, and therefore remember better, have been discussed earlier in this chapter under the related topic "Developing Listening." Here are some addiitonal suggestions for increasing a pupil's memory span.

1. Making certain that the work is on the level of the pupil.
2. Making the work interesting enough so that the pupil will have reason to want to pay attention.
3. Varying the activities frequently enough so that the child's power of attention will not be overtaxed. At the same time children should be helped to develop an ever longer span of attention.
4. Developing in pupils the desire to remain with an activity until it is completed, unless there is good reason not to do so, through helping them recognize the wastefulness of effort when, for little reason, they discontinue an activity before its planned completion.
5. Keeping reasonable orderliness conducive to good attention in the room.
6. Giving boys and girls the opportunity to play "memory games." For example, they might note the articles displayed on a table or on a tray. Then one child leaves the room while an object is removed from the collection. When the child returns, he tries to tell which article is missing.

Remembering a Sequence of Ideas

To help the boys and girls remember a sequence of ideas encountered in reading or listening, the teacher may wish to follow some of these suggestions:

1. After the teacher or a pupil has told a story, the teacher may ask such questions as: "What was the first thing Nancy did when she saw that her dog had followed her?" "What did she do next?"
2. After the teacher has given directions for a simple experiment, such as

showing that plants need light, he may ask the pupils: "What is the first thing we need to do?" and "What do we need to do next?" After the experiment has been completed, the pupils may be asked to enumerate the steps that were followed.

3. The boys and girls, with the assistance of the teacher, might build a topical outline for the dramatizing of a story. The pupils decide on the events to be included in the dramatization and the teacher lists these on the chalkboard. They could then arrange these events in logical sequence.

4. The teacher might place on a flannel board, in mixed-up order, a series of pictures illustrating a story known to the boys and girls and then ask the pupils to rearrange the pictures in correct order.

5. The group may make a "movie," either to illustrate a story that the teacher has told or read to them or to portray activities in which they have engaged. Such an activity furnishes excellent practice in remembering events in sequence and cultivates other abilities important in reading, such as critical thinking, good work habits, skill in following directions, and ability to work with others.

Steps in planning a "movie" on a story told to the class may be these:

Discussing the story
Deciding to make a "movie" of the story
Retelling the story
Deciding on pictures to include
Working out a sequence of the pictures to be drawn
Assigning pictures to be drawn
Drawing the pictures
Deciding on captions or longer explanations of the pictures to be recorded for the "movie" by the teacher
Arranging the pictures and the writing in the proper sequence
Fastening the pictures and the writing to a roll
Practicing telling the story of the "movie"

If the story of "The Three Billy Goats Gruff" were made into a "movie," these are pictures that might be drawn:

Three billy goats at the side of the hill
The green hill that they saw in the distance
The stream they would have to cross
The bridge they would have to cross
The ugly troll who lived under the bridge
The youngest billy goat starting to cross the bridge
The troll roaring at the youngest billy goat
The youngest billy goat talking with the troll
The youngest billy goat feeding on the hillside
The second billy goat starting across the bridge

The troll roaring at the second billy goat
The second billy goat talking with the troll
The second bill goat going across the bridge
The first and the second billy goats feeding on the hillside
The big billy goat starting across the bridge
The troll roaring at the big billy goat
The big billy goat talking with the troll
The fight between the big billy goat and the troll
The end of the troll
The big billy goat going across the bridge
The three billy goats feeding on the hillside

Following Directions

The ability to follow directions involves considerable skill in remembering. To facilitate learning, the teacher's directions should be clear. Although at first the directions should be very simple, they should become more complex as pupils develop in ability to remember sequential directions. At times the teacher may need to demonstrate how to follow a rather involved set of directions. At other times he can help pupils by having the class follow directions together.

Stimulating Growth in Critical and Creative Thinking

An important component of effective reading is the ability to think critically and creatively. Encouragement for the development of this power can and should be given during the prereading period, as well as on all subsequent levels in learning to read.

A discussion of critical and creative reading is included (see Chapter 7A, "Comprehension," p. 163), and suggested activities for helping boys and girls increase in power to do reading of this type are listed (see Chapter 7B, p. 190). For background for the next few paragraphs the reader may at this time wish to refer to those pages. Reference is made below only to a few procedures for stimulating the pupils' power of critical and creative thinking—and subsequent reading—including some that are especially appropriate for use in the prereading and early reading stages.

The teacher can help boys and girls increase in ability to think critically and creatively by asking thought questions when he reads or tells stories to the class. For example, as he reads the story *Millions of Cats* by Wanda Gág, he may ask: "What do you think the little old woman will say when the little old man comes home not with one cat, but with millions of cats?" Or after the teacher has told *The Tale of Peter Rabbit*, he may ask: "Why was Peter Rabbit happy at the end of the story even though his mother had punished him?"

The following are a few additional ways in which the children can be encouraged, through stories told or read to them, to do critical or creative thinking.

1. They can draw a picture of a character in a situation described in the book.
2. They can synthesize or combine their ideas in such a manner that the outcome is novel, though somewhat resembling that of the author who created an imaginary character. For example, after hearing the story *The Funny Thing* by Wanda Gág which tells about a dragonlike creature fed on jum-jills, they may enjoy experiences in which they are encouraged to be inventive in making up their own strange characters. After hearing about *Chitty-Chitty-Bang-Bang* by Ian Fleming, they may wish to invent a magical car.
3. They can pantomime or dramatize stories, giving rein to the exercise of their interpretive powers.

To encourage critical and creative thinking, it is not enough that the teacher ask suitable questions; boys and girls, too, should be encouraged to ask thought questions. To provide such encouragement the teacher will need to respect the questions they ask. The teacher can show his respect by providing opportunity for this kind of questioning and by listening attentively to the questions. At times he may wish to help the boys and girls record their questions. Care needs to be taken in any attempt at improvement that the altered question continues to express what the child has in mind. Praising a child when he asks a pertinent question beyond the factual level is another way in which thought questions can be encouraged.

Critical thinking can also be stimulated through application of something read to real-life problems. For example, in stories about handicapped children, the class might consider ways in which they have observed individuals with handicaps make adjustments to daily routines of living. Or they might tell of ways in which other people have accommodated those with disabilities.

The teacher can encourage critical thinking by giving the boys and girls a part in planning activities, in deciding on the better course of action in a given situation, in determining why some of their actions were wise or unwise.

Some of the suggestions given in Chapter 7A under "Questioning as a Technique for Improving Comprehension" (see p. 176) are apropos to this discussion on "Stimulating Growth in Critical and Creative Thinking."

Orienting to the Left-to-Right and Top-to-Bottom Sequence

Some children entering kindergarten or first grade require help in observing a left-to-right and top-to-bottom sequence in reading pictures or print. Some need to be shown which is their right and which is their left hand. Others, who do know left from right, have not yet discovered that reading, in English, proceeds from left to right and from top to bottom. Special practice in left-to-right and top-to-bottom reading may sometimes be needed.

The following are suggestions for helping children develop this directional orientation to reading.

1. As the teacher reads a book to the class, he can point out where he starts reading and in what direction he progresses.
2. As the teacher or children reread from charts or the chalkboard stories that have been dictated, the teacher can run his hand rhythmically under the lines. Or he can ask a pupil to point to the word with which he should begin reading. In time, a pupil can sweep his hands below the line he is reading from a chart or from the chalkboard. Care must be taken in the latter case that word pointing with consequent "word calling" does not result.
3. At times, when the teacher writes on large sheets of paper or on the chalkboard, he can ask the pupils where he should begin writing and in what direction he should proceed.
4. As some pupils are placing a picture story on a flannel board, they may need guidance in arranging the pictures from left to right in each row and from top to bottom by rows.
5. To emphasize the left-to-right order, boys and girls could be shown a series of possibly three pictures illustrating different actions, with the pictures not in the sequence of the activity illustrated. For example, the pictures might illustrate a boy leaving his home. The first one might show him outside the door of his home, the second running when he is already a distance from home, and the third running when he is still farther from his home. The pupils could then be asked to arrange the pictures in order in a left-to-right sequence on a chalkboard tray.

Developing and Maintaining Interest in Reading

One of the major objectives of the prereading and early reading stages should be to guide the boys and girls so that they will develop or maintain an interest in reading. Unless boys and girls have strong motivation for reading, many of the other suggestions given in this and succeeding chapters will be futile or almost futile. The power of interest must not be overlooked or minimized.

The importance of access to an abundance of interesting reading materials has already been stressed in this book. Other ways in which the teacher can try to interest the children in books are: taking them to the school or public library where they can browse among the books and where, probably, the librarian will be willing to tell them a story; inviting one or more children from a second or third grade to entertain the first grade by reading an interesting story to them; reading stories and informational material to the class.

The sharing period, discussed earlier in this chapter, can serve to interest children in reading. They can be encouraged to show and talk about books they like. Some of these may be picture books for which the child reporting makes up the story. Or the books may contain a simple text, which someone has read beforehand to the pupil reporting.

Use of little booklets containing children's stories, written by the teacher at the dictation of the pupils, gives added incentive to learning to read. In these booklets may be recorded reports planned by the class as a whole on an activity in which they have engaged, such as a trip to a farm. Or the material may consist of individual accounts about each child—as to who the members of his family are, of his interests, and the like. Reports on the work of each child's father or mother or guardian can be written by the teacher as the child "dictates" the content. Then the child can illustrate the book. Teachers, too, can make up stories for booklets to be read by the pupils, in which the vocabulary can be well controlled. Although making such books is time-consuming, it can be a worthwhile use of time in which children observe the preservation, in writing, of valued thoughts.

Illustrations of Work Involving a Language-Experience Approach

To make clearer how work can proceed when a language-experience approach is used (see Chapter 4, "An Overview of Reading Instruction," p. 42), an illustrative procedure for a prereading group or for an early learning-to-read group is given here.

Procedures for Work on an Experience Chart about a Party

To illustrate how, step by step, the points concerning work on an experience chart (see "Teaching Procedures," p. 44) can be followed, a description of possible, though imaginary, procedures in the development and use of a language-experience chart is included here.

Early in the year, after the first-grade boys and girls had been on a listening walk, they made an experience chart on which were recorded some of the sounds they heard while taking the walk. At that time the teacher suggested that they might want to make a chart of all especially interesting activities in which they would take part during the year. The idea received an enthusiastic reception. The teacher pointed out that such charts could help the children remember what they had done during the school year. He also suggested visitors might like to read them. Consequently, the day after the Halloween party, it was easy to interest the boys and girls in making a chart reporting on it.

The teacher helped the boys and girls decide on the title for the chart.

When "Our Party" was suggested, he asked if anyone could think of a title that would tell what kind of party it was. When a boy responded by suggesting "Our Halloween Party," the teacher wrote the title on the chalkboard. Then the pupils discussed some of the points they wanted to include in the report. Comments such as these were made:

We will want to tell that we had a Halloween party.
We should tell that we had candy.
We want to tell that we were dressed up.

As the pupils suggested the wording of the sentences, the teacher helped them with sentence structure. Furthermore, he watched the vocabulary used on the chart so that some of the "new words" were repeated frequently enough to assure the pupils' increased likelihood of learning them. He also guided the children so that their thoughts were recorded in logical sequence. Thus, the following sentences, which the teacher wrote on the chalkboard, evolved:

Our Halloween Party[1]
We had a party.
We played games at our party.
We had Halloween cookies at our party.
We also had Halloween candy.
We wore Halloween costumes.
We had fun at our party.

Fun, a, at, and *played* were words used on the chart that the children had previously acquired as part of their reading vocabulary. "New words," which the teacher planned to teach in connection with the work on this chart, were *we, had, our,* and *Halloween.* These words, excepting *Halloween,* were found in the first-grade reading books the children would later be reading.

Next followed practice in "reading" the chart. First the teacher read it alone. Then he and the pupils read it together.

For an illustration on the chart several suggestions came from the children. Someone recommended cutting a picture of a goblin out of an old magazine. Another pupil suggested that a picture of a goblin be cut freehand. Still another child thought that drawing a picture of one would be better. After further discussion it was agreed that each pupil should cut out of construction paper, freehand, a picture of something that would go well with the chart. It was also agreed that each pupil could then decorate his cutout as he saw fit. A committee, it was decided, was then to select one for the chart that the teacher agreed to have ready by the following day.

The next day the teacher brought the chart to class with him, along with separate strips of tagboard on which were written the title and each

[1]Adapted from the wording of a chart on page 36 of *Bulletin Boards* by Martha Dallmann (Darien, Conn.: The Educational Publishing Corporation, 1959), p. 36.

of the sentences used on the chart, and cards on which the "new words"—*we, had, our* and *Halloween*—and the "review words"—*fun, a, at,* and *played*—were written.

Practice was then given in reading the new materials. First the teacher alone read the chart as he moved his hand under each line of writing. After the pupils had read it twice in concert, several children read it alone. Then the pupils matched the sentence strips with the chart, holding each strip next to the corresponding sentence on the chart and reading it. As the teacher read a sentence out of its normal order in the story, a pupil found the correct strip and read it orally.

To give practice with the words on the cards, the teacher began by asking someone to find the word *our* in the title. Then the pupils pronounced the word *our* as the teacher showed the class the word card for it as he placed it in a card holder. A pupil pointed to the word *our* as it appeared in some of the sentences of the report and pronounced it. In a similar manner the teacher presented the words *we* and *Halloween*. When he introduced the word *had*, before telling the pupils the word, he wrote *house* and *had* on the chalkboard, explaining that the "new word" began with the same sound as the word *house*, which the class had already learned to read. After the class had identified the *h* sound in *house*, the teacher pronounced the word *had* and asked the pupils to note that both of these words began with the /h/ sound. Next, the pupils named other words beginning with the same sound—such as *hat, home,* and *Harry*—which the teacher wrote on the chalkboard. As the teacher showed the cards for the "review words" *fun, a, at,* and *played*, the pupils named them and found them on the chart. The word cards containing the new words and the review words were then mixed, and pupils, individually, named them as the teacher showed the cards. Before the period was over several children again "read" the chart.

For follow-up work, on the third day of the lesson the teacher brought to class duplicated copies of the chart, one for each child, on paper $8\frac{1}{2}$ x 11 inches. He also had sheets of paper of the same size on which were the four "new words"—*we, had, our,* and *Halloween*. Above the word *Halloween* space was provided in which the pupils then drew illustrations of things that might suggest Halloween. The teacher also distributed to each boy and girl a piece of construction paper on which the pupils could paste the freehand drawings they had cut out of paper two days before. The pupils made all the sheets into booklets, fastening them with brass fasteners. Several children then read the story orally. The rule was made that, as soon as a child could "read" the story without error, he could give his booklet to his parents and "read" it to them. The boys and girls who did not have an opportunity to "read" the booklet orally on that day were given a chance to do so within the next few days, either during class time or at other times. When need for additional practice was indicated, it was provided.

FOR FURTHER STUDY

Alexander, J. Estill, ed., *Teaching Reading* (Boston: Little, Brown, 1979), Ch. 2, "Readiness," by N. Knight.

Burns, Paul C., and Betty D. Roe, *Teaching Reading in Today's Elementary Schools*, 2d ed. (Skokie, Ill.: Rand McNally, 1980), Ch. 2, "Prereading Experiences for Children."

Bush, Clifford L., and Mildred H. Huebner, *Strategies for Reading in the Elementary School*, 2d ed. (New York: Macmillan, 1979), Ch. 3, "Readiness for Reading."

Durkin, Dolores, *Teaching Them to Read*, 3d ed. (Boston: Allyn and Bacon, 1978), Ch. 6, "Readiness," and Ch. 7, "Kindergarten Reading."

————, *Teaching Young Children to Read*, 2d ed. (Boston: Allyn and Bacon, 1976).

Furth, Hans G., and Harry Wachs, *Piaget's Theory in Practice: Thinking Goes to School* (New York: Oxford University Press, 1974).

Hall, Maryanne, *Teaching Reading as a Language Experience*, 2d ed. (Columbus, Ohio: Charles Merrill, 1976).

Heilman, Arthur, *Principles and Practices of Teaching Reading*, 4th ed. (Columbus, Ohio: Charles Merrill, 1977), Ch. 2, "Assessing and Developing Reading Readiness."

Hittleman, Daniel R., *Developmental Reading: Psycholinguistic Perspective* (Chicago: Rand McNally, 1978), Ch. 6, "Strategies for Developing Readiness for Reading Instruction."

Karlin, Robert, *Teaching Elementary Reading: Principles and Strategies*, 3d ed. (New York: Harcourt, Brace, Jovanovich, 1980), Ch 6, "Reading Readiness."

Ollila, Loyd O., *The Kindergarten Child and Reading* (Newark, Del.: International Reading Association, 1977).

Zintz, Miles V., *The Reading Process: The Teacher and the Learner*, 3d ed. (Dubuque, Iowa: Wm. C. Brown Company Publishers, 1980), Ch. 9, "The Assessment of Prereading Skills."

Questions and Comments for Thought and Discussion

1. What do you regard as some of the criteria that would help teachers identify at kindergarten level "high-risk" children—those in danger of failing when they are exposed to formal education? What suggestions do you have for trying to prevent their failure?

2. At the present time, what is your attitude toward the role of reading or readiness-for-reading programs on the kindergarten level? Give reasons for your stand. What evidence, in addition to that which you now have, will you want or need to obtain either to substantiate or negate your current point of view in regard to reading or pre-reading activities in the kindergarten?

3. If you were a first-grade teacher, what would you want to do at the beginning of the school year to assess the degree of readiness for reading that each of your children had acquired? Or in the case of those who already were reading, to ascertain the level of their achievement?

4. If you were a first-grade teacher who at the beginning of the school year found he had a pupil who was far behind the others in the classroom as far as "reading readiness" was concerned, while you were helping the other pupils with the learning-to-read process, what strategies could you use with the child who is less ready than the others?

5. In this chapter many suggestions are given for developing educational

readiness for reading. What additional suggestions on any of these topics can you make?

6. Can you think of any points that would be of value in a checklist for
   readiness for beginning reading instruction beyond those listed in the
   one included in Chapter 5A? If so, word your additions so that they fit
   in with the format of the checklist given in this chapter.

6A

Word Recognition

Reading involves much more than word recognition, although the ability to recognize recorded words is basic to the reading process. Without skill in associating word forms as given in writing with word sounds and meanings, no one can be an effective reader. Persons in the field of reading accept without question that this ability to recognize words is essential to the development of maturity in reading. On this point there is no argument. There are, however, many points of controversy among laymen and among educators concerning how word recognition should be taught.

The current debate on word recognition, among those in the reading field, primarily focuses on the question of how it should be taught during the beginning stages of learning to read. The issue is whether the emphasis in the initial stages of reading instruction should be on learning the sounds represented by the written letters or whether, without much or any attention to the letter-sound relation, the effort should be concentrated on helping pupils to acquire the meaning of the written message. In other words, the point of contention is whether a code approach or a meaning approach to reading instruction should be used.

The code approach emphasizes the need of the child in beginning reading to learn the sounds associated with each letter or combination of letters. It is so named because the aim of the teacher employing the method is to help the learner acquire facility in the use of the code of the letter-sound relation. The meaning approach, on the other hand, places major emphasis on the meaning of what is read and gives little, if any, attention to developing in pupils skill in recognizing relations between the letters and sounds they represent. This approach is also known as the *whole-word approach.* There are also various combina-tions of the two methods, with some placing almost equal emphasis on deciphering the code and acquiring meaning. In practice, neither is generally used to the exclusion of the other; thus an eclectic approach is used.

Many people, both professional and lay, would state that the issue in beginning reading instruction is the *phonic approach* versus the *"look-say" approach.* The phonic approach is a code approach, since it is by means of phonics that the child learns what sounds are represented by the letters of the alphabet. The "look-say" method refers to the practice by which the pupil, without learning to focus on the letters of the alphabet and their sounds, centers his attention on the whole word. Typically he looks at the word as someone tells it to him and then he repeats it ("says" it). When the "look-say" method is used, emphasis is usually placed on the meaning of what is read. Consequently, for practical purposes this approach is classified as a meaning approach. Thus, the question of the phonic versus the "look-say" approach can be thought of as roughly paralleling that of the code versus the meaning approach.

Historical Perspective

Gaining an historical perspective on the problem of whether a code or a meaning approach should be emphasized in beginning reading instruction may be helpful in understanding why teachers sometimes fail to see the importance of both these aspects of reading.

In the history of reading instruction in the United States at times one method and at times another has been the prevailing one. In Colonial times and throughout much of the nineteenth century and even into the twentieth, a code-deciphering approach to reading instruction was generally used. The child learned the names of the letters of the alphabet and the sounds they most commonly represented. He combined sounds to make syllables and words of more than one syllable. Thus, a synthetic phonic approach was used, in which the learner synthesized the sounds of the syllable or word as a way of learning to recognize a word.

A strong reaction to the use of phonics then set in. The criticisms leveled against phonic methods were numerous. Important among them were the following:

1. The English language is not based on an easily acquired letter-sound relation, for some letters are associated with more than one sound (for example, c, with its soft and hard sounds) and some sounds are represented by more than one letter or letter combination (for example, the sound of /s/, which is represented not only by the letter s but also frequently by the letter c).
2. Phonics when used as the initial approach to reading instruction tends to produce slow word-by-word readers.
3. Use of phonics as a beginning method places the emphasis on the mechanics of reading rather than on thought getting.
4. A phonic approach is likely to make learning to read an uninteresting experience.

Early in the twentieth century the whole-word or sight method became popular. Some teachers advocated using a sentence method, in which an entire sentence was read to a child and then his attention drawn to some of the words that comprise it. Others favored a story-method approach, with a very short story read to the pupils and subsequently their attention directed to some of the sentences and words comprising the story. It will be noted that the language-experience approach is representative of some aspects of the story method. The whole-word method, the sentence method, and even the story method, including the experience chart, were popular during the period when the progressive education movement was at its height in this country. It was frequently suggested that the beginner should learn about fifty to seventy-five words by the sight method, with someone telling him each word, before beginning work on phonics. It was also recommended that when phonics was used it should be analytic phonics rather than synthetic phonics. In other words, instead of beginning with the sounds represented by letters and combining them into syllables the learner should start with the word and from it derive the phonic elements that make it up. For example, when the child knew the word *mother*, because he had been told the word, the teacher might through phonic analysis have him identify the sound with which the word begins and then ask him to name other words that begin with the same sound.

Proponents of the phonic method for beginning reading instruction have not been lacking at any time during the century. However, little attention was paid to them by leaders in the field of elementary school education for several decades before the publication of *Why Johnny Can't Read*.[1] In this book the word method is severely criticized and a phonic approach strongly advocated. Widely read and highly acclaimed by the public, Flesch's book was the target for much criticism by professional educators. However, in spite of the denunciation of the book by various profes-

[1] Rudolph Flesch, *Why Johnny Can't Read and What You Can Do about It* (New York: Harper & Row, 1955).

sional persons, it had a significant effect on the teaching of reading. Undoubtedly it has been instrumental in causing phonics to be given greater attention in educational literature even by teachers who strongly disagree with much of the book.

Significant Research

Although an exceedingly large amount of research has been done in the area of the teaching of reading, with much of it dealing with approaches to learning to read, most of these have been rather piecemeal. The studies have typically been isolated ones made by individuals working independently without the help of financial backing for authoritative investigations in the field. Two of the studies that are exceptions to this rule are: (1) the Cooperative Research Program on First-Grade Reading Instruction, sponsored by the U.S. Office of Education[2] and (2) the study by Jeanne Chall reported in the book *Learning to Read: The Great Debate*.[3] Both of these studies deal, in part, with the question of whether a code or a meaning approach or a combination of the two should be used in beginning reading.

Basic conclusions from the *Final Report, Project No. X-001*[4] sponsored by the U.S. Office of Education relevant to the question of whether the initial approach in reading instruction should be a code-deciphering process, in which letters of the alphabet are matched by the learner with the sounds

they represent, are indicated in the following quotations from that report:

> From the evidence reported concerning the use of phonics in teaching children to read earlier there can be little doubt that phonics should be an important part of the reading program. However, there is disagreement on the type of phonic approach which should be used and on the amount of phonics which should be included in the reading program. It seems apparent, from the studies reviewed, that phonics does not contribute much to children's comprehension of what is read.
>
> Indications are that the initial reading vocabulary should be selected with a greater balance between phonetically regular words and high utility words. It is likely that introducing words solely on the basis of frequency of use presents an unusually complex decoding task for the beginning reader.
>
> Word study skills must be emphasized and taught systematically regardless of what approach to initial reading instruction is utilized.
>
> Combinations of programs, such as basal program with supplementary phonics materials, often are superior to single approaches.[5]

In the book *Learning To Read: The Great Debate*,[6] Jeanne Chall reports on the results of her extensive investigation made under a grant from the Carnegie Foundation for the Advancement of Teaching. Her findings were revolutionary in that they are in rather direct opposition to many of the points of view about beginning reading instruction commonly held by specialists in the reading field. She throws a bombshell among those who believe that a code-deciphering approach, one in which the grapheme-phoneme relation is emphasized from the very beginning, is undesirable. In fact, the author even makes it seem rather professionally embarrassing that, according to her claims, her investigation indi-

[2]Guy L. Bond and Robert Dykstra, *Final Report, Project No. X-001* (Washington, D.C.: Bureau of Research, Office of Education, U.S. Department of Health, Education, and Welfare, 1967).

[3]Jeanne S. Chall, *Learning to Read: The Great Debate* (New York: McGraw-Hill, 1967).

[4]Bond and Dykstra.

[5]Bond and Dykstra, p. 210.

[6]Chall.

cates that Rudolph Flesch as well as the many laymen—often irate parents—urging a phonic approach to reading instruction are probably right, and that many professional writers on the teaching of reading are, for the most part, wrong in their premise that learning to read in the initial stage of reading instruction through a code approach is undesirable.

To be sure, Jeanne Chall has not been without critics. However, her study has had a great impact on the teaching of reading in that enthusiasts for the code approach can cite her research as justification for that approach.

Ways of Developing in Ability To Recognize Words

We will now turn our attention to four major ways in which ability in recognizing words in print can be developed. These can be classified as:

1. Learning words by means of the sight method
2. Using context clues
3. Using phonic analysis
4. Studying words structurally

Many persons favoring a code approach to reading deny the value of the first-named skill; and some greatly question the use of context clues as a means of word recognition or identification.

All four skills are discussed here in turn, although often more than one is employed simultaneously in an attack on a given word. For example, in the sentence "Dick is playing with his dog," the child may use several clues for recognizing the word *playing*. If the word is not already a part of the child's sight vocabulary, he can use context clues, study the word through phonics, and

note the structure of the word as he takes cognizance of the *ing* ending. Nor should the fact that consideration of the use of phonics in this discussion precedes that of the study of words through attention to their structure be interpreted as recommendation for teaching most of the phonic word attack skills before teaching those of structural analysis or synthesis. Some of the latter may well be taught before many of the former type. Similarly, all the emphasis on learning to recognize words through context clues should not precede, in classroom practice, all work on identifying words either through phonics or through the study of the structure of words.

Learning Words by Means of the Sight Method

The predominant method of teaching reading seventy-five and more years ago was to teach the child the individual letters first and then to teach him how to combine these letters into syllables and words. The reading of phrases and sentences was presumed to follow naturally. This method seemed the simplest and most logical. In the terminology of today a code approach was used, namely, phonic synthesis. In fact, the approach had some similarity to code approaches used today by an increasing number of persons.

Justification for teaching words as wholes has been based in part on early research on perception, which many believe revealed that most people tend to recognize the larger visual shapes first and examine details only when the total configuration cannot be readily identified. Thus, advocates of the whole-word method could claim that it is easier for a child to recognize the word *dog* as a unit than to discover the phonic values of the letters of the word and combine them. They could argue that as the child recognizes his pet dog without adding up the colors and characteristics of the individual parts—legs, ears, eyes, and the like—so can he learn to recognize a word. Furthermore, the argument could be that only when dogs resemble each other in most details does one look more closely at the parts to make an identification and that similarly often the learner needs to analyze the difference between words only when it is not a marked one.

Presentation of new words to be added to the pupil's sight vocabulary can be made both in meaningful context and out of context. The purpose is to make the pupil's response automatic when he sees the word. In this connection the chalkboard and teacher-made or commercial charts are useful. Labeling of objects in the room is helpful if it is made functional. Thus, the shelves in the cupboard may be labeled *Scissors*, *Paste*, *Brushes*, and *Cloths* to aid the child in finding or storing materials. Words learned out of context should as soon as possible be encountered in context. Reading-card exercises in which whole words are presented should be preceded and/or followed by the use of these words in reading. The task is made easier if the words are selected from those the child uses in his own speech and from those "service words"—such as prepositions, pronouns, and connecting words—that account for a majority of all words read.

The basis of the procedure is repetition of the desired words in different situations. If the child's reading vocabulary is consequently impoverished, as many critics of the sight-word method complain, the use of abundant voluntary reading in nontextbook books for children can serve as a supplement, adherents of the meaning approach can claim.

It used to be recommended rather generally by persons favoring the sight method that a stock of between fifty and seventy-five words learned by this method is necessary before work in phonics can be successfully begun (see p. 109). However, many people who currently favor the sight method for use in beginning reading instruction agree that there is no reason why teaching by this method cannot be accompanied earlier by some help from phonics. In fact, many recommend an eclectic approach almost from the beginning, with work on one or more phonic elements of many of the words being learned.

It is important that only a rather limited number of new words be presented at one time by the sight method. Individual differences among the children should determine the number attempted, and the teacher should not inhibit the gifted reader in a successful quest for a growing reading vocabulary, whatever the method of teaching. For the average pupil, however, a firmer foundation is laid if only a few words are thoroughly fixed in mind from day to day.

Some persons draw attention to the value of noting the general configuration of a word as an aid to recall. After a pupil has been told a word, it is claimed, he may at times find it helpful in recognizing the word when he encounters it again if he observes the outline of the word or other matters of form.

Observation of the configuration of a word can be a valuable procedure, it is asserted, not only during the periods of reading readiness and initial reading instruction but in all stages of reading, including adult reading. In fact, for rapid reading it may be essential. Through noting the outline of the word the reader is saved, it is argued, from the necessity of painstakingly deciphering many words that he meets, especially if this clue is used in conjunction with the verbal context in which a word appears. Furthermore, people favoring this procedure could claim that attention to the configuration can be given to good advantage along with a study of phonics. One way in which the child in the early stages of learning to read can be aided in developing skill in the use of the configuration clues is through questions and comments by the teacher concerning the length of a word. If a child reads *mother* when he sees the word *man*, the teacher may say: "This word could not be *mother*, for *mother* is a longer word than this."

The following cautions should be observed in using the configuration of a word as a method of recognition.

1. Pupils should not be expected to remember a large number of words through configuration clues only, for many words closely rememble one another in general appearance. Overuse of this practice is likely to result in guessing.

2. The teacher should be on guard against making wrong use of the striking characteristics of a word as a means to word recognition. To try to help a child remember the word *look* by referring to the two *o's* as windows, for example, is a confusing practice for many words besides *look* are spelled with a double *o*.

One more concern should be mentioned pertaining to the use of a sight method of teaching reading. Recent research tends to refute earlier findings concerning how much a beginning reader can see at a single eye fixation (a stop of the eye while reading). Spache and Spache[7] conclude that contrary to early research a child often needs more than one fixation to see a whole

word. Stated in a different way, a beginning reader frequently sees or recognizes less than one whole word at one fixation. If this conclusion is true we need to reconsider methods currently used and approved in teaching words by the sight method. Undoubtedly more research is needed on this point.

Using Context Clues

Like the sight method, the use of context clues is severely criticized by many advocates of a code approach to beginning reading instruction. It has been ridiculed as a "guessing" method, but its adherents persistently claim that intelligent guessing is often a desired procedure.

Let us note how context clues are often used as a method toward achieving independence in word recognition.

A teacher may use the sight method plus the method of visual context when he helps a pupil learn the word *mother* as it appears with a picture of a woman with a child. When using both of these procedures in teaching a child to identify the word, he may tell him the word is *mother* and then lead the child to notice that the word goes with the picture. Or he may ask him what the word under the picture might be. If the child says *mother*, the teacher needs to let him know that he is right.

A word can also be presented by the sight method combined with the use of verbal context clues. For example, if the pupils know all the words except *ball* in the sentence, "Bob has a new bat and ball," the teacher might tell them that he thinks many of them can figure out the new word in the sentence as they read it to see what word would fit where the new word appears. If the pupils suggest that the word might be *ball*, he will need to tell them that they are right. If the pupils do not name the

[7]George D. Spache and Evelyn B. Spache, *Reading in the Elementary School* (Boston: Allyn and Bacon, 1969), pp. 7–12.

correct word, the teacher should tell them the word and help them see that *ball* fits with the meaning of the rest of the sentence.

In spite of the critics of the use of context clues, many persons consider skill in making use of verbal context clues significant to all stages of reading, including adult reading. Arguments for use of context clues include:

1. In the earlier stages it is of great help in providing boys and girls with needed practice on words they have identified at a previous time but which they still do not recognize instantly without other aids.
2. Before the pupils have learned to identify and remember words through word analysis or synthesis, they can, by means of skill in the use of verbal clues, frequently receive from the context aid in recalling the word that they need.
3. Even after the readers have developed facility in the use of structural and phonic analysis and synthesis, they can be aided in increasing their rate of reading through efficient use of verbal context clues. Often through context a reader can recognize a word faster than through analytic or synthetic methods. For example, a person who comes across the sentence "Geometry is one branch of mathematics in which I am greatly interested," may be able to recognize, by means of the context, the word *mathematics*, providing he knows the other words in the sentence and has a background for understanding the sentence.
4. There are many words in English whose pronunciation depends on the context, such as *read, lead, bow, refuse.*

We have noted in number 3 that an adequate background of experience is essential for success in the use of context clues. A person who does not know what geometry is would receive little help from context in the sentence: "Geometry is one branch of mathematics in which I am greatly interested." Consequently, it is the teacher's responsibility to provide sufficient experiences with the subjects about which the pupils will be reading. The teacher can help boys and girls get the needed background by a variety of means—discussions, explanations, demonstrations, experiments, field trips and other visual aids, and reading. After a pupil has read fairly easy material on a given subject, he can often be helped to understand more difficult material that he reads subsequently on the same topic. At times guidance can be given just before the class begins reading a selection in which concepts are discussed with which the pupils are unfamiliar. At other times, preparation for the reading may have taken place days or even weeks before. A wide background of experience is one assurance that the child will have less difficulty not only in reading in general but also in making intelligent use of verbal context clues.

If a reader is to be expected to get help through the verbal context in the identification of a word, the proportion of unfamiliar to familiar words should be kept small. If a first-grade child comes to the sentence, "The boy has a bat and ball," without recognizing either *boy* or *bat* or *ball*, no intelligent use of context clues can be made. The exact ratio of unknown to known words, as far as recognition of the words is concerned, cannot be ascertained; it may differ, among other factors according to the difficulty of the concepts discussed, the intelligence, maturity, background, and reading ability of the reader, and the skill of the teacher.

The identification of a word does not necessarily have to take place in context in order that the pupil may recognize it later by context clues. A teacher may write the word *mother* on the chalkboard when he tells the child the word, and later on, when the child again encounters the word in his readings, help him make use of the context to recall the word. Sometimes it is desirable first to present a word in isolation, since more attention can then be given to its characteristics.

Until recently little was done to help boys and girls learn how to use context clues in connected discourse, although advocacy of the techniques dates back for at least half a century. In 1965 Wilber Ames[8] developed a classification scheme of value in comprehending the meaning of unknown words in contextual situations. His classification of types of context clues which might be taught systematically include the following fourteen categories.

1. Clues derived from language experience or familiar expression
2. Clues utilizing modifying phrases or clauses
3. Clues utilizing definition or description
4. Clues provided through words connected or in series
5. Comparison of contrast clues
6. Synonym clues
7. Clues provided by the tone, setting, and mood of a selection
8. Referral clues
9. Association clues
10. Clues derived from the main idea and supporting details pattern of paragraph organization
11. Clues provided through the question-and-answer pattern of paragraph organization
12. Preposition clues
13. Clues utilizing nonrestrictive clauses or appositive phrases
14. Clues derived from cause-and-effect pattern of paragraph and sentence organization

How application of some of the items on the list can be made is illustrated later in this book (see p. 193).

Using Phonic Analysis and Synthesis

Let us clarify the terms *phonics* and *phonetics*, two terms that are often wrongly used interchangeably. *Phonetics* pertains to the science of speech sounds, whereas *phonics* refers to the relationship that exists between a spoken speech sound and the written symbol which represents it. The word *phonics* should be used when we are speaking of the particular word attack skill known as decoding, the process used when translating a written symbol to the sound that it represents.

The place of phonics in reading instruction, as noted earlier, has been the subject of heated controversy and of much experimental research. Not only has the subject been discussed by teachers for many years but it has also in recent times excited partisan interest not only within the teaching profession but among the public at large. This increased participation in the controversy is undoubtedly due in part to the publication of such books as *Why Johnny Can't Read* and the increased and easy availability to the lay public of commercial phonics teaching materials.

The teaching of phonics is based on the need of an understanding of the relation

[8]Wilbur Ames, "The Development of a Classification Scheme of Contextual Aids," *Reading Research Quarterly*, vol. II, no. 1 (Fall 1966), pp. 57–82, with quotations from pages 66–67.

between the written symbol (the grapheme) and the sound it represents (the phoneme). This understanding is predicated on recognizing the written symbol and then translating it into the sounds represented. For example, the learner makes use of this process as he recognizes the letter *c* in *can* as symbolizing the /k/ sound. In order to make the transition from the graphemes to their phonemes, an individual needs, of course, to know the sounds represented by the various letters. In other words, in order to make this translation, he needs to know the code of equivalence between the written symbols and the sounds they represent.

A problem involved in decoding in reading is that the English language is far from being based on a one-to-one sound-symbol correspondence. The grapheme-phoneme relation in English is, indeed, a complicated one. As stated earlier (see p. 109) some letters or combinations of letters represent different sounds in different words, and some sounds are represented by more than one letter or combination of letters. For example, let us note again the letter *c*. As indicated earlier the grapheme *c* can stand for an /s/ sound or for a /k/ sound. Furthermore, the /k/ sound can be represented by the graphemes *c, k, ck, qu* (as in *antique*). We designate this lack of consistency in the code in the English language as a lack of a one-to-one relation between the letter and the sound it represents, between the grapheme and the phoneme.

So far in our discussion of coding, we have referred only to decoding. We need to recognize also the process of encoding. At times the latter term is used to refer to the act of translating the oral symbol (the spoken word or part of it) into the written symbol. It is the process used when writing, as the writer decides on the letters to use to represent the needed sound. In a sense encoding is the opposite of decoding, if we

think of decoding as the process of substituting the phoneme for the grapheme (as in reading.) But there is yet another meaning of the term *encoding* as it refers to the language arts. As used by some persons, it refers to the mental process which permits the reader to interpret meaning as he uses, at the same time, his knowledge of the relation between phonemes and the graphemes which represent them. Although it is not possible to see this process, the teacher can ascertain what meaning the child has derived by asking a selected number of questions on the content or by asking him to summarize what he has read. Which of these two interpretations of the term *encoding* is being used by a writer or a speaker needs to be determined through the context in which it appears.

Points of Dispute

Probably few persons in the field of the teaching of reading would disagree with the point of view that no one becomes an efficient reader who has not learned—either by himself or with the aid of another person, most likely the teacher—at least part of the code giving the relation between the written symbols and the sounds represented by them. The dispute about teaching phonics, therefore, is not over the *whether* but over the *how*, the *when*, and the *what*.

A point of much debate, as noted earlier, is whether a code emphasis or phonic approach rather than an analytic or meaning approach should be the basis for beginning reading instruction. Those who believe in the analytic method favor presenting children with whole words first and then teaching them to analyze those words into the sound elements which comprise them. In other words, the analytic approach starts with sight vocabulary and then makes use of the phonic analysis of words.

A point of difference, which arises among those subscribing to an analytic approach in beginning reading instruction, is the question of whether instruction in phonics should be systematic or incidental. Granted that there is an essential body of phonic skills to be mastered, should these skills be taught sequentially to all children, with whole words deliberately chosen to illustrate a phonic principle? Or should the phonic principles be taught to each child as the need arises in his reading? Many reading specialists and classroom teachers prefer a combination of these two approaches.

An objection to the sequential, isolated teaching of phonic principles is the fact that many alert young readers discover the principles themselves in the course of highly motivated, meaningful reading, and for them class instruction in phonics may be wasteful. On the other hand, in individualized reading programs there is danger that many children will fail to encounter or to master essential phonic elements.

Advocates of the code-emphasis approach favor teaching the relationship between the letters or graphemes and the sounds or phonemes they represent, first. Two methods of teaching these sound-symbol relationships exist. First, an individual letter can be related to an isolated sound. This technique exemplifies a synthetic approach. One of the difficulties involved when attempting to teach letter-sound relationships in isolation is that it is extremely difficult, if not impossible, to pronounce consonant sounds in isolation without adding a vowel sound. For example, if an attempt is made to reproduce in isolation the sounds represented by b, a, and t, in an effort to recognize the word bat, they would probably be given as /bu/, /ah/, /tu/. In an attempt to blend those sounds into a word, they would probably be pronounced bu-au-tu, and thus the result-

ing vowel distortion might be a source of confusion for a learner.

A second method of teaching sound-symbol relationships in a code emphasis approach is one in which the association is learned not in isolation but within a word. Most current phonics methods of teaching beginning reading are code-emphasis approaches that use variations of the "sounds-within-words" technique.

One method of using the "sounds-within-words" technique is through the use of key words. For example, the child might be given a card for the letter b. On the card might be a picture of a $ball$, the word $ball$, and a b and a B as shown in this illustration:

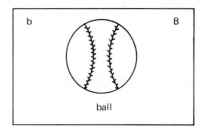

The child would learn that the word $ball$ is printed on the card under the picture of the ball and the first sound heard in the word $ball$ as it is pronounced is the sound represented by the letter b, which is printed in both upper- and lower-case letters at the top of the card. By substitution, then, the sound represented by the letter b could be transferred to other words in which the letter b occurs.

Over the years, children have learned to read by various methods, including both the analytic and synthetic. The problem has been one of finding an approach that would be most appropriate for each individual—one that would lead to effective reading and encourage strong and continuing interest in reading throughout life. Many people will concede that an intelligent, able, sympathetic teacher, one who is flexible enough to adapt his procedure to individual needs, is more important than the method—whether it is the analytic or the synthetic. However, this fact in no way relieves us of the necessity of weighing the relative advantages of one method over another.

Principles of Teaching Phonics

With the great divergence of opinion concerning the role of phonics in reading instruction, there are but few generalizations having to do with teaching by this method that will be accepted by the two opposing factions other than that phonics is important in learning to read. Other principles, though less commonly accepted, to which, however, a large number of educators adhere, are listed here:

1. The phonics taught should be of use to the learner Only those generalizations about differences and likenesses of words should be taught to beginning readers which apply to the simple words they encounter in reading or in presentations by the teacher.

2. For most pupils, instruction in phonics should be systematic The progression should be from the simpler, more widely used elements and generalizations to the more difficult and less generally applied learnings, with well-distributed practice.

3. The work in phonics should be adapted to individual differences Any program in word recognition should be geared to the developmental level of the children. Pupils within a given grade may be expected to be on varying levels in many

respects, including the various phases of phonic analysis. Some will not be ready as soon as others. Some will be able to deal with simple abstract learnings; others will profit more from concrete experiences. Moreover, progress will vary greatly after initial instruction has begun. Some pupils will need practically no help beyond that provided by the material they are currently reading, while others will benefit greatly from additional practice in workbooks or teacher-made materials and games or drills that focus attention on certain needed skills.

4. Rules and generalizations should frequently be taught inductively By presenting three or more familiar words that have the same initial, medial, or final letter, the teacher can call attention to the similarity and help the pupil to fix the appropriate sound in mind in such a way as to enable him to recognize the same sound in another word. For example, if the pupil has learned the similar beginning of the words *make, mother,* and *man,* he is equipped to attack the word *many* by applying a generalization to a new grouping of letters. Chalkboard, chart, and workbook can supply practice in making such applications, and, of course, the rule, which the pupil himself has been led to formulate, can then be used in his own "silent" reading. Similar generalizations can, for example, be made and applied with the medial vowel in words ending in a silent *e.*

It is unwise to expect that all generalizations about phonics should be learned inductively. Children can also learn through deductive teaching. While it seems desirable that often they should be helped in reaching conclusions in the form of rules or generalizations, to follow the inductive procedure at all times would slow the process of learning. Furthermore, much learning in life outside of school takes place without use of an inductive method. Children learn to profit from deductions made from generalizations presented to them.

Elements of Phonics To Be Taught

One point of disagreement concerning the teaching of phonics is the question of what should be taught. It is not the purpose of the writers to state authoritatively what the phonic content of the reading program should be. Most reading systems emphasizing phonics and most basal readers indicate clearly what they recommend as the minimum of phonics that should be taught. The listing given here includes only those elements that are rather commonly accepted as important.

It should be noted that several of the generalizations here given are not without exception as far as the universality of their application is concerned.

1. Some consonants represent one sound; they are:

b	*d*	*f*	*h*	*j*
big	dot	fun	hat	jump
bat	day	fig	hold	jelly

k	*l*	*m*	*n*	*p*
kitten	lay	man	now	pin
king	limb	more	not	put

r	*t*	*v*	*z*
run	tin	vice	zebra
rap	tire	van	zinc

2. Some consonants represent more than one sound; they are:

s	*s*	*s*	*s*	*x*
(s)	(z)	(sh)	(zh)	(gz)
set	is	sure	pleasure	exit
sun	was	sugar	measure	exam

x	*x*
(ks)	(z)
mix	xylophone
box	xenia

3. The letter *q* in a word is followed by the letter *u*. The *qu* may represent either the *k* or *kw* sound, as in:

qu	*qu*
/k/	/kw/
antique	quick
critique	qualify

4. A *c* or *g* before an *e*, *i*, or *y* usually represents the soft sound; before an *a*, *u*, or *o*, they represent the hard sound as follows:

c	*c*	*g*	*g*
(soft)	(hard)	(soft)	(hard)
city	came	gym	gate
cent	cone	giant	goat

5. Consonant blends are combinations of two or three consonants blended in such a way that each letter in the blend keeps its own identity. Examples of words containing consonant blends are:

br	*cr*	*dr*	*fr*	
bring	cry	drive	fringe	
brought	crude	drink	fright	

gr	*pr*	*tr*	*bl*	*cl*
grass	price	trim	black	clown
grain	prune	train	bland	climb

fl	*gl*	*pl*	*sl*	*sp*
fly	glass	play	slow	spice
flake	glide	plan	slide	spot

sc	*sk*	*sl*	*sm*	*sn*
scale	skate	slow	smile	snow
scout	sky	slide	smell	snake

st	*sw*	*sch*	*scr*
stay	swing	school	scram
stop	swim	schedule	scrub

spl	*spr*	*str*
splash	spring	string
splice	sprout	strong

6. Consonant digraphs are written or printed symbols made up of two or more consonants representing one speech sound, such as:

sh	*wh*	*gh*	*tch*
ship	white	tough	watch
shrink	which	rough	pitch

7. Some consonant digraphs may represent more than one speech sound, such as:

ch	ch	ch
(ch)	(sh)	(k)
charge	machine	chasm
chain	chef	character

th	th
(voiced)	(unvoiced)
that	think
this	thought

8. A single vowel usually represents the short sound if it is in a closed syllable (syllable ending in a consonant), such as:

a	e	i	o
bat	fed	fin	bond
apple	better	finish	cottage

u	y
luck	gym
butter	myth

9. If a final e in a word is preceded by a single consonant, a single vowel preceding the consonant is usually long and the e is silent as in words, such as:

a	e	i	o	u
ate	Pete	ride	hope	cute
made	delete	pine	pole	flute

10. A single vowel usually represents the long sound if it is in an accented open syllable (syllable ending in a vowel), such as:

a	e	i	o
table	me	pilot	open
maple	secret	rival	local

u	y
pupil	my
tulip	cyprus

11. Vowel digraphs are combinations of two vowels representing one speech sound, such as:

ai	ay	ee	oa	ie
pain	may	street	boat	pie
mail	clay	fleece	toad	cried

12. Some vowel digraphs represent more than one speech sound, such as:

ea	ea	ea
(ā)	(ē)	(ĕ)
great	each	head
steak	creak	bread

13. The sound represented by a single vowel preceding an r is usually modified by the r, as in:

ar	er	ir
car	her	shirt
marble	certain	thirsty

or	ur
corn	hurt
order	furnace

14. The sound represented by a single a preceding an l, w, or u, or ll is neither long nor short, as in:

u	w	l	ll
caught	saw	talk	ball
caustic	drawn	always	call

15. Diphthongs are written or printed symbols representing two vowels so nearly blended that they almost produce a single speech sound, as in:

oi	oy	ou	ew	ue
oil	boy	ouch	new	blue
moist	employ	found	chew	true

Sequence

One caution needs to be expressed at this point. The listing of phonic elements and generalizations as given in this chapter is not to be considered as the sequence in which they are to be taught.

Grade levels are undesirable criteria for determining sequence. Since the accomplishments of boys and girls and their readiness for any phase of reading instruction varies so much from grade to grade, it is better to express the sequence of phonic skills to be studied in terms of levels of achievement.

There is no one best sequence for teaching the various aspects of phonic analysis. Numerous acceptable orders of presentation have been worked out. The succession should be based on principles such as these:

1. There should be progression from the simple to the more complex.
2. Other things being equal, the more frequently used elements and generalizations should be taught before the less frequently used.
3. Provisions should be made on each level for the maintenance of skills acquired, at least in part, on the preceding level.

One of the best sources of suggestions on the sequence to follow in phonic analysis is to be found in the teachers' manuals accompanying series of readers. Any teacher using one of these series should acquaint himself with the program outlined in the manuals. However, the suggestions should not be followed slavishly. The recommendations are, for the most part, made in terms of the average child in a grade. The teacher must make adaptation to individual differences. An example of a sequence for phonics instruction follows.

1. Provide needed work on auditory and visual discrimination.
2. Teach the sounds of consonants before those of vowels. Start with the single consonant sounds that have but one sound, namely, *b, d, f, h, j, k, l, m, n, p, r, t, v,* and *z.* Teach them as they occur in initial and then in final positions in words, before teaching them in medial positions. Later teach common consonant digraphs, then two-letter consonant blends, and then, three-letter consonant blends.
3. Teach the vowel sounds with the short sounds first and then the long.

4. Teach vowel digraphs and diphthongs and silent letters.
5. Teach rules governing long and short vowels.

Studying Words Structurally

Phonic analysis is not the only type of word analysis. A second method of analyzing words is through the use of structural analysis. While in phonic analysis the reader deciphers a word by means of sounds represented by the letters or combination of letters in a word, in structural analysis he recognizes the meaning or pronunciation units of a word.

Structural analysis deals with both word variants and word derivatives. By a word variant is meant a word that deviates from the root word according to the case, number, and gender of nouns; the tense, voice, and mood of verbs; and the comparison of adjectives and adverbs. Thus, variants of the noun *prince* are *princes* and *princess;* of the verb *walk* are *walks, walked, walking;* of the adjective *small* are *smaller* and *smallest.* Word derivatives are words formed from root words through the addition of prefixes and/or suffixes—for example, *likable* and *uncomfortable.* Learning compound words—for example, *something* —through identification or recognition of the parts of polysyllabic words through the aid of syllabication is also part of structural analysis.

The question may be asked: "Why teach structural analysis of word variants or word derivatives when these words could be studied through phonic analysis or synthesis?" To be specific: "Why should the teacher bother teaching children to use structural analysis or synthesis when learning the word *unhappy* if they can analyze the word through phonics?" The answer is that phonic analysis is a slower form of word analysis than structural analysis. The child who has learned to recognize instantly the prefix *un* in *unhappy* does not have to engage in the uneconomical procedure of first analyzing by means of phonics. The reader who can quickly identify the common prefixes and suffixes reads with more speed than the one who has to use phonics in this process.

In succeeding paragraphs the following questions will be discussed:

1. What are the basic principles that should be observed in teaching structural analysis?
2. What should be taught to boys and girls in the elementary school about structural analysis?
3. In what sequence and at what levels should the various elements of word structure be taught?
4. What are some additional suggestions for teaching children to identify and recognize words by means of structural analysis?

The fourth question will be answered primarily in the following chapter (see Chapter 6B, "Developing Skill in Word Recognition," p. 145).

Principles of Teaching Words Structurally

The following principles warrant special emphasis in relation to analyzing or synthesizing words by means of their structure.

1. Overemphasis on structural analysis should be avoided Structural analysis should be seen in relation to other methods of word recognition. When a word can be recalled by means of quicker methods, such as configuration or context clues, the reader should not resort to word analysis. If too much attention has been paid to locating root words, prefixes, and suffixes, it is possible for reading to become ineffective because the reader approaches too many words by trying to locate word parts. It may be undesirable to have all "new words" analyzed either structurally or through a phonic approach.

2. As rule, the reader should examine a "new word" to see if he can analyze it structurally before he tries to unlock it by means of phonics This principle is sound because structural analysis is usually a quicker method of word recognition than phonic analysis. Consequently, rate in reading as well as quality of comprehension can be improved if the more tedious methods involving phonics are employed only when other means fail.

3. The analysis of "new words" should not, as a rule, be isolated from reading as a meaningful process Frequently it is advisable to present in context a "new word" that is to be analyzed structurally. The context can help the reader decide what the word is. For example, if the reader comes across the sentence, "Sam is walking home," and he knows the root word *walk,* he can often tell without really studying the ending that the "new word" is *walking,* not *walks* or *walked.* At times a word might be presented without context but later be used in a functional setting.

4. The sequence in teaching a "new word" by means of structural analysis should, as a rule, be from the whole word to the word part and then back to the whole word Specifically, it is often desirable to present the word first—for example, *walking*—next to ask the pupils to identify the root word and the ending, and then to have them combine the root with the ending. This procedure is recommended because it more nearly resembles the situation in which the pupil is likely to encounter a word. Nevertheless, occasional special practice in which a child forms variants or derivatives of a word is helpful, as, for example, having the pupils form the words *walks, walked,* and *walking* from *walk.*

5. Structural analysis should not be confused with "finding little words in big words" One rather common method used to help boys and girls analyze words structurally is to ask them to "find little words in big words." This practice may be misleading. For example, finding *at* in *rat* could lead a child also to look for *at* in *rate* and therefore confuse him. A child accustomed to searching for "little words in big words" might pronounce *together* as *to-get-her* or *some* as *so-me,* and in the word *furthermore* he might be led to a wrong identification if he isolates *the* or *he* or *her.*

6. Generalizations should be developed with the pupils They should not be presented as rules to be memorized. Usually when teaching that words ending in *y* preceded by a consonant change the *y* to *i* before adding *es,* the teacher may write on the board a few nouns ending in *y,* some preceded by a consonant, others by a vowel, like *boy, boys; lady, ladies; day, days; candy, candies;* and *toy, toys.* The pupils may observe how the plural of each of the singular nouns in the list was formed, writing in one column the singular words ending in *y* preceded by a vowel and in the other the singular words ending in *y* preceded by a consonant. Next the pupils may summarize their observation that to the words in the first column ending in *y* preceded by a vowel, an *s* only was added. The teacher may then explain that this sum-marization holds true in other cases. Similarly the boys and girls may summarize their finding that in the words in the second column—those ending in *y* preceded by a consonant—the *y* was changed to *i* before *es* was added. The teacher may then explain that this summarization, too, holds true in other cases. To make this original learning permanent, the pupils should be helped to note the application of these rules in their later reading and in their spelling. This method of procedure in developing a generalization is much more likely to be effective than that in which the teacher gives the rule and the pupils memorize it.

7. There should be a developmental program that provides for training in structural analysis Skill in analyzing words structurally is such a significant phase of skill in word recognition that it cannot be left to chance. While incidental methods should be used when they help foster a better understanding of words on the part of boys and girls, the teacher should make certain that all the essential elements of structural analysis are presented and that provisions are made for the maintenance of these skills through meaningful distributed practice. Suggestions as to the elements to include in such a program are given in the next paragraphs.

A Developmental Program

Exactly which elements and generalizations in structural analysis should be taught in the elementary school is a question that has not been determined. In trying to decide on the points to be studied, the teacher should bear in mind: (a) the frequency of occurrence of the structural form; (b) the ease with which the learner can identify the form; and (c) the value of the element to the development of speed and independence in word recognition.

The following elements in structural analysis of words are frequently considered important enough to be taught somewhere in the elementary school:

1. Recognizing word endings in words in which the root is known to the reader, such as:

s	ed	y	er
cats	walk*ed*	rain*y*	wid*er*
windows	hopp*ed*	milk*y*	fatt*er*

es	ing	able	al
watch*es*	ring*ing*	work*able*	politic*al*
wash*es*	walk*ing*	desir*able*	electric*al*

ful	ness	like
hand*ful*	sick*ness*	life*like*
help*ful*	new*ness*	child*like*

less	ment
help*less*	pay*ment*
thank*less*	amuse*ment*

Pupils should be familiar with the application of the following generalizations about the endings of word.

Words ending in *y* preceded by a consonant change the *y* to *i* before adding *es* to form variants of the root word. (baby, babies)

Words ending in *y* preceded by a consonant change the *y* to *i* before *ed, er, est,* or *ly* is added. (marry, married; tiny, tinier; funny, funniest; merry, merrily)

Many words ending in a consonant preceded by a vowel double the final consonant before *ed* or *ing* is added. (run, runner; flap, flapping)

Many root words ending in *e* drop the *e* before adding *ing* to form a variant. (take, taking)

2. Recognizing prefixes which modify the meaning of the root word, such as:

re	im	de
return	*import*	*deflate*
reclaim	*immature*	*dethrone*

dis	un	pre	com
discolor	*unhappy*	*pretest*	*compress*
disarm	*untie*	*preset*	*compact*

The more advanced pupils in the elementary school may also be helped to recognize the fact that a variation of the prefix *im* occurs in words such as *illegal* and *illegible,* where instead of the *m* of the prefix *im,* the first consonant of the root of the word is doubled so that the consonant preceded by *i* forms the prefix to the root of the word.

3. Identifying or recognizing compound words where one or both parts of a compound word are known to the reader.

mail box	door mat	hand bag
blue bird	motor boat	sea side

4. Identifying or recognizing the possessive form when the word without the possessive ending is known to the reader.

dog's   wife's   boys'   cat's   husband's   girls

5. Identifying or recognizing common contractions, such as

I am—I'm	you are—you're
it is—it's	they have—they've
I will—I'll	let us—let's
do not—don't	we are—we're

6. Identifying or recognizing polysyllabic words partly by means of syllabication

It is not essential to the recognition or pronunciation of a word to know exactly where some of the breaks between syllables occur. For instance, a child does not need to know whether the division of syllables in the word *making* comes before or after the *k* in order to pronounce the word correctly, even though for written syllabication purposes that knowledge is important.

In the absence of scientific proof as to the role of generalizations for syllabication on ability to recognize words, the teacher may consider which, if any, of the following generalizations he would think important to develop with his pupils.

If the initial vowel in a word is followed by two consonants, the first of the two consonants usually ends the first syllable of the word, as in *big ger.*

If the initial vowel in a word is followed by a single consonant, the consonant usually begins the second syllable of the word. (v/cv) If the last syllable of a word ends in *le,* the consonant preceding *le* usually begins the last syllable, as in *ta ble.*

VC/CV	V/VC	Consonant "le"
big ger	o pen	ta ble
win dow	ma jor	puz zle

7. Recognizing the schwa sound (ə) For interpretation of diacritical marks it may be important for the pupil to know facts such as these about the schwa sound: The vowel/symbol correspondence in an unaccented syllable is not the same as in an accented syllable. Frequently the same sound is heard in the unaccented syllable regardless of the vowel with which it is spelled. This sound is called the schwa sound. Examples of the schwa can be heard in:

about bedlam beautiful beaten beckon

Sequence

The order in which the elements significant in structural analysis should be taught cannot be stated authoritatively for all grades or for all individuals within a grade. Factors such as the following will need to be taken into consideration in working out the sequence in which the elements should be taught. (a) The items included in a list of points to be developed in stressing facility in word recognition through structural analysis should not be taken up in the order in which they are listed in this book. (b) One factor that

should help determine the order of development is the occurrence or presentation in the reading textbook of words representative of the form to be studied. (Most basal reader series for the elementary school provide definite guidance in the teachers' manual for a program of word recognition.) (c) The difficulty of a point to be learned should be one of the criteria for deciding upon the order in which the items should be taught. Other things being equal, those points easier to learn and to apply should be taught first.

Linguistics and Word Recognition[9]

Let us first of all clarify the meaning of the word *linguistics,* which has been defined in various ways. It has been referred to as the study of language. LeFevre[10] calls it "a scientific method of studying language." Fries defines linguistics as:

> . . . a body of knowledge and understanding concerning the nature and functioning of human language achieved by the scientific study of the structure, the operation, and the history of a wide range of very diverse human language.[11]

Linguistics is not a new field of inquiry and research. Interest in the nature of language

[9]This discussion of linguistics is, in part, an adaptation of information given in *Teaching the Language Arts in the Elementary School,* 3d ed. (Dubuque, Iowa: William C. Brown Company, Publishers, 1976), by one of the authors of this book, Martha Dallmann.

[10]Carl A. LeFevre, "The Contribution of Linguistics," *Issues and Innovations in the Teaching of Reading,* (Chicago: Scott, Foresman, 1967), pp. 199–205.

[11]Charles C. Fries, "Linguistic Approaches to First Grade Reading Programs," *Reading Instruction: Selected Materials,* Althea Berry, Thomas C. Barrett, and William R. Powell, eds. (Boston: Allyn and Bacon, 1969), pp. 372–382. The article is a reprint from *First Grade Reading Programs, Perspectives 5,* (Newark, Del.: International Reading Association, 1965), pp. 45–53.

dates back to ancient history. It is only of late years, however, that the question of the application of the findings of linguists to teaching elementary-school subjects has been given much consideration. Understandably the point of inquiry is focused primarily on the bearing that the view of linguists can or should have on the language-arts program. In this connection questions such as these are of concern to the teacher of reading.

> Should the reading program be linguistically oriented?
> How can effective application of linguistics be made to the teaching of reading?

These questions are particularly relevant as they apply to the teaching of word recognition and comprehension.

No attempt is made in these pages to present the reader with enough data to answer intelligently the puzzling questions concerning the teachings of linguists in their application to reading instruction. What is attempted is to provide him with some basic information on the topic, of use in further reading and study.

Claims of Linguistically-Oriented Educators

During the past few decades, suggestions for the application of phonetic principles to the teaching of reading have been made by a number of eminent linguists, among them Leonard Bloomfield[12] and C. C. Fries.[13] They emphasize the point that reading and writing are derived from spoken language. They regard the study of speech sounds as central to any defensible theory of reading instruction.

Persons interested in making application of the knowledge in the field of linguistics to the teaching of reading have many points of agreement. As a rule they place much emphasis during the initial period of reading instruction on the importance of selecting words for mastery on the basis of the spelling pattern, not on frequency of use. An example of a spelling pattern is the consonant-vowel-consonant arrangement occurring in words such as *hut, bat, can.* Another illustration is the consonant-vowel-consonant-final *e* arrangement, as in *date, fame, line.* In general, persons advocating a linguistic orientation agree that the aim of beginning reading instruction should be word recognition through the study of words with like spelling patterns, in series such as *can, fan, ran, ban, man, tan, van.* Some even advocate the inclusion in such lists of "nonsense words" to provide added practice.

Many educators favoring a linguistic approach to learning are united in their highly critical attitude toward phonics teaching. They condemn it on the allegation that the study in our schools typically proceeds from the sound to the word rather than from the word to the sound. They believe that in the former approach untrue sounds are produced as, for example, when the child sounds the *h* in *hat* as *huh.* So they propose that the learner be introduced, for example, to the grapheme *h,* with its corresponding phoneme, by his attention being drawn to the *h* in a large number of words of the same spelling pattern beginning with the letter *h,* such as *hat, ham, had, has.* However, Emans[14] points out that linguists when criticizing the teaching of phonics are unaware of the fact that phonics is typically not taught as linguists claim it is. Emans also draws at-

[12]Leonard Bloomfield, "Linguistics and Reading," *The Elementary English Review,* vol. 18 (Apr., May 1942), pp. 125–130; 183–186.
[13]Charles C. Fries, *Linguistics and Reading* (New York: Holt, Rinehart and Winston, 1963).

[14]Robert Emans, "Linguists and Phonics," *The Reading Teacher,* vol. 26, no. 5 (February 1973), pp. 477–482.

tention to the fact that while linguists in general are highly critical of a phonic approach, they seem to be unaware of his contention that a linguistic approach to reading instruction is a phonic (sound) approach, since emphasis is placed on the identification of sounds, though it is in spelling patterns.

Another criticism by linguistically-oriented educators is that the teaching of phonics, as it is done in many of our schools, is poorly organized, with gaps in learnings to be acquired and with a defective sequence in the development of the desired learnings. They are also in general agreement in their opposition to much use of the sight method (the whole-word method). An objection they have to this method is that when used as a means of learning to recognize words, every word needs to be "memorized." It is interesting, in the light of this objection, to note that the child is, after all, learning by a whole-word method, even when he learns words, as recommended by linguists, consistent in spelling patterns, as he names words such as *hen, den, men, ten,* and possibly including nonsense words such as *gen, ren, jen.* Fries' explanation pertinent to this claim is that "in the spelling-pattern approach it is the pattern itself (not the particular word) that is repeated frequently using a variety of words and matrixes."[15]

We have noted some of the points on which many linguists or linguistically-oriented educators interested in the field of the teaching of reading are in agreement. Let us next consider some points of disagreement among them.

1. Not all believe that the very first "lessons" should consist of study of lists of words with the same spelling pattern

While Bloomfield and many other linguists are of that opinion, Henry Lee Smith, Jr., for example, advocates that the child's first reading instruction, before he turns his attention to lists of words arranged in spelling patterns, should be given through the use of experience charts.

2. They differ in their lists of recommended words arranged according to spelling patterns There are wide differences in this respect from one series of linguistically-oriented readers to another.

3. There is variation among them as to their recommendation concerning the length and number of lists of words that should be presented to the beginning reader, according to spelling pattern, before he should be supplied with material using words in sentences In fact, some linguists recommend that sentences should be the unit of instruction even in the initial stages.

4. Some are opposed to the use of pictures to accompany the text in beginning reading instruction; others favor that practice Those against their use fear that the child might be reading pictures rather than mastering the grapheme-phoneme equivalence.

Evaluation of Linguistically-Oriented Programs

As the teacher evaluates the many linguistically-oriented reading programs and the so-called "linguistics programs," he should try to determine:

1. The linguistic theories on which the material or program claims to be based
2. The correctness of the claims made in terms of whether they are actually a significant part of the program or materials

[15]Fries, "Linguistic Approaches to First Grade Reading Programs," pp. 45–53.

3. The desirability of the theories on which the system or the materials are based
4. The ways in which application of the theories is made
5. The teacher's judgment of these methods (and materials) in terms of acceptability in general and in terms of practicality for his teaching situation.[16]

The Reading Vocabulary

Writers of most textbooks have tried to include almost exclusively only those words in books for the primary grades that are a part of the understanding and speaking vocabulary of the child. Unfortunately, they have not found it possible to include the many dialects and linguistic variations employed by children in so vast and diverse a country as the U.S. This is one reason why often the reading textbook fails to meet the needs of children in the many geographic sections, among various ethnic groups, and in some socioeconomic levels. How, for example, can the youngster on a Nebraska farm, in a New York ghetto, or on an Alabama plantation meet on common terms with a boy or girl who has grown up in a Cleveland suburb? All this is not to suggest, however, that a reading series designed for the children of a large nation must provide a homogeneous reading diet, but it does suggest that the pluralistic nature of our society is not duly recognized in basal reader series.

The selection of words for inclusion in the pupil's reading vocabulary, especially in the primary grades, is a matter of considerable consequence. It is for this reason that authors of textbooks in reading have spent time and effort in the selection of words used in their books. They have rightfully insisted that it is unwise to try to teach beginning readers to read words with which they are unfamiliar, when there are several thousand words in their understanding vocabulary that they cannot recognize in print. It is not until the later primary grades that most authors of basal readers try to introduce many words that will extend the child's understanding vocabulary. In order to provide a vocabulary suitable for the child to read, authors of reading series have frequently based their vocabulary selection in part on carefully compiled lists of words, which, however, represent the vocabulary of the middle-class Caucasian population.

Word Lists

Various word lists have been compiled, among them lists by Edward L. Thorndike,[17-18] Arthur I. Gates,[19] Clarence Stone,[20] Edward W. Dolch,[21] Henry Rinsland,[22] H. Kucera and W. N. Francis,[23] John Steck,[24] Albert J. Harris and Milton D. Jacobson,[25] Wayne Otto and Robert Chester,[26] and Dale Johnson.[27] Of note also is the *American Heritage Word Frequency Book.*[28]

---

[16]Martha Dallman, *Teaching the Language Arts in the Elementary School*, 3d ed. (Dubuque, Iowa: William C. Brown Company, Publishers, 1976), p. 40.

[17]Edward L. Thorndike, *A Teacher's Wordbook of 20,000 Words* (New York: Teachers College Press, 1935).

[18]Edward L. Thorndike and Irving Lorge, *A Teacher's Wordbook of 30,000 Words* (New York: Teachers College Press, 1944).

[19]Arthur I. Gates, *A Reading Vocabulary for the Primary Grades* (New York: Teachers College Press, 1935).

[20]Clarence R. Stone, *Stone's 1941 Graded Vocabulary for Primary Reading* (St. Louis, Mo.: Webster Publishing Company, 1941).

[21]Edward W. Dolch, *Methods in Reading* (Champaign, Ill.: The Garrard Publishing Co., 1955), pp. 373–374.

[22]Henry Rinsland, *A Basic Vocabulary of Elementary School Children* (New York: The Macmillan Company, 1945.)

Of the lists that have been published, the one most used by teachers is Dolch's *A Basic Sight Vocabulary*, consisting of 220 words, exclusive of nouns, which are used with greatest frequency in reading books for the primary grades. Since no nouns are given in this list, Dolch has compiled a separate list of 95 nouns commonly used in the lower grades in basal readers. Dolch's study shows that approximately two-thirds of the words in reading material for the primary grades are among the 220 words listed by him. Almost as large a percentage of words found in the intermediate-grade reading books that were examined in the Dolch study are in the list. Because of the frequency of the use of the words, they are words that many teachers think every child should learn to recognize with facility during the initial period of reading instruction.

Although a great service has been done by the compilers of word lists, these points should be considered.

1. When making use of word lists based in part or in entirety on occurrence of words in writing of or for adults, the teacher should not conclude that the words used most frequently in writing for adults are the ones that should appear in the books for children in the lower grades.

2. If a word list is based on the material written for adults as well as on some for children, unless the two parts of the study are kept discrete, it is questionable to what extent the list is useful in determining the vocabulary that should be used in reading material for children.

3. Whenever a new reading series bases its vocabulary extensively on a list that expresses current practice in vocabulary selection among materials already in print for children, there is the likelihood that whatever imperfections in vocabulary there are in other books will be perpetuated.

4. There is danger of a lack of rich content if the vocabulary is too strictly controlled. A problem confronting writers in the content areas, such as social studies and science, is that it is difficult or even impossible to express in a highly limited vocabulary, some of the complex concepts to be developed. Consequently, as a rule, the books for children in the content areas have a greater vocabulary burden than those in basal reader series. While in some respects this situation is fortunate, cognizance needs to be taken of the resulting reading problems.

The Vocabulary Burden

No conclusive research is available on the optimum number of new words per page, but it is questionable whether it is desirable to introduce on the average more than one new word per page in preprimer material and more than two per page in the primer and first reader stages. The number of new words to be presented on a page,

[23]H. Kucera and W. N. Francis, *Computational Analysis of Present-day American English* (Providence, R.I.: Brown University Press, 1967).

[24]John Steck, *A Word Count of Spoken English of Culturally Disadvantaged Preschool and Elementary Pupils* (Kansas City, Missouri: University of Missouri, 1973).

[25]Albert J. Harris and Milton D. Jacobson, "Basic Vocabulary for Beginning Reading," *The Reading Teacher*, vol. 26, no. 4 (January 1973), pp. 392–395.

[26]Wayne Otto and Robert Chester, "Sight Words for Beginning Readers," *Journal of Educational Research*, vol. 65 (July-August 1972), pp. 435–443.

[27]Dale D. Johnson, "The Dolch List Reexamined," *The Reading Teacher*, vol. 24 (February 1971), pp. 449–457.

[28]Peter Davies, Barry Richman, and John B. Carroll, eds. *The American Heritage Word Frequency Book* (Boston: Houghton Mifflin Company, 1972). (Published jointly by American Heritage Publishing Company and Houghton Mifflin Company.)

however, is dependent on so many factors that it is doubtful whether research can establish the optimum number for any level. It is usually conceded that as the child progresses in his ability to read, he can encounter, without reaching a level of frustration, more new words in proportion to the running words than he could earlier. In this connection it is important to bear in mind that while the number of new words given on a page in an intermediate-grade book is often considerably larger than the number in first-grade books (one reason being that the average length of the page increases from the primary to the intermediate grades), in reality many of the so-called "new words" in the intermediate-grade reader are new only insofar as they have not been used before in the series; they may be words which the pupils have identified through other reading.

A bright child may not need nearly as many repetitions as the average child. Furthermore, the method of presentation of a new word by the teacher determines in part how many repetitions are desirable. It would seem that probably in the books for the primary grades, when they are supplemented by additional word study, adequate repetition is provided for the average child reading on his instructional level—the level on which he can read without frustration when given proper instruction. However, many reading textbooks for the intermediate grades do not repeat words often enough for many boys and girls to be able to learn them without undue difficulty. This point is particularly serious when the words are new not only to the child's reading but also to his understanding vocabulary. A teacher can, however, solve this problem in part by supplying significant supplementary practice on the words, most of which should as a rule be done in context.

The proportionate number of new words and the amount of repetition desirable should not be determined mechanically, without reference to the individual, to the method of presentation of words, and to the supplementary reading that the child does. The learning of words should not be dependent solely on repetition in a textbook. If considerable emphasis is put in reading instruction on developing power to decipher new words and on meaning, it becomes less important to rely greatly on word lists.

What we have said in the preceding paragraphs is relevant to the determination of words, providing that a basal reader, in which frequently there is a rather rigid vocabulary control, is used. Some authorities question the need even in reading textbooks for as much control over vocabulary as is now exercised in most series. Authors of general books for boys and girls, including those for beginners, have typically seldom shown much concern about word count. And careful count of "new words" in language-experience charts might defeat a major purpose of that approach, namely that of providing boys and girls with the opportunity to express themselves in the material they dictate to the teacher for future reading by them.

6B

Developing Skill in Word Recognition

Specific suggestions for classroom practice in developing skill in word recognition are presented in this chapter. As the reader notes them it is hoped he will keep in mind the importance of having the learner see motives for performing suggested activities. Without convincing motivation, felt by the boys and girls, much of their work on the skills of word recognition or any other reading skill is likely to be of less than maximum value. The reader should also bear in mind that much of the work on word recognition can best be done in meaningful reading situations, rather than through isolated practice exercises.

Teaching Words as Sight Words

The following suggestions may be helpful to teachers when using the whole-word method as one of the means of helping boys and girls grow toward independence in word recognition.

1. **Presenting new words before reading a selection** Let us assume that the new word to be encountered is *summer.* The teacher has written it on the chalkboard in manuscript and now points to it, saying it clearly. He invites the class to repeat it with him in unison. He turns next to a cardholder or to word cards placed on the chalk ledge and asks individual children or the class as a whole to select the word *summer* from among the words listed. On the chalkboard are several sentences, one or more of which include the word *summer.* Children are called on to select those sentences containing the word and to point to the word. They then find the word in the selection to be read.

2. **Studying new words after a selection has been read** At times the teacher may prefer to have the children read a selection before he helps them with the new words in it. He is justified in doing so if he has reason to believe that the pupils will be able to figure out the new words by themselves. If the selection to be read contains many new words, however, it is usually advisable not to rely on children's ability to deal with them independently. After the reading, the children may be asked to identify the words with which they had difficulty, so that the teacher may present them in the manner suggested in the preceding paragraph. When using this procedure, however, the teacher should keep in mind the fact that frequently boys and girls, especially those with many problems in the recognition of words, may not respond to the suggestion that they designate the words they do not know. The teacher will, therefore, frequently want to select for practice, words with which he thinks one or more children may have difficulty.

3. **Presenting new words before reading a selection and providing further practice on them after the reading** In many instances work on words either before or after reading a selection may be insufficient to as-

sure needed control of the new vocabulary. Consequently, at times the teacher will want to present the "new words" before the reading and then provide additional practice on them after the reading. The latter reinforcement of the learning may frequently be planned in such a way that the boys and girls become more familiar not only with the word in question but also with other forms of the word and of words that have elements in common with it. For example, if the "new word" *talk* has been presented before the reading, after the selection has been read, the boys and girls might work on variants of the word, such as *talks, talked, talking*. Or if the word *cat* has been presented, after reading the story or part of it, the pupils might work on words similar to *cat* in all respects except the initial letter, such as *hat, fat, pat, rat, sat*.

4. Distinguishing between words of similar length and shape   Words that bear a general resemblance to each other in the eyes of a young child may be placed on the board in a row, with all the words alike except the one that is to be distinguished from the others. Or in the following list of words, pupils may be asked to draw a circle around each word that "says" *where*.

when   where   where   when   where   when

The exercise may be repeated for the identification of the word *when*. Brief exercises may be arranged for other words of similar general appearance, such as *say* and *may, man* and *can, make* and *cake, mat* and *sat*.

5. Distinguishing between words presented in pairs   Words often confused by young readers may sometimes be presented in pairs. Thus the following words may be written on the board together:

when, where   thought, through
then, there   went, want.

The teacher points to each pair in turn, saying the words and calling on pupils to draw a line under the appropriate word or pair of words. Or he may write an incomplete sentence, calling on pupils to supply the missing words.

I _____ a new ball.   *(went, want)*

6. Matching words and pictures   Both to provide practice in recognizing words and to test the ability to do so, the teacher can provide each pupil with a sheet of paper giving a column of words and another of pictures. Pupils can then be asked to draw lines from the words to the matching pictures. Or, instead of single words, groups of words or whole sentences can be supplied along with matching pictures. For example, pupils may be asked to draw a line from a picture of a boy with a ball to the one of three sentences such as these written near the picture:

Mary has a ball.
Tom has a ball.
Tom has a bat.

7. Using individual word cards   When pupils have individual cards, similar to the larger ones suitable for group work, for practice on words, they might hold up their word cards that correspond to the ones the teacher shows. Then one of the pupils could name the word on the card.

8. Labeling objects in the room   After the teacher has made labels for various items in the classroom, the pupils can be asked to place the labels with the objects. In some cases the labels may be placed on or near the objects, and in other instances they may be attached to the objects with tape. Labels can be used to designate objects in an exhibit, owners of lockers, contents of shelves or cupboards, library books, and the like.

9. Pantomiming words   Pantomime can be used effectively for practice on sight words that are difficult to illustrate in some other ways. Verbs and prepositions are among these. The pupils might illustrate by actions, as the teacher points at the written words—verbs such as *hop, walk, run, smile, laugh* and prepositions such as *under, between, over.*

10. Using a flannel board   To a flannel board might be attached, for practice on sight words, various cutouts illustrating "new words." These may be selected in terms of words "new" in a given story or in terms of those used in connection with a given topic, such as Christmas, Thanksgiving, birds, or space. On a table near the flannel board might be placed word cards (backed by a strip of flannel or felt) to accompany each of the cutout figures. The pupils could attach the cards to the appropriate illustrations. They could check their work by referring to a chart that is provided, on which the words are given next to the illustrations of them.

11. Using "helper charts'   "Helper charts," on which are indicated lists of duties to be performed by members of the class, possibly illustrated, could have a parallel column with names of persons to perform the tasks. For example, the direction *Water plants* in the first column could have a card to the right of it with the name *Sally* attached to the chart. Or the only words on the chart could be the children's names. In that case a picture of a waste basket, for example, could indicate that David is to pass it during the week that his name is on the chart opposite the illustration.

12. Following directions given on a chart   Practice in learning some words or groups of words by sight can be provided by listing on a chart some directions that the pupils have frequent occasion to follow, for example: *Get ready to go home. Put on your coats. Get ready for storytelling.* As the teacher points at a direction, the pupils respond by following it.

13. Illustrating words for a booklet   To help pupils remember words that can be illustrated, the teacher might prepare a worksheet for every child on which in each quarter of the sheet is written in manuscript a word to be illustrated. These sheets can be assembled in a booklet.

14. Distinguishing between homonyms   The sight-word method can be used in teaching homonyms. To gain practice in using newly acquired knowledge of the words, pupils might be given exercises in which they are to supply the correct homonyms. In sentences such as the following, the pupils might be asked to write the correct word given in parentheses.

John _____ the ball to the catcher.   *(threw, through)*
_____ you please open the window?   *(Wood, Would)*

Developing Word Recognition through Context Clues

Context clues are often most effective when they are employed along with other methods of word attack. The following suggestions should be read with this point in mind.

Using Picture Clues

Below are ways in which pictorial clues can serve as aids to word recognition:

1. Using pictures in connection with the presentation of a word   If the teacher wishes to present the word *ball* to the young child, he may first show a picture of a ball and carry on a brief conversation about it. In this way he is able to create in the child's mind the impressions of reality that give meaning to the verbal symbols. First comes the referent, then the symbol for it. The symbol can then evoke the referent when the reader encounters it in verbal context. To reinforce the visual image, the teacher may call attention to the length and contour of a word and present the reader with sentences in which it is used.

2. Introducing new words, in advance of reading, with the aid of pictures   Before either the class or one individual begins to read a selection, the attention of the children may be called to an accompanying picture in the book. Discussion of the picture can naturally lead to the new word in the text, which can be pointed out and emphasized. In such preliminary discussions, the teacher may encourage the class to anticipate the story from an examination of the pictures.

A variation of this method is having pupils find the picture that completes a part of a sentence that the teacher has written on the board among various ones placed on the chalkboard. Then the teacher can write the word with the rest of the sentence or show a word card with it.

3. Using picture-word cards   Some teachers have quite successfully made extensive use of picture-word cards in teaching word recognition. Sets of cards, each one of which carries on one side a picture with the appropriate label and on the other word alone, are given to all pupils for practice. Larger versions of the picture cards can be placed along the walls, and the children can make a game of matching their own card with those they find there. It should be emphasized that such games in word recognition should be combined with abundant experience in encountering the words in sentence context.

4. Using picture clues on the bulletin board The bulletin board should be a source of constant pleasure and stimulation to the pupils. Pictures—clipped from magazines, drawn by pupils, or secured from various other sources—are a most effective means of introducing children to the printed word. For example, a picture of a Christmas tree, attractively labeled, can be used as a device for drawing attention to the appearance of familiar words and for leading into a brief study of the structure of those words.

5. Giving the pupils duplicated pictures on which various words that they are learning are illustrated For example, there could be a picture of a Christmas scene, with these words illustrated in it: *mother, father, tree, book, doll, candy, ball.* The words could be written along the sides and bottom of the picture. The pupils could then draw a line from each of the words to the part in the picture illustrating that word.

6. Using other visual aids Some reading series are accompanied by films or filmstrips that introduce children to new concepts and new words. Teacher-made slides, based on the reading materials, can also prove to be effective in helping children cope with new vocabulary.

Using Verbal Context Clues

Following are suggestions for using verbal context clues as an aid to word recognition.

1. Using questions to help pupils learn words If, for example, in the sentence, "Betty bought a present for her mother," all words but *bought* are known by the reader, the teacher may ask: "How do you think Betty got the present that she gave her mother?" If the child says that she found it, the teacher may ask him to name words other than *found* that could fit into the sentence, or he may tell the pupil that the word begins with the letter *b* as a clue to the "missing word."

2. Anticipating meaning through completion exercises Pupils can be asked to supply words that might fit in a blank in an incomplete sentence, such as, "Dick _____ home after school." When the word to be supplied is *ran*, if the pupils suggest *walked, ran, hurried, hopped,* or any other words that would fit into the space, the teacher might say: "Yes, each of those words would fit into the sentence, but the one that belongs there begins with the /r/ sound. What word is it?" The correct word is then written in the blank. A variation from this type of exercise is one in which the pupils choose from a group of words the one that fits the meaning, for example:

Sam played _____ .   *(ball, boy, bat, work, sing).*

3. Anticipating words when listening Training in the use of context clues may occur if the teacher pauses at suitable places as he reads orally and asks the class to tell what they think the next word is. For example, he may read a sentence such as "The cat climbed up a _____" and then ask what word might come next.

4. Discussing with the class appropriate techniques for identifying words through context Although the suggestions will necessarily vary with the pupil's stage in learning to read, certain general hints may prove helpful to children in various grades: (a) Read the entire sentence before trying to determine the meaning of the new word. (b) Look at the beginning and ending sounds of the word to note whether these match a word that would make sense in the context. (c) Read for meaning—if your first impression of a word does not make sense, give it a second and more careful look. (d) If sentence clues do not help, read the whole paragraph; the broader context may provide the key.

5. Becoming acquainted with words related to the theme of the selection If the teacher will introduce children to interesting new words in advance of the reading, vocabulary difficulties may be substantially diminished. Thus, in a story about Eskimos, a preliminary discussion of such words as *igloo, kayak, whale, walrus, glacier,* and *frigid* may markedly reduce the child's word-recognition problems.

6. Learning to recognize synonyms and antonyms Word meanings may frequently be obtained from reference to neighboring words. Thus, in the sentence, "These are the nomothetic, or institutional dimensions of our goal-structure, as distinguished from the idiographic, or individual dimensions," we have both synonymic and antonymic clues to the unusual words, *nomothetic* and *idiographic.* Phonic and structural clues are essential, and an elementary knowledge of Greek would help us a great deal, but the sentence contains its own built-in keys to the new words. At the child's level, the following sentences illustrate the value of contextual clues in the form of synonyms and antonyms.

The picture showed an *ocelot,* a member of the cat family, in a charming pose.

While the princess moved among the guests with a friendly smile for everyone, the prince offended many with his *dour* expression.

As the game was about to begin, the principal announced over the loudspeaker that the coach and *mentor* of the team would be present, after all.

Unlike the *torrid* winds of his homeland, the cool breezes from this picturesque harbor invigorated and inspired Sapu.

For various and *sundry* reasons, the squire delayed building his new home.

Neither the rich nor the *indigent* failed to find a welcome at the bishop's home.

7. Having pupils find the word in a group of words which means the opposite or almost the opposite of the first word in the row.

kind: sad   happy   good   mean

8. **Giving riddles, in written form, for the pupils to solve**   A number of simple riddles such as the following might be written on the chalkboard:

I give milk.
I eat grass.
What am I?

Opposite the riddle might be placed a number of words—such as *cow, cat*—from which the children are to select the one that answers the riddle.

9. **Taking advantage of typographical aids**   Among the various types of context clues, some of the most helpful are the mechanical typographical devices. Punctuation marks, italics, bold print, parentheses, indentations, footnotes, and other similar devices provide helps in the recognition and interpretation of new words.

Developing Word Recognition through the Use of Phonics

Suggestions given here for the use of phonics in the teaching of word recognition are intentionally confined to a relatively small number. The teachers' manuals that accompany the better reading series contain many excellent suggestions for applying the phonics principles stated in Chapter 6A. These suggestions are based on the special vocabularies which are a part of the developmental programs followed in specific series. Methods of teaching phonic skills described in the following paragraphs should be adapted to the specific needs of children, whether or not a basal reader series is used.

1. One of the most elementary of the phonic skills is that of knowing the sounds commonly associated with single consonants in the initial position in a word. In the first work on phonics the teacher should teach consonants that, unless they are "silent letters" or blended with others, can be depended on to have the same sound always—such as, *b, h, j, l, m*. Practice can be provided by means of procedures such as these:

    a. The boys and girls might make sentences in which the initial sound of many words in a given sentence is the same, such as:
        Polly picked peas and put them near the flower pot.

    b. As the teacher names a word, the pupils might write the letter representing the sound with which the word begins.

    c. As the teacher names a word beginning with a consonant in initial position, the pupils might point at objects in the room, the names of which begin with the same sound. The game "I Spy," in which the leader says, "I spy something that begins with the same sound as the word _____," can be played.

    d. A phonic tree may be made by placing a small branch of a tree in a jar of sand. The "tree" could be whitewashed and the stand, if not colorful, painted green. To the top of the tree could be attached a card with a letter to be emphasized. If the letter *t* is used, the boys and girls might hang pictures of words beginning with that letter to the branches of the tree. Similarly, a tree could be used for practice on consonants in ending positions, on blends, on various vowel sounds, and on phonograms such as *ake, air, at.* The children can look for the pictures or they can choose appropriate ones from a box containing many pictures selected on the basis of use for help in phonics. The tree should be changed frequently if maximum learning is to be achieved through use of this device.

2. To get practice in application of what they know about consonants in initial position in a word, as well as about the use of context clues, pupils could tell what word fits into sentences such as this one, where only the initial consonant of the word is given:

    Dan gave his d_____ a bone.

Or the boys and girls might draw pictures to illustrate words missing in sentences of that type.

    Similar types of practice might be provided for pupils to strengthen their recognition of the sounds of consonants in final position in a word.

3. Practice could be provided in making substitutions of consonants in words. For example, if the pupil knows the word *fun,* he has merely to substitute the consonant *r* for *f* to be able to recognize the word *run.* The teacher can ask boys and girls who know the word *man,* when they come to the "new word" *can:* "What word that we know looks the same as this word except for the beginning letter?" When the boys and girls have replied *man,* the teacher can write *man* on the chalkboard directly below the word *can* and then ask with what sound that word (pointing at *can*) begins. He can continue by saying: "Let's name a word that begins with the *c* (hard c) sound and rhymes with *man.*" Opportunity might also then be given for the boys and girls to name other words that are like *man* and *can* except for the beginning letter, such as *tan* and *ran.* Attention needs to be drawn not only to the possibility of substitution of consonants in initial position but also in ending and medial position in a syllable as a possible means of deciphering a new word. In such cases a similar procedure may be followed. The same method can also be used with words in which substitution of a vowel in a syllable is a possible means of identifying a new word, as when, for example, *sit* is recognized if the word *sat* is known.

4. Some boys and girls who can use phonic clues secured through the

recognition of consonants at the beginning and ending positions of a word may be uncertain what to do when a consonant comes in a medial position within a syllable, as for example, in the word *late.* As a rule, in the case of monosyllabic words not much practice is needed on consonants in medial position if the pupils know well the role of the consonants in the initial and ending positions. Nevertheless, an indication should be given to the child fairly early in his training in phonics that consonants can occur in other than beginning and ending positions.

5. As boys and girls meet in their reading consonant blends such as *st, gr, tr, cr,* and *br,* they should learn that these and other consonant combinations are sounded in such rapid succession that they do not make two entirely separate sounds. They could be asked to name words beginning with whatever blends they are then studying or have studied. A phonic wheel like the one illustrated can help provide occasional practice not only on beginning consonant blends but also on initial single consonants.

   The wheel can be made of two circles of tagboard, one a little smaller than the other, fastened together in the middle by a brass fastener so that the smaller wheel can spin around. Since the wheel here illustrated is to give practice on *st* in initial position in a word, the letters *st* are written on the inner circle next to an indentation in that circle made by cutting out a piece of the tagboard. The cutout part should be of sufficient size so that endings such as *ore* (to go with the *st* to from *store),* *one, op,* and *ick* written on the outer circle can be seen when the slot is moved in such a way that the opening in the smaller circle is opposite the place where the ending in the larger wheel occurs. Then, as the child spins the smaller circle, he can read the words that begin with *st,* such as *store, stone, stop,* and *stick.*

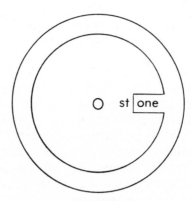

6. Another phonic device that helps provide practice needed by some pupils is that of listing either consonant blends or single consonants on

slips of tagboard about one inch square, with the consonant or consonant blend written at the right of each of these cards. Attached by brass fasteners to the bottom of the pile of these smaller cards could be a larger one, possibly 1 × 5 inches, that contains all of the letters of a word except the beginning consonant or consonant blend. If, for example, on the longer card the ending *ake* were given, then on the smaller cards might be written, *b, r, c, t, m, f, l, s, and w.* To form different words for recognition, the pupils can lift up one small card at a time and thereby make a number of words ending in *ake.*

7. After boys and girls have learned the sound of *th*, both voiced as in *there* and voiceless as in *thin*, the teacher may wish to write on the board a list of words beginning with *th*, some with the voiced and some with the voiceless sound, such as *the, that, thick, think.* Then as the pupils pronounce each word they could, for example, put a star in front of every word that begins with the sound of the *th* in *thin.*

8. When teaching vowel sounds the teacher may, for example, ask the pupils to identify the sound of the /a/ in words such as *at, bat, man, sand.* Or he may ask the boys and girls which words in a series such as the following has an *a* with the same sound as the *a* in *at: ate, cat, am, air, can, arm, late, bat.*

   Another, but similar, type of practice could be provided by asking the children to indicate which in a series of words listed on the chalkboard or on paper contains a given sound that is identified as the long sound or the short sound of a vowel. For example, the pupils might select words with the long *e* sound from among a group of words such as the following, included among which are words with the long *e* sound, words with the short *e* sound, words with other sounds of *e*, and words with the silent *e: be, set, late, been, he, she.*

   Another procedure is to have the pupils make new words by changing the vowel in a word to form other words, as when they substitute for the *a* in *hat*, the letters *i, o,* and *u* to form *hit, hot,* and *hut.*

9. Further practice on vowels could be provided through procedures such as the following:

   a. After the teacher has written on the board a word containing one vowel, for example, *bell,* he asks questions that involve changing the vowel of the given word so that another word is formed. For example, if the word *bell* has been written on the chalkboard, the teacher might ask the pupils what change would need to be made in that word so that the "new word" names something with which boys and girls play.

b. In two columns words containing various vowel sounds could be listed, with one word in each column having the same vowel sound as a word in the other column. The pupils can be asked to match the words with similar vowel sounds.

take at
and end
eat seat
ten say

10. To provide practice in identifying the sound of a vowel—for example, the sound of long and short *a*—the boys and girls could be given a sheet of paper on which are drawn squares about 2 × 2 inches. In each of the squares is a picture illustrating a short word containing the long or short sound of the letter *a*. Also in each square the teacher could write four or more words, some of which contain the long *a* and some the short *a* sound. The pupils could then be instructed to draw a line under every word in a square that contains the same sound of the *a* as in the word illustrated by the picture. One row of the pictures with accompanying words might look like this:

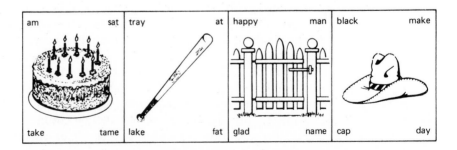

As a variation of the exercise just described, the pupils could indicate which words in a row, such as the following, have the same sound of the vowel *a* as it has in the first word in this row:

bat   rat   rate   made   sat

11. The pupils may write on small slips of paper the vowels on which practice is being provided, one vowel per piece of paper. If the practice is to be on the vowels *a* and *e*, for example, the pupils may hold up one of these two letters that is represented by a sound in each word as the teacher names it. Thus, when the teacher says *name*, the pupils hold up their slips of paper with the letter *a* written on them.

12. To teach the boys and girls the sound of *ar, or, er, ir,* and *ur,* the teacher could have them give the sound of these letters in words such

as these on the board: *color, murmur, burglar, fir, orator.* Next the
pupils can give the sound of those combinations of vowels with *r.*
Then they can name other words containing an *ar, or, er, ir,* or *ur*
combination. They should be helped to realize that a vowel preceding
an *r* does not necessarily indicate such a combination, as, for example, in the words *rare, figure, mire, deer, clear.*

In a similar manner the teacher can proceed to develop inductively
the generalization about the modified sound of *a* when it precedes a
w or an *l,* as in *claw* and *fall.*

13. After the boys and girls have learned that in vowel digraphs—such as
ea, oa, ai, ay, ee, and *ei*—the sound of the first letter forming the
digraph is often long and the second silent, the teacher may list on
the board examples that the pupils name. Then they can mark words,
given on a list distributed to each child, that contain one of the digraphs that follows the rule. Some of the words in this list might be
each, oats, may, eel. What words are used will depend in part on the
reading level of the learner. In a similar manner pupils could practice
on diphthongs such as *oy, oi, ou,* and *ow.*

The pupils should be cautioned that the generalization regarding
vowel digraphs is not, by any means, an invariable rule.

14. The teacher may wish to develop generalizations about silent letters.
To teach inductively the generalization that a final *e* in a syllable preceded by a single consonant is usually silent, the teacher could place
on the chalkboard a numbered list of three or four words that are
governed by the rule, such as, *rate, tame, hope, rule.* With each word
the pupils could be asked to: (a) pronounce the word; (b) tell with
what letter the word ends; (c) tell whether the *e* is silent; (d) indicate
what kind of letter—vowel or consonant—precedes the vowel; and (e)
state how many consonants precede the vowel. As a summary the pupils could answer these questions about all the words in this list:

With what letter does each word end?
Is the *e* silent?
What kind of letter—vowel or consonant—precedes the final *e*?
How many consonants precede the final *e* in each of the words?

Next the teacher could tell the pupils that usually, when the final
letter in a word is *e,* the *e* is silent if it is preceded by a single consonant. He could then give the pupils opportunity for applying this generalization. They could tell in which words in a list of words such as
these the rule applies: *came, ride, male, riddle, table.*

15. To help pupils remember sounds of letters they could make individual
booklets in which there is a page for each letter or letter sound that
they have studied. On these pages they could paste pictures illustrating words that contain these sounds.

16. To get further practice in associating the written symbol with its
sound(s), a box containing slips of paper with various consonants or

consonant blends on them could be used. As a child draws a letter out of the box, he might name it and find objects in the room the names of which begin with that letter. Or the pupils might match the written symbols with pictures of objects, arranged around the room, that begin with a given sound. Or, as the teacher holds up a picture, the children might hold up a card with the letter or letters with which the name of the object in the picture begins.

17. Rhyming words can be used in teaching phonics with procedures such as the following:

   a. The teacher repeats a nursery rhyme and asks the pupils to listen for words that rhyme.

   b. The boys and girls complete jingles that the teacher makes up, such as:

   At recess time on this day
   All the children will want to _____.

   c. The pupils name pairs of rhyming words.

   d. As the teacher names various words in pairs, some of which rhyme and some of which do not rhyme—such as *meat, seat—* and *take, talk*—the pupils tell which pairs rhyme.

   e. The teacher presents orally sets of three words, two of which rhyme. The pupils tell which words rhyme.

   f. The pupils make card files of rhyming words. For example, one card could consist of words rhyming with *play*, such as *day, hay, lay, may, pay, ray, say, stay, today, way*. Pupils may wish to refer to the cards when writing original poetry.

   g. The teacher places on the chalkboard ledge a series of pictures, the name of each of which rhymes with the name of some other object or person pictured in the collection. For example, he might place on the chalkboard pictures of a boy and of a toy, of a hat and of a bat. As a leader points to one of the pictures, another pupil finds a picture the name of which rhymes with the name of the one at which the leader pointed.

18. After the boys and girls have had work on blends, the teacher may draw three or more large circles on the chalkboard, on one of which he has written, for example, the word *clock*, on another the word *tree*, and on still another *store*. Then as he gives from a word card the name of a word beginning with the sound of the *cl* in *clown*, a child can take the card and put it on the chalkboard ledge near the circle in which the work *clock* is written. Similarly, when the teacher pronounces the word *stove*, a pupil should place the word card under the circle with the word *store*.

19. When the boys and girls are ready to learn the diacritical markings of words, it is important to begin slowly enough so that the work will not be confusing to them. After they have worked on the long and short sounds of the vowels, the teacher may tell them that there is a

way of indicating the sound of a letter in writing. Then he can tell them the marking frequently used for the long and short vowels and provide practice in their interpreting and writing these markings for words. At this time he may also wish to draw attention to the fact that in some systems of marking the short vowel sounds are not indicated by markings and explain that the assumption is that when words are marked diacritically, if no marking occurs over a vowel, the vowel is short. One way in which he may wish to help boys and girls use diacritical marks is by asking them to mark all the long and short vowels in a list of words of which they already know the pronunciation. Later they can learn to decipher words by means of markings.

Since more than one set of diacritcal markings is in common use, the system selected for practice should be the one most used in the pupils' glossaries or dictionaries. In the intermediate grades, however, boys and girls should be helped to decipher words when a system different from one they have been employing is used. They should know that at the bottom of the pages of a dictionary the guide to pronunciation that will help them interpret the markings of the words in that book is given.

Developing Word Recognition through Attention to the Structure of Words

Without resorting to the undesirable practice of having boys and girls "find little words in big words"—such as *do* in *dog*—the teacher can in many ways aid pupils in developing through structural analysis a method of identifying and recognizing some words more rapidly than possible through phonic analysis.

Study of Roots of Words, Prefixes, Suffixes, and Inflectional Endings

A few ways are suggested here by means of which boys and girls can be helped in the recognition of words through attention to the roots of the words, prefixes, suffixes, and inflectional endings.

1. The boys and girls can make a list of words containing a given root, such as *walk, walks, walked, walking.*
2. When the pupils come to a word such as *unwise*, if they have had the word *wise*, the teacher can draw a line under *wise* and ask what that part of the word is. The pupils can then give the prefix and, next, combine the prefix with the root of the word. Having the boys and girls make a list of common prefixes—such as, *mis, im,* and *ir*—with

words in which they form a prefix—such as *misuse, impossible* and *irresponsible*—can help them both in word recognition and in word meaning.

3. On a sheet of paper each child can write the base words of a list of words containing either prefixes or suffixes or both that have been written on the board.

4. The teacher may write on the board a list of words with prefixes that mean *not*—like *unahppy, impossible,* and *irresponsible.* Then the boys and girls could name words to add to the list. Next they could draw a line under the different prefixes that mean *not.*

5. The boys and girls can supply the correct prefix for each word in a list such as the following, for which the meaning of the word to be formed has been given:

    _____ known   not known
    _____ like   not to like
    _____ kind   not kind

6. The pupils can be helped in the development of the generalization that many root words ending in *e* drop the final *e* before adding *ing,* as, for example, *make, making.* They can name words to which this generalization applies.

7. Each pupil can be given a card with a prefix or suffix or inflectional ending, while the teacher has a series of cards containing root words to many of which a prefix or a suffix on a pupil's card could be added. As the teacher holds up a card, all pupils who have a card with a prefix or suffix that can be combined with the root word stand. Next the pupils who have the appropriate prefixes or suffixes can write on the chalkboard the words that can be formed from the root word with addition of their prefixes or suffixes.

8. The class might make a chart with three columns in the first of which are listed common prefixes. In the second column could be given a meaning of each prefix, and in the third column examples of words in which the prefix has the designated meaning.

9. The pupils could be asked to draw a line from a root word given in one column to a prefix that can be used with that word in another column.

    form   dis
    happy   re
    interested   un

10. The pupils may be asked to draw a line from each prefix given in one column to a common meaning of that prefix found in a second column.

    un   back
    ex   under
    re   out
    pre   before
    sub   not

11. The pupils could be asked to indicate whether a given group of letters at the beginning of a series of words is a prefix. A few possible words for such a list follow. (The pupils should be helped to realize that the pronunciation of a word may be a clue as to whether a given group of letters at the beginning of a word forms a prefix.)

  *un*important
  *un*ion
  *dis*appear
  *dis*aster
  *re*volution
  *re*write

Attention to Compound Words

To help boys and girls gain facility in recognizing compound words, these suggestions may be followed:

1. The boys and girls can make a collection of compound words for posting on the bulletin board. To the right of each compound word, the words of which it is composed can be written.
2. A crossword puzzle could be made by the teacher or pupils in which a number of compound words would serve as answers. Part of each word could be supplied in a numbered list, while the other part could be chosen from an unnumbered list that is supplied with the puzzle.
3. Each pupil in the room might be given a card on which is written part of a compound word that can be combined with the word on another pupil's card to form one word. The children find their word partners and then each pair tells the class what was formed.

Syllabication as an Aid to Word Recognition

As the boys and girls acquire the essentials of syllabication, they should learn to divide words into syllables—first of all, as an aid to word recognition and, second, as a help in writing words when it is necessary to divide them into syllables. (See Chapter 6A, "Word Recognition," p. 124, for some generalizations about syllabication, of value in word recognition.) Suggestions for work on syllabication are also given below.

1. To provide assistance in syllabication the pupils might be given a list of words, some with one, others with two, and still others with more than two syllables. The boys and girls could indicate after each word the number of syllables it contains.
2. The boys and girls might be given a list of words with more than one syllable, which they are to look up in a dictionary to find out how the words are divided into syllables.

3. After the boys and girls have learned inductively a few important generalizations about syllabication, they could be given a list to match with words governed by these rules.

Other Means of Studying the Structure of Words

A few other means of word study through attention to the structure are here given.

1. The class could make a list of contractions, with the words that were combined to form each contraction given opposite each.
2. The boys and girls could make or solve a crossword puzzle constructed by the teacher, the answers to some of which are contractions. The words from which the contractions are formed could constitute part of the numbered list of words for the puzzle.
3. The boys and girls could be given a list of words, some of which are possessive pronouns and some of which are contractions, such as the following: *its, it's, there's, theirs, I'll, hers.* They can be asked to tell which are possessive pronouns and which contractions. They might also use the words in sentences.

Using Picture Dictionaries

The term *picture dictionary* usually refers to books in which a picture is used with every word entry to help the child identify and recall words. To illustrate the letter *a,* a large picture of an apple, along with the word *apple,* and a sentence containing the word may be given. Often, but not always, the words are arranged in alphabetical order.

Brief descriptions, quoted in part or in entirety from the publishers, of a few picture dictionaries are given below. They provide added information about these aids to learning.

Courtis-Watters Illustrated Golden Dictionary for Young Readers by Stuart A. Courtis and Garnette Watters, published by the Golden Press. This picture dictionary is designed for middle elementary grades. Not all words are pictured, but pronunciation and word division are indicated for all words. A section in the book contains maps, days of the week, months, seasons, holidays, names of oceans and continents, abbreviations, various measures, largest cities in the world, longest rivers in the world, and many other useful items of information.

Picture Dictionary for Boys and Girls by Alice Howard Scott, published by the Garden City Publishing Company. The author is mindful of present-day youthful interest in technical inventions and equipment. Contains over 1700 lively illustrations in color and over 3600 words.

Child's First Picture Dictionary by Lillian Moore, published by Grosset & Dunlap. It contains words of a child's own world. Only the present tense of verbs is listed. Contains 302 words suitable for first and second grades.

The Golden Picture Dictionary by Lillian Moore, published by Simon and Schuster. It contains 800 words for beginning readers. Pictures are well within a child's realm of experience. It is suitable for grade two through four.

Golden Dictionary by Ellen Walpole, published by the Golden Press. It is geared to second through fourth grades. Color is on every page.

The Picture Dictionary for Children by Garnette Watters and Stuart Courtis, published by Grosset & Dunlap. All pictures are in black and white. It includes pictures, comparisons, contexts, print, and script in ways that very young readers enjoy. Suitable through the third grade, it contains 2177 basic words and an index of defined and undefined words compiled to aid teachers.

The Rainbow Dictionary by Wendell Wright, published by the World Publishing Company. This dictionary is suitable for children five to eight years old. It uses various methods in helping children to learn meanings of words, such as the picture with its caption, the simple explanation of a word, the use of the word in a sentence, the use of the words and a synonymous word or phrase in two otherwise identical phrases, the use of the word with its antonym, or the use of the word in a quotation. Simple pictures are used.

The following are some additional picture dictionaries:

McIntire, Alta, *The Follett Beginning-To-Read Picture Dictionary* (Chicago: Follett Publishing Company).

Monroe, Marion, and W. C. Greet, *My Little Pictionary* (Glenview, Ill.: Scott, Foresman).

O'Donnell, Mabel, and Wilhelmina Townes, *Words I Like to Read, Write and Spell* (New York: Harper & Row).

Parke, Margaret B. *Young Reader's Color-Picture Dictionary for Reading, Writing, and Spelling* (New York: Grossett & Dunlap).

Scott, Alice, and Stella Center, *The Giant Picture Dictionary For Boys and Girls* (Garden City, New York: Doubleday).

Some suggestions for the selection and use of picture dictionaries are:

1. For younger children stress simplicity of arrangement of words and of illustration of the words as you select a picture dictionary.
2. Be sure to make ample time available for the use of the picture dictionary.
3. Take time to help children in the use of the picture dictionary.
4. Use the picture dictionary primarily as a pupil self-help device.
5. Make the picture dictionary easily available and display it attractively.
6. Have the pupils make their own picture dictionaries. One type of picture dictionary is one in which the children either draw or paste a picture representing an entry word and then write the word, often used in a simple sentence, on the same page with the picture. These pages can be arranged to good advantage in alphabetical order by means of a looseleaf notebook. As the pupil is learning a new word that can be

illustrated, he writes it on a sheet of paper and pastes on the same sheet a picture that he has found or draws one himself. Sometimes the picture dictionary is a group project; at other times each pupil makes his own.

A picture dictionary may be in the form of cards, instead of sheets of paper, that contain the words and the illustrations of words. These cards can be arranged in a file, which can be expanded as the class progresses in knowledge of words. Another variation of the picture dictionary is often made in connection with the words that can be illustrated that occur in a story or a section of a book. As the pupil is learning new words that can be illustrated in a given story or unit in a reader, he illustrates each one; he then can refer to the word as he finds the need of doing so. For example, if in a story the child is introduced to the words *rabbit, tree, ran, squirrel,* and *into,* he may divide a sheet of paper into four parts, using one of the four parts for the word *rabbit* under a picture and reserving another of the four parts for each of these words: *tree, ran,* and *squirrel. Ran* he may illustrate by a boy, a dog, or a rabbit running. Since words such as *into* do not easily present themselves in a pictorial illustration, that kind of word is often omitted from a picture dictionary. However, in a card file these words might be alphabetically arranged as "words we often use."

Another example of a pupil-made adaptation of the picture dictionary is one that deals only with words used in a science or a social studies unit of study.

As the pupil uses the picture dictionary to recognize words, the teacher can help him derive other benefits from it. Some of these values are (a) help in spelling; (b) development of interest in words; and (c) development of skill in finding words in alphabetical order. If the picture dictionary is pupil-made, these are additional values: (a) practice in arranging words in alphabetical order and (b) development of skill in arranging words and pictures neatly on a page.

Games and Word Recognition

In connection with the role of games in relation to the development of power in word recognition, these questions frequently concern teachers: (a) Under what conditions are games desirable? (b) What are some games that can aid in word recognition?

Criteria for Selection of Games

In determining the role of games in developing power in word recognition, the teacher needs to have his purposes clearly in mind. If the major purpose is to help the boys and girls become more skillful in identifying and remembering words, then a game, to be acceptable, must satisfy the requirements for effective practice or reinforcement. If the chief aim is to furnish recreation, then it is not essential that the characteristics of effective drill be present. Games that are not primarily designed to give help in reading can be scheduled during times of the school day set aside for recreational activities, such as before school, during the noon hour, and during other periods when recreation is the primary aim.

One criterion for effective practice that is often not observed when games are used in learning to read is, "Other things being equal, that method of reinforcement is the better of two that provides the more practice on the skill in question in a given length of time." Other criteria for playing games used primarily as learning activities are:

1. The atmosphere in the classroom should be a relaxed one.
2. The boys and girls should be cognizant of the purpose served by the game.
3. The game should be on the interest level of the participants.
4. If competition is an element of the game, it should be chiefly competition with self rather than with others.
5. When presenting a game the teacher should show enthusiasm.
6. The directions for a game should be so simple that the children can easily comprehend and follow them.
7. After directions for a "new" game have been given, it may be desirable to have a few pupils demonstrate it before the group plays it.
8. The game should be a means to an end, not an end in itself.

Games can be educational tools. (Roger Rouch)

9. If a game involves group competition, all children should have an opportunity to win in some games.

List of Games Commercially Available

Some reading games are available through publishing companies, in variety stores, and in department stores. Use of most of these can be justified chiefly as recreational activities that may, however, provide opportunity for growth in reading. Many teachers like to place such games on a reading table, so that they will be accessible to the children in free periods.

The following list of games is merely illustrative of the large number now available.

1. *"Phonic Lotto." by E. W. Dolch (The Garrard Publishing Company).* "Phonic Lotto," a game for two to ten players, consists of ten cards $7^1/_2 \times 5^1/_2$ inches, and sixty smaller cards, $2^1/_4$ inches square. Each of the larger cards is divided into six squares on which there is printed a vowel or vowel combination accompanied by a picture, the name of which contains the vowel or vowel combination given in the square. The sixty smaller cards show pictures of objects whose names contain one of the vowel sounds found on the squares of the large cards. The sounds on which there is drill are the long and short vowel sounds, *a, e, i, o, u;* the digraphs, *ai, ay, ee, oa;* the diphthongs, *oi, oy, ou, ow, ew, oo;* and the vowels with the letter *r,* namely, *ar, er, ir, or, ur.* In the game the purpose is to match the small cards so that the pictures on them are placed on the pictures on the large card, the names of which contain the same vowel sounds.

2. *"Group Word Teaching Game," by E. W. Dolch (The Garrard Publishing Company).* The game consists of nine sets of cards each containing six similar cards. On the cards of each set are listed 24 of the 220 basic sight words compiled by Dolch. The game is played much like "Lotto." As a word from a printed list is read by the leader, the players cover the word on their cards with small oblong pieces of paper.

3. *Group Sounding Game," by E. W. Dolch (The Garrard Publishing Company).* There are six cards, similar to "Lotto" cards, in each of the following sets: Set A—initial consonants; Set B—short vowels, *a, e,* and *i;* Set C—all short vowels; Set D—harder consonants; Set E—blended consonants; Set F—consonant digraphs; Set G—long vowels; Set H—vowels with *r;* Set I—diphthongs; Set J—miscellaneous consonants; Set K—closed syllables; Set L—open syllables; Set M—prefixes and suffixes; Set N—three syllables; and Set O—three syllables. The game can be played by six players, who cover the words the leader calls from a list of words on a given "set" that they are furnished.

4. *"What the Letters Say," by E. W. Dolch (The Garrard Publishing Company).* This game, also called "A Beginning Sounding Game," consists

of cards on which one sound for each letter is illustrated by a picture and a word. In the game the child gets practice in associating the name of a letter with one of its sounds and with three different words on different cards that illustrate the sound.

5. *"Take," by E. W. Dolch (The Garrard Publishing Company).* This is a self-teaching phonics game in which the pupils match the sounds of the beginning, middle, or ending of words with cards on which a picture and the name of that picture are given. This game is for boys and girls in the third grade and up.

6. *"The Syllable Game," by E. W. Dolch (The Garrard Publishing Company).* In "The Syllable Game" there are three decks of 64 cards each, with two-syllable words in two decks and with words up to four syllables in the third deck. It is a game that a child can play either alone or with another person while learning to recognize many common syllables.

7. *"Phonic Rummy" (Kenworthy Educational Service, Inc.).* "Phonic Rummy" comes in four sets: one for grades one and two; another for grades two and three; still another for grades two, three, and four; and a fourth for grades three, four, and five. In each set there are two packs of 60 cards. With these cards a game in matching vowel sounds can be played.

8. *"Junior Phonic Rummy" (Kenworthy Educational Service, Inc.).* This game, similar to "Phonic Rummy," is also a matching game in which words used widely in first-grade readers are matched for vowel sounds.

9. *"Doghouse Game" (Kenworthy Educational Service, Inc.).* "Doghouse Game" comes in 12 game envelopes, on the face of each of which are printed 35 phonograms as well as rules for pronunciation and 64 consonants and consonant blends. A variety of games can be played with the cards.

10. *"A B C Game" (Kenworthy Educational Service, Inc.).* This game—designed for teaching letter, word, and picture recognition—is played by matching the cards in the set, on each of which are a picture, the name of the picture, and the letter with which the word begins. The game is played somewhat like "Old Maid," as the players try to find the mate for every card that they have until every player, excepting the person who has the card entitled "Mr. ABC," has given up all of his cards.

11. *"Phonic Quizmo" (Beckley-Cardy Company).* This is another game that is similar to "Lotto." The pupils cover on their cards the words beginning with the same letter or letter combination found in words that the teacher reads from a list supplied with the game.

12. *"Phonetic Word Wheel" (Beckley-Cardy Company).* Various games can be devised with the phonetic word wheel in which the pupils are provided with practice in recognizing vowels, consonants, and blends.

13. *"Make-a-Word Game" (Beckley-Cardy Company).* With the 65 green cards with consonants or consonant blends and the 65 orange cards with phonograms that are supplied, matching games can be played.

14. *"Go Fish" (The Remedial Education Center).* "Go Fish," a consonant word game, consists of a series of three cards for each consonant, of three different colors, with a picture on each, the name of which begins with a consonant sound, the letter for which is also given on the card. Each player is given 6 cards, while the remaining cards are placed into the fish pile in the center. Each player in turn asks any other player for a card that begins with the consonant sound that he gives. If the player is unsuccessful in his attempt to get the desired card from a player, he goes to the fish pile to see if he can draw it from that. If he does not get the card at his first attempt, he loses his turn. Whenever a player has acquired all three cards beginning with the same consonant sound, he places the three cards in a pile in front of him, forming a "book." The person with the largest number of "books" wins the game.

15. *"Vowel Dominoes" (The Remedial Education Center).* To play this game, cards $1^{1}/_{2}$ by $2^{1}/_{2}$ inches, resembling dominoes, are used. On half of each card is a vowel and on the other half a picture of a word containing a vowel sound. For example, on half of one card is the letter *o* and on the other half a picture of a drum, to represent the *u* sound. The game can be played much like dominoes. For example, a card with the letter *a* and a picture of a safety pin can be placed next to a card with the letter *i* and a picture of a top, so that the half of the first card on which the safety pin is drawn is next to the letter *i* of the second card. Thus the picture of a word with the *i* sound is placed next to the letter *i*.

Other Reading Games

Many games other than those produced commercially can be used to develop reading skills. It is hoped that those listed here can suggest to the teacher others that might be particularly suitable to the needs of his pupils.

1. Word Baseball. One way in which to play "word baseball" is to designate one corner of the room as "home" and the other three corners as first, second, and third bases. If the pupil who is "up to bat" can pronounce the word that the teacher shows him, he can go to first base. If he can also say the next word, he may go to second base. If he can go on through third base to home, he scores a "home run." However, if he is unable to pronounce his first word, he is "out" and an "out" is recorded for his team. If he cannot pronounce a word, other than the first one given to him when his turn comes, he proceeds to second base when the next batter on his side has pronounced the first word given to him. A similar procedure determines the length of his stay on third base. Scoring can be done in a variety of ways.

2. A Reading "Spelldown." The class can line up in two teams as they do for other "spelldowns." One child can be appointed scorekeeper. The teacher should have a large number of word cards with words that the pupils have studied but on which they need further practice. As the teacher holds up the first card, the first pupil tries to pronounce it and use it in a sentence. If he is able to pronounce the word and use it in a sentence, he scores a point for his team; he then takes his place at the end of the line. If he cannot pronounce a word and use it in a sentence, he stays where he is and a score is recorded for the opposing team. In that case the card is shown to a member of the other team. If he, too, does not know the word or cannot use it in a sentence, the word "comes back" to the next pupil on the team who was first given the word. Each time a word is missed, the opposing team gets a point.

3. Action Sentences. The leader, who may be the teacher, places in a word holder or on a chalk ledge several sentences with directions such as "Get a book from the table." After a pupil has performed one of the directions, another child points to the sentence that tells what the other child did. He reads the sentence as he points to it.

4. Ten-pins. Ten-pins can be set up on the floor. From a stack of word cards placed face down, players take turns in picking up the top card. If a player can pronounce the word on his card, he gets a turn at trying to knock pins over with a ball. If he cannot pronounce a word, the person whose turn it is next, pronounces it. Score is kept in terms of the ten-pins that are dislocated. This game is chiefly for recreational, not reading, purposes.

5. Ring-toss. A variation of ten-pins is ring-toss. In this game the person pronouncing his word correctly gets a turn at trying to toss a ring onto a hook. The winner is the one who has hooked the most rings by the time the hooks are filled. The chief value of this game is recreational.

6. Sentence Game. Each player places his cards on the table or desk, word side up. The teacher reads a sentence using words appearing on the cards. Every child who has a card on which a word used in that sentence is written goes to the front of the room. A pupil designated as "sentence maker" makes the sentence by arranging the children with their cards in the proper order as the teacher repeats the sentence. If a sentence maker forms the sentence incorrectly, another pupil is appointed in his place. The pupil who does not recognize that he has a needed word in his possession, or who thinks that he has one when he does not, can be "penalized" by having to put his card into the center pile, from which the "sentence maker" selects the word if it is again needed for a sentence.

Distributors of Games

Teachers interested in securing reading games may, in addition to canvassing stores, wish to write to publishing companies for catalogues describing their reading games. Some companies that distribute games are:

Beckley-Cardy Company (10300 West Roosevelt Road, Westchester, Ill. 60153).

Developmental Learning Materials (3505 North Ashland Avenue, Chicago, Ill. 60657).

Educational Games, Inc. (P.O. Box 3653, Grand Central Station, New York, 10017).

Educational Reading Service (East 64 Midland Avenue, Paramus, N.J. 07652).

Garrard Publishing Company (1607 North Market Street, Champaign, Ill. 61820).

Highlights for Children, Inc. (2300 West Fifth Street, Columbus, Ohio 43216).

Holt, Rinehart and Winston (383 Madison Avenue, New York, 10017).

Houghton Mifflin Company (2 Park Street, Boston, Mass. 02107).

Judy Publishing Company, The (Box 5270, Main P.O., Chicago, Ill. 60680).

Kenworthy Education Service, Inc. (Box 3031, Buffalo, New York 14205).

McCormick-Mathers Publishing Company (300 Pike Street, Cincinnati, Ohio 45202).

McGraw-Hill Book Company (1221 Avenue of the Americas, New York, 10036).

Remedial Education Press (Kingsbury Center, 2138 Bancroft Place, NW, Washington, D.C. 20008).

Science Research Associates (259 East Erie Street, Chicago, Ill. 60611).

Steck-Vaughn Company, The (Box 2028, Austin, Texas 78767).

For Further Study

Burns, Paul C., and Betty D. Roe, *Teaching Reading in Today's Elementary Schools*, 2d ed. (Skokie, Ill.: Rand McNally & Company, 1980), Ch. 3, "Basic Reading Skills: Word Recognition."

Durkin, Dolores, *Teaching Them to Read*, 3d ed. (Boston: Allyn and Bacon, Inc., 1978), Ch. 11, "Phonics: The Content," and Ch. 12, "Phonics Instruction."

Goodman, Yetta M., and Carolyn Burke, *Reading Strategies: Focus on Comprehension* (New York: Holt, Rinehart and Winston, 1980).

Heilman, Arthur W., *Phonics in Proper Perspective*, 3d ed., (Columbus, Ohio: Charles E. Merrill Publishing Co., 1976).

Hittleman, Daniel A., *Developmental Reading: A Psycholinguistic Perspective* (Chicago: Rand McNally College Publishing Company, 1978), Ch. 9, "Strategies for Vocabulary Development and Word Recognition."

Karlin, Robert, *Teaching Elementary Reading; Principles and Strategies* 3d ed. (New York: Harcourt Brace Jovanovich, 1980), Ch. 6, "Teaching Word Recognition."

Lamb, Pose, *Linguistics in Proper Perspective* (Columbus, Ohio: Charles E. Merrill Publishing Co., 1977).

Ransom, Grayce A., *Preparing to Teach Reading* (Boston: Little, Brown and Company, 1978), Ch. 9, "Teaching Word Recognition Skills."

Tinker, Miles, and Constance M. McCullough, *Teaching Elementary Reading*, 4th ed. (Englewood Cliffs, N.J.: Prentice-Hall, 1975), Ch. 8, "Word Identification and Recognition."

Zintz, Miles V., *The Reading Process: The Teacher and the Learner*, 3d ed. (Dubuque, Iowa: Wm. C. Brown Company Publishers, 1980), Ch. 9, "Word Recognition Skills."

Questions and Comments for Thought and Discussion

1. In Chapter 6B many suggestions are given for developing word recognition skills. Try to find suggestions for additional activities that might be of value in teaching word recognition by each of these methods: the sight method, the use of context clues, phonics, the study of the structure of words. Teachers' manuals or guidebooks accompanying basal readers are one good source for such suggestions.
2. You may find it profitable to examine several picture dictionaries. If you do, evaluate them in terms of what you know about means of developing word recognition.
3. Some teachers believe that workbooks are an essential part of the basal reader program, while others severely criticize them. However, it is frequently claimed that such criticism may be the result of the misuse of the workbooks, rather than the material itself. What suggestions do you have for the use of workbooks accompanying basal reader series? If you would not want to use workbooks, be able to state your objection(s) to them.
4. You may find it helpful to devise a series of practice exercises for use in helping children develop a word-recognition skill. For example, you may want to plan an exercise designed to help boys and girls recognize prefixes in words, by noting which in a series of words have and which do not have prefixes. It is recommended that you include in your list some words, such as *distant*, in which letters appear at the beginning of a word that do not form a prefix but which are spelled like a common prefix. Indicate for which grade level you are preparing the exercise.
5. Suggestions are given in this chapter as to how illustrative materials can be used as teaching aids for the development of word-recognition skills. You may find it profitable to make some illustrative material that might be used in the development of skill in word recognition.

Comprehension

The importance of skill in recognizing words is pointed out in preceding chapters. While it is impossible for a person to read without being able to recognize words, word recognition does not constitute all of reading. It is merely a tool for reading. Unless the reader comprehends what is recorded on the page, he is engaging in an exercise in recognizing words, not in reading as the word *reading* is used in this book.

Although there are differences of opinion as to how to define comprehension as it refers to reading, there is general agreement that by reading with comprehension is meant constructing meaning from what is being perceived in writing. In fact, reading without understanding should not be called reading, for reading necessarily involves comprehending.

A passage can properly be read with varying degrees of understanding. The scale of comprehension ranges from practically no meaning to what might be referred to as complete understanding. The degree of comprehension will depend not only on the difficulty of the material, on the physical condition of the reader, and on his skill in reading but also on his purpose. All he may want as he reads a selection is to get the general idea of what is written. On the other hand, he may set out to read the material in order to test every point made in terms of its applicability to a problem confronting him. He may read every detail of the directions for performing an experiment, but may read the society column of a newspaper only to find out whether anyone he knows is mentioned in it. One of the marks of the efficient reader is the extent to which he can adjust the degree of his comprehension to his objective.

The level on which comprehension takes place can be classified in a variety of ways. One classification recognizes that comprehension may be on: (a) the factual level; (b) the interpretive or inferential level; or (c) the evaluative or critical level. This is the plan of organization followed in this chapter. In the chapters on interests of boys and girls, Chapter 11A and Chapter 11B, the authors recognize a fourth level, namely the appreciation level. Reading on the factual level refers to understanding what is actually written on the page. Reading on the interpretive level designates reading in which the reader comprehends the meaning that is not expressed "in so many words," but can be implied or inferred. In evaluative reading the reader evaluates what he reads through mental activities such as judging the authenticity of the material in terms of the qualifications of the author, predicting outcomes, determining the correctness of the conclusions reached by the writer, associating what he is reading with his own experiences, past or contemplated. The understanding with which a person reads may also be thought of as: (a) getting the facts; (b) making inferences from what he reads; and (c) applying what he reads by means of associational processes. Yet another means of classifying the type of comprehension is to divide it into: (a) the factual level; (b) the level of generalization, where the reader generalizes on what he reads; and (c) the critical level, where the reader evaluates what he reads in terms of the purpose of the author and the reliability and validity of the material.

In the classifications given there is no basic contradiction concerning what reading comprehension should include. All of these classifications throw light on the process of reading with understanding. One trend in current thinking, which is reflected in the categories into which comprehension has been divided, is the placing of increased emphasis on the nonfactual level of comprehension.

Comprehension Skills

There is controversy among leaders in the field of the teaching of reading as to whether or not reading is a general ability. Some claim that it is, while others think of reading as a combination of various specific skills, such as getting the main idea or predicting outcomes, which should be identified for the purpose of helping the learner improve in ability to comprehend what he reads. Part of this argument is probably one of semantics, since comprehension could be described as a general ability even by those who believe that there are specific skills that comprise the general ability. Where the point of view does make a difference, however, is in the application to a teaching-learning situation. Those who believe that there are specific abilities that constitute effective comprehension will probably want to pay definite attention to these skills in their instructional procedures; others who do not share this view are likely not to place much, if any, emphasis on the acquisition of these various abilities. To the authors of this book it seems important that help be given to many boys and girls in acquiring such skills as noting details that support the main idea of a selection, judging the authenticity of a report, and making generalizations on the basis of what is read. Rationale for this position lies, in part, in the fact that improvement in ability to perform one of these activities does not necessarily bring about improvement in others. For example, greater skill in noting details significant for achieving a purpose the reader has in mind may not have any effect on judging the authenticity of a report. Consequently, various comprehension skills are here identified and described.

Skills Classified according to Purpose of the Reader

The specific skills that form a part of the ability to comprehend what is read may be classified rather loosely according to (a) the purpose of the reader and (b) the length and nature of the selection read. We consider first the skills dependent upon the reader's purpose.

Reading on the Factual Level

Reading on the factual level pertains to skill in understanding the information that is directly stated in the written material. Understanding at this level is closely related to the ability to read inferentially and critically. Among the skills required for reading at the factual level are: (a) knowing the meaning of words; (b) reading to find the main idea; (c) reading to select significant details; and (d) reading to follow directions.

Knowing the Meaning of Words If a large number of words in written material are unknown to the reader, comprehension suffers. A special problem frequently exists in the case of words with multiple meanings, as for example, the word *walks* in the sentence, "The people in the crowd were from all *walks* of life." Teachers from the beginning stage of reading instruction on should help boys and girls become aware of various ways in which individual words are used.

Finding the Main Idea One of the most common reasons for reading is to get the general idea of a selection. This may often legitimately be the goal in reading fiction or even in reading other types of material, such as science. For instance, in science the primary-school child may read a page to find out whether it tells about helicopters.

The more mature reader in an elementary school may read to find out whether it is advisable to include a certain chapter in a bibliography that he is preparing on "Adventures in Space." The ability to determine the main idea of a part read is basic also to many other comprehension skills, such as the ability to summarize and organize. Skill in finding the main idea in a paragraph or in a longer selection and in not mistaking a detail for the major point needs to be developed in many pupils not only through incidental means but often also through practice exercises.

Selecting Significant Details The ability to note important details is closely related to skill in finding the central thought or main idea of a selection. To be proficient in this respect, the reader needs to do more than differentiate between main points and supporting details; he must also be able to decide what points are important for the purpose he has in mind. In regard to *Miss Hickory* by Carolyn Sherwin Bailey, the story about the little doll whose body is a twig of an apple tree and whose head is a hickory nut, the person who tells the story may want to remember exactly where the story takes place. However, the child who is reading the book solely for his own enjoyment may satisfy his purpose without taking special note of this detail. The reader who gives equal attention to all details that are presented may find himself so encumbered that he loses perspective. Practice may be needed to help him decide which details are worthy of special note and which should be ignored. Their relation to the main idea of the selection will often determine their value; the purpose of the reader will be another determinant. As the pupils work for improvement in noting details, they should be helped to realize that details are of value as they support a main idea or assist in arriving at a conclusion or serve some other purpose of the reader beyond that of merely taking note of details.

Care must be taken that practice in noting details does not decrease the ability to find the main idea or to generalize. Constant emphasis should be placed on the fact that details should be fitted into a setting in which they serve a purpose.

Following Directions The ability to follow directions is usually a combination of many reading skills. The ability to note details, to organize, and to note the sequence of points are among the learnings essential to this type of reading skill.

Reading on the Interpretive or Inferential Level

Interpretative or inferential reading is also referred to as "reading between the lines." In other words, in reading on this level the reader is able to understand what is implied though not directly stated. Included in this category are the following skills: (a) reading to summarize and organize; (b) reading to arrive at generalizations; and (c) reading to predict outcomes.

Summarizing and Organizing Both the ability to select the main idea and to choose significant details are basic to another commonly sought-after goal of reading— that of summarizing and organizing. However, to make an adequate summary or to organize what has been read, it is not enough for the reader to know the main idea and the significant details. He must also be able to sense the relation between the main point and the details, as well as the relation among the details. Furthermore, he often needs to know either how to make these relations clear to others or how to record them for later rereading.

Frequently, the efficient reader makes summaries and organizes what he reads without doing any writing. The person who reads a chapter and then asks himself what the main points are, what material constitutes signficant details, and how all these parts are woven together is making a summary and organizing what he reads. In fact, skill in organizing or summarizing is ordinarily put to use without the writing of summaries or outlines. Practice in summarizing and organizing may lead to such skill in these activities that frequently the reader almost unconsciously summarizes and organizes what he reads.

Arriving at Generalizations Formulating generalizations is in a sense a specialized form of summarizing. To arrive at generalizations the reader needs to note specific instances and then decide whether the data presented are sufficient to warrant a significant conclusion. If they are of the type on which a sound conclusion can be based, he must determine what the deduction from the instances discussed should be. If, for example, he reads about children in Holland who wore wooden shoes, he should realize that he would be wrong if he made the decision that Dutch children always wear wooden shoes. On the other hand, if a typical scene in a schoolroom in China were described, and if the author indicated that the scene is representative, the reader may correctly conclude that Chinese schools in many respects are unlike the school he is attending.

One danger for the person not skillful in making generalizations is that he may generalize without sufficient evidence. Another is that he will make too broad a generalization. To avoid errors due to both of these causes a teacher can give specific guidance not only with material read but also with observations made in other situations.

Predicting Outcomes Another important comprehension skill is that of predicting outcomes. This skill may manifest itself in a variety of ways. For example, if the reader sees the sentence, "The farmers set no traps for any of the animals on the grounds, for they like animals," he can anticipate (unless a break of thought is indicated by words such as *but, however,* or *nevertheless*) that the next sentence in the paragraph will not contradict the thought that the farmers were kind to animals. This skill is in effect an aspect of what we call "active reading," in which the reader assumes an attitude of anticipation.

Skill in predicting outcomes is useful in helping the reader note when he has misread a word or a group of words or a sentence. It is also of value because the person who is adept at predicting outcomes as he reads can usually get the thought more quickly than others. This skill is helpful also in remembering what is read, for it enables the reader to take special note only of those points that are new to him or are different from what he would have expected. The burden of recall is thereby lessened.

Reading on the Evaluative Level

One of the most significant comprehension skills is that of making evaluations of what is read. By critical evaluation is not meant the attitude of suspecting every statement read of being false. The power of critical evaluation in reading involves numerous factors. The reader needs to learn to ask such questions as these: Is the material relevant? Can the alleged facts be verified? Is the author qualified to discuss the subject? Do the statements harmonize with what I know to be true? Does the author draw valid conclusions from the facts? Is the author omitting or suppressing any important facts? Are the statements expressions of fact or of opinion? Does the material contain any unstated assumptions? Can I accept these assumptions? Should I revise my own assumptions in the light of what I have read?

Critcal discrimination in reading calls for a background of knowledge concerning the subject under discussion. Literally, the word *criticism* means the application of criteria or standards of judgment. Such criteria can come only from some previous contact with the subject. The reader has no way of judging the truth of the statement, "Polio is seldom fatal," if he has not had some earlier knowledge about polio. He must then be entirely dependent on the reliability, competence, and credibility of the author. Moreover, critical reading involves the capacity for making comparisons and appraisals. Critical reading is active, creative reading. Children should begin developing the skills of critical independence in reading at the outset.

The levels of criticism will vary with the age and maturity of the pupil. A primary-school child may be asked to pick out a false statement in a series, such as "Penguins live near the North Pole," while a sixth-grade pupil may be called on to find editorial statements in a news story. Critical discrimination in reading can be cultivated through skillful training.

It should be noted that critical reading is essential, too, to some of the comprehension skills discussed in this chapter, such as reading to find the main idea, reading to predict outcomes, reading to arrive at generalizations.

Skills Classified according to Structure or Length of Reading Unit

We turn now to another kind of classification of comprehension skills. Getting meaning from or through the printed page involves the ability to perceive and understand words *in relation* to other words. It is to be hoped that in the future application of learnings from the science of linguistics will throw light on the complex problems connected with comprehending the relations between words and groups of words so that the reader can be helped more adequately to comprehend phrases, sentences, paragraphs, and longer selections.

Phrase Meaning

Since a phrase can be said to be more than the sum total of the words in it, skill in comprehension of phrases is not synonymous with skill in word meaning. The expression *in the long run*, for example, means more than *in* plus *the* plus *long* plus *run*, even though the meaning of each of the words contributes to the total thought. Especially in the case of idiomatic expressions there is need to note the words in their composite setting in a phrase. Another cause of difficulty in phrase comprehension is that frequently an immature reader does not recognize a phrase as such and, therefore, does not read it in a meaningful grouping. In the sentence, "At long last the tired men arrived," if the reader pauses after the word *long* because he does not recognize the word *last* as belonging to the phrase, he may not get the meaning. Therefore, it is necessary in the case of many learners to focus attention on the recognition and interpretation of the meaning of phrases.

Sentence Meaning

What has been said about a phrase being more than the sum total of the words comprising it can also be said about a sentence. While the comprehension of many sentences is often almost automatic with persons who are reading on their proper level, with others it is not. A reader might understand every word of a long or involved sentence without getting the meaning of the sentence. The understanding of sentences as thought units may be fundamental to the comprehension of a complex sentence. For this reason, a study of the interrelationships of the parts of a sentence may be of value. Because sentence comprehension is more than word recognition and because an understanding of sentences is essential to the comprehension of longer selections, the reader should become skillful in reading sentences as whole units.

Paragraph Meaning

Many of the problems involved in the comprehension of paragraphs have already been referred to in the discussion of skills in finding the main idea, selecting significant details, and following directions. Some of the suggestions given in connection with summarizing and organizing, arriving at generalizations, predicting outcomes, and evaluating also apply to paragraph comprehension. Frequently it is through reading a paragraph that the outcome can be predicted. The paragraph may be one to be evaluated critically or to be summarized. Some problems of comprehension involve skills that are peculiar to the paragraph rather than to phrases or longer selections. Finding the topic sentence, if there is one, is one such problem. Another is that of seeing the relation between the topic sentence and the other sentences. A realization of the purpose of each sentence in a well-constructed paragraph is still another. Because of these and other considerations unique to paragraph comprehension, special attention should be given to the means of understanding the paragraph.

Comprehension of Longer Selections

Selections longer than paragraphs—such as articles, stories, chapters, or books—may present special problems. Among these are questions as to how to get the most value from center headings, side headings, and transitional words and phrases, or how to study the interrelationships between various types of paragraphs. Problems of sustained attention, too, arise with reading of this type. Since there are skills peculiar to comprehension of longer selections, special attention needs to be paid to the means of reading stories, articles, chapters, and books.

Factors Affecting Comprehension

The teacher must understand the factors that affect comprehension if he is to help individuals overcome their shortcomings in comprehending what they read. Moreover, knowledge of the causes may help the teacher to prevent the occurrence of serious deficiencies. These are typical of problems of individuals who have difficulty in understanding what they read: "I am not able to concentrate as I read." "I have difficulty in figuring out the meaning of a selection because there are so many words that I do not recognize." "I often have trouble getting the meaning of the first page or two when I start reading. Sometimes I have to read for a few minutes without really knowing what I am reading before it makes sense to me." "I can understand what I read but I cannot give a satisfactory summary of it."

Difficulty of Material

One of the major causes of lack of comprehension on the part of boys and girls is that teachers expect them to read materials beyond their level. Methods for determining various reading levels of individuals—the independent, instructional, and frustration levels—and of the corresponding reading level of written materials are discussed in Chapter 12.

Intelligence

A child's ability to comprehend in reading is sometimes limited by the conceptual "load" that his mental ability enables him to carry. All the mechanical reading skills in the world will not enable him to read materials involving abstractions beyond the level of his mental development. While we should never underestimate a child's powers, we should adjust the task to his capabilities. The slowest learner can grow in comprehension, but we must expect the growth to be slow. The reader whose IQ is 65 may learn how to find the answer to a simple question, but he should not be required to interpret a complicated graph.

Environment

Noisy surroundings, inadequate lighting, high or low temperatures, stimulating or distracting surroundings may interfere with maximum comprehension. The extent to which the environment affects comprehension varies with individuals. The same person may at one time not be bothered by factors that other times decidedly decrease his comprehension. Interest on the part of the learner is one of the determinants of the effect of potential distractions.

Emphasis on Word Recognition

Methods of teaching that concentrate on the recognition of individual words but neglect attention to meanings that can be derived from connected discourse may account for deficiences in comprehension. Some children make the transition from word to phrase to sentence to paragraph to longer selections with ease and with little aid from the teacher. Many boys and girls, however, are baffled by the task of finding meaning in word groups. They need to be encouraged to move rapidly on the line in order to discover what happened or to find the answers to their questions. Exclusive use of phonic methods, for example, may result in mere word calling rather than intelligent reading. The aim is to equip the pupil with a variety of methods of attacking new words and at the same time to develop in him the power to get larger meaning from the printed page.

Emphasis on Oral Reading

Oral reading can have either a desirable or a detrimental effect on comprehension. At times oral reading of a selection that is particularly difficult for the reader may increase his understanding of it, since he then not only sees but also hears what he reads. Furthermore, in effective oral reading, if there is an audience, the reader is required not only to understand what he reads but also to interpret his understanding to others. In this process increased attention needs to be placed on comprehension.

Unfortunately, oral reading, if not done well, can have an undesirable effect on comprehension. The reader can become so conscious of his audience that he will fail to understand what he is reading. Over-emphasis on oral reading may also make a child so self-conscious while reading to others that his concentration may be on how, rather than on what, he is reading. There is a point to the familiar story of a child who, after he had read a passage orally, was asked by his teacher a question about the content of the selection. His response was,

"I don't know. I wasn't listening; I was reading."

Background for Reading a Selection

A frequent cause of poor comprehension is lack of an experience background essential to the understanding of what is being read. A city child who has never been on a farm may have difficulty in fully comprehending a story about country life. A boy in the upper elementary school who has little experience in working with science materials may not be ready to follow the directions given for an experiment. Lack of knowledge of the words used and of understanding of the concepts involved are limitations to comprehension. Semantic problems of pupils who know only one meaning of words such as *fair, spring, plain* may also cause difficulties in comprehension.

Adjustment of Reading Techniques to Purpose and Type of Material

Effective reading requires a flexible approach to the printed page. A person who has been reading a great deal of fiction and deriving great pleasure from the experience, may encounter problems in reading comprehension because he might read it at the rate he would read a story. On the other hand, a child who is a meticulous reader of science materials, may fail to derive real satisfaction from reading stories because he uses the same reading methods for narrative material that he has been accustomed to employ with factual and expository prose. Similarly, a child may be unable to recognize the main idea of a passage because he is too absorbed in noting concrete details. There should be versatility in adapting the reading method to the reading purpose and to the nature of the material being read.

Rate of Reading

In the preceding paragraph reference is made to the fact that failure to adjust reading rate to the type of material is a cause of difficulty in comprehending what is being read. In the next section of this chapter, "Reading Rate and Comprehension," we will explore the relation between rate of reading and comprehension.

Reading Rate and Comprehension

We have emphasized the fact that "reading" without comprehension cannot properly be called *reading.* The question of the interrelationship between rate and comprehension is clarified somewhat if we think of *reading rate* as meaning *rate of comprehension.* If we believe that the better of two readers is the one who can more quickly comprehend the meaning of a given passage, we can easily dispense with much of the debate about rate versus comprehension.

Appraisal of Reading Rates

In order to plan an effective program of reading instruction that will help each child learn to read at appropriate rates, careful appraisal should be made of every pupil's reading rates.

Since an effective reader has more than one reading rate, it is not a simple matter to make an appraisal. Consequently, a variety of means needs to be used. *Informal observation* is one. The classroom teacher has many opportunities to note the characteristics of a pupil's reading rates. He can observe whether the child wastes time while reading. By studying the child in reading situations he can gather evidence as to whether the pupil is able to adjust his rate of reading to his purpose and to the difficulty of the material. He can note whether he skims parts of it and reads other parts more carefully.

Sometimes important evidence about a pupil's reading habits as they affect rate of reading can be secured through conferences. The teacher can often discover by this means whether the pupil knows that variations in rates are necessary to good reading. Answers to questions as to the type of situations in which skimming or slow reading is required can also be illuminating to the teacher desirous of learning more about a pupil's rate of reading. Tests, too, can furnish valuable data. Some of the standardized reading tests contain subtests for determining rate, among them the following: the *Sangren-Woody Reading Test* (Harcourt Brace Jovanovich), the *Iowa Silent Reading Tests: Elementary Test* (Harcourt Brace Jovanovich), the *Gates-McGinitie Reading Tests* (Teachers College Press, Columbia University), and *Diagnostic Reading Tests* (Committee on Diagnostic Testing). However, tests in which rate is measured in only one type of situation do not give a clear index of an individual's rate of reading. For this reason tests need to be supplemented by other means of appraisal. Because of these limitations in the measurement of rate, many teachers like to make tests of their own. Suggestions for ideas for teacher-made tests are indicated in some of the exercises given in Chapter 7B.

Whenever a pupil is timed while reading, whether he is taking a standardized or nonstandardized test, allowance should be made for the fact that the results may be inaccurate because the pupil knows he is being timed. No matter how hard a teacher may try to keep the testing situation free from strain, some children, as soon as they know they are being timed, show the effects of working under pressure. There are many children who cannnot do their best under such conditions.

One type of record that the teacher may find it advantageous to keep is a *checklist* on which he indicates change or persistence in attitudes or habits or skills concerned with the improvement in reading rates. By means of a checklist the teacher can be spared the necessity of depending on his memory as to the reading skills of each of his pupils. Questions such as the following may be on the checklist: (1) Does the child recognize the need of variation in rate? (b) Is he able to adjust his rate to his purpose and to the material he is reading? (c) Does he know when to skim?

Charts, graphs, and tables are useful in appraising growth in the ability to read at appropriate rates. In keeping this type of record, the teacher should be sure to compare only those data that are truly comparable. Rate in skimming an article should not be compared with rate in reading a selection of similar difficulty, with different purposes on the part of the reader, when more detailed examination is required. For skimming, a reading rate of 400 words per minute may be slow for a given student, while a work-type rate of 200 words per minute may be fast. Rate of reading two selections that are not alike in difficulty or type cannot be directly compared.

Another point is that, if rates in reading are charted, they should be recorded over a relatively long period of time. In many situations there are too many rather insignificant variations in rate from day to day to make a short-term study of rates of reading of much value. It often takes more than a few days of successful practice to show measurable improvement, even when real progress is being made from the beginning.

Furthermore, the learner himself should be informed of his progress. If, as a rule a child is old enough to try to improve his rate of reading, he is old enough to understand a simple record of his performance. The learner's concern should be the improvement of his own skill, not a desire to equal or surpass others or to attain a norm.

National norms on standardized tests are not very helpful to teachers who wish to evaluate their pupils' reading rates. Different tests may show different medians for the various school grades, in part because of the wide variation in difficulty and type of content they present.

Causes of Problems Related to Reading Rates

The rate at which a person reads is determined by various factors. Low intelligence, which leaves its impact on all reading skills, can have a marked effect on rate of reading. Poor health also seems to have a detrimental influence on the rate at which an individual reads, although it must be noted that some people in poor health are among the most prodigious and most rapid readers. Additional causes of unduly slow reading are lack of skill in word recognition, vocalization or excessive subvocalization, pointing to words, overemphasis on oral reading, lack of sufficient practice in reading at different rates, and lack of interest and purpose.

Lack of Skill in Word Recognition

The person who has difficulty in recognizing words quickly and accurately is likely to be a slow reader. He is at a special disadvantage when he wishes to find the answer to a question. He is also handicapped when he tries to read study-type materials that contain words not easily recognized by him.

Often the methods by which an individual has been taught to recognize words play an important role in reading rate. The person who habitually analyzes words by phonic methods will have slower habits of word recognition than one who has learned to analyze words only if he cannot quickly identify them as wholes. This fact should not be interpreted to mean that a knowledge of phonics is detrimental to speed of reading. Rather, it suggests that misuse of phonics may have an undesirable effect on rate of reading. Phonics is an important aid to word recognition only when faster methods fail to bring results. Moreover, the person who can identify a large number of words through effective use of methods of word attack other than phonics, such as recognition of a sight word or use of context clues or structural analysis, may often be the one who can more speedily accomplish his purpose in reading.

Vocalization

Early stress on speech sounds in reading instruction inevitably creates strong associations in the mind of the child between the sight of a word and its sound. The sound image is intended to serve as a bridge between visual perception and the apprehension of meaning, and normally the child becomes less and less conscious of language sounds as he seeks meaning on the printed page. Exclusive preoccupation with sounding in the initial stages of reading tends to cause lip movements and possibly excessive subvocalization in later stages. Speed of reading may then be restricted to approximate the rate of oral reading. Under these conditions the child

needs to unlearn habits deeply fixed in the beginning.

Closely related to the habit of vocalization is the feeling some readers have that they must "read" every word in order to comprehend. In many types of reading, as in skimming and scanning, the good reader finds the key words and supplies the intervening words with sufficient accuracy to derive the meaning intended by the author. In these cases the reading materials are not simply a continuity of symbols intended to correspond to the spoken language; they are, rather, a set of clues, a sort of shorthand, designed to communicate meaning without the need for vocal articulation of all the words.

Pointing to Words

Another practice likely to arrest development in rate of reading is pointing to each word as it is being read. In early reading instruction in the first grade, when it usually takes the reader longer to recognize a word than to say it, pointing with the finger may not reduce reading rate. However, the practice can have a detrimental effect later on speed of reading, for the habit may become established, with the result that the pupil persists in its use after he should be reading at faster rates than are possible when pointing at each word.

Many first-grade teachers supply the children with markers in the form of heavy strips of paper, often about the length of a line of print and about an inch in width. With these markers, which the boys and girls keep under the line being read, the children can often keep their place more easily than they otherwise could. Probably if a marker is used only for a very limited length of time it can serve as a helpful crutch. The danger is that children may get into the habit of needing some means other than their eyes and mind to keep the place.

Like all other crutches, markers should be discarded as soon as they have helped a person over a difficult situation.

Overemphasis on Oral Reading

Oral reading has its proper place in reading programs, but a program dominated by oral reading practice is almost certain to produce habits of slow silent reading. Even in the initial reading period children should be encouraged to read words silently much of the time. In general, it is recommended that children be asked to read a passage silently before they are called on to read it orally. By this means silent reading habits are established, and the subsequent oral reading will be improved because of increased comprehension of the material read. The practice of children following in their books while someone is reading the same material orally to them is to be discouraged after the pupils have learned to read more rapidly silently than orally. Otherwise they may tend to reduce their silent reading rate to be more equal to their oral reading rates.

Lack of Sufficient Practice in Reading at Different Rates

An error of omission in some instructional programs is the lack of emphasis on differential rates of reading. Many boys and girls need considerable guidance in acquiring versatility or flexibility in reading rates and sufficient time to practice this skill. Unless boys and girls are supervised in time afforded for this practice, there is likely to be little positive effect from admonishing them to read slower or faster.

Lack of Interest and Purpose

The ability to read rapidly is only in part a matter of habit and skill. Perhaps even more important is the attitude of the reader. If the pupil knows what he is looking for on the printed page, he will be impatient until he finds what he wants. He will not dawdle over the passages that are only secondary to the goals he is seeking or that are irrelevant to them. Clear purposes are, therefore, basic to the improvement of both comprehension and rate.

The daydreaming pupil makes little progress in reading. But when his interest has been kindled, when the action in a story moves toward a climax, when the narrative brings smiles or tears, he races down the lines to learn the outcome. The scene before him will not be obscured by laborious struggles with printed words. With the well-selected story, the words, the page, even the immediate environment may fade from consciousness and only the people and the places and the actions in the story remain. For many children the key to reading speed is interest. Abundant, highly motivated reading will do what no tachistoscopes or flashmeters can.

Controlled Reading

Various machines for regulating the speed at which the printed page is exposed to the reader are commercially available. The basic principle of most of these devices is that of an instrument known in psychological laboratories as a tachistoscope. This is a contrivance that flashes words or phrases on a screen at a controlled rate. The use of the tachistoscope and similar instruments in reading instruction is sometimes called controlled reading.

The chief purpose of these instruments is to increase the reader's ability to perceive whole words and phrases quickly in a single fixation. Through intensive and prolonged practice a child may be able to perceive—that is, recognize and identify— words and phrases with progressively greater speed. The theory is that such training will transfer to the printed page and will result not only in improved reading rate but also in better comprehension, because meaning is usually derived from whole words and words in combination rather than from individual letters.

Some of the devices that employ "pressure methods" are the SRA Reading Rate Accelerator (Science Research Associates, Chicago), the Keystone Reading Pacer (Keystone View Division/Mast Development, Davenport, Iowa), the Renshaw Tachistoscopic Trainer (Stereo Optical Company, Chicago), and the Shadowscope Pacer (Lafayette Instrument Company, Lafayette, Indiana). The Keystone Tachistocope, also available through the Keystone View Division of the Mast Development Company, is another device for increasing rate of perception of individual letters and words. All of these and similar machines present printed matter at controlled rates of speed. Faced with a gradually increasing rate of exposure, the reader is pressed to "take in" meaningful units on the line at a pace that can be constantly accelerated.

Unquestionably, the reading machines have been effective in improving reading rate in many cases. How permanent the improvement has been is a matter of conjecture. Quite possibly the machines have an initial advantage in that they provide novelty and interest in the improvement of reading. Unfortunately, after a time the novelty may wear off, and consequently one of the chief reasons for the success reported with instruments of this type may no longer operate.

In controlled reading, emphasis is placed primarily on the improvement of rate. Programs of improvement in reading should also place stress on comprehension. Although many research studies indicate either that there was no loss in comprehension or that slight gains were made, the little increase in power in comprehension has not always been commensurate with the amount of time and energy spent on attempts at improvement of reading.

The use of mechanical aids for controlling the rate of reading does not eliminate the need for an attack on the underlying causes of inappropriate rates of reading. The machines may discourage dawdling habits of reading, but in themselves they do not eliminate the chief causes of unsatisfactory rate of comprehension, such as lack of skill in methods of word recognition, lack of skill in selecting details, difficulty in organizing what is read, failure to read material critically, and inability to locate information rapidly. In fact, controlled reading can even have a detrimental effect on some of these factors. For example, the person whose chief cause of slow reading is a difficulty in recognizing words may develop even poorer habits of word recognition because he is not given time to apply sound means of word identification. Nor can the efficient reader employ the flexible habits of reading that are needed to get meaning quickly. When he comes to a word that he must analyze, he will need to stop for a longer pause. He may find it advisable to make regressive movements if he discovers that he has just finished reading a point that he should note carefully. He will want to vary his rate in accordance with this purpose in reading, rather than follow the operation of mechanical shutters that compel him to read every line or part of a line in the same time as the preceding ones.

Guidelines for Assisting Pupils in Reading at Appropriate Rates

To assist the teacher further in helping boys and girls to read at appropriate rates, guidelines that should be kept in mind by the teacher are now discussed. Only those generalizations are presented on which there is little, if any, disagreement among specialists in the teaching of reading.

1. Growth in ability to read at appropriate rates is subject to training Assistance can be given the person who is not reading at appropriate rates. Studies show that remarkable increases in rate have been achieved in a brief period of time in many clinical situations, supervised reading courses, and classroom situations where this phase of reading has been stressed. In fact, there is reason to think that almost all readers could make valuable increases in the speed with which they read, without loss in comprehension, if they were given appropriate help and if they put forth needed effort. Emphasis on increase of reading rates should usually be postponed until the intermediate grades, when pupils have ordinarily gained proficiency in reading skills basic to the development of greater speed.

2. Reading rates should vary with the purpose of the reader, the type and difficulty of the material, and the reader's background knowledge The desirable rate may vary—even within a given selection—from one part to another. Both the teacher and the learner should be aware of this fact. In the first grade the teacher will usually set the purpose for reading. He may ask a pupil to read the next page to find out what Bobby did when his mother told him want she wanted for her birthday, or he may ask the pupil to glance over the next page to find the "new word" *mother*, which has been presented on the chalkboard or on a word card. The teacher may show the pupil that in the latter assignment it is not necessary for him to read every word and

that consequently it might not take him as long to read that page as it would if he read the page to answer a question about it. Thus, an early beginning can be made in helping boys and girls learn to read at different rates and for different purposes.

Later in the development of skill in reading, the learner should be given increasing opportunity to decide on suitable purposes himself and to determine what rate of reading he will need in order to accomplish his objective.

A somewhat arbitrary classification of reading rates may help to clarify for boys and girls and for the teacher the ways of adapting speed to the nature of the material and the purpose for reading it. Reading rates have been divided into three categories: rapid reading, moderately rapid reading, and slow reading. Scanning and skimming can be considered two kinds of rapid reading; however, a person can be reading rapidly without engaging in either scanning or skimming. In scanning, as the term is used here, the reader rapidly searches the page for specific information. He may be scanning as he glances at the contents to see if it gives information on a given topic. Scanning is done when a person looks at a page of a table of contents to find the title of a given chapter so that he can tell on which page the chapter begins, or when he looks over the words on one or more pages of a dictionary in order to locate an entry word. A person is skimming when he reads a paragraph or longer selection rapidly to get the main idea and possibly a few supporting facts.

Rapid reading is also appropriate, as, for example, when the reader looks at a newspaper to find out what is going on in the world or reads a magazine article just for fun. Moderately fast reading is called for when the reader wishes to note some details. Slow reading is advisable in a study-type of situation or when appreciation of the beauty of style or of the unfolding of the details of a situation or of the personality of the characters is desired.

3. Teachers and pupils should have clearly defined goals for the improvement of reading rates General objectives are not enough. The teacher should try to find out the needs of the pupils in order to help them overcome their difficulties. The aims should be specific—for example, to learn when to read at the different rates, to read study-type material more slowly so as to have an opportunity to get the thought of the selection, and to read fiction rapidly while maintaining the desired amount of comprehension.

The pupil, too, should have clearcut objectives. Results are better when the learner is consciously seeking specific goals.

4. Development of ability to read at appropriate rates should not interfere with development of other reading skills Rates of reading should not be increased at a sacrifice of comprehension. To be sure, when a pupil has been reading more slowly than his immediate purpose warrants, rate should be increased. Increase in rate sometimes brings about a better degree of comprehension, if teaching methods eliminate defects in rate and comprehension simultaneously. It requires insight on the part of the teacher to know when rate and when comprehension should be stressed the more.

5. Neither haste nor undue tension should characterize the efforts to read at appropriate rates All practices in an effective program of developmental or remedial reading should be in harmony with the principles of mental health. Studies of child development have shown the harmful effects of creating pressures which result in anxiety and fear of failure. However, this fact should not be interpreted to mean that at times measures should not be taken to prod a person whose poor achievement, below his expected level, is due to dawdling habits or to lack of effort. Not only are haste and undue tension undesirable from the point of view of maintaining an emotional equilibrium but they are also detrimental because they interfere with success in learning. Consequently, the child should be encouraged to do his best without becoming frantic when he fails to achieve his goal.

6. The marked difference in children's ability to read at appropriate rates should be recognized Part of the variation among children results from differences in training received in school and practice outside of school. A further cause lies in the variations in innate capacity of individuals to master the intricacies of learning to read at the appropriate rates. Some will never become as skillful as others in reading at desirable rates.

An effective program for helping pupils to acquire skill in reading at appropriate rates recognizes these variations among individuals. The teacher needs to know what stage of learning to read each child has reached, and he must work out a program that is adapted to the needs of individual children. He should not be satisfied with averages. Some children who read with less than average speed for their grade in all types of reading situations may still be working up to capacity or even straining themselves to do good work beyond their capacity. On the other hand, some children, although surpassing norms in rate of reading, may, nevertheless, be reading below their potential.

General Procedures for Improving Comprehension

Improvement in comprehension skills can be brought about in the same manner that growth in almost all other reading abilities can be stimulated. It can be achieved through reading in context during the regular reading period, through reading activities during other parts of the school day, and through reading out of class, as well as through the use of practice exercises specifically set up to provide improvement in the skills. Activities other than reading, too, can serve as an important means of improving comprehension in reading. Because of the close relation between comprehension of material presented orally and comprehension of material in written form, some procedures beneficial to the former type are also valuable in the development of the latter. Whatever types of activities are used, the power of motivation should be recognized and provisions made for stimulating purpose on the part of the learner. Without it many of the procedures and activities suggested in this and other chapters might easily turn out to be sterile exercises.

Improvement through Incidental Means

If the term *incidental means* is used to refer to all types of reading situations other than those involving practice exercises, there are many ways in which comprehension skills can be improved during the regular reading period by such means. Much of the reading of beginners, for example,

deals with reading to answer questions. The boys and girls may read a story in their textbooks in order to answer a question that either the teacher or a pupil has raised. Or after the pupils have read a story they may practice selecting the main point by suggesting titles for a puppet show that they plan to base on the story. Similarly, practice in summarizing can be given when a pupil who has time to finish reading a selection summarizes the ending of the story for a child who has not completed it. During the process of reading a story there can be discussion as to what the children think will happen next. Skill in predicting outcomes can also be acquired by discussion of why certain developments in a story were the ones likely to take place. If a child reads the story of *The Three Billy Goats Gruff*, after he knows how the little Billy Goat Gruff was allowed to cross the bridge, he can be asked what he would imagine the middle-sized Billy Goat Gruff would say when the troll threatened to eat him.

Group assignments can serve as follow-up to direct instruction. (Roger Rouch)

In classes other than reading much opportunity can be given for improvement of comprehension skills simultaneously with learning the content. In the social studies there is almost unlimited chance for meaningful practice in reading maps. Boys and girls can be helped not only in reading political maps but also physical maps, temperature maps, rainfall maps, population maps, product maps, and others. Growing out of the work in social studies may be projects such as this in which one fifth grade engaged. The teacher placed on a big bulletin board a variety of maps and a sheet of paper on which were listed significant and interesting questions under a caption such as, "Can You Find the Answers to These Questions?"

The many tables given in books in the area of social studies can be made to serve an important purpose in comprehension. Boys and girls who need to learn when to use a table and how to use it can be helped to acquire that learning during classes in the social studies and science. In these classes they can learn the importance of noting the titles of tables and the significance of the names of the columns and rows in a table. They may at times be asked to see how many of the questions that they have raised are answered in a table or graph or map in their own textbooks. They may also use a reference book, such as a young people's encyclopedia, to find out what information bearing on their problems they find there in maps, tables, charts, or graphs. Use of literary maps in phases of literature for children can improve skill in using pictorial materials of that type and at the same time enhance the study of literature.

There are also many ways in which the teacher can encourage the pupil to acquire skill in various types of comprehension outside of the classroom. He can stimulate the pupil to read widely and extensively. Incentive to note main points and significant details and to organize and summarize can be given by providing the children opportunity to report on some of the outside reading in a variety of ways. The reports may take the form of telling in a few sentences the gist of a book they have been reading or of describing in detail some favorite scene. Planning dramatizations based on books, giving puppet shows or television programs, or making "movies" can help the learner to read with more comprehension.

The teacher can help the boys and girls develop many of the comprehension skills through activities other than reading. He can ask the children to predict events in stories that he is telling or reading to them. He can encourage them to summarize reports they have heard, to enumerate in order the steps they followed in performing an experiment, to make plans for a project in which they are about to engage, to come to valid conclusions when they have listened to a series of remarks on related topics, and to decide whether certain information given to them orally is factual or a matter of opinion. The teacher's insistence on better concentration on whatever the children are doing can also bring about rewarding results. The individual who does not concentrate in nonreading activities may find it difficult to refrain from letting his mind wander while reading.

Improvement through Practice Exercises

For some boys and girls a program of improvement in comprehension skills similar to the type just described will be sufficient. However, many will profit greatly if they are also given direct practice in the form of exercises to help them develop skills in comprehending what they read. Some pupils may need direct practice on all of the major types of comprehension skills, while others will require such help with only some or one of the skills. Ability in diagnosis on the part of the teacher is therefore necessary as he tries to determine which boys and girls need special practice in developing some or all of the comprehension skills.

In the use of practice exercises, the teacher must keep in mind certain basic principles:

1. *The teacher should have a clearly defined goal to be accomplished with each of the practice materials he uses.* He should decide what skills require direct practice and then provide the best type of exercises possible for achieving his goal economically.
2. *The boys and girls should know the purpose of each practice exercise.* Unless they know why they are doing a certain exercise, they are likely to get inferior results and lose interest.
3. *The boys and girls should be helped to see the importance of the skill to be developed by means of a given exercise.* If pupils are not helped to appreciate the worthwhileness of an activity, they may perform it halfheartedly and consequently achieve poorly. In fact, it may often be valuable to let them help determine, with teacher guidance, the number and types of exercises they need.
4. *Both the teacher and the pupil should know what, if any, progress is being made.* Knowledge of results, especially if they are encouraging, seems to be a real incentive for learning. Through a study of results the teacher can also profit directly by securing evidence on the effectiveness of methods and procedures used.

Questioning as a Technique for Improving Comprehension

Questions raised by teachers and students can serve as one of the most effective means of improving comprehension, both of the spoken and written word. Although it is with reading that we are here primarily concerned, we recognize the interrelationship between what is read and what is heard.

Informal observation of classroom practice as well as statistical reports clearly show that questioning is one of the most common procedures employed during the school day. In fact, the number of questions asked during a typical day leads one to the conclusion that, if anything, questioning is over-used, rather than under-used, as a teaching tool. A major problem lies in the type of questions being asked, not only on the factual level of comprehension but also on the other levels.

Earlier in this chapter (see p. 159) we have referred to several ways in which levels of comprehension have been designated. We have also stated that the plan the writers are following in this book is this division: (a) the factual level; (b) the interpretive or inferential level, and (c) the evaluative or critical level. To this basic categorization we have added the appreciation level, which we are considering in the chapters on interests of children, namely Chapter 11A and Chapter 11B. We need to bear in mind, however, as we add the appreciation level that it is not a discrete level but that there is overlapping between it and the other three included in our organizational scheme.

Principles Underlying Skill in Questioning

Some of the principles that can serve as guides in determining questioning procedures are here listed.

1. *Questions should be asked on all levels of comprehension.* A large majority of the questions asked in classrooms, both in oral and in written form, are on the factual level. That is a regrettable situation. While obviously it is valuable under many circumstances to ask questions on that level, questioning of literal comprehension should not be so extensive that questioning on other levels is not given due attention.

2. *Even kindergarten children can profit from questioning on all levels of comprehension.* Erroneously some people have assumed that questioning beyond the factual level is above the developmental stage of young boys and girls. Psychology does not accept the premise that the young child is unable to make judgments or inferences or come to conclusions. In fact, it is through exercise of his reasoning powers that he is likely to grow in ability to reason. Through answering appropriate questions other than only factual ones, he can be expected to grow in ability to give intelligent responses to more and more difficult thought questions.

3. *Three major purposes that questions can serve are to interest persons in reading a selection, to increase comprehension, and to check it.* Unfortunately a large percentage of questions teachers ask are for the last-named purpose. That fact is true not only as it applies to test questions, but also to many other occasions for asking questions.

4. *As a rule, boys and girls should be cognizant of the purpose of questions addressed to them, either orally or in written form.* That statement should, however, not be interpreted as meaning that every time a question is asked, an explanation needs to be given as to why it is asked. Rather, it means that boys

and girls should be able to realize that there is reason for asking questions of them, whether it is, for example, to test their ability to read, their memory, their skill in selecting main ideas and supporting details, to give them background for a selection to be read, or to help them make application of what they have read.

5. *Respect should be shown to pupils' responses to questions on all levels.* Showing respect, however, is not synonymous to accepting incorrect answers to factual questions or to refrain from helping boys and girls improve upon inferences they have made or conclusions at which they have arrived. While there is no excuse for the teacher to show lack of respect for a child when, wrong answers are given to factual questions, it is especially important that all responses the student makes which involve the higher thought processes—his own reactions—are dealt with understandingly and sympathetically.

6. *Questions should be within the learner's capability to answer.* Asking boys and girls a series of questions many of which they cannot answer invites a frustrating experience for the learner—one that may result in unwillingness in the future even to try to respond to questions. If a pupil is unable to answer a question as originally asked, the teacher may be able to follow it up with one that will be of help to him in answering the question first asked. If pupils are given a series of study questions to which to respond either in writing or orally, care needs to be taken that they can read the questions and are able to find the answers without undue difficulty.

7. *Questioning should be adapted to individual differences within a group.*

With the disparity in ability and in background experiences of boys and girls within most class groups, care needs to be taken that questions are neither too easy for some nor too difficult for others. Application should be made of what the teacher knows about adapting instructions to individual differences. When responses to questions are given orally, easier questions can be addressed to the less able. In written work, too, questions that are easier to answer can be given to some.

8. *Boys and girls should be encouraged to ask questions and be helped in improving the quality of questions they formulate.* The atmosphere of the classroom should be such that pupils will have assurance that they will not be ridiculed by the teacher or classmates when they ask what to them are bonafide questions. The standard response of some teachers to questions they themselves cannot answer is that the person asking the question might look it up in a reference book and then report to the class. Such a suggestion may discourage a student from asking questions in the future.

A questioning technique involving the learner as questioner is referred to as "reciprocal questioning" (REQUEST). When this procedure is followed, the teacher and the students alternate in asking questions on what has been read. As Turner[1] points out, this technique, according to Anthony Manzo,[2] has its greatest usefulness when used with the opening paragraphs of a selection. Turner[3] also states that considerable use of this technique may be of value in remedial reading.

Types of Questions

In an attempt to improve the quality of teachers' questioning and encourage questions of various types, questions have been classified into different categories by authors. Parsons and Shaftel[4] submit this categorization of questions: (1) rhetorical; (2) information recall; (3) leading questions; and (4) probing questions. An example of each type follows.

Rhetorical: I would have been afraid of the consequences, wouldn't you?

Information recall: What did Lincoln say when he saw slaves sold at an auction?

Leading question: What was wrong about _____'s method of trying to solve his problem?

Probing question: Do you think there are ghosts?

We can also recognize different types of questions as to levels of comprehension according to the pattern of organization the authors of this book are following, namely (a) the factual, (2) the interpretative or inferential, and (3) the evaluative or critical. Examples of some questions on these levels are here given.

Factual level: (1) In what year did the Pilgrims come to America? (2) What was the Mayflower Compact?

---

[1]Thomas J. Turner, Ch. 8, "Questioning Techniques: Probing for Greater Planning" in *Teaching Reading,* edited by J. Estill Alexander (Boston: Little, Brown, 1979), pp. 162–3.

[2]Anthony Manzo, "The Request Procedure," *Journal of Reading,* vol. 13, (Nov. 1969), pp. 123–216.

[3]Ibid., p. 163.

[4]Theodore W. Parson and Fannie R. Shaftel, "Thinking and Inquiry: Some Critical Issues" in The Thirty-seventh Yearbook of the National Council for the Social Studies, *Effective Thinking in the Social Studies,* edited by Jean Fair and Fannie R. Shaftel (Washington, D.C.: National Council for the Social Studies, 1967), p. 129.

Interpretive or inferential level: (1) Why didn't any of the Pilgrims return to England in the spring of 1621 when the Mayflower made its return voyage to England? (2) Why were some of the Indians unfriendly to the Pilgrims?

Evaluative or critical level: (1) Do you think the Pilgrims treated the Indians fairly? (2) Are we correct in calling the Thanksgiving of 1621 "The First Thanksgiving?"

References on Questioning

The following references deal with questioning. Further bibliographical data on the books here named are given under "For Further Study" at the end of Chapter 7B.

Chapter 8, "Questioning Techniques: Probing for Greater Meaning" by Thomas N. Turner in *Teaching Reading* edited by J. Estill Alexander.

Pages 47–81 of Ch. 3, "Reading Comprehension" in *Teaching Reading in the Middle Grades* by Richard J. Smith and Thomas C. Barrett.

Pages 153–78 of *Teaching Reading Comprehension* by David Pearson and Dale D. Johnson.

The section on "Levels of Thinking and Questioning Techniques" in *Reading Instruction in the Secondary School* by Betty D. Roe, Barbara D. Stoodt, and Paul C. Burns; pp. 155–165 of Ch. 6, "Comprehension."

Use of Cloze Procedure

A technique to which considerable attention has been paid recently by some persons in the field of the teaching of reading is the cloze procedure. When this technique is used, the reader is confronted with the need of supplying words that have been omitted—words that fit the meaning of the passage. Thus, it requires him to put meanings together in the process of reading as compared with the question-answer technique where conclusions or answers come as a result of reading a passage in its entirety, without any parts omitted.

A teacher can design materials for use with the cloze technique by selecting passages from the pupils' reading materials. Any number of variations of the technique can be used. For example, the teacher can delete every tenth word (in fact, every *nth* word). Or he might decide that only certain words, such as nouns, will be omitted. He can determine the kind of word, the frequency of deletion, the difficulty of the written material, and the responses acceptable.

An example of an item of a cloze exercise in which every tenth word is omitted is as follows:

Since the leaves had fallen and the birds had _____ southward, the day had seemed a dreary one to _____ little girl as she walked slowly to the home _____ one of her best friends.

The same sentence, rewritten with every noun omitted, would read thus:

Since the _____ had fallen and the _____ had flown southward, the _____ had seemed a dreary one to the little _____ as she walked slowly to the _____ of one of her best _____.

Following are a few of the multilated statements from Char's[7] "Experimental Context Clues Test," in which only one word is omitted in each item.

John was always late to school, but he decided to turn over a _____leaf and come on time this year.

Jim lost his lunch money because

[5]Permission was given to reproduce by the author of the test (unpublished) Lynette Y.C. Char

there was a hole in the _____ of his jeans.

Forests are important. They provide lumber and things made from it. And think of all the birds and animals that need the forest for their _____ , home, and protection.

The flat roof was made of logs side by side and plastered together. In the roof was a small chimney hole, and fitted in the hole was a piece of a hollow tree trunk. The trunk was the

_____ .

The cloze procedure, so far used chiefly for testing purposes and for determining the difficulty of reading material, has also been shown to be of value as a teaching procedure, for use in the development of ability to note details, to determine main ideas, and to make inferences, though seemingly at a sacrifice of rate of reading.

What are the assumptions underlying the use of the cloze procedure? For its use as a testing tool and as a means of checking the readability of material, the assumption is that the ability of the performer to determine from the remaining context (sometimes called the "mutilated" material) what words have been deleted is indicative of his power to comprehend. When the procedure is used as a teaching technique, the assumption is that practice in supplying the correct words helps the reader increase his power of comprehension.

7B

Developing Comprehension

Procedures for Developing Comprehension
Skills Classified According to Purpose of the Reader
Developing Skill in Finding the Main Idea
Learning To Select Significant Details
Learning To Follow Directions
Developing Skill in Reading To Answer Questions
Developing Skill in Making Summaries and Organizing Material
Developing Ability To Arrive at Generalizations and To Come to Conclusions
Improving Ability To Predict Outcomes
Developing Skill in Evaluation
Skills Classified According to Structure or Length of Reading Unit
Developing Skill in Acquiring Word Meanings
Developing Skill in Getting the Meaning of Phrases
Improving Skill in Sentence Comprehension
Developing Skill in Paragraph Comprehension
Developing Skill in Understanding the Meaning of Longer Selections
Skill in Reading at Appropriate Rates of Comprehension
Developing Skill in Reading at a Rapid Rate
Developing Skill in Reading at a Moderately Rapid Rate
Developing Skill in Reading at a Slow Rate

Development of Comprehension Skills through Reading Lessons
Using a Story at the Lower-Primary Reading Level
Finding the Main Idea
Selecting Important Details
Following Directions
Summarizing and Organizing
Arriving at a Generalization

Predicting Outcomes
Answering Questions
Sentence Comprehension
Comprehension of a Longer Selection
Using a Story at a More Advanced Reading Level
Finding the Main Idea
Selecting Important Details
Outlining and Organizing
Arriving at Generalizations or Coming to Conclusions
Predicting Outcomes
Evaluating What is Read
Word Meaning
Phrase Meaning
Sentence Meaning

This chapter suggests ways in which information on comprehension given in the preceding chapter can be put into practice. The lists in this and other B-chapters should be used as references from which those that appear appropriate for use can be selected. It is hoped that many of them will suggest to the teacher additional practices that might be valuable for use in the classroom. Some of the suggestions can be followed when systematic or incidental instruction in reading is given; others are of value primarily during the phases of the reading program that deal with the development of skills. In all cases, however, if the activities are to be of maximum value, boys and girls should see purpose in them—purpose that they can accept as worthwhile.

Procedures for Developing Comprehension

The suggested procedures are here divided as to: (a) skills classified according to purpose of the reader; (b) skills classified according to structure or length of reading unit; (c) skill in reading at appropriate rates of comprehension.

Skills Classified According to Purpose of the Reader

Suggestions for developing the following types of skills are given:

1. Finding the main idea
2. Selecting significant details

3. Following directions
4. Answering questions
5. Making summaries and organizing material
6. Arriving at generalizations and coming to conclusions
7. Predicting outcomes
8. Evaluating

Developing Skill in Finding the Main Idea

Activities such as the following may help the learner to find the main idea of a passage:

1. Matching a series of pictures with the paragraphs they illustrate
2. Stating the main idea of a selection
3. Selecting the best title from a list
4. Naming a title to fit a given paragraph or longer selection
5. Reading a story to find out whether it is suitable to tell or read to others for a given purpose or to dramatize
6. Noting certain phrases such as *the first* and *the most important* to see if they point out a main idea
7. Locating topic sentences in paragraphs that contain topic sentences
8. Changing each of the side headings of a longer selection to a question answered by the part following

Additional Activities   The following are illustrations of practice exercises based on some of the preceding suggestions.

1. Direction: After you have read the story, put an x on the line to show which one would make the best title.

We made plans for our book fair. We decided to decorate our classroom. Each boy and girl will make a book cover. We also decided to have a parade of book characters. We will march into the other classrooms. We will invite other children to our book fair. When they come to our room, we will tell them stories.

_____ (a) Our Plans for Our Book Fair

_____ (b) Our Parade

_____ (c) Our Book Covers

_____ (d) Reading in Our School

2. Direction: On the line below the story write a good title for it.

Sir Edwin Landseer was one of the greatest animal artists of modern times. When he attended art school, he divided his time between his classes and the zoo, where he studied animals and drew pictures of them. Although Landseer drew pictures of many animals, probably his most famous ones are those of dogs. The best-known one undoubtedly is the one named "The Old Shepherd's Chief Mourner." It is the picture of a devoted dog sadly guarding the coffin of his master, a shepherd.

Learning To Select Significant Details

By performing activities such as the following, boys and girls can get practice in noting details and choosing those that are significant for their purposes.

1. Indicating which of a series of ideas listed are included in a given selection
2. Telling which of a series of details support the stated main idea of a selection
3. Completing sentences, copied by the teacher from a selection, in which blanks were left for words that will test the comprehension of details
4. Showing which word in a series of sentences or paragraphs does not belong in a paragraph
5. Looking at a picture and then describing it
6. Drawing a picture illustrating details of what has been read
7. Making a list of details that occur in a story, as preparation for dramatizing the story
8. Composing a paragraph by supplying details to support a main idea that has been selected as a theme
9. Deciding which details are important to remember in terms of a stated purpose
10. Taking notes on points read in order to report them to others in a group in connection with a unit of work
11. Reading reference materials to answer questions raised by the class or by a committee in order to get information needed for a project
12. Showing through outlining the relation between details and a main point
13. Reading material in science and mathematics in which careful note needs to be taken of many points in order to comprehend the meaning, and then answering questions on the material or using it in other ways
14. Writing a main idea for a paragraph and then writing details to support it
15. Writing a paragraph describing a given object, which other pupils are to guess

Additional Activities   Two types of procedures that can be used in order to develop skill in selecting details are illustrated in the following exercises:

1. Directions: After you have read the following paragraph, write *M* on the line to the left of the topic listed that expresses the main idea of the paragraph. Write *D* to the left of each topic that expresses a detail mentioned in the paragraph. Write *O* to the left of any item not mentioned in the paragraph.

One of the most interesting animals in the world is the great gray kangaroo, found in great numbers in Australia. One of its characteristics of special note is its size and shape. It is sometimes 10 feet in length from the tip of the nose to the end of the tail and weighs as much as 200 pounds. Its long, strong tail is used as a prop when the kangaroo stands on its two hind legs. The kangaroo is a very swift runner. It can clear as many as twenty feet at one leap. It runs on its hind legs only. The development and care of the young is very interesting. Upon birth the baby kangaroo is only about an inch in length. It is then taken care of in the pouch to the front of the mother's hind legs. In this pouch it receives its nourishment from the milk of the mother. After the baby has lived in the pouch for about four months, it leans out of the pouch to eat grass while its mother, too, is grazing. Then for months thereafter, usually till the baby is about ten months old, the young kangaroo returns to the protection of the pouch even though it spends much of its time in the world outside. In fact, the baby likes the pouch so much that it stays in it until its mother refuses to carry it any longer.

_____ (a) The claws of the kangaroo

_____ (b) The kangaroo, an interesting animal

_____ (c) Australia, the home of the kangaroo

_____ (d) How the kangaroo takes care of its young

_____ (e) The leap of the kangaroo

_____ (f) The value of the kangaroo

2. Directions: The main topic of a paragraph is the food of the camel. Some of the sentences that are listed below are on that topic. Others do not deal with the topic and therefore should not be included in a paragraph on the food of the camel. Write *yes* on the line to the left of each sentence that can correctly be included in the paragraph and write *no* on the other lines.

_____ (a) The camel eats thistles that grow in the desert.

_____ (b) The camel is a lazy animal.

_____ (c) The mother camel is very tender toward her baby.

_____ (d) The camel likes to eat baskets or saddles or newspapers.

Learning To Follow Directions

These methods may be helpful for an individual who is trying to improve his skill in following directions:

1. Repeating directions
2. Observing written directions, such as: "Make one ball yellow. Make the other ball blue"
3. Following written or oral directions for making things, such as a folder for papers or a papier-mache globe

4. Drawing a picture from directions given orally or in writing
5. Writing directions for doing or making something
6. Reading directions for a game and then following them
7. Reading directions for doing tricks and then performing them
8. Arranging in correct order the sentences for directions to do or make something
9. Finding directions for experiments and carrying them out in front of the class
10. Following directions for preparing a dish, such as jello, apple sauce, lemonade

Developing Skill in Reading To Answer Questions

Proficiency in finding the answer to a question can be helpful in a variety of reading situations. It is important at times in order to choose the main idea, to note details, to predict outcomes, to form generalizations, to follow directions, and to perform other activities connected with reading.

Answers are relatively easy to find when the questions are partly couched in the exact words of the writer. With the immature reader or the one who has difficulty in reading to find the answer to a question, this type of question may be used at first. If the writer says, "Susan's father gave her a kitten for her birthday," the teacher may ask, "What did Susan's father give her for her birthday?" A sample of a question to which the answer can be found less easily is: "What reasons can you find for the actions of the heroine?" or "Why do you think the heroine acted as she did?" The formulation of questions the teacher asks can encourage or discourage critical thinking.

Not only should the pupils gain skill in finding answers to questions that are stated by others but to avoid overdependence on the teacher they also need to develop in ability to formulate significant questions for themselves as purposes for reading. Questions by the teacher should serve chiefly as steppingstones to questions that the reader raises himself.

Practice that can be of value in developing skill in answering questions can be secured by performing activities such as the following:

1. Reading to answer questions stated by the teacher
2. Indicating which of a series of questions listed by the teacher are likely to be answered in a given selection and then checking the responses after reading the selection
3. Indicating which of a series of questions that may possibly be answered in a given selection are formulated clearly, and rewording those that are not
4. Reading to answer questions stated at the end of a selected reading
5. Reading to answer questions brought out by viewing a film or filmstrip
6. Formulating questions to be answered by classmates

Developing Skill in Making Summaries and Organizing Material

Skill in summarizing and organizing what is read can be developed through activities such as these:

1. Telling which of several summaries best summarizes a paragraph or longer selection
2. Writing headlines for a class paper
3. Taking note of words such as *first, second, third* as they occur in context
4. Classifying materials in the room for functional purposes; for example, placing all the books on one topic on a specified table or assembling pictures on different topics for use on two or more bulletin boards
5. Telling what items belong in classifications such as *food, clothing, shelter*
6. Arranging pictures in the order in which events illustrated by them occurred in a story
7. Organizing steps in a process demonstrated on a field trip, under topics such as, for example, "Steps in Baking Bread" or "The Manufacture of Flour"
8. Placing subtopics, given in mixed-up order, under a list of main topics that are specified
9. Arranging in correct order paragraphs dealing with one topic, given in mixed-up order
10. Selecting the sentences that do not belong in a paragraph containing some irrelevant sentences
11. Making charts giving information about topics studied, such as "How We Travel," "Famous Americans," "Greek Contributions to Civilization"
12. Studying a table of contents to note the organization of a book
13. Learning where a topic sentence, if there is one, is often found in a well-constructed paragraph
14. Planning pictures for a "movie" or mural on a story or article read
15. Filling in main topics and subtopics of a selection when suggestions are given as to the number of main topics and the number of subtopics under each main topic
16. Learning the form for making outlines, including numbering and lettering, indentation, capitalization, and punctuation
17. Telling what is wrong with an incorrect outline that some pupil has made or one that the teacher has intentionally written incorrectly
18. Making an outline, such as the following, of points to be included in book reports:
    The title and author of the book
    What the book is about
    Two or three interesting parts of the book

How the reporter liked the book

Where the book can be obtained

19. Checking a series of true-false statements such as the following, to indicate which give good advice for making notes. (a) Take your notes, as a rule, in your own words, rather than in the words of the writer. (b) If you do not understand what something means, be sure to include the point in your notes.

20. Checking a list of notes to determine which are appropriately recorded and which are not

Additional Activities   Two additional ways in which practice can be given in summarizing or outlining are indicated in these exercises.

1. Directions: The sentences in this paragraph are not in the correct order. Write 1 on the line to the left of the sentence that should come first. Write 2 on the line to the left of the sentence that should come second. Number the rest of the sentences in the same way.

_____ Stephen heard something call, "Caw! Caw!" _____ There lay a baby crow. _____ Stephen looked around. _____ One day Stephen went to the woods with his father. _____ When Stephen saw that the crow could not walk, he took it home with him. _____ The crow had a broken leg. _____ Stephen always took good care of his crow.

2.   As the boys and girls are studying about the Missouri Compromise, they could be asked to fill in subtopics in this beginning of an outline on the Missouri Compromise:

A. Events leading up to the compromise

1. _____

2. _____

B. Provisions of the compromise

1. _____

2. _____

C. Effects of the compromise

1. _____

2. _____

Developing Ability To Arrive at Generalizations and To Come to Conclusions

In addition to the following suggestions for activities that can be valuable in developing the ability to arrive at generalizations and come to conclusions, some of those recommended in the preceding listing, under "Developing Skill in Making Summaries and Organizing Material" can be used.

1. Making and guessing riddles
2. Checking which ones of several conclusions are warranted by data given, and explaining why the unsound conclusions are invalid
3. Stating as specific a conclusion as possible after reading data presented in a paragraph or longer selection and explaining, in some cases, why no broader conclusion could be reached
4. Matching a fable with a proverb it illustrates
5. Discussing questions such as the following after reading a story: (a) "Why do you think _____ made his decision to go West?" (b) "Under what conditions do you think _____ would have been friendly to strangers?"
6. Telling which of a list of statements are generalizations and which are specifics
7. After making a generalization based on what has been heard or read, checking it against experiences or finding additional support for it or experimenting to see if the generalization applies
8. Discussing the effect that certain events in a story or in history had on individuals
9. Stating the generalization that is justified on the basis of given facts
10. Discussing the ideas contained in several stories to see if they give generalizations that were brought out in a story
11. Formulating titles that indicate the generalization brought out in a series of stories

Additional Activities   These exercises indicate how some of the above suggestions can be carried out.

1. Directions: Pupils can make up and guess riddles such as the following:
   a. I have two legs and two wings. I can fly high into the air. I sing songs. I lay eggs. What am I?
   b. I lived in Minnesota when I was a boy. I was an aviator. I made one of the most famous airplane flights that has ever been made. My wife enjoys flying. What is my name?

2. Directions: Below the following paragraph is a list of statements in the form of conclusions. On the blank to the left of each statement write *yes* if you think the reader can correctly come to that conclusion after reading the paragraph. Otherwise, write *no.* If a conclusion is not correct for the paragraph, in the space provided state why you think it is not a sound conclusion. When you give your reasons, make certain to write the number of the conclusion to which you are referring.

On my last visit to the zoo, I spent part of my time watching two mother camels and their little colts. Both of the mothers stood near their young as if they wished to protect their babies from all harm. It seemed to me that there was a look of tenderness on the mothers' faces as they were looking at the little camels. I then remembered that my father had told me that the mother camel is often very kind to her young.

_____ 1. The camel is very gentle toward other animals.

_____ 2. The camel is very gentle toward people.

_____ 3. The mother camel is often very kind to her baby.

_____ 4. The mother camel is a very gentle animal.

Reasons: _____

_____

_____

_____

_____

_____

Improving Ability To Predict Outcomes

Some of the suggestions given in the preceding listing may be added to the following list of activities for improving the ability to predict outcomes.

1. While looking at the pictures of a story, stating what the outcome of the story is likely to be
2. Telling what is likely to happen next in a story or article, with or without the help of multiple-choice questions
3. Discussing why things happened as they did in a story or other account
4. Making up endings for stories, orally or in writing
5. Comparing our present situation with a previous one in history and deciding what might happen as a result of present conditions
6. Predicting what will happen next after having listened to part of the account of an experience another pupil has had
7. Predicting, after reading a current news report, what will happen and then the following day checking to see if the prediction was correct

Developing Skill in Evaluation

The ability to evaluate what is read may require any of the following skills:

1. Distinguishing between fact and opinion
2. Telling what is real and what is fanciful
3. Determining the qualifications of the author and his purpose and attitude
4. Noting how up-to-date the information presented is
5. Deciding whether propaganda is being spread
6. Examining critically the generalizations made

The reader is referred to the discussions of "Reading on the Evaluative Level" (see p. 163) and of "Developing Abilty To Arrive at Generalizations and To Come to Conclusions (see p. 188). Below are additional suggestions for developing skills listed on the preceding page. It should be noted that some suggestions applicable to evaluation of what is read are listed on preceding pages under other topics dealing with the development of comprehension.

Fact or Opinion   To gain proficiency in distinguishing between fact and opinion, the pupils might do the following:

1. Analyze newspaper reports to determine whether they present facts or opinions.
2. Study news reports and editorials to determine the essential differences in the two types of writing.
3. Locate statements of opinion found within a given selection.
4. Indicate which of a series of statements express facts only and then rewrite those that are not purely factual so that they do not express an opinion.
5. Rewrite statements of fact that are mixed with statements of opinion in such a way that instead of showing sympathy toward a person or event they will show antipathy (and vice-versa).

Real or Fanciful   In order to become more adept at judging whether or not written material is of a fanciful nature, pupils might perform activities such as these:

1. Find examples in stories of means by which the author indicated that the story is fanciful.
2. Draw up a list of expressions often used in stories to show that the stories are fanciful, such as, "Once upon a time."
3. Decide whether a story is real or fanciful and indicate the reason for the decision.
4. Read a story that is fictional but based in part on fact and then determine which statements are likely to be true and which are more likely to be fictional.

The Author   In order to become more able to decide on the qualifications of an author or his purpose or point of view, the pupil might, for example:

1. Decide how each of two persons, both qualified to speak or write on a given subject but with a different experience background, might express himself on that subject.
2. Discuss which of two authors whose qualifications are stated would be better qualified to write on a given topic.
3. Decide with classmates on questions that, if answered, might help a reader determine the qualifications of an author, for example: (a) Does

the author have much information about the subject? (b) Has he a good reputation as a writer? as a person? (c) Is there reason why he would be likely to push one point of view at the expense of another?

4. Decide on the purpose of an author in writing a given selection.
5. Indicate which sentences in a list reveal a sympathetic attitude and which an unsympathetic one toward a person or a situation.

Up-to-dateness   Activities such as these might be of value in helping boys and girls decide on the up-to-dateness and the need of up-to-dateness in regard to writings:

1. Noting the copyright date of books
2. Indicating which books written long ago are valuable for a stated purpose and which are not
3. Finding an item of information as it is reported in a book with an old copyright date and in one with a recent copyright and then comparing the two
4. Making a list of questions on which information in a book with an old copyright date would be as useful as one with a recent copyright
5. Answering questions or following directions such as these, when pupils have available to them a number of books, including those to which reference is made in the directions or questions, some with old and some with recent copyright dates: (a) Is your social studies book written recently enough so that it can report on events that occurred during the past five years? (b) What is the copyright date of Virgil Hilyer's book, *A Child's Geography of the World?* (c) Find two items of information in the book *A Child's Geography of the World* that are out of date. Find two items of information given in that book that are still true today.

Propaganda Techniques   Activities such as the following may help a person detect propaganda when he sees it in print or hears it:

1. Indicating which statements present only so limited a part of the truth that an incorrect impression is given
2. Indicating which of a series of words—such as *native land, house, home folks*—often arouse emotion
3. Noting types of words often used to arouse emotions of sympathy or love or anger
4. Writing a paragraph using one or more propaganda techniques
5. Noting how an author who says he is presenting both sides of a controversial matter slights one side of the question
6. Reading a report on an event in two newspapers, one of which is known to be sensational, and then comparing the reports
7. Writing headlines that might be included in a newspaper or magazine known for sensationalism, and rewriting these headlines as they might appear in a paper or magazine not given to sensationalism.

Skills Classified According to Structure or Length of Reading Unit

So far in this chapter we have been noting how skills classified according to purpose of the reader can be developed. Now we will turn our attention to skills classified according to the structure or length of a reading unit.

Developing Skill in Acquiring Word Meanings

While in the early stages of learning to read the words in the reading material should be some that are in the learner's understanding vocabulary, there comes a time when reading should serve as a means of developing growth in word power. To stimulate such development, activities by the pupils such as the following can be provided by the teacher:

1. Before reading a selection, finding the meaning of words through class discussion, studying the words written in context on the chalkboard, looking up the words in the dictionary
2. Making class or individual word files in which cards are kept for the "new words" acquired that the class decides to include or that an individual (in case of a personal file) wishes to include in his list. The type of information that the pupil will want to give on a file card will depend in part on his stage of development. For less advanced readers nothing more than the word, an explanation of it, and a sentence with the word illustrating a common meaning of it might be included on a card. For more adept readers the phonetic spelling, the plural forms of nouns, various explanations of the word, and sentences containing the word showing different meanings could also be recorded.
3. Deciphering the meaning of words in exercises constructed by the teacher illustrating some of the points in Wilbur Ames' classification scheme, which categorizes types of context clues that might be taught systematically (see p. 115). An illustration of three of his fourteen types is given below:
    + *Synonym clues or appositives.* A *peccary*, a wild pig native in both North and South America, is a blackish animal with whitish cheeks and an indistinct white collar.
    + *Clues utilizing definition or description.* His behavior was *inexplicable.* No one could explain why he was tardy.
    + *Comparison of contrast clues.* She was much more gregarious than her friend who preferred being alone much of the time.
4. Giving illustrations of some of the types of context clues identified by Ames (see number 3 above).

Developing Skill in Getting the Meaning of Phrases

Skill in the comprehension of phrases can be developed by means of the following activities:

1. Matching phrases in one column with words with similar meaning in another column
2. Finding in a selection phrases that answer certain questions, such as, "What group of words tells that Frank is happy?"
3. Discussing the meaning of commonly used idiomatic expressions
4. Interpreting figures of speech
5. Underlining the complete phrase in an exercise where the first word of the phrases is underlined
6. Playing a game in which pupils read what is written on a phrase card
7. Completing sentences by matching the beginnings of sentences given in one column with appropriate endings in a column of phrases

Additional Activity   An exercise such as this might be used, for which the directions are: "Each sentence in this exercise contains an expression that is italicized. To get the meaning of the expression, note the meaning of each word in it and study the context. If necessary consult your dictionary. Then, in the space provided, explain what the expression means."

1. When the explorers came to the end of the path, they saw a *veil of spray* coming down from the falls more than a hundred feet in height.

_____

2. General Grant asked his opponents for *unconditional surrender.* ____

_____

Improving Skill in Sentence Comprehension

Some pupils may find the following activities of value in improving their comprehension of sentences.

1. Drawing a line under one of a series of sentences that is illustrated by a picture in a workbook or teacher-made practice exercise
2. Picking out in connection with an illustrated story the sentences that are well illustrated by a picture
3. Arranging in correct order the parts of scrambled sentences
4. Listing the sentences in a selection that help prove a given point
5. Finding in a book a sentence that suggests an appropriate title for a story or picture
6. Answering with *yes* or *no*, questions on which readers will agree if the meaning is clear to them, such as: (a) Is winter a colder season than summer? (b) Do all good people live in warm houses?
7. Making sentences that show variety in structure, such as: (a) "Quickly the boys ran home." (b) "The boys ran home quickly."
8. Studying the thought of sentences in which the subject and predicate are in inverted order, and constructing some of that type
9. Finding sentences that answer given questions
10. Answering questions about a sentence with which the pupils have difficulty and indicating which part of a sentence answers each question

11. In connection with a long sentence that presents comprehension difficulties, making a sentence for every idea contained in it
12. Deciding on the meaning of some sentences through the study of punctuation marks

Additional Activity The boys and girls can be provided with practice in reading for meaning by using cloze techniques or variations of them (see p. 179). Two items, developed by Lynette Char, for each of six categories based on Wilbur Ames' classification of context clues (see p. 115) are given here as examples.[1] A practice exercise containing cloze items can be made for each of the categories of context clues. It should be noted that cloze items can be used for either practice or testing purposes.

1. *Definitions and descriptions*
    + The boys were playing a game of _____ in the park. It was very exciting when a player caught a high pass and made a touchdown.
    + She was always _____. She meant well and had a good clock, but somehow she could never get started on time. Something always seemed to happen at the last minute to delay her.
2. *Words connected or in series*
    + The two children never minded the three-mile walk to school. The forest always offered them something new to _____, hear, smell, or touch.
    + Forests are important. They provide lumber and things made from it. And think of all the birds and animals that need the forest for their _____, home, and protection.
3. *Direct referrals*
    + She was bothered about something. She tried to think that the something did not matter. She was going to laugh and forget about it. But she couldn't laugh and she couldn't _____.
    + The name *raccoon* comes from an old American Indian word that means *one who scratches with his hands*. Raccoons have front paws that look like little _____, and they often scratch around on the ground looking for insects to eat.
4. *Modifying phrases/clauses*
    + Jim lost his lunch money because there was a hole in the _____ of his old blue jeans.
    + Since we're probably _____, I wonder if anyone else has arrived yet.
5. *Familiar expressions*
    + We wanted to give Tommy a surprise birthday party, but someone let the _____out of the bag and told him about it.

[1]Lynette Y. C. Char, *The Ability of Sixth-grade Pupils To Use Certain Verbal Context Clues in Listening and Reading,* unpublished doctoral dissertation (Minneapolis, Minn.: University of Minnesota, 1968). By permission of the author.

+When John had done something well and someone told him about it, Grandpa used to say that he was as _____ as a peacock.

6. *Comparisons or contrasts*

+Neither the reader who reads everything rapidly nor the one who reads everything _____ is really a good reader.

George was very sure that he was right, even when everyone else knew he was _____.

Developing Skill in Paragraph Comprehension

Many suggestions for improving comprehension of paragraphs are considered earlier in this chapter. A few additional ones are here given:

1. Finding the paragraph that answers a question or contains a specified thought
2. Studying the topic sentence of a paragraph to help get the main idea of the paragraph
3. Using the topic sentence of a paragraph as an aid when organizing, as well as when skimming
4. Writing paragraphs on specified topics
5. Matching a series of paragraphs with summaries of these paragraphs

Additional Activity The following exercise can be particularly helpful since it is based on reading in the children's books. At least one of the paragraphs used in this exercise should have a topic sentence and at least one should not.

Directions: Read the three paragraphs in your (name of textbook supplied) on page _____ to answer these questions and to follow these directions. (The same questions as those given for the first paragraph should be asked about the other paragraphs.)

Paragraph 1. Does it contain a topic sentence? _____ If so, write the first three words of the sentence: _____

If there is a topic sentence in the paragraph, do all the details given in the paragraph support the topic sentence? _____

If the paragraph does not contain a topic sentence, would the paragraph be improved if it had one? _____ Give reasons for your answer. _____

_____

If the paragraph has no topic sentence and if the paragraph could be improved if it contained one, write a sentence that would make a good topic sentence for the paragraph. _____

_____

Developing Skill in Understanding the Meaning of Longer Selections

Since many suggestions for development of skill in comprehending longer materials are given under a variety of topics discussed earlier in this chapter, we list here only the following types of activities that some pupils could profitably perform to gain more skill in comprehending materials of this type.

1. Finding the place in a story or article or book where specified parts begin
2. Reading a story or article to decide where it can be divided into parts
3. Taking a pretest, before reading a selection, on questions based on the selection and then, after reading it, taking the test again.

Additional Activity   To help boys and girls make adequate use of center heads and sideheads, an exercise such as this may prove of help.

Directions: Read the headings given in this exercise. Study them to find out which of the questions listed below the headings you would expect to find discussed under each. Then in the space to the right of each question write the number of the center head and the letter of the sidehead under which you would expect to find the answer discussed. Write an *N*, for *not discussed,* in the space to the right of each question that you do not expect to find under any of these headings.

Center head: 1. *The Boyhood of Columbus*
Sideheads: a. Birthplace
                   b. Work of his father
                   c. His early interest in the sea

Center head: 2. *The Plan of Columbus*
Sideheads: a. His beliefs about the shape of the earth
                   b. His disbelief in the stories of the dragons of the sea
                   c. His belief that India could be reached by water

Center head: 3. *Columbus in Search of Aid*
Sideheads: a. Refusal of Spain to help him
                   b. Plan to ask France for aid
                   c. The help of the abbot
                   d. Promise of help by Queen Isabella and King Ferdinand

Center head: 4. *Getting Ready for the First Voyage*
Sideheads: a. Getting men
                   b. Getting ships and supplies

Center head: 5. *First Voyage*
Sideheads: a. Fears of the sailors
                   b. Scarcity of food
                   c. Length of the voyage
                   d. Threat of mutiny
                   e. Seeing land
                   g. Exploring the land
                   h. Return to Spain

Center head: 6. *Later Voyages and Death*
Sideheads: a. The second, third, and fourth voyages
                    b. Return to Spain in chains
                    c. Last days and death

1. Why were the sailors afraid they would fall off the edge of the earth?
    _____
2. How did the Spanish court treat Columbus upon his return after his
    fourth voyage? _____
3. Did the Norsemen discover America? _____
4. What did Columbus believe, even before 1492, was the shape of the
    earth? _____
    _____
5. Why did Spain at first refuse to give aid to Columbus? _____
6. Why was it hard to secure good men for the first voyage? _____
7. How many ships did Columbus have with him on his first voyage?
    _____
8. When was land first seen? _____
9. What did Columbus do to keep his men from mutinying on the first
    voyage? _____
10. Where did Columbus die? _____
11. What parts of America did the French explore? _____

Skill in Reading at Appropriate Rates of Comprehension

The purpose of this section is to illustrate how the teacher can help children to develop reading rates appropriate to the various types of materials
and purposes for reading. Reading rates are here grouped, as they are in
the preceding chapter, into three categories, namely, rapid reading, moderately rapid reading, and slow reading. Each of these types of reading is
desirable under certain circumstances and undesirable under others. The
efficient reader knows not only how to use these but also when.

Some activities performed by pupils can be helpful for increasing rate
whether fast, moderately fast, or rather slow reading is called for by the
purpose of the reader and the material. The following are illustrative:

1. Discussing the importance of reading at the fastest rate possible in
    keeping with the aim of the reader and the nature of the material
2. Discussing the importance of maintaining a desired level of compre-
    hension as rate is increased
3. Explaining that some readers read too fast to achieve the comprehen-
    sion level they wish to attain
4. Explaining the importance of purpose in reading, in order to help pu-
    pils understand the optimum speed at which the material with a stated
    purpose should be read
5. Explaining the relation between type and difficulty of material and the
    optimum speed at which the material should be read

6. Estimating the speed (in terms of fast, moderately fast, and slow) at which materials of designated types and difficulty should be read
7. Reading while being timed and later checked for comprehension
8. Keeping a record of progress in reading at appropriate rates
9. Discussing importance of freedom from interfering movements, such as vocalization in supposedly silent reading and pointing to words when reading

Developing Skill in Reading at a Rapid Rate

Activities such as the following may be of value in the development of skill in skimming or scanning. Some of them are applicable, too, to other rapid reading.

1. Discussing in what situations scanning can properly be used, as, for example, when the reader wishes to ascertain whether information on a given topic or an answer to a question is provided
2. Scanning a paragraph to find out whether a named topic is discussed or to find the sentence that answers a stated question
3. Scanning a table of contents to find out on what page a chapter on a given topic begins
4. Scanning parts of an article in an encyclopedia to find a desired fact
5. Scanning a page in a book to find a given "new word" that has been presented
6. Scanning a page to find the answer to a question based on that page
7. Finding a word in the dictionary
8. Scanning a telephone directory to find the name of a person whose telephone number is desired
9. Scanning a selection to find proof for a point made
10. Discussing in what situations skimming can properly be used, as, for example, when the reader wishes to get only a general impression of what is discussed in the selection
11. Skimming a page while consciously moving the eyes rapidly across and down a page, without stopping to note details
12. Skimming a book to find out whether one would like to read it
13. Skimming a selection after a more thorough reading to see if any points to be remembered have been forgotten by the reader
14. Skimming a story after previous reading to determine what characters are needed for a dramatization of the story
15. Explaining how the eyes may move on a page when scanning or skimming. It may help some of the boys and girls to know that in scanning and in skimming the eyes do not need to move from the very end of one line to the very beginning of the next, but that often they take in only part of each line as they move rapidly over the page.
16. Timing oneself or being timed while engaging in many of the types of activities that are here suggested
17. Reading a paragraph in which some words have been omitted, words

without which a reader can get the general thought of the paragraph. The pupils can be told not to try to guess the missing words but to see if they can understand the paragraph as it is written while reading it rapidly

The following are ways in which improvement may be brought about in reading at an effective rate when reading fast, but when neither skimming nor scanning is desired, as is often the case when reading a magazine or a book of fiction:

1. Explaining when fast reading other than skimming or scanning should be used
2. Identifying situations in which fast reading, other than skimming or scanning, is desired
3. Getting practice in reading rapidly easy material or material with which the reader has some familiarity
4. Getting practice in selecting the main idea of a paragraph, without intent to note details, as rapidly as possible
5. Timing oneself or being timed while reading rapidly

Practice Exercises

Some pupils can be helped to acquire appropriate reading rates by means of practice exercises. Material in workbooks, accompanying basal readers or independent of them, can be adapted for such use. However, the teacher may also find it desirable to construct exercises of his own such as the one given here. The following exercise is representative of some that may encourage either skimming or rapid reading without skimming. An exercise such as the following, especially if timed, is particularly helpful to pupils inclined to use too much time in locating the main thought in a paragraph or longer selection.

Directions: This exercise is to help you learn to locate rapidly a certain sentence in a paragraph. You will be timed while you are doing this exercise. Preceding each paragraph there is a sentence. You are to find the sentence in the paragraph that expresses the thought of that sentence. When you have located the sentence in the paragraph, draw a circle around the first word of it and continue with the next paragraph.

Sentence: The Indian elephant has a lighter skin than the African.

There are many differences between the two kinds of elephants, the African and the Indian. The African elephants grow larger than the Indian elephants. As a rule, both the male and the female of the African elephant have tusks, but only the Indian male has them. The tusks of the African elephant are larger than those of the Indian. The ears of the African elephant are also larger. The elephant in Africa has two knobs at the end of its trunk, but the Indian has only one. The elephants from Africa are darker than those from Asia. Even the texture of skin of the two animals is different, for that of the Indian elephant is not as rough as that of the African.

Developing Skill in Reading at a Moderately Rapid Rate

In order to develop skill in reading moderately easy material with the purpose of finding the main ideas, as well as numerous details, activities such as the following may prove helpful:

1. Discussing in what situations moderately fast reading should take place
2. Getting practice in selecting the main ideas and some supporting details rapidly
3. Being timed or timing oneself while reading
4. Reading a page of a book to find the words that complete sentences written on the chalkboard or on a sheet of paper
5. Reading a paragraph in which one or two words do not fit the meaning of one or more sentences. When these words are located, the children should circle each incorrect word and write a more suitable word in the margin
6. Telling for which of a series of listed purposes one would ordinarily engage in moderately fast reading. The list might be similar to this:
   a. Reading to get the general idea of living conditions in the South during the last year of the Civil War
   b. Looking for a word in the dictionary
   c. Reading a report in the society column of a newspaper to find out where a certain party was held
   d. Studying in a science book about how heat travels in order to be able to draw a series of pictures for an accordionlike folder that would illustrate conduction, radiation, and convection
7. Answering questions that the teacher asks about something read to or by the pupils that can be answered in phrases. For example, the question might be: "Why did Snipp, Snapp, and Snurr want to find work?" The pupils could choose the correct phrase from a list such as this and read it out loud: (a) "to go to the show," (b) "to buy a present," (c) "to buy a dog."

Practice Exercise

Stories are well adapted for use as exercises—for example, the following—in fairly rapid reading of rather easy material. The story should be one that the children do not already know.

Directions: Read as rapidly as you can the story of *The Shoemaker and the Elves* so as to be able to answer fairly easy questions that you will be asked on it. Your teacher will time you while you are reading the story.

Questions on the story. (These questions are to be answered in as few words as possible.)

1. How many pairs of shoes did the shoemaker find the morning after the night when he had cut out leather for just one pair of shoes? _____
2. Why did the shoemaker and his wife decide to sit up one night shortly before Christmas? _____

3. Where in the room were the shoemaker and his wife hiding the evening when they sat up? _____

4. How many elves came to do the work for the shoemaker? _____

5. What did the shoemaker and his wife do to show their gratitude to their elves? _____

6. How did the elves like their presents? _____

Developing Skill in Reading at a Slow Rate

Many elementary school children, especially in the intermediate grades, need help in reading for study purposes. Often they also need to learn how to adjust their reading rate for directions which they are asked to follow. Although the rate of reading for such purposes is necessarily relatively slow, pupils should nevertheless be helped to do such reading as rapidly as possible to attain their objectives. Many can probably profit from taking part in some activities such as the following:

1. Discussing in what situations fairly slow reading is called for
2. Identifying situations in which slower reading should take place
3. Reading, under timed conditions, materials that require careful understanding of what is read
4. Memorizing a significant line or longer part of a paragraph or poem
5. Selecting all points that support a stated main topic
6. Reading a selection in order to report on it

Development of Comprehension Skills through Reading Lessons

All of the comprehension skills can be developed in part through reading lessons without recourse to definite practice exercises. This section of the chapter is devoted to demonstrating how growth in the various skills can be encouraged in these lessons. The suggestions are based on selections from two reading series, one for boys and girls reading on a lower primary-grade level and the other for those on a more advanced level. The comprehension skills that a teacher will decide to develop in either of these lessons should depend on the total developmental reading program, based on the needs of the boys and girls. The suggestions listed in connection with either of these lessons are not necessarily the ones to be used. They are merely suggestive of the many possible ones from which a selection may be made. Nor should nearly all of the recommendations be used for any one selection, for the number is too large and there is overlapping among them. Excellent suggestions for the development of power in comprehension are listed in the manuals for the teacher accompanying the basal readers.

Using a Story at the Lower-Primary Reading Level

For an example of how various comprehension skills can be highlighted in a story at the lower-primary reading level suggestions are based on "The Three Little Pigs"[2] as retold by John Lowell.

Finding the Main Idea

The pupils may read the story to decide whether it would be a good one to read to another group or whether it would be suitable for a dramatization, a puppet play, or a home-made "movie" if they had been planning to engage in one of those activities.

Selecting Important Details

If the pupils decide to dramatize the story or to give a puppet play or to make a "movie" of it, they may need to read the story carefully in order to decide what details and actions to include.

Following Directions

The teacher may write on the chalkboard directions such as these:

1. Read the rest of the story.
2. Write the word *wolf.*
3. Write the word *pig.*

Summarizing and Organizing

Although most work on writing summaries is usually postponed until boys and girls are on a higher reading level than the one for which this story is geared, some children who read it might wish to include a brief summary of stories they like particularly well in a large looseleaf notebook, possibly 18 x 24 inches. For such a notebook the group could cooperatively plan a brief summary on this order. "Three little pigs built their own houses. One little pig made his house of straw. Another little pig made his house of sticks. The smart little pig built his house of bricks. The wolf blew down the straw house. He blew down the house made of sticks. He could not blow down the brick house. The wolf went down the chimney of the brick house. He fell into some hot water. That was the end of the big bad wolf."

If the pupils decide to put on a play, they can help determine what the parts of the play should be. The division might be as follows:

1. The mother pig tells her little pigs to build houses.
2. The little pigs build their houses.
3. The wolf blows down the house of two little pigs.

[2]Leo Fay, Ramon Ross, and Margaret LaPray, *Red Rock Ranch*, The Young America Basic Reading Program, Level 6 (Chicago: Lyons and Carnahan, 1974), pp. 106–117.

4. The wolf tries to blow down the house of the third little pig.
5. The wolf falls into hot water.

Then the pupils can decide on the details to be portrayed in connection with each part.

Arriving at a Generalization

After the group has discussed how the first two little pigs showed they were foolish and how the third little pig showed he was wise, the teacher might ask the boys and girls what lesson they think the first two pigs may have learned from their experiences with the bad wolf.

Predicting Outcomes

During the course of reading the story, the teacher may at appropriate places make comments and ask questions such as these: (1) The wolf had no trouble blowing down the straw house. Do you think he will be able to blow down the house made of sticks? (b) Why did the little pigs put some hot water in the fireplace and more wood on the fire when they saw the wolf was coming down the chimney? Or after the boys and girls have read the first two sentences of the page where the wolf said, "I will get the three little pigs," the teacher might ask them what they think the wolf's plans were.

Answering Questions

After the boys and girls have read the page that tells the reader the big bad wolf said, "Ummmmm, I like little pigs," the teacher might ask the class what they think the big bad wolf meant when he said that.

Sentence Comprehension

If the pupils have difficulty in comprehending the rather long sentence, " 'Please, man, give me some of your bricks to build a house,' said the little pig," the teacher may ask them to tell in their own words what the little pig asked the man. Practice in formulating good sentences as they discuss what they read or as they make a summary can also indirectly help boys and girls in the comprehension of the meaning of written sentences.

Comprehension of a Longer Selection

On the basis of a story such as this, pupils can be helped in learning to read longer selections more effectively by performing such activities as these: (1) finding where each of the parts of the story that were enumerated earlier in connection with this story under "Summarizing and Organizing" begins or (b) telling the story to another group of boys and girls.

Using a Story at a More Advanced Reading Level

In *Joys and Journeys,*[3] one of the upper-level books of the *Read Series,* is the selection "Benny by the River," the story of the boy Benny, son of a displaced family that had escaped from behind the Iron Curtain. Requested to "be nice to Benny" by the parents of the gang to which the boy who is the narrator of the story belongs, the boys in the group tried but all they did was to tolerate him and let him tag along with them. To the boys Benny seemed queer because of his speech, his clothes, his haircut, his shyness. They looked on him with disdain after, shaken with terror, he had sobbed when he approached the bridge that led to the boys' swimming place. Then when Benny's mother had explained to the narrator of the story that Benny's fear stemmed from the day when, as they were fleeing from behind the Iron Curtain, guards shot and killed his brother who had helped him across a river, the narrator planned to tell the other boys the terrible story, so that they would understand why Benny had acted as he did. But the explanation was not necessary, for that very evening, as the boys were skating on the river, Benny, endangering his own life, saved one of the group who had broken through the ice.

Finding the Main Idea

After the boys and girls have read the story, they may suggest other titles for it, or they may choose the appropriate title from a series of possible titles such as: (a) Leaving the Iron Curtain behind Us; (b) Ridiculed by the Gang; (c) Courage Undaunted.

Selecting Important Details

Pupils may enumerate the details which indicated that the boys' attitude toward Benny before his heroic act had been one of tolerance or less than tolerance.

Outlining and Organizing

The boys and girls might think of this dramatic story as an excellent one for a play and then determine what scenes could be portrayed in a dramatization. The following is one possible plan of organization:

1. Treatment of Benny by the boys before the bridge episode
2. The bridge episode
3. The changed attitude of the boys following Benny's reaction at the bridge
4. The mother's visit
5. The rescue
6. A change in treatment of Benny

[3]Marjorie S. Johnson, Roy A. Kress, John D. McNeil, and Pose Lamb, *Joys and Journeys, The READ Series,* Level J (New York: American Book Company, 1971), pp. 280–290.

Arriving at Generalizations or Coming to Conclusions

The story provides excellent opportunities to help boys and girls develop in their ability to make generalizations. Attention can be drawn to the fact that the boys had come to an incorrectly inferred conclusion that Benny was cowardly. The importance of deferring generalizations until enough evidence is available can be stressed. The class might also discuss the appropriateness of the conclusion stated in the last sentence of the story: "That Benny Wlodarski is some guy."

Predicting Outcomes

After the pupils have read to the point where Benny, terrorized at the thought of crossing the bridge, left the other boys, pupils could be asked how they imagined the boys would treat Benny after that episode.

After finishing reading the story, they could predict how the boys would treat Benny in the future. They could base their prediction in part on the sentences: "Benny didn't need any help. He'd won a place for himself without it."

Evaluating What Is Read

The ability to evaluate what is read can be developed by considering the true-to-life quality and the justifiability or wrongness of actions portrayed by sentences such as the following: (a) If he had been anyone else, we would have yelled the roof down at the stunts he did—but we remembered too clearly that day by the river. (b) My mom always called Benny "that poor little foreign boy," and she'd told me to be nice to him. The other kids heard the same from their folks, so we let Benny tag around with us; but we weren't really friendly to him.

Word Meaning

This story provides much opportunity to help boys and girls develop their reading and speaking and understanding vocabulary. They can probably learn through the context the meaning of some words formerly unfamiliar to them, such as, possibly, those given in italics in the following sentences: (a) "November had been as cold as October'd been *balmy*;" (b) "I *peered* toward the shadows, and I could see Benny's figure."

Phrase Meaning

The story contains many idiomatic expressions, the meaning of which the class could discuss. In some cases they might like to substitute other words for a phrase and then compare the forcefulness of the sentences in the book with those that they suggested. Some of the phrases that might be studied are: (a) the water's edge; (b) yelled the roof down; (c) strike out.

Sentence Meaning

Development of skill in sentence comprehension might be brought about through questions and directions such as these:

1. What did Benny's mother mean when she said: "And is all. Paul, my son"?
2. Give in your own words the meaning of the statement by Mrs. Wlodarski: "We have not say much about when we leave old country."
3. Why are complete sentences not necessary to give the thought of the last six words of these comments made by the narrator: "I thought of Benny that day with us, crying. Remembering another bridge. Remembering a bullet"?

For Further Study

Alexander, J. Estill, ed., *Teaching Reading* (Boston: Little, Brown, 1979), Ch. 7, "Comprehension: Reading for Meaning" by Thomas N. Turner; Ch. 8, "Questioning Techniques: Probing for Greater Meaning" by Thomas N. Turner; Ch. 9, "Critical and Creative Reading" by Thomas N. Turner; and Ch. 10, "Study Skills" by Arnold R. Davis.

Bush, Clifford L., and Mildred H. Heubner, *Strategies for Reading in the Elementary School*, rev. ed. (New York: Macmillan, 1979), Ch. 5, "Comprehension: Basic Factors," and Ch. 6, "Comprehension Skills."

Durkin, Dolores, *Teaching Them to Read*, 3d ed. (Boston: Allyn and Bacon, 1978), Ch. 15, "Comprehension."

Friedman, Myles I., and Michael Rowls, *Teaching Reading and Thinking Skills* (New York: Longman, 1980), Part III, "Reading Comprehension."

Goodman, Yetta M., and Carolyn Burke, *Reading Strategies: Focus on Comprehension* (New York: Holt, Rinehart and Winston, 1980).

Harris, Larry A., and Carl B. Smith, *Reading Instruction: Diagnostic Teaching in the Classroom*, 3d ed. (New York: Holt, Rinehart and Winston, 1980), Ch. 8, "Reading Comprehension: Experiental and Language Factors," and Ch. 9, "Reading Comprehension: Cognitive and Affective Factors."

Page, William D., and Gay Su Pinnell, *Teaching Reading Comprehension: Theory and Practice* (New York: Teachers College Press, 1979).

Pearson, P. David, and Dale D. Johnson, *Teaching Reading Comprehension* (New York: Holt, Rinehart and Winston, 1978), Ch. 8, "Questions."

Ransom, Grayce, A., *Preparing to Teach Reading* (Boston: Little, Brown, 1978), Ch. 11, "Teaching Comprehension Skills."

Roe, Betty D.; Barbara D. Stoodt; and Paul C. Burns, *Reading Instruction in the Secondary School*, rev. ed. (Chicago: Rand McNally College Publishing Company, 1978), section on "Levels of Thinking and Questioning Techniques," pp. 155–65.

Sanders, Norris, *Classroom Questions: What Kinds?* (New York: Harper and Row, 1966).

Smith, Frank, *Comprehension and Learning: A Conceptual Framework for Teachers* (New York: Holt, Rinehart and Winston, 1975).

Smith, Richard J., and Thomas C. Barrett, *Teaching Reading in the Middle Grades* (Menlo Park, Cal.: Addison-Wesley, 1976), Ch. 3, "Reading Comprehension."

Spache, George D., and Evelyn B. Spache, *Reading in the Elementary School*, 4th ed. (Boston: Allyn and Bacon, 1977), Ch. 13, "Developing Comprehension and Critical Reading Skills."

Tinker, Miles A., and Constance M. McCullough, *Teaching Elementary Reading*, 4th ed. (Englewood Cliffs, N.J.: Prentice-Hall, 1975), Ch. 9, "Comprehension and Interpretation"; Ch. 10, "Comprehension and Study Skills"; and Ch. 12, "Speed of Reading."

Zintz, Miles V., *The Reading Process: The Teacher and the Learner*, 3d ed (Dubuque, Iowa: Wm. C. Brown, 1980), Ch. 10, "Comprehension Skills"; Ch. 11, "Study Skills"; and Ch. 12, "Developing Critical Reading Abilities."

Questions and Comments for Thought and Discussion

1. In the past, teachers and research workers in reading have given a great deal of attention to word perception and general reading comprehension skills on the literal and interpretive levels. But in recent years the development of critical reading skills has come to be of increasing concern. Do you believe that critical reading can be taught in the early grades? If so, can you describe a situation in which conditions would appear to be conducive to the development of critical reading ability during one of the first years in the elementary school?

2. The term *creative reading* has come to mean many things. It may mean an attitude of suspended judgment with regard to reading materials, the ability to read above and beyond the obvious, the ability to see or perceive relations, the ability to recognize authors' intentions. At what level would you try to develop such abilities? How would you embark on such a venture?

3. Some suggestions are given in this chapter (see p. 192) for assisting boys and girls in recognizing propaganda techniques. In what additional ways could the teacher assist his pupils in becoming aware of the use of such techniques as they are reading or viewing television or listening to the radio or to people talk?

4. Many suggestions are given in this "B" chapter for developing various comprehension skills, and some examples of exercises are included. You may wish to plan an exercise to help boys and girls, on any level of reading development, to improve in any one of these skills—such as predicting outcomes, recognizing propaganda techniques, judging the qualifications of an author.

5. If you have access to teachers' guidebooks or manuals to be used with basal readers, you may wish to examine them to find useful suggestions for helping boys and girls grow in the ability to comprehend what they read.

6. It has been asserted that a flexible reader selects the speed best suited to his purpose and to the reading material. Sometimes teachers direct students to vary their rate, shifting to a higher or lower rate when encountering easier or more difficult ideas or when comprehension needs differ. Does saying, "speed up," "slow down," "shift gears" really accomplish much? How would you go about achieving your ends as a teacher?

7. You may decide to read part or all of one of the references on questioning given on page 179 and then report to your classmates on significant points of view you learned through the reading.

8. Based on the information you currently have, what is your reaction as to the usefulness of "reciprocal questioning" (REQUEST)?

Oral Reading

Sixty years ago reading instruction in most elementary schools was instruction in oral reading. Numberous educators had called attention to the sterility of the exclusively oral approach. Thus, Edmund B. Huey wrote in 1908:

> Reading as a school exercise has almost always been thought of as reading aloud, in spite of the obvious fact that reading in actual life is to be mainly silent reading. The consequent attention to reading as an exercise in speaking . . . has been heavily at the expense of reading as the art of thoughtgetting . . .[1]

In this statement Huey confirmed the views of earlier educational leaders such as Horace Mann and Francis W. Parker. It was not until the early 1920s, however, that a widespread shift of emphasis from oral to silent reading took place. In this period a great quantity of published materials, including a yearbook of the National Society for the study of Education, numerous research reports, textbooks on the teaching of reading, reading manuals, and series of basal readers stressed the need for instruction in silent reading.

The chief arguments in favor of silent as against oral reading were based chiefly on two considerations:

1. Most reading outside of school is silent reading.
2. Silent reading emphasizes meaning rather than sound. Psychologists of many schools—behaviorist, gestalt, organismic, and others—were concerned with the ways in which communication takes place between the writer and the reader.

Experimentation with various methods of teaching reading and the rise of the test and measurement movement further strengthened the trend toward silent reading instruction.

The Importance of Oral Reading

As teachers began to emphasize silent reading many of them, unfortunately, began to neglect oral reading. Especially in the intermediate grades little attention was paid to oral reading. It may be true that not more than about 1 percent of out-of-school reading is oral. However, frequency of use should by no means be the sole determiner of the emphasis to be placed on the development of any ability. Such factors as the value of the skill and the relative difficulty of mastering it should also play an important part in any decision concerning what is to be included in the curriculum. Oral reading is a valuable skill, one that is not automatically learned in an effective program of silent reading instruction. Rather, in the case of a large number of boys and girls—probably the great majority of them—specific attention is required on the part of the teacher if adequate skill in oral reading is to be acquired.

Values of Oral Reading

A point being stressed, even at times overstressed, by linguists and some educators that is influencing the teaching of reading is the primacy of oral over written communication. With this emphasis has come a higher valuation on oral reading and on its accompanying skill, listening, especially in the early stages of learning to read.

One important value of oral reading that is often not given due attention is that it

---

[1]Edmund B. Huey, *The Psychology and Pedagogy of Reading* (New York: Macmillan, 1908), p. 359.

can produce beneficial results in the social and emotional development of children. The growth in literary appreciation that can come as boys and girls read orally to each other is in itself justification for oral reading instruction. Furthermore, sympathetic relations among members of a group may often be created or strengthened by means of the oral reading experience. A boy or girl may acquire a much-needed feeling of acceptance in his group by being able to contribute a story, a joke, or an interesting fact by reading aloud from a book, a magazine, or a newspaper. Pupils who do not excel in other activities may find recognition in superior performance in oral reading. Moreover, oral reading may help them develop self-assurance and poise.

Many additional values can be achieved through oral reading. Oral reading can help pupils:

1. To communicate ideas
2. To provide enjoyment for others

Reading can be a cooperative venture. (Washington School, St. Cloud, Minnesota)

3. To add to the reader's understanding of what he reads
4. To diagnose problems in silent reading
5. To increase vocabulary
6. To improve speech

Functional Situations for Oral Reading

At all times when oral reading is included in the day's program it should serve a purpose that is considered worthwhile not only by the teacher but also by the pupils. Frequently the function should be in relation to the ongoing activity of the classroom. Opportunities for purposeful oral reading are exemplified by the following activities, which are merely suggestive of many others:

1. Reading captions under pictures on bulletin boards and flannel boards
2. Giving oral reports or reading stories orally, including original ones by the boys and girls, to another group, possibly within the context of a program consisting of a variety of activities
3. Putting on a make-believe radio or television program
4. Rereading orally short selections that have been read silently, with the purpose of clarifying the meaning
5. Reading parts from a book to illustrate a point or to base a discussion on it with classmates
6. Preparing an oral interpretive reading selection in which the reader assumes the part of a narrator and the participants in the dialogue
7. Participating in a panel that is reading a series of short stories or a longer story in parts
8. Giving a play in which the "conversation" is read
9. Reading reports

10. Reading the minutes of a meeting
11. Reading announcements
12. Taking part in choral reading

Although, as a rule, oral reading should find its purpose in the need or suitability for such reading within the ongoing classroom activities, sometimes the main function of oral reading may be practice to increase the pupils' skill in oral reading. At such times, it is advisable that boys and girls recognize the objective to be served by the practice. The aim may be to help them read more effectively in programs that they may present to their classmates or to a larger segment of the school population. At other times the goal for the practice may be stated in less specific terms, such as becoming better oral readers in any situation requiring them to read orally. In such practice sessions attention might be focused on maintaining or acquiring contact with the audience, on effective phrasing, and on skillful interpretation of the mood the writer seems to wish to portray. Exercises in the form of practice in pronunciation, enunciation, and variation of voice are also valuable for many boys and girls. Among the suggestions listed under "Instructional Practices" (see p. 222), are included some that provide specific practice in attaining these and other desirable skills of oral reading.

Relation between Oral and Silent Reading

Almost all the skills that are important in silent reading are also needed in effective oral reading because in a certain sense all oral reading is preceded by silent reading. A word in print cannot be given orally unless the reader has recognized the word and

by that very act has read it silently. Consequently, skill in word recognition, possession of a suitable meaning vocabulary, and the ability to comprehend what is read are essentials of both oral and silent reading. Even rate of reading is a factor in both types because the individual who cannot read silently as rapidly as he can say the words he is reading is handicapped in his oral reading.

The efficient oral reader possesses many of the skills important to silent reading as well as many additional abilities peculiar to oral reading. One of these is correct pronunciation of words. In silent reading the pupil must recognize the word and know its meaning, but it is not essential that he know how to pronounce it. Clear articulation, a pleasing and well-modulated voice, and proper contact with the audience are additional concerns of the oral reader. Furthermore, in oral reading thought getting, common to both oral and silent reading, must be followed by vocal interpretation because it is necessary to convey to the audience the reader's grasp of the meaning of the passage, at times both the literal meaning and an inferred meaning. Thus oral reading, if done well, becomes a highly complex skill.

The effective oral reader possesses many of the skills important to silent reading as in the eye-movement studies of the first part of the century. The studies of the eye-voice span (the distance between the word the reader pronounces and the point on which his eyes fixate), for example, showed that in oral reading the eyes of the effective reader run well ahead of his voice. When reading silently he is not delayed as in oral reading by the mere physical act of articulation. The silent reading rate of the efficient reader exceeds that of his oral reading. In the later elementary school years the average pupil may read silently from one and a half to two times his oral reading rate, or even more.

Oral reading can serve as an aid to silent reading in many ways, some of which are illustrated later in this chapter and in the "B" chapter that follows. Oral reading, for example, helps in the diagnosis of difficulties in silent reading. As a pupil reads a selection orally, the teacher can frequently detect the types of errors that keep the pupil from reading well silently. Difficulties such as the following, common to both oral and silent reading, often are revealed: omission of words or phrases; insertion of words or phrases; substitution of letters, words, or phrases; skipping lines; repeating lines; and phrasing so inadequately that it interferes with thought getting and interpretation (see Chapter 12, "Classroom Diagnosis of Reading Ability").

Learning to read well orally, then, is more difficult in some respects than learning to read well silently. Not only must the oral reader have a good grasp of the meaning of the material he reads but he must have many other abilities besides. He needs not only, as in silent reading, to get the thought but he must also interpret or convey it to his listeners. He must know his listeners—their interests and probable attitudes toward the material read as well as their capacity to understand it—and he must be sensitive to their reactions as he reads to them. He must be fluent enough to focus his mind on the thought rather than the recognition and pronunciation of individual words. He must reproduce in his reading the mood and intention of the author, recognizing irony or pathos, happiness or depression, excitement or pensiveness. To accomplish his purpose he must know how to use pauses effectively. He must have skill in using his voice. He must

be free of mannerisms that might detract attention from the message he brings. He must make a poised appearance.

It is important that the person who is to read orally to a group be given, as a rule, the opportunity to read the material silently before he reads it to others. Silent reading preceding oral reading is desirable in order that the reader be given the opportunity in his first reading to solve problems of word recognition and pronunciation that he may have. Furthermore, the reader will be likely to interpret the meaning of the writer more accurately if he has the chance to get the meaning himself before he is confronted with the task of interpreting. In oral reading the reader is in the limelight in a social situation, and he may become uncomfortable unless he has the security of knowing the material he is to present to his audience. Even the adult reader usually likes to read beforehand that which he is to read to others, whether the material consists of minutes of a meeting written by someone else, a story from a magazine, or an article from the newspaper. However, there is also a legitimate place for sight reading.

The term *sight reading* is here used to refer to oral reading when the reader has not previously read the material either silently or orally. As indicated in the preceding paragraph, such procedure is usually undesirable for the reasons given. However, it can be used advisedly at times, for example, when the teacher is the only listener. The purpose in having a pupil read to the teacher might be diagnostic.

Occasionally, too, sight reading may be justified for another purpose. The boys and girls may be reading orally without previous practice in silent reading in order to have practice in sight reading in an audience situation. The teacher may want to explain to the pupils that sometimes people do get called on to read something orally without having had the opportunity to read it beforehand. It can be made clear to the boys and girls that practice in sight reading may help them to feel at ease if sometime someone asks them to read orally without their having the chance to precede the oral reading by silent reading.

It is important when pupils do sight reading in front of their peers than an atmosphere of understanding and good will permeate the situation. A child required to read by sight to an audience, unless the situation is one that is well controlled to eliminate problems, is in a precarious position. In an atmosphere lacking in good will and mutual understanding, he may become frustrated and otherwise emotionally upset to the extent that he develops a dislike for reading. Such an attitude may result in serious reading retardation.

Oral Reading in the Early Stages of Learning To Read

The role of oral reading in the early stages of learning to read has been and continues to be a point of argument. The debate, however, no longer centers on whether there should be any oral reading at that time. Nor does it turn on the question of whether there should be silent reading in the first grade. The issue is primarily how oral reading, as part of the developmental program of the first grade, should be conducted. Some would argue that from the very beginning the child should not read orally without having read the material silently beforehand. Arguments of proponents who are against oral sight reading at that early stage are stated below.

1. Before a child is asked to read in front of an audience material which he has not previously read either orally or silently, he should have developed basic reading skills to the extent that he will not, with easy material, be confronted with problems of word recognition or of comprehension in what he may be called on to read to a group. If he lacks such skills, he will have difficulty in interpeting the written message to an audience, and when required to perform the task in front of others, may suffer emotionally.

2. When the beginning reader reads orally material he has not previously read silently, he may read it word by word and thus develop into a reader who habitually reads in that manner.

3. When an immature reader who is unprepared for reading reads to a group, he may cause his audience to be bored.

A somewhat questionable practice in many beginning-to-read groups is that of having the pupils read around the class orally while the rest of the boys and girls are supposedly following in their books. Even when boys and girls have read the selection silently beforehand, if considerable time has elapsed between the silent reading and the oral, reading is likely to be done in a halting manner and thus be harmful to the oral reader and uninteresting to the audience. Moreover, incentive for interpretation of the written message by the oral reader is not likely to be strong. The audience is then in danger of getting practice in half-listening and half-reading, since the boys and girls may lack whole-hearted purpose in both reading and listening. Even greater harm is likely to result if this practice is engaged in after the pupils have learned to read more rapidly silently than orally, for then the rate of silent reading may be affected adversely. When the learner can read more rapidly silently than orally, there is danger that his silent reading rates may be reduced, to accommodate the slower speed of oral reading.

There is, however, an important place for oral reading in the first grade. It has been pointed out that probably many boys and girls in the first grade do not get the feeling that they are reading unless they are reading orally. At a stage in reading instruction when attitudes concerning reading are of the greatest significance, to deprive the child of the opportunity to do oral reading may prove disastrous as far as his future success in reading is concerned. It may even affect adversely his personality development when the importance of reading is emphasized as much as it usually and rightly is in the typical first-grade room.

How then does oral reading fit into the beginning reading program? Here are a few suggestions:

1. The boys and girls can read the story in a basal reader silently, in short segments. In the beginning days of reading instruction the teacher might ask them to read silently only one sentence at a time. For example, the boys and girls might be asked to read a designated sentence to find out what Tom said to his mother. Thereafter, the teacher might ask a pupil to read the sentence orally as he thinks Tom said it. To be sure, every sentence that is read silently should not be read orally. At times the teacher may ask questions about what was read. At other times he may ask the boys and girls to point to a word or words he names. At still other times the pupils might discuss what they have just read. Or they might predict what they think will happen next.

2. Reading a selection by parts is also, after previous silent reading of the selection, good reason for oral reading. It is advisable that pupils to whom parts have been given have the opportunity to reread the material silently after the assignment of lines has been made.

3. Even in first grade, occasionally one or more pupils might read to the class material the group has not read. The persons doing the reading should practice beforehand both silently and orally the material they will read. The teacher can do much to make such reading a real occasion, a program for the listeners.

4. The children can read orally the language-experience charts they have helped construct.

5. Oral reading at home by the pupils should be encouraged. (See p. 220 of this chapter for suggestions as to how parents can help in the oral reading program.)

Proportion of Time for Oral and Silent Reading

What should be the proportion of oral to silent reading? A precise answer to this question cannot be given for each grade, for the apportionment depends on a variety of factors. One of these is the length of the reading period in schools that set aside time daily for reading instruction. There is wide variation in the same grades in various schools, and often there are differences within the same building if there is more than one room of the same grade or level. Moreover, even when the reading periods in two rooms of the same grade are of equal length, the time spent in oral reading may vary greatly. In one room more time may be spent in silent reading during study periods than in the other. Furthermore, the amount of oral and silent reading done during other class periods, such as social studies or science, will influence the question of the proportion of time to be devoted to each. Reading at home, too, will affect the division of the reading period between the two types of reading. Factors such as individual differences among children, their past training, and the methods of instruction used by the teacher will also need to be considered.

Recommendations concerning the proportion of oral to silent reading at times state that it should decrease as the child progresses through the elementary school. In many first-grade rooms perhaps approximately half of the time of the reading class is spent in oral reading. In the next year the proportion may have decreased to a 1 to 2 ratio, with still less attention paid to oral reading in succeeding years, where it may reach a 1 to 4 ratio or even much less.

Oral reading in the lower grades is abundantly justified by the extreme pleasure that many children experience when they read to others or listen to others read to them. Although oral reading exercises can prove boring to all concerned, many children look forward to the opportunity to read aloud to the teacher or classmates when there is an atmosphere of approval. It would seem unwise to deprive children of a satisfying experience that strengthens the desire to learn to read. Every avenue to genuine reading interest should be utilized.

Appraising Skill in Oral Reading

Before the teacher attempts to appraise the oral reading of his pupils, he will advisedly have in mind the characteristics of the efficient oral reader.

Characteristics of the Efficient Oral Reader

The teacher who undertakes to evaluate children's growth in oral reading will look for signs such as those here indicated:

1. The pupil recognizes common words at sight.
2. He pronounces the words correctly.
3. His posture is erect and dignified without being overly formal.
4. He handles his book effectively.
5. He shows that he knows the meaning not only of the words but of the entire selection.
6. He uses variety and appropriateness of tone, pitch, force, and speed.
7. He enunciates clearly.
8. He appears at ease while he reads.
9. He is free from interfering mannerisms.
10. He is responsive to the reactions of the audience.
11. He exhibits interest and enthusiasm when he reads.
12. He gives his own interpretation of the selection through his oral reading.

Comprehension is a primary requisite to efficient oral reading. As explained earlier in this chapter, this fact constitutes one important reason why pupils should not ordinarily be encouraged to read a passage aloud until they have first read it silently and have understood it. Good phrasing, effective expression, and appropriate emphasis all depend on the reader's grasp of the meaning. It is sometimes possible for a skillful reader to read orally without giving full attention to the content, but for most children good comprehension is a requirement for accurate, intelligible oral reading. Meaning will determine the correct selection of word accents, the sound values of letters, and the intonation appropriate to the purpose of the writer.

The physical behavior of the oral reader, while distinctly secondary to the problem of comprehension, requires some attention on the part of the teacher. Formal restrictions that were once imposed with respect to the position of the feet and hands are no longer observed. Children are encouraged to stand erect, to assume a natural, relaxed position, and to avoid leaning against a desk, table, or chair. The book or magazine should not shield the face of the reader. Ideally, contact with the audience is maintained by frequent upward glances toward the listeners, but such contact should usually result from a feeling of ease and an eagerness to communicate, rather than conscious effort or deliberate practice.

It is recommended that pupils know what traits are considered important for effective oral reading. In the intermediate grades, and probably even in the upper primary, the boys and girls can take part in drawing up a checklist of the qualities of a good oral reader. These points may be recorded on a chart. If there is not enough display space in a classroom to keep the chart up all the time, it could be stored until it is to be used, namely, when the pupils are reading orally or are preparing for oral reading.

The points to be included in a checklist for use by the boys and girls will necessarily vary from grade to grade. In the lower grades a brief listing couched in simple language will be all that is desirable. In the upper elementary school the list of items may be similar to the one recorded on page 236.

Checking Oral Reading

Informal observation of a pupil's performance in the oral reading situation, especially with the aid of a checklist, is one of the best methods of evaluating growth in the skills peculiar to oral reading. Defects such as bad posture, finger pointing, and poor intonation are easily noted by the alert teacher who is interested in improving the oral reading performance of his pupils. A record may be kept of the diagnosis in a manner similar to that suggested in III–D on page 236. Boys and girls can participate in the appraisals made. It is recommended that the suggestions for improvement given in class be leveled, as a rule, not at any one individual but that they serve as points for consideration by all the pupils who have read orally on a given day as well as others in the class.

Mention is frequently made of standardized oral reading tests. Such tests, however, are in reality devices to determine a pupil's skill in silent reading. They are helpful in revealing to the teacher the specific difficulties that a pupil encounters when dealing with words and sentences. They are necessarily tests to be administered individually. Valuable information can be obtained for use in the diagnosis of reading problems from reading tests such as the following:

Diagnostic Reading Tests (oral reading sections) (Committee on Diagnostic Reading Tests)

Gates Oral Reading Test (Teachers College Press, Columbia University)

Gilmore Oral Reading Tests (Harcourt Brace Jovanovich)

Goodman and Burke Reading Miscue Inventory (Macmillan Publishing Company)

Gray Oral Reading Check Tests (Bobbs-Merrill Company)

Slosson Oral Reading Tests (Slosson Educational Publications, East Aurora, New York).

These tests measure points such as reversals of letters and words, substitutions of letters and words, omissions, and incorrect return sweeps of the eyes as they move in reading from the end of one line back to the left side of the page to the next line of writing.

While oral reading tests can provide some insight into what is occurring as the reader reads silently, it must not be assumed that the excellences or the difficulties in oral and silent reading are exactly the same. Qualities such as shyness or nervousness or self-consciousness may interfere in oral reading but have no or practically no effect on silent reading—in fact, may not be present. Similarly, a child who reads too rapidly silently to get the meaning of what he reads may have a problem that will not show up in oral reading.

An effective way of diagnosing oral reading is by making a tape recording of a pupil's oral reading. Not only can the teacher, through this means, check the reading but the pupils also can profit by listening to the tape and evaluating the reading with the help of the teacher. In fact, a tape can also be used effectively while the pupil is taking a standardized oral reading test.

For an indication of the pupil's skill in reference to points peculiar to oral reading—such as phrasing, expressiveness, and reaction to the audience—the teacher must rely on his own careful observation of pupil performance and such cumulative anecdotal records as he may find time to keep. (See Chapter 12, "Classroom Diagnosis of Reading Ability," p. 337 for more information on the evaluation of reading ability, some of which pertains to or is applicable to oral reading.)

Causes of Deficiencies in Oral Reading

Reference was made earlier in this chapter to some of the manifestations of pupil difficulties in oral reading. These overt signs of trouble—such as omission of words, reading at too rapid a rate for effective interpretation, or nervousness while reading—are often indexes of underlying problems. Among the factors that frequently contribute adversely to oral reading are: (a) an undesirable audience situation; (b) unsuitable material; (c) lack of skill in some abilities important in silent reading—such as skill in recognizing words and power of understanding what is read; (d) need of specific help in development of skills peculiar to oral reading—such as desirable posture, correct handling of the book, and effectiveness of interpretation; and (e) insufficient preparation for the reading of a given selection.

Failure of the eyes of the reader to focus ahead of the words he is reading orally can contribute to problems in oral reading (see page 212). If the eyes of the person reading orally were fixating on the word he speaks, there would be danger of word-by-word reading, with its accompanying lack of interestingness and clarity of interpretation. For most readers it is probably conducive to smooth oral reading if their eyes are, as a rule, a few words ahead of the voice, far enough so that the reader can read every word with proper interpretation because he knows the context in which it occurs. If the eye-voice span is too long, however, the reader may forget some of the words before he has read them orally, with resulting difficulties—such as substitutions, ommissions, or additions. Problems related to the length of the eye-voice span can best be approached indirectly. For example, familiarity with the material, appropriate level of the difficulty of it, desire to communicate to the audience the meaning of the passage—all help in the establishment of a suitable span between the word on which the eye fixates and the one being spoken.

Another difficulty some boys and girls have in reading orally is that their rate is not suitable—either too fast or too slow. The desirable speed depends on factors such as the material to be read, the purpose in reading it, and the size of the audience. A rule-of-thumb is that the rate for oral reading should be approximately the same, under given circumstances, as it should be for talking.

General Suggestions for the Improvement of Oral Reading

Chapter 8B presents specific suggestions for procedures planned to help boys and girls become better oral readers. In this section of the present chapter are listed and explained some general recommendations on which the details of procedure can be based. The part that follows includes suggestions for alleviating the causes of deficiencies in oral reading, which are given in the preceding section.

1. **Children should be given many opportunities to do oral reading and they should be encouraged to make use of these opportunities** The fact that apparently it is possible for children to learn to read for meaning without oral reading experiences in the classroom does not justify depriving them of the chance to engage in oral reading. Children's motives for oral reading, on which the teacher can build, are of many kinds. The boys and girls may

read aloud to the teacher to show their progress in mastering the printed page; they may do so to share a poem or a story with other children; they may read orally to prove a point or to raise a question. They may engage in additional activities of the type suggested earlier in this chapter.

2. **The skills of oral reading can be improved through instruction** Successful experiences in oral reading may give needed self-confidence to the shy child. Approval by teacher and class may help him to take needed further steps toward self-assured oral reading. Teachers can help boys and girls toward overcoming problems such as monotony of rate or pitch and to read literary materials aloud with feeling and animation.

3. **The teacher's example can be a model for the oral reading of the boys and girls** Not all teachers are skillful oral readers, but all can learn to read aloud with good enunciation, appropriate volume and emphasis, and an interesting variety of pitch and rate. Teachers in all grades should cultivate this ability if they are deficient in it.

4. **Ordinarily the pupils should be encouraged to listen to the reader without following him in their own books** Reasons for this generalization were given earlier in this chapter (see p. 214).

5. **Children should have access to a wide variety of suitable materials for oral reading** Such materials should be easy and interesting and often include dialogue. They should include stories and poems, both published materials and the children's own work. Stories or articles cut out of discarded books and magazines make excel-

lent material for oral reading. On special occasions, such as holidays or the birthdays of famous persons, stories about the exploits of national heroes and the meaning of the holidays may be used. Humorous anecdotes are especially suitable for oral reading.

6. Oral reading should take place only when there is a receptive audience The reader must be eager to communicate, and the audience must be eager to listen. Until such conditions exist, it might be better to postpone the oral reading. The group might set up simply-worded standards of behavior that an audience should meet. They might also discuss what characteristics of the reader make it easy for an audience to be good listeners.

7. Adverse criticism by members of the audience should usually not be directed against one individual reader (see p. 217) but should be stated as applicable to some or all of the group unless the spirit of the classroom is such that none will be likely to be embarrassed by the suggestions from his peers However, suggestions for improvement by the teacher, given privately, are in order.

8. The cooperation of the parents should be enlisted whenever possible Although parents should not be expected to help teach the skills of oral reading, they can encourage children to read aloud to them and to other children in the home. Such experiences effectively supplement the limited opportunities the school can provide for oral reading. At meetings of the Parent Teacher Association (PTA) teachers might well suggest ways in which parents can help with reading, oral reading included. At these meetings suggestions can be given as to what standards in oral reading should be expected from boys and girls. Recommendations for a program of home reading, where the parent reads to the child and the child to the parent, can also profitably be given. Since problems in reading differ from grade to grade, home-room meetings of the PTA are especially suitable for group conferences with parents about how they can be of help. Brief bulletins to parents about their possible role in the program of oral reading can also be of value.

8B

Developing Skill in Oral Reading

In order that the child may learn to interpret the written page effectively to others, he should be given abundant opportunity to read meaningful material aloud. To provide the boys and girls with this opportunity is one of the most important ways in which the teacher can help them become skillful oral readers. However, although experience in reading in purposeful situations is basic, some direct instruction is also at times important.

Instructional Practices

Below is a classified listing of some illustrative teaching practices that may prove helpful in providing instruction in oral reading.

Improvement in Pronunciation

1. Stressing the importance of correct pronunciation through class discussion and comments by the teacher
2. Using rhyme to illustrate correct pronunciation, as in "*Just* rhymes with *must*, not with *best!*"
3. Teaching the interpretation of diacritical marks

Improvement in Enunciation

1. Stressing the importance of clear enunciation
2. Having pupils practice the enunciation of words in which the endings *ing, ed,* and *t* are often slurred
3. Giving the pupils opportunity to listen to recordings in order to note examples of excellent enunciation
4. Having pupils make tape recordings of their voices to note the quality of their enunciation

Improvement in Phrasing

1. Having pupils listen to the teacher read a sentence with good phrasing and say it back to him. (This suggestion should, as a rule, be observed as the teacher works with one child at a time.)
2. Contrasting good and poor phrasing in the reading of a sentence
3. Having pupils note proper places for pausing
4. Teaching the role of punctuation marks in determining where the pauses should come

Improvement in Skill in Interpretation

1. Explaining to the pupils the role of the reader as interpreter
2. Explaining some of the points that have bearing on effective interpre-

tation, such as those pertaining to: (a) reading a selection beforehand; (b) making certain that one understands what is to be read orally; and (c) reading with expression

3. Providing pupils with sentences for oral reading that express strong emotions—such as love, fear, sadness, surprise, anxiety
4. Demonstrating to the class the need for variety of tone, pitch, and rate in oral reading, by contrasting monotonous with interesting expression
5. Providing practice in expressing different moods through changes in voice qualities
6. Having pupils find the words in a sentence that are especially significant in the context and then read the sentence to emphasize these words
7. Encouraging pupils to prepare a sketch in which varying inflections are used when saying the same expression in order to produce different meanings. For example, the sentence, "What a day!" could be given so as to express more than one reaction to the day

Miscellaneous Suggestions

1. Having pupils look for answers through silent reading of a passage and then read the appropriate parts aloud
2. Emphasizing the importance of having a clear purpose for any oral reading
3. Helping boys and girls overcome individual mannerisms that draw attention away from the message
4. Providing opportunity for pupils to listen to speakers who use their voices effectively
5. Arranging for pupils to read in concert with others, as for example, in choral reading
6. Discussing with a class what a reader can do to make it easy for an audience to listen attentively
7. Encouraging the beginning reader to read at home to interested parents or sisters and brothers material he has read at school. Duplicating copies of a language-experience chart for each child to take home, after he is able to "read" it, is one way of making it possible for the child to demonstrate his skill.

Oral Reading by the Teacher

Frequent oral reading by the teacher is highly desirable. This practice makes it possible for pupils to become acquainted with and to appreciate literature of genuine worth that is too difficult for them to read by themselves. Moreover, the teacher, serving as model of a fluent oral reader, can thus set standards of reading to which the pupils can aspire.

Naturally, not all teachers are equally skillful in oral reading. For many it is desirable to precede the reading to the class with careful preparation through prior silent reading of the selections or even rehearsal of the oral reading activity itself. Such preparation includes also careful consideration of the material to be used. Stories read to children should be of high quality but on the level of their appreciation. They should be of the kind that lend themselves to oral reading. For younger children, especially, stories with much conversation in them are likely to have the greatest appeal. In addition to fiction, the reading material may include selections from poetry, social studies, current events, and science.

A procedure that the intermediate-grade teacher may find valuable is one in which the boys and girls alternate with him in reading a rather lengthy story, possibly an entire book. Fifteen or twenty minutes daily might be spent thus. The pupil or pupils, whose turn it is to read orally on a given day, should beforehand have practiced carefully reading orally the part of the selection assigned to them. Often it is advisable in reading of this type that the teacher serve as reader most of the time in order that the interest of the audience will not be lost.

Teachers sometimes ask, "When and how should the pictures be shown when a book is read to the class?" The answer must depend on the circumstances. Many picture-story books are poorly adapted to reading to a group. Such books are more suitable for individual reading or reading shared by two or three children. Most of the modern picture books for

The teacher can set standards for oral reading. (Suzanne Szasz)

young children have more illustrations than text; indeed, the central message is in the pictures while the text is chiefly commentary. In such cases, it is best to have pupils grouped as closely as possible around the teacher. The teacher reads the text material on a page and holds up the book to show the picture, turning it so that everyone may see. The children should have time to see and enjoy each scene as the story progresses. To help the pupils' observation, the teacher may at times decide to point out details in some of the pictures as the story goes along. If the class is too large for convenient showing of the pictures to all pupils, the story should be read to children in smaller groups. No child should be deprived of seeing the pictures. And after the reading, the book should be put on display or added to the room collection, if possible, where individual pupils can reexamine it at leisure.

Oral Reading by Children in Small Groups

In both primary and intermediate grades, the children can be divided into small groups of three or four or five who will meet in various parts of the room to read orally to one another. If this procedure can be carried out effectively in a room, much of the problem of finding time for everyone to get as much practice in oral reading as is desirable can be solved. Care must be taken that the material read is very easy and very interesting. Furthermore, in each group there should be at least one person who can serve as chairman and help the others with words they cannot recognize. So that an orderliness conducive to work prevails, it is usually necessary to work out rules of procedure for group reading, designating such points as order of reading, responsibilities of the chairman, responsibilities of the reader, and duties of the listeners. If possible, there should be a rotating chairmanship, but no child who is unable to perform the duties of a chairman should be selected for this task. The teacher can spend his time going from group to group, observing points that he may wish to bring up at a later time so as to provide for improvement in routine. This plan works only when pupils can read the material they have fairly well and when the teacher is able to maintain the desired orderliness even when he is not at all times in direct contact with each group.

Practice in reading in small groups can be especially valuable when the various groups read in order later on to give information to the rest of the class on a problem that the class is studying. At times, the boys and girls, as they are working in small groups, might be practicing reading selections, possibly stories in a basal reader that they may later wish to read to their parents at home.

Marguerite Goens, formerly a first-grade teacher in Indianapolis, worked out an excellent plan for small-group reading with the help of a third grade in her building. In this cooperating third grade several of the better read-ers went to the first-grade room twice a week for twenty minutes to take charge of oral reading groups consisting of three or four pupils each. While the assistants were working with the children, the room teacher circulated from group to group giving needed assistance. In order to make certain that the reading material was of worth and on the level of the readers and that it fulfilled the requirements of oral presentation, everything that was to be read, including material that pupils brought to school, had to be approved by the teacher before it was read orally. The group work did not take the place of the developmental reading classes, but it did serve as a vital adjunct to it.

Reading Poetry Orally

One of the neglected areas of oral reading in many schools is that of poetry reading by boys and girls. It is an art so filled with rich opportunities for developing appreciation that much more emphasis should be placed on it than is commonly the case. Unfortunately, when poetry is read orally, it is often done so poorly that the results actually interfere with its enjoyment.

As a rule, the child who does the reading should be well prepared. There are occasions when the boys and girls might read, without preparation beforehand, in order to be given specific help in reading poetry more effec-tively. But when the aim of the teacher is to have the audience get enjoy-ment from the reading, the pupils should be able to read the poetry so as to arouse appreciation in their listeners. At all such times the pupil should practice reading his poem orally before he appears in front of his audience. If possible, the teacher should help him while he is practicing. He can do so by assisting the reader in getting the meaning of the poem through questioning, through comments, and through reading orally part or all of the poem himself. All the other elements essential to effective oral reading of prose, such as skill in word recognition and handling the book with facility, are also requirements for reading poetry. The child must have a feeling of confidence and poise as he comes in front of this audience, a becoming self-assurance that results from knowledge of being well pre-pared and having a worthwhile contribution to make. Some pitfalls in reading poetry that the teacher must try to help the child avoid are "sing-song" reading, lack of discrimination between commas that represent grammatical structure and those that represent rhetorical phrasing, and overdramatic reading.

The poetry should be well selected. Even for young children there is much poetry of superior quality. An examination of the excellent antholo-gies of literature for children will suggest many poems and will give the names of poets whose work, other than that quoted in the anthology, is worth investigating. At times the teacher may choose the poems to be read, but no pupil should be forced to read a poem that he himself does not enjoy, or one that he does not want to read to the group. When a boy or girl has a voice in choosing the poem, however, the selection should not be left entirely up to him. The teacher is responsible for seeing that no poem chosen is of poor quality. Furthermore, in the choice of poems the ability of the reader to interpret and of the audience to enjoy must be considered.

The reading of poetry should be done in a suitable setting. Sometimes the teacher should help create the mood needed for enjoyment even before the pupil begins reading. The teacher can at times do this by means of questions or discussion. For example, before a child reads the poem "The Swing" by Robert Louis Stevenson, the teacher may give the audience a chance to tell whether they like to be up in a swing and how they feel when they are swinging. At other times a picture may help children get into the right mood for a poem. Before a pupil reads "The Duel" by Eugene Field orally, a picture of a gingham dog and a calico cat, with a discussion as to how the two look at each other, may get the pupils interested in finding out how the gingham dog and the calico cat in the poem got along. Printed pictures that express the mood of the poem well are sometimes available. At other times the reader may wish to draw or ask someone to draw beforehand a picture that he thinks will make the audience want to hear his poem. Interest in the poem may be aroused by posting the picture on a bulletin board even as long as a few days before the poem will be read. A question written near the picture, such as "What is happening in this picture?" might arouse curiosity.

The audience should often have more access to a poem than is afforded by one reading. Poems that are read orally may be posted on a bulletin board so that everyone can read them. Or they may be put into a booklet placed on the library table, easily accessible to all the children. Oral rereading of the poem by the person who had earlier read it to the class is often effective. When a series of poems has been read, the pupils may be asked to specify a few that they would like particularly to hear again.

Choral Reading

Choral reading, in its simplest terms, can be defined as the reading of poetry or prose by several or many voices either in unison or by parts, with at times solo work included.

Values of Choral Reading

Many values may be found in choral reading at its best. One of these is the beneficial effect it can have on personality development. The shy child may become more self-confident when he can, inconspicuously, contribute to a shared undertaking. Similarly the "show-off," even in solo parts, can learn to make his contribution complementary to the group's effort and find satisfaction in so doing.

Another value that can result from choral reading is an understanding and appreciation of poetry and poetic prose. This, obviously, can be expected only if literature of enduring quality is used for choral reading purposes.

A third value is the beneficial effect choral reading can have on the speech and the oral reading of the child. The emphasis placed in choral reading on voice quality, interpretation of meaning, enunciation, and articulation can affect oral reading favorably. Furthermore, the poise and self-assurance that it aims to develop, and under favorable conditions achieves, are essentials of effective oral reading of any type.

It is not the purpose of this chapter to give a comprehensive treatment of how to teach choral reading. The description that is given, as well as the suggestions for teaching it that are included, will serve, it is hoped, to make clear the relation between choral reading and other oral reading.

Background for Choral Reading

Before the teacher begins choral reading with his class, whether he teaches in the primary or intermediate grades, it is advisable that he ascertain whether or not the boys and girls have been introduced to a variety of worthwhile poems. If the field of their appreciation of poetry is narrow, his first step should probably be reading or—better yet—saying poems to the class. As he repeats a poem, pupils may wish to join him on whatever lines or parts of lines they remember. At other times he may want to precede the reading of a poem by giving a brief background for the poem, to set the mood for it or to provide valuable information that may add to the appreciation of the poem. He may accomplish this purpose by comments he makes or by class discussion. After reading a poem or saying it to the class, if the boys and girls are able to read it, they might read it orally with him. Help can be given with the rhythm of the poem so that it adds to the words, not detracts from them through sing-song reading. To some poems children could beat time or walk or run or skip as the poem suggests. Music that harmonizes with the theme of a poem could be played. Pictures in the room suggesting the mood of some poems, books of poetry in which the illustrations add to the significance of the words, flowers, or other objects of beauty through the sight of which the pupils may catch the spirit of poem could be used to help interest boys and girls in good poetry. Flannel boards and bulletin boards can serve as means of displaying illustrations of some favorite poems. A poetry corner in the classroom may serve as further motivation. In the upper primary and in the intermediate grades pupils might bring to school poems that they find particularly enjoyable. In one class every boy and girl selected a favorite poem, which the teacher typed and then combined into a class booklet. The table of contents gave not only the title of the poem but also the name of the person who selected it. Enthusiasm for reading the booklet ran high, partly because the boys and girls wanted to read the choices of their classmates.

To succeed in laying a suitable background for the appreciation of poetry, the spirit of the classroom must be one in which thoughts of poetry are encouraged. It must be one in which creativeness and imaginativeness have a place. It must be one in which teachers and pupils work together cooperatively; one in which, to paraphrase Samuel Crothers in his book, *The Gentle Reader,* the birthright of imagination is not sacrificed for a mess of knowledge.

Grouping for Choral Reading

While a background for choral reading is being laid, it is usually advisable with beginners in the art to have pupils attain some skill in saying poems in concert before any attempt is made at grouping for choral reading. It is wise at that time for the teacher to take note of the characteristics of the voices of the various individuals as he hears them talk or read—usually, if not always, without the boys and girls being conscious of the fact that he is testing for grouping. Since the simplest grouping is a two-part division of voices, into the high and low, the teacher may want to note mentally which voices belong in each group. Sometimes he may also employ a more direct method as he tests voices by having pupils repeat a sentence or sing a tune or count to ten. He may wish to enlist the help of the boys and girls in doing the grouping. After the pupils have had some practice in two-group speaking, the teacher may wish to organize a third group, including in it the pupils whose voices are on the borderline between high and low.

Care must be taken when grouping that no misunderstandings result. Some girls may be inclined, unless caution is exercised, to think that it borders on the disgraceful to have a low voice and be in a group with many of the boys. Similarly, without care on the teacher's part, some boys might consider it "girlish" to be in a group with many of the girls. The teacher should point out that in the elementary school in two-part grouping there are often some boys and some girls in each of the groups. He could also point out that the blend of the voices of both boys and girls in each division can contribute a great deal to choral reading. It should be made clear that the grouping done before much time has been spent on choral reading is subject to change later. Reasons for change may be that the child's voice has changed or that the testing situation produced inaccurate results. The need for more pupils in one of the groups with different poems may also result in reassignment of groups. It is important that a pupil be happy in the group to which he has been assigned. Better that the reading of a poem be poor than that one child be made unhappy by his role in an activity that should bring joy to all participants!

Casting

After grouping comes casting. By casting a poem is meant dividing the lines of a poem or prose selection into parts and assigning these parts to individuals or groups of individuals.

It should probably be pointed out that a poem can be read in unison for choral reading, with high and low or with high, intermediate, and low voices saying the same lines. Such reading is more difficult than that in which the several groups speak different lines. Reading in unison as choral reading is not to be confused with concert reading in which there is no division into types of voices. Because of the difficulty of effective reading in unison, that type of choral reading is usually not attempted in the elementary school, although concert reading, with all boys and girls saying the same lines without grouping of voices, is common practice.

There are several types of casting commonly used in elementary schools. The reading may be done in a solo-chorus combination, as, for example, when the teacher or other leader reads alone all parts excepting the chorus parts, in which the entire class participates. The dialogue type of choral reading can be done by two individuals who take the parts or by two choruses saying alternate lines or groups of lines or by an individual and a chorus. The line-a-child casting differs from the dialogues by two persons in that lines are assigned to three or more individuals. Similarly, line-a-choir reading differs from dialogues participated in by two choruses in that three or more groups say the lines. The use of various combinations of these types in reading a single long selection makes possible considerable variation of pattern of reading. Which type should be used will be determined in part by the ability of the group, the selection itself, and the objectives to be accomplished. Frequently the children, under the guidance of the teacher, should have a voice in deciding on the type of casting to be done and the assignment of parts.

Selection of Material

The final responsibility for selecting material for choral reading lies with the teacher. While it is desirable that boys and girls, especially those somewhat experienced in choral reading, be encouraged to help in the choice, it should be clear to them that their recommendations will not necessarily be accepted. The teacher will not want to subject the class to poorly chosen verse or prose for choral reading because one or more pupils suggested it.

There are certain standards that should be observed in the selection of material. If boys and girls participate in the selection, standards should be applied by them, too. However, in a pupils' checklist the wording might be different from that in a list such as the following, which is prepared for the teacher. These points should be noted about a poem to be used for choral reading:

1. It should have literary value.
2. It should be on the pupils' level of understanding.
3. It should be one the boys and girls will enjoy.
4. It should be one that the teacher will enjoy teaching.
5. It should have a rhythm.
6. It should fill a need of the class.
7. It should be adaptable to choral reading of the type that the boys and girls are capable of doing.

Books containing poems chosen for their suitability for choral reading, with suggestions for casting, can be of value to both teachers and pupils. Some such books are *Choral Speaking Arrangements for the Lower Grades* by Louis Abney and Grace Bowe (The Expression Company), *Choral Reading for Fun and Recreation* by Helen A. Brown and Harry J. Heltman (Westminister Press), and *Let's Say Poetry Together* by Carrie Rasmussen (Burgess Publishing Company). Poems listed in such books, however, are not necessarily the most suitable for any given group of boys and girls. Wide acquaintance with poetry, access to the best anthologies of poetry for children, as well as books of poetry by single authors, will keep the teacher and, to some extent, the pupils from being limited by poems suggested in books designed specifically for choral reading. One such book is *Time for Poetry* by May Arbuthnot and Shelton L. Root, with Scott Foresman as publisher.

Additional Suggestions

Following are additional points that the teacher should bear in mind as he helps boys and girls in choral reading:

Choral reading should be pleasurable. If it is not, the major reasons for doing it will probably not be accomplished.

Boys and girls should be helped, if help is indicated, to comprehend the meaning of the material they use for choral reading. This does not mean that the child must know every word in a selection or that he must have the depth of insight into a poem that an adult might have. However, problems in vocabulary should not be allowed to interfere with the interpretation of meaning. Nor should comprehension of the poem be limited by lack of sufficient insight to make it meaningful to the child. Fortunately, there is no reason why the teacher cannot help boys and girls with problems of word meaning and of comprehension of poems that present difficulty in these two respects. He can frankly approach the pupils with the thought that attention to some of the words will enhance their understanding and hopefully their enjoyment of a poem. Or such a comment might follow a brief period of word study. Similarly, through questions and comments, the teacher can help the members of the class with the meaning of a poem.

Boys and girls should be aware of the importance of good posture in choral reading and they should be stimulated to want to assume such a posture. Practice in desirable posture might be valuable. Discussion of the need of good breath control and of the relation between breath control and posture might be helpful.

The teacher might well emphasize with the boys and girls the importance of good speech. He can show them, through illustration and demonstration, the difference between slovenly and clear enunciation. In fact, a group of boys and girls could put on an informal dramatization depicting both faulty and good enunciation.

A good leader is essential to effective choral reading. The leader can show the speakers or readers when the different parts should come in, when the voices of a group should be softer or louder, happier or sadder, faster or slower. During practice periods at times a pupil might serve as leader so that he can deal inconspicuously and competently with any problem that may arise.

Costuming is to be discouraged in choral reading. The wearing of costumes might detract from the beauty of the interpretation as presented by children's voices. Some teachers like to have their pupils wear uniform apparel when engaging in choral reading before an audience, possibly having the boys wear light shirts and dark trousers and the girls white blouses and dark skirts. But what could be as effective as boys and girls dressed in their better school clothes as they interpret in their unsophisticated way a worthwhile message from a poem that is of lasting value to them!

Recordings can be made of choral readings. Sometimes recordings can be made for practice purposes, to provide the participants with opportunity to note their strengths and weaknesses. At times, too, in a program of choral readings part of the program might be presented through tapes. As a rule, tapes should be used for only a relatively small part of the program, for one of the marked values of choral reading is that it provides the boys and girls with an opportunity to appear before an audience and thus to achieve, at least in part, some of the values listed earlier in this chapter.

Dramatization and Oral Reading

Dramatization can serve various important purposes in the elementary school, one of which is improvement in oral reading. It is true that oral reading is not a part of many types of dramatizations by elementary-school children. Frequently, plays planned by boys and girls are given somewhat impromptu, without any lines recorded and without, therefore, any reading to be done. However, under some circumstances oral reading has a legitimate part in dramatization. Some situations in which oral reading is used are as follows:

1. Sometimes when boys and girls make up their own plays the lines are recorded, the parts assigned to children, the lines practiced as the children read their parts orally, and finally the play is read to an audience.
2. Some reading series contain dramatic selections not designed for memorization, but planned for oral reading.
3. Some printed plays, later to be memorized by the pupils, are read by them orally in early practice periods.
4. Narrators of plays can read their parts to the audience.
5. Frequently the lines for a puppet play are read orally. Sometimes they are read by characters behind the scene. At other times they may be read by a person, in view of the audience, who plays a role similar to that of the narrator.

Puppetry and Oral Reading

Puppetry affords many excellent opportunities for oral reading. It is discussed here briefly.

Puppetry can serve as an adjunct to the reading program. (Piney Woods School, Piney Woods, Mississippi)

Values of Puppetry

Puppetry can serve many valuable objectives, among them the following:

1. It can be used as a means of motivation for school work in various areas. For example, a puppet show based on some phase of colonial life, such as the colonial school, can play a significant role in interesting the boys and girls in that period of history.
2. It can be a means of giving information. For example, a well-planned and well-executed puppet show featuring some important phases of Benjamin Franklin's life may give the members of the audience and the participants in the puppet play valuable information about Franklin.
3. It can be used when giving oral reports. For example, in a report on *Miss Hickory* by Caroly Sherwin Bailey, the child giving the report may decide to have puppets tell the last part of the story, where Squirrel finally gets the hickory nut head that he had so long coveted.
4. It serve as a means of self-expression.
5. It can provide boys and girls with the experience of making puppets, designing and making the stage, sewing or painting the backdrop, and making the furniture.
6. It can develop into a happy leisure-time activity for the child who will make of puppetry a hobby.
7. It can provide opportunity for oral reading in a functional and interesting setting.

Puppets and Puppet Stages

A few suggestions are here given as to kinds of puppets and puppet stages that can be used. For more suggestions on the topic, the teacher is referred to books on literature for children and on the teaching of the language arts, which frequently include a section on puppetry. Additional references include: *The Puppet Theater Handbook* by Marjorie Batchelder (Harper & Row), *Puppets and Plays—A Creative Approach* by Marjorie Batchelder and Virginia Comer (Harper & Row), *Puppets into Actors* by Olive Blackham (Macmillan), *Shadow Puppets* by Olive Blackham (Harper & Row), *A Handbook of First Puppets* by Alexander Ficklen (Lippincott), *Puppet and Pantomime Plays* by Vernon Howard (Sterling), *First Book of Puppets* by Moritz Jagendorf (Franklin Watts), *The Puppet Book* by Shari Lewis (Citadel Press), *Easy Puppets* by Gertrude Pels (Crowell), *The Puppet Do-It-Yourself Book* by Lois Pratt (Exposition Press), *Puppetry, Marionettes, and Shadow Plays* by Loren Taylor (Burgess Publishing Company).

Puppets should be distinguished from marionettes. It is customary to apply the term marionette to those lifelike creatures that are controlled by strings; the term *puppet* is often reserved for figures that are not manipulated by strings. Because of the difficulties in handing many types of

B. Noting points to watch during oral reading
1. The teacher (referring to the chart in *III-C*) states that the boys and girls on the committee have tried to watch those points as they practiced reading the stories beforehand.
2. Two pupils put on a two-minute skit demonstrating good and poor posture while reading orally, and the class briefly names points of excellence and of criticism in the two types of posture demonstrated.
3. The pupils discuss what "remembering the audience" means, stressing the fact that while "looking at the audience" is important, it should not be done mechanically.
4. The pupils indicate what a good listener does. (The teacher makes reference to the aim listed as *II-A.)*
C. Statement of the procedure to be followed
The teacher explains that after a few introductory remarks the members on the committee will read the stories listed on the chalk board, to which reference is made in III-A.
D. Reading of the stories by the children preceded by an introductory remark or a question on each story by the teacher or by the reader
E. Brief discussion of the content of the stories
F. Pupils' evaluation of the reading
1. Pupils name the points on the chart *(see III-C)* that they think were watched particularly well.
2. Pupils name the points on the chart *(see III-C)* in which they need improvement.
G. Forward look
1. Group discusses means by which they can improve upon the points referred to under F-2 above.
2. The teacher states that later he will individually discuss with each committee member the quality of his reading as they use the individual cards *(see III-D)* in making the analyses.

Explanation of the Plan

Each of the following points is discussed here to explain further to the reader of this book the plan outlined above and to indicate a few of the many possible variations in procedure that can be made: *(a)* preparation before class; *(b)* deciding upon the aims for the period; *(c)* reference to the points observed in the oral reading; *(d)* announcement of the plan of procedure in reading; *(e)* reading of the selections; *(f)* discussion of the story; and *(g)* evaluation of the reading.

1. Preparation before class. Preparation should include choosing the readers, selecting the materials to be read, practicing reading the selections, providing for the materials needed during classtime, and making seating arrangements.

a. Choosing the readers. It is recommended that, as a rule, no pupil be chosen for a second turn at participating in an oral reading program before everyone in the room has had the opportunity to take part in one. Furthermore, it is usually advisable that pupils of varying ability appear on each program. While it would be relatively easy to keep a program interesting if all participants were good readers, it might be difficult to hold the interest of the audience if only the poorer readers performed.

The question may be asked: "Should the poor reader really be expected or allowed to take part in an audience reading program?" The answer is: "Yes, as a rule," If a pupil is not permitted to read because he has decided difficulties in reading, he may feel slighted, even though often he may act as if he were pleased that he did not have to read. Moreover, it is the poorer reader, more than the excellent one, who needs the practice. The teacher can help save the former from feelings of inadequacy in the oral reading situation by giving him shorter selections than most others in the group so that he can prepare thoroughly what he reads. It is probably good policy to give some of the better readers relatively brief selections, too, so that the one who is less able will not think of the brevity of his reading as a stigma attached to his performance. Also, the teacher can see to it that the child who cannot read as well orally as the others has very easy material to read. Help from the teacher in preparation for the reading can often preserve the ego of the reader, with a minimum of undesirable emotional reactions. At the same time, in this way the pupil can get real help in becoming a better reader. Some teachers, rather than depriving a poor reader of the opportunity to read orally, wisely help him all but memorize his selection before class so that he may perform well before his peers.

b. Selection of material. The material to be read orally should be selected with particular care. Sometimes the teacher will make the selection by himself, always remembering that the material should be at the level of the pupils' interest. At other times pupils should have the opportunity to choose from a variety of selections presented by the teacher. When children make their own suggestions, the teacher, perhaps in consultation with a pupil committee, will advise as to the suitability of the selections.

The material selected should be easy for the reader to read orally and easy for the audience to comprehend. Often it is advisable to select material for audience reading that is a grade or so lower in difficulty level than the reader's silent reading level. Effective oral reading requires ability in silent reading plus the complex skill of interpreting to others what is read.

A variety of suitable materials is available. Stories, both humorous and serious, fanciful and realistic, are one source. Anecdotes make very good reading. Work-type materials of the kind that requires more than one reading or very careful attention have no legitimate place in an oral reading program. Sometimes each child on the program may have a separate, very short, selection to read. At other times a longer one may be apportioned to two or more, or even all, of the persons who will be reading. Appropriate selections are easily available in most situations because only one copy of a book or magazine article is needed. This is true even if more than one pupil is preparing material out of the same book or magazine, since they can practice at different times and since no one should be reading silently while someone is reading orally. Many teachers like to cut materials out of books that are ready to be discarded or magazines that are not being saved. Mounted material can often be handled better while it is being read and can be kept in better condition when filed for later use.

c. Preparation of the reader. Each reader should be thoroughly prepared for the reading. As a rule, silent reading of the selection beforehand is not enough. The pupil should read it orally one or more times, either to the teacher or to someone else who can help him not only with word recognition but also with problems of interpretation. If several children are to read parts of the same selection, at times they can help each other during the practice period. But the teacher is always responsible for seeing to it that no one comes before the class inadequately prepared. Furthermore, each pupil should know exactly where his selection is to begin and end if he is to read only part of an article or story.

d. Provision for materials and equipment. Careful provision should be made, often with the help of the boys and girls, so that supplies and equipment needed during the class period will be available. Included may be material placed on the chalkboard, as in the case of the plan reproduced in this chapter. If a plan like this one were used, the program for the period could be listed on the board, with the title of each story to be read and the names of the persons who were to read each in the order of appearance. Sometimes, boys and girls like to make duplicates of the program on paper to distribute to the audience at the beginning of the class period.

A chart similar to the one referred to in the teaching plan (see p. 236), which gives the points the pupils will watch in their oral reading, can be displayed. So that the pupils may wholeheartedly accept the skills for the improvement of which they work, it is usually advisable to have the list worked out cooperatively by the pupils and teacher. The wording should be meaningful to the pupils. If the word *enunciation* is used, as it is on the list given in the plan, the teacher should make certain that the boys and girls know what it means. The list can be drawn up early in the school year and can then be reproduced on chart paper. For easy reference, it could be either kept posted in the room at all times or else exhibited whenever pupils give reading programs.

Each pupil could be provided with a card similar to the one illustrated on page 236. These cards could be kept by the teacher or the child. The record should not be kept for competitive purposes, and only the teacher and the owner of a card should have access to it. A check may be placed on the chart after each item on which the child does well and a minus sign may be placed after each item on which he needs to improve. Although provision is made for checking seven different times on the card reproduced here, the number could vary. A place is left for the date of each reading. Space for comments can be on the back of the card.

Sometimes other materials may be needed. A map often adds to the value of the reading by enabling the pupil to locate places about which he reads. At times pictures help the audience to visualize what will be read. Realia, too, may profitably be exhibited, if they help accomplish the purpose set for the oral reading. For example, pupils in the fifth or sixth grades can be aided in getting into the mood of the story about Nancy Hanks, the mother of Abraham Lincoln, if a replica of a log cabin is shown as representative of the type in which Lincoln lived when he was a boy.

    e. Room arrangements. Arrangements should be made before class for proper seating of the audience and of the participants in the program. Sometimes all that is needed is to reserve seats near the front of the room for those who will read. At times, the seats can be rearranged so as to make it as easy as possible to have a desirable audience situation.

2. Deciding on the aims for the period. The aims can be suggested by the pupils who prepare the oral reading or by the teacher. No matter who states them, it is important that they are objectives that the class can wholeheartedly accept. In the teaching plan given on page 236 two aims were listed. The second aim, the aim of the readers, "To try to read so that our listeners will enjoy hearing us read," should be determined before class as the boys and girls practice reading. The first is a suggested objective for the members of the audience.

The audience is entitled to have a reason for listening. If the children have no purpose, they will often pay inadequate attention to what is read. Therefore, a suggestion as to what the purpose might be could be given either by the pupils who will read or by the teacher. At times the purpose may deal with entertainment and at other times it may be to get information. It is not necessary that in every oral reading lesson the audience specifically decide that they will try to be good listeners. After a while it should be taken for granted that this will always be an objective. Nevertheless, occasionally additional elements may well be stressed for observation as far as the conduct of the audience is concerned. It is often advisable that each person who reads have in mind a particular point that he wishes to observe especially well.

As a rule the number of expressed aims should be greatly limited, probably to three at the most. It is to be assumed that the pupil will always have certain objectives in mind in reading of this type, without mention being made of them. A large number of stated aims is likely to result in diffusion of effort.

3. Reference to the points to be observed. It is not necessary that the points to watch in oral reading should be discussed in each audience reading situation before the boys and girls begin reading. Sometimes they may be taken up after the reading only, and at other times no class mention needs to be made of them. Several factors should enter into the decision as to whether they should be discussed, either before or after the reading. One is the time available for discussion during the lesson. Another is whether the mood to be portrayed through the reading can better be created if no mention is made of the skills to be developed.

4. Announcement of the plan of procedure in reading. Although in the plan given the teacher made the announcement, often the teacher can remain entirely in the background and a pupil, appointed as chairman of the meeting, can make the announcement. At other times, when the pupils are handed copies of the program, no mention of the order needs to be made.

5. Reading of the selections. It is essential that the atmosphere of a program should be maintained throughout the time set aside for reading.

The teacher should not correct or prompt the reader unless it seems necessary for the continuance of the program. Interruptions should probably be made no more often than in an assembly program. Possibly the only occasion when the teacher is justified in intervening arises when the child stops reading because he does not know the next word even though previously he had been instructed to proceed as best he could.

6. Discussion of the story. Sometimes the discussion of the story may be omitted—certainly in cases in which the mood created by the story might be destroyed by talking about it. Usually, if there is discussion, it should be brief. It might be led by the teacher or by a pupil. Occasionally, if the aim is to see how well the boys and girls have comprehended the information given, they might check themselves on their ability to answer written questions on what was presented.

7. Evaluation of the reading. If checking on cards, such as the one on page 236, does not inhibit reading, then the teacher can do so while the boy or girl reads. It should be kept in mind that not everyone is made self-conscious by such a practice, although some might be. There is also a danger in this practice that over-emphasis could be placed on

techniques rather than on interpretation. Playbacks of tape recordings of the student's reading can be used for evaluation. The pupil and the teacher should listen to the tape together, and at that time the written evaluation can be recorded on the pupil's card.

Hard and fast rules about evaluation should not interfere with occasional informal comments on the success with which a pupil has mastered specific skills of oral reading. However, usually it is most effective to discuss group progress in general terms at the end of the reading period. Individual pupils may be encouraged to keep their own scores and compare them with the teacher's judgments in private conference. No child should feel that he is going on trial when he rises to read.

For Further Study

Burns, Paul C., and Betty L. Broman, *The Language Arts in Childhood Education*, 3d ed. (Skokie, Ill,: Rand McNally, 1975), Ch. 5, "Oral Composition."

Bush, Clifford L., and Mildred H. Huebner, *Strategies for Reading in the Elementary School*, 2d ed. (New York: Macmillan, 1979), Ch. 7, "Oral Reading."

Harris, Albert J., and Edward R. Sipay, *How to Increase Reading Ability*, 6th ed. (New York; McKay, 1975), Ch. 9, "Assessing Reading Performance, II."

Harris, Larry., and Carl B. Smith, *Reading Instruction: Diagnostic Teaching in the Classroom*, 3d ed. (New York: Holt, Rinehart and Winston, 1980), Ch. 8, "Reading Comprehension: Experiential and Language Factors," and Ch. 9, "Reading for Appreciation and Enjoyment."

Karlin, Robert, *Teaching Elementary Reading: Principles and Strategies*, 3d ed. (New York: Harcourt Brace Jovanovich, 1980), Ch. 9, "Reading for Appreciation and Enjoyment."

Kean, John M., and Carl Personke, *The Language Arts, Teaching and Learning in the Elementary School* (New York: St. Martin's, 1976), Ch. 5., "Oral Language in the Elementary School."

Smith, E. Brooks; Kenneth S. Goodman; and Robert Meredith, *Language and Thinking in School*, 2d ed. (New York: Holt, Rinehart and Winston, 1976), Ch. 13, "Strategies for Teaching the Art of Communication."

Smith, James A., *Adventures in Communication: Language Arts Method* (Boston: Allyn and Bacon, 1972), Ch. 5, "Adventures in Listening," and Ch. 6, "Adventures in Oral Expression"

Tinker, Miles A., and Constance M. McCullough, *Teaching Elementary Reading*, 4th ed. (Englewood Cliffs, N.J.: Prentice-Hall, 1975), pp. 236–248, "Reading Aloud."

Zintz, Miles V., *The Reading Process: The Teacher and the Learner*, 3d ed. (Dubuque, Iowa: Wm. C. Brown, 1980), Ch. 13, "Oral Reading."

Questions and Comments for Thought and Discussion

1. If you have had any experiences with choral reading, either as participant or as a member of an audience, what values of choral reading have you recognized? What difficulties, if any, in the use of choral reading have you detected?

2. As a special project one or more members of your class may wish to compile a list of poems well adapted to choral reading in the elementary school and to indicate one desirable casting for a few of the poems.

3. If you have the opportunity, you may wish to observe a reading lesson in an elementary school. If you do, note ways in which oral reading is used effectively. Also take cognizance of any undesirable practices related to oral reading that you may be observing.

4. One objective of teaching listening should be to develop the ability to listen appreciatively. Many opportunities arise during the school day to use this important listening ability. Teachers should be aware of ways to cultivate and improve it. What are some effective ways?

5. Members of your class may wish to construct a variety of kinds of puppets, or one or more members of your group may decide to work on a display of various types of stages for puppetry.

Locating Information and Using It

The development of the ability to locate information in printed sources has become an increasingly important concern of the school. In earlier days in the United States, pupils used relatively few books and were usually directed to the exact locations of the material to be studied. In this day of abundant newspapers, magazines, encyclopedias, dictionaries, almanacs, and other kinds of printed matter, skill in finding information is becoming ever more imperative. The increasing complexity of modern life has helped bring this new need into focus.

Unfortunately many children as well as adults, including college graduates, have only limited skill in locating information. For this reason many people simply make no effort to look for some of the information they need or desire. Often people who have access to dictionaries and who want to know the meaning of a word do not look it up because they have difficulty in making efficient use of this indispensable reference aid.

Happily, teachers are beginning to meet the challenge presented by changing needs, by making a persistent effort to help boys and girls receive the needed information and practice in locating materials economically and efficiently and in making effective use of them. Almost all professional books on the teaching of reading stress the importance of these skills and make suggestions for their development. Basal textbook series for boys and girls provide for growth in these skills, and the teachers' guidebooks which accompany the children's books abound in excellent recommendations as to how these skills can be developed. Many of the workbooks provide helpful exercises.

Basic Locational Skills

Basic to effective use of reading materials from various sources are skill in:

1. Finding words arranged in alphabetical order
2. Finding a specified page quickly
3. Finding an entry word
4. Deciding on key words
5. Knowing the types of content found in reference books
6. Interpreting information
7. Making use of information

Skill in Finding Words Arranged in Alphabetical Order

Skill in finding words arranged in alphabetical order is needed in many types of situations, as in locating information in the index of a book, in the card catalogue, in the dictionary, in an encyclopedia, and in other reference books. Unfortunately, many elementary-school teachers have often wrongly assumed that the pupil has the following skills or learnings essential to locating words arranged in alphabetical order.

1. Knowledge of the sequence of letters in the alphabet
2. Ability to tell which letter precedes and which follows another without repeating part of the alphabet either orally or silently
3. Instant knowledge of the part of the alphabet—the first, middle, or last—in which a letter occurs
4. Knowledge of the fact that in indexes, dictionaries, and card catalogues the words are arranged in alphabetical order
5. Understanding of and skill in arranging

words in alphabetical order when the first letter of each word is different

6. Understanding of and skill in arranging words in alphabetical order when the first letters of the words are alike but the second different

7. Understanding of and skill in arranging words in alphabetical order when the first two or more letters of the words are alike but subsequent letters are different

8. Knowledge of how to arrange words in alphabetical order when situations such as these and others exist:
   a. Words beginning with the syllable *Mc* or *Mac*
   b. Titles beginning with *the, a,* or *an*
   c. Words such as *grand* and *grand-mother* in which all the letters of one word are given in the same sequence in the first part of a second word
   d. Names of persons when both the first and the last names are given

Skill in Finding a Specified Page

Another skill basic to many types of reading is finding a given page in a book or magazine quickly. Many pupils need to be taught that there are quicker ways of finding a page than to start at the beginning of the book and leaf through it until they come to the page they want. They also need practice in opening a book in the vicinity of the page they want. Development of this skill should be encouraged, as a rule, even in the first grade. Much of the practice in finding a specified page can be provided in the ongoing instructional program without the use of practice exercises.

Skill in Finding an Entry Word

Skill in finding an entry word is needed in using a dictionary, an encyclopedia, and other reference books. In order to find an entry word quickly, pupils need to know the following facts about guide words:

1. In dictionaries, guide words are usually listed at the top of each page of the main part of the books.

2. Guide words indicate the first and the last entry words listed on a given page.

3. By glancing at the guide words in a dictionary the reader can tell whether the word for which he is looking is on that page.

4. Similar provisions are made in some of the other reference books, so that the reader can quickly ascertain whether the topic for which he is looking belongs between the first and last topics found on a given page.

It is not enough, however, for children to know what guide words are and where they are found. They should also develop skill in using guide words to locate entries quickly.

Skill in Deciding on Key Words

Another locational skill needed is that of knowing under what word to look for the desired information. This skill is often referred to as the ability to decide on key words. Lack of it causes much waste of time and frequently is the reason why reference books are not used more. Skill can be developed step by step through a gradation of difficulties, beginning with work on finding a topic in an index or reference book when the topic is worded in the same manner as the entry in the book. Later, pupils may be given practice in deciding which one of a variety of words is the most likely entry under which the needed information would be found. Use of subtopics in indexes should also be taught as an aid in finding key words.

Knowledge of Content of Reference Books

Many pupils need guidance in learning what type of information is contained in different kinds of books and magazines. For example, a pupil will need to learn what types of information to look for in social studies books, science books, and health books. He will also need to learn what types of information he can expect to find in various encyclopedias for children, in the *World Almanac,* in an atlas, in a dictionary, and in other reference books. As he develops skill in the use of these books, he will continue to discover new types of information. He cannot learn about them all at once. In the case of the dictionary, for example, he will usually first learn that it yields the meaning of words. Only later will he discover that he can find the pronunciation of words and, still later, that it contains information about syllabication and other matters.

Interpreting Information

After the reader has located information, he must be able to interpret it. Sometimes interpretation is an easy process, requiring neither special effort nor skill. At other times particular alertness is needed.

Pupils need to develop skill in learning to interpret the abbreviations given in reference material. Knowledge of many abbreviations is essential to effective reading of reference books. Pupils should know where to look for a key to the abbreviations and how to apply the information given in the key.

Common to several types of reference materials are the references to additional material designated by *see* or *see also.* The boys and girls need to know before they leave the elementary school what is meant by these directions, as well as how to use them. It is also important for them to know when they should follow the *see* or *see also* direction. Speed in locating the cross reference and in deciding whether it contributes to the topic also needs to be developed.

Another problem in the use of reference materials is selecting the points that have bearing on the purpose that the reader has in mind. How to interpret charts, tables, maps, graphs, and diagrams given in reference books is only part of the task. The pupil needs to know how to find the desired information given in words, groups of words, sentences, and paragraphs speedily and correctly.

Making Use of Information

After the reader has found and interpreted the information he wants, he may use it for a variety of purposes. He may compare what he has learned in one reference with what he has read in another or with what he already knows. He may take notes on it, write a summary, or make an outline in order either better to remember the data himself or to assist him as he tries to impart the information to others through informal conversation, reports, panel discussions, or illustrations. Sometimes he may compile a bibliography for his own or others' use. How to take notes, make summaries and outlines, and perform some of the other activities for purposes of retention and comprehension are discussed in other parts of this book.

Ability To Find Information in Various Types of Books

The types of books in which boys and girls should learn to find information with efficiency can be classified under three categories: (a) nonreference books, (b) the dictionary, (c) reference books other than the dictionary.

Ability To Find Information in Nonreference Books

Elementary-school children should learn to use the following parts of books or features in books effectively in order to locate information quickly in their textbooks and in general books:

1. The preface
2. The introduction
3. The table of contents
4. Lists of maps and illustrations
5. Chapter headings, center headings, and sideheadings
6. The glossary
7. The index

Pupils should know where each of these parts is found, what its function is, and how to use it. Furthermore, the teacher should try to develop in them the desire to make effective use of the various parts.

Preface

Boys and girls should learn the following facts about the preface:

1. It is found in the front part of the book.
2. It is written either by the author or the editor of the book.
3. It tells the author's purpose in writing the book and often indicates any special features of the book.
4. It is useful in indicating whether a given topic or question is likely to be treated in the book.

Introduction

If the introduction is studied, the pupils should know that the terms *introduction* and *preface* are sometimes used interchangeably. They should learn that some books contain both a preface and an introduction. As they examine these two parts of a book, they should know that, although a study of the introduction may help them to decide whether information that they want is given in the book, its primary purpose is not to serve as a locational aid.

Table of Contents

Boys and girls can begin using the table of contents almost as soon as they start reading books. When a simple table of contents is given, as in many primers, the pupil can find the "new story" in the table of contents with the help of the teacher. Reference can also be made to the page. If the pupil cannot read the page number by himself, the teacher may say, pointing to the page, "This number *10* tells us that our story begins on page *10*." Then he can help the pupils find the page.

Somewhere in the elementary school the boys and girls should learn that the table of contents, in many instances, not only indicates the contents but also the plan or organization of the book, providing it is divided into various units or sections with subheadings. Through examination and explanation they should acquire familiarity with some of the possible formats in which tables of contents can be written.

List of Maps and Illustrations

Pupils should learn the following about maps and illustrations:

1. A list of maps and illustrations, when included in a book, may be found either in the front or back part of the book.
2. Textbooks in social studies, science, and health are much more likely to provide a list of maps or illustrations than general books.

3. The list of maps and illustrations gives the captions used with the maps and illustrations and also the page on which they are found.

Chapter Headings, Center Headings, and Sideheadings

Pupils should be taught the value of various kinds of headings in locating material and should be given practice in their use. As soon as side and center headings are provided in the textbooks that pupils read or in the reference books they use, some help should be given in making effective use of these aids as a means of locating information.

Glossary

If some of the books the pupils are using contain a glossary, they should note that it is found in the back part of the book and that special terms and words used in the book are explained in this section. They should notice that the words are listed alphabetically.

Index

The following are some of the points the pupils should learn about the index of a book:

1. Where the index is located
2. How the topics are arranged in an index
3. How subtopics are listed

The following skills should be developed:

1. Deciding upon what entry word to use when trying to gain information on a given point
2. Finding an entry with dispatch
3. Making effective use of subtopics in an index
4. Finding the part on a page indicated in the index that gives the information desired

Ability To Use the Dictionary

One of the outstanding developments in materials of instruction for the elementary school has been the dictionary for children. Pupils in the early part of this century often had access only to a large, unabridged dictionary and/or to one or more smaller ones that were also published chiefly for adults. For many elementary-school boys and girls these dictionaries were unsuitable.

Dictionaries for the Elementary School

In addition to the picture dictionaries (see Chapter 6B, "Developing Skill in Word Recognition," p. 148), the following dictionaries are used in the elementary school:

Beginning Dictionary (Scott, Foresman and Company)

Giant Golden Illustrated Dictionary, Stuart A. Courtis and Garnette Watters, eds. (Golden Press, Inc.), six volumes.

The Holt Basic Dictionary of American English (Holt, Rinehart and Winston).

The Holt Intermediate Dictionary of American English (Holt, Rinehart and Winston).

Macmillan Beginning Dictionary (Macmillan)

Macmillan Dictionary for Children (Macmillan)

Thorndike-Barnhart Beginning Dictionary, Edward L. Thorndike and Clarence L. Barnhart, eds. (Scott, Foresman).

Thorndike-Barnhart Junior Dictionary, Edward L. Thorndike and Clarence L. Barnhart, eds. (Scott, Foresman).

Webster's A Dictionary for Boys and Girls (American Book).

Webster's New Elementary Dictionary (American Book).

The Winston Dictionary for Schools, Thomas K. Brown and Wiliam D.

Lewis, eds. (Holt, Rinehart and Winston).

The World Book Dictionary, Clarence Barnhart, ed. (World Book—Childcraft International, Inc.), two volumes.

Dictionary Skills

The skills to be learned in using a dictionary in the elementary school can be summarized thus:

1. Ability to locate a word quickly
2. Ability to learn the pronunciation of a word
3. Ability to find the spelling of a word and related abilities, including: (a) spelling; (b) syllabication; (c) hyphenation; (d) abbreviations; and (e) capitalization
4. Ability to learn the meaning of a word
5. Ability to use the parts of the dictionary preceding and following the main part of the dictionary, both in the pupil's dictionary and in an unabridged dictionary

The teacher must bear in mind that many of the skills listed as dictionary skills are important in other reading activities as well. For example, to be able to locate a word quickly may be of value when skimming, when using an encyclopedia, when finding a telephone number. Furthermore, the pupil should not get the impression that the dictionary is the only source through which some of the skills mentioned can be acquired. Item 4 of the preceding listing "ability to learn the meaning of a word" can best be and should be acquired in a variety of ways, through listening to conversation and explanations, through watching television, through reading, for example. Help frequently needs to be given in effectively using these other sources of vocabulary development.

Locating a word in the dictionary In order to locate a word in the dictionary quickly, the pupil needs to know more than how to find a word in a list arranged alphabetically and how to make use of guide words. The difficulty in which one fifth-grade girl found herself illustrates the need for more information. This girl's teacher had told her pupils that the unabridged dictionary in their room contained every word in the English language. One day, while the teacher was busy with another group, this girl ran across the word *busied* in her reading and was puzzled as to the meaning of the word. Had the word been *busy* she would have recognized it in print, and had she heard the word *busied* pronounced, she might have had no difficulty with its meaning. However, when she saw the word *busied* in context, she thought it would be pronounced *bu si' ed,* giving the s an s instead of a z sound and the i a long sound. She therefore went to the big dictionary and looked for the entry *busied.* When she could not find *busied* listed as an entry word, she had no idea that she might find it under another form. Consequently, she could hardly wait until she could tell her teacher about her amazing "discovery" that the dictionary did not contain every word in the language. When the teacher asked her which word she did not find, she told her *busied,* pronouncing the word as *bu si' ed.*

Many boys and girls need direct teaching in order to learn how inflected forms can be located in the dictionary. Emphasis on structural analysis can serve as an aid in recognizing inflected forms.

Learning the pronunciation The elementary-school child can learn to find the pronunciation of a word by means of respellings and diacritical marks, as interpreted in the key to pronunciation at the bottom of the pages in the dictionary. It is suggested that he be helped to become so familiar with the key that he will find it unnecessary to refer to it often. The child should also learn that there is lack of uniformity among compilers of various dictionaries in the system of diacritical marks that they use.

The significance of the syllabication of words and of the marking of the accent should be made clear to the boys and girls somewhere in the elementary school. They should understand that if two pronunciations are given for a word, each pronunciation is correct. At times the difference may be in accent, as, for example, in the case of the word *record,* which as a noun has the accent on the first syllable but as a verb on the second. Furthermore, the boys and girls should be taught that if no specification is given as to which of two pronunciations should be used under given circumstances, it is wrong to assume that the first of the two is the preferred one. Often the two pronunciations may be equally acceptable, but since one must be written before the other, the acceptability is not necessarily indicated by the order in which the pronunciations are given.

Finding the spelling Reference has already been made to the fact that teachers, at times, wrongly assume that a student is ready to look up the spelling of words in the dictionary. It is a difficult feat for many individuals, even for some adults, to find a word in the dictionary without being certain of the spelling. The pupil should be given guidance and practice in this skill. Merely to say to a child, "Look up in the dictionary the words that you do not know how to spell," is inviting frustration. Pupils should learn how the plurals of nouns and other inflected forms are indicated. They need to know that some words pronounced alike—homonyms—have different meanings for different spellings. For writing purposes it is also at times necessary to know how words can be divided into syllables and whether they are hyphenated. Consequently, the pupil needs to know the key for the division into syllables and hyphenation. Some dictionaries show syllabication by means of space left between syllables; others show it by a hyphen, which must not be interpreted as a sign that the word is a compound word. The symbols for hyphenation also vary. In some dictionaries the hyphen is used to show hyphenation, and in others the double hyphen, one line above the other, is used for that purpose. Often the pupils need help in finding out what the symbols in a given dictionary indicate.

Another problem in spelling deals with the abbreviation of a word if it can be abbreviated. Boys and girls should know that the dictionary gives abbreviations of words, and they should learn where they can be found.

By means of the dictionary pupils in the elementary school can learn how to find out whether a word is always written with a capital letter. They might learn where and how dictionaries give information about capitalization.

Learning the meaning In order to acquire skill in learning the meaning of words through the use of a dictionary, the pupils need to be able to:

1. Select the meaning that fits into the setting in which a word is used.
2. Make effective use of pictorial illustrations given for some words.
3. Make effective use of the verbal illustrations given, knowing which meaning fits a given context.
4. Understand information given about inflected forms.
5. Interpret symbols for the parts of speech they have studied.

6. Make use of information given about idiomatic expressions.
7. Understand what is meant by synonyms
and antonyms, and how the dictionaries
they use give this type of information.

**Making use of information given in the
parts that precede and follow the main
part of the dictionary** If there is an unabridged dictionary in the schoolroom, the
teacher in a fifth or sixth grade may wish
to introduce pupils to some of the types of
information given in the part preceding
and following the main section of the dictionary. They may be interested to know
that by turning to an unabridged dictionary they can find illustrations of flags of
all the countries of the world, that the dictionary gives biographical data on important persons, and that it has a very helpful
section dealing with geographical locations.
Even some of the dictionaries designed for
boys and girls in the elementary school
contain materials of great value in the front
and back portions. Familiarity with all the
parts of one's own dictionary might be an
objective that is accomplished some time
during the elementary school.

Ability To Use Reference Books Other than the Dictionary

Enclyclopedias and other suitable reference
materials for boys and girls can serve at
least two very important purposes, that of
helping the child gain needed information
and that of opening for him a source of information that can continue to serve his
needs throughout life. More and more
schools are ordering sets of encyclopedias
as well as other reference material for the
various rooms in their school system.
If there are no adequate reference books
in an intermediate-grade room, the teacher

should discover whether some can be obtained for his classroom. However, even if
the desired reference books are not available in the classroom, they may often be
found either in school or in public libraries.
Some boys and girls have sets of encyclopedias or other reference books at home
which they should utilize.

The quality of reference materials for
boys and girls in the elementary school has
greatly improved. There are the well-known
Compton's Pictured Encyclopedia (F. E.
Compton and Company), *The World Book
Encyclopedia* (World Book-Childcraft International, Inc.), *Britannica Junior Encyclopaedia* (Encyclopaedia Britannica Educational Corporation), and *Our Wonderful
World* (Grolier, Inc.)

Other encyclopedias for boys and girls,
some limited in scope, include:

The Book of Popular Science (Grolier,
Inc.)
The Children's Hour (Spencer Interna-
tional Press)
The Golden Book Encyclopedia (Golden
Press)
*The Golden Book Encyclopedia of Nat-
ural Science* (Golden Press)
*The Illustrated Encyclopedia of the An-
imal Kingdom* (Grolier, Inc.)
Makers of America (Encyclopaedia Bri-
tannica Educational Corporation,
with William Benton publisher)
Merit Students Encyclopedia (Crowell-
Collier Educational Corporation)
My First Picture Book Encyclopedia
(Grosset & Dunlap)
*The New Book of Knowledge: The Chil-
dren's Encyclopedia* (Grolier, Inc.)
*Pictorial Encyclopedia of American His-
tory* (United States History Society,
Inc.; The Children's Press, Inc., Mel-
mont Publishers)
Young People's Science Encyclopedia

Horizons can be expanded through the use of reference books. (World Book photo. © 1981 World Book-Childcraft International, Inc.)

(The Children's Press, Inc., Melmont Publishers)

A fifteen-volume resource library designed especially for preschool and primary-grade children and their teachers that is filling a decided need is *Childcraft: The How and Why Library* (World Book–Childcraft International, Inc.).

There are several other types of reference materials that some boys and girls in the upper elementary school can learn to use effectively. One is the *World Almanac*, published yearly, which gives concise data, chiefly in the form of isolated facts, on a large variety of topics, such as government, sports, and industry. It is especially valuable for the statistics recorded in it. The child can find the answer to many questions of interest to him, for example: "What is the population of the United States?" or "Which is longer, the Mississippi River or the Congo River?" Parts of *Goode's School Atlas*, with its variety of types of maps, constitute an excellent supplement to maps given in geography books. Familiarity with

the *Subject Index to Poetry*, if a copy of it is available, can also serve the needs of some boys and girls in the fifth and sixth grades. Some pupils in the intermediate grades would profit from an introduction to *Who's Who* and *Who's Who in America*.

In the first part of this chapter there is an enumeration of skills basic to the use of many types of reference material, for example, ability to find words when they are arranged in alphabetical order, ability to use cross references, and ability to utilize information found in reference books. All of these skills are needed for effective use of encyclopedias and other specialized reference books. In addition to these skills, pupils need the following in order to use materials of this type efficiently:

1. Knowledge of what is contained in the reference books
2. Knowledge of the organization of the reference books
3. Ability to decide in which reference book the desired information is likely to be found
4. Skill in finding the information

Ability To Locate Materials in the Library

In order to be able to locate materials effectively in a library or learning resource center the pupil needs to know how to use the card catalog, how to locate books on the shelves, and, possibly in the case of a few pupils, how to use sources such as the *Readers' Guide to Periodical Literature*. The help given in learning how to locate books in a library should be in terms of the library to which children have access. If none is located in the community, a miniature classroom library can serve as substitute.

Using the Card Catalog

Almost all libraries have card catalogs that serve as indexes to their book collections. Pupils should know that the term *card catalog* is applied to the collections of drawers in which are filed three-by-five-inch cards which give data on all the books in the library. They should learn that the cards are arranged alphabetically in the drawers and that the progression of the drawers is from the top toward the bottom drawer of one stack of drawers to the top drawer of the next stack.

In order to acquire skill in the use of a card catalog, one must be familiar with these three types of cards that the card catalog contains—namely, the author card, the title card, and the subject card. They also need to know that on an author card the alphabetical arrangement is according to the last name of the author, on a title card according to the first significant word of the title, and on a subject card according to the subject of the book. The pupils should also realize that if an individual knows the first and last name of the author of a book, it may be timesaving to look for the book under the author card. If the name of the author is not known but the exact title is, it is expedient to look for the title card. If neither the name of the author nor the exact title is known, one should look for the subject card. The children should also learn that by means of the subject card they can find out what other books are available in the library on a given subject.

Guidance should be given in observing the data found on all three types of cards. The terms *B* for *biography* and *J* for *juvenile,* if these are used, should also be explained. The pupils should learn the significance of the call number and the use they can make of it in locating a book in the library.

Finding Books on Shelves

If the library accessible to the child has open stacks, the pupils should learn something about the arrangement of books.

Most small libraries use an adaptation of the Dewey decimal system of classification. If the library has that system of classification, the pupil should learn to use it. While pupils should not be asked to memorize the categories, they should have general familiarity with the system and know where in a library they can find the classification chart. The Dewey decimal system employs the following number classifications:

000–099	General works, including bibliography and general periodicals
100–199	Philosophy, psychology, ethics
200–299	Religion, Bible, mythology
300–399	Sociology, economics, education, political science
400–499	Philology, dictionaries, grammars
500–599	Natural science, including mathematics, chemistry, physics
600–699	Applied science, including useful arts, medicine, agriculture, manufacturing
700–799	Fine arts, music, recreation
800–899	Literature
900–999	History, biography, travel

A variation from the Dewey decimal system that many libraries make is in the classification of fiction and biography. Frequently fiction is arranged according to the last name of the author, while biography is classified under *B.*

Increasingly, libraries—chiefly the larger ones—are changing from the Dewey decimal system to the Library of Congress classification. It is recommended that in the elementary school boys and girls be introduced to the latter system only if they use a library that has that method of classification. The A to Z classes, without subdivisions, of the Library of Congress Classification, are here reproduced.

A General Works: Polygraphy
B Philosophy and religion
C History: Auxiliary Sciences
D History: General and Old World
E-F History: America
G Geography, Anthropology, Folklore, and so on
H Social Sciences
J Political Science
K Law
L Education
M Music
N Fine arts
P Philology and Literature
Q Science
R Medicine
S Agriculture, and so on
T Technology
U Military Science
V Naval Science
Z Bibliography and Library Science

Using Indexes to Magazines

The number of children's magazines of excellent quality is increasing. Children at all levels of the elementary school enjoy looking at, if not reading, magazines on their levels. As soon as they are ready for instruction in the use of a subject index guide to periodicals for children, providing one is available in the library they use, they should be assisted in using it so their interest can be pursued systematically beyond simply perusing current issues.

Some boys and girls in the upper elementary school can be taught how to locate magazine articles by means of the *Readers' Guide to Periodical Literature*. The teacher, possibly with the help of the librarian, may decide to teach the child such facts as the following:

1. Where the *Readers' Guide to Periodical Literature* is located
2. How often it is published
3. Method of cumulation
4. Type of information it contains
5. How to locate information in it

Locating Other Materials in the Library

Increasingly, there will be an urgent need for boys and girls even in the elementary school to learn to locate materials other than books and magazines both in their classroom and in central libraries or learning centers. With the greater supply of films, filmstrips, slides, tapes, and records, those in charge of libraries are finding it imperative to store these aids according to a system that will facilitate their use. With growing individualization of work in many schools and with libraries increasingly being used as learning centers, it is becoming all the more important that boys and girls know where to find these materials. The system of storage used will vary considerably from library to library. If time is to be saved and use of the materials encouraged, elementary-school pupils will need to be familiarized with whatever method of organization is used in libraries to which they have access.

Undoubtedly, in the near future guidance not only in locating materials in learning centers but also in making use of newer media will be essential in an elementary-school program. If predictions concerning the library of the future come true, then skill in making use of audiovisual aids of many kinds and of operative systems, such as storage banks and dial access, will be a decided asset to learning.

Principles Underlying the Teaching of Locational Skills

An overriding principle that should be observed when determining procedures for helping boys and girls acquire skill in locating information and using it is that the need for learning these skills should arise, when possible, out of the daily lives of the pupils. Additional guidelines include:

1. Not nearly all boys and girls in the elementary school should be expected to learn all the locational skills listed in this chapter Some are too difficult for the slow or retarded learner to acquire. And many would be of little or no value to some of them.

2. Readiness for a locational skill facilitates learning In part, readiness for this type of skill, as for other learnings, is a matter of maturation. However, to a considerable extent it is closely related to the experience background of the learner. Fortunately, the background of experience can be broadened, and the teacher is in a key position to help. No teacher needs to wait complacently for a child to become ready to learn how to locate material in print. Readiness can be achieved through a well-planned sequence of activities, preferably those that relate to problems for functional use of printed sources.

3. The optimum grade placement of a skill either for initial presentation or for practice purposes has not been ascertained It is generally agreed, however, that although the bulk of the work in developing skill in locating information should be done in the intermediate grades, work in the primary grades can make a significant contribution in this area. In the

first three grades help can be given in locating some of the information that children wish to find in books and magazines. Furthermore, in the primary grades a stable foundation can be laid for skills that can be developed in the intermediate grades.

The following are some of the skills in locating information that can be developed, at least in part, in primary grades:

1. Looking at the pictures to get an idea as to the content of a book
2. Noting the titles of stories as they appear in the main part of the book
3. Finding page numbers
4. Reading the titles of stories as listed in the table of contents
5. Looking at the titles of stories in order to see which ones are likely to deal with a given topic
6. Knowing where, in the room or school or public library, books of interest to them can be found
7. Learning alphabetical order
8. Arranging letters and words in alphabetical order
9. Knowing how to use a picture dictionary
10. Using a glossary in a textbook
11. Learning some facts related to using a dictionary for children
12. Finding material and looking at pictures in an encyclopedia for younger children, for example, *Childcraft*
13. Looking at pictures and getting information through the teacher's reading from encyclopedias such as *Compton's Pictured Encyclopedia, The World Book Encyclopedia, Britannica Junior,* or *Our Wonderful World*
14. Getting information from atlases, yearbooks, and the *World Almanac*

4. Opportunity should be provided to make use of skills learned Closely related to the problem of readiness for learning a skill is that of making use of what is learned. Since the pupil is, as a rule, more receptive to learning if he knows he will find it of value, those abilities of real worth to a child before he is an adult should be stressed. Fortunately, many skills that are needed by adults are also important to children. By providing the child with an opportunity to make real use of his skill, the teacher can furnish him with distributed practice, important in the learning of any skill.

5. Provison should be made for evaluating skill in locating information One way of appraising the skill of intermediate-grade boys and girls in locating information is use of standardized tests. Unfortunately, most standardized reading tests for the elementary school do not test skill in locating information. Tests that do devote sections to this skill are the *Iowa Silent Reading Test*, the *Iowa Every Pupil Test*, and some forms of the *California Achievement Tests*.

The teacher can also appraise skill through more informal means, such as teacher-made tests, observation of pupils while doing practice exercises designed to develop skills in locating information, and observation of pupils when they look up information while not taking tests or doing practice exercises. An advantage of the teacher-made tests over standardized tests is that the locational skills not tested in the commercially produced tests can be included. A further point in favor of teacher-made tests is that the teacher has the opportunity to devise test items that apply specifically to what the pupils are or will be studying. As he observes boys and girls in nontesting situations, he can note not only their skills but also their attitudes toward finding information and utilizing it. For example, expressions showing dislike of look-

ing up words in a dictionary tell the teacher something he ought to know for planning future strategy.

In making evaluations it is important to observe these criteria:

1. Evaluation should be made in terms of the objectives. Before a teacher begins instruction in locating information a survey test giving information on the pupil's abilities in a variety of locational skills may be given.
2. Both teacher and pupils should take part in evaluation procedures. If the pupil has a voice in planning the means of appraisal, he is more likely to try to improve in the skills that are being taught. Furthermore, his attitude toward the tests will probably be more favorable.
3. Evaluation should be a continuous process. It should not be confined to appraisal when work on a skill is begun and when the time to be spent working on it systematically is ended. Throughout the period of learning, checks should be made on how successful the teaching and learning have been.

6. Systematic instruction should be given in the development of the locational skills While it is possible that for a small minority of the boys and girls in the elementary school no instruction beyond the incidental will be essential, in many instances even such children will profit from lessons definitely planned to help them acquire greater facility in the locational skills. For a large number of pupils, much floundering and inefficiency will result unless they are given direct help in the development of the ability to locate information. How these skills can be developed incidentally in the content subjects is discussed in part of Chapter 10B. To supplement such instruction, direct assistance can, and in most cases should, be given by providing presentation lessons, in which the pupils are taught locational skills, and practice lessons in which they can strengthen their command of the skills. In the following chapter suggestions as to types of practice desirable are given.

7. Materials of instruction should fit the needs of the individuals Many teachers are not aware of the excellent materials that are available for the development of locational skills. Teachers' guides accompanying many of the basal reader series give suggestions for developing such skills on various levels of reading ability.

9B

Developing Skill in Locating Information and in Using It

Anyone with ordinary intelligence and average reading ability should have no difficulty in acquiring many locational skills. Unfortunately, however, because of inadequate instruction, many persons who have graduated from high school are deficient in this area. A teacher who puts into practice the principles set forth in the preceding chapter can do much to help pupils attack their problems of finding information in printed materials. The following pages will illustrate ways of putting these principles into practice.

Developing Basic Locational Skills

Basic to the development of skill in locating information in various types of books and magazines are supportive skills in:

1. Finding a given page in a book quickly
2. Finding words arranged in alphabetical order
3. Deciding on key words
4. Interpreting punctuation marks, diacritical marks, abbreviations, and symbols
5. Selecting points that have bearing on a given problem
6. Utilizing information gained

Finding a Given Page in a Book Quickly

Pupils can be given help in quickly finding a given page in books of various types by means of activities such as the following:

1. Telling the pupils in the first grade where to find page numbers in a book
2. Teaching the pupils how to turn the pages of a book
3. Having the pupils try to open a book as near as possible to a given page before they begin turning pages
4. Having pupils estimate to which page the teacher opened a book

Finding Words Arranged in Alphabetical Order

Finding words in lists arranged alphabetically is a basic skill in locating information. The following methods are illustrative of the means by which this skill may be developed:.

1. Having the pupils memorize the letters in alphabetical order
2. Writing the letters in alphabetical order on the board with some letters missing and asking the pupils to supply the missing letters
3. Having the pupils state in which part of the alphabet—first, middle, or last—given letters are found. Some teacher may prefer making the

skill is that of making use of what is learned. Since the pupil is, as a rule, more receptive to learning if he knows he will find it of value, those abilities of real worth to a child before he is an adult should be stressed. Fortunately, many skills that are needed by adults are also important to children. By providing the child with an opportunity to make real use of his skill, the teacher can furnish him with distributed practice, important in the learning of any skill.

5. Provison should be made for evaluating skill in locating information One way of appraising the skill of intermediate-grade boys and girls in locating information is use of standardized tests. Unfortunately, most standardized reading tests for the elementary school do not test skill in locating information. Tests that do devote sections to this skill are the *Iowa Silent Reading Test*, the *Iowa Every Pupil Test*, and some forms of the *California Achievement Tests.*

The teacher can also appraise skill through more informal means, such as teacher-made tests, observation of pupils while doing practice exercises designed to develop skills in locating information, and observation of pupils when they look up information while not taking tests or doing practice exercises. An advantage of the teacher-made tests over standardized tests is that the locational skills not tested in the commercially produced tests can be included. A further point in favor of teacher-made tests is that the teacher has the opportunity to devise test items that apply specifically to what the pupils are or will be studying. As he observes boys and girls in nontesting situations, he can note not only their skills but also their attitudes toward finding information and utilizing it. For example, expressions showing dislike of looking up words in a dictionary tell the teacher something he ought to know for planning future strategy.

In making evaluations it is important to observe these criteria:

1. Evaluation should be made in terms of the objectives. Before a teacher begins instruction in locating information a survey test giving information on the pupil's abilities in a variety of locational skills may be given.
2. Both teacher and pupils should take part in evaluation procedures. If the pupil has a voice in planning the means of appraisal, he is more likely to try to improve in the skills that are being taught. Furthermore, his attitude toward the tests will probably be more favorable.
3. Evaluation should be a continuous process. It should not be confined to appraisal when work on a skill is begun and when the time to be spent working on it systematically is ended. Throughout the period of learning, checks should be made on how successful the teaching and learning have been.

6. Systematic instruction should be given in the development of the locational skills While it is possible that for a small minority of the boys and girls in the elementary school no instruction beyond the incidental will be essential, in many instances even such children will profit from lessons definitely planned to help them acquire greater facility in the locational skills. For a large number of pupils, much floundering and inefficiency will result unless they are given direct help in the development of the ability to locate information. How these skills can be developed incidentally in the content subjects is discussed in part of Chapter 10B. To supplement such instruction, direct assistance can, and in most cases should, be given by providing presentation lessons, in which the pupils are taught locational skills, and practice lessons in which they can strengthen their command of the skills. In the following chapter suggestions as to types of practice desirable are given.

7. Materials of instruction should fit the needs of the individuals Many teachers are not aware of the excellent materials that are available for the development of locational skills. Teachers' guides accompanying many of the basal reader series give suggestions for developing such skills on various levels of reading ability.

6. Make use of information given about idiomatic expressions.
7. Understand what is meant by synonyms and antonyms, and how the dictionaries they use give this type of information.

Making use of information given in the parts that precede and follow the main part of the dictionary If there is an unabridged dictionary in the schoolroom, the teacher in a fifth or sixth grade may wish to introduce pupils to some of the types of information given in the part preceding and following the main section of the dictionary. They may be interested to know that by turning to an unabridged dictionary they can find illustrations of flags of all the countries of the world, that the dictionary gives biographical data on important persons, and that it has a very helpful section dealing with geographical locations. Even some of the dictionaries designed for boys and girls in the elementary school contain materials of great value in the front and back portions. Familiarity with all the parts of one's own dictionary might be an objective that is accomplished some time during the elementary school.

Ability To Use Reference Books Other than the Dictionary

Enclyclopedias and other suitable reference materials for boys and girls can serve at least two very important purposes, that of helping the child gain needed information and that of opening for him a source of information that can continue to serve his needs throughout life. More and more schools are ordering sets of encyclopedias as well as other reference material for the various rooms in their school system. If there are no adequate reference books in an intermediate-grade room, the teacher

should discover whether some can be obtained for his classroom. However, even if the desired reference books are not available in the classroom, they may often be found either in school or in public libraries. Some boys and girls have sets of encyclopedias or other reference books at home which they should utilize.

The quality of reference materials for boys and girls in the elementary school has greatly improved. There are the well-known *Compton's Pictured Encyclopedia* (F. E. Compton and Company), *The World Book Encyclopedia* (World Book-Childcraft International, Inc.), *Britannica Junior Encyclopaedia* (Encyclopaedia Britannica Educational Corporation), and *Our Wonderful World* (Grolier, Inc.)

Other encyclopedias for boys and girls, some limited in scope, include:

The Book of Popular Science (Grolier, Inc.)

The Children's Hour (Spencer International Press)

The Golden Book Encyclopedia (Golden Press)

The Golden Book Encyclopedia of Natural Science (Golden Press)

The Illustrated Encyclopedia of the Animal Kingdom (Grolier, Inc.)

Makers of America (Encyclopaedia Britannica Educational Corporation, with William Benton publisher)

Merit Students Encyclopedia (Crowell-Collier Educational Corporation)

My First Picture Book Encyclopedia (Grosset & Dunlap)

The New Book of Knowledge: The Children's Encyclopedia (Grolier, Inc.)

Pictorial Encyclopedia of American History (United States History Society, Inc.; The Children's Press, Inc., Melmont Publishers)

Young People's Science Encyclopedia

familiar with the key that he will find it unnecessary to refer to it often. The child should also learn that there is lack of uniformity among compilers of various dictionaries in the system of diacritical marks that they use.

The significance of the syllabication of words and of the marking of the accent should be made clear to the boys and girls somewhere in the elementary school. They should understand that if two pronunciations are given for a word, each pronunciation is correct. At times the difference may be in accent, as, for example, in the case of the word *record,* which as a noun has the accent on the first syllable but as a verb on the second. Furthermore, the boys and girls should be taught that if no specification is given as to which of two pronunciations should be used under given circumstances, it is wrong to assume that the first of the two is the preferred one. Often the two pronunciations may be equally acceptable, but since one must be written before the other, the acceptability is not necessarily indicated by the order in which the pronunciations are given.

Finding the spelling Reference has already been made to the fact that teachers, at times, wrongly assume that a student is ready to look up the spelling of words in the dictionary. It is a difficult feat for many individuals, even for some adults, to find a word in the dictionary without being certain of the spelling. The pupil should be given guidance and practice in this skill. Merely to say to a child, "Look up in the dictionary the words that you do not know how to spell," is inviting frustration. Pupils should learn how the plurals of nouns and other inflected forms are indicated. They need to know that some words pronounced alike—homonyms—have different meanings for different spellings. For writing purposes it is also at times necessary to know how words can be divided into syllables and whether they are hyphenated. Consequently, the pupil needs to know the key for the division into syllables and hyphenation. Some dictionaries show syllabication by means of space left between syllables; others show it by a hyphen, which must not be interpreted as a sign that the word is a compound word. The symbols for hyphenation also vary. In some dictionaries the hyphen is used to show hyphenation, and in others the double hyphen, one line above the other, is used for that purpose. Often the pupils need help in finding out what the symbols in a given dictionary indicate.

Another problem in spelling deals with the abbreviation of a word if it can be abbreviated. Boys and girls should know that the dictionary gives abbreviations of words, and they should learn where they can be found.

By means of the dictionary pupils in the elementary school can learn how to find out whether a word is always written with a capital letter. They might learn where and how dictionaries give information about capitalization.

Learning the meaning In order to acquire skill in learning the meaning of words through the use of a dictionary, the pupils need to be able to:

1. Select the meaning that fits into the setting in which a word is used.
2. Make effective use of pictorial illustrations given for some words.
3. Make effective use of the verbal illustrations given, knowing which meaning fits a given context.
4. Understand information given about inflected forms.
5. Interpret symbols for the parts of speech they have studied.

division of the alphabet into the first, second, third, and fourth quarters.

4. Having the pupils arrange letters in alphabetical order
5. Asking the pupils to arrange in alphabetical order a series of words in which the first letters are different; in which the first letters are alike but the second letters are different; in which the first two letters are alike but the third letters are different; etc.
6. Helping pupils to discover that persons' names are usually listed according to the last names and that when two or more persons have the same last name, the order in which the names are arranged is determined by the alphabetical sequence of letters of the first names. For example, the order for the following three names should be given as (a) Smith, Dan; (b) Smith, James; and (c) Smith, Marilyn.
7. Asking the pupils to arrange in alphabetical order the names of the boys and girls in their class
8. Explaining to the class that as the teacher shows each word card of a set, a pupil is to respond by naming a word beginning with the letter immediately preceding, in alphabetical order, the letter with which the word on the card begins. A variation of this procedure is to have a pupil give a word beginning with the letter immediately following, in alphabetical order, the letter with which the word on a given card begins.
9. Guiding pupils to note the placement and function of guide words in the dictionary and in many other reference books
10. Having the pupils indicate whether a given word comes between two stated guide words
11. Asking the pupils to name words that are expected to be found as entry words on a page in the dictionary for which the guide words are stated

Practice Exercises

Below are samples of practice exercises that can be used in teaching boys and girls to find words or write words in alphabetical order.

1. Directions: Write the letters that come immediately before and after, in ABC order, each of the following letters:

1. ___ *t* ___   5. ___ *o* ___
2. ___ *f* ___   6. ___ *w* ___
3. ___ *d* ___   7. ___ *v* ___
4. ___ *q* ___   8. ___ *k* ___

2. Directions: Write *yes* on the line to the left of each number if the words in that item are arranged in alphabetical order. Otherwise write *no*.

___ 1. camel, cat, lion, fox
___ 2. bay, gulf, lake, ocean
___ 3. Talk, tear, tease, take
___ 4. James, Jones, Johnson, Jacobson

3. Directions: Put an x through each word that is not in alphabetical order in the lists that follow:

apples, bananas, pears, oranges, plums
stone, brick, granite, marble, wood

4. Explanation: In providing pupils with practice in arranging words in alphabetical order, the easiest type of exercise is one in which the first letters of the words are different. More difficult is an exercise in which only some of the first letters of the words are different, so that the alphabetical order of the word needs to be determined in part by the second letter of the words; still more difficult is an exercise in which the third and fourth letters of a word help to determine the alphabetical order. (In the exercise that follows the third letter of *bluebirds* and *blackbirds* determines which word comes first.)

Directions: Write 1 to the left of the word that should come first in alphabetical order, 2 to the left of the word that should come second, and so on.

_____	bluebirds	_____	doves
_____	blackbirds	_____	chicadees
_____	bobwhites	_____	cardinals
_____	ducks	_____	cranes

5. Directions: On one page of a dictionary the guide words are *Nashville* and *nature*. Write yes to the right of the following words that you would expect to find on that page. Write no to the right of the others

narrow	_____	net	_____
nail	_____	neck	_____
nature	_____	needle	_____
nation	_____	nurse	_____
name	_____	navy	_____

Deciding on Key Words

One of the more difficult locational skills is to decide on the key words under which certain information can be found. Through a progression of activities from the less to the more difficult, and from the known to the unknown, this ability can be developed. Some methods that can prove helpful in developing this skill are:

1. Asking the pupils to tell under what key word in an index a reference may be found for a question such as: "In what year did George Washington become president of the United States?"
2. Providing the boys and girls with an exercise in which they will choose the one of three or four words under which a reference is the most likely to be listed that gives information on a stated topic

3. The list of maps and illustrations gives the captions used with the maps and illustrations and also the page on which they are found.

Chapter Headings, Center Headings, and Sideheadings

Pupils should be taught the value of various kinds of headings in locating material and should be given practice in their use. As soon as side and center headings are provided in the textbooks that pupils read or in the reference books they use, some help should be given in making effective use of these aids as a means of locating information.

Glossary

If some of the books the pupils are using contain a glossary, they should note that it is found in the back part of the book and that special terms and words used in the book are explained in this section. They should notice that the words are listed alphabetically.

Index

The following are some of the points the pupils should learn about the index of a book:

1. Where the index is located
2. How the topics are arranged in an index
3. How subtopics are listed

The following skills should be developed:

1. Deciding upon what entry word to use when trying to gain information on a given point
2. Finding an entry with dispatch
3. Making effective use of subtopics in an index
4. Finding the part on a page indicated in the index that gives the information desired

Ability To Use the Dictionary

One of the outstanding developments in materials of instruction for the elementary school has been the dictionary for children. Pupils in the early part of this century often had access only to a large, unabridged dictionary and/or to one or more smaller ones that were also published chiefly for adults. For many elementary-school boys and girls these dictionaries were unsuitable.

Dictionaries for the Elementary School

In addition to the picture dictionaries (see Chapter 6B, "Developing Skill in Word Recognition," p. 148), the following dictionaries are used in the elementary school:

Beginning Dictionary (Scott, Foresman and Company)

Giant Golden Illustrated Dictionary, Stuart A. Courtis and Garnette Watters, eds. (Golden Press, Inc.), six volumes.

The Holt Basic Dictionary of American English (Holt, Rinehart and Winston).

The Holt Intermediate Dictionary of American English (Holt, Rinehart and Winston).

Macmillan Beginning Dictionary (Macmillan)

Macmillan Dictionary for Children (Macmillan)

Thorndike-Barnhart Beginning Dictionary, Edward L. Thorndike and Clarence L. Barnhart, eds. (Scott, Foresman).

Thorndike-Barnhart Junior Dictionary, Edward L. Thorndike and Clarence L. Barnhart, eds. (Scott, Foresman).

Webster's A Dictionary for Boys and Girls (American Book).

Webster's New Elementary Dictionary (American Book).

The Winston Dictionary for Schools, Thomas K. Brown and William D.

Lewis, eds. (Holt, Rinehart and Winston).

The World Book Dictionary, Clarence Barnhart, ed. (World Book—Childcraft International, Inc.), two volumes.

Dictionary Skills

The skills to be learned in using a dictionary in the elementary school can be summarized thus:

1. Ability to locate a word quickly
2. Ability to learn the pronunciation of a word
3. Ability to find the spelling of a word and related abilities, including: (a) spelling; (b) syllabication; (c) hyphenation; (d) abbreviations; and (e) capitalization
4. Ability to learn the meaning of a word
5. Ability to use the parts of the dictionary preceding and following the main part of the dictionary, both in the pupil's dictionary and in an unabridged dictionary

The teacher must bear in mind that many of the skills listed as dictionary skills are important in other reading activities as well. For example, to be able to locate a word quickly may be of value when skimming, when using an encyclopedia, when finding a telephone number. Furthermore, the pupil should not get the impression that the dictionary is the only source through which some of the skills mentioned can be acquired. Item 4 of the preceding listing "ability to learn the meaning of a word" can best be and should be acquired in a variety of ways, through listening to conversation and explanations, through watching television, through reading, for example. Help frequently needs to be given in effectively using these other sources of vocabulary development.

Locating a word in the dictionary In order to locate a word in the dictionary quickly, the pupil needs to know more than how to find a word in a list arranged alphabetically and how to make use of guide words. The difficulty in which one fifth-grade girl found herself illustrates the need for more information. This girl's teacher had told her pupils that the unabridged dictionary in their room contained every word in the English language. One day, while the teacher was busy with another group, this girl ran across the word *busied* in her reading and was puzzled as to the meaning of the word. Had the word been *busy* she would have recognized it in print, and had she heard the word *busied* pronounced, she might have had no difficulty with its meaning. However, when she saw the word *busied* in context, she thought it would be pronounced *bu si' ed,* giving the *s* an *s* instead of a *z* sound and the *i* a long sound. She therefore went to the big dictionary and looked for the entry *busied.* When she could not find *busied* listed as an entry word, she had no idea that she might find it under another form. Consequently, she could hardly wait until she could tell her teacher about her amazing "discovery" that the dictionary did not contain every word in the language. When the teacher asked her which word she did not find, she told her *busied,* pronouncing the word as *bu si' ed.*

Many boys and girls need direct teaching in order to learn how inflected forms can be located in the dictionary. Emphasis on structural analysis can serve as an aid in recognizing inflected forms.

Learning the pronunciation The elementary-school child can learn to find the pronunciation of a word by means of respellings and diacritical marks, as interpreted in the key to pronunciation at the bottom of the pages in the dictionary. It is suggested that he be helped to become so

9B

Developing Skill in Locating Information and in Using It

Anyone with ordinary intelligence and average reading ability should have no difficulty in acquiring many locational skills. Unfortunately, however, because of inadequate instruction, many persons who have graduated from high school are deficient in this area. A teacher who puts into practice the principles set forth in the preceding chapter can do much to help pupils attack their problems of finding information in printed materials. The following pages will illustrate ways of putting these principles into practice.

Developing Basic Locational Skills

Basic to the development of skill in locating information in various types of books and magazines are supportive skills in:

1. Finding a given page in a book quickly
2. Finding words arranged in alphabetical order
3. Deciding on key words
4. Interpreting punctuation marks, diacritical marks, abbreviations, and symbols
5. Selecting points that have bearing on a given problem
6. Utilizing information gained

Finding a Given Page in a Book Quickly

Pupils can be given help in quickly finding a given page in books of various types by means of activities such as the following:

1. Telling the pupils in the first grade where to find page numbers in a book
2. Teaching the pupils how to turn the pages of a book
3. Having the pupils try to open a book as near as possible to a given page before they begin turning pages
4. Having pupils estimate to which page the teacher opened a book

Finding Words Arranged in Alphabetical Order

Finding words in lists arranged alphabetically is a basic skill in locating information. The following methods are illustrative of the means by which this skill may be developed:.

1. Having the pupils memorize the letters in alphabetical order
2. Writing the letters in alphabetical order on the board with some letters missing and asking the pupils to supply the missing letters
3. Having the pupils state in which part of the alphabet—first, middle, or last—given letters are found. Some teacher may prefer making the

3. Asking pupils to indicate the word in a list of proper names consisting of more than one word, such as the following, which would serve as a key word when locating information on the person or place: *Thomas Edison, United Nations, West Germany, Hawaiian Islands*
4. Providing guidance as the pupils consult an index to find out whether a given problem is discussed, and then report on the procedure they used in locating the reference giving the information desired.

Practice Exercise

The following part of an exercise shows how practice in deciding on key words can be provided. The value of such exercises can usually be greatly increased if the pupils are given a chance to discuss their reasons for making their selections.

Directions: Draw a line under the key word after each of the following questions that seems to you the most likely entry word in an index of a nonreference book or in a reference book such as an encyclopedia under which you would find an answer to the question:

1. What is one of the chief exports of the Philippines? (export, island, Philippines, products)
2. What was the color of the uniform of the soldiers of the South during the Civil War? (Civil War, South, uniform, war)

Interpreting Punctuation Marks, Diacritical Marks, Abbreviations, and Symbols

Since in indexes, dictionaries, and other reference books punctuation marks are used in different ways and since the abbreviations and symbols used vary somewhat from one book to another, it is suggested that much of the work on this topic be taken up as each new reference book is studied. The following are ways in which these interpretive skills can be developed:

1. Helping the pupils find out how syllabication of words is indicated in their own dictionaries and how the hyphen between compound words is represented
2. Asking the pupils to look up in the dictionary words or terms such as *bluejay, Sunday school,* and *good-by* to find out which are hyphenated
3. Providing practice in pronouncing words for which the pronunciation is shown by diacritical markings, as well as for words in which the pronunciation is indicated by respelling
4. Having the pupils study the key to abbreviations and to symbols used in a reference book
5. After helping the pupils learn how division into syllables is shown in

their dictionaries, asking them to divide words into syllables after consulting a dictionary

6. Providing practice in interpreting accent marks by having pupils pronounce words that are not always accented in the same way, such as *pres ent* and *pre sent*

7. Teaching the abbreviations for words commonly used and then testing the pupils on them

Selecting Points That Have Bearing on a Given Problem

After the necessary reference pages have been located, skill in selecting points that have bearing on a given problem can be developed through various activities such as:

1. Asking the class questions that are phrased in words similar to those used in the text that serve as an answer to them and later asking questions when the answers are not phrased in the same way as in the text

2. Asking pupils to find the answer to a question or a direction such as the following, in which the answer consists of two or more sentences referred to in various parts of a paragraph: "Name three reasons why many cranberries are produced in Massachusetts."

3. Asking the pupils to list items they would expect to find under a certain topic

Utilizing Information Gained

After the exact information needed has been located, skill in utilizing it can be acquired through activities such as the following:

1. Having the pupils judge whether a statement is reliable by considering who wrote it or in what book it appeared

2. Giving pupils practice in deciding which of a series of statements are relevant to their problem

3. Having pupils compile a bibliography of information helpful on a topic

4. Providing opportunity for the pupils to give a talk or write a paper on information they have gathered

5. Giving the pupils opportunity to explain to others what they learned, by putting on puppet shows or making friezes or "movies"

6. After the pupils have looked up a topic in an encyclopedia, giving them time to write a small number of interesting and significant facts that they learned and then having others in the class read those sentences

7. Having pupils compare the information on a given subject gained from one encyclopedia with that on the same topic in another encyclopedia

Developing Skill in Using Nonreference Books

Below are indicated some ways which the teacher can help boys and girls acquire skill in using the various parts of a book for locating information.

The Table of Contents

1. Having pupils turn to the table of contents of their beginning readers to find the story they will read
2. Asking boys and girls to answer questions by examining the table of contents in their readers. The following questions are suggestive of types that might be asked:
   a. Is there a story in this book about a rabbit?
   b. On which page does the story about a fox begin?
   c. What is the title of another story about an animal?
3. After the pupils have examined the table of contents of several books, having them make a list of books in which information is given on a specific topic in which they are interested
4. Having the pupils construct a table of contents and an index for a class notebook they are making—for example, one on "Explorers in Space"

The Index

1. Asking the boys and girls questions concerning the index, such as: (a) In what part of a book is the index found? (b) How are the main entries of an index arranged?
2. Helping boys and girls understand the paging system followed in an index. For example, they may need assistance in understanding that an indication of pages such as 400–405 means that a certain topic begins on page 400 and extends to page 405; or that 400, 406 indicates that the topic is discussed on page 400 and on page 406.
3. Asking the boys and girls to underline what key word in an index they would look under first to see whether information is found in the book for answering a given question such as: (a) In what year was George Washington Carver born? (b) Do all male elephants have tusks?
4. Giving the pupils practice in finding the answer to a given question in the main part of the book, after they have consulted the index to find the page on which the answer is given.

Various Parts

1. Having pupils examine the various parts of a book to find out where they are located, what they contain, and how the data given in them are arranged.

2. Helping pupils make a chart in which they list the important points to remember about each part of a book. An example of such a point is: "The index is found in the back part of a book."
3. Having the pupils find answers to questions about the various parts of a book, as, for example, "What is the purpose of the preface?"
4. Providing practice for the pupils in examining the preface of a book to see if the book is likely to contain information needed on a given general topic.

Developing Skill in Using the Dictionary

Some procedures that can help in the development of skills essential to the effective use of the dictionary are listed below.

1. Having the pupils record the dictionary page number on which each in a list of entry words is found. (This exercise could be a timed one.)
2. Having the pupils make a list of the types of information given for an entry word
3. Asking the pupils to find the answers to questions such as the following by using the dictionary: "Are the American robin and the European robin alike?"
4. Providing practice in which the pupils select from a dictionary the meaning of a word that is appropriate in a given context
5. Providing the pupils with sentences in each of which a word is underlined and asking them to restate each sentence without using the underlined word. An example of such a sentence is: "The boys and girls do not *anticipate* a big crowd."
6. Having the pupils make a list of sentences illustrating all the meanings of a word that they can think of or that they can find in a dictionary, as, for example: I can *run* fast; He can *run* the machine.
7. Having the pupils explain, with the help of the dictionary, the meanings of words that are homonyms, and then having them use the words in sentences
8. Having the pupils name words containing common prefixes and suffixes
9. Having the pupils find the meanings of words that are often confused, such as *suppose* and *expect*
10. Providing practice in pronouncing words that according to the dictionary have two correct pronunciations and using the two pronunciations in sentences they give orally
11. Asking the pupils to look up in the dictionary a list of words often mispronounced, such as *handkerchief,* and providing them with practice in pronouncing the words correctly

a library that has that method of classification. The A to Z classes, without subdivisions, of the Library of Congress Classification, are here reproduced.

A General Works: Polygraphy
B Philosophy and religion
C History: Auxiliary Sciences
D History: General and Old World
E-F History: America
G Geography, Anthropology, Folklore, and so on
H Social Sciences
J Political Science
K Law
L Education
M Music
N Fine arts
P Philology and Literature
Q Science
R Medicine
S Agriculture, and so on
T Technology
U Military Science
V Naval Science
Z Bibliography and Library Science

Using Indexes to Magazines

The number of children's magazines of excellent quality is increasing. Children at all levels of the elementary school enjoy looking at, if not reading, magazines on their levels. As soon as they are ready for instruction in the use of a subject index guide to periodicals for children, providing one is available in the library they use, they should be assisted in using it so their interest can be pursued systematically beyond simply perusing current issues.

Some boys and girls in the upper elementary school can be taught how to locate magazine articles by means of the *Readers' Guide to Periodical Literature*. The teacher, possibly with the help of the librarian, may decide to teach the child such facts as the following:

1. Where the *Readers' Guide to Periodical Literature* is located
2. How often it is published
3. Method of cumulation
4. Type of information it contains
5. How to locate information in it

Locating Other Materials in the Library

Increasingly, there will be an urgent need for boys and girls even in the elementary school to learn to locate materials other than books and magazines both in their classroom and in central libraries or learning centers. With the greater supply of films, filmstrips, slides, tapes, and records, those in charge of libraries are finding it imperative to store these aids according to a system that will facilitate their use. With growing individualization of work in many schools and with libraries increasingly being used as learning centers, it is becoming all the more important that boys and girls know where to find these materials. The system of storage used will vary considerably from library to library. If time is to be saved and use of the materials encouraged, elementary-school pupils will need to be familiarized with whatever method of organization is used in libraries to which they have access.

Undoubtedly, in the near future guidance not only in locating materials in learning centers but also in making use of newer media will be essential in an elementary-school program. If predictions concerning the library of the future come true, then skill in making use of audiovisual aids of many kinds and of operative systems, such as storage banks and dial access, will be a decided asset to learning.

Principles Underlying the Teaching of Locational Skills

An overriding principle that should be observed when determining procedures for helping boys and girls acquire skill in locating information and using it is that the need for learning these skills should arise, when possible, out of the daily lives of the pupils. Additional guidelines include:

1. Not nearly all boys and girls in the elementary school should be expected to learn all the locational skills listed in this chapter Some are too difficult for the slow or retarded learner to acquire. And many would be of little or no value to some of them.

2. Readiness for a locational skill facilitates learning In part, readiness for this type of skill, as for other learnings, is a matter of maturation. However, to a considerable extent it is closely related to the experience background of the learner. Fortunately, the background of experience can be broadened, and the teacher is in a key position to help. No teacher needs to wait complacently for a child to become ready to learn how to locate material in print. Readiness can be achieved through a well-planned sequence of activities, preferably those that relate to problems for functional use of printed sources.

3. The optimum grade placement of a skill either for initial presentation or for practice purposes has not been ascertained It is generally agreed, however, that although the bulk of the work in developing skill in locating information should be done in the intermediate grades, work in the primary grades can make a significant contribution in this area. In the first three grades help can be given in locating some of the information that children wish to find in books and magazines. Furthermore, in the primary grades a stable foundation can be laid for skills that can be developed in the intermediate grades.

The following are some of the skills in locating information that can be developed, at least in part, in primary grades:

1. Looking at the pictures to get an idea as to the content of a book
2. Noting the titles of stories as they appear in the main part of the book
3. Finding page numbers
4. Reading the titles of stories as listed in the table of contents
5. Looking at the titles of stories in order to see which ones are likely to deal with a given topic
6. Knowing where, in the room or school or public library, books of interest to them can be found
7. Learning alphabetical order
8. Arranging letters and words in alphabetical order
9. Knowing how to use a picture dictionary
10. Using a glossary in a textbook
11. Learning some facts related to using a dictionary for children
12. Finding material and looking at pictures in an encyclopedia for younger children, for example, *Childcraft*
13. Looking at pictures and getting information through the teacher's reading from encyclopedias such as *Compton's Pictured Encyclopedia, The World Book Encyclopedia, Britannica Junior,* or *Our Wonderful World*
14. Getting information from atlases, yearbooks, and the *World Almanac*

4. Opportunity should be provided to make use of skills learned Closely related to the problem of readiness for learning a

12. Helping the pupils get meaning from illustrations in a dictionary by asking them questions about a picture or by having them explain how a given picture supplements the verbal explanation
13. Drawing the attention of pupils to aspects of an illustration that give an indication of the size of what is pictured
14. Helping boys and girls study the key to pronunciation used in their dictionaries
15. Asking the pupils to mark vowel sounds in a list of words of which they know the pronunciation, according to the key to pronunciation on which the markings in their dictionary are based
16. Providing practice in looking up the spelling of a word in the dictionary by helping the pupils decide on probable spellings of it and then looking for these in the dictionary
17. Providing practice in finding out through the dictionary the possible parts of speech of a word such as *effect* and using it in those ways in a sentence

Practice Exercises

The following are examples of exercises for developing skill in using the dictionary.

1. Directions: Look up in your dictionary the following list of words that are often mispronounced. On the line to the right of each write the respelling of the word with markings, including the accent, as given in the dictionary. Your teacher may give you an opportunity to pronounce some of the words to your classmates.

1. athletic _____
2. adult _____
3. handkerchief _____
4. little _____
5. often _____
6. library _____

2. Directions: To the right of each sentence write the spelling of the italicized (or underlined) word. If necessary, consult your dictionary to get the correct spelling.
1. I think that this trip was really *necess____ry.* _____
2. Did you *rec____ve* my message? _____
3. The boys and girls will leave in two *sep____rate* groups. _____

3. Directions: Some of the following compound words, which are divided into syllables, should be separated by a hyphen and others should not. Consult your dictionary before you write the words correctly on the lines left for the purpose. Study the spelling of the words so that you can write them if your teacher dictates them to you.

an y body _____
green house _____
out of date _____
sis ter in law _____
shell fish _____
steam ship _____
two edged _____
ex pres i dent _____

4. **Directions:** Here are some of the meanings found in a dictionary for the word *head.* On the line to the left of each sentence given below write the letter appearing before the meaning of the word *head* that the word has in each of the sentences: (a) The part of the body of man and most animals which contains the brain, eyes, ears, nose, and mouth; (b) mind, intelligence; (c) top part; (d) front end; (e) round, tight top part of a plant; (f) picture or sculpture of a head; (g) topic of title; (h) knob on top of a tool, etc.

_____ 1. Mother bought a head of lettuce.
_____ 2. Our teacher asked one of the boys to be at the head of the line.
_____ 3. Mr. Jones carved a granite head of the President.
_____ 4. The head of the hammer was securely fastened.
_____ 5. Jimmy has a good head for numbers.

Developing Skill in Using Reference Books Other Than the Dictionary

Skills needed in order to locate material in reference books other than the dictionary can be developed through activities such as the following:

1. Providing opportunity to use as many as possible of the following reference books: *Childcraft, Compton's Pictured Encyclopedia,* the *World Book Encyclopedia, Junior Britannica, Our Wonderful World,* the *Junior Book of Authors,* the *Index to Poetry,* the *World Almanac,* and a standard atlas

2. Providing the pupils with a list of topics on which they are to check those that are likely to be found in an encyclopedia

3. Having pupils answer a list of questions, the answers to which are found in one or more of the reference books listed in the first item above

4. Having pupils give information found on one or more of the maps contained in an atlas to which they have access

5. Asking pupils to tell in which volume of a set of encyclopedias information on a specified topic would be likely to be given. For this purpose the information on the labels on the back of the encyclopedias can be written on the board or duplicated on paper.

6. Explaining the use of the index volume of a set of encyclopedias and providing pupils with practice in using it
7. Giving pupils a list of questions to answer in one word or a few words after consulting an encyclopedia
8. Having pupils make a chart to indicate in what reference books they would try to locate information on specific problems
9. Providing pupils with an opportunity to report on any topic of interest to them on which they found information in a reference book and to state what reference book they consulted
10. Having a "quiz program" based on information found in reference books. It would be helpful, in some instances, to have the pupils indicate in which reference book the answer to each question was found.

Practice Exercises

Following are a few of the many types of practice exercises that can be used in order to develop skill with reference books.

1. Directions: Find the answers to these questions in the *World Almanac.*

Is the population of the village, town, or city in which you are living given in the *World Almanac?* If so, what was it according to the last edition of the *World Almanac?*
Where was Thomas Edison born? _____
What is the state flower of Minnesota? _____
What state leads in the production of cotton? _____
When was Florida admitted to the Union? _____
What is the state bird of Ohio? _____
In what building did Abraham Lincoln die? _____

2. Directions: Place an x on the line to the left of each of the following topics that you would expect to be found in an encyclopedia:
_____ 1. The population of your home town
_____ 2. An account of the Battle of Gettysburg
_____ 3. Early attempts at aviation
_____ 4. The spelling of the word *necessary*

3. Directions: Below the questions is a list of different kinds of books that are lettered from *(a)* through *(g)*. On the line to the right of each question, write the letter or letters given to the books in which you would expect to find an answer to the question:
What was the population of Delaware, Ohio, during the past year? ____

_____

What were the chief exports of France during the past year? _____

_____

How often should a person clean his teeth? _____
_____

What causes a dental cavity? _____
_____

What is the origin of the word *belfry*? _____
_____

What part of speech is the word *produce* when the accent is on the second syllable? _____
_____

Books
a. *Compton's Pictured Encyclopedia*
b. *The World Almanac*
c. *Junior Book of Authors*
d. *Reader's Guide to Periodical Literature*
e. A dictionary
f. An atlas
g. A hygiene book

Developing Skill in Locating Material in the Library

Some procedures effective in learning to locate material in the library are:

1. Taking the children on a trip to the library
2. Displaying and explaining to the children a chart giving the Dewey decimal system of classification if that method of classification is used in their library
3. Asking the pupils to write a subject card, an author card, and a title card as you give them the necessary bibliographical data on a book
4. Asking pupils to list facts given in a card catalog in addition to the author and the title of a book
5. Asking pupils to suggest subjects under which they may be able to find on a subject card references to the answer to a given question; for example, "What was travel like in the country in 1865?"
6. Having pupils put on a skit that illustrates "do's" and "don't's" of library behavior
7. Having a pupil act as librarian and explain to his audience the meaning and use of a call number
8. Explaining to the boys and girls the plan of cumulation followed in the *Reader's Guide to Periodical Literature* and having them find entries on articles included in various volumes
9. Asking pupils to explain every part of an entry found in the *Reader's Guide to Periodical Literature*
10. Helping pupils make a card catalog of the books in their own room

library. Guide cards should be included in the catalog and *see also* cards.

11. Having pupils gather from reference books information needed for work on a unit in science or social studies

12. Providing time for pupils to examine and read various magazines in the library and then to give reports on them

Practice Exercises

Following are suggested activities for developing skill in locating material in the library.

1. Explanation: After the teacher or one or two pupils have drawn a diagram of a card catalog on a chart, the pupils could be asked questions concerning it, such as these:

In which drawer would you look for a book by Louisa M. Alcott?
In which drawer would you look for the title of another book by the author of *The Story of Doctor Doolittle?*
What uses can you make of a card catalog besides finding out what books are in the library?

2. Directions: Find the answers to the following questions by consulting the card catalog in your library.
What is the call number of the book *Up a Road Slowly?* _____
What books written by the author of *The Singing Tree* are in your library? _____

_____

What is the title and call number of a book in your library on early pioneer life? _____

_____

What facts other than the title and author are given on the subject card for the book *Call It Courage?* _____

_____

3. The pupils could be given a diagram of the library they are using that shows the location of the various stacks and tables and racks where books or magazines are kept. The various positions should be numbered so that the pupils can refer to them by number. Make certain that pupils understand the diagram.

Directions: On the diagram showing the arrangement of your library, the bookshelves and tables are numbered. Answer the following question by writing the number of the bookshelf or table used in the diagram. If you do not know the answer to a question, study the arrangement of the library before you try to write an answer.

Where are the books for very young children kept? _____
Where are the books on biography kept? _____
On what table are some of the newest books for boys and girls placed?
Where are the books on American history placed? _____
Where are the encyclopedias for boys and girls kept? _____

For Further Study

Burns, Paul C., and Betty D. Roe, *Teaching Reading in Today's Elementary Schools*, 2d ed. (Skokie, Ill: Rand McNally, 1980), Ch. 6, "Reading/Study Skills."

Harris, Albert J., and Edward R. Sipay, eds., *Readings on Reading Instruction*, 2d ed. (New York: McKay, 1972), article no. 58, "The Development of Locational Skills" by Martha Dallmann.

Harris, Larry A., and Carl B. Smith, *Reading Instruction: Diagnostic Teaching in the Classroom*, 3d ed. (New York: Holt, Rinehart and Winston, 1980), Ch. 11, "Teaching Reading for Life—Content Reading."

Durkin, Dolores, *Teaching Them to Read*, 3d ed. (Boston: Allyn and Bacon, 1978), "Locating Information," pp. 531–541.

Hittleman, Daniel R., *Developmental Reading: A Psycholinguistic Approach* (Chicago, Ill: Rand McNally, 1978), "Strategies for Locating Information and Using Reference Materials," pp. 339–345.

Zintz, Miles V., *The Reading Process: The Teacher and the Learner*, 3d ed. (Dubuque, Iowa: Wm. C. Brown, 1980), Ch. 11, "Study Skills."

Questions and Comments for Thought and Discussion

1. What is your position on the following controversial statement? Be able to state your case.

   Dictionary skills are an inseparable part of the language arts program in general and the reading program specifically and need not, in fact, should not, as a rule, be taught in isolation.

2. Some persons have urged that we pay more attention to the concept of "dictionary readiness." They name as prerequisites such matters as readiness for locating words, readiness for deriving the meaning, readiness for determining pronunciation. What, in part, constitutes each of these facets of readiness?

3. When children learn how to use reference books certain problems almost inevitably arise. For example, there is the problem of children copying when gathering data in a reference work. Or there is the concern that children not use the encyclopedia until they know how to outline or write material in their own words. Imagine you are a sixth-grade teacher and you have to deal with one of these problems. How would you proceed?

4. In considering the role and function of the elementary-school library, certain questions in terminology arise. Should the library be called an instructional materials center, a learning resource center, an educa-

tional media center, or just a library? Be able to give reasons for your preference.

5. You may find it helpful to devise a series of practice exercises for use in teaching part of one or more locational skills. If so, you may wish either to model them after some exercises given in this chapter or to use your own ideas in deciding upon the general pattern of the exercises.

Reading in the Content Areas

Many teachers in the upper elementary school claim that a major reason for failure of boys and girls in the content areas is lack of skill in reading the material. Teachers of mathematics in the elementary school have long known that inability to read the "story problems" of arithmetic constitutes a real problem for many pupils. In science, in health, in literature—in whatever area a considerable amount of reading is expected of the pupils—a low degree of reading skill poses a serious handicap.

Obviously one reason for the problem some boys and girls encounter when reading in the content areas is their failure to acquire the skills essential to all reading. If a pupil has failed to develop skill in word recognition, in comprehension, in reading at appropriate rates, and in other essentials of reading of all types, he will be unable to read effectively in the content areas. However, some boys and girls who are efficient readers in their reading textbooks or who read many kinds of general books with ease have decided problems when reading in the content areas. The problem may be that they read all materials as they would read that given in reading textbooks or in books for recreational reading. Their difficulty may be that they cannot effectively meet those problems in word recognition, comprehension, and other aspects of reading that are somewhat peculiar to reading in the areas of history, geography, science, or mathematics. Furthermore, often little motivation is required to interest boys and girls in the story-type material of the basal readers, while incentive for reading the study-type material in the content areas may frequently need to be provided.

Special Problems in Reading in the Content Areas

The problems of reading in the content areas differ from other reading not so much in type as in their frequency and cruciality. Important among the problems in reading in the content areas are those in vocabulary, in comprehension, in reading at appropriate rates, and in locating information and utilizing it. Yet another one is that of stimulating the interest of boys and girls in independent reading in the content areas.

As we note how attention to problems of reading in the content areas can affect favorably the learning in those areas, we must also bear in mind that effective reading in the content areas can improve reading ability in general. The advantage of paying attention to special problems in the content areas, thus, can have a two-way benefit, helping in teaching the content subjects and helping in the improvement of reading.

Problems in Vocabulary

Often the problem in the content areas for a child who reads up to the norm for his grade in a reading textbook is one of vocabulary. In the social studies the pupil encounters such new words as *isthmus, latitude, legislature, emancipation, adaptation, culture.* In elementary-school science many words occur of which the child previously may have had no knowledge, such as *planetarium, solar, convection.* In books about music and art words such as *percussion, bas relief, perspective* may give difficulty. Words unfamiliar to the reader will be found in any reading material likely to help the child increase in knowledge and power with words. In fact, textbooks in reading beyond the beginning stages of reading instruction are designed to present some words that are new to the child. The special point of difficulty in vocabulary in reading in the content areas is that the child is often confronted with a large proportion of words unknown to him, a proportion larger than in the basal readers.

Frequently, too, in the content areas a word may have a different meaning from the one that a child may have been accustomed to associate with it. Neither the word *cape* as found in *Cape Cod* nor the word *gulf* in *Gulf of Mexico* has the meaning that many children may previously have associated with it. Also, the *draft* of the Constitution and the *cradle* of civilization can be confusing to the child who has given other interpretations to those words. Homonyms also are often a source of trouble. The *steppes* of some near-polar regions are not likely the steps with which the pupil has had associations.

Another vocabulary problem lies in the number and difficulty of the concepts presented. Expressions such as *no taxation without representation* or the *consent of the governed* need to be made meaningful to many pupils before they can comprehend the material they read in the social studies. The teacher, however, cannot expect the children to comprehend the full meaning of many of the concepts all at once. *Liberty* can acquire added meaning for the child as he reads about and discusses from year to year more and more situations in which liberty or lack of it is evident. It will mean more and more to him as again and again, with increasing insight, he notes the beneficial effects of environments characterized by a spirit of liberty and the deleterious results of regimentation. The boys and girls will grow in ability to note the difference between liberty and license. They will, hopefully, in time come to realize that lib-

erty should be sought not only for self but also for others.

Problems in Comprehension

There are problems of understanding besides those pertaining to vocabulary—including concept building—that confront many pupils when reading in the content areas and that, therefore, necessitate careful reading. To be sure, not all reading in the content areas should be of the study type. However, much of the material in these areas requires more meticulous reading than that which the pupils need in basal reading textbooks or books of fiction. This point is especially true of many of the problems presented in mathematics. Following directions for performing an experiment in science also requires attention to detail that is often unessential—in fact, even undesirable—for reading many other types of materials. In the social studies, where material often shows a bias, critical evaluation is frequently needed. Reading with the intent to remember for a long time or possibly always is also often demanded of the reader who wishes to accomplish worthwhile objectives that he may set for himself when reading in the content areas. The many references to names and places may put a tax on memory. Referrals to maps and pictures, helpful though they may be, can interfere with the sequential reading by the person unaccustomed to reading material in which many references of that type are made. Charts, graphs, maps, and diagrams often need to be studied in order to make the text meaningful.

The organization of the material in the social studies is at times more complex than that to which the pupil is accustomed in much of his other reading. In the basal reader and the story book, chronological order usually has been the simple determinant of the organization. In the social studies cause-effect relationships, inverted sequence of time, and progression from incidents to generalizations or from generalizations to incidents many times form the basis of the organization. Center heads, sideheadings, and other organizational clues—helpful when their use is understood—can be of little or no assistance or possibly even a stumbling block for the reader not skilled in their use.

For the reasons stated in the preceding paragraphs, and others, the pupil may have problems in comprehension as he reads in the content areas unless he is given help in meeting difficulties as they arise.

Friedman and Rowls[1] point out yet another source of difficulty for many students in reading a social studies textbook. These books are written in an expository style rather than in the narrative, which students have been accustomed to read. Friedman and Rowls[2] state:

> Expository materials, like social studies textbooks, contain a great deal of information, in comparison to more narrative materials, and require close reading and different reading strategies.

Remembering What Is Read

The expectation that pupils should remember a good deal of what they read in the content areas, especially in textbooks, forms one of the chief problems in reading in those fields. When reading in reading textbooks, the child usually does not need to retain for a long time what he reads. When reading in the content areas, however, it is often important for him to remember many points. Some should be remembered for a short time, but others for

a long time. Frequently, unless a pupil can keep in mind important points about what he reads on one day, his understanding of what he reads on a later day may lack in meaningfulness for him.

In the social studies names of persons, places, and events, which in many textbooks in that area occur in great numbers, are often a special cause of difficulty. The problem may be two-fold. The reader may be unable to determine what to try to remember and/or he may not know how to proceed to fix in his memory points he recognizes as being of importance. Consequently guidance in discerning that which is worth remembering is often essential, as well as help in remembering such points.

In science, too, it is often imperative that the boys and girls be given help in determining what points should be retained. The pupil who one day reads and understands what *convection* is but does not remember what he learned may be at a loss when at a subsequent time reference is made to it, possibly in the same textbook, with the assumption by the author that the pupil remembers what is meant by the term. His problem in remembering may be caused by the fact that he never really understood what he read. Or it may be that he tries to remember every fact without relation to the generalization that can at times be drawn from facts. Lack of purpose in reading, other than possibly to answer factual questions, may be the cause of much undesirable forgetting of what is read. Another cause of inability to remember what is read may be failure to do what is sometimes referred to as *associational reading.* Many boys and girls seem to make relatively few, if any, associations with past experiences, either firsthand or vicarious, as they read in the content areas.

In mathematics both immediate and long-time recall is often essential. Whenever

[1]Myles I. Friedman and Michael D. Rowls, *Teaching Reading and Thinking Skills* (New York: Longman, 1980), pp. 462–63.

[2]Ibid., p. 463.

there is a problem to be solved, the pupil must remember the conditions stated until he has solved it. Some children do not do so; they forget what they have read even before they have finished the sentence or group of sentences that give the terms of the problem. Long-time recall in solving practice problems in mathematics is often not necessary or desirable. As a rule, the reader does not need to remember the information presented in a problem after he has correctly solved it, although the method of solution may warrant remembering. However, there are many points learned in mathematics that should be remembered permanently and should be remembered with exactitude. The child who has noted that twelve inches equal one foot needs to learn that fact so that he remembers it all his life and so that he remembers exactly how many inches equal one foot.

Organizing What Is Read

Another problem that confronts many pupils when reading in the content areas is understanding the organization of a book and organizing in their own minds material they have read. Frequently in both the social studies and science the organization followed by the author is indicated through center headings, sideheadings, and divisions subordinate to the second order of classification. (Sometimes the major divisions of the material are indicated by center headings, with sideheadings as the first order of division of the center headings; at other times the major divisions of the topic are shown by sideheadings, with center headings as the first subdivision of sideheadings.) Since such organizational clues are there to help the reader, failure to make adequate use of them can greatly increase the difficulty of reading the material with comprehension.

The ability to organize what is read by means of summarizing it is often needed in reading in the content areas—more often than in reading textbooks, in which boys and girls often have had most of their reading instruction. One way of summarizing information is through making an outline. Outlining is usually not needed when reading books of fiction or basal readers. To be able to outline, however, can be a decided aid when reading for certain purposes in the content areas.

Understanding Cause-Effect Relationships

Reading materials in the social studies and in science abound in important references to cause-effect relations. For example, in history the understanding of the relation between slavery and secession and the Civil War may be essential to intelligent reading of material dealing with this subject. In geography the causes of erosion may constitute the theme of a selection. Understanding in science may be based on the effect of a law of motion in a situation described. Failure to recognize the relation may interfere with comprehension and later with recall.

Even though it may be clearly stated that one event caused a second one, the pupil may not understand how the one caused the other. At times, too, the reader may erroneously attribute such a relation to two events that do not have a causal relation but are both the cause or the result of a third event. Failure to comprehend a cause-effect relation or to assume one when there is none may seriously interfere with comprehending what is read in the content areas.

Making Generalizations

There is considerable danger in the area of the social studies, when reading or when observing situations firsthand, of coming to conclusions without adequate evidence. This difficulty the pupils should recognize so that if they see, for example, one or two or three or even a score of persons of a particular age group acting improperly, they will not generalize that that is the way persons of that age act. Similarly, as they read about the causes of a war, they should not make an overgeneralization on the data presented by concluding that quarrels or disputes among nations should be settled through war.

There are several other dangers in arriving at generalizations, which boys and girls should be helped to avoid, namely: (a) undergeneralization on data given; (b) failure to distinguish between generalizations and data given to support them, with a resultant possible confusion of a detail with a generalization and/or a generalization with a detail; (c) inability to detect when a generalization made in a book is too broad for the data presented; (d) inability to apply generalizations to situations with which the pupil may be confronted at a future time.

Judging the Authenticity of Statements

Especially in the social studies is there much need to consider whether or not statements are authentic. A pupil needs to note, for example, when certain information was published. A statistic on the population of New York City in a book published in 1970 should indicate to the pupil that to learn how many people are presently living in New York City, he needs more recent information. When controversial issues are discussed, the reader needs to be able to take into consideration who made the claims in order to detect on the part of the writer possible prejudice, lack of information, or a reputation for accuracy or inaccuracy. When reading some types of social studies materials, he needs to be able to judge whether a fact or an opinion is being expressed. For reading historical fiction the ability to determine which points are historical and which are embellishments on actual happenings is needed.

In science, too, it is important to have or to develop skill in judging the authenticity of what is read. Who makes the claim as to the achievements of the Americans or of the Russians in space ventures may make a difference in what is recorded. Whether the person writing an article is likely to have sufficient information to speak with the authority he assumes is another point that needs to be considered in reading science materials. Surely, with the vast explosion of scientific knowledge during recent decades, the date on which a report was written is of great importance in some areas of science. However, along with developing skill in judging statements through examination of the date when they were made, the pupil needs also to be aware of the fact that some information in the area of science recorded many decades ago is as authentic now as then. An illustration is the statement that many animals have protective coloring. Another example is the fact that Benjamin Franklin invented the Franklin stove.

Interpreting Graphs, Tables, Charts, and Maps

Books on both the social studies and science for older boys and girls contain many graphs, tables, charts, and maps. Frequently these are essential to full understanding of the text. They are likely to be especially valuable for the reader when the writer draws attention to certain aspects of the illustrations. For example, in connection with a map showing the Polar route, the reader may be asked to compare the distance between two cities when the Polar route is followed by a plane, with the distance between the two cities if a plane followed a parallel of latitude. It is not suggested, however, that the reader study in detail all illustrative material presented, for its value will depend in part on the purpose of the reader. If he is, for example, reading a selection to answer a certain question, he will not need to refer to a table illustrating some other point.

Many boys and girls are not aware of the value of illustrative materials and consequently do not attempt to interpret them. Others, though recognizing their worth, lack skill in interpreting them and consequently do not take time to "read" them. Still others make errors when trying to understand them. Since very little "reading" of this type is required in basal readers and in books of fiction, the teacher should recognize the likelihood of need for special instruction as pupils read in the content areas. With the increasing production of graphical and tabular materials, skill in interpreting them has become more important than ever before.

Problems in Reading at Appropriate Rates

Reading of material in the content areas at inappropriate rates may be due to lack of skill in comprehending what is read. Or it may result from factors such as lack of skill in word recognition, vocalization, pointing to words, overemphasis on oral reading, lack of interest and purpose, or insufficient practice in reading at different rates. A special problem pertaining to the rate of reading in the content areas is that some pupils who have done most of their reading in material easy to comprehend and for purposes that could well be achieved through rapid reading try to read more difficult material

for study purposes at the same rate at which they had previously been reading. The premium that some teachers often erroneously place on speed of reading may cause the better readers to have a handicap when studying in the content areas. The problem in reading at appropriate rates in the content areas is essentially that of learning to read as rapidly as possible without tension or undue strain materials of all types in the content areas, in harmony with the difficulty of the material and the purpose of the reader.

It is wrong to assume that all reading in the content areas is study-type material. If that is the only kind of reading the pupil does, his range is too limited. For some of the materials in the content areas—such as reports in newspapers or magazines—the most desirable rate to accomplish the purpose of the reader might be skimming. At times, rapid reading but not skimming or scanning might be the rate at which the reader's purpose is best attained as, for example, when he is reading an interesting anecdote about Abraham Lincoln. Reading at a moderate rate might be desirable when the pupil is reading fairly easy material in his textbook in order to answer questions he has been given. At times, however, to find answers to questions, especially when the material is rather difficult, the slowness of careful study might be the most suitable rate. Thus, the need for flexibility of rate should be recognized. Furthermore, a pupil may need to be warned against dawdling habits when reading at any of the rates indicated. It is possible to dawdle when skimming, that is, not skim as rapidly as one could for the purpose in mind. It is possible to dawdle when doing careful study-type reading. At each of the levels of reading rates the pupil should be encouraged to read as rapidly as he can commensurate with the fulfillment of his purpose in reading.

Problems in Locating Information and in Using It

When the single textbook was the vogue in social studies classes and in science classes, the need for locating information when studying was not nearly as great as it is now when a variety of reading materials is utilized in those areas. To be sure, even when only one textbook is used, pupils can often benefit from guidance in using the table of contents, the index, the appendix, and other special features of the textbook. However, in classrooms in which one textbook does not constitute the curriculum source of a content subject, it is imperative that boys and girls know how to locate information from various sources and how to make use of it. The teacher who merely tells a pupil, when making an assignment for outside reading, that he should look up information on a given topic is not giving the help that many children need. For greatest effectiveness there is need of guidance in locating information and utilizing it along all the lines indicated in Chapters 9A and 9B. These skills include, among others: (a) developing the basic skills of finding words arranged in alphabetical order, deciding on key words, and discovering what types of information are given in various kinds of books; (b) interpreting punctuation marks, diacritical markings, abbreviations, and symbols; (c) selecting points that have bearing on a given problem; (d) utilizing information gained; (e) developing skill in using nonreference books; (f) developing skill in using the dictionary; (g) developing skill in using reference books other than the dictionary; and (h) locating materials in a library.

As in the case of guidance in the use of other special skills needed for reading intelligently in the content areas, the content subjects afford excellent opportunity for teaching skill in locating information. They serve three purposes. They present situations that require knowledge of how to locate information, thereby furnishing an incentive for learning needed skills. They provide practice needed for perfecting a skill that is being learned. They help the child obtain information in the content areas.

Interesting Pupils in Independent Reading in the Content Areas

The reader is referred to chapters 11A and 11B for suggestions on how to interest boys and girls in reading material in history, geography, science, and other content areas. Others are given below.

Unfortunately often in the past, pupils' independent reading has been largely confined to books of fiction. With the excellent array of books for children in the areas of the social studies, science, art, and other content areas, it is, indeed, unfortunate if the pupils in an elementary school do not read them. Books on history, minority cultures, biography, far-away lands and people, health, music and art can give boys and girls insight into themselves and the world around them. It is regrettable if a child chooses to read none or only a few of the books of this type.

A major problem in relation to independent reading in the content areas is providing boys and girls with suitable books. Another is helping boys and girls develop skill in evaluating the authenticity of the material they are reading. Still another is helping pupils to differentiate between fact and fiction—between what is historical background, for example, and that which is an embellishment of the facts of history.

Guidelines for the Teacher

In the preceding chapters of Part II guidelines are given for meeting the problems related to the skills of reading as they apply to reading in general. The guidelines given below are especially applicable for fostering growth in reading in the content areas.

1. Interesting the student in learning in the content areas is a key to effective teaching Unless the teacher secures the interest of the class in learning, regardless of what sound teaching procedures he may otherwise use, little, if any, learning will take place.

2. Many reading skills are appropriately taught in the content subjects The teacher should help boys and girls develop skills in the meaningful setting provided. This principle applies not only to the so-called study skills, such as locating information, but also to other reading skills, among them skill in recognizing words, understanding what is read, and reading at appropriate rates.

3. The material to be read should be on the reader's level Too frequently we expect children to read material which is much too difficult for their level of reading ability. To determine the approximate reading level of written material, readability formulas can be used. Among the available readability formulas are the following: (a) The Spache Readability Formula for Primary-Grade Material[3] (b) The Dale-Chall For-

mula for Predicting Readability,[4] (c) SMOG Grading,[5] (d) Fry Readability Graph.[6]

4. Every teacher of the content subjects should consider himself a teacher of reading In departmentalized set-ups teachers of content subjects often fear that the time they might spend on helping pupils to read better in their field is time lost to them for teaching the subject matter of their area. Their fears in many instances are groundless. Effective teaching of reading skills important to a content subject should improve the pupils' comprehension of the subject matter.

5. The teacher of the content subjects, whether or not he is the homeroom teacher who has the pupils for all subjects, should have clearly in mind reading objectives for his area of learning These goals should include primarily those skills particularly important for reading in the area. For example, one objective might deal with guiding the child in learning the specialized vocabulary that he encounters in his subject.

6. The program for guiding boys and girls to read more effectively in all of the content areas should include various types of approaches Among these approaches are: (a) presentation lessons in which the pupil is helped to understand how he can improve in some skill needed

---

[3]George Spache, "A New Readability Formula for Primary-Grade Reading Material," *Elementary School Journal*, vol. 54 (1953), pp. 410–413.

[4]Edgar Dale and Jeanne Chall, "A Formula for Predicting Readability," *Elementary Research Bulletin*, vol. 27 (January 21, 1948), pp. 11–20,28.

[5]G. Harry McLaughlin, "SMOG Grading—A New Readability Formula," *Journal of Reading* (May 1969), pp. 639–646.

[6]Edward Fry, "A Readability Formula That Saves Time," *Journal of Reading*, vol. 11 (April 1968), pp. 513–516; 575–578.

for effectiveness in reading in a given area; (b) practice exercises in which special help is provided in the maintenance of a needed skill; and (c) incidental means of strengthening the skills needed which could be supplied by activities in the on-going school program.

7. The readiness principle applies with special force to reading in the content subjects Before a pupil is asked to read a chapter or a part of a chapter in a textbook, he should be mentally prepared for the task. The words he encounters on the printed page may be abstract symbols to him unless he can bring a body of experience to the reading. Moreover, often he should have had prior experience with words that symbolize the images and concepts he is to learn.

8. The teaching-learning procedure should be adapted to individual differences In a nonhomogeneously grouped classroom, as a rule, the textbook in a content subject, if suitable for most of the students, is too difficult for others. To help toward the solution or minimization of this problem one or more suggestions such as these might be followed: (a) Give more help, before the pupils read a selection in the textbook, to those who need it. (b) Substitute easier material from other sources for those parts in the textbook read by the "average student."

9. Pupils should learn to approach a reading assignment in the content areas with clearly conceived purposes They should know what they are looking for, and why. Such purposes may arise out of previous class discussions, demonstrations, or experiments.

10. A textbook in the content areas should not be followed slavishly It is not necessary that it be studied "from cover to cover." The teacher should choose only those parts of the book that he believes best contribute to the accomplishment of his objectives. At times, too, the teacher may decide that certain objectives can best be achieved through use of visual aids, reading from other books, dramatic activity, special reports, teacher explanation, and the like.

11. Visual aids should be used to help boys and girls achieve the objectives in a content area Displays can add greatly to the understanding of and interest in many topics. Pictures, slides, motion pictures, models, maps, supplementary books, realia—these and others are useful in science and in the social studies as well as other content areas.

12. Opportunity for pupil evaluation of growth in needed reading skills should be provided For evaluation to be most beneficial it is important that the pupils have goals to be achieved in mind.

13. An effective program of reading in the content subjects should stimulate boys and girls so that they will want to read in those areas during leisure time as part of their independent reading Unless the boys and girls are stimulated to read such materials outside of school and in later years, the program will not have been entirely successful.

10 B

Stimulating Growth in Reading in the Content Areas

In the last part of the preceding chapter are listed guidelines for stimulating growth in reading in the content areas. In this chapter specific suggestions are given indicating methods and procedures that can be used in harmony with these guidelines.

Suggestions for Meeting Problems of Reading in the Content Areas

In this section are suggested ways in which the teacher can help boys and girls meet problems they encounter in reading in the content areas—problems in vocabulary, in comprehension, in reading at appropriate rates, and in location of information and in its utilization.

Problems in Vocabulary

It is hoped that suggestions such as the following will stimulate the teacher to think of additional ones that may be especially adapted to the needs of at least some of the boys and girls in his class.

1. **Explaining the meaning of a word before reading a selection containing that word** Before the pupils begin reading a selection, the teacher might write on the chalkboard, frequently in context, the words with which he thinks his pupils will be unfamiliar. For example, he might have on the chalkboard the words *taxation without representation,* using the expression within the context of a sentence. The sentence might be, "The colonists were opposed to *taxation without representation,*" with the phrase to be studied underlined. He might then say to a fifth-grade class that he imagines everybody knows what taxes are and that consequently they will have no trouble with the word *taxation* (at which he points in the sentence on the chalkboard). He might then ask the class to read the sentence silently to see if anyone can figure out what the word *representation* means in the sentence. If no one can give an adequate explanation, he might explain the word or might tell the boys and girls that as they read a certain part of the social studies work for that day he thinks they may be able to find out what is meant by the expression *taxation without representation.* After the class has read silently the selection in which the term occurs, discussion should follow. Pupils might make up meaningful sentences of their own from which it is evident that they know the meaning of the term.

2. **Arriving at the meaning through the context of a paragraph** Sometimes the teacher may wish to draw the pupils' attention to a word that occurs in a selection that they will read even though he may decide

not to help them with its meaning. For example, when they are about to read a paragraph explaining how sometimes, instead of buying and selling goods, people engage in bartering, the teacher may say something to this effect as he points at the word *barter* on the chalkboard: "In the next paragraph this word *barter* is used. I think you may be able to explain what the word means after you have read the paragraph." Then, after the boys and girls have read the paragraph, it would be desirable to have one or more pupils state what they think *barter* means.

3. Making word cards   Instead of a word chart the pupils might make picture word cards on each of which is written a word and an illustration of it. For practice purposes, on one side of the card might be written the name of the word with a picture, while on the other the word only. If a pupil looks at the latter side first, he may be able to test himself by looking at the other side of the card to find out whether his response was correct.

4. Making a picture book   Especially in the lower grades picture books made by the class illustrating various terms learned in the social studies, science, or mathematics can serve a helpful purpose. A notebook may deal only with the words learned in one unit of study or it may include any terms used frequently in the social studies, science, or mathematics during the course of the school year. Words such as *teacher, school, boys, girls, playground, principal, nurse* could be included in connection with a unit in the lower grades on the school. With older boys and girls words such as *valley, plateau, colonization, jet propulsion, pollination, area, circumference* can be illustrated, explained, and used in sentences to clarify the meaning. If a loose-leaf notebook is used, the words can be arranged alphabetically.

5. Clarifying words through construction activities   Pupils like to show ingenuity in making things that will clarify to them and others the meaning of words. To show what the word *portage* means, a pupil might make a reproduction of one of papier mâché. Similarly objects explaining words such as this could be made: *portcullis, plateau, isthmus, irrigation, summit, steppes.* Sometimes before a word is encountered in reading, one of the pupils could make the illustrative material and then show it to the class immediately before they come across the word in their reading. At other times, after a series of new terms have been studied, the class might decide to have various members make reproductions that will help them visualize and remember some terms. An interesting and instructive exhibit can be made in this manner.

6. Doing practice exercises At times practice exercises in which pupils are given the opportunity to concentrate on various phases of vocabulary building are valuable for some boys and girls. Examples follow.

+ The pupils may be given these directions: "On the lines below each sentence copy the explanation in your dictionary that best fits the italicized word in the sentence." Illustrative sentences of the type that might be used are given below, with space indicated for the pupil responses.

The Panama Canal has six pairs of *locks*, three near the Atlantic side and three near the Pacific side.

_____

_____

After much argument, the two parties reached a *settlement*.

_____

_____

+ The directions for this exercise might be worded thus: "After studying each of the paragraphs below, explain, on the space allowed, what you think the underlined word means. Then look it up in the dictionary. If you can then improve upon your explanation, do so. If your first explanation was correct, write nothing on the last two lines below the paragraph."

A *compromise* was reached. It was agreed that Missouri should enter as a slave state, but that all states that might in the future be carved out of the rest of the Louisiana Territory north and west of the southern boundary line of Missouri should enter the Union as free states.

Explanation: _____

_____

Corrected explanation: _____

_____

7. Solving and making crossword puzzles Pupils' interest in crossword puzzles can be capitalized upon in the intermediate and upper grades. The puzzles might be teacher-made, on words or concepts or other information in relation to a topic being studied. Students, too, may enjoy making up crossword puzzles for their classmates to solve. Points such as these might be included in a puzzle for a unit on colonization:

(1) Name of the first permanent colony in America
(2) An agreement between two groups of people.
(3) Name given to the early settlers of Plymouth.

8. Learning through a variety of audio-visual aids These are a few of the ways in which boys and girls can improve their understanding of words and concepts used in the content areas: (a) seeing films and slides; (b) going on field trips; (c) listening to a speaker; (d) interviewing people.

Problems in Comprehension

A few recommended procedures are listed below that may help boys and girls increase in power to read with comprehension in content areas. Suggestions are given relative to: *(a)* remembering what is read; *(b)* organizing what is read; *(c)* understanding cause-effect relationships; *(d)* making generalizations; *(e)* judging the authenticity of statements; and *(f)* interpreting graphs, tables, charts, and maps.

Remembering What is Read

One reason why boys and girls have difficulty in remembering important points when reading in the content areas is that they fail to see the relationship of the details to one another and to main points. Furthermore, they are often unable to decide which details are important to remember for a given purpose. Following are a few suggestions for the teacher that may help some boys and girls toward overcoming these two difficulties and some others in connection with remembering what is read.

1. Have the pupils list details stated in a paragraph that support the main idea of a paragraph.
2. Provide practice exercises to help the pupils in remembering what is read to them. Below are given the directions, with an accompanying paragraph, of one type that might be useful.

   Directions: The main idea of this paragraph is keeping our lunchroom a pleasant place. Some of these sentences are on that topic. Others are not. Put a plus sign (+) on the line to the left of each sentence that tells about keeping the lunchroom a pleasant place. Put a zero (0) on the line preceding each sentence that does not keep to the main idea of the paragraph.

   Paragraph: _____ We are trying hard to keep our lunchroom a pleasant place. _____ We have decided to keep it quiet enough so that we can all enjoy eating in a peaceful place. _____ Last year Jim and Herb had a fight in the lunchroom. _____ We will keep our tables and chairs orderly. _____ We will put up some pictures showing the foods we should eat. _____ My mother serves good meals. _____ We will try to talk only about happy and pleasant subjects. _____ We will wait patiently for our turn in the lunchroom line.

3. Assist the pupils in determining which details are important to illustrate in a mural on a theme such as the history of transportation or the story of rubber.

4. Ask the pupils to select the details that throw light on how a character should act in a skit or play the class is planning to give on a subject such as the first Thanksgiving in Plymouth or on the topic "Man Walks on the Moon."

5. After the pupils have read a problem in mathematics silently, have them answer questions on information given, without recourse to the problem, such as: (a) Was the house sold at a gain or a loss? (b) What are we to find in this problem?

6. For a social studies class, make a chart listing all the people important enough for the pupils to remember. Have the class decide on an important sentence about each, one that summarizes the work of the person. Then, from time to time, have pupils give the important sentence to be remembered about each person. So that the boys and girls can review the statements by themselves, they might be given a duplicated list of the sentences decided on or they might copy the sentences into a notebook. Illustrations of possible sentences to remember are:

> De Soto discovered the Mississippi River.
> George Washington was the first president of the United States.

Instead of important people, the chart might be made on important dates or on important events. summarizing sentences such as these might be decided on for the chart on dates:

> In 1607 the first permanent English settlement in America was made in Jamestown, Virginia.
> In 1789 Washington became president.

Organizing What Is Read

In order to develop skill in organizing what is read in a content subject, the pupils might perform some of the following activities:

1. Check the correspondence between: (a) the center headings and the sideheadings of a given selection in a social studies or science book and (b) the parts of an outline the teacher has made.

2. Use the center headings and the sideheadings of books in the social studies or sciences, for practice in predicting what might be included under each heading, and later, after having read the selection, for summarizing what is actually found under each.

3. Make an outline for a report to be given on data collected from more than one source.

4. Make an outline of a selection using the center headings and the sideheadings of a well-organized selection as determiners of the outline.

5. Make a chart summarizing the main points learned on a field trip or in the study of a unit.

6. Group the questions the boys and girls have set for study of a unit of work. For example, the teacher could list on the chalkboard whatever questions they would like answered, in whatever order the pupils name

them in a study of the problem, "In what ways is Mexico a land of contrasts?" Next the teacher could explain that it may be easier to find answers to the questions if the class organizes them around main topics. Then the pupils can decide on the grouping, under the guidance of the teacher.

7. Decide upon scenes for a play that the class might be planning to give.
8. Write headlines for the front page of an imaginary newspaper written during the period of time being studied. Headlines such as these might be written: "Two Oceans United" (the opening of the Panama Canal); "Indian Woman Aids Explorers" (Sacajawea); "Salem Freed of Witches" (The Salem Witch Hunt).

Understanding Cause-Effect Relationships

To help the boys and girls gain in proficiency in understanding cause-effect relationships, as they come across them in their reading in the content areas, they might engage in activities such as the following:

1. Explaining how a given event caused another
2. Stating what they think might have happened had a given event not occurred in the manner that it did
3. Making a list of cause-effect relations stated in material assigned
4. Matching a cause with its effect as given in a two-column exercise, in which in column A are given the causes the effects of which are listed in a different order in column B. For example, one item in column A might be *secession*, to be matched with *Civil War* in column B

Making Generalizations

The teacher might help the pupils acquire skill in making generalizations when reading in the content areas by:

1. Having the pupils test stated generalizations in terms of the details given to support them
2. Asking the pupils to select among a list of details the one that does not contribute to the generalization reached
3. Having the pupils write a generalization that can be made from a list of facts presented
4. Giving pupils an exercise such as the following:

Directions.   Decide which of the following sentences contain generalizations about Benjamin Franklin and which contain facts that might help support a generalization. If a sentence contains a generalization, write the letter G (for *generalization*) on the blank to the left of it; if it contains a detail that might support a generalization, write the letter D (for *detail*) on the blank.

_____ He invented the Franklin stove.

_____ He was ambassador to France.

_____ He helped draft the Constitution.

_____ He did much to help his fellow men.

_____ He helped frame the Declaration of Independence.

5. Asking the pupils to find details that support a given generalization
6. Having pupils compile a list of generalizations of questionable validity in a given content area that they have heard. The pupils could be asked to give reasons for their questioning of each generalization.
7. Stating a generalization that can be deducted from given facts which can serve as details to support an unnamed generalization. For example, sentences such as these about life in Sparta could be given:
   + In Sparta every new-born baby was inspected by an official of the government who decided whether or not the child was well enough to be allowed to live.
   + As young boys the Spartans were taken from their parents and trained by the government.
   + The boys early received military training.
   + Spartan girls were required by the government to have rigorous training.
   + Spartan men had to serve in the army from the time they were 20 till they were 60.
   + Men between the ages of 20 and 60 had to eat and sleep in public barracks.

Judging the Authenticity of Statements

Through suggestions such as some of those in the preceding list under "Making Generalizations," the teacher can also help boys and girls judge the authenticity of some types of statements. Following are additional ways in which he can do so:

1. Having the pupils compare two somewhat contradictory reports in newspapers on a current event, as they note points of contradiction and as they try to explain them
2. Asking the pupils to read a report on a political issue that is controversial and have them decide what sentences would probably be deleted or changed if a person on the other side of the controversy were to report on the issue
3. Reading the qualifications of two people writing on the schools of Russia. The background of one, as described, should be such that it would be highly probable that he could write with authority on the subject, while the background of the other would be such that his report would not bear the weight of that by the other writer.
4. Rewriting an article about American or Russian successes in the space race appearing in an American paper so as to express the point of view that might be taken in a Russian newspaper
5. Deciding whether an account is a presentation of facts. After the pupils have read a selection dealing with the social studies, they can decide

whether the account is a presentation of facts. If it is not factual in entirety, the boys and girls can point out parts that are not factual or based only in part on facts. They can also be asked to give reasons for arriving at their conclusions.

6. Determining whether the writer of statements presented was in sympathy with the situation or person(s) he describes. If the pupils think a quotation shows that the writer was sympathetic toward the situation or person(s), the teacher might ask them to rewrite the passage as a person might write it who has the opposite point of view. For example, in one account a person may be referred to as *spy* and in another as *patriot*.

Interpreting Graphs, Tables, Charts, and Maps

The following types of activities may prove helpful in teaching boys and girls to read graphs, tables, charts, and maps with greater understanding:

1. Making a map of the community
2. Studying a map and map legend and then answering questions based on them
3. Showing information of various types—for example, surface features, population centers, political divisions—on maps that have been duplicated
4. Making, in answer to a question, a list of important points that can be gained for a stated purpose from a given map, table, graph, or chart
5. Studying an exhibit placed on the bulletin board of various types of graphs—including line graphs, bar graphs, circular graphs, and pictorial graphs—and answering questions also posted on the bulletin board of significance in the content areas that can be answered through a study of the illustrative material
6. Using charts, graphs, tables, and maps as the boys and girls give special reports, if through use of them they can add to the clarity of the presentation
7. Having a quiz program in which questions are asked about a content area that can be answered through examination of graphic or tabular aids
8. Making charts that clarify some important learning the class has acquired while studying a topic in a content area—such as, for example: (a) the proportion of persons on earth belonging to each of the races, (b) the territorial expansion of the United States, (c) the work of parents of the boys and girls in the class, (d) the increase or decrease in the cost of living

Problems in Reading at Appropriate Rates

The following list of activities indicates how pupils can get practice in reading at appropriate rates in the content areas. (See Chapter 7B, "Developing Comprehension," p. 198, for some ideas that are also applicable to reading in the content areas.)

Developing Skill in Rapid Reading

Some of the ways in which boys and girls can get helpful practice in skimming or other rapid reading are:

1. Glancing at a list of books dealing with science or with social studies, to determine which ones they would like to read
2. Skimming an article in an encyclopedia to note whether it contains information that they could use for a report
3. Skimming a page of a book to find out whether or not it contains information about a given person

Developing Skill in Reading When a Moderately Fast Rate Is Required

The following are activities in which boys and girls might engage in order to get practice in reading when a moderately fast rate is the optimum:

1. Reading a selection in a social studies textbook in order to find an answer to a question, which can be found rather easily in that selection
2. Reading in a book that is quite easy to read, in order to tell the class a few points of interest

Developing Skill in Reading When a Slow Rate Is Required

Opportunity to help pupils read efficiently when a rather slow rate is required may be provided in situations such as the following:

1. Studying directions for a construction activity related to the social studies or science
2. Studying the history of a period or of a country in order to obtain background information for making a mural on the topic

Problems in Locating Information and in Using It

Many of the suggestions given in the next paragraph and in the two sections following may be of value in helping the pupil meet problems locating and using information in the content areas. (See also Chapter 9A, "Locating Information and Using It," p. 244, and Chapter 9B, "Developing Skill in Locating Information and in Using It," p. 259.)

In unit work carried on in the social studies or science many situations arise in which the need for locational skills becomes evident and in which practice in improving these skills can be given. As the possibilities for the development of locational skills in connection with a unit are considered, it is important for the teacher to bear in mind that only those activities dealing with locational skills should be performed in connection with the unit work that really help toward the accomplishment of the objectives set for that work. If more work on any of the skills is needed than is provided by activities that help in the attainment of the objectives for the unit study, this practice should usually be given at other times through exercises and lessons specifically designed for the development of these skills. Otherwise it is probable that the work on the problem of study will lack the unity which the very name *unit* implies.

Developing Locational Skills in a Unit on Community Workers

Even in a unit of work planned for the primary grades, many locational skills can be developed as problems that arise in connection with the unit are being solved. The following list suggests some ways in which a unit on community workers can be instrumental in developing skill in locating information and using it.

1. The pupils could look for books on the various community workers they are studying.
2. They could examine the table of contents of some of the books on community workers to find out on what page information is given on a worker.
3. The members of a committee or one individual could look for information in a book that will give the answer to a specific question, for example: "What does a fireman do when he hears a fire alarm?"
4. They could compile a list, arranged in alphabetical order according to the last name of the author, of books on community workers. They could use three-by-five-inch cards to be filed or sheets of paper on which they could list a number of references.
5. Before drawing pictures for a "movie" or a frieze on community workers, they could look in books for pictures that would give them some needed background information.
6. For a booklet that the group could make, the pupils could write a table of contents, a preface, and an appendix. In the appendix they might include: (a) a table showing the work of each of the workers studied; (b) a picture of each community worker, showing the type of uniform or clothes he wears; (c) a diagram showing where the workers work. This diagram could indicate, for example, the location of the post office, the fire station, bakeries, and police headquarters.
7. The more mature pupils could find information that deals with the topic in *Compton's Pictured Encyclopedia* or the *World Book Encyclopedia*. Younger ones could find information in *Childcraft*.
8. The pupils could be helped to find in their picture dictionaries the spelling of words needed for writing.
9. They could look for poems useful for the unit and make an index of poems found.

10. They could collect songs about community workers and make a file showing in which books the songs are printed.

11. They could get help in interpreting charts and graphs that are of value in connection with the unit and they could show graphically such data as: (a) the number of milkmen, policemen, postmen, firemen, bakers, and doctors in the community; (b) the number in each of the categories of community workers who are fathers or mothers of the boys and girls in the room; (c) the increase in the number of firemen in the community during various intervals in the past few decades. Pictorial graphs could be made to show some of the suggested data.

Developing Locational Skills in a Unit on the Western States

Skill in the location of information can be developed in a large variety of situations in connection with a unit on the Western states, work frequently taken up in the fifth grade. The following ways in which locational skills can be learned in such a unit will, it is hoped, suggest many others.

1. A committee of boys and girls could look up material in encyclopedias and in history books other than the textbook preparatory to putting on a skit on an interesting episode in the settlement of the West. Topics might be: the work of Sacajawea, the building of the first transcontinental railroad, traveling westward by covered wagon, the discovery of gold in California. An activity of this type could provide boys and girls with practice in such locational skills as the following: (a) clarifying the problem that they wish to investigate; (b) deciding in what books to look for information; (c) learning to locate the books they wish to use; (d) using the table of contents; (e) deciding on possible key words and looking for these words in an index or in an encyclopedia; (f) locating the information needed on a page; (g) making an outline of the information gathered from various sources; (h) using the outline to prepare the skit.

2. The pupils could make a collection of pictures dealing with the Far West and file them alphabetically, using guide cards to indicate their position in a filing drawer.

3. Individuals, committees, or an entire class could make a notebook on some phase of the Western states and include in it a preface, an introduction, an appendix, and an index. Some topics that might be chosen are: beauty spots of the West, the opening of the West, the coming of missionaries, and famous men and women in the settling of the West. A few suggestions for the content of the appendix are: (a) a list of important dates; (b) a page giving biographical data about the famous people connected with the Far West; (c) a sheet giving data in tabular form about the national parks of the West.

4. Many locational skills could be used in making a frieze showing the means of communication used in pioneer days of the West, such as the

wagon, clipper ship, stagecoach, pony express, overland stage, railroad, and telegraph. Some of the locational skills that could be used in a project of this type are: (a) finding pictures of the various means of communication; (b) using encyclopedias and history and geography books for wide reading; (c) selecting the points that have bearing on a given problem; (d) finding the dates when a given means of communication was used so that the correct sequence of events will be known; and (e) making use of the information found.

5. A large variety of locational skills could be used in giving a talk on topics on the Western states, such as, for example: (a) any one of the states of this section of the country; (b) famous pioneers such as John C. Fremont, Marcus and Narcissa Whitman, Buffalo Bill; and (c) important events, such as the discovery of gold in California.

6. The pupils could make a card file on books of value in connection with the study of the West. They could make subject cards, title cards, and author cards. Guide cards, similar to those used in the card catalog, could also be made.

7. When drawing pictures to show, for example, the life history of a salmon, they could consult various textbooks and reference books—encyclopedias, an atlas, and history and geography books.

8. Making an illustrated dictionary of words and phrases learned while studying the unit could involve such locational skills as: (a) arranging words in alphabetical order; (b) looking words up in a dictionary or other reference books; (c) finding illustrations of the terms; (d) using a dictionary to determine the spelling of words.

Interesting Boys and Girls in Independent Reading

One of the chief responsibilities of the teacher is to interest pupils in reading in these areas and to try to get "the right book to the right child." The latter involves knowing the child—his interests both in books and in nonreading situations—and knowing books.

Guidelines for Choosing Books for Independent Reading

Books in the content areas should be equal in quality to those of other types. (See "Book Selection," p. 308, "Book Awards," p. 310, and "Book Club Selections," p. 311.) For example, in historical fiction, as in all fiction, there should be a worthwhile theme, a strong plot, and convincing characters. However, certain criteria pertain in particular to books in the content subjects designed for independent reading. Some of these are:

1. If the book is historical fiction, it should be historically accurate. While many of the details of this type of book will understandingly not report actual happenings, the background on which the story is based should be in harmony with what history records.
2. The story elements should not be sacrificed in historical fiction. It should tell a good story.
3. Any book on history should give the pupil improved perspective of happenings in the past.
4. Fiction based primarily on a geographical background, such as *Heidi,* should give the pupil a clearer portrayal of life in a region than he had before reading the book. The differences among people should be emphasized less than the likenesses—in needs, in longings, and in hopes. Nor should generally outmoded customs, such as the wooden shoes of the Netherlands, be presented as typical of a country.
5. In science books the points presented as facts must be scientifically accurate. Unless science books deal primarily with one or more phases of the history of science, the information given should be at least fairly up-to-date.

Ways of Interesting Boys and Girls in Independent Reading

A few suggestions are listed here for promoting independent reading in the content areas. (See Chapter 11B, "Promoting Children's Interests in and through Reading," p. 315.)

1. To interest boys and girls in books on aviation a sign written in white letters on a blue background (to simulate sky writing) with the words *All about Aviation* could be placed near a number of books on that topic. The writing could be done in cursive writing, with a flourish to resemble that of sky writing. A small airplane could be drawn on the sign to attract further attention.
2. A pupil-made model of the home of one or more animals could be placed near books on animals. The home of the beaver might, for example, be made of papier mâché. One illustration could show the exterior of the home, with considerable emphasis on the unique surroundings of the beaver's habitat. A second model of the home might be a cross-sectional view, showing the interior. A pupil or a group of pupils might explain their production to the rest of the class and refer them to additional books about beavers and other animals.
3. As a pupil gives a report on a book of historical fiction in order to interest his classmates in reading it, he might add to the interest of his report by showing the class a time line which he has drawn to illustrate the events of history that occurred during the time when the story took place.

Use of the Textbook in the Social Studies

In the majority of the schools of this country a textbook is used in the area of social studies in the upper years of the elementary school. With the many excellent textbooks on the market this practice is not to be criticized. Much of the criticism that has been hurled against textbooks in the elementary school should be directed not against the use of textbooks but against the misuse of them.

Cautions in the Use of Textbooks

The following are some of the cautions to be observed when using a textbook in the social studies or in science:

1. One textbook should not constitute the curriculum.
2. Many books other than the basic textbook should be made available. In some rooms boys and girls have ready access to a few copies of each of several textbooks. Well-selected general books on varying levels of difficulty should also be available to the pupils, some in the home room and others in the school library or learning center.
3. Magazines and current events papers should be part of the classroom or school library.
4. An abundance of audiovisual aids to learning should be utilized. Films, filmstrips, slides, transparencies, still pictures, cassette recordings, records—these as well as many others can richly complement or supplement reading.
5. Pupils should not, as a rule, be asked to read a textbook without help being provided in the comprehension of material presented. The material in a textbook is not to be "covered," but, as someone has said, it is to be "uncovered" with the guidance of the teacher.
6. Use of the study-recitation type of procedure should be avoided, as a rule.
7. Reading orally the material from the textbook by a pupil while others in the class presumably follow in their books is an undesirable procedure. It is to be criticized for various reasons, among them: (a) the reader has little incentive for reading well orally when a true audience situation is lacking; (b) the persons not reading are likely to half-listen and half-read, thereby getting poor practice in both those facets of the language arts; (c) the subject matter of a textbook for a grade usually is not adapted to oral reading or to hearing it read orally.
8. Not all the material in a textbook needs necessarily to be read by the pupils, especially not if the large number of worthwhile activities other than studying the textbook make it impossible to do justice to them and to all the reading material in the textbook. It is important that some topics in the social studies be studied in much more detail than

is presented in the textbook. Consequently, the teacher, to save time for those additional types of activities, might present essentials related to other topics in the textbook without requesting all to read everything given in the textbook on those topics.

Suggested Procedures for Using a Textbook in the Upper Elementary School

Although the procedures suggested in the pages following are geared to teaching with the use of an intermediate-grade social studies textbook, many of the ideas might also be adapted for use with primary-grade pupils. Many, too, can be utilized when reading textbooks in science.

One of the points emphasized in the preceding list of cautions to observe when using a textbook in the social studies or science is that the teacher should help the boys and girls with the study of the textbook. As a rule, parts of the textbook should not be assigned for study during a period preceding a class period. Rather, during class time the boys and girls should be helped with the study of the textbook. Nor is it enough, as a rule, to give the pupils some help preliminary to their reading the entire selection for the day and then have them discuss afterward what they have read. To provide more help with textbook reading in the social studies, when most of the day's work is based on a textbook, the reading material for the day could be divided into several parts, possibly three or four. Help could then be given preceding and following reading of each of these parts. An outline that might be followed with such a lesson, when the textbook material is divided into three parts, could be such as this:

1. Introduction to the work of the day. This part might include any of the following: (a) connecting the work for the day with that which preceded and/or which is to follow; (b) interesting the pupils in the work of the day; (c) statement of the aim(s) for the day's work.
2. Word study and/or location of places
3. Initial study of the first part of the textbook to be studied that day, consisting of: (a) an activity or activities preceding the silent reading of the part; (b) silent reading of the part for a stated purpose; (c) an activity or activities following the silent reading
4. Initial study of the second part of the textbook to be studied that day (to be studied as indicated under 3)
5. Initial study of the third part of the textbook to be studied that day (to be studied as indicated under 3)
6. Follow-up activity or activities. Possible activities are giving a report, having a panel discussion, summarizing.

There are many ways in which the pupils can be prepared for silent reading of a selection. These are but a few of them: (a) giving the pupils an opportunity to tell what they already know about the topic; (b) helping them with the vocabulary; (c) telling the class points of significance about the topic; (d) showing pictures relating to the selection; (e) posing questions to which the pupils can find answers in the selection.

Following the reading of a selection these are some of the activites in which the boys and girls might engage: (a) answering or asking questions; (b) reading orally answers to questions; (c) giving additional information, possibly in the form of a report, and/or listening to some the teacher gives; (d) viewing pictures or listening to records or cassette recordings; (e) evaluating what has been read; (f) giving a demonstration.

In a typical classroom there are usually a few pupils for whom the reading of the textbook is on the frustration level. These boys and girls deserve the serious attention of teachers (see Chapter 13, "Recognizing the Uniqueness of the Learner," p. 367, for some suggestions). It is hoped that some of the procedures suggested below will help the teacher in meeting the needs of the boys and girls for whom the reading of the textbook in the social studies or science is too difficult. With each of the suggestions, one difficulty with the procedure is stated, not to discourage the reader of this book from trying to do something about the problem but to forewarn him of the shortcomings of the situation.

1. Finding parallel reading material for the slower readers. (However, day in and day out it is difficult for the teacher to find such material.)
2. Helping the poorer readers while the rest of the class reads silently. (Care needs to be taken, if this procedure is followed, that the rest of the class is not deprived of some of the attention of the teacher to which they are entitled.)
3. Having a better reader read the material to a slower reader. (While this practice may be all right at times, it cannot be followed repeatedly without "short-changing" the able reader, whose time should be spent primarily in self-improvement, not chiefly in tutoring.)

For Further Study

Bond, Guy L.; Miles A. Tinker; and Barbara B. Wasson, *Reading Difficulties, Their Diagnosis and Correction*, 4th ed. (Englewood Cliffs, N.J.: Prentice-Hall, 1979), Ch. 14, "Overcoming Specific Comprehension Limitations."

Burns, Paul C., and Betty D. Roe, *Teaching Reading in Today's Elementary Schools*, 2d ed. (Skokie, Ill.: Rand McNally, 1980), Ch. 6, "Reading/Study Skills."

Durkin, Dolores, *Teaching Them to Read* (Boston: Allyn and Bacon, 1978), Chapter 17, "Content Subjects and Study Skills."

Friedman, Myles I., and Michael D. Rowls,

Teaching Reading and Thinking Skills (New York: Longman, 1980), Part VI, "Teaching Content Reading."

Hittleman, Daniel R., *Developmental Reading: A Psycholinguistic Perspective* (Chicago: Rand McNally College Publishing Company, 1978), Ch. 10, "Developing Strategies for Content Area Reading."

Karlin, Robert, *Teaching Elementary Reading: Principles and Strategies*, 3d ed. (New York: Harcourt, 1980), Ch. 7, "Reading in the Content Fields."

Ransom, Grayce A., *Preparing to Teach* (Boston: Little, Brown, and Company, 1978), Ch. 13, "Reading in the Content Fields."

Smith, Richard J., and Dale D. Johnson, *Teaching Children to Read*, 2d ed. (Reading, Mass.: Addison-Wesley, 1980), Ch. 14, "Teaching Children How to Read Content Area Materials."

Questions and Comments for Thought and Discussion

1. Special problems in reading in the content areas are discussed in some detail in this chapter. Can you give illustrations of how these or others were a real problem to you or someone else? What, if anything, was done toward their solution in the case or cases to which you can refer? What might have been done if nothing actually was done?

2. How could the teacher set about to try to develop pupil interest in a topic through eliciting their questions? What might be the strengths of such procedure as compared to one in which pupils were to keep in mind facts presented to them? What might be some of the weaknesses of this strategy and how might they be reduced or overcome?

3. Several suggestions are given in this chapter for helping boys and girls remember what they read in the social studies. Can you think of others or of ways of implementing those that are suggested in the book?

4. Examine several elementary-school science or social studies textbooks. What problems might a boy or girl meet when reading them? How could the teacher help in the partial solution of these problems?

5. You may decide to rewrite a passage in a textbook on a content subject for the middle grades so that its readability level is considerably lower.

6. Writing a teaching plan based partly on a textbook of your choice in the social studies or in science may help you crystallize some of the points stressed in this and in the preceding chapter. You may wish to follow an outline such as this:

    A. Topic
    B. Objectives
        1. Teacher's
        2. Pupils'
    C. Material needed
    D. Outline of procedure
    E. Means of evaluation.

Children's Interests in Reading

The development of keen and continuing interest in reading is not only one of the basic aims of reading instruction as a means to insure well-rounded growth in reading ability, but also an essential means to transfer the reading habit to continuous and life-long learning. We must, therefore, discover and nurture the interests that impel the child to seek meaning from the printed page.

For this reason, what is variously called "free" reading, "recreational" reading, and "personal" reading has come to occupy a place of first importance in the school program. While not long ago teachers tended to regard this kind of reading as peripheral to the instructional program—a kind of extracurricular activity—today "reading for fun" is considered a legitimate and desirable activity for school hours. The systematic study and support of children's interests has thus become a central part of the instructional program in reading.

The Aims of Guidance in Wide Voluntary Reading

The great importance of wide voluntary reading can be seen from an examination of some of the major purposes of this type of reading.

1. Providing leisure-time activities Perhaps the first, though not necessarily the most important, purpose is the development of the habit of reading in leisure time. Children should have much leisure time, and they should have abundant resources for its constructive use. Certainly some of these resources should take the form of sports, hobbies, and social activities. But reading good books and magazines should also be a source of much pleasure. Developing the love for good reading is one of the greatest benefits that we can provide for children. The leisure hour can be an hour of magic, enchantment, relaxation, and relief. It can help the child to see the wonder and the beauty in the "commonplace" world all around him.

2. Expanding the horizons of children in space and time Most children, like most adults, live in a circumscribed world. It is true that radio, television, and motion pictures have expanded the world immeasurably in our generation, but the new media have not supplanted print as a means of broadening our horizons. Each of the new media has something unique to give, but each has its limitations. Only the printed word can offer to the reader the world of the past in a mood of reflection and reminiscence and interpretation. New symbols evoke, through the various electronic media, the excitement of the possibilities of the future. But the book is highly important in unfolding the meaning of that future in words which supply the reader with the means to communicate to others his aspirations for the life of tomorrow.

3. Providing vicarious experience Closely related to the objective of the widening horizon is that of the vicarious enrichment of experience. The materials and methods employed in the achievement of this objective will be substantially the same as those used in the effort to expand young people's intellectual horizons, but the direction the instruction will take will vary in essential particulars. Here the purpose will be to build a stock of impressions that the child's direct experiences cannot provide. To a large extent it is by means of the rapidly growing, well-organized mass of experience with people, places, things, and processes that the child or youth develops the ability to comprehend what he reads, to converse interestingly, to discuss intelligently, to make constructive use of his leisure, to maintain an active mentality, to live comfortably with himself in hours of solitude.

The peculiar advantage of children's literature is that it can offer an emotionalized approach to reality which enables the reader to identify himself personally with his subject. It is a means of seeing the world through other people's eyes for a time, and it multiplies a hundredfold the experiences and insights of each person who reads widely.

4. Developing aesthetic sensitivity

Many complaints have been made about the general level of taste of the American people. The banality, transparency, and even venality of typical radio and television programs have been widely commented on. The public taste in motion pictures has been criticized with equal severity. The run-of-the-mill picture makes its appeal to people of limited intelligence and crude taste, and producers say that these are the films that show most profit at the box office. There is reason to believe that the case has been overstated, since the public has often responded enthusiastically on those rare occasions when a really superior picture is offered. Nevertheless, it is clear that for multitudes of people the area of aesthetic sensitivity has scarcely been cultivated. Good literature for children can help in the development of discrimination among aesthetic values if the children can be introduced to it in an atmosphere conducive to such development.

The development of aesthetic appreciation was the earliest of the school's stated objectives in the teaching of literature, and for a long time it was the only one. Today, although we see many other valuable uses for literature, literary judgment, enjoyment,

and appreciation remain among the most important.

5. Helping children to understand themselves and others

Evelyn Wenzel, in *Elementary English* (February 1952), discussed the "Little House" books of Laura Ingalls Wilder. This fine series of stories certainly possess great literary merit, but Professor Wenzel in this article considers these books from another viewpoint. She has recognized them as being a means of helping young people meet their personal needs. She finds in Mrs. Wilder's work many situations dealing with:

1. Young people's need for security: material security, emotional security
2. Young people's need for achievement: physical, intellectual, spiritual, and moral achievement, growing up, overcoming fears and misunderstandings, overcoming sibling troubles, meeting the problems of an expanding world, dealing with adolescent problems and the problems of courtship and marriage, and gaining insight into some of the mysteries of life.
3. Young people's need for change and escape.

Professor Wenzel's analysis is one that might be made of many other writers.

As children grow up, they have the need to understand and accept differences in others as well as in themselves. They must learn to accept the handicapped member of the class without derision, condescension, or fear. Actually, most children can do this quite unconsciously, but often their attitudes have been poisoned by bigoted adults. Teaching good human relations, therefore, is not so much a matter of developing new attitudes as of having children unlearn acquired ones.

In the case of acceptance of differences in ethnicity and national origin there is much need for special attention. Fortunately for the teacher, there are now appearing many guides to children's literature dealing with personal and human-relations problems. *Reading Ladders for Human Relations*, published by the American Council on Education, provides lists of children's and young people's books dealing with four human-relations themes. The Children's Book Center of the University of Chicago publishes a monthly list of the best new children's books, annotated and classified according to theme.

In dealing with acceptance of multi-ethnic differences in classrooms, also discussed in Chapter 13, the teacher will find the following resources useful:

Cortes, Carlos, et alera, *Understanding You and Them: Tips for Teaching about Ethnicity* (Boulder, Colo.: ERIC Clearinghouse for Social Studies, 1976).

Garcia, Ricardo, *Fostering a Pluralistic Society through Multi-Ethnic Education.* Fastback #107 (Bloomington, Ind.: Phi Delta Kappan Educational Foundation, 1978).

National Council for the Social Studies, *Ethnic Studies.* Curriculum Guidelines Taskforce. Guidelines for Multi-Ethnic Education (Washington, D.C.: National Council for the Social Studies, 1976).

6. Helping boys and girls develop a greater sense of values The work of Lawrence Kohlberg[1] has gained wide attention for its scholarly research and focus on the value of human life. He depicts moral stages of development in a three-stage, six-level conceptual framework, which has been used to discuss character development in books as well as in real-life situations. Certainly these ten basic moral values that he believes common to all human societies deserve the attention of the teacher serious about helping pupils gain a greater sense of values:

1. Laws and rules
2. Conscience
3. Personal roles of affection
4. Authority
5. Civil rights
6. Contract, trust, and justice in exchange
7. Punishment
8. The value of life
9. Property rights and values
10. Truth.

For analysis of moral stages of development in pupils or in analysis of character development in stories, the teacher is referred to:

Oliver, Hugh, ed., *How to Assess the Moral Reasoning of Students.* A Teacher's Guide to Use with Lawrence Kohlberg's Stage-Development Method. Profiles in Practical Education. No. 8. (Toronto, Ontario, 252 Bloor Street West: The Ontario Institute for Studies in Education, 1972).

Lickona, Thomas, ed., *Moral Development and Behavior: Theory, Research, and Social Issues.* "Moral Stages and Moralization: The Cognitive-Developmental Approach" (New York: Holt, Rinehart and Winston, 1976), pp. 34–35.

Studying the Interests of Children

In order that we may effectively guide the reading of children, we must know a great

[1]Richard H. Hersch, Diana Pritchard Paolitto, and Joseph Reimer, *Promoting Moral Growth, From Piaget to Kohlberg* (New York: Longman, 1979), p. 84,

deal about their reading and their nonreading interests.

Nonreading Interests

Reading interests are the product of the general interests of children and youth. Often, therefore, the process of stimulating reading interests involves the expansion and enrichment of the child's general interests. In this section we shall examine the various interests that have been found to be characteristic of boys and girls at various age levels.

Hobbies

The teacher who discovers the hobbies of the boys and girls in his classroom will realize that often children progress through a series of hobbies and diverse intellectual interests. One talented boy, for example, was successively preoccupied with the following topics from ages five to fourteen: animals, stamps, rocks, magic, chemistry, medieval heraldry, military strategy, photography, maps, hunting and fishing, navigation, locksmithing, and science fiction. Subsequently he developed an interest in hot rods, but fortunately for his safety pursued it only in magazines. In the fishing stage his involvement was limited to the purchase of equipment with the small sums he earned as a newspaper carrier. Because no fishing waters could be found in a reasonable distance from his home, his fishing hobby was strictly an activity of the imagination. But what is important is that during this phase he read *Field & Stream* and other outdoor-life magazines. In each of these stages his hobby was enriched through the reading of weekly armloads of library books, which opened new worlds to him in his chosen field of interest. Only in his sports interests did he confine himself generally to the physical activities themselves.

Television

The mass media of communication, especially television, are extremely popular with children. Research indicates that television has maintained its popularity with elementary-school children throughout the years that it has been available on a large scale. It is the favorite leisure-time activity of young boys and girls. Richard L. Tobin[2], Communications editor of the *Saturday Review*, reported that Gerald L. Looney of the University of Arizona found that on the average the prekindergarten child in his study "spends more than 3/5 of his waking hours watching television." He stated that by the time the child enters kindergarten he will have spent, on the average, "more time watching television than a student spends in four years of college classes."

Complaints about the quality of many television offerings for both children and adults are numerous and vigorous. That they are, indeed, justified can be seen from a survey by staff members of the *Christian Science Monitor*, also quoted by Tobin. The staff recorded in seventy-four hours of viewing during one week "217 incidents and threats of violence and 125 killings and murders in full view of the video audience."

Although the conditions reported in these studies may not be representative of populations other than the ones investigated, undoubtedly the situation is serious. Teachers have a choice of encouraging boys and girls to spend much time reading worthwhile books or, by default, having them continue present-day practices in viewing television of the type and to the extent that many now do. However, in our zeal for reform we must remember that there are also highly desirable programs for boys and girls.

---

[2]Richard L. Tobin, "Murder on Television and the Fourteen-year-old," *Saturday Review*, January 8, 1972, p. 39.

A much-discussed question is whether television stimulates or inhibits the development of interest in reading. The answer probably is that for some children it stimulates and for others it inhibits such interest. While many parents and teachers report that children on the whole read less today than they did before the advent of television, many librarians report an increase in the reading of children's books. Certainly the many long hours that children spend with television each week are diverted from time that in an earlier day might have been spent with good books. On the other hand, some television programs open new avenues of interest to children, who then seek books on those subjects and read them with increased interest and comprehension. The relation between television and reading appears to depend, to a considerable extent, on the nature of the program. Travelogues, science programs, and biographical and historical presentations probably serve to encourage some children to read more widely.

Reading Interests

Children differ widely in the degree to which they are interested in reading. Some read no books at all on their own, while others read several books a week. In order to discover what kinds of books will interest children, it is necessary to examine the voluntary choices of those who do like to read. Many such studies have been made.

As one might expect, pictures help a great deal to interest children in books. Children especially prefer colored pictures. However, the picture merely serves as a bridge to the content of the book. If the subject of the picture interests the reader, it will lure him to the book; if it does not, it will be ineffective.

In judging whether a book will interest a child, we must be careful not to be limited to adult standards. Children obviously do not always like books that adults consider superior. It is possible for adults to remember books they liked as children, and to assume that modern children will like them too. In some cases this is true. *Little Women, Heidi, Black Beauty, The Five Little Peppers,* and *Treasure Island* are perennially popular with children; *Robinson Crusoe, A Christmas Carol, Hans Brinker,* and *The Adventures of Tom Sawyer* also fall into this category. But many books for children of the past deal with topics and express attitudes that were of interest in their day but seem inappropriate or even ludicrous in our time. The same holds true for the element of literary style.

It is encouraging to note the many paperbacks of good quality for children that are flooding the market. An excellent listing of titles of paperbacks is given in the catalogue *Paperbacks and Selected Media, K–14* of the E & R Development Company (A Division of Hertzberg-New Method, Inc., Vandalia Road, Jacksonville, Illinois 62650.)

Magazines are popular with children eight years of age and older. They appeal to them because the selections are short and usually well illustrated and because they are expendable, timely, and varied. Yet magazines represent a much-neglected resource of the elementary school.

One of the best-known and most reliable sources of information about children's magazines is Laura K. Martin's *Magazines for School Libraries* (The H.W. Wilson Company). Ruby E. Cundiff's *101 Magazines for Schools* is available from the Tennessee Book Company (Nashville). The National Council of Teachers of English has published a committee report entitled *Using Magazines* (Urbana, Illinois). A monthly mimeographed periodical called *Subject Index to Children's Magazines*, edited by Meribah Hazen, serves as a kind of juvenile

Reader's Guide to Periodical Literature (301 Palomino Lake, Madison, Wisconsin).

When we read generalizations about children's interests in reading, we must always keep in mind that each child has his own individual pattern of voluntary reading. Some average children read more than some bright children. Some able readers read very little; some children of limited reading ability read a great deal. Some children continue to increase in the amount of reading as they reach adolescence. Some children read excessively, or compulsively, because of emotional maladjustment; others avoid reading for the same reason. It is the particular combination of experiential and personality factors that come together in the life of an individual child that determines his voluntary reading habits. There can be no substitute for the painstaking study of individual children to discover the extent and nature of their reading interests.

A useful tool for teachers in supporting children's varied reading interests is David Krathwohl's *Taxonomy of the Affective Domain*, which enables teachers to assess intensity of interest on different levels. Excellent suggestions for use of his scale are given in these books:

> Barrett, Thomas C., ed., *Evaluation of Children's Reading Achievement.* "Evaluating the Affective Dimensions of Reading" by David Darling (Newark, Del.: International Reading Association, 1967), pp. 127–141.
>
> Smith, Richard J., and Thomas C. Barrett, *Teaching Reading in the Middle Grades* (Reading, Mass.: Addison-Wesley Publishing Company, 1974), pp. 101–5.

The above-named books well supplement the taxonomy given in *Taxonomy of Educational Objectives: Handbook II, Affective Domain* (New York: David McKay, 1964).

Books for Children

Not only does the teacher who wishes to give guidance to children need to know their interests, but he must also know which books will nurture those interests.

Book Selection

With the exception of those who are experts in literature for children, few teachers are able to keep up with the great outpouring of books for children, and fewer still can judge with ease which of the new titles are suitable for them. Teachers are, therefore, to a considerable extent, dependent on the recommendations of specialists. Even when teachers and media specialists use various sources of book reviews in order to select new titles to balance holdings in school media centers, care needs to be taken to insure responsible selection of appropriate titles. For different reasons the incidence of censorship attempts has risen in recent years. Since allegedly the defense of books as a primary tool for educational purposes is at issue, teachers are well advised to familiarize themselves with problems associated with book selection and the possibility of having complainants formalize their dissatisfaction with a work because of language usage, illustrations, or the content of materials used as textbooks as well as supplementary reading.

A teacher may wish to write to the Office for Intellectual Freedom, American Library Association, (50 East Huron Street, Chicago, Illinois 60611) for the 1976 revision of "Policies and Procedures for Selection of Instructional Materials," adopted by the American Association of School Librarians. The National Council of Teachers of English (1111 Kenyon Road, Urbana, Illinois 61801) also publishes information on censorship in schools and suggestions for dealing with this widespread phenomenon.

Of interest to the teacher, too, may be the article by Larry Mikulecky entitled "Censorship and Reading Instruction" (*Reading Teacher*, 33:3–6, October 1979), which gives a position statement regarding censorship, prepared by the Intellectual Freedom Committee of the International Reading Association.

Following are additional references on censorship of reading materials that are particularly appropriate:

Broderick, Dorothy M., "Censorship: A Family Affair?" *Top of the News*, Spring, 1979.

Carlson, Ken, "Censorship Should be a Public, Not a Professional Decision," *Social Education*, 42, 1978, pp. 118–22.

Davis, James E., ed., *Dealing with Censorship*. ERIC Document ED 168 039 (Bethesda, Md.: ERIC Document Reproduction Service, 1979).

Glatthorn, Allan, "Censorship and the Classroom Teacher." *English Journal*, 66:12–5, Feb. 1977.

National Council of Teachers of English, *The Students' Right to Read* (Urbana, Ill.: National Council of Teachers of English, 1972).

National Council of Teachers of English Committee, "Censorship: Don't Let It Become an Issue in Your Schools," *Language Arts*, 55, 1978, pp. 230–242.

The numerous booklists now available can be sources of valuable aid to teachers in planning their periodic requests for books. There are a few standard lists that should seriously be considered as part of the reference collection of an elementary school library. These include:

A Basic Book Collection for Elementary Grades (Chicago: American Library Association).

Children's Books for Schools and Libraries, Phillips B. Steckler, ed. (New York: Bowker).

The Children's Catalog, Ruth Giles and others, comp., Standard Catalog Series (New York: H. W. Wilson, Supplements).

The Elementary School Library Collection, Mary Virginia Gaver, et al. (Newark, N. J.: The Bro-Dart Foundation)

Interracial Books for Children, published eight times a year by the Council on International Books for Children (1841 Broadway, New York, N.Y. 10023) is a source of information on a timely concern.

The following are publications, printed periodically, that evaluate currently written books for children.

The Atlantic (Atlantic Monthly Company)

The Booklist (American Library Association)

Book Review Digest (H. W. Wilson)

Bulletin of the Center for Children's Books (University of Chicago Press)

Chicago Sunday Tribune

Childhood Education (Association for Childhood Education, International)

Horn Book Magazine (Horn Book, Inc.)

The Instructor (The Instructors Publications, Inc.)

Junior Libraries (Bowker)

Language Arts (National Council of Teachers of English)

New York Herald-Tribune Book Review

New York Times Book Review

Parents' Magazine (Parents' Magazine Press)

Publisher's Weekly (Children's Book Number, Bowker)

Reading Teacher (International Reading Association)

School Library Journal (Bowker)

Teacher (Macmillan Professional Magazines, Inc.)

Wilson Library Bulletin (H. W. Wilson)
Young Readers Review (Box 137, Wall Street Station, New York, N. Y. 10005).

The Children's Book Council (67 Irving Place, New York, N. Y. 10003) distributes a folder entitled "Choosing a Child's Book." A copy is available free when a stamped, self-addressed envelope is sent with a request for it.

Book Awards

The books selected for awards are worthy of careful consideration for possible recommendation to boys and girls.

The two awards in the field of literature for boys and girls that are best known are the Newbery Medal and the Caldecott Medal. The Newbery Medal has been given since 1922 when Frederic C. Melcher provided for the award to be made yearly for the book judged the most distinguished in the field of literature for children. Himself a publisher, Melcher named the award in honor of the famous publisher of books for children, John Newbery. In 1939, also through the generosity of Melcher, the first Caldecott Medal was awarded. It was named after Randolph Caldecott, well-known illustrator of books for children. This award is given annually to the book judged to be the most distinguished picture book for children published during the year. The selection of both the Newbery Medal and the Caldecott Medal books is made by members of the staff of the American Library Association.

Quite a number of additional awards are now being made. Some of these are:

The Jane Addams Children's Book Award (established by the United States Section of the Women's International League for Peace and Free-

dom, 345 East 46th Street, New York, N.Y. 10017, for books with constructive themes).

The Aurianne Children's Book Award (established by a bequest of Augustine Aurianne, a former librarian, to be given to writers of books for children between eight and fourteen, encouraging kindness to animals, selected by the American Library Association).

The Mildred L. Batchelder Award (established in honor of a former executive secretary of the American Library Association, to be given to the American publisher of an outstanding book for children originally published abroad in a language other than English).

The Lewis Carroll Shelf Award (given by the School of Education, University of Wisconsin, with the cooperation of state organizations).

Child Study Association of America Children's Book Award (awarded by the Children's Book Committee of the Child Study Association of America).

Thomas Alva Edison Foundation National Mass Media Awards (given by the Thomas Alva Edison Foundation National Mass Media Awards, 8 West 40th Street, New York, N.Y., for four types of books).

Charles W. Follett Award (given by the sons of Charles W. Follett, the Follett Publishing Company).

The Edgar Allen Poe Award (given by the Mystery Writers of America, for the best mystery story for boys and girls of the preceding year—providing one is considered worthy of the award).

The Laura Ingalls Wilder Award (given by the American Library Association).

Two books that give additional information on awards are *Literary and Library*

Prizes (published by Bowker, latest edition), and *Children's Books: Awards and Prizes* (published periodically, available through the Children's Book Council, 67 Irving Place, New York, N.Y. 10003).

Book Club Selections

Selections made by commercially sponsored book clubs for children also merit consideration by the teacher. During recent years they have gained in popularity. They have the advantage and disadvantages rightly associated with book clubs for adults. A few of the clubs are named below. For a longer list and for information on each club included in the listing, the reader is referred to *Literary Market Place*, published by Bowker, a copy of which is available in many libraries. Sponsors of the clubs will send details of membership to any interested person.

    Arrow Book Club (Scholastic Book Services, 50 West 44th Street, New York, N.Y. 10036).

    The Bookplan (921 Washington Avenue, Brooklyn, N.Y. 11225).

    Junior DeLuxe Editions Club (A division of Doubleday, Garden City, N.Y. 11530).

    Junior Literary Guild (247 Park Avenue, New York, N.Y. 10017).

    Lucky Book Club (Scholastic Book Services, 50 West 44th Street, New York, N.Y. 10036).

    Parents' Magazine's Read Aloud Book Club for Little Listeners and Beginning Readers (A division of Parents' Magazine Enterprises, 52 Vanderbilt Avenue, New York, N.Y. 10017).

    See-Saw Book Program (Scholastic Book Services, 50 West 44th Street, New York, N.Y. 10017).

    Teen Age Book Club (Scholastic Book Services, 40 West 44th Street, New York, N.Y. 10017).

    The Weekly Reader Children's Book Club, Primary and Intermediate, one for each of these two levels (245 Long Hill Road, Middletown, Conn. 06457).

    Young America Book Club (245 Long Hill Road, Middletown, Conn. 06457).

    Young Readers of America, a branch of the Book-of-the-Month Club (345 Hudson Street, New York, N.Y. 10014).

Periodicals for Boys and Girls

Although the great storehouse for reading and for reading instruction is found in books, periodicals, too, are a treasury of printed materials for boys and girls.

Listings of Periodicals

The following sources are among those that list periodicals for boys and girls:

    Association for Childhood Education, International, *Guide to Children's Magazines, Newspapers, Reference Books*, Nancy Nunnally, comp. (Association for Childhood Education, International).

    Dobler, Lavinia G., and Muriel Fuller, *The Dobler World Directory of Youth Periodicals* (Citation Press).

    Graves, Eileen P., ed., *Ulrich's Periodicals Directory* (Bowker, published periodically).

    Martin, Laura K., *Magazines for School Libraries* (Bowker).

    H. W. Wilson, *Reader's Guide to Periodical Literature* (H. W. Wilson).

Periodicals for Class Use

Two publishing companies that provide wide circulation of periodicals designed for class use are the American Education Publications (245 Long Hill Road, Middletown, Conn. 06457) and Scholastic Magazines, Inc. (902 Sylvan Avenue, Englewood Cliffs, N.J. 07632). The former publishes *My Weekly Reader* in the following editions:

Weekly Reader Surprise (for Kindergarten)
Buddy's Weekly Reader (for Grade 1)
Weekly Reader News Hunt (for Grade 2)
Weekly Reader News Patrol (for Grade 3)
Weekly Reader News Parade (for Grade 4)
Weekly Reader Eye (for Grade 5)
Senior Weekly Reader (for Grade 6)

American Education Publications also publishes for Grades 7–9 *Current Events, Current Science,* and *Read Magazine;* for Grades 2–3, with a reading-ability level of 2.0–3.0, *Know Your World Extra;* and for Grades 3–5, with reading-ability level of 3.0–5.0, *You and Your World.*

The Scholastic Magazines, Inc., publishes the following editions of its newspaper for boys and girls in the elementary school:

News Pilot (for Grade 1)
News Ranger (for Grade 2)
News Trail (for Grade 3)
News Explorer (for Grade 4)
Newstime (for Grades 5 and 6)

Other Periodicals

The following are some of the periodicals widely read by boys and girls. Some are designed for boys and girls; others, though primarily written for older people, are also read by many boys and girls in the later years of the elementary school.

American Girl, The (Girl Scouts of the United States, 830 Third Avenue, New York, 10022).

American Junior Red Cross News (American National Red Cross, 17 and D Streets, N. W., Washington, D.C. 20006).

Arts and Activities (Jones Publishing Company, 8150 North Central Park Avenue, Skokie, Ill. 60076).

Audubon (National Audubon Society, 1130 Fifth Avenue, New York, N.Y. 10028).

Boys' Life (Boy Scouts of America, New Brunswick, N.J. 08903).

Calling All Girls (The Parents' Institute of *Parents' Magazine,* 52 Vanderbilt Avenue, New York, N.Y. 10017).

Child Life Magazine (Child Life, Inc., 36 Federal Street, Boston, Mass. 02110).

Children's Digest, combined with *Humpty Dumpty's Magazine* (The Parents' Institute of *Parents' Magazine,* 52 Vanderbilt Avenue, New York, N.Y. 10017).

Children's Playmate Magazine Children's Playmate Magazine, Inc., 3025 East 75th Street, Cleveland, Ohio 44104).

Cricket (Open Court Publishing Company, Walnut Lane, Boulder, Colo. 80321).

Golden Magazine (Western Publishing Company, Inc., 1220 Mound Avenue, Racine, Wis. 53404).

Highlights for Children (Highlights for Children, 2300 West Fifth Avenue, Columbus, Ohio 43216).

Humpty Dumpty's Magazine, combined with *Children's Digest* (The Parents' Institute of *Parents' Magazine,* 52 Vanderbilt Avenue, New York, N.Y. 10017).

Jack and Jill (Curtis Publishing Company, Independence Square, Philadelphia, Pa. 19105).

Junior Natural History Magazine (American Museum of Natural History, Central Park West at 79th Street, New York, N.Y. 10024).

Junior Scholastic (Scholastic Magazine, Inc., 50 West 44th Street, New York, N.Y. 10036).

Model Airplane News (Air Age, Inc., 551 Fifth Avenue, New York, N.Y. 10017).

National Geographic Magazine (National Geographic Society, 17th and M. Street, Washington, D.C. 20036).

Peck-of-Fun (Clapper Publishing Company, P.O. Box 568, Park Ridge, Ill. 60068).

Plays (Plays, Inc., 8 Arlington Street, Boston, Mass. 02116).

Popular Mechanics (Popular Mechanics, 575 Lexington Avenue, New York, N.Y. 10022).

Popular Science (355 Lexington Avenue, New York, N.Y. 10017).

Summertime (Scholastic Magazines, Inc., 33 West 42nd Street, New York, 10036).

World (National Geographic Society, 17th and M. Street, Washington, D.C. 20036).

A rather unique recent addition to magazines for children is *Kids Magazine*,[4] published by Kids Magazine (Box, 3041, Grand Central Station, New York, N.Y. 10025). It is written by and for children.

Guidelines

With an awareness of the interests of the children and with a knowledge of books, how can we guide boys and girls to grow in appreciation of literature and in enjoyment of other types of worthwhile reading? Below are some guidelines.

[4]Staff of *The Reading Teacher,* "Adults Talk about Kids," *The Reading Teacher,* vol. 25, no. 2 (November 1971), pp. 60–61.

1. Interests are acquired and, like other acquired traits, are amenable to training or teaching. They are responsive to the home and school environments and are conditioned by experience.

2. In any group of children there will be wide variations in the children's tastes and interests. It is the task of the teacher to discover, so far as possible, what these tastes and interests are.

3. Reading interests and life interests bear a reciprocal relation to each other. A child will read, or can be induced to read, about the things he is interested in; through reading he will become interested in more things.

4. In order that we may help a child broaden his interests and elevate tastes in reading and in other activities, we must begin at his present level. No matter how limited or immature his interests may be, they are all we have to build upon. We cannot usually advance the child from Mickey Mouse to *Robinson Crusoe* in one leap. Normally we progress by easy stages. The speed will depend on the child and the circumstances.

5. The literature program should be a balanced program. It should include many themes and areas of interest, many literary types, many media, and both factual and imaginative material.

6. Many children who read widely will oscillate between books of high and low literary merit. All printed matter is grist for their mill. The measure of their growth is the highest literary level to which they respond with comprehension and pleasure. The reading of some material of lesser quality is in itself no evidence of immaturity.

7. In the evaluation of children's reading interests, every effort should be made to ascertain the child's genuine prefer-

ences rather than his perception of what the teacher considers worthwhile.

8. The techniques of improving a child's voluntary reading habits should in general be those of enticement and persuasion rather than those of coercion.

9. The aim of the literature program should be the development of enduring worthwhile interests in and through reading.

10. In the development of reading interests, as in all other instruction, the teacher is the key factor. If the teacher feels affection for the children, exhibits a sincere interest in their problems and interests, is accepting, gives encouragement, and demonstrates genuine enthusiasm for books, he can create an atmosphere that is favorable to reading. But a generalized attitude of friendliness and good rapport with children is not enough. Since the task of the teacher is to bring child and book together, he must know a great deal about the child and he must have a wide acquaintance with books.

11. An inviting setting to encourage reading should be provided. Experienced teachers believe that attractive surroundings help in encouraging children to read. For many children, especially those who have little interest in reading, an attractive room provides a setting in which reading seems the natural thing to do. An inviting reading corner—with a table, comfortable chairs, and perhaps a reading lamp—may attract children who have completed their other work.

12. Home and school cooperation is of great value in the cultivation of desirable reading interests on the part of children.

13. Through reading children's interests in nonreading areas can be developed.

11B

Promoting Children's Interests in and through Reading

In Chapter 11A are presented: (a) points concerning both children's reading and nonreading interests; (b) information about books and periodicals for children; and (c) guidelines for the teacher as he seeks to assist the boys and girls in the development of their interests in and through reading. In this "B" chapter specific suggestions are given as to ways in which such guidance can be given.

The title of this chapter indicates that the aim is not only to suggest ways in which the teacher can help promote children's interests in reading but also through reading to develop in breadth and depth their nonreading interests. This dual aim the reader should keep in mind in connection with suggestions given in this chapter, even when it is not explicitly stated. For example, the teacher might not only help the child grow in interest in reading about peoples of other lands, but also, simultaneously, guide him so that he will become more interested in people about whom he reads. Thereby, his attitudes may be affected beneficially and his behavioral reactions toward all people improved. Or as the teacher helps the child develop interest in biography, he can also try to help the child desire to emulate the admirable characteristics of those about whom he is reading.

Helping boys and girls to develop nonreading interests through reading may at times tax the ingenuity of the teacher. It is hoped that the following illustrations and those scattered throughout the chapter will suggest to the teacher many other means by which he can help his pupils.

1. After the children have read about sea shells, the teacher may be able to interest some of them in developing a hobby of collecting shells.
2. After the boys and girls have read one or more books dealing with nature, some children may find, with the teacher's guidance, incentive for discovering the beauties of the neighborhood in which they live.
3. After the boys and girls have been reading about the history of our country, the teacher may be able to interest some of the children in finding out more about the history of their own community.
4. A suggestion from the teacher after one or more pupils have read about the native American may serve as stimulus for participation on the part of some children in areas such as folk music, pottery, weaving.
5. Books about exploration in space may stimulate, with or without guidance by the teacher, some children to make models of aircraft.
6. Through reading poetry the teacher may interest some boys and girls in creative writing.

It should not be expected that every type of reading will elicit, even with excellent guidance, new interests on the part of all boys and girls. In fact, it would be highly undesirable if it did. It would be likely to result in a confusion of interests and in lack of desired concentration on any if a child would develop new and deeper interests through every type of independent or recreational reading that he does. Guidance in this phase of reading as

Sustained independent reading can develop life-long reading habits. (Lincoln Elementary School, Honolulu, Hawaii)

in all teaching needs to be geared to the capacities and needs of the individual child.

A Planned Literature Program

Let us consider next how a planned literature program for the elementary school can be put into operation.

A proposal of a planned literature program for the elementary school should not be interpreted by the reader as negation of the voluntary reading program. While voluntary reading should be a significant part of the literature program, the acquaintance the child develops with literature should not be only incidental. While many of the values to be gained from literature can be achieved through the voluntary reading program without much structure, a well-structured program of literature to supplement the incidental can help insure a balanced reading diet.

A literature program in the elementary school should aim to achieve the goals mentioned earlier in various parts of the preceding chapter. In addition, it should have as objective that:

1. Every boy and girl in the elementary school become acquainted with the various types of literature for children.
2. The pupils have an understanding of the characteristics of good literature of the various types.

3. The children have the ability to evaluate, on their level of appraisal, the various kinds of literature to which they have been introduced.

Nor are acquaintance and the power to evaluate sufficient. The goal should also be to help each boy and girl appreciate the various types of literature and, more important still, benefit from literature so that their lives will be made richer and more fulfilling.

Curriculum Designs

A curriculum should be set up on a school-wide basis. The dangers of rigidity need to be guarded against in planning the program. It should make allowance for individual differences among teachers, as well as among pupils. And yet it should have a design. One such pattern is reported in detail by Charlotte Huck and Doris Kuhn.[1] This reference, entitled "A Taxonomy of Literary Understandings and Skills," is well worth study by teachers interested in setting up or helping set up a program in literature. Reported below are the main divisions and first-order subdivisons of that taxonomy.

Understands Types of Literature
    Differentiates fiction from nonfiction
    Differentiates prose from poetry
    Recognizes folk tale
    Recognizes fable
    Recognizes myth
    Recognizes realistic fiction
    Identifies historical fiction
    Identifies fantasy
Understand Components of Fiction
    Recognizes structure of plot
    Recognizes climax of story
    Recognizes character delineation and development
    Recognizes theme of story
    Recognizes setting—both time and place
    Describes author's style or use of words
    Recognizes point of view
Understands Components of Poetry
    Interprets meaning
    Looks for imagery in poem
    Can describe diction (poet's choice of words)
    Recognizes sound effects of poetry
    Identifies various forms of poetry

[1]From *Children's Literature in the Elementary School*, 2d ed. by Charlotte S. Huck and Doris Young Kuhn, pp. 688–91. Copyright © 1961, 1968 by Holt, Rinehart and Winston. Reprinted by permission of Holt, Rinehart and Winston.

Evaluates Literature
  Understands authors write to achieve purpose
  Evaluates setting
  Evaluates plot
  Evaluates characterization
  Evaluates style of writing
  Evaluates point of view
  Evaluates theme
Applies Knowledge of Literary Criticism
  Uses criteria for type of literature
  Asks appropriate questions to analyze writing technique
  Sees relationships among literary selections
  Recognizes similarities and differences in works of one author or illustrator
  Asks appropriate questions for understanding large meanings
  Recognizes that literature gives insight into human thought and action
  Applies insights gained through literature to his own life
  Continues to seek new understandings

An increasing number of books as well as articles in professional journals contain annotated bibliographies of books grouped by thematic emphasis. This resource makes it possible for teachers to plan approaches focusing on universal themes such as life's cycle or paralleling emphases on different cultures. Two references which contain annotated bibliographies on thematic emphases are:

Rudman, Marsha Kabakow, *Children's Literature: An Issues Approach* (Lexington, Mass.: Heath, 1976).

Sadker, Myra Pollack, and David Miller Pollack, *Now upon a Time: A Contemporary View of Children's Literature* (New York: Harper and Row, 1977).

The teacher may also find the following books helpful in implementing a thematic approach:

Huck, Charlotte S., *Children's Literature in the Elementary*, 3d ed. (New York: Holt, Rinehart and Winston, 1976), pp. 702–60.

Stewig, John Warren, *Children and Literature* (Chicago; Rand McNally College Publishing Company, 1980), Ch. 14, "The Curriculum: More than Books," pp. 517–49.

Steps in Planning a Literature Curriculum

The steps in planning a literature curriculum are similar, in broad outline, to those that can effectively be followed in setting up any other curriculum (see p. 407). Probably the first step would be that of interesting the faculty in planning the curriculum. This step can be accomplished through helping them realize the importance of a program and the practicality of devising one. The groundwork is often done by the person responsible for curriculum development. But interest in the project might be triggered by a teacher or group of teachers greatly concerned about the need for the program, possibly by teachers who have attended a summer school or a workshop on the theme of curriculum development or on literature in the elementary school. Next, might come a period of general faculty orientation to the work of developing a literature program. Speakers, study groups, films—these are among the means by which this phase of the work can be carried on. Fairly near the outset a committee whose chief responsibility would be to draw up a curricular plan should be formed. A curriculum specialist or other ex-officio member of the staff might serve as chairman, or a member of the teaching staff might be so designated. Released time or summer employment is at times given to particularly interested teachers capable of giving leadership in planning a curriculum. Although the major responsibility may lie with the committee, members of that group should draw heavily for suggestions on all members of the staff. After a tentative curricular plan has been developed, it is usually desirable to present it to the faculty for suggestions. Then needed changes can be made.

A trial period for the curriculum is, in many cases, of value. Either the entire elementary school can participate in this phase or only one or a few teachers can serve as directors of the pilot program. After the trial period, the curriculum can again be subjected to critical evaluation and to revision if the latter is indicated. Provisions should be made, during the planning period, for continuing improvement of the program throughout the time when it will be in operation.

Included in the curricular guide, which should be in written form, parts such as these could serve teachers well: objectives of the program, means of implementing it, titles of books and book lists, names of other materials (such as visual aids) of value in the program, means of evaluating the program, a bibliography on published reports on literature programs for the elementary school.

Teaching-Learning Techniques for Promoting Children's Interests

The suggestions for teaching-learning techniques given in the following pages can be of value in the planned literature program and in the supplementary voluntary reading program. They are classified as they pertain to: (a) oral communication, (b) written communication, (c) audiovisual presentations, (d) recordkeeping, and (e) miscellaneous activities.

Promoting Children's Interests through Oral Communication

Let us first consider techniques of oral communication of value in the literature program.

Oral Reading by the Teacher

One of the best ways in which the teacher can interest boys and girls in reading is by reading to the class orally. If the objective is to interest the pupils in worthwhile reading, as it should be, the materials selected for oral reading must be of that quality. This requirement does not, however, exclude that which is not utilitarian in a somewhat narrow sense of the word. Reading material can be worthwhile when it is purely for enjoyment. Furthermore, in the eagerness of the teacher to read only suitable material, he needs to remember the level of appreciation of the boys and girls, since they cannot be *forced* onto higher planes of enjoyment. Taking the boys and girls step by step from where they are, without resorting to the cheap and tawdry, to ever and ever higher levels is the challenging task of the teacher. Fortunately there are available many excellent books for boys and girls on various levels of appreciation. (See Chapter 11A, "Children's Interests in Reading.") There are also available many aids to the teacher for selecting books (see p. 308).

Many teachers like to set aside a time in the school day when they read to the boys and girls. The teacher may wish to read to the class only the beginning of a book, such as *The Family under the Bridge* by Natalie Carlson and then stop at an especially interesting place and ask who would like to have the book to finish reading it. If the book is suited to the reading levels and interests of the boys and girls, it may well be that everyone or almost everyone in the class will indicate that he wants to read it. In such a case a schedule for the loan of the book needs to be made out. The teacher may wish to read some books in entirety, possibly devoting fifteen or twenty minutes daily to such reading.

Oral Reading by Boys and Girls

Interest in literature can also be stimulated through oral reading to the class by boys and girls. The material should be worthwhile. Furthermore, when the purpose is to interest the boys and girls in good literature, care needs to be taken that the oral reading is done with the degree of excellence that it can provide enjoyment to both the reader and to his audience. Thus the material needs to be suited to the individual who does the reading and to his listeners. It is recommended that each reader practice reading his selection orally before he reads it to his peers.

Choral Reading

There is also choral reading (see p. 227) of materials of literary value— of "Someone," of "Who Has Seen the Wind?," of "Little Orphant Annie," or of "Why Do Bells for Christmas Ring?" Through choral reading a feeling of oneness can be created similar to that achieved through group singing. Tape recordings of pupils' choral readings can be an effective means of giving pleasure and satisfaction to an audience.

Storytelling

Storytelling by an adult is one of the most ancient of all the means by which young people have become aware of the heritage of literature. While good storytelling is an art, it is one that can be successfully cultivated by any teacher of young children. Valuable hints may be found in the pamphlet "Once Upon a Time" prepared by the Picture Book Committee of the Children's and Young People's Section of the New York Library Association. Another source is *Stories to Tell to Children* compiled by Laura E. Cathon and others (Pittsburg Carnegie Library). An excellent book, containing many examples of good stories to tell to children, has been written by Ruth Tooze.[2]

There are those who maintain that storytelling with boys and girls as an audience should be done only by adults. Excluding boys and girls from the role of the storyteller is based on the assumption that storytelling is too difficult an art for a child to engage in if the effect on the audience is to be the main consideration. Critics with this conviction would limit storytelling to such persons as the teacher, the librarian, or a college student taking a course in literature for children. The argument supporting this point of view could be that just as appreciation of music is not likely to be fostered through a poor rendition of a musical number, so love of literature will probably not be encouraged through ineffective storytelling. Many teachers, however, do not share this opinion—that storytelling should not be participated in by boys and girls. Regardless, however, of who tells the story, it should be one worth hearing.

Dramatization

Dramatization, like storytelling, can be of value not only to the participants but also to the listeners as a means of interesting them in reading stories.

Children who have read the same book may wish to dramatize scenes from it. The dialogue may be taken directly from the book or it may be improvised. This latter "creative" kind of dramatics is usually more fun and is less likely to be stilted and overformal. However, the nature of the story and especially the vocabulary used and the purpose for the dramatization should determine the type of dramatization selected. In either case it may be possible to record the dramatization on tape, to be replayed for other classes.

[2]Ruth Tooze, *Storytelling: How To Develop Skills in the Art of Telling Stories to Children* (Englewood Cliffs, N.J.: Prentice-Hall, 1959).

There are rich opportunities for dramatization not only through the usual type of play but also through puppetry, pantomimes, and charades. Puppetry (see p. 233) is being used increasingly in connection with literature for children, especially with interpretations of folklore. Charades, representing an important event in a story, a book title, or a character's name can be effective. Pantomime of stories, possibly used as a basis for guessing games, can also be a means of interesting boys and girls in reading.

Book Discussions and Informal Book Reports

When a child likes a book, he wants to talk about it with someone. He should have an opportunity to discuss it with the teacher, and he should be encouraged to tell the class about it during discussions in the story hour if time permits. Or he may give a report on the book.

Many teachers react negatively to a suggestion that book reports be given. An apology for good reporting on books is not in order. It is the poor ones that should be avoided. As boys and girls report on books they have enjoyed, they can provide a joyous learning experience for the listener. Through listening to book reports members of the audience can be interested in reading some of the books reported upon.

When giving a report, it will be helpful for many pupils to have in mind an outline to follow—maybe one worked out by the group—such as this:

1. Telling, in a few sentences, what the book is about
2. Describing or relating a few significant incidents
3. Giving the reporter's evaluation of the book

There should be no requirement that any one outline be followed rigidly. There are many ways in which variety can be shown in oral book reports, these among them.

1. The reporter can give the review in the first person.
2. He can show an object representative of the book, such as a thimble for *Thimble Summer*, a wooden doll for *Miss Hickory*, a strawberry—possibly one from a variety store, in the form of a pincushion—for *Strawberry Girl.*
3. He can, either alone or with one or a few of his classmates as helpers, put on a brief dramatization of an incident in the story.
4. He can be dressed as the main character of the book. A cap or felt hat with a feather stuck into it at a pert angle is enough to add zest to a report on Howard Pyle's *Robin Hood.*
5. He can show pictures he has drawn to illustrate his book.
6. He can record on tape his report either while giving it to the class or beforehand for playing to the class.
7. He can use a transparency he has made related to his talk.

Book Programs by Children on Radio and Telvision

Some radio and television stations, especially in smaller communities, welcome school groups to their programs. The opportunity to present a discussion of books for children on radio or television can serve as powerful motivation for children to read many of the best current books for young people. They can be presented as single projects or in a regular series during the school year.

With younger children it is sometimes effective to have a storytelling period with a make-believe microphone. Such simulated "broadcasts" may serve to encourage the shy child who normally would hesitate to speak before a group. Programs may take the form of dramatizations, interviews, or direct storytelling. Visits to local radio studios will furnish ideas for procedures and physical settings. Later on, the children may be ready to participate in real broadcasts on radio and television. Meanwhile the focus will be on the books themselves and on the exciting activity of sharing book experiences.

Promoting Children's Interests through Written Communication

As in the case of oral book reports, written reports have often been a means of discouraging, rather than encouraging, interest in reading. But this need not be the case. It may be desirable to work out a standard form, similar to one suggested for the oral report, but variations should be welcomed. Here are some ideas to make written book reports functional and to make written reporting interesting to boys and girls.

1. A simple file of cards on books read by the boys and girls, including among other points the reader's reaction to the book, can be kept.
2. A class notebook can be made in which on each right-hand page are given the title and the name of the author. Below the title every child, after he has read a given book, can write a brief comment on it and sign his name to his statement(s).
3. A class or individual looseleaf notebook can be kept in which are filed alphabetically, a sheet per book, brief written reports on books read, possibly illustrated.
4. Reports may take the form of an imaginary diary of a character in a book, of an imaginary letter written by one book character to another, or of an imaginary conversation between characters in different books.
5. Each pupil may make a two-page booklet on a book he likes. It could be a large sheet of construction paper folded, with the title, name of the author, and possibly an illustration on the cover. On the second page, on the inside of the folder, a review written on white lined paper could be pasted, and on the page opposite it an illustration could be drawn or quotations from the book cited. These reports could be placed on the library table for all to read.

6. So-called "category notebooks" could be made by organizing in looseleaf files the reports on books being read into categories such as mysteries, historical fiction, science fiction, fables, myths. One might be called "Miscellaneous." As a child finishes reading a book he can sign his name to the page on which the title of the book he read appears.

Promoting Children's Interests through Audiovisual Presentations

Audiovisual aids are a very effective means of awakening the children's desire to read. These aids may include records, radio and television programs, films, filmstrips, slides, and pictures.

Dramatic recordings of books that have won the Newbery Award are now available. The discs may be obtained direct from Newbery Awards Records, New York. Complete teaching aids, including background information, vocabulary lists, suggestions for prelistening and follow-up activities, and other data accompany the records. The dramatizations are expertly directed and are performed by professional actors. The famous Landmark Book Series, published by Random House, is accompanied by dramatizations based on the books. The records may be secured from Enrichment Records, Inc., New York. Other publishers produce records that dramatize children's books. Thomas Y. Crowell, for example, has issued a record of *Harriet Tubman, Conductor on the Underground Railroad* by Ann Perry, and Ginn and Company has an album of LP recordings entitled "Let's Listen." Record companies have issued recordings of many of the children's favorites. Camden (R.C.A.-Victor) has one on *The 500 Hats of Bartholomew Cubbins* by Dr. Seuss, read by Paul Wing, and another on *A Christmas Carol.* Spoken Arts Records provides unusual recordings of literature. Of particular interest to teachers of young children are the *Just So Stories of Kipling, You Read to Me, I'll Read to You* by John Ciardi, and *Grimm's Fairy Tales.* A catalog may be obtained from Spoken Arts, New Rochelle, New York. Folkways Records presents songs, folktales, and poetry. A catalog may be secured from Folkways Records, New York. The playing of such records, both before and after reading of the books, gives the children a sense of the reality of the story and may make the reading itself an irresistible activity.

The use of records and recordings has numerous advantages. First, it is possible for the teacher to listen in advance to a record in order to determine its suitability for a class. Second, it is possible to stop a record at any time to discuss aspects of a story or to answer children's questions. Third, it is possible to play a record over and over, as often as the teacher or the children may desire.

As the record appeals to the ear, so the slide, filmstrip, and film appeal to the eye. Like the record, however, the visual media require careful preplanning by the teacher. Especially in the case of the slide and the filmstrip, the teacher should be familiar with the content in advance. Some filmstrips come provided with guidelines for the teacher which explain each frame and focus attention on the significant ideas in the series. As a rule it is desirable to discuss with the class in advance what is to be looked for in the still or moving pictures and to follow up the presentation with questions, interpretations, and summaries.

An example of filmstrips suited to the elementary grades is the series "Our American Heritage of Folk Music," produced by the Society for Visual Education, Inc., Chicago, Illinois. This is a series of long-playing records accompanied by filmstrips on "Songs of the Sea," "Songs of the Cowboy," "Songs of the Mountains," "Songs of the Plains," "Songs of the Railroads," and "Songs of the Civil War." Each filmstrip consists of about fifty frames. The records and filmstrips together provide a pleasant stimulus to the reading of children's books dealing with these themes.

Certain radio and television programs can be recommended in connection with developing children's interest in reading. Some stations conduct "book hours" to which we can call children's attention.

Although television is a relatively new medium, it has grown with unprecedented speed (see p. 306). A large body of professional literature on the subject of children and television has come into being. Two interesting pamphlets may be recommended: *Children and TV—Making the Most of It,* a publication of the Association for Childhood Education International, Washington, D.C., and *Your Child, Radio, and TV* by Paul Witty, published by Science Research Associates, Chicago, Illinois.

Not all audiovisual aids are as formal as those described in the preceding paragraphs. Many miscellaneous aids may be used to good advantage. Bulletin boards offer almost limitless opportunities for interesting children in books. Some can be planned to interest them in reading any good books, with a caption such as "Reading Can Be Fun"; others are useful in stimulating interest in a certain type of book, such as tall tales; still others advertise only one book. Sometimes the pupil who has made an illustration for a bulletin board might inform his audience of some other episodes in the book that he thinks might be of special interest to the listeners. It is strongly recommended that a copy of the book that is illustrated be available in the classroom at the time of the exhibit so that the children can have ready access to it. Suggestions for types of displays for bulletin boards are given in this listing:

1. Children's original illustrations of favorite stories
2. Picture strips that highlight the development of the plot of a story
3. Posters that urge more reading or that feature particular books
4. Jackets of new books.

Additional suggestions include:

1. Having a "Who Am I?" bulletin board in which pictures of main char-

acters are to be matched with their names or with the titles of the books

2. Making a bulletin board that will challenge the child's curiosity by posing questions which he can answer after further reading
3. Posting poems that encourage reading
4. Making a bulletin board with the title "Around the World in Twenty [or any other number of] Books," of which the central feature is an outline map of the world, around which are arranged book jackets connected by ribbon or lines to the points of their geographical setting. Or illustrations representative of the books can be drawn onto the map; or on a table in front of the bulletin board can be placed books connected by streamers to the appropriate spots on the map

Many other types of exhibits can serve as motivation. In one room copies of favorite books of individuals were placed on display. The name of the child recommending a book was given; thus, it was possible for others to ask him about the book. Displays of recent acquisitions by the school are of special value if provisions are made for scheduling the loan of books. Attractive displays of good reading lists are also useful. Other worthwhile displays include:

1. Miniature figures dressed as book characters
2. Clay models of book characters and settings
3. "Peep shows" of scenes from books
4. Diorama and panorama scenes from books

In Chapter 15 (see p. 415) are listed guides to the selection of audio-visual aids.

Promoting Children's Interests through Recordkeeping

Although cumulative reading records are often regarded as devices for evaluation, they can also serve as incentive for reading. They take many forms, to some of which reference was made earlier in this chapter. Following are a few additional ideas for keeping records of books read and thus, hopefully, developing greater interest in reading.

1. A "book tree" can be made to which are attached drawings illustrating books enjoyed by one or more pupils. The "tree" can be a fairly large branch of a real tree, probably three or four feet in height, stabilized in a flowerpot by clay. The names or initials of the pupils who enjoyed a given book can be written on the back of the drawing.
2. A tree trunk and branches can be cut from brown construction paper. Individual leaves can be made from green paper or in the fall from colors suggestive of autumn leaves. As books are read, the title and author can be written on the "leaf," as well as the name of the pupil who read it.
3. Older boys and girls can make use of a four-page leaflet called *My Read-*

ing Design (published by *The News Journal,* North Manchester, Indiana), which provides for listing of book titles and insertion of numbers in a pie graph representing different themes and types of books.

Promoting Children's Interests through Miscellaneous Activities

The teacher who is enthusiastic about books and reading will find many other ways of interesting children in books. Teachers can cooperate with children's librarians who organize reading clubs that meet regularly in the public library. The activities of such reading groups may include film showings, book reviews by the members or by adult counselors, tours of historical sites or places of local interest, sessions in which records or cassettes are played, and discussion of reviews in magazines and newspapers.

Classroom activities may include recommending favorite books to children in lower grades, conducting imaginary conversations among well-known characters from different books, visiting the public library, writing letters of appreciation to authors of books that were especially well liked, writing brief reactions to stories that made a special impact, identifying story sites on a world map, making posters on books, and having each child assemble his own poetry anthology.

Other activities that have been suggested include decorating book jackets; writing a movie script for an adventure story; giving an illustrated lecture about a travel book; using postcards, slides, magazine clippings,

Reading can be reinforced through construction activities. (Piney Woods School, Piney Woods, Mississippi)

and other pictorial matter; making a "movie" of a book by means of a series of pictures on a paper roll attached to rollers; supplying a different ending to a story; telling the class one of the most humorous or exciting incidents from a book; writing a letter to the librarian or a friend recommending a book; making a mural based on a story; listening to radio or television reviews of children's books; collecting pictures to illustrate a book of verse; making a scrapbook about a subject treated in a book; stretching a cord across the room and mounting on it paper-doll-like representations of characters from books; modeling soap figures illustrating characters or objects or scenes from books.

Boys and girls can also be motivated to read good literature through puzzles, riddles, and games such as these:

1. A child represents some well-known fictional character as he appears before a panel which tries to guess his identity by questions requiring direct *yes* and *no* answers. A pupil, with one or several helpers, may put on a skit in which the audience is given a clue as to the character he is representing or the book he is portraying.
2. Each pupil prepares a short description of a character in a book which he has read, and, as he gives his description to the class, the class tries to guess who the character is and the title and the author of the book in which he appears.
3. The teacher and/or pupils make a rebus of titles of children's books or stories. These are among those on a chart of rebuses published by the Children's Book Council:
   Pinocchio: a picture of a pin, the letter *o*, a picture of a key, the letter *o*.
   Robin Hood: a picture of a robin, a picture of a hood.
   Treasure Island: a picture of a treasure box, a picture of an eye, the letter *l*, the *and* sign (&).
4. Children solve and make crossword puzzles based on books.
5. The pupils construct time lines of events within a given book. These lines are particularly adapted for use in connection with books of historical fiction or of biography.

A Miscellany of Other Considerations

In this part of the chapter these additional topics are briefly considered: (a) Book Week activities, book festivals, and book fairs; (b) the school library or learning resources center.

Book Week Activities, Book Festivals, and Book Fairs

In order to stimulate interest in children's books on a nationwide scale, the Children's Book Council each year sponsors National Children's Book

Week. The Council, composed of the editors of books for children of leading publishing houses, is located at 67 Irving Place, New York 10003. It supplies schools with a Book Week poster, usually designed by a distinguished illustrator of books for children, streamers with themes related to books for children, full-color bookmarks reproducing the Book Week posters, records, picture quizzes, and other Book Week aids. Local schools throughout the country celebrate Book Week with special assemblies, open-house, plays, radio programs, or other activities.

Another development in the field of children's books is the book fair or book bazaar. The book fair is usually a community project involving the schools, libraries, churches, civic groups, and various organizations interested in literature and the arts. Interest in local book fairs has been stimulated by the Children's Book Council, which also publishes a volume, *The World of Children's Books*, that includes a chapter on "How to Run a Book Fair." The book fair is usually set up in cooperation with a local bookseller or jobber who supplies the books and allows a commission on direct sales and orders taken at the fair. Such proceeds from book sales are commonly applied to some educational project, often the expansion of the school library. An extensive list of books for display at the fair has been compiled by the Publisher's Liaison Committee. It may be secured without cost from the Children's Book Council.

The School Library or Learning Resources Center

In some schools the library has been made into a "materials center" or a "learning resources center." As such what was formerly the library serves as a central clearinghouse for all instructional materials, including audiovisual aids, pamphlets, textbooks, and the like. Since library books are only one kind of instructional material, it seems logical to many that there should be a center for all kinds of teaching aids. However, some objections have been raised to the use of the library as a materials center. It is pointed out that the work of a materials center may become chiefly a mechanical and routine activity and will add to the many responsibilities of the librarian. Moreover, fears are expressed that some of the appropriations for audiovisual and other materials will be deducted from the expenditures for books. Furthermore, the expert handling of instructional material will add to the training needed by the qualified librarian. These are valid considerations.

The idea of the materials center should, therefore, probably not be introduced unless the school is prepared to add a specialist in audiovisual aids and sufficient clerical staff, and to provide the necessary additional space and equipment without reducing in any way the appropriation for library books and library maintenance. In the discussion in the following three paragraphs the term *library* is used since we are here dealing only with materials formerly associated with libraries.

Since the textbook has ceased to dominate instruction in modern elementary schools, greater reliance than ever is being placed on the library. The library provides an extensive and well-selected variety of recreational books, geared to many interests and levels of reading ability. It has fine reference books such as *Compton's Pictured Encyclopedia*,[3] *The World Book*,[4] and *Britannica Junior*,[5] as well as sets such as *The Pictorial Encyclopedia of American History*.[6] The library helps children to develop new interests and hobbies, and introduces them to the use of community libraries and bookstores. It serves also as a central repository for books that are loaned to teachers for classroom use.

In view of the great importance of a good school library to the reading program, it is indeed regrettable that so large a percentage of American elementary schools have inadequate libraries, or none at all. When pressures from increased enrollments call for ever more classroom space, the library room, if one has been provided, is often among the first to go. Administrators and teachers should do all in their power to convince boards of education and the public that a good library is essential to a good school. Far from being a luxury, it is a facility without which the school cannot function efficiently.

Requirements for an elementary-school library will vary with the size of the school. If the school has no library, the staff should see to it that a beginning, however modest, is made, and that improvement and expansion are provided for each year. The school should be provided with the statement of school library standards of the American Library Association (*Standards for School Library Programs* by the American Association of School Librarians, Chicago). This report describes standards for personnel, equipment, and materials for school libraries in schools of various enrollments.

For Further Study

The following are a few of the many books on the teaching of reading that contain parts relevant to the topic of Chapter 11A, "Children's Interests in Reading" and/or to this chapter on "Promoting Children's Interests in and through Reading."

Alexander, J. Estill, ed., *Teaching Reading*, 2d ed. (Boston: Little, Brown and Company, 1979), Ch. 15, "Attitudes and Interests," by J. Estill Alexander.

Barrett, Thomas C., ed., *The Evaluation of Children's Reading Achievement* (Newark, Del.: International Reading Association, 1967), "Evaluating the Affective Dimensions of Reading," by David Darling, pp. 127–41.

Burns, Paul C., and Betty D. Roe, *Teaching Reading in Today's Elementary Schools*, 2d

[3]F. E. Compton Company, Chicago.
[4]World Book—Childcraft International, Inc., Educational Division, Chicago.
[5]*Britannica Junior*, Chicago.
[6]Children's Press, Inc., Chicago.

ed. (Skokie, Ill.: Rand McNally & Company, 1980), Ch. 8, "Developing Literary Appreciation and the Affective Domain."

Bush, Clifford L., and Mildred H. Huebner, *Strategies for Reading in the Elementary School*, 2d ed. (New York: The Macmillan Company, 1979), Ch. 8, "Children's Interests."

Dallmann, Martha, *Teaching the Language Arts in the Elementary School*, 3d ed. (Dubuque, Iowa: William C. Brown Company Publishers, 1976), Ch. 10, "Guiding Growth in Independent Reading," and Ch. 11, "Creativity through Dramatic Expression and Choral Speaking."

Fisher, Margery, *Who's Who in Children's Books: A Treasury of the Familiar Characters of Childhood* (New York: Holt, Rinehart and Winston, 1975).

Harris, Albert J., and Edward R. Sipay, *How to Increase Reading Ability*, 6th ed. (New York: David McKay Co., Inc., 1975), Ch. 18, "Fostering Reading Interests and Tastes."

Hittleman, Daniel R., *Developmental Reading: A Psycholinguistic Perspective* (Chicago: Rand McNally College Publishing Company, 1978), Ch. 11, "Developing Strategies for Literature Reading."

Karlin, Robert, *Teaching Elementary Reading:*

Principles and Strategies, (New York: Harcourt Brace Jovanovich, Inc., 1980), Ch. 7, "Reading for Appreciation and Enjoyment."

Landeck, Beatrice, *Learn to Read/Read to Learn: Poetry and Prose from Afro-Rooted Sources* (New York: David McKay Co., Inc., 1975).

Rudman, Marsha Kabakow, *Children's Literature: An Issue Approach* (Lexington, Mass.: D.C. Heath & Company, 1976).

Tanyzer, Harold, and Jeal Karl, eds., *Reading, Children's Books, and Our Pluralistic Society* (Newark, Del.: International Reading Association, 1972).

Tichenor, Tom, *Tom Tichenor's Puppets* (Nashville, Tenn.: Abingdon Press, 1971).

Tiedt, Iris M., ed., *Drama in Your Classroom* (Urbana, Ill.: National Council of Teachers of English, 1974).

Tinker, Miles A., and Constance M. McCullough, *Teaching Elementary Reading*, 4th ed. (Englewood Cliffs, N.J.: Prentice-Hall, Inc., 1975), Ch. 15, "Interests and Tastes."

Zintz, Miles V., *The Reading Process: The Teacher and the Learner*, 3d ed. (Dubuque, Iowa: William C. Brown Company Publishers, 1980), Ch. 14, "Developing Permanent Reading Habits."

Questions and Comments for Thought and Discussion

1. How can the teacher help a child, through books, to grow in understanding of himself as an individual and as a member of society?
2. It is not unusual to see children being singled out for having read many books over a given period such as the summer vacation. What do you think of this practice? What, if anything, in this respect is done at the local level?
3. It is widely assumed that improved reading interests and habits result from a careful study of children's present interests and from a varied school program for developing more desirable reading habits and tastes. Do you know of such a program? If so, what are some of its salient features?
4. For enjoyment boys and girls as well as adults will read that in which they are interested. Consequently, in order to encourage a child to read as a leisuretime activity, it is deemed important that the teacher know his interests. How might you set about trying to discover these inter-

ests of boys and girls in your charge and then apply this knowledge as you guide them in forming lifelong habits of reading worthwhile materials for enjoyment?

5. What is your attitude toward the controversial subject of censorship of reading materials for pupils in the elementary school?

6. Many people think it is desirable for an elementary school to have both a school library and a library in each classroom. What is at the present time your opinion in this respect? What reasons can you give for your opinion?

7. How can you as elementary school teacher keep yourself informed about recent books for boys and girls?

8. You may wish to make one or more visual aids of the type boys and girls might make that would help to interest them and/or others in worthwhile independent reading.

9. To start an organized file or scrapbook on suggestions for teachers to interest children in leisure-time reading may be a profitable activity for you.

10. You may wish to make a list of poems you consider suitable for presentation to pupils of the age group in which you are particularly interested. It is recommended that you record the title, the poet, and, unless the poem is well-known to you, brief notes on it. Also it would be desirable to indicate a source in which each poem is recorded.

Part III

The Reading Program in Action

Classroom Diagnosis of Reading Ability

One of the fundamental themes we have been emphasizing is the importance of trying to fit the program of instruction in reading to the needs of the learner. If we are to be successful in adapting instruction to individual differences, we must necessarily have clearly in mind what the needs of the various individuals are. To locate and define them is the purpose of diagnosis, if we think of diagnosis as the means of ascertaining not only the weaknesses in reading but also the strengths of each pupil. Unless we have identified these needs our teaching will be lacking in effectiveness.

The extent of a person's acquisition of the ability to read is determined to a large degree by the level of his mastery of the various skills essential to excellence in reading. Thus, it becomes the task of the teacher to ascertain how far each child has progressed in the development of these skills and to provide for him instruction that gives the most promise of helping him make further progress. The teacher who, after having made a diagnosis of the learner's reading ability, bases his teaching on the pupil's requirements, is providing him with what various writers refer to as *diagnostic instruction.*

The almost exclusive emphasis placed in this chapter on the diagnosis of reading skills should not be interpreted as indicating that the skills of reading should constitute the total of the teacher's concern in diagnosis. That assumption would, indeed, be an erroneous one. The child's interests and tastes in reading, in fact the level of his recreational reading, should, as discussed earlier, be a matter for diligent investigation by the teacher. Furthermore, the teacher who views as an objective of the reading program the development of the individual, who believes that reading should lead to desirable action will also want to search for signs that indicate whether reading has really carried over into action that is socially useful and individually satisfying. Appraisals of such goals must not be overlooked. If they are, some of the primary reasons for teaching reading are lacking in the diagnosis. Outcomes such as these are difficult to measure. However, through procedures such as informal observation, pupil conferences, and at times pupils' writing, insight can be gained that might give trustworthy evidence as to whether an individual is making constructive use of his ability to read. Important though such study is, it is not the subject of this chapter, which deals with the diagnosis of reading skills.

Guidelines for Diagnosis

Several guidelines that the teacher should keep in mind when making or interpreting diagnoses of reading ability are indicated in the preceding paragraphs. Additional points of general applicability to classroom diagnosis are given below.

1. Diagnosis of reading ability should not be confined to the poor reader Each child has the right to instruction based on a knowledge of his strengths and weaknesses on the level of his reading ability. However, in many instances, it would not be practical, with limited time and personnel, to make detailed analyses of the reading ability of all boys and girls in a room. They are an essential for those pupils who seemingly are not profiting to the extent of their capacity from the reading program as it is being conducted.

2. The teacher should try to discover the causes of any difficulties in reading that the learner may have Since understanding the reasons for the existence of a problem can give insight into the course of action to be followed in remedying an unsatisfactory situation, the teacher will want to search for factors that contribute to the problem. For example, background data on the level of the child's intelligence, his physical welfare, his mental health, his motivation for reading (or lack of it) can provide valuable information on which to base diagnostic instruction. Nor should the search for causes cease when the teacher has discovered one cause, for usually causation of difficulties in reading is multiple.

3. Diagnosis should be made in terms of the objectives for the reading program The teacher who makes his diagnosis in terms of his goals will be more likely to establish a comprehensive plan for diagnosis than the teacher who knows but vaguely what he wants to accomplish.

4. Diagnosis should be a continuous process Obviously the teacher should not be giving tests nor using checklists daily. But every day, during reading class and at other times, the teacher should be aware of clues that provide insight into the child's reading strengths and weaknesses.

5. Boys and girls should be helped to recognize the purposes of diagnoses that are being made of their reading ability The extent to which the pupils should be informed will depend on various factors, such as the intelligence of the learner, his age, his interest in reading and in reading improvement. Even the beginning reader, when being checked, for example, on words on a list, can be told simply: "Let's see which of these words you know. I want to help you with those you don't know."

6. Boys and girls should be given an opportunity to engage in self-evaluation With the help of the teacher the child might keep a record of "new words" mastered in a primer or first reader, of the number of days on which he did not move his lips (while the teacher observed him) when reading silently, of the number of questions answered correctly on comprehension tests set up uniformly to make comparability from one testing to another easily possible.

7. The depth of the diagnosis to be made should be determined, in part, by the nature of the problem The seriousness of the problem should be one determining factor. Another should be the ease with which a problem can be analyzed. By far the large majority of boys and girls will require only the depth of diagnosis that the classroom teacher is capable of making through formal and informal testing and through use of techniques, such as individual conferences, observation, group inventories. However, others should, ideally, be referred to a clinician or other reading specialist for further diagnosis.

8. When making diagnoses of students with divergence in cultural background, the teacher should try to ascertain whether the evaluative instruments are culture-fair If they are not, the teacher should take that point into consideration when making the evaluation of a student.

9. The teacher should recognize that diagnostic procedures even at best are imperfect Research has not established the most propitious means of arriving at a knowledge of the status of a child's reading ability. It is generally agreed that a combination of various types of diagnostic techniques brings better results than the use of only one. All of them have shortcomings, but since not all techniques have the same weaknesses or defects, hopefully when more than one is used, the disadvantages of one may be offset somewhat by the strengths of others.

10. Diagnosis should result in action
We are reminded of the school administrator—hopefully a fictitious character—who reportedly complained that though he had given standardized tests repeatedly to the boys and girls in his school, they were no better achievers than previously. Though none of us would be as naive about the purpose of testing as this individual, there are schools in which the results of diagnosis are not used adequately as determiners of future teaching. Diagnosis beyond the level that will be used in the improvement of instruction is a waste of time and energy and money.

Determining the Expectancy Level

As the teacher diagnoses the reading strengths and weaknesses of a child, he will want to determine the teaching procedures he will employ in the light of what can be expected of the learner. He can obtain a rough indication of reasonable expectations by means of informal methods (see Chapter 5A under "Subjective Data on Mental Maturity," p. 71). The intelligence quotient (mental age divided by chronological age) can be used as a rough index for computing what is known as the *expectancy level*. A ten-year-old with an intelligence quotient of 100 can be expected to read on the level of a ten-year-old; if he has an intelligence quotient of 80, his expectancy level can be thought of as eight years (80% of 10). However, the index of expectancy level will be no more accurate than the intelligence quotient upon which it is

based. Various ways of figuring the expectancy level have been suggested. Bond and Clymer, as reported by Bond and Tinker,[1] have devised this formula for obtaining the estimated expected reading level: (number of years in school × IQ) + 1.0. Using this formula, a pupil with an intelligence quotient of 90, who is beginning his third year of school, would have a reading expectancy of 2.8 (2 × .90 + 1.0). In other words, according to this formula, the teacher can expect him to read as well as the average child in the eighth month of the second grade. A child with an intelligence quotient of 120, who is in the third month of the fifth year of his schooling, would have a reading expectancy of 6.2 (4.3 × 1.20) + 1.0 = 6.16 or, rounded off, 6.2.

Durkin[2] suggests still another formula for computing what she and some other writers refer to as the *reading achievement expectancy*, namely: Mental age (M.A.) − 5. It is based on the assumption that the average child in the first grade has a mental age of about six, in the second grade of seven, and so on. According to this method of computing reading expectancy, with a mental age of eight, a child, regardless of his grade placement, could be expected to read on the third-grade level. One with a mental age of ten would have a reading achievement expectancy at the fifth-grade level. In explaining the formula Durkin rightly points out that to the extent that factors other than mental age affect reading ability, the reading achievement age calculated according to her formula becomes inaccurate. She also draws attention to the fact that the concept of *grade level* is lacking in precision. However, use of any

[1]Guy L. Bond and Miles A. Tinker, *Reading Difficulties: Their Diagnosis and Correction.* 4th ed. (New York: Appleton, 1979), pp. 62–63.
[2]Durkin, *ibid.,* p. 407.

of the formulas for computing expectancy levels, when other factors are then taken into consideration, can help point out to the teacher the differences in learning ability and rate which exist in every classroom, and can serve as index to him of the expectations on which he should plan the program of instruction.

Assessment of Reading Ability through Standardized Reading Instruments

Since, in the chapters on readiness for beginning reading instruction, we have discussed standardized and nonstandardized procedures for assessing readiness for reading, we will now limit our considerations to only those instruments that test beyond that level.

Standardized reading tests can be classified as survey tests and diagnostic tests. The former provide an average score; the latter undertake to break down the reading into specific strengths and weaknesses.

While standardized reading tests, when used with great caution, can be of decided value, they must be interpreted with a clear recognition of their shortcomings.[3] At best they test only a limited number of factors important in reading. Another serious limitation lies in timed comprehension tests. The scores obtained from them give erroneous impressions to the interpreter of the test who is not cognizant of the fact that many such tests give scores that are a mixture of rate of reading and comprehension. An additional fact to note is that the grade-

equivalent scores provided by the publishers of tests often are not reliable indexes of the level at which the reader normally functions.

Survey Tests

The scores on a survey test purport to tell the teacher how well a pupil can perform on a given test in comparison with other pupils of the same age or grade to whom the test was given in the process of standardizing it. Some survey tests are divided into subtests dealing with various reading skills—such as rate of reading, word recognition and word meaning, comprehension of sentences and of longer selections, skill in locating materials—while other survey tests have but one part. Neither kind provides specific information as to the needs of a person examined, although unfortunately some teachers group pupils for instruction according to scores obtainable from these tests. In reading groups formed on the basis of the limited information available from survey tests, since the exact needs of the pupils as far as reading skills are concerned are unknown, the instruction cannot be specific enough to meet the requirements of each individual.

In some survey tests reading is only one of the skills checked, as for example, in the *Iowa Every-Pupil Test of Basic Skills* (Houghton Mifflin) and in the *California Achievement Tests* (California Test Bureau). In other survey tests, such as the *Gates-McGinitie Reading Test* (Teachers College Press), only reading is tested.

From a survey test the teacher can get an indication of whether a class or an individual is below, at, or above the average of the norm group (the group on which the test was standardized). The comparison is usually made in terms of the percentile rank (P.R.) or the grade equivalent score. By

[3]Paul A. Witty, "Rate of Reading: A Crucial Issue," *Journal of Reading,* vol. 13, no. 2 (November 1969), pp. 102–106.

means of the percentile rank a comparison of the score of a pupil is made with the norm group by indicating what percent of the individuals in that group he surpasses.

The grade-equivalent score is also found by consulting tabular data furnished by the publishers of a test. If a pupil has a score on the test representing the average received by pupils at the beginning of the fourth grade in the norm group, his grade-equivalent score is 4.0. If he has the score that represents the average made by a pupil in the fifth month of the sixth grade, his grade equivalence is 6.5 Teachers frequently misinterpret the grade-equivalent score. They are under the erroneous impression that a child in fourth grade, for example, who received a grade-equivalent score of 6.8 reads as well as a high sixth-grade child. All such a score indicates is that the child on that reading test scored higher than the average sixth-grade child taking the test.

In recent years publishers have frequently been using the *stanine* as a test norm. When this comparison of scores is used, the distribution of scores on a test is divided into nine parts, with points on the scale falling between 1 and 9. A score of *5* (the midpoint) indicates average performance; of *9*, very high; and of *1* very low. A stanine of *8* is high; *7*, well above average; *6*, slightly above average; *4*, slightly below average; *3*, well below average; *2*, low.[4]

In making a selection of standardized reading tests, either survey or diagnostic, the teacher should study carefully the teachers' manuals supplied with them. Manuals will tell the *validity* of a test, which indicates the degree of accuracy with which the test measures what it is in-

tended to measure, and the *reliability* of a test, which indicates the degree to which a test yields consistent results. The teacher should keep in mind also the purpose for which he intends to use the test. For example, tests that consist chiefly of vocabulary items may not adequately measure the degree to which a pupil is able to deal with words in context. The length of the test and the time available to teachers and pupils may also be important factors. Finally, the relative recency of the test may have a bearing on the suitability of the selections used as test items.

Diagnostic Tests

We have already discussed one type of diagnostic test, the so-called oral reading test, which is designed to test primarily, through oral reading, the silent reading of a pupil (see p. 217). In the next two paragraphs are described two of the many diagnostic tests that assess growth in word recognition, namely the *Stanford Diagnostic Reading Test* by Bjorn Karlsen, Richard Madden, and Eric Gardner (Harcourt Brace Jovanovich, Inc.) and the *Doren Diagnostic Reading Tests of Word Recognition Skills* by Margaret Doren (American Guidance Service, Circle Pines, Minnesota). It is hoped that a description of these tests will give the reader insight into the purpose and nature of diagnostic tests.

The *Stanford Diagnostic Reading Test* can be administered either to an individual or a group. Different levels of the test are designed for use with different age groups ranging from boys and girls in the latter part of grade 1 through community college students. Depending upon the level used, the skills measured include auditory discrimination, auditory vocabulary, word recognition, phonics and structural analysis, literal and inferential comprehension, read-

[4]Caroline E. Massad, "Interpreting and Using Test Norms," *The Reading Teacher*, vol. 26, no.3 (December 1972), p. 291.

ing rate, and skimming and scanning.

The *Doren Diagnostic Reading Tests of Word Recognition Skills* is a group test measuring decoding skills normally associated with primary reading levels. The subtests are on: (a) letter recognition; (b) beginning sounds; (c) whole-word recognition; (d) words within words; (e) speech consonants; (f) ending sounds; (g) blending; (h) rhyming; (i) vowels, (j) sight words; (k) discriminate guessing. Like the *Silent Reading Diagnostic Tests* this one by Margaret Doren provides a profile which can be helpful in assessing areas of weakness in the use of word-attack skills. Although it is a very useful instrument, the length of time needed for administering it—nearly three hours—will deter some teachers from giving it.

Criterion-Referenced Tests

Lately a type of test, frequently referred to as a *criterion-referenced test*, has become increasingly popular. Not all persons in the field of education will agree as to how the term *criterion-referenced test* should be used, but there is fairly general agreement among educators that such a test sets out to ascertain what the person tested knows or can do relative to the specific area of the subject matter checked by the test. For example, a criterion-referenced test could be designed to check the learner's knowledge of and skill in finding quickly words arranged alphabetically. Such a test might contain items testing skills such as: (a) knowledge of the sequence of letters of the alphabet; (b) ability to arrange letters alphabetically; (c) ability to arrange words alphabetically when the first letters of the words are different, when the first letters are alike but the second letters are different, and so on; (d) knowledge of which word of a compound proper noun (such as

the name of a person, place, society) is the one that determines the alphabetical order of the name. A criterion-referenced test could check the number of words as well as which words on a word list the learner knows. The learner's knowledge and application of the knowledge of some generalizations in phonics could be tested by an item-by-item sampling of the various specific points of information and skills desired when teaching the generalizations being tested.

Unlike the survey test, the criterion-referenced test is not given to compare a pupil's level of learning with that of others. Like the usual diagnostic test, it is administered to find out what the person tested knows or can do in a specified, circumscribed area of learning. While diagnostic tests are given primarily to discover the weaknesses of a learner, the criterion-referenced test is used to find which knowledge or skills in the area being tested the learner has acquired and which he has not. In a sense we could think of the criterion-referenced test as one type of diagnostic test, since it shows mastery or lack of it of points considered significant in the area under study.

A successfully constructed criterion-referenced test should clearly define the area of learning being investigated. It should be based on a reliable analysis of the types of information or skill that constitutes the components of needed learnings in that area. The omission of some essential points in the test might give the interpreter of the test the erroneous impression that the child is in possession of information or skill in a given area that has not been tested.

Criterion-referenced tests can be designed by the teacher. However, they are also available in print. Science Research Associates (259 East Erie Street, Chicago,

Ill. 60611) has developed what it calls Criterion-Referenced/Diagnostic Tests. Other companies that are developing or have developed criterion-referenced tests are the Educational Testing Service (Princeton, N.J. 08540), the Instructional Objectives Exchange (Box 24095, Los Angeles, Calif. 90024), McGraw-Hill (1221 Avenue of the Americas, New York, N.Y. 10036), and Random House (201 East 50th Street, New York, N.Y. 10022).

Assessment of Reading Ability through Nonstandardized Procedures

Standardized tests, in spite of their value, have their shortcomings, some of which can be counterbalanced in part by informal diagnosis.

Informal Observation

A method that the alert, sympathetic teacher has always used is that of informal observation of the child's overall performance, his attitude toward books and reading, his play interests, his hobbies, and his reading interests. The observation may take place in nonreading as well as in reading situations. For example, a child may unintentionally reveal a dislike for reading while working with classmates on a model airplane or while discussing what he would like for his birthday. The teacher may note the kinds of book choices a child makes during the free reading period. He may observe the child's behavior as he reads a book—whether he squints, whether he stops often in his reading, whether he assumes good or poor posture as he reads.

Since few teachers are able to keep in mind the developing characteristics of many children over a period of time, it is helpful to keep an informal record of the day-by-day observations. A file folder should be kept for each pupil suspected of having difficulty in reading; in fact, teachers will find it helpful to keep such a folder for every pupil in the class. In this folder the teacher should insert, from time to time, any material that may throw light on the child's reading problems. The folder should include samples of the child's writing and drawing as well as reading exercises he may have performed. But perhaps the most important material is the teacher's report of the child's observed behavior. This may be in the form of a sentence or two for a given day (the date should be noted), such as: "Today Alex spent 15 minutes in uninterrupted reading of *The Little House in the Big Woods*. He has never concentrated before for so long on his reading, as far as I know." The notations should usually not be of a general nature, as "I think Alex is improving." The anecdotal record should essentially be a behavioral record. In the course of six months it should be possible to discover from the record in what direction the child is moving with respect to significant aspects of reading growth. The type of information described in this paragraph cannot be secured from even the best of the standardized reading tests.

The Informal Reading Inventory (IRI)

Informal reading inventories have been designed in various ways and for a variety of purposes. The one described here, like most that are used by classroom teachers, is an instrument for finding a pupil's independent, instructional, and frustration reading levels. The *independent reading level* is determined by the highest level of reading material that the child can read effectively without assistance from the teacher or others. The *instructional reading level* is indicated by the highest level of reading material that he can handle with effectiveness when he receives help. The *frustration reading level*, the level immediately above the instructional level, is established by the level of reading material at which the reader is unable to proceed effectively even with assistance.

Because giving an informal reading inventory is rather time-consuming, the teacher may not wish to give one of the type here described to all of his pupils; he may decide to use it only with pupils who are showing undue difficulties in reading. If a teacher does use an informal reading inventory with all his pupils, he may find that he needs to interpret with special caution the scores obtained when checking the average or the better-than-average reader, for scores made by such readers on these inventories are often erratic and therefore questionable.

Construction of the Testing Materials

Typically, an informal reading inventory consists of a number of reading passages taken from a basal reader series or other graded material. Some reading inventories also include a word list for testing word recognition.

The reading passages are usually arranged in order, two at a level, ranging from the preprimer through at least the sixth-reader level and extending as high as the ninth-reader level. Some basal readers use number or letter designations instead of terminology such as *primer* or *first reader* to indicate the level of the book in that particular series. Comparatively, though, *level 3*, *Level C*, or the name *primer* might refer to books of the same degree of difficulty. In this book we refer to designations such as *preprimer, primer,*

and *first reader*. While no exact specifications as to the length of each selection can be given, it is probably advisable to include in each passage on the preprimer level between 30 and 40 words and to increase the number at each succeeding level until at the sixth-reader level the passages contain between 150 and 175 words. Since the difficulty of materials in basal reader series varies, it is recommended that the readability level of each passage be checked. About five questions are recommended for the preprimer- and primer-level passages. The number should be increased for subsequent levels. Some teachers like to use ten questions for all levels beyond the primer because of the ease of figuring percentages on a base of ten. Questions should check factual comprehension, interpretive skills, and critical reading.

Each passage selected for the testing, with accompanying questions, should be placed on a separate sheet. The pages can then be compiled into a booklet for use by the examiner, arranged in a progression from preprimer to the highest level used (sixth-reader level or beyond). A summary sheet for recording test results can serve as cover for the booklet. It is recommended that if possible the examinee read directly from the book from which the passages for the teacher's booklet are taken. When, however, a copy of the book is not easily available for use by the child, separate booklets containing only the reading passages—not the questions nor the answer sheet nor the record sheet included in the teacher's booklet—can be used by the pupil.

Administration of the Test

Obviously it would be a waste of time to start each child being examined with passages on the preprimer level. The examiner can begin with the level which he thinks would be only a little below the child's independent reading level. If the teacher's estimate is found to be too high, he then can ask the child to read at a lower level till he finds the passage representing the child's independent reading level. Then the child continues reading on higher levels till his frustration reading level is also located.

The child reads both passages on a level, one orally and the other silently. As the child reads a passage orally, the teacher records the errors made in the teacher's booklet. It is recommended that an error be counted even though the child corrects it immediately. After a child has read a selection, either orally or silently, the teacher asks the questions on the passage and keeps a record of the number answered correctly.

There is no one system of recording errors that is superior to all others. What is important is that a given type of error be marked consistently in the same manner. When this requirement is followed, it becomes readily apparent, by looking at the recording the teacher has done, what types of errors the child made and with what frequency he made each type. The record can then be very useful in developing an instructional program based on the child's needs. Below is suggested one listing of types of errors to which attention may be given, along with a possible code for indicating them:

Interpretation of the Test Results

After the IRI has been administered, the word-recognition and comprehension scores are determined for each passage. The word-recognition percentages are computed by dividing the number of words in the oral reading selection into the number obtained when the number of errors are substracted from the total number of words in the selection.

Example: 40 (words in the oral passage)
            −6 (errors)
            34 (words minus errors)

$$\frac{.85}{40)\overline{34.00}} = 85\% \text{ (word recognition)}$$
$$\underline{32\ 0}$$
$$2\ 00$$
$$\underline{2\ 00}$$

Obviously no word-recognition scores are obtained from silent reading passages. Comprehension scores are found for both oral and silent reading passages, as illustrated in the following example.

Example: If ten questions are used for a passage, each is valued 10 points. If one question out of ten is answered incorrectly the comprehension score is 90. (In other words, dividing the number of correct responses by the total number of questions gives the percentage correct.) Oral and silent reading comprehension scores are then

Error	Marking System	Explanation of Marking System
1. Substitution	horse ~~house~~	Mark out the word which is not pronounced correctly and write the substitute word above it.
2. Addition	had ∧	Write in the added word.
3. Omission	◯	Circle the omitted word.
4. Repetition	——	Draw a line over a repetition of two or more successive words.
5. Reversal	⌢	Draw a half-moon mark over reversed words.
6. Unknown word(s)	✕	Cross out unknown word(s).

Level	Word Recognition	Oral Comprehension	Silent Comprehension	Average Comprehension
PP	100	100	100	100
P	100	100	80	90
1	95	90	90	90
2	97	80	80	80
3	91	80	70	75
4	88	70	60	65
5	80	60	40	50
6	68	30	30	30

Independent Reading Level: P
Instructional Reading Level: 2
Frustration Reading Level: 3

averaged. Both the word recognition and comprehension scores are next transferred to a summary sheet. A sample of a summary for a third-grade pupil is given here.

From this table it is possible to identify the independent, instructional, and frustration reading levels of the pupil being tested, as shown below the table. Specialists in reading differ somewhat in the percentages correct that should be required for some of the levels. Those recommended here and used in arriving at the levels indicated above are:

The *independent reading level,* sometimes referred to as the recreational reading level, is the highest level of passages read with a rating of at least 99 percent in word recognition and at least 90 percent for the average of the two comprehension scores. This is the level of material the learner can handle for pleasure reading.

The *instructional reading level,* the level of material which should be used for instruction in reading, is the highest level of passages read with 95 percent word recognition and 75 percent comprehension (average of the oral and silent reading comprehension scores).

The *frustration reading level* is reached when the pupil's scores fall below either 95 percent word recognition or 75 percent comprehension (average score) and do not again reach a point beyond that level in testing on

later levels. In materials of this degree of difficulty the learner is likely to be frustrated because of the numerous errors he makes.

Zintz identifies a fourth level, the capacity level. Of it he says:

The capacity level for reading is the *highest* level at which the child can understand the ideas and concepts in information material that is read to him. In determining this level, the teacher begins reading to the student at the level of difficulty at which he stops oral or silent reading because of reaching his frustration level. The same questions prepared to ask if he read the material are also appropriate to ask him after the teacher reads the material. Comprehension of 75 percent, the same proportion used for establishing instructional level, is the figure used for establishing capacity level. It is important to determine a child's capacity level so it can be compared to the child's instructional level. If the instructional level is only second level of second grade (2^2) and the capacity level for reading is fourth grade, the child's reading retardation is 1.5 years. This is one indication that the child has the innate ability to read much better than he or she is reading.

Now let us look again at the IRI table at the top of this page. According to the percentages given in the preceding para-

[5]Miles V. Zintz, *The Reading Process: The Teacher and the Learner,* 3d ed. (Dubuque, Iowa: William C. Brown Company Publishers, 1980), p. 451.

Level	Word Recognition	Oral Comprehension	Silent Comprehension	Average Comprehension
PP	100	100	80	90
P	100	100	100	100
1	96	90	90	90
2	95	100	90	95
3	96	80	80	80
4	96	90	80	85
5	90	80	70	75
6	87	70	70	70

Independent Reading Level: 2
Instructional Reading Level: 4
Frustration Reading Level: 5

graphs for each of the three levels, it will be noted that the independent reading level of the individual whose scores are recorded is the primer level, because at the first-reader level recorded in the table the word recognition score is below 99 percent. The instructional reading level of the pupil is second-reader, since beyond that point his word recognition scores fall below 95 percent. The frustration level is automatically the next level above the instructional level.

When selecting reading material for a pupil whose reading levels have been ascertained, we should not, if he is reading below his grade level, ask him to read a basal reader on the level indicated; we should give him other materials on that level. Imagine the chagrin of a sixth-grade boy whose instructional level is found to be a second-reader, if he were given a second-grade reader for study! What he needs is other material written on second-reader level.

Not all informal reading inventories are as easily interpreted as the previous example. The following pattern of scores is often obtained. Without caution confusion in their interpretation can arise.

At first glance it might appear that we have misinterpreted the scores. Fourth-reader level would be the instructional reading level since it is the highest point where at least 95 percent word recognition and 75 percent average comprehension are found. Fifth-reader level is also the frustration level. However, we do not have at least 99 percent word recognition and 90 percent average comprehension at second-reader level, which has been indicated as being the independent reading level.

According to a very strict interpretation of the scores this child would have to be placed at primer level for independent reading. The question becomes, "Should we place a boy or girl with an instructional level of four all the way back to primer level for recreational reading material?" The answer is, "Usually, no." The interest level in those materials is generally far below what the child wishes to read. We suggest that when there is such a great spread between the instructional and independent reading levels, according to the IRI, it is usually advisable to drop back no more than two levels below the instructional level for independent reading materials. In most instances books at that level will be easy enough for the child to read and still enjoy.

Yet another pattern of scores often obtained is as follows:

Level	Word Recognition	Oral Comprehension	Silent Comprehension	Average Comprehension
PP	100	100	100	100
P	95	100	100	100
1	91	100	80	90
2	97	90	80	95
3	95	80	60	70
4	97	80	70	75
5	95	80	70	75
6	87	70	50	60

Independent Reading Level: 3
Instructional Reading Level: 5
Frustration Reading Level: 6

If we look carefully at the scores we find some throughout the profile which are below acceptable points (level one word recognition and level three comprehension). In these instances, however, the low scores can be disregarded since it is reasonable to say that, if the child could read the words at level two, he certainly was capable of doing so at level one and, if the material was understandable at level four, it was also understandable at level three. Low scores such as these often occur when giving informal reading inventories. Perhaps the child was distracted, was thinking about something else, or simply did not like the story. In any event, those low scores are not indicative of reading difficulty.

One further comment about this set of scores. As in the previous example, the independent reading level is placed two levels below the instructional level even though using a very strict interpretation of the scores we would have to go to pre-primer level.

One additional pattern of scores needs to be illustrated:

Level	Word Recognition	Oral Comprehension	Silent Comprehension	Average Comprehension
PP	100	100	100	100
P	100	100	100	100
1	99	100	80	90
2	91	80	80	80
3	92	80	80	80
4	91	85	75	80
5	85	80	70	75
6	78	70	50	60

Independent Reading Level: 1
Instructional Reading Level: 3
Frustration Reading Level: 4

The problem in interpreting this set of scores is that no definite instructional level can be easily identified. The word recognition scores at levels 2, 3, and 4 are all in the low 90s and never reach the desired criteria of 95%. The average comprehension scores at those levels, however, are satisfactory for instructional-level reading.

The highest level in this example where the desired minimums of 95% word recognition and 75% comprehension, which would indicate the instructional reading level, are found is level 1. In reality, the scores actually found at level 1 are high enough to indicate that this level is the independent reading level. Consequently, a better choice for the instructional reading level would be the middle level of those three levels where the low 90s word-recognition scores occur; hence the reason for selecting level 3 as the instructional reading level.

Additional Information

These additional points may be of value to the reader:

1. A rough index of a child's instructional level can be ascertained from his grade-equivalent score as found through a survey test. To find it, one year should be subtracted from the child's grade-equivalent score. For example, a pupil with a grade-equivalent score of 6.0 has an estimated instructional level of 5.0.
2. Standardized reading inventories are also available commercially. Recommended are the *Botel Reading Inventory* (Follett Publishing Company), the *Classroom Reading Inventory* (William C. Brown Company), and the *Standard Reading Inventory* (Pioneer Printing Company).
3. For variations of procedure in constructing test materials for an informal

reading inventory, for administering it, and for interpreting it, the reader interested in pursuing the topic is referred to the following books:

Betts, Emmett A., *Foundations of Reading Instruction*, 2d ed. (New York: American Book, 1957), pp. 438-485.

Bond, Guy L., and Miles Tinker, *Reading Difficulties: Their Diagnosis and Correction,* 4th ed. (New York: Appleton, 1979), Ch. 7, "Specific Approaches to Diagnosis."

Burns, Paul C., and Betty D. Roe, *Teaching Reading in Today's Elementary Schools*, 2d ed. (Chicago: Rand McNally, 1980), pp. 355–363.

Cheek, Martha C., and Earl H. Cheek, *Diagnostic-Prescriptive Reading Instruction* (Dubuque, Iowa: Wm. C. Brown, 1980), pp. 57–70.

Durkin, Dolores, *Teaching Them to Read*, 2d ed., (Boston: Allyn and Bacon, 1970), pp. 498–503; 507–513.

Ekwall, Eldon E., *Diagnosis and Remediation of the Disabled Reader* (Boston: Allyn and Bacon, 1976), Ch. 11, "Using Informal Reading Inventories and the Cloze Procedure and the Analysis of Oral Reading Errors."

Sebesta, Sam L., and Carl J. Wallen, eds., *Readings on Teaching Reading* (Chicago: Science Research, 1972), "The Informal Reading Inventory: How to Construct It, How to Use It," by Frazier Cheyney, pp. 225–228.

Zintz, Miles V., *The Reading Process*, 2d ed. (Dubuque, Iowa: Wm. C. Brown, 1980), Ch. 19, "The Informal Reading Inventory."

Other Nonstandardized Techniques

Among other nonstandardized techniques that can be used for purposes of diagnosis are: (a) assessment of word-attack skills; (b) use of teacher-made criterion-referenced tests; and (c) use of the cloze technique.

Assessment of Word-Attack Skills

It is possible, and in many instances advisable, for the teacher to construct his own evaluative instruments to assess growth in any of the skills of reading. The following, for example, are points that might be included in a teacher-made test on the use of word-attack skills: (a) visual discrimination; (b) auditory discrimination; (c) letter names; (d) consonant sounds; (e) consonant blends; (f) consonant digraphs; (g) short vowel sounds; (h) long vowel sounds; (i) vowel digraphs; (j) compound words; (k) inflectional endings; (l) prefixes and suffixes; (m) syllabication.

An example of such a test is the Informal Word Analysis Survey given in Appendix B (see p. 433). Included in this appendix are: (a) the teacher's copy; (b) the pupil's copy; (c) a description of test items; (d) instructions; and (e) individual and class profile sheets. (The authors of the Survey hereby give permission to anyone to duplicate it, if he so desires.)

Use of Teacher-Made Criterion-Referenced Tests

Teachers can construct their own criterion-referenced tests in accordance with points included in the discussion on such tests presented earlier (see p. 343). When devising items for these tests care needs to be taken that:

1. The area (or "domain," as it is sometimes called) to be tested is clearly defined
2. The items test all phases of the "domain" being tested
3. The items are so stated, along with the direcions, that they test what they pur-

port to test, not ability to interpret directions

Use of the Cloze Technique

The cloze technique (described in Chapter 7A, "Comprehension," p. 179) as a teaching device, is increasingly used also as an instrument for testing comprehension. The form of the cloze items when used for testing is the same as that which can be used for teaching purposes. Every nth word of a passage can be omitted, as in the following paragraph in which a blank has been left for every tenth word. Or every noun or verb or other part of speech can be deleted.

> Did you know that the state flag of Alaska _____ seven major stars of the Big Dipper and the _____ Star on a field of blue? When Alaska was _____ a territory, before it became a state, a contest _____ held to design a flag. It was open only _____ school children. An Indian orphan boy won the contest. _____ design is still used for the state flag of _____

Use of a cloze exercise to test comprehension is based on the theory that the pupil who can better surmise the missing words from the remaining context is reading with the greater understanding. Various studies[6] have indicated the validity of this hypothesis, though research to date has not established the extent to which reliance can be placed on this technique either as a teaching procedure or as a testing tool. So far its value has not been demonstrated for use in the development or testing of some comprehension skills, such as judging the qualifications of an author or noting propaganda techniques. However, it seems to be of value in the development or testing of skills, such as noting details, getting the main idea, or predicting outcomes.

[6]Wesley J. Schneyer, "The Cloze Procedure for Improving Reading Comprehension," *The Reading Teacher*, vol. 19 (December 1965), p. 174.

The percent of correct responses in a cloze exercise is also being used for ascertaining readability (difficulty) of passages and for subsequent use in determining the independent, instructional, and frustration levels. Zintz[7] suggests the following range of correct responses for each of these levels: (a) fewer than 40 percent correct responses indicates the frustration reading level; (b) between 40 percent and 50 percent correct responses indicates the instructional reading level; (c) over 50 percent correct responses indicates the independent reading level.

New uses for the cloze procedure are also being discovered. Mary K. Gove[8] used this technique "as one means of encouraging beginning readers to apply their understanding of 'how language works' to written language" and Genevieve S. Lopardo[9] has found the cloze procedure useful in working with disabled readers.

Assessment of Readability Levels

It is extremely important that we find the reading abilities and disabilities of the children whom we teach. It is of equal importance that we know the reading level of the materials we ask children to read. In other words, it does little good to know that a child can read fourth-reader level material independently if we then ask that child to read a book written at sixth- or seventh-grade level.

It is almost impossible, without much experience, to pick up a book, look at it, and give an accurate estimate of the reading level at which it is written. Rather, we suggest that the teacher become acquainted with and use readability formulas on the books he uses in his classroom.

The Graph for Estimating Readability, by Fry,[10] which is relatively easy to use, is one example of such a formula. The graph, with directions, follows.

Directions for Using the Readability Graph

1. Select three one-hundred-word passages from near the beginning, middle, and end of the book. Skip all proper nouns.
2. Count the total number of sentences in each hundred-word passage (estimating to nearest tenth of a sentence). Average these three numbers.
3. Count the total number of syllables in each hundred-word sample. There is a syllable for each vowel sound; for example: cat (1), blackbird (2), continental (4). Don't be fooled by word size; for example: polio (3), through (1). Endings such as -y, -ed, -el, or -le usually make a syllable, for example: ready (2), bottle (2). It may be convenient to count every syllable over one in each word and add 100. Average the total number of syllables for the three samples.
4. Plot on the graph the average number of sentences per hundred words and the

[7]Miles V. Zintz, *Corrective Reading*, 3d ed. (Dubuque, Iowa: William C. Brown Company Publishers, 1977), p. 80. Data in this reference are an adaptation of an article by John R. Barmuth entitled, "Comparable Cloze and Multiple-Choice Comprehension Test Scores," *Journal of Reading*, 10 (February 1967), 291–299.

[8]Mary K. Gove, "Using the Cloze Procedure in a First-Grade Classroom," *The Reading Teacher*, vol. 29 (October 1975), p. 36.

[9]Genevieve S. Lopardo, "LEA-Cloze Reading Material for the Disabled Reader," *The Reading Teacher*, vol. 29 (October 1975), p. 42.

[10]Edward Fry, "A Readability Formula That Saves Time," *Journal of Reading*, vol. 11, (April 1968), p. 513.

Graph for Estimating Readability

by Edward Fry, Rutgers University Reading Center

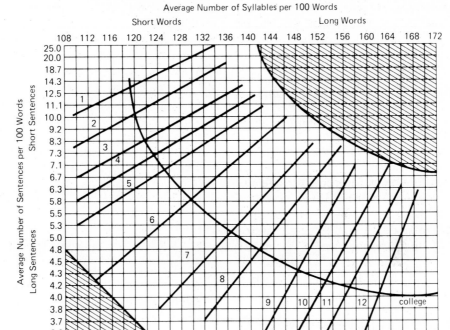

Average Number of Syllables per 100 Words

average number of syllables per hundred words. Most plot points fall near the heavy curved line. Diagonal lines mark off approximate grade-level areas.

Plotting the data given in the example below we find they fall in the fifth-grade area; hence the book is about fifth-grade difficulty level. If great variability is encountered either in sentence length or in the syllable count for the three selections, then randomly select several more passages and average them in before plotting.

Interesting information can at times be obtained from looking at the range of the reading levels of the three passages checked before they are averaged. Frequently, cer-

Example

		Sentences Per 100 Words	Syllables Per 100 Words
100-word sample	Page 5	9.1	122
100-word sample	Page 89	8.5	140
100-word sample	Page 160	7.0	129
		3)24.6	3)391
	Average	8.2	130

tain parts of a book are significantly more difficult to read than others.

When using readability formulas it should be kept in mind that they do not take into consideration the motivation and the experience background of the reader nor the concept load of the passage.

For Further Study

Bond, Guy L., and Miles A. Tinker, *Reading Difficulties: Their Diagnosis and Correction*, 4th ed. (New York: Appleton, Century, Crofts, 1979).

Burns, Paul C., and Betty D. Roe, *Teaching Reading in Today's Elementary School*, 2d ed. (Chicago: Rand McNally & Company, 1980), Ch. 9, "Assessment of Pupil Progress."

Bush, Clifford L., and Mildred H. Huebner, *Strategies for Reading in the Elementary School*, 2d ed. (New York: The Macmillan Company, 1979), Ch. 13, "Methods of Appraisal."

Fry, Edward, *Reading Instruction for Classroom and Clinic* (New York: McGraw-Hill, Inc., 1972).

Harris, Albert J., *How to Increase Reading Ability*, 6th ed. (New York: McGraw-Hill, Inc., 1975).

Harris, Larry A., and Carl B. Smith, *Reading Instruction: Diagnostic Teaching in the Classroom*, 3d ed. (New York: Holt, Rinehart and Winston, 1980).

Howards, Melvin, *Reading Diagnosis and Instruction: An Integrated Approach* (Reston, Va.: Reston Publishing Company, 1980), Ch. 2, "Diagnosis and Misdiagnosis," and Ch. 3, "Administering and Interpreting the IDA."

Karlin, Robert, *Teaching Elementary Reading: Principles and Strategies* 3d ed. (New York: Harcourt Brace Jovanovich, Inc., 1980), Ch. 2, "Diagnostic Teaching of Reading."

Silvaroli, Nicholas J., *Classroom Reading Inventory*, 3d ed. (Dubuque, Iowa: William C. Brown, 1976).

Zintz, Miles V., *Corrective Reading* (Dubuque, Iowa: William C. Brown, 1977).

Questions and Comments for Thought and Discussion

1. We have noted that standardized reading tests are sometimes classified as survey tests and diagnostic tests. How can the scores of reading survey tests be of value to the teacher who is making a diagnosis of a child's reading? What cautions should the teacher have in mind when interpreting scores on a survey test?

2. Why is it important for classroom teachers of reading to be proficient in the adminstration of group psychological, physiological, and skill-assessment tests?

3. Both an informal reading inventory and a standardized reading achievement test can be used to find a pupil's instructional reading level. How can the two instruments supplement one another?

4. You may wish to construct part of an informal reading inventory according to suggestions given in this chapter. (Unless you are competent to check the readability of passages you use by means of a readability formula, it is suggested that you take the passages for your inventory from a basal reader series.) Or you and other students may wish to

construct all the materials for an informal reading inventory and each of you test a child with it, write a summary sheet on your findings, and give your interpretation of the results orally to your class.

5. After studying again the part that deals with the cloze technique (as described in Chapter 7A, "Comprehension," p. 179) and after reviewing the comments made in this chapter on that technique as a testing tool, you may wish to construct an exercise using this procedure.

6. An oft-repeated emphasis is that all teaching should be based on diagnosis. What implication do you see in this claim for the classroom teacher? What is your reaction to the claim?

7. What advantages or disadvantages do you see as you compare a test such as the "Informal Word Analysis Survey" reproduced in Appendix B (see p. 433) with a reading achievement test?

8. You may wish to check for readability levels some elementary-school books in the area of the social studies and/or science. What might you do to help some children better understand the content of such books?

Recognizing the Uniqueness of the Learner

Children differ not only in their achievement levels and their rates of learning but also in almost every identifiable human characteristic. They differ in physical, emotional, and tempermental characteristics, in their mental potential, in their social attitudes, in their interests, and in their special talents. They differ also in their ways of "unlocking words". No system of instruction could possibly do full justice to all these differences in all their aspects. An important principle to remember is that differences are normal and that in many respects they contribute to the appeal as well as to the difficulty of teaching.

Reading and Linguistic Diversity

Every human being is a member of a cultural and ethnic group, which may or may not be in predominance in a given geographic area. It is imperative to consider that while there are many likenesses among people of varying ethnic backgrounds, there are also marked differences. Even when linguistic diversity is not widespread or apparent in a community, the teacher should strive to broaden and deepen the students' appreciation and acceptance of the differences in language usage as a needed reality in the nation and in the world.

Basic Considerations

All people are surrounded by a cultural context upon birth. The word *culture* may refer, for example, to the American culture (more accurately to the culture of the United States when referring only to that country in the North and South American continent) as compared with the European culture. However, one may also refer to cultures that distinguish regions, for example, the Southern culture. Similarly, when discussing peoples who live within different regions in any part of the nation, we may distinguish culture as it pertains to membership in an ethnic group. For instance, citizens of the United States living in New Prague, Minnesota, may experience the influence of both the culture of the United States and of the ethnic manifestations of Czechoslovakian culture. And, a Chinese-American child living in San Francisco may absorb the "American" culture of his ethnic heritage. Important for the teacher to real-

357

ize is that there are not only differences *among* ethnic groups but also *within* them. In other words, while there are important differences, let us say, between the North American Indians and the Scandinavians, there are also highly significant cultural differences among the members of each of these groups. The likenesses among ethnic groups may be vastly greater than those within any one group. Furthermore, an individual may or may not identify strongly with ethnic group membership, after having through the process of assimilation or enculturation adopted the culture of the predominate group where his heritage is of an ethnic minority. The error in overgeneralization on characteristics of any ethnic group is thus evident.

We use the term *ethnically different* or *ethnically divergent* in this chapter to refer to children from homes in which the ethnic background is unlike that of the group most predominate in numbers in their vicinity. We characterize those boys and girls as *socioeconomically disadvantaged* regardless of ethnic origin whose home background is low on the socioeconomic scale as defined in our society. The lack of cultural advantages may be found in any ethnic group whose socioeconomic circumstances are impoverished. This lack is often referred to as the culture of poverty as contrasted with the culture of affluence. In each of these situations it is not ethnicity which is advantaged or disadvantaged, but the attainment or lack of attainment of economic success, which allows for mobility on the social scale. When deprivation or lack of opportunity for economic betterment is related to intolerance and misunderstanding of ethnic divergence and minority group status in a multicultural society, it is referred to as prejudice on the part of individuals and as discrimination when the practice is institutionalized.

Necessarily the treatment given in this chapter to a consideration of ethnic differences in relation to the teaching of reading cannot be extensive. We will therefore consider only two of the special problems of teaching reading to children from ethnically divergent backgrounds. One concerns dialect speech; the other deals with learning to read when English is the child's second language. As the reader notes the suggestions given under both of these topics, he should keep in mind the fact that basic to an effective program of teaching reading to a child of any ethnic origin, is the teacher who has the undergirding conviction that differences among ethnic groups are not synonymous with inferiority. A deep-seated respect for an individual of any group is essential.

Increased awareness of linguistic diversity in our nation's population has resulted in and from a growing body of literature which provides an ample resource for teachers of reading. A sample of references is listed at the end of this section.

Dialect Speech

One of the major points of concern in the focus on the linguistic development of the child from an ethnically divergent home has been his dialect (see p. 18). As in the case of other concerns about his language, it has often not been dealt with judiciously. Contributing to this problem has been the lack of understanding of what standard English refers to and the absence of clarity with which the word *dialect* is often used.

Standard Speech versus Dialect Speech

That which is designated as standard English is a form of speech considered appropriate for a particular context. In spoken form, standard English is congruent with the written linguistic pattern in most textbooks in regard to word order, complexity of grammatical syntax, and choice of vocabulary. Consideration of what constitutes dialect speech, a divergence from standard English, can throw further light on what standard English represents. An explanation, rather than a definition, of the term *dialect speech* is probably the more illuminating for our purpose.

Dialect speech has characteristics which are associated with geographical region, social class, or national origin. Typically, the term *dialect speech*, when referring to the speech of children, has been used to designate that of the immigrant child from a non-English-speaking country and that of one born in the United States from a non-English-speaking home. Also the speech of many boys and girls from English-speaking families, whose speech differs markedly from so-called standard English, is usually considered dialect. But, in a sense, all native-born Americans speak a dialect of English. This statement may come as a surprise to some. An anecdote illustrative of the inability of persons to recognize the pervasiveness of dialects in our country is reported by H. Rex Wilson[1] who states:

> A recent addition to American folklore tells of a Texan who welcomed the presidency of Lyndon Johnson with the comment, "At last we have a President who doesn't talk with an accent."

Although attitudes toward speakers of a different dialect than our own are often negative, a basic understanding of what constitutes dialect speech makes this attitude prejudicial and, therefore, rationally untenable. Using the same language (whether, for example, English, Spanish, or

Chinese) dialect speakers—which include all of us—speak in distinctive ways for several reasons. These reasons may be classified as regional, social, and cultural.

Regional dialects are what make a Bostonian's pronunciation of the word *supper* different from that of a Midwesterner's. Also, the influence of a regional speech community is what accounts for reference to a skunk as a polecat depending on where one lives.

Social dialects refer to distinctions noticed in speech patterns which often result from the extent of formal education. The degree of sophistication and of complexity in language usage is different, for example, between an academician and someone whose need of formality in language usage is less. Or there may be a stylistic variation in speech chosen by an individual from a repertoire useful in adapting to a given situation, for example, such as using baby-talk when speaking to an infant.

Fostering Understanding of Dialect

It is apparent that teachers of reading must be aware of dialect differences among pupils in order to teach reading effectively. They must recognize whether a pupil will experience interference because of differences in sounds, morphological variations (words with affixes), word order, and vocabulary usage. Although different approaches have been used in the teaching of reading to the linguistically divergent, there is general agreement regarding the need of the teacher to be sensitive to individual differences which must be diagnosed to effect success in learning to read.

The extent to which teachers are knowledgeable about dialect differences in part determines the strategies which will be applied in teaching reading. These strategies range widely from insistence that standard English be learned prior to beginning read-

[1]H. Rex Wilson, "The Geography of Language," *Linguistics in School Programs.* The Sixty-Ninth Yearbook of the National Society for the Study of Education, Part II, Albert H. Marckwardt, ed. (Chicago: The University of Chicago Press, 1970), p. 64.

ing instruction to teaching reading initially solely through the use of non-standard, dialect materials. Between these two disparate approaches there are a number of methods less extreme which have been used with varying degrees of success. The reader is referred to the research literature for assistance in determining what strategies might be most appropriate and effective for a given local situation or region. However, research to date has not presented unequivocal evidence on this complex matter.

Although research has not given a conclusive answer in regard to many matters concerning the teaching of reading to children with speech divergent from that which is taught in school, there are several points of view on which there is some agreement among a signigicant proportion of the teaching profession. Many educators, agree—the writers of this book among them—that it is not necessary to change the dialect of an English-speaking child in order to teach him to read. The child speaking a divergent dialect reads the sounds of his own speech as he reads English. The learner's natural dialect, unchanged, can be the immediate bridge to the skills of literacy without forcing him to learn a new dialect as a prerequisite. However, he should be richly provided with "reading-readiness" activities that extend his background of experience, that help increase his auditory perception and his ability to make auditory discriminations, that increase his power over language. To deprive a child of the experience of learning to read for an indefinite number of months or even a year or longer is a highly questionable procedure.

Since it is not necessary for a child to change his divergent dialect when he is beginning to learn to read, the teacher should allow him, when reading orally, to read in his dialect the material written in "standard English." Later when the learning-to-read process is well under way, the child may acquire, at his learning pace, "standard English" as a "second language."

It is the point of view of the authors of this book that since standard English (the predominate form used in textbooks and formal communication in commerce) is the form recognized for social mobility and for acceptance in various vocational and professional areas, standard English should, in time, be taught to children whose speech patterns may not conform. However, it is essential that the teaching proceed without denial of the dialect spoken by the child, but with acceptance and understanding of it. Modeling of standard English by teachers and allowing the child to use his own pattern of speech communication as a prerequisite to extending his range of communication can be effected without negative judgment of whatever variant form of English may be considered non-standard. It should be remembered that variant forms exist because of their utility in communicating appropriately in the contexts in which they were learned.

English as a Second Language

In recognition of the continuing need of teachers to accommodate pupils who are not native speakers of English, the government of the United States in 1967 enacted legislation referred to as Title VII, which officially sanctioned and supported bilingual education. It was intended primarily for Mexican-Americans since Spanish is the second most spoken language in the United States. In 1968 the Bilingual Education Act was amended to include all non-English-speaking children and to provide for various forms of assistance including teacher education.

The problems encountered in implementing various bilingual education programs have been reviewed by Pamela and Iris Tiedt[2] in terms of these areas: (1) the language of both the students and their teachers; (2) the language reflected in curriculum materials used, and (3) basic goals of the programs with respect to language. The reader is referred to the reference by Tiedt and Tiedt as source of an excellent treatment of factors to be considered in designing and implementing bilingual education programs.

In recent years, with growing social consciousness and the arrival of new immigrants such as the Indo-Chinese and Cuban refugees, the responsibility of the public schools to provide an appropriate education has been accentuated. The cultural and linguistic backgrounds even within these two populations is sufficient to suggest the enormity of the task which lies ahead in dealing with cultural pluralism, that has existed in the United States since the beginning of its nationhood. The basic issue in provision of bilingual education currently debated is whether the intentions of the programs of the federal government are to maintain both the native language of the speaker and English as a second language or gradually to replace the native language with English.

The maintenance of both languages (native and second) has advantages when basic instruction is first received in the speaker's native tongue. The non-English-speaking student can experience success and a positive self-concept when English-speaking students also are given an opportunity to learn another language and know about another culture. Furthermore, students need not painfully experience the learning of a second language in high school, the period of the students' education to which the teaching of a second language to the English-speaking student is now generally deferred. In the contemporary world, bilingualism is an asset and one enjoyed by other citizens throughout the world where often English is one of several languages learned.

It is important also to view difficulties in implementing bilingual education. Some educators have discussed the erosion of nationalism as a possible consequence of bilingual and bicultural education. This view should be considered with caution in the light of the fact that other nations have maintained unity because of governmental policy to respect language divergences among their populations. In some other countries, for example, Canada, the challenge is being given serious consideration in an attempt to maintain unity. Given a futuristic orientation, however, world affairs have sufficiently demonstrated that international relations in the world community increasingly suggest the need for improved communication between and among culturally and linguistically different peoples.

Although problems are numerous in accommodating the language diversity of pupils in a pluralistic society, yet, in keeping with the spirit of American public education to provide for individual differences among the learners, gradual resolution of the problem as would be appropriate in various areas of the country is a reasonable expectation. It should be observed, however, that in the past in times of national crises, for example, during World War II and the post-Sputnik era, governmental policy has not been consistent. Teachers of reading if not already prepared to meet the challenge,

[2]Pamela L. Tiedt and Iris M. Tiedt, *Multicultural Teaching: A Handbook of Activities, Information and Resources* (Boston: Allyn and Bacon, 1979) Appendix A, "A Linguistic Evaluation of Bilingual Education Programs," pp. 324–5.

can find numerous resources in the literature to learn strategies for accommodation of linguistic diversity among pupils.

References

The selected references here listed include consideration of both dialect and other language differences.

Paul C. Burns and Betty D. Roe, *Teaching Reading in Today's Elementary Schools* (Chicago: Rand McNally College Publishing Company, 1976).

Joshua Fishman, *Bilingual Education: An International Sociological Perspective* (Rowley, Mass.: Newbury House Publishing Company, 1976).

Daniel R. Hittleman, *Developmental Reading: A Psycholinguistic Perspective* (Chicago: Rand McNally College Publishing Company, 1978).

James L. Laffey and Roger Shuy, eds., *Language Differences: Do They Interfere?* (Newark, Del.: International Reading Association, 1973).

Pose Lamb and Richard Arnold, *Teaching Reading: Foundations and Strategies*, 2d ed., (Belmont, Calif.: Wadsworth Publishing Company, 1980).

Diane Lapp and James Flood, *Teaching Reading to Every Child* (New York: Macmillan, 1978).

Carmen O'Brien, *Teaching the Language-Different Child to Read* (Columbus, Ohio: Charles E. Merrill, 1973).

Grayce A. Ransom, *Preparing to Teach Reading* (Boston: Little, Brown and Company, 1978).

Richard J. Smith and Dale D. Johnson, *Teaching Children to Read*, 2d ed. (Reading, Mass.: Addison-Wesley Publishing Company, 1980).

Pamela L. Tiedt and Iris M. Tiedt, *Multicultural Teaching: A Handbook of Activities, Information, and Resources* (Boston: Allyn and Bacon, 1979).

Reading and the Exceptional Child

Special consideration should be given to some of the concerns related primarily to teaching reading to the exceptional child. We will consider the needs of (a) the gifted, (b) the slow learner, and (c) the child who achieves below his potential.

Reading and the Gifted

The neglect of the gifted child in terms of special provisions to accommodate his needs is one of the acute problems of the day. Avowed interest in individualizing instruction to provide for different needs has not been followed up by establishment of a large number of programs to implement specialized instruction for the gifted. Fortunately, special attention is increasingly being given to their education. However, isolating the gifted from other students throughout the school day has lost favor.

Need of Special Attention to the Gifted Child

Since the school in a democratic society regards all children as being of equal worth, it must not in its distribution of effort deliberately discriminate against any group because of low, average, or high academic aptitude and achievement. There are compelling reasons why all should learn to read as well as their capacities permit. Nevertheless, because teachers are human and fallible and because time and resources are not unlimited, they cannot always do complete justice to all the children in their classes. Many teachers find that work with retarded and average pupils is so time-consuming and the needs of these children so apparent that they tend to neglect those who obviously are superior in academic ability. The growing concern about the gifted child is therefore justified.

The type of instruction required by the bright child does not differ greatly from that given to other children. The physical, sensory, emotional, and other factors essential to good reading, as well as the specific skills of reading, are important to all. The difference is to be found in the range and level of difficulty of the materials and in special problems peculiar to the bright child.

One difference, for example, is the fact that bright children often acquire many of the reading skills independently and almost unconsciously in the course of extensive, highly motivated reading. Special lessons and exercises in these reading skills can and should be by-passed for them. What the teacher needs to do in such situations is to be sure that these skills have been mastered.

Specialists in the education of the gifted child recognize that social maturity does not necessarily go hand in hand with academic achievement. There is no evidence that bright children as a group are less mature socially than other children. In fact, intellectual maturity is commonly accompanied by social maturity. It would not be surprising, however, if we found that some very bright children were less conforming, that they demanded reasons for rules of behavior, and that they exhibited some impatience with other pupils less well endowed.

A degree of nonconformity is a desirable personality trait. Independence of mind is essential to social and scientific progress and to artistic creation. But it is of the greatest importance that our ablest individuals learn early in life to act responsibly and to be concerned about the well being and happiness of others. The codes of the physician, who places the well being of his patient first, and of the scientist, who weighs the effect of his discoveries on society, may have their origins in the early face-to-face experiences of childhood. In our fascination with a child's brilliance we cannot afford to forget the great influence for good or evil that he can have upon society. Reading is one of the potent means at our disposal to lead the child on the road to responsible and constructive effort.

The present-day drive toward "academic excellence" is overdue, but it must not be permitted to distort the humanistic goals of education. The child who reads about people in other cultures and other lands should be cultivating the art of unlimited kinship with people. In fact, he should be developing in all desirable characteristics.

Unfortunately, discussions of the problems of educating the gifted child rarely concern themselves with questions relating to emotional growth and attitude formation. They are concerned chiefly with the conservation of intellectual talent now so often going to waste because of unfavorable home and community environments and school programs not sufficiently adapted to the needs of the gifted child. One difficulty is that emotions are hard to discover and measure; it is almost impossible to formulate succinct education objectives with regard to them, except as they result in serious and persistent antisocial behavior. Nevertheless, any consideration of the teaching of reading and literature which does not embrace the emotional dimension is necessarily incomplete and distorts any valid conception of the teacher's task.

The bright child usually has little difficulty in learning to interpret the literal and figurative meaning of a selection appropriate to his general maturity. What we cannot be so sure of is that the child will know how to identify with situations he reads about or utilize what he reads in building a mental image of the social and human consequences of conditions and events. Speed and comprehension in the reading of a poem, for example, are not enough. There must be moments of contemplation in which the reader visualizes a scene, thinks with wonder about a deed of heroism, and possibly laughs or weeps with a character in a story. Speed tests in reading do not measure these capacities for feeling. Social sensitivity and human understanding should occupy a high place among our objectives in reading instruction.

Identifying the Gifted Child

What shall we call those whose gifts are many and great? Many terms have been used. These children have been called "able," "bright," "talented," "academically superior," "children of high academic aptitude," "intellectually gifted," "academically talented," among other expressions. These terms sometimes have different meanings; in some cases they are applied to children with special aptitudes in art, music, or mechanical activity, and in other cases to children whose intellectual potential amounts to genius. At times an individual with an IQ of 130 or above has been considered gifted—even genius or near genius. However, an IQ of 130 or slightly higher is probably lower than that of a person whom we would ordinarily designate as genius or near genius.

There are, in fact, no sharply defined boundaries among these groups although the problems of instruction may differ as we go up on the scale. Any dividing lines must be arbitrary. In our discussion we shall deal with the largest group of superior learners, and for convenience draw the line at approximately 130 IQ. We shall use some of the terms mentioned above interchangeably.

The usual methods of identifying bright children involve the use of individual and group tests of intelligence, achievement tests, and teacher observation. Individual intelligence tests are probably the most accurate of the methods, but they are time-consuming and require trained examiners. Group intelligence tests and achievement tests are useful as screening devices, but they may be quite inaccurate in assessing an individual's true capabilities. Teacher observation is an essential part of the evaluation process because it may reveal aspects of a child's mental powers not reflected in any test. It is not unusual for a group test to rate as many as 25 percent of the gifted children below their true intelligence level.

Often in the past the description of the gifted child has been limited to the one with a high intelligence quotient but, fortunately, current definitions are more inclusive. There has been growing evidence to support the contention that if the only criterion used for designating giftedness were an intelligence quotient of 130 or above, some of the most creative pupils would not be detected. Investigators supporting this claim that items on intelligence tests do not help identify some of the differentiating characteristics of the gifted, such as originality, imagination, or divergent thinking channeled toward constructive outcomes. In harmony with this point of view Paul Witty,[3] who has through the decades made

[3]Paul Witty, Alma Freeland, and Edith Grotberg, *The Teaching of Reading: A Developmental Process* (Boston: Heath, 1966), p. 340.

extensive study of the gifted, proposes that "any child whose performance is consistently or repeatedly remarkable in a worthwhile line of human endeavor might be considered gifted." Such a broadened definition allows for the inclusion of pupils not only with verbal facility but also those whose talent could be fostered in the arts, sciences, mechanics, and social leadership.

Gifted children with high intelligence quotients are generally accelerated in academic attainment. They often read early and are verbally gifted. Contrary to a stereotyped view, the intellectual giftedness of these pupils does not restrict them, as a group, from being socially as well as emotionally more mature than their peers. Moreover, the gifted child has been found to be physically better developed than the average child of his age group. Other observable characteristics, which help to distinguish the intellectually gifted from the average, include these: rapidity of learning, good memory, marked reasoning ability, wide scope of information, large vocabulary, superior reading ability, keen power of comprehension.

It is interesting to note that characteristics descriptive of pupils whose giftedness is identified through their verbal ability differ considerably in some respect from those of the gifted creative children. The latter are described more often as encountering problems in social adjustment, as being original in their thinking but highly impatient with routine, and as frequently being disruptive in classrooms. But, like the verbally gifted, they are often early readers. Because of their interest in reading it is frequently possible to assist them in wide reading so as to extend their interests and to enable them to identify with worthy persons similar to those whose biographies are part of the literary heritage.

Creating the Conditions for Maximum Learning

The key to good teaching is the teacher himself. Materials and methods are important, but no amount of pedagogical theory, library resources, audiovisual aids, laboratories, auditoriums, or testing programs can compensate for the lack of the competent, resourceful teacher.

All children need teachers who are above average in intelligence. But the bright child needs a teacher who is distinctly superior in mental ability. His IQ need not be as high as that of the brightest child in his class, but he should be bright enough to feel secure in his relations with the child and to command his respect. He should be willing to learn from the bright child and sometimes to let the child teach the things the teacher does not know as well.

Statements by gifted children describing teachers they like reveal that they want teachers who know their subjects, related fields, and current events; who use humor and illustrative material to add interest to the subject; and who are skillful in relating the subject to other fields and to the pupils' lives. They want teachers who require them to learn, to work together on class projects, to discuss problems together, and to assume initiative and responsibility. They like teachers who are versatile, fair, even-tempered, and patient.

The teacher of the gifted can and should be more permissive in his assignments to gifted children than to those of more limited abilities, who usually desire and need definite and detailed instructions for a task. Gifted children are more likely to ask questions about the *why* of the methods employed by the teacher; and the teacher should freely discuss his reasons and objectives with them. If the pupil is egotistic or immature because of coddling at home, the teacher should set challenges and require performance that will result in the development of a more mature self-image on the part of the child. In short, the teacher of the academically superior child should have all the qualities of any good teacher, and some of them to a high degree.

Next to a good teacher in importance is the provision of abundant reading materials difficult enough and diversified enough to provide a genuine challenge and to appeal to the wide range of interests so characteristic of the bright child. For truly gifted children the book and magazine resources of many elementary schools are inadequate. Public libraries, state traveling book collections, and possibly the paperback selections in supermarkets and elsewhere need to be utilized to meet this child's interests. Academically superior pupils tend to be omnivorous readers, particularly when suitable reading materials are readily accessible. They are attracted, also, to encyclopedias, atlases, dictionaries, and other types of reference materials. As a consequence, the school library assumes great importance in the reading guidance of gifted children. Failure to provide proper library facilities in elementary schools must necessarily result in great waste of the precious resources represented by the learning potential of these children.

The need for more and better reading materials implies also the necessity of a wide knowledge of literature for children on the part of the teacher. No teacher can possibly have read all the books that gifted children are likely to read or should read, but fortunately there are excellent guides and booklists which should be available to the teacher in the school library.

In providing books for individual reading, teachers should make certain that they include titles that will challenge the able reader. Many superior readers in the upper elementary grades enjoy reading books generally considered adult fare. They should be encouraged to read suitable books on that level.

Planning Reading Programs for Gifted Children

Studies of the reading habits of verbally gifted children reveal that they spend many hours a day reading, that they have wider interests and do more voluntary reading than the average child, and that about half of the highly gifted read before they enter school. Significantly, they learn to read by a great variety of methods, and it may be assumed that in their cases the method employed is far less important than the versatility and skill of the teacher and the availability of suitable reading materials.

Plans employed for meeting the needs of gifted children in general fall into three main categories: (a) enrichment; (b) acceleration; and (c) special grouping. Of these, perhaps the most popular plan is that of enrichment. In an enrichment program provision is made for individual differences in ability within the setting of the regular classroom. The gifted child remains with his age-mates, but is encouraged to take on more complex tasks. More emphasis is placed on original thinking and problem solving. In the case of reading, the academically superior child is expected to choose books calling for higher levels of comprehension than those possessed by other members of the class.

A promising form of enrichment is the unit organization of instruction, especially in the middle grades. In this plan the teacher may propose a number of topics for study from which all the pupils make a choice. With the aid of the teacher, the class assembles a bibliography for the chosen area of study, using the various reference aids in the classroom and library. The teacher then assists the pupils in developing the topic. Some of the reading selections may be read and enjoyed by all the pupils, but the abler members of the class should also select reading materials commensurate with their abilities. A task of the teacher in the content areas is to assist all pupils, regardless of ability, to grow toward increased maturity in reading.

The policy of acceleration may take different forms. One of these is early admittance to school of the bright child. Certainly there is nothing sacred about age six as the earliest entering age, particularly since the differences among children of the same chronological age are so wide. In schools with a nongraded primary division it is possible to permit bright children to complete the three-year period in less time, especially if they are socially and emotionally well adjusted. Double promotion is another plan of acceleration, but one to be used with great caution to avoid the danger that the child will miss basic steps in skill development or the building of background information.

Many parents and school officials are reluctant to adopt a policy of acceleration because of the fear that the accelerated child will have difficulty in making a good adjustment in a group of older children. Research studies have indicated that, in general, pupils have benefited from programs of acceleration and that the fear of social maladjustment because of acceleration is usually unfounded. Nevertheless, the needs and social maturity of each child should be carefully studied before he is advanced to a group of older children.

Special classes for gifted children have been organized in a sizable number of elementary schools. An alleged advantage of such classes is that they enable gifted children to enjoy the opportunity of working with their intellectual peers and so to benefit from the give-and-take of planning and discussing with other children equally alert and eager to think and to explore. But in this kind of segregation they miss early associations with children less gifted, with whom they will be living as adults. Better than total division of the gifted from other boys and girls, in the opinion of many educators, is the practice engaged in at some schools in which the gifted are in special classes only part of the school day and are kept with their age-mates for the remainder of the day, usually for such activities as music, art, and physical education.

Reading and the Slow Learner

The slow learner, as the term is used here, is not to be confused with the underachiever in reading, to whom attention is given later in this chapter. When we speak of the slow learner we are referring to the individual who has below-average mental ability for performance in academic areas. We designate him as an underachiever in reading only if he is not reading up to the level at which, with his intelligence, he could be expected to read. Although, on the very basis from which intelligence quotients are derived, the average IQ is 100, usually a range of ten or fifteen points above and below that figure is considered within the area of normalcy. Thus, in terms of intelligence quotients, we are categorizing as slow learners those boys and girls with IQ's of less than 85 or 90. We do not refer to the mentally retarded, however, when we use the term *slow learners*. In the following excerpt[4] is shown a legislative designation of *mentally retarded:*

> "Mentally retarded" means significantly subaverage general intellectual functioning existing concurrently with deficits in adaptive

[4]*Federal Register* 41:56977, (1976).

behavior and manifested during the developmental period, which adversely affects a child's educational performance.

One of the greatest impediments to successful performance, in accordance with the capacity of the slow learner, is the attitude toward him of those with whom he comes into contact—his parents, his teachers, other adults, his peers. Many parents, especially those with average and above-average intelligence, find it difficult to accept the slow learner at full worth, as an individual entitled to the same rights to the pursuit of happiness as the brightest among us. Some are ashamed that they are the parents of a child below average in learning capacity. Often this attitude is perceived even by the slowest among the slow. Some parents even use epithets such as *stupid* to the child's face!

Teachers have not been innocent of maltreatment of the slow learner on the affective level. Many prefer having the bright child in their classrooms. Often unintentionally on the part of the teacher, yet insidiously, that attitude carries over into their actions, and the boys and girls who are slow learners sense it. Teachers who frequently praise high academic performance of the average and above-average child may not realize what a depressing, discouraging effect such references must have on the one who never can achieve academically up to the level that the teacher deems praiseworthy. Another example of inhuman treatment is urging the slow learner to reach levels impossible for him to attain. Nor has homogeneous grouping in spite of the best of intentions on the teacher's part, had a salutary effect, in many instances, on the ego of the children in the lowest group.

Teachers of reading are, at times, too eager to get a child to become a good reader, regardless of other consequences. At various points throughout this book we are stressing that it is less important that a child develop into an effective reader than that he become a well-balanced individual who can lead a socially useful and personally satisfying life. To the extent that reading contributes to this objective it is important; when it begins interfering with it, its value is less than questionable. While the teacher will, indeed, want to strive to help the slow learner read up to his capacity, he should not have that as his highest aim. Usually there needs to be no conflict between means of accomplishing both of these objectives—between reading up to capacity and becoming a well-rounded individual; in fact, we can expect a positive correlation between the two.

The teacher who accepts the slow learner along with his problems with understanding and respect and appreciation is in a key position to help make a better world for the child. His influence on parents can be of great moment as he points out to them the need of accepting the child as he is, of not expecting too much from him academically, of noting his achievements both in academic and nonacademic areas, of letting him know that his accomplishments are recognized. The teacher can affect the attitude of other adults through casual conversation, through parent-teacher conferences, through group meetings with parents. He can favorably influence the peer group through day-in, day-out classroom actions as they observe the teacher in his treatment of the slow learner, as they hear him emphasize the contributions of each child, as they realize they are in a classroom in which an atmosphere of friendliness and of respect for one another prevails.

As important as the attitude that others

show toward the slow learner is that with which he regards himself—his self-concept. The latter can be determined by the former. The child who is treated as if he were inferior is usually quick to develop the belief that he is of lesser value, that he is tolerated rather than accepted in a group, that there is no use trying to do anything well since he considers any attempts he might make as doomed to failure. No wonder that the learners are often an unhappy group of human beings, robbed by their fellow men of the satisfaction of many of their innate needs—of a feeling of accomplishment, of a knowledge that they are wanted in the groups to which they belong, of the blessing of loving and being loved. And yet we as teachers have wondered why the slow learner has not been quicker to respond to our teaching, forgetting that we ourselves, in a state of even temporary discouragement, find it difficult to develop incentive for achievement or stamina for work!

When we refer to the matter of self-concept in its relation to success in reading, we are referring to a healthy self-concept, which enables the child to accept himself realistically, without undue concentration on himself. With such an attitude he will view his limitations with understanding. It will also help make it possible for him to attribute to himself the dignity deserved by every human being. He will pay due attention to his accomplishments and will focus on his possible future attainments. He will be sensibly competitive with his own past record of achievement rather than with those of others. What the teacher will do to assist the child with inferior ability—or any other child, for that matter—in achieving such a perspective can be of value to the child not only as he faces the developmental task of learning to read but also as he approaches other situations confronting him.

The Reader Who Achieves below His Potential

A child who is reading under his level of mental ability is underachieving regardless of whether he is reading above, at, or below his grade or age level. The gifted child, as well as the slow learner, can be underachieving. So can the great number of boys and girls with average intellectual ability.

Causes of Underachieving in Reading

Knowledge of the causes of unsatisfactory progress in reading is valuable from two standpoints. Such understanding can help the teacher (a) prevent retardation and (b) deal intelligently with difficulties as they arise. The task is to look behind the symptoms and find the causes. These will usually be a combination of several elements; indeed, multiple causation is a basic principle of remedial reading. The causes of reading difficulty are usually numerous, complex, and interrelated. (See Chapter 12, "Classroom Diagnosis of Reading Ability.")

Because of their interrelatedness, the search for causes should not end when one apparent cause has been found. Frequently, a primary cause of retardation in reading, especially if the difficulty is one of long duration, results in one or more secondary causes, which may in turn greatly influence the effectiveness of the reading program. Thus, for example, illness, with consequent irregularity of school attendance, may be at the root of a child's reading difficulty. It may result in lack of interest in learning, which by itself is significant enough to bring about serious problems in learning to read.

Reading Deficiency and Personality

Reading problems are often associated with personality problems. Since reading is so important in the life of every child, failure in this activity may be expected to cause anxieties, feelings of insecurity, and even aggressive behavior. On the other hand, children who come to school with a sense of inadequacy, a feeling of being unloved, or an unconscious hostility against the adult world may lack the necessary incentive to learn to read or may be prepared to resist efforts on the part of the teacher to teach them. The factors of personality problems and reading problems are no doubt frequently reciprocal. For this reason, it is commonly necessary to provide personal guidance along with corrective instruction in reading. Certainly the teacher needs to consider the total development of the child, not merely his reading needs.

Reading Deficiency and the Home Situation Various investigations show that situations in homes or poor family relations are contributing causes to poor progress in reading. However, the emotional stresses resulting from conflict or deprivation in the home are only one source of reading retardation as far as the home is concerned. Indifference on the part of parents toward a child's reading may be responsible for a lack of incentive to learn to read. Paradoxically, oversolicitude on the part of parents may also create tensions that impede reading progress. If there is hostility between child and parent, the very eagerness of the mother and father to note reading progress may serve as a motive for holding back. More typically, the desire of the child to gain parental approval results in fears that inhibit normal and felicitous growth in reading.

The reading background provided by the home is a potent factor in determining how well the child will succeed in school. When parents show an enthusiastic interest in their children's reading, when they read

stories to them and show them the pictures, when they discuss the contents of the books with them, they are laying strong foundations for pleasurable, independent reading. Important, too, is the presence in the home of a variety of attractive, appealing books for children. Time for quiet reading provided at home and a reasonably comfortable place for reading also help to start the child on the road to the enjoyment of books.

Fortunately, many children who come from impoverished or otherwise unpromising home environments nevertheless become excellent readers. Perhaps in a few instances the very lack of favorable home surroundings may serve as an incentive for greater effort in learning to read. The example of Abraham Lincoln comes to mind. Such cases, however, are exceptional. As a rule, when children from unfavorable home environments become good readers, it is in spite of, not because of, their early deprivation.

Reading Deficiency and Early Experiences with Reading Children's first experiences with reading will in great measure determine their later progress. If they are faced with reading tasks for which they are not ready, they may build antagonistic attitudes toward reading which interfere with normal growth. Moreover, they may develop inappropriate habits of word attack or sentence reading which will cause trouble throughout the formative years.

Examples of such habits are many. The child may develop the habit of sounding the words without giving attention to the meaning. Or he may feel that partial recognition of words is satisfactory. Word pointing may serve too long as a crutch in silent or oral reading. Such devices may be harmless or even helpful at the very beginning, but children should soon learn to do without them if they are to read for meaning and develop appropriate speed. The same may be said about the use of markers (strips of paper moved from line to line during reading). The child should be encouraged as early as possible to develop independence in making accurate return sweeps from line to line. Extremely slow rate of reading, word-by-word reading, and overanalytical methods of word attack may also be responsible for unsatisfactory growth in reading.

Reading Deficiency and the School Climate The general atmosphere of the school can be an important factor in children's success in reading. If there is a feeling of tension or pressure, if the child senses that the school authorities are anxious about his reading, he may develop harmful attitudes toward the reading process. On the other hand, if there is a bright, relaxed atmosphere, reading tends to take on the aspect of a delightful challenge. Such an atmosphere is created primarily by the ways in which teachers talk about reading, by their reactions to children's successes and failures, and by the variety of stimulating activities going on in the school. Physical surroundings, too, play a part in forming children's attitudes toward reading. Dreary, unstimulating classrooms lacking in suitable reading materials may inhibit the reading growth of pupils who might burgeon in a more evocative environment. Overcrowded classrooms, regimented instruction, antiquated textbooks, and lack of good school libraries may be responsible to a degree for much of the reading retardation found in our schools.

Reading Deficiency and the Quality of Instruction It is not pleasant for those of us who are teachers of reading to be reminded of the fact that reading deficiency is frequently due to the quality of the instructional program. However, if much is to be done to improve on the present situation in reading, that point must be faced squarely and procedures for altering it introduced.

Reading Deficiency and Other Factors Basically the causes of reading deficiency must be sought in the presence or absence of the elements important to growth in reading, discussed in Chapter 3, "The nature of Reading," under the topic "Elements Important to Growth in Reading" (see p. 27). Physical well-being, visual and auditory acuity, intelligence, experience background, mental health, and interest and purpose in reading are essential factors to be investigated when the child fails to make expected progress in reading. The process of exploring causes of reading retardation is essentially one of finding out which of these essential elements are lacking to a significant degree.

Teaching the Child Who Underachieves and Reads below His Age Level
Perhaps the first thing a teacher should keep in mind in teaching the child who reads below his level is the need to enlist his enthusiastic effort in the process of improvement. Most pupils who have had severe and persistent difficulty in learning to read have developed negative attitudes toward reading. They have, for one reason or another, experienced repeated frustration in a task that they recognize as the most important challenge facing them day after day. The result may be fear or hostility or indifference. Sometimes the awareness of parents' concern or annoyance pursues them to the schoolroom. They may feel that the good opinion of the teacher or classmates depends upon their performance.

Such children are in great need of "success experiences." The school day must be a day of achievement. The teacher should patiently seek out opportunities to enable the retarded reader to excel in some activity, whether in singing or dancing, in making something, or in reporting an everyday experience. Sometimes a disabled reader may do very well in taking part in a dramatic activity. The child must feel that he belongs, that he is respected. He should have something good to report when he returns home.

The experience of success is of greatest consequence to the disabled reader. If the materials he is called upon to read, or the phonics and other reading exercises are chosen with a view to his abilities, he will be emotionally prepared to take the first step. He need not be praised for every correct response, but he must know when he has done well.

Every effort should be made to stimulate the child's desire to read independently in books of his own choosing. It is quite possible to cultivate in disabled readers an interest that will lead to lifetime habits of reading. The use of pictures, dramatizations, conversations about books, and other devices for arousing interest are doubly important in the case of the retarded reader. Easy, well-illustrated books and magazines should be attractively displayed on the book table and the magazine rack.

Another consideration in the planning of work with the disabled reader is the role of the parent. Teachers who have responsibility for large numbers of children cannot be in frequent communication with all the parents, but in the case of the severely retarded reader such communication is essential. The personal interview is the most effective form, but in the absence of opportunity for face-to-face discussions the letter report can be most useful. Parent and teacher have much to learn from each other about the child. The teacher needs to know as much as possible about the child's home situation and his behavior with respect to play, TV habits, sleeping habits, and his reading at home. On the other hand, the parent needs to have advice as to methods of reinforcing the efforts of the teacher in providing appropriate reading guidance.

In some instances the parents are indifferent to the child's school problems. In others, they are overconcerned and competitive and place undue pressure on the child. Sometimes the parent adopts a punitive attitude toward the child who is not doing well in reading. The parent should be informed early about any important difficulty a child is having, so that he or she will not be shocked or agitated to discover that the child needs special help. As a rule, parents should be discouraged from attempting to give reading instruction at home; they should be encouraged to provide the environment, the stimulation, and the good example that will strengthen the teacher's efforts to build constructive attitudes toward reading on the part of the child.

Finally, appropriate guidance for the child who underachieves should extend to the work in the content subjects. Gains achieved in the reading period can be quickly canceled out if the child is confronted in science, social studies, hygiene, and other subjects with regimented textbook materials that yield little meaning for him. Habits of partial comprehension acquired in the course of the school day may nullify whatever has been learned in remedial reading sessions. Careful preparation in the way of concept formation, explanation of new terms and old terms with specialized meanings, and the use of diversified reading materials at many different levels of difficulty are some of the procedures required by all pupils but particularly by those who are seriously deficient in reading ability.

The following are some additional suggestions for working with the child who is underachieving and who is reading below his level. Many of them can be applied, with or without modification, to teaching the slow learner regardless of whether he is also underachieving.

1. Be encouraging, but not beyond the point of truthfulness While every good teacher tries to encourage all children, optimism is especially important in the case of the backward reader. Frequently, the retarded reader is a discouraged person. Again and again, without success, he has tried to learn to read. Often he has come to think of himself as a failure not only in reading but in almost everything. Consequently, primary emphasis sometimes needs to be placed on providing an activity in which the child can perform with superior results.

The teacher must, however, guard against encouragement that belies facts. A child should not be given the impression that it is going to be easy for him to become a good reader, for, unfortunately, such is usually not the case. As a rule, learning to overcome ineffective habits of reading is a slow and laborious task. The child who has been promised an easy path to learning to read will be discouraged when he later discovers that it is a difficult one.

2. Interest the pupil in reading Frequently the child who achieves poorly lacks interest in reading; repeated failure or inability to read as well as his peers is not conducive to the development of such interest. Consequently, one of the first problems, and one of the most difficult, is to inspire the reader to want to read. Some-

times an interest in reading is stimulated through assurance to the child that he can most likely learn to read. Another means is surrounding him with books that contain many pictures on topics in which he is interested. Since often he cannot read these books, the teacher should devote some time daily in telling him points of significance about one or more of them. Another device often used is having some of the pupils tell about points of special interest they have learned from books as they are showing them to their classmates.

Everything that has been recommended earlier in this book as a means of interesting boys and girls in reading also holds, at least to some extent, in the case of the retarded reader. It should be remembered, however, that it is usually much harder to develop reading interest in the retarded reader than in the average or superior reader.

3. Use appropriate materials of instruction Teachers of retarded readers often point out that not enough suitable material is available on the child's level of development and at the same time on his reading level. The complaint is justified. A fourteen-year-old boy with a reading ability of a typical second-grade child is not going to care much about reading a second-grade reader. However, the problem is no longer quite as acute as it used to be. A large number of general books, on subjects of great interest to children throughout the intermediate grades, are written so simply that many retarded readers can enjoy them, especially with some help. Some sets of readers, too, are especially designed for the retarded reader.

A number of reading lists have been prepared to aid the teacher in locating suitable books for slow readers or underachievers in the elementary school. The problem of finding appropriate materials is more serious with the child who has so small a reading vocabulary that he cannot even recognize the words in a preprimer. Books that are challenging in thought to a nine-year-old child who cannot read on the preprimer level are not available. Sometimes, with the intelligent child who cannot read, the teacher can explain that at first he will find the books decidedly below his level of interest. He should also then be made to feel that his chief interest should be in the results he accomplishes on his road to becoming a good reader, rather than in the subject matter. A teacher who showed a child some books in a series that he had selected for the pupil's reading explained that while the earlier books lacked subject matter that would be challenging to him, the later ones contained many selections of interest. The teacher might also tell the child that he may find, as many adults do, that sometimes it is fun to read subject matter that is chiefly designed for younger readers.

Teacher-made materials sometimes contribute to the solution of the problem of what to have the retarded child read, particularly in the early stages of learning to read. The teacher can often write material, either dictated by the pupil or written by the teacher without contributions from the child. It is too time-consuming, however, for the teacher to continue to write much of the material that a child will be reading.

4. Decide on the methods to be used on the basis of a careful diagnosis The teacher who uses the same methods of procedure with all retarded readers will usually not get satisfactory results. Considerable time spent on diagnosis can be very valuable if the results are utilized in planning the program.

5. If a method does not seem to work well with a pupil, change your procedure after you have given the method a fair trial No one method has been proved to be so much superior to all others that the teacher should persist, in spite of lack of results, in using it with any child. Even if the teacher has used a given procedure effectively with many other children whose needs seem to be similar, he should change his plans with a specific pupil if they are not productive of results with the child. However, he should not shift from one method to another without persisting long enough with the first to be quite confident that it will not be successful. Some children take a long time to learn by any method. Too much change in method, here as in other learning situations, is likely to result in confusion.

6. Use a variety of methods The use of one method, no matter how good, to the exclusion of others usually does not produce the best results. No one method alone is likely to be best fitted to the needs of any individual, for reading is so complex a process and retardation in reading is ordinarily caused by such a multiplicity of factors that various types of approaches are needed. It is especially important that a variety of methods be used when several persons are being taught as a group. Frequently one method, although helpful for all, is not the most felicitous one for every individual in the group.

There is, however, also danger in too much variety of method. The number should be limited somewhat so that it will not be necessary for the child to expend an unwarranted amount of time and energy in becoming accustomed to various ways of learning to read. Best results are usually attained only after a person has had considerable experience with a particular method.

7. If instruction is given in group situations, make certain that it is provided under the best circumstances possible

Some work with retarded readers can be done satisfactorily only if help is given on an individual basis. At other times, however, work in small-group situations seems advisable. Furthermore, there are instances when sheer lack of time on the part of the teacher makes is necessary to give help to two or more persons at one time.

The following suggestions may prove helpful when grouping seems desirable: (a) *Group the pupils according to their needs.* For skill development the grouping should be according to the type of skill in which they are deficient. All those of approximately the same level of reading ability who need help in word recognition of a given type may be taught together, while those whose major difficulty is a specific phase of comprehension may form another group. (See Chapter 14, p. 388, for a discussion of diagnostic grouping.) However, boys and girls of widely different ages should not be placed in the same group because of the unhappiness it might cause the older children. (b) *Keep the groups flexible so that changes can quite readily be made as needs change.* The administration of any program for helping the disabled reader should allow for the maximum of change from one group to another, whenever such a shift would be to the best advantage of the learner. (c) *In group work pay special attention to the needs of each person.* Even when the teacher is helping several children at the same time, much can be done to individualize the work. A child who has more skill than the others in his group in oral reading could be asked to read orally the more difficult parts of a selection. (d) *Help each individual to realize that he is an important member of the group.* The attitude of the teacher has much to do with whether a child feels important. The teacher can find many ways to show each child that he considers him of real value as a contributing member of the group. Even the boy or girl who cannot read can be helped to feel his worth if he can show pictures of interest to others or tell of experiences that his age-mates recognize as valuable contributions.

Helping the Bright Child Who Underachieves but Does Not Read below His Age Level

In a sense almost everyone underachieves. We tend to perform up to full capacity only under pressure. The pressure may consist of a drive or ambition, a keen but perhaps transitory interest, circumstances that demand the full exercise of our powers, or a strong desire to win the approval of others in certain situations. Some children are driven to high achievement in school subjects by a desire to compensate for a real or fancied deficiency in physical skill or in general social adjustment.

What concerns the teacher of reading, however, is persistent failure of a bright child to perform up to his full potential in reading and to achieve the kind of growth that may reasonably be expected of him. It is of great importance that the causes of his inadequate performance be discovered as early as possible.

The possible causes of underachievement in some bright children are numerous, and for the most part they do not differ in kind from the causes of underachievement among average and below-average children. Among these causes is the familiar one of a lack of a strong foundation of reading skills—such as methods of attack on unfamiliar words, getting the main idea of a passage, reading at appropriate rates. Although many able learners acquire some of these skills without much, if any, assistance, others do not. Like most children who fail to learn the basic skills early, the bright child may develop negative attitudes toward reading which persist throughout the elementary school and beyond. Indeed, the bright child may to be more sensitive than others to his unsuccessful efforts in reading during the initial stages.

In some instances conditions in a bright child's home may be responsible for underachievement in reading. If parents do not place a high value on academic excellence, if the home has few books or magazines of quality, if the child is not given encouragement or opportunity to read at home, he may never realize his own potential or set himself goals commensurate with his abilities. It then becomes necessary for the school to compensate for the impoverished cultural environment at home by providing intellectual and cultural stimulation through an abundance of direct and vicarious experiences.

Some bright children, perhaps *because* they are bright, enter school before they are matured sufficiently to cope with the adjustments and the tasks required by the school situation. Others are handicapped by being transported from one school situation in which they felt secure to another in which the surroundings are strange, the methods different, and a teacher's personality in contrast to the one he had before. Frequent absence from school because of illness or other factors is detrimental to the educational progress of most able pupils, as it is to that of average or slow learners.

Emotional problems, often stemming from discordant family relations, may in-

terfere with satisfactory growth in reading. Children who experience continued anxiety, feel rejected, or show hostility toward the adult world frequently suffer a lack of self-confidence that is necessary for learning; they are emotionally distracted when they should be concentrating on their reading. However, by no means are all bright children who underachieve emotionally disturbed nor do emotional difficulties always result in underachievement. The teacher should, however, be alert to the presence of emotional factors as a possible block to the full realization of the bright child's reading potential.

It has been estimated that as many as 25 percent of the gifted children in a typical class achieve below their ability. Whatever the true proportion may be, we cannot afford the waste of talent arising from any child's failure to reach attainable goals in reading. We must do all we can to discover the obstacles to maximum growth and, so far as possible, to remove them.

Reading and the Socioeconomically Disadvantaged Child

Although cultural differences, when honored as assets, can serve as rich resources for the curriculum, poverty constitutes a decided disadvantage. When the impact of poverty distinguishes children, damaging effects on learning usually result. The extensiveness of poverty and the dire situation of children born into this tragedy raise challenges to education that must be met.

Basic Considerations

Before we discuss socioeconomic factors influencing success in reading, let us consider the terms *culture* and *ethnocentricism* in order to clarify further the problems which arise when there is failure to distinguish *cultural diversity* (an asset and a rich resource) from the inappropriate term, *culturally deprived* (an ethnocentric status judgment). Although there are hundreds of definitions of culture, anthropologists generally agree to the following characteristics of culture:

1. It is not innate, but learned.
2. The various facets of culture are interrelated.
3. It is shared and defines the boundaries of different groups.[5]

Since culture is invisible, only the manifestations of it can be examined.

Because each person identifies with a culture, no matter how consciously or unconsciously, ethnocentric behaviors result. According to LeVine and Campbell,

> Ethnocentrism has become a familiar word most generally understood, in parallel with "egocentrism," as an attitude or outlook in which values derived from one's own cultural background are applied to other cultural contexts where different values are operative.[6]

In understanding culture and ethnocentric behaviors that are a natural result of ethnic identification, it can be seen that educators must avoid associating the disadvantages of lower socioeconomic status with cultural heritage, in which we can all take pride. It is the circumstance which perpetuates inequities in basic and equal opportunity to benefit from education that requires focus. In order to be effective in teaching all pupils, the teacher who is likely to be in a predominant cultural group and a member of the middle socioeconomic group must be especially cautious not to adopt an attitude that substitutes ethnocentric judgment for genuine appreciation of cultural diversity.

Educational and Societal Problems

Although there are still many poor people living in nonmetropolitan areas, the steady migration of the poor to the cities has become a marked sociological factor. Unfortunately the influx to the cities of the unskilled and semiskilled workers from farms, reservations, mountains, and other regions seems to have increased the incidence of poverty. It has come at a period of time when there is less need for the kinds of work being replaced by technological advances. To add to the disastrous condition of the poor migrating to the cities, the requirements for securing work even in the so-called unskilled labor category have become higher.

One factor contributing greatly to the problems connected with educating the underprivileged lies in the cyclic nature of the disadvantages accruing from being born into poverty and from growing up in it. The uneven chances in metropolitan settings of gaining employment, even at wages lower than others, are receiving for the same work, are partly related to less than equal opportunity of experiencing quality education. Undereducation as a result of high drop-out rates prior to high school graduation results in poorer qualifications to compete in the labor force. Thus the cycle begins with the children of the poor starting out at a disadvantage and increasing the likelihood of the perpetuation of the cycle of near-despair due to poverty. Many underprivileged give up hope for success and join the ranks of the destitute.

[5]Edward T. Hall, *Beyond Culture* (New York: Anchor Press/Doubleday, 1976), pp. 13–14.
[6]Robert A. LeVine and Donald T. Campbell, *Ethnocentrism: Theories of Conflict, Ethnic Attitudes, and Group Behavior* (New York: John Wiley & Sons, Inc., 1972), p. 1.

The attempts of the socioeconomically disadvantaged to achieve economic success with its attendant privileges are thwarted partly because access to the means of gaining success through educational achievement is more difficult for them than for others. This difficulty is partly related to the failure of education to adopt adequate strategies to insure success for these learners with different needs and learning styles. When the plight of the poor is both deplored and ignored by the more affluent members of society (teachers among them), whose perception of the problem may be that it results from the "failure of the home" to assume its rightful responsibility, an attitude of denial of equal opportunity to benefit from public education exists. This attitude is inexcusable when associated with teacher behavior. Such an inadvertent projection of blatant ethnocentric values denies the learner of being culturally identified when socioeconomically deprived, and therefore in greater need of the advantages of education. This form of denial of equal access to the benefits of public education, when found in the school milieu, must be arrested if a real understanding of motivation to achieve is to be gained.

The deprivation of the poor has its effect upon reading ability of their offspring. While many children who are not socioeconomically disadvantaged experience difficulty in learning to read, the incidence of lack of achievement among the poor and certain ethnic minorities is much greater than it is among other children. Because of the close relationship between an individual's concept of himself and teacher expectation (see "Self-Concepts," p. 14) and because of the danger that underprivileged children may have a low concept, it should be the concern of the teacher that schools not perpetuate this feeling of low esteem.

Prior to diagnosis of reading problems, the teacher should scrutinize his own behavior for both ethnocentric bias and identification with middle socioeconomic status in relation to the effect this self-perception would have upon learners who are different. Teacher expectations with regard to achievement of pupils are especially detrimental to learning conditions when IQ scores and achievement scores of culturally different groups are compared without careful analysis of the underlying economic conditions which perpetuate basic inequities in institutional structures. Only when a teacher relates to all children with a studied appreciation of cultural pluralism can there be an authentic high regard for each person's need for equal opportunity to learn and thereby to gain access to the self-esteem that may result in motivation for achievement to the fullest limits of human potentiality. The examination of materials and the diagnosis of reading problems are secondary to the establishment of empathy or rapport in the teaching-learning process.

The inextricable nature of the effects of education and economics upon each other call for massive changes in society not possible only within institutional structures.

Large-scale Attempts To Ameliorate Educational Problems Associated with Poverty

Fortunately many people and many agencies are deeply concerned with the problems faced by boys and girls who are socioeconomically disadvantaged. Individuals, private organizations, foundations, and city and federal agencies have studied or are studying the problems in the hope of coming up with recommendations for solutions.

One of the major attempts to help improve the education of the underprivileged has been in the form of what is often referred to as compensatory programs. These programs are designed to help boys and girls from socioeconomically disadvantaged families by compensating them for growing up in poverty and for the ineffective teaching they have received in many of their schools. The programs were developed in the 1960s as large-scale attempts to recognize the plight of the poor in the United States. Basic compensatory programs aimed at the preschool level may be categorized as programs of intensification or programs of intervention. In both types, the approaches are geared to promote accelerated language facility and the development of cognitive thinking or concept development. Some of the programs have characteristics of both these types. Many were designed to accelerate educability at different levels in the schools through specific and direct concentration on crucial language skills.

Operation Head Start, which is probably the most popular of the anti-poverty educational programs, was designed to give children, before entering first grade, a "head start" in schooling planned for their needs. It was begun in 1965. In late 1967 it was followed by a pilot program, *Project Follow-Through*. *Follow-Through* came into existence because many studies convinced educational and government leaders that *Head Start* "graduates" seemed to benefit from early education. It was found that these pupils began regular school only slightly behind their middle-class schoolmates and well ahead of other impoverished children who had not had preschool experience. Unfortunately, however, it appeared that the educational advantage of *Head Start* youngsters faded after six or eight months in the public schools. A somewhat related type of endeavor, *Project Upward Bound*, provides special services for economically deprived youths with considerable potential, in order to help prepare them for education beyond high school. Statistics seem to indicate that the great majority of those who have been enrolled in *Upward Bound* programs have gone on to further study.

The experience with *Operation Head Start* and *Project Follow-Through* seems to endorse earlier findings that a special feature of the learning difficulty of the educationally deprived child lies in the difference between his language and that used in school. Since verbal ability or disability unquestionably permeates all areas of academic learning, a closer examination of this condition is imperative. It is not enough simply to assume that a child is "nonverbal" or "less verbal."

That educators would differ as to procedures to be followed in compensatory programs is not at all strange; we find similar differences in opinion among persons connected with other phases of the educational program. Sad it is, however, to note that after years of federal subsidy to upgrade educational achievement of disadvantaged pupils, there is still little evidence that the problem is being overcome. In fact, pupils in the inner cities are falling farther below the national averages.

In spite of deficits in current programs for helping the underprivileged, we as teachers cannot wait for greater effectiveness of programs or surer means of evaluation. We need, without delaying our attack on existing problems, to look to differential strategies in reading instruction as one of the avenues toward helping the underprivileged immediately or in the very near future. The challenge to the teacher remains greater than ever to examine the manner in which educators purport to teach so as to favor cultural diversity as a resource.

Materials of Instruction

Increasingly books have been appearing on the market designed to accommodate the uniqueness of the individuals comprising the school population. We will next note some of these types of books.

Books Dealing with Variations in Ethnic and Cultural Backgrounds

Many educators believe that the inner-city child, like the children from all socioeconomic levels and cultures, when beginning to learn to read, should be given material based on his background of understanding. It is generally conceded that the content of most reading books for beginners fails to meet this criterion for the disadvantaged child. Usually the life style portrayed in the readers is not that with which the underprivileged child is familiar. The difference may make him resentful of the fact that he is shut out from the happy world frequently pictured by the family life of the boys and girls filling the pages of such books. In fact, the content, remote from his own experiences, may seem alien to his perception of reality.

The question of what context of life familiar to the disadvantaged child should be a part of the material of the basal reader is still largely a matter of conjecture. Another question in urgent need of investigation is: "How long after the learner has passed the stage of initial reading instruction should the content of reading textbooks be chiefly confined to subjects dealing with an environment familiar to the child?"

In increasing numbers the multiethnic and multi-cultural reader has been appearing on the market. The selections in these readers deal with life situations typical of those in which boys and girls of various cultures and races living in our country find themselves. The pictorial illustrations give a sympathetic portrayal of the characters and the ways of living described in the text. These readers are designed for children of all socioeconomic levels and ethnic groups portraying rural and urban life, in the hope that the boys and girls reading these books will not only develop a better understanding of themselves and their own way of life but also of boys and girls unlike themselves in background.

Books for Retarded Readers

There have been available for some time books written with the retarded reader in mind. However, it is only of late that a large number have been published. Books for the retarded reader, though necessarily written with a limited vocabulary, must be on his interest level and on his intelligence level. (However, it must not be assumed that all retarded readers have low intelligence.)

Sources of information on books for the retarded reader include:

Annotated Bibliography of Selected Books with High Interest and Low Vocabulary Level (Indianapolis Public Schools)

Books for Slow Readers (Holiday House)

Gateway to Readable Books: An Annotated Graded List of Books for Adolescents Who Find Reading Difficult, Ruth Strang (H. W. Wilson Company)

Good Reading for Poor Readers, George D. Spache (The Reading Laboratory and Clinic of the University of Florida, Gainesville, latest edition)

A Graded List of Books for School Libraries, which contains a section on books for slow learners (Harcourt Brace Jovanovich)

Some of the publishers who market books with high interest-low vocabulary are:

Beckley-Cardy Company (Benefic Press)
The Bobbs-Merrill Publishing Company
Bowmar Publishing Corporation
The Children's Press
Doubleday and Company
Follett Publishing Company
Garrard Publishing Company
Harper & Row
D. C. Heath and Company
Holt, Rinehart and Winston
The Macmillan Company
Melmont Publishers (Children's Press)
Random House
Reader's Digest Association
Science Research Associates
Scott, Foresman and Company
Webster Publishing Company
Wheeler Publishing Company
World Book—Childcraft International, Inc.

Information on series for retarded readers can be secured from the publishers on request. Only a few of the many well-known ones are named here.

Air Space-Age series (Benefic Press, Beckley-Cardy Company)
American Adventure series (Harper & Row)
Basic Vocabulary series (Garrard Publishing Company)
Beginning-to-Read Biographies (G. P. Putnam's Sons)
The Checkered Flag series (Field Educational Publications)
The Cowboy Sam series (Benefic Press, Beckley-Cardy Company)
I Want to Be series (Melmont Publishers, Children's Press)
The Jim Forest Readers (Field Educational Publications)
Landmark Books (Random House)
New Reading for Independence series (Scott, Foresman and Company)

Pleasure Reading series (Garrard Publishing Company)
Reader's Digest Skill Builders (Reader's Digest Services)
Reading Incentive Program (Bowmar Publishing Company)
Space Age Books (Bowmar Publishing Company)

"Easy-to-Read" Books

Books referred to as "easy-to-read" books are intended not primarily for the slow reader but for the beginning reader. Among the best known of these books are those by Dr. Seuss, such as *Green Eggs and Ham* (published as one of the Beginner Book series by Random House) and *The Cat in the Hat* and *The Cat in the Hat Comes Back* (published by Houghton Mifflin Company). "Easy-to-read" books are written with a controlled vocabulary in sentences that are simple in structure. The books range in difficulty, with some on the independent reading level of boys and girls in the last half of the first grade, while others have as high as a third-grade readability level. They have become increasingly popular in schools where independent reading is emphasized even during the early years of school.

There are critics of the "easy-to-read" books who are disturbed that the books are not of higher literary value. However, some educators argue that books that beginners can read can hardly be expected to be of high literary quality, due to the necessity of controlled vocabulary. They contend that as long as the "easy-to-read" books are not of poor quality, their use should be encouraged if through them boys and girls become more interested in reading. It should be noted that in order to supplement the reading of these books by boys and girls, the teacher should read to them the classics that are the literary heritage of childhood.

The following are among the publishers, in addition to Houghton Mifflin Company and Random House (mentioned in connection with the Dr. Seuss books) who supply books of the "easy-to-read" type: American Book Company; Benefic Press (Beckley-Cardy Company); Follett Publishing Company; Grosset & Dunlap; Harper & Row; Holt, Rinehart and Winston; Kenworthy Educational Service; David McKay Company; Oxford Press; Steck Company; Southwest Regional Laboratory for Educational Research and Development (Inglewood, Cal.).

A valuable reference for the teacher is the revised edition of *Books for Beginning Readers* by Elizabeth Guilfoille, published by the National Council of Teachers of English.

For Further Study

The reader is referred to the books listed on page 362 that deal in part with a consideration of dialect and/or other language differences.

Broderick, Dorothy, *The Image of the Black Child in Children's Fiction* (Ann Arbor, Mich.: R. R. Bowker Company, 1973).

Bush, Clifford L., and Mildred H. Huebner, *Strategies for Reading in the Elementary School*, 2d ed. (New York: The Macmillan Company, 1979), Ch. 14, "Challenging Every Reader."

Ching, Doris C., *Reading and the Bilingual Child*, (Newark, Del.: International Reading Association, 1976).

Figurel, J. Allen, ed., *Reading Goals for the Disadvantaged* (Newark, Del.: International Reading Association, 1970).

Fishman, Joshua, *Bilingual Education: An International Sociological Perspective* (Rowley, Mass.: Newbury House Publishing Company, 1976).

Hall, Edward T., *Beyond Culture* (New York: Anchor Press/Doubleday, 1976).

Harber, Jean R., and Jane N. Beatty, compilers, *Reading and the Black English Speaking Child*. An annotated bibliography (Newark, Del.: International Reading Association, 1978.)

Harris, Albert J., and Edward R. Sipay, *How to Increase Reading Ability*, 6th ed. (New York: David McKay Co., Inc., 1975), Ch. 5, "Meeting Individual Needs in Reading."

Harris, Larry A., and Carl B. Smith, *Reading Instruction: Diagnostic Teaching in the Classroom*, 2d ed. (New York: Holt, Rinehart and Winston, 1976), Part VI, "Individualizing Reading Instruction in the Classroom."

Heilman, Arthur W., *Principles and Practices of Teaching Reading*, 4th ed. (Columbus, Ohio: Charles E. Merrill Publishing Co., 1977), Ch. 11, "The Culturally Different Child as a Learner."

Hittleman, Daniel R., *Developmental Reading: A Psycholinguistic Perspective* (Chicago: Rand McNally College Publishing Company, 1978), Ch. 12, "Strategies for Pupils with Special Needs."

Johns, Jerry L., *Literacy for Diverse Learners: Promoting Reading Growth at All Levels* (Newark, Del.: International Reading Association, 1974).

Lapp, Diane, and James Flood, *Teaching Reading to Every Child* (New York: The Macmillan Publishing Company, 1978), Ch. 13, "Understanding Bilingual Speakers as Readers."

Musgrave, G. Ray, *Individualized Instruction: Teaching Strategies Focusing on the Learner* (Boston: Allyn and Bacon, Inc., 1975).

Ransom, Grayce A., *Preparing to Teach Reading* (Boston: Little, Brown and Company, 1978), Ch. 14, "Linguistically Different Children."

Smith, Richard J., and Dale D. Johnson, *Teaching Children to Read*, 2d ed., (Reading, Mass.: Addison-Wesley Publishing Company, Inc., 1980), Ch. 12, "Meeting the Needs of the Linguistically Diverse."

Spache, George D., *Good Reading for the Disadvantaged Reader* (Champaign, Ill.: Garrard Publishing Co., 1974).

Thonis, Eleanor Wall, *Literacy for America's Spanish-Speaking Children* (Newark, Del.: International Reading Association, 1976).

Tinker, Miles A., and Constance M. McCullough, *Teaching Elementary Reading*, 4th ed., (Englewood Cliffs, N. J.: Prentice-Hall, Inc., 1975), Ch. 14, "Individual Differences," and Ch. 18, "Individualizing the Reading Experiences of Boys and Girls."

Witty, Paul A., ed., *Reading for the Gifted and Creative Student* (Newark, Del.: International Reading Association, 1972).

Zintz, Miles A., *The Reading Process: The Teacher and the Learner*, 3d ed., (Dubuque, Iowa: Wm. C. Brown Company Publishers, 1980), Part Five, "Provision for All Children."

Questions and Comments for Thought and Discussion

1. Have you observed instances in which the gifted child tried not to let his peers know that he liked school work and that he was doing well in it? What suggestions do you have for the teacher to help prevent such an unfortunate situation?

2. Have you observed instances in which the teacher in an elementary school neglected the gifted? If so, suggest ways in which the teacher might have been more helpful to them without shortchanging other children in the classroom.

3. What differences in instructional procedures do you recommend for these classifications of pupils who are achieving in reading below their intellectual capacity: (a) the ones who are reading below their age or grade level; (b) the ones who are reading at their age or grade level; (c) the ones who are reading above their grade level?

4. Explain why the person who underachieves in reading is not necessarily a slow learner.

5. *Culturally different* and *economically deprived* are not synonymous terms. What are the implications of this fact for teaching?

6. Sometimes people apply the term *disadvantaged* to boys and girls from non-English-speaking homes even though the cultural aspects of the home environment show no deprivation. Such boys and girls do not belong to the group called *disadvantaged* any more than the reader should be labeled as a *disadvantaged* person if he were going to school in a country in which he did not know well the language spoken in the school. He would *be at a disadvantage*, but he would hardly be called a *disadvantaged individual*. What difference do you see between the two terms?

7. What implications for teaching reading to the disadvantaged do you find in Chapter 2, "Language Development and Reading"?

8. What specific preparation should teachers of socioeconomically deprived children have?

9. What are factors in a socioeconomically disadvantaged home that may interfere with desired progress in learning to read? In what ways might the school be able to offset in part some of them?

10. What are some of the specific experiences that economically deprived children often lack that you think will cause difficulty for them as they

progress through their educational experiences?

11. Even if you become a teacher in a suburban community, you may well find that you have one or more children in your room who are culturally different from the others. What plans could you make to help them learn to read if you are a first-grade teacher? If you are teaching in the later years of the elementary school?

12. Have you observed teachers who have a healthy attitude toward the socially disadvantaged child? If so, what were some of the characteristics they possessed and the techniques they used?

13. How might programs such as Operation Head Start better prepare disadvantaged children for school? Do you know of any efforts on the local community level to help prepare them better for their later educational experiences? If so, describe them.

Organizational Patterns, Including "Mainstreaming," for Accommodating the Uniqueness of the Learner

In Chapter 13 we have discussed the uniqueness of the learner in relation to the instructional program in reading. We identified types of divergent learners and emphasized their respective needs, with suggestions for meeting them. In this chapter we pay particular attention to organizational patterns for adapting instruction to these needs.

Providing for Individual Differences through Grouping

Various methods of grouping to decrease heterogeneity are used. Several of these, with overlapping between them, are described here.

Grouping within a Classroom

A widespread method of dealing with individual differences within a single class is to subgroup children according to ability, often on three levels. Advocates of this plan justify it by facts such as these, which are supported, in essence, by various studies:

At the first-grade level, the range of achievement in a class can be expected to be two or more years.

At the fourth-grade level, the range of achievement in a class may be four years or more.

At the sixth-grade level, the range of achievement in a class may be six years or more.

Grouping within a room is not without its limitations. The three-group plan, commonly used, or any other plan for homogeneous grouping may make the children and their parents conscious of differences in achievement and create pressure on a child to measure up to others in reading. Indi-

vidual differences remain within the groups, and there is some danger that the teacher will assume that the differences have been cared for by the mere fact that the three-level plan is in operation. Certainly the problem is not solved if the teacher uses the same material with all pupils, allowing only for a difference in the speed with which the groups are expected to read them. However, when he uses different material for the groups, his needed daily preparation of work is increased decidedly; and there is a limit to the amount of work that can be expected even of an excellent teacher.

Much of the effectiveness of subgrouping within the class will depend on the children's understanding of the purpose for which they are assigned to the groups. Great importance should be attached to how the teacher and the children feel about the group. Many writers emphasize the need to keep the groups flexible. Classification of children in groups should frequently be determined by specific purposes. For example, groups may be organized for the express purpose of providing instruction in developmental reading, and individual children should be regrouped as their performance requires. In other cases, a group may be devoted to the study of specific skills, regardless of the general proficiency of the members. Research groups may be formed for pupils who wish to investigate a similar problem. Other groups, interested in the same theme—such as pets, airplanes, plants, farm life, railroads—may plan presentations to the whole class. In some instances groups may be formed in which the better readers help the slower ones—all, of course, under the supervision of the teacher.

Especially in the case of the beginning reader, there is the problem of what to do with groups not under the immediate direction of the teacher. No group should be left to itself without some specific task. If a group is asked to spend a period in silent reading, the teacher should make sure that each child has found a suitable book to read or is in the process of finding one at the book table or elsewhere. If a group is planning a project such as, for example, a display or a report to the class, the nature of the task should be clear to everyone, and any questions to be asked and answered should be well formulated in advance. In no case should a group be left with mere busy-work. Games and seatwork should be carefully planned to provide needed reinforcement in skills previously taught.

Teachers who follow the practice of subgrouping within the class should be keenly aware of the limitations and dangers of the method. First, it has been estimated that dividing pupils into three groups may reduce variability in achievement by much less than half of that in normally organized groups. Second, the tests commonly employed in the classification of pupils measure only a small, although signiqicant number of the desired competencies. Third, the relative performance of individuals within the groups will change as the instruction proceeds. Fourth, studies have shown that academic progress under a system of ability grouping is only slightly greater than under a system of heterogeneous grouping.

More important, perhaps, than any of the foregoing considerations is a concern for the overall psychological effect of grouping on the child. If the grouping is flexible and if the child understands why he is a member of a certain group at any specified time, grouping may be quite harmless, even helpful. If the grouping stigmatizes a child with himself or others, the effect may be more serious than any loss in reading progress. Reading ability is valuable only insofar as it contributes to the general happiness and well-being of the individual and his functioning in society. We must not sacrifice the child to our desire to exhibit favorable reports of reading scores.

Division into Classrooms according to Abilities of Pupils

In some schools in which there are more children in a grade than can be taught in one classroom, the practice is followed of organizing for greater homogeneity through division of the pupils into rooms of relatively equal ability. The pupils who are considered better equipped intellectually or academically are placed in one classroom and, if there are only two rooms to the grade, the others are placed in another room. In larger schools there may be one or more rooms with intermediate groups. In this plan of organization the pupils in the more academically advanced group, for example, would be assigned to one teacher and the other groups to other teachers throughout all or most of the school day.

Fortunately this method of classification is no longer used frequently. It is to be condemned as a form of segregation that is likely to keep "low-track" children in the elementary school from having the same educational opportunities as others.

Homogeneous Grouping for Reading on a Multiage or Multigrade Basis

Some schools are organized so that boys and girls are assigned to reading groups without regard to their exact grade. Frequently this type of organization in the elementary school is limited to the middle grades. The plan can be followed even if there is only one fourth-grade, one fifth-grade, and one sixth-grade room within a building. During most of the school day the boys and girls are in their own grade room, but for reading class they are assigned to a room of their approximate reading level. For reading instruction pupils lowest in achievement in reading among the middle-grade pupils will be with one teacher, regardless of their regular grade placement. Thus, a sixth-grade pupil might be reading in the lowest of the three groups. Similarly, the pupils among the highest in reading achievement may be taught by another teacher regardless of whether regularly they are in the fourth, fifth, or sixth grade. Obviously, if there are more than three middle-grade teachers within a building, the children can be divided into four or more ability groups for reading instruction.

It is not difficult to recognize some advantages of homogeneous grouping for reading on a multiage or multigrade basis. A major superiority over that of grouping for all activities by rooms is that the stigma of assignment to a lower-level group is likely to be less if a child is in a lower group for reading only but in the same room with classmates of a variety of abilities in other areas of the curriculum. The stigma is also likely to be less because the child sees that others in the school—not only his own classmates—may be in need of instruction lower than grade level. There are, however, significant shortcomings to this system of classification, some of which are noted for other types of homogeneous grouping earlier in this chapter. Even when ability in reading is the basis for classification, there will be considerable variation within a group. The children may be fairly alike in ability to comprehend what they read but may differ greatly in skill in reading at appropriate rates or in locating information in print. Furthermore, when boys and girls are assigned to different teachers for reading, there is danger of divorcing reading in-

struction from reading activities other than those in reading classes, as, for example, from reading in the social studies. Lack of correlation of activities during the reading class with nonreading activities during other times of the school day constitutes another shortcoming. The danger is that the teacher who teaches only reading to a child, and therefore does not know him as well as he could if he were his regular classroom teacher, may be more interested in the learning acquired than in the learner.

Diagnostic Grouping

Increasing attention is being paid to a promising technique, that of diagnostic grouping, as an organizational basis for diagnostic instruction which focuses upon the specific skill needs of individual learners. Grouping in reading is determined by the needs of the pupils, as revealed by careful diagnosis of each child's level of achievement in reading, including both strengths and weaknesses. Through this kind of grouping some of the major criticisms rightfully made of many other grouping practices can be met. Since the groups focus on the specific needs of the learner, when a child no longer requires special help in the skill that forms the differentiating concern of the group, he is dismissed from it. When none of the boys and girls in the group is in need of additional help of the type for which the group was organized, it is disbanded. Thus, flexibility in grouping is one of the major assets of the plan. It is possible when using this grouping technique to meet the needs of the more capable, as well as the less able, reader during the same reading period. It can then be of help in the solution of a problem that has long frustrated teachers.

Let us illustrate how the theory of diagnostic grouping can be implemented in a

Small-group instruction can be directed toward diagnosed needs. (Washington School, St. Cloud, Minnesota)

classroom setting. We will assume that the pupils in a classroom have been tested with instruments designed to find their independent, instructional, and frustration levels in reading and their problems in word recognition. That information can be tabulated on a class summary sheet similar to the one illustrated here, where data for part

	Independent Level	Instructional Level	Auditory Discrimination*	Letter Names	Letter Sounds	Short Vowels	Silent "e"	Long Vowel (open syllable)	Inflectional Endings	Affixes	Syllabication	Silent Letters
Tom	1	2	✓	✓	✓				✓			
Sally	3	3	✓	✓	✓	✓	✓	✓	✓			✓
Fred	2	4	✓	✓	✓	✓	✓	✓	✓		✓	✓
Mary	P	2	✓	✓	✓							
Elaine	4	5	✓	✓	✓	✓	✓	✓	✓		✓	✓
Ralph	3	5	✓	✓	✓	✓	✓	✓	✓	✓	✓	✓
Norma	3	4	✓	✓	✓	✓	✓	✓	✓		✓	
Steve	2	4	✓	✓	✓	✓	✓	✓	✓	✓		

* *Check indicates no need of special attention.*

of an imaginary class are recorded. On the basis of information, such as that presented in the table, groups for both the development of comprehension and word recognition skills can be formed. In the illustration given, Sally, Fred, Norma, and Steve could constitute a group in which material at their instructional level of fourth reader would be used for purposes of increasing comprehension skills. Tom and Mary could form another group organized for the same purpose, but using material on the second-reader level, while Elaine and Ralph could be in a group reading on the fifth-reader level. Similarly, groups could be formed for the development of word-attack skills. Sally, Fred, Mary, Elaine, and Norma could, for example, be in a group to learn more about affixes.

Other Grouping Practices

Some teachers successfully employ several types of grouping within the same classroom, so that for some purposes an individual is a member of one reading group and for other purposes he is a member of another group. A child may be in one group based on the diagnosis of his needs for skill development and in another organized according to his interests in reading. For example, he may be in a group wanting to read tall tales or biographies. Or the grouping can be in connection with a subject taken up in a content area. For instance, when the class is studying about the homes of children around the world, the group investigating homes in cold countries might include above-average, average, and below-

Instruction can be adapted to the needs of the individual. (Learning Resources Center, St. Cloud State University)

average readers. Care needs to be taken that each child has ready access to material on his level of reading, even when he is in a group not based on his diagnosed needs.

Individualizing Instruction without Grouping

With the growing dissatisfaction with the lock-step system of instruction prevalent in many schools during the first few decades of the century and in earlier times, educators sought to devise means by which reading and other skills could be taught to meet the needs of individuals better. Some turned to grouping; others put their faith in individualization without grouping; still others saw the benefits that could be derived from use of both plans, realizing that instruction can be individualized both in group and in nongroup situations.

In the pages that follow we will give consideration to three means of individualizing instruction without grouping, namely: (a) "reading laboratories," (b) automated reading, and (c) programed reading instruction.

"Reading Laboratories"

One example of the current interest in the individualization of instruction in reading is the popularity of "reading laboratories." These "laboratories" consist of kits of practice materials for different elementary school levels. In addition to the reading selections, they may contain answer keys, check test pads, student record books, and a teacher's handbook. In some, other supplies are included. Materials on each level, in many instances, vary in difficulty from easy to hard. Pupils are expected to move ahead as fast as their learning rates and capacities will permit. An important element of many of the "laboratories" is that they provide for checking by the learner. Emphasis is placed on the successful response and the use of intrinsically interesting materials.

Science Research Associates has published the *SRA Reading for Understanding Laboratory*, which deals primarily with the development of comprehension skills, and is planned for grades 3 through 12, and the *SRA Reading Laboratory*, which places emphasis on various reading skills, including reading rates, and is designed for grades 1 through 13. Phonics is emphasized in the lower levels of the *SRA Reading Laboratory*. Also available on the market are the *SRA Schoolhouse* materials, for the primary and the middle grades, and reading programs of the Imperial International Learning Corporation, based, in part, on tapes in cassette form. R. H. Stone Products (13735 Puritan, Detroit, Mich. 48227) publishes various programs, among them a cassette reading program. Other reading laboratories include:

BFA Comprehension Skills Laboratory (BFA Educational Media, Division of CBS, Inc., 2211 Michigan Avenue, Dept. 866, P. O. Box 1975, Santa Monica, Calif. 90406).

Building Reading Power (Charles E. Merrill Publishing Company).

The Literature Sampler (Redgrave Publishing Company, Division of Docent Corporation, 430 Manville Road, Pleasantville, N. Y. 10570).

The Reading Clinic (McGraw-Hill Book Company).

The Reading Practice Program (Harcourt Brace Jovanovich).

Automated Reading

In recent years we have seen a proliferation of mechanical devices designed for classroom reading instruction. One need only browse through the reading aids exhibited at the annual meeting of the International Reading Association to witness the "machine explosion." Some manufacturers of such devices advertise their products as aids to instruction while others claim the reading program can be conducted primarily through the use of their machines. One device for automated reading, the Borg-Warner System 80, will be discussed briefly.

System 80 is an instrument somewhat resembling in appearance a television set. Lessons for this machine are provided in kits. They are available in various areas, among them reading, spelling, mathematics, bilingualism, and French. Each kit contains a series of sequenced lessons. In working through a lesson the child takes a lesson card from the kit and inserts it in the machine. The child both sees and hears the various segments of the lesson and responds to each part. Progress checks are made after each lesson. After the progress check is completed, the child can repeat a lesson if necessary or proceed to the next lesson in the sequence.

Machines, such as those described, can be quite helpful to a busy teacher. They can be used for reinforcement of lessons taught and are certainly a good source of motivation for some children, but in the opinion of the writers, they are not sufficient for a total reading program.

Programed Reading Instruction

Programed instruction can be carried on with or without machines. Many programs, for which machines are not used, are written in booklets which resemble workbooks in appearance. The idea behind programed reading instruction does not differ fundamentally from plans for individualization

described under "Reading Laboratories." In fact, the latter are often the means for programed instruction.

In programed instruction the pupil is presented with instructional materials that enable him to learn on his own. The exercises, presumably prepared after careful editing and experimentation, are graduated in very small steps, so that hopefully even the slow learner can, at his own rate, arrive at the desired generalization. An exercise, or "frame," usually presents an explanation followed by a sentence containing a blank to be filled in, or, if a machine is used, by a button to be punched or a lever to be moved. The correct answer, given immediately below or on a page to which the pupil is referred, enables the pupil to compare his own answer with the correct one, so that he is "reinforced" if the answer is right or corrected if it is wrong. A program, or a sequence of frames, is selected for the individual in terms of his specific stage of learning. The method is termed "self-teaching" although teacher guidance is not unnecessary. In the case of reading, the programs may deal with the basic skills of word recognition—such as phonic analysis, context clues, and structural analysis—or with comprehension and location of information.

Following are examples of "frames":

The *gh* in the word *rough* has the sound of the letter _____.   *f*

The *ou* in the word *rough* has the short sound of the letter _____.   *u*

The meaning of the word *bark* in the sentence: *The bark of the birch tree is white* is _____.   *a*
   a. part of a tree
   b. sound a dog makes

Without doubt programed learning will continue to be the subject of debate among educators. It will be examined not only from the point of view of its efficiency in achieving academic objectives, but especially from the point of view of its total effect on the pupil. Certainly in theory it has much to commend it, particularly in its stress on the principle of success in learning and on self-activity. It is recommended that teachers and administrators acquaint themselves with programed materials.

"Mainstreaming"

"Mainstreaming" can be thought of as an accommodation of individual and special needs within a regular classroom setting when it provides a setting which is least restrictive for the learner. "Mainstreaming" is a coined word that many persons apply to the act of nonsegregation of the handicapped into special rooms throughout the school day, but it also refers to nonsegregation of the gifted throughout the school day.

Around the turn of the century a movement began to emerge to segregate the handicapped from their peers for instructional purposes. Prior to that such children had often been ignored in educational settings. The movement to segregate the handicapped grew until the 1950's and 1960's, when marked dissatisfaction with this plan arose as new insights and understandings came to light. Research evidence began to show that segregating the handicapped had not been as effective as had once been thought. Many schools began to accept handicapped children in the "main stream" of the classroom setting, for instructional purposes.

Federal Legislation

Culminating the movement toward teaching the handicapped within the regular classroom, rather than segregating such students into special rooms, have been efforts of the federal government to insure all children equal educational opportunity.

Laws Concerning Educating the Handicapped

Three important separate pieces of federal legislation regarding equal opportunity for education were enacted in the mid seventies. The first of these legislative acts was mandated in Section 504 as part of P.L. 93–112,[1] the Vocational Rehabilitation Act Amendments of 1973. Section 504[2] reads in part:

> No otherwise qualified handicapped individual in the United States shall, solely by reason of his handicap, be excluded from the participation in, be denied the benefits of, or be subjected to discrimination under any program or activity receiving Federal financial assistance.

The second of the legislative acts was P.L. 93–380, the Education Amendments of 1974. Included in this act was the guarantee of due process procedures and the assurance of education for the handicapped in the least restrictive environment.

The third piece of legislation, which was enacted in November 1975, P.L. 94-142, the Education for All Handicapped Children Act, is the law which presently has the most impact on education in regard to providing equal access to educational opportunities for handicapped children in the United States. Basically, it includes:

> . . . provisions which are designed to assure that all handicapped children have available to them a free appropriate public education,

---

[1]P.L. 93–112 is to be interpreted as the law enacted by the 93rd Congress and that it was the 112th law which the President signed during the session of that Congress.

[2]*Federal Register* 41:56971, (1976).

to assure that the rights of handicapped children and their parents are protected, to assist States and localities to provide for the education of handicapped children, and to assess and assure the effectiveness of efforts to educate such children.[3]

Since federal financial assistance will not be granted to school districts not in compliance with P.L. 93–112, P.L. 93–380, and P.L. 94–142, most school districts are attempting to comply with the provisions spelled out in the three previously mentioned acts, but are most concerned with P.L. 94–142.

Provisions of P.L. 94–142

In this part of the chapter we shall give excerpts from P.L. 94–142 and explanations concerning regulations enacted in that legislation as we consider these topics: (1) Determining who is handicapped; (2) Provisions for a "least-restrictive" environment; (3) The Individualized Education Program (IEP); and (4) Guidelines for In-service education.

Determining Who Is Handicapped. The term "handicapped children" is explained as follows:

"Handicapped children" means those children evaluated . . . as being mentally retarded, hard of hearing, deaf, speech impaired, visually handicapped, seriously emotionally disturbed, orthopedically impaired, or as having specific learning disabilities, who because of those impairments need special education and related services.[4]

If a teacher suspects that a student in his classroom should be considered "handicapped," appropriate testing must be initiated to determine if he is indeed, "handicapped." Written permission of the parent or guardian must be obtained prior to testing. We quote here guidelines given for the testing, for many of them provide excellent suggestions for testing a child, regardless of whether it is to be done to accomplish the purpose for which the guidelines were constructed. They are:

State and local educational agencies shall insure, at a minimum, that:

(a) Tests and other evaluation materials:

    (1) Are provided and administered in the child's native language or other mode of communication, unless it is clearly not feasible to do so;

    (2) Have been validated for the specific purpose for which they are used;

    (3) Are recommended by their producer for the specific purpose for which they are used; and

    (4) Are administered by personnel who meet applicable certification or licensure requirements under State law;

(b) Tests and other evaluation materials include those tailored to assess specific areas of educational need and not merely those which are designed to provide a single general intelligence quotient;

(c) In test selection and administration, if a test is administered to a child with impaired sensory, manual or speaking skills, the test results accurately reflect the child's aptitude or achievement level or whatever other factor the test purports to measure, rather than reflecting the child's impaired sensory, manual, or speaking skills (except where those skills are the factors which the test purports to measure);

(d) No one test or type of test or other means of evaluation is used as the sole criterion for placement;

(e) Information from sources other than

---

[3]*Federal Register* 41:56996, (1976).
[4]*Federal Register* 41:56977, (1976).

ability or achievement tests, including information concerning physical condition, sociocultural background, and adaptive behavior in home and school, is gathered and considered and the weight given to each of these sources is documented;

(f) The interpretation of the evaluation data and the subsequent determination of the child's educational placement are made by a team or group of persons knowledgeable about the child. The meaning of the evaluation results, the placement options, and the personnel available to provide special education and related services; and

(g) If the information derived either from ability and achievement tests or from other sources results in a showing that the child does not, because of a disability, need instruction in a special setting, the child is not placed outside the regular instructional setting.[5]

Provisions for a "Least Restrictive Environment." One intent of the legislative acts was that handicapped children should be educated in the "least restrictive environment." "Least restrictive" is interpreted to mean that a major goal of our educational system should be to provide, to the extent possible, instructional programs for handicapped children in classrooms with nonhandicapped children. This interpretation does not imply that special educational programs for some handicapped students will not take place outside the regular classroom. Such segregation can occur but only if the nature or severity of the handicap is such that the goals of education cannot be met in the regular classroom even with the help of supplementary aids and services.

Special education is defined in P.L. 94–142 as:[6]

. . . specially designed instruction, at no cost to parents or guardians, to meet the unique needs of a handicapped child, including classroom instruction, instruction in physical education, home instruction, and instruction in hospitals and institutions.

In some instances part of the handicapped student's day may be spent outside the regular classroom because of certain instructional needs, such as special help in reading and/or mathematics. However, the rest of the school day is to be spent in a classroom with nonhandicapped children. Important to remember is the fact that, to the maximum extent possible, the handicapped student's education is to take place with nonhandicapped children.

The Individualized Education Program (IEP). If testing of a handicapped child indicates that special education is needed, an individualized education program (IEP) must be developed for that child. At least four people must be involved in the development of an IEP. They are: (1) a representative of the local education agency who is qualified to provide or supervise specially designed instruction to meet the needs of handicapped learners, (2) the child's teacher, (3) the parent or guardian of the child, and (4) whenever appropriate, the child.

The individualized education program must include:

(a) A statement of the child's present levels of educational performance, including academic achievement, social adaptation, prevocational and vocational skills, psychomotor skills, and self-help skills.

(b) A statement of annual goals which describes the educational performance to be achieved by the end of the school

[5]*Federal Register* 41:56991, (1976).

[6]*Federal Register* 41:56978, (1976).

year under the child's individualized education program;

(c) A statement of short term instructional objectives which must be measurable intermediate steps between the present level of educational performance and the annual goals;

(d) A statement of specific educational services needed by the child, (determined without regard to the availability of those services) including a description of:

    (1) All special education and related services which are needed to meet the unique needs of the child, including the type of physical education program in which the child will participate, and

    (2) Any special instructional media and materials which are needed;

(e) The date when those services will begin and length of time the services will be given;

(f) A description of the extent to which the child will participate in regular education programs;

(g) A justification for the type of educational placement which the child will have;

(h) A list of the individuals who are responsible for implementation of the individualized education program; and

(i) Objective criteria, evaluation procedures, and schedules for determining, on at least an annual basis, whether the short term instructional objectives are being achieved.[7]

Parent permission for testing and involvement in the development of the IEP is required. The following guidelines for parent participation are included in the Act.

(a) Each local educational agency shall take steps to insure that one or both of the parents of the handicapped child are present at each meeting or afforded the opportunity to participate, including scheduling the meeting at a mutually agreed on time and place.

(b) If neither parent can attend, the local educational agency shall use other methods to insure parent participation, including individual or conference telephone calls.

(c) A meeting may be conducted without a parent in attendance if the local educational agency is unable to convince the parents that they should attend. In this case the local educational agency must have a record of its attempts to arrange a mutually agreed on time and place, such as:

    (1) Detailed records of telephone calls made or attempted and the results of those calls.

    (2) Copies of correspondence sent to the parents and any responses received, and

    (3) Detailed records of visits made to the parent's home or place of employment and the results of those visits.

(d) The local educational agency shall take whatever action is necessary to insure that the parent understands the proceedings at a meeting, including arranging for an interpreter for parents who are deaf or whose native language is other than English.[8]

Guidelines for In-service Education. In many instances the training of teachers has not adequately prepared them to work with handicapped students. Retraining is needed. Because of this lack of preparation P.L. 94–142 requires that local educational agencies institute in-service training programs which will help teachers learn

[7]*Federal Register* 41:56986, (1976).

[8]*Federal Register* 41:56986, (1976).

needed skills. Guidelines for in-service training programs mandated by P.L. 94–142 follow:

(a) As used in this section, "inservice training" means any training other than that received by an individual in a full-time program which leads to a degree.

(b) Each annual program plan must provide that the State educational agency:

    (1) Conducts an annual needs assessment to determine if a sufficient number of adequately and appropriately prepared and trained personnel are available in the State; and

    (2) Initiates innovative and experimental inservice personnel development programs based on the assessed needs of State-wide significance related to the implementation of the Act.

(c) Each annual program plan must include the results of the needs assessment under paragraph (b)-(1) of this section, broken out by need for new personnel and need for retrained personnel.

(d) The State educational agency may enter into contracts with institutions of higher education or other agencies, institutions, or organizations (which may include parent or other advocacy organizations), to carry out experimental or innovative personnel development programs, development or modification of instructional materials, and dissemination of significant information derived from educational research and demonstration projects.

(e) Each annual program plan must provide that the State educational agency insures that ongoing inservice training programs are available to all personnel who are engaged in the education of handicapped children, and that these programs include:

    (1) The use of incentives which insure participation by teachers (such as released time, payment for participation, options for academic credit, salary step credit, certification renewal, or updating professional skills);

    (2) The involvement of local staff; and

    (3) The use of innovative practices which have been found to be effective.

(f) Each annual program plan must:

    (1) Describe the process used in determining the inservice training needs of personnel engaged in the education of handicapped children;

    (2) Identify the areas in which training is needed (such as individualized education programs, nondiscriminatory testing, least restrictive environments, procedural safeguards, and use of parent surrogates in due process hearings);

    (3) Specify:

        (i) The groups requiring training (such as special teachers, regular teachers, administrators, psychologists, speech pathologists, audiologists, physical education teachers, therapeutic recreation specialists, physical therapists, occupational therapists, medical personnel, parents, volunteers, hearing officers and parent surrogates) and

        (ii) The estimated number in each group,

    (4) Describe the content and nature of training for each area under paragraph (f) (2) of this section;

    (5) Describe how the training will be provided in terms of (i) geographi-

cal scope (such as State-wide, regional, or local), and (ii) staff training source (such as college and university staffs, State and local educational agency personnel, and non-agency personnel);

(6) Specify:
   (i) The funding sources to be used,
   (ii) The cost of the training, and
   (iii) The time frame for providing it; and

(7) Specify procedures for effective evaluation of the extent to which program objectives are met.

(g) Each annual program plan must include a description of changes the State educational agency expects to make in the provision under paragraph (f) of this section during the three years after the annual program plan takes effect.[9]

Implementation of a Program for the Handicapped

The laws which govern the implementation of educational programs for the handicapped are very explicit. They are designed to protect the rights of children and their parents. Non-compliance with the laws by a school system can mean the loss of any federal funds that the system is receiving.

[9]*Federal Register* 41:56987, 56988, (1976).

As is to be expected, school systems differ somewhat in the procedures they follow in implementing Section 504 of P.L. 93–113, P.L. 93–380, and P.L. 94–142. We will next note how several school districts have cooperatively worked out a means of implementation. We refer to the Child Study System, designed and used by the Benton-Stearns [County] Special Education Cooperative.[10]

The Child Study System provides a vehicle through which special education and classroom school personnel can make decisions about the special educational needs of students in the Benton-Stearns Special Education Cooperative. This system provides the process by which referrals to Special Education are reviewed, evaluations completed, services provided, and the progress of the students reviewed. There are seven basic steps involved: Referral, Referral Review Staffing (Initial Staffing), Observation, Assessment, Team Planning Conference, IEP Implementation, and Periodic Review.

[10]The Benton-Stearns Special Education Cooperative, located in Central Minnesota, consists of school districts located in the towns of Cold Spring, Foley, Holdingford, Kimball, Sartell, and Sauk Rapids, all of which are located in either Stearns or Benton County. Permission to use the Child Study System has been granted by Michael Leigh, superintendent of the cooperative.

Child Study System of the Benton-Stearns Special Education Cooperative

I. Referral System: Procedure by which a parent, classroom teacher, special education staff, or other sources can submit a student's name for review by the Initial Staffing Team.

A. Referral

School personnel who detect or are informed of an academic, behavioral, or social difficulty will complete the Referral Form, making certain that all demographic data is correct. Route the Referral Form to the building principal for his/her approval. If referral is considered appropriate, it is signed and forwarded to appropriate special education staff.

B. Referral Review Form

This review form is recommended as a tool for building principals, classroom teachers, special education staff and other essential personnel for the collection of data that will be completed and presented at the referral review staffing.

II. Referral Review Staffing (Initial Staffing): The purpose of the Referral Review Staffing is to review all currently available information regarding the presenting problem, decide what additional information is needed, and who is responsible for gathering those data. Team members responsible for the collection of the data will present their findings at a forthcoming Team Planning Conference.

A. In attendance: classroom teacher, special education teacher, building principal, and other essential personnel.

B. Review all available data (example: cumulative file, past testing, teacher feedback, Referral Review Form).

C. Determine need for additional data and who will be responsible for gathering of such data. Determine who will serve as case manager.

D. Time line set for case work-up.

E. Request to Conduct Formal Educational Assessment Form completed.

1. phone contact prior to mailing

2. forms sent home

3. phone contact in five (5) days, if no parental response

4. request to conduct Formal Educational Assessment Form received

5. conciliatory steps taken if negative reply or no response has been made

III. Observation: The most recent directive from the State Department of Education requires a formal observation of all prospective Special Learning Disability (SLD) students. In order to assure that the cooperating districts are in compliance with this directive, the Benton-Stearns Special Education Cooperative has provided a Written Report Form. This form will outline the necessary questions to be answered, as well as provide space for observation notes.

It is recommended by the Benton-Stearns Special Education Cooperative that observation be made in all areas of special education.

Consideration should be given to the fact that the observation should be made by someone other than the classroom teacher and that it be made in the environment in which the child is having difficulty. (Example: If the child is having difficulty in math, the observation should be made during math period, not art or some other unrelated subject areas.) In other words, the observation should correspond to the area of difficulty identified on the Referral Form or the Referral Review Form.

A. Designate staff responsible for making observation.

B. Observation completed in area child is having difficulty.

C. Written Report Form completed through item 2 by observer on date of observation.

D. Observation findings disseminated at team planning conference, Written Report Form completed and signed by team member.

IV. **Assessment:** An assessment must be conducted when, because of a person's performance in the present educational placement or presentation of possible handicapping conditions, he or she is thought to be in need of possible initiation or change in the placement or program. The assessment must be in compliance with all statutes. The assessment will be completed within thirty (30) school days after receipt of verification of parent/guardian written authorization for assessment.

A. Verification of parent/guardian written authorization.

B. Complete data collection, (example: home visits, classroom observations, testing, extended diagnostic teaching assessment, and obtaining information from outside agencies are all activities which might be accomplished during this period). Assessment must be completed within thirty (30) school days.

C. Case manager notifies in writing staffing team and parents of upcoming team planning conference.

D. Case manager must record all attempts/contacts to notify parents of team planning conference. When parent(s) initiate request for assessment and it is the decision of the Child Study Team to refuse to conduct an assessment written notification shall be sent to the parent.

V. **Team Planning Conference:** This conference will determine whether special education involvement is warranted and, if so, develop individualized education program (IEP).

A. Team members: parents, building principal, classroom teacher, special education teacher, other essential personnel, and when appropriate, the student.

B. Team members present findings.

1. The review of available assessment information may indicate a need for more extensive assessment or other additional information before a team decision or appropriate educational plan can be developed.

C. Written Report Form completed by team.

D. Determine existence of handicap.

1. If handicap is not established, discuss options outside of special education.

2. If handicap is identified, proceed to program recommendations.

E. Participants present program recommendations.

F. Set goals, objectives, and criteria for evaluation.

G. Determine level of service.

H. Future review date will be determined.

I. Complete Individualized Education Program Plan.

VI. I.E.P. Implementation: Following the Team Planning Conference and after the parents have indicated their approval of the program plan, implementation of the Individualized Education Program Plan begins.

A. Written parent authorization required for initial program placement.

B. Appropriate forms must be completed prior to program change or I.E.P. renewal and sent to parents (ten school day timeline in effect prior to change without parent authorization).

C. Conciliatory steps taken if negative reply or no response has been made in the case of initial placement.

D. Implement Individualized Education Program Plan.

VII. Periodic Review: The purpose of the review staffing will be to determine if the goals and objectives established for a given student are appropriate and are being met, or whether there is a need to modify/change the Individualized Education Program Plan. It may also determine whether termination of services is appropriate.

A. Inform parent(s) in writing of date, time, place . . . and invite to meeting.

B. Review and answer questions on Report of Periodic Review Form.

C. Inform parent(s) in writing of review findings if they are not in attendance.

D. If the decision made at the review staffing is to continue with the basic Individualized Education Program Plan as it was in the original team staffing (no significant change in programming), parent permission is not necessary for this continued placement.

E. *Change of Placement/Program:* If the decision is to significantly alter the education programming/placement, a new Individualized Education Program Plan must be written by the Team, and a Request to Initiate or Change Placement Form is completed by the case manager and forwarded to the parents. If termination of special education services has been decided, complete Special Notice of Intent to Terminate Service and send to parent(s) for signature.

1. If parents have not responded within five (5) school days, the case manager will contact them by telephone to determine whether they have received the form and answer any questions which the parent(s) might have.

2. Proposed change in programming will be initiated unless a negative response is received in writing by the school within ten (10) school days. In the event a negative response is received a conciliation conference will be set up with parent(s).

F. *Termination of Service.* If the decision at the review staffing involves termination of special education services, it is necessary that the case manager present to the parent(s) a Notice of Intent to Terminate Special Services Form asking for their written permission to terminate special education services.

1. If the parent(s) do not respond on this form within five (5) days, a phone call will be made by the case manager to determine if they received the form, or have questions regarding the recommended termination of service.

2. If the parent(s) return Response Form to School's Proposed Action indicating their refusal to accept this termination, the case manager will contact the parents to schedule a conference or home visit to discuss the reasons for proposed termination of special services and, when appropriate, obtain written parent permission to terminate. When ten (10) school days have passed with no response, the case manager will establish contact with the parent to obtain their response.

G. *Reassessment:* Clarification of reassessment policy may be found in the *Benton-Stearns Special Education Cooperative Handbook.* Appropriate forms shall be used for reassessment. The reassessment procedure will be conducted if the parent does not object or does not respond within ten (10) school days.

1. Every two years for primary placement in special education.

2. Every three years for primary

placement in regular classroom.

3. As the result of team decision.

4. At the request of the parents.

H. *Follow-up:*

1. The written follow-up review must be completed within (12) months after a special education program or service has been terminated. This review is conducted to determine the student's current performance, and to determine if the student is making satisfactory progress without the special education program or service.

Strengths and Weaknesses of Programs for the Handicapped

As there are likely to be both strengths and weaknesses in any comprehensive, widely-used educational program, so we find them in those worked out by school systems in accord with federal regulations.

Strengths of Programs

The following are among points made in favorable assessment of the laws governing the education of the handicapped and the implementation of them.

1. The intent of the laws is humanitarian in that the regulations purport to give all boys and girls—regardless of handicaps they may have—the right "to a free appropriate public education."[11] It guarantees to them the right to be educated in the least restrictive environment.

2. The laws aim to protect the rights of children and their parents. Legal provisions assure the parents a voice in the evaluation of their children's aptitudes and, in part, in the implementation of

[11]*Federal Register* 41:56996 (1976).

the program. There seems no place for autocratic determination, by school personnel alone, as to best interests of the child. Furthermore, the frequently talked about parent-teacher cooperation, but not so widely or wisely inaugurated into many school programs, becomes a reality.

3. The laws repudiate the practice, to the extent possible, of providing for the handicapped students in special-education classes. In many instances in the past a special class for handicapped students has been little more than a convenient means of excluding those students from the regular classroom setting. It sometimes seemed that the philosophy of "out of sight, out of mind" was in operation. The laws legislate against preventable isolation and, in many cases, the rejection which the handicapped have experienced.

4. The nonhandicapped students have the opportunity to profit by association with their less fortunate fellow-students. Thus they come into contact with experiences that would be likely to give them increased perspective of the world of reality.

5. The laws require that for each handicapped child an individualized education program be worked out and recorded in writing. This insistence on giving more than lip-service to the principle of individualizing instruction aims to favorably offset lack of such adaptation that has frequently characterized education of the handicapped both in the regular classrooms and in special-education rooms.

6. The law provides for the assessment of the program, and it designates criteria on which the evaluation is to be based. This mandate seems in contrast with many educational programs that fall short of effective and justifiable means of evaluation.

7. There is strong reason for complying with the laws since federal funds are to be withheld from all public school systems not complying.

Weaknesses of Programs

Among the alleged weaknesses that occur in the program for the handicapped are the following.

1. There is a problem of adjustment in schools when children who have been in special-education rooms are entering the regular classroom for the first time. This adjustment problem affects not only the handicapped boys and girls but also other classroom pupils and the teacher.

2. There is danger that the programs implemented for the handicapped will be highly skills-oriented—to the neglect of the human-relations component so desperately needed. To be sure, careful scrutiny of the Individualized Education Program required to be submitted for each handicapped child should indicate the general orientation of the program, as well as specifics of it. Thus the IEP should serve as one guard against overemphasis on skill development.

3. Most teacher-education programs are presently not geared toward helping prospective classroom teachers become acquainted with the needs of handicapped boys and girls. This situation must be corrected or at least, be alleviated. Furthermore, in-service programs for practicing teachers can also provide some needed guidance to remedy this situation.

4. Unless a child's educational program is well geared to suit his individual needs, there is danger of the child facing frustration in a room where the majority of

the students are doing work on a level decidedly above his. Because of such frustration a pupil may be unwilling to try to do work on his level.

5. There is danger that the emotionally disturbed child may disrupt the classroom. Undoubtedly even in a special-education room he might interfere with the learning of other boys and girls in the room. However, in the regular classroom, due to the larger number of pupils, the undesirable impact might be greater.

6. There is danger that the nonhandicapped child will be given less attention and consideration in a classroom in which there are handicapped children than he would otherwise receive. This problem is especially likely to occur since by legislative mandate an Individualized Education Program has to be worked out for each handicapped child though there is no such stipulation for the nonhandicapped student.

7. The program might place an undue strain on teachers. Unless a classroom teacher has adequate assistance, he may find that doing justice to the handicapped and the nonhandicapped overtaxes him.

8. Some parents of non-handicapped students are critical of the program. They believe their children suffer in the "mainstreaming" of the handicapped into the classrooms.

9. With reduction in budgets for education, some people fear that with the amount of money to be spent on fulfilling the requirements of the law in relation to the handicapped, there will result an unjustifiable curtailment of money for the education of the nonhandicapped. Undoubtedly care needs to be taken in budgetary planning to avoid any tendency in this respect that might exist.

For Further Study

For references on the topic of this chapter, we refer the reader to the Education Index. Many articles have been appearing that deal with this topic. Also the reader is referred to the many books dealing with special education of the handicapped—physically, mentally, and emotionally handicapped. Some recent general books on the teaching of reading include significant parts on the education of the handicapped. The reader is referred to the listing of titles under "For Further Study" in Chapter 13 (see p. 382), some of which deal in part with teaching the handicapped, the gifted, and the socioeconomically deprived.

A new journal, *Education Unlimited,* is a resource for regular and special educators, parents, and others who work with students with special needs (the handicapped, gifted, and talented) in the least restrictive educational environments. (The address is: Education Unlimited, 1834 Meetinghouse Road, Boothwyn, Pa. 19061).

Questions and Comments for Thought and Discussion

1. One problem with ability grouping is that pupils in low groups may feel a stigma attached to them. What, if anything, can be done to offset or minimize the danger of reluctance in being a member of such a group?

2. What do you see as the main strengths of diagnostic grouping? Do you notice any weaknesses in the procedure? If so, what are they?
3. How can reading be individualized in group situations?
4. If you have an opportunity to see a teacher teach reading in an elementary-school classroom in which the pupils are grouped, try to determine the basis for grouping, ways in which the instruction seems to be adapted to individual differences, and the effectiveness of the teaching.
5. If you have the opportunity to visit a school system in which considerable progress has been made in implementing the recent federal regulations regarding the education of the handicapped, you may find such a visit highly profitable. You may wish to note and discuss with the teacher or other staff member points such as these: drawing up of IEP's and examination of some such programs; problems involved in organizing a classroom according to the mandates of the recent laws; classroom organization; the role of the reading specialist.
6. In this chapter are listed alleged advantages (see p. 402) and alleged weaknesses (see p. 403) in the implementation of federal legislation regarding the handicapped. Which of the points in both those listings are, in your opinion, defensible? Which are indefensible?
7. Can you name points of strength and/or points of weakness other than those listed in this chapter (see p. 402 and p. 403) concerning federal regulations in educating the handicapped and in implementing these rulings?
8. The question of the extent to which the federal government should control education in the various States is almost unceasingly a matter of concern to teachers and to the lay public. Can you give arguments for and/or against the federal government designating in detail matters concerning the educating of the handicapped? At the present stage of your knowledge of these laws and the ramifications that have arisen, or may arise, do you believe the federal government, rather than state or local governmental bodies, should draw up specifications such as those contained in the recent rules?

Implementation of the Reading Program on a Schoolwide Basis

Excellence in the teaching of reading in a school requires more than superior teaching in each classroom. There must be a certain unity in the total reading program, though there may be, in fact, advisedly should also be, recognizable dissimilarities in the classrooms of the school. Such differences should be the result, however, not of ignorance on the part of the teachers as to how others are teaching but studied variations that seem best suited to individual teachers and to the boys and girls they are teaching.

An effective program of reading instruction in a school calls for intelligent, knowledgeable, and capable leadership. Strong support and leadership from the building principal is a necessity. So is careful overall planning. In this chapter we are considering: (a) what steps can be followed in developing a schoolwide program; (b) in what ways the program can be interpreted to parents; and (c) how the program can be evaluated. Part of what is discussed here is a summary or an application of principles taken up earlier in this book.

Steps in Planning a Schoolwide Reading Program

The initiative in undertaking a schoolwide program of reading instruction may come from any one or more of many sources. Sometimes a series of newspaper articles or a critical book may focus attention on the problem and hence lead to thoughtful reexamination of current practices in reading instruction. Sometimes an enthusiastic administrator or a teacher freshly returned from a leave for professional study sparks the program. A study may emerge from faculty discussions of a commonly felt need. Whatever its impetus, the program can be successfully undertaken only if a large pro-

portion of the teaching staff recognizes the need for it and is interested in participating in it.

Determining the Reading Status of Pupils

"How are we doing?" is the first question to ask when the teaching staff plans the schoolwide program. Teachers need to know whether their present program is getting results, whether the achievements are above or below national norms, whether the students are reading up to their capacity, and, especially, what the strengths and weaknesses are. Although many teachers, without taking an inventory, know that many of their pupils do not read as well as they could be expected to read, they will, nevertheless, find it helpful to have specific information as to the range of their reading abilities and the degree of reading retardation, in terms of deviations from national standards, that exist in their schools. The first step in a general reading program, therefore, is a careful study of the existing situation with respect to pupils' reading.

Although standardized reading tests have definite limitations and should never be regarded as infallible barometers of reading ability, they are useful indicators of the presence or absence of important reading skills. They are especially valuable as general screening and classification devices and as measures of the overall effectiveness of the reading program. However, in interpreting the ratings on standardized tests, the effectiveness of the program should be judged in relation to the nature of the individuals being taught—their intelligence and their background of experience. When interpreted with due caution, tests are one important means of determining the approximate reading status of large groups of pupils.

The standardized tests reveal what pupils can do in a test situation. Of equal importance are the extent and quality of the voluntary reading activities of the pupils. Reading ability is of no value unless it is used. For this reason, a survey of reading attainments in a school or school system could well include a study of the cumulative reading records kept by pupils of their personal, voluntary reading. Such a study does not lend itself so readily to statistical summary and analysis as data from standardized tests do, but it is no less important. In the interpretation of the records, the *nature* of pupils' choices should be given as much consideration as the number of books read.

Since so much of contemporary reading is done in the mass media, the preliminary survey should include an inquiry into the newspaper and magazine reading habits of older children. The inquiry should deal not only with the amount of time spent in a day or week in the reading of newspapers and magazines but especially with the pupils' preferences among the various features and the range of their interests. (See Chapter 12, "Classroom Diagnosis of Reading Ability," for a somewhat detailed discussion on evaluation and also see p. 311, "Periodicals for Boys and Girls.")

Deciding on General Procedure for the Study

The staff will need to consider the general organizational procedure to be followed when planning the program and on guidelines to determine their study and deliberations. Some of the suggestions for developing a literature program (see p. 317) may be helpful to the reader in understanding procedure that can be followed in planning a new program in any curriculum area.

Organizational Plan

In line with customary procedures when curricular programs are being planned, the faculty may decide that on some phases of the study the entire staff will take part while other work will be done by committees or individuals. The entire faculty can meet in order to listen to lectures on the teaching of reading, view movies, observe demonstration lessons, hear reports from committees or from one or more staff members, express opinions, make recommendations or decisions. The group may also endorse the acceptance of responsibility by the entire staff for participating in any way in which committees may solicit their help—such as taking part in short-range action research, filling out questionnaires, and making other reports. Committees can explore various areas of professional information needed for intelligent decision-making during the process of setting up the program. Topics such as these may be recommended by the staff for thorough investigation by committees: the objectives of the reading program, instructional procedures and practices, materials of instruction, plans for evaluation of the program. Additional study by individuals, usually reporting to committees, can involve reading, school visitation, attendance at conferences and workshops, writing the curriculum for reading that was accepted in principle by the faculty.

Guidelines for the Planning Period

Though the most desirable structure for work on planning a program will vary from one school system to another, the following suggestions, of rather general applicability, are some a staff may wish, with or without modifications, to accept as guidelines.

1. Since an excellent reading program in any school requires the cooperation of

all teachers, every teacher should have the opportunity and the responsibility to participate in the planning** Special teachers, in fields such as music, art, physical education, have a stake in any schoolwide program. While they should not be expected to carry as much of the load as the teachers of classes that deal to a great extent with reading activities, their participation should be of value to them as teachers of their specialties. They can also make a contribution to the total program through suggestions they may offer, especially following study of problems involved.

Because the planning of the program can advisedly be the in-service project for the school year, participation in the orientation and planning period can justifiably be a requirement for all teachers. This statement is made with the assumption that a program of this magnitude and far-reaching effect will not be undertaken unless it has the enthusiastic support of a large number of the teachers.

2. The plan for reorganization of a schoolwide reading program should be in harmony with what can reasonably be expected the school will be able to carry out with success A too-ambitious program may spell failure from the outset. A technique frequently employed in curriculum revision, which makes feasible some programs that otherwise might be too far-reaching for practical purposes, is that of not putting all phases of the program into operation simultaneously. Sometimes the first stage is a pilot program, carried on by only a few teachers, usually by those particularly interested in it. At other times during the first phase all teachers might concentrate in particular on only one part of the planned program, such as means of vitalizing the teaching of reading or use of audiovisual aids to teaching reading or

strategies for teaching word recognition and identification.

3. Change for the sake of change should not be advocated Change can mark progression or retrogression; it can be beneficial or harmful. Only those changes should be recommended which give substantial promise of being advantageous over practices followed at the time by a school.

4. Care should be taken when planning a program for reading instruction that it will not interfere with the fulfillment of other important goals of the school A program in no area of the curriculum can be justified if it curtails the accomplishment of equally justifiable objectives in other areas of study. Nor should it affect adversely, to the best of our knowledge of child development, the harmonious growth of the learner in all aspects—physical, emotional, social, spiritual.

5. Compensatory provisions should be made for those teachers who are delegated to spend a great amount of time in planning the schoolwide program While part of the responsibility of every teacher is to grow professionally and to assist in the improvement of the instructional program, no teaching member of the staff should be expected, without compensatory arrangements, to give an excessive amount of time to a schoolwide project. However, principals and supervisors, who often carry major responsibility and devote much time to the instigation of a program, can consider their contributions as part of their regular workload. Various plans are used to assure that, for some classroom teachers, their work on program revision will not constitute an unreasonable task. In some cases they are given a reduced load during part of the school year. A substitute teacher may be engaged to free the regular teacher one or more days a week or one or more forenoons or afternoons during a week. Some school systems engage a limited number of classroom teachers to devote six weeks or so of the summer months for work on the curriculum. Such provisions, whether in terms of released time from regular classroom duties or additional remuneration during vacation months, seem appropriate. However, it would, indeed, be unfortunate if any group of teachers, because such or similar provisions could not be made, would refrain from undertaking needed curriculum revision.

6. When planning a schoolwide program, the staff should recognize that some of the plans will necessarily involve all the teachers while others could be followed by one or more teachers, but not by others For example, if individualized instruction is to be engaged in, it will not be necessary to involve the total staff. One or two or more teachers could, for example, adopt a plan similar to that recommended by Jeannette Veatch (see p. 53) if they wished, while others would structure their program in other ways.

7. Even as early as the planning stage, means of evaluating the program after it is in progress, should be considered Criteria should be established for evaluating the program in line with the objectives agreed on. Means of making application of these standards should also be a point of deliberation and decision-making during the general planning period.

8. Time should be devoted during the planning period for deciding on the general procedures for making changes, if necessary, in a program after it is in op-eration Provisions should be made for needed additions or alterations or deletions following evaluations made after the program is in progress. Sometimes it may be advisable to lay alternative plans from the beginning in case the ones decided on for the program later appear not to be the best possible. Or supplementary plans that might possibly be incorporated in later stages of the program can be considered during the planning period.

9. Plans should be laid for continuing study by the staff of problems related to the teaching of reading If some of the plans require administrative approval, the possibility of obtaining such approval could be investigated and the ground work laid for later incorporating the plans as part of the in-service program.

Acquiring Background for Decision-Making

To be qualified to make recommendations for a schoolwide reading program and to put them into operation, the teachers must be knowledgeable in the area of the teaching of reading. Such understanding must include familiarity with the nature of the reading process, means of fostering growth toward maturity in reading through emphasis on needed skills and on reading for enjoyment, strategies for diagnosing and making provisions for the needs of individuals. There is no substitute for such knowledge. Without it no program can be successful. In addition, it is desirable that teachers be informed on topics such as the following, some of which are primarily organizational and others chiefly instructional in nature: behavioral objectives; reading stations; services of auxiliary personnel; the structure of the reading program; individualized reading; grouping practices; programed reading instruction; instructional materials, equipment, and special facilities. Since programed instruction, individualized reading, and grouping practices have been discussed earlier in this book, they will not be included in the discussion that follows.

Behavioral Objectives

Objectives for any instructional program should be clearly stated as guides to action. While general objectives can serve as basic guidelines, they need to be translated into specific goals of significance in day-by-day teaching. Furthermore, they should: (a) reflect a broad and comprehensive view of the reading process and of the values that can accrue from learning to read and (b) be worded so that they can be the basic structure for both teaching and evaluation.

Based on the philosophy of education that emphasizes that learning implies a change in the behavior of the learner, attempts have in recent years been made by teachers in many subject fields and at all levels of instruction to formulate objectives, not as topics to be studied, as has been common practice, but in terms of observable effects of learning on the learner. These objectives are worded so that the attainment of an objective is revealed if the learner can show competence through satisfactory performance of the given tasks. They are referred to as behavioral objectives because the emphasis is on what the pupil can do—on the behavior he can exhibit—not primarily on what he knows. A behavioral objective might be stated as "The pupils can arrange the following words alphabetically: . . ." rather than "To know how to arrange words alphabetically."

One problem in stating objectives behaviorally for the total reading program is that as yet there is no known way of identifying as observable objective behavior all the desired goals of a comprehensive reading program. The inclusion of some objectives but not others may result in serious omissions of very important components of reading. Another problem lies in the laboriousness of even attempting to identify behaviorally all known goals for teaching reading. Another shortcoming is that as the child becomes more and more conscious of the points on which he is being evaluated through behavioral objectives set by the school, he may degenerate or, at least, not develop adequately in power to establish his own objectives for reading.

Lists of behavioral objectives are available. If members of a teaching staff decide to draw up their own list of objectives for a schoolwide reading program, they should clearly recognize that an arduous task confronts them. Unless the staff is willing to spend the vast amount of time required and unless it considers itself competent to make such a listing after much study, it should, providing it wishes to state objectives behaviorally, confine such a statement of objectives to only a few phases of the total reading program and word the objectives for other phases topically. Behavioral objectives might, for example, be stated for (1) learning to alphabetize, (2) using the index, (3) dividing words into syllables. In fact, there are sound reasons why a staff should not spend a large amount of time in working out the objectives for a program as preliminary to other work toward launching a reading program.

A proposed program of schoolwide dimensions can fail to come to successful fruition because the group spends so exorbitant an amount of time working on objectives that interest in the total project wanes because of long postponement of work beyond the somewhat theoretical. While at the beginning of the planning period it may be beneficial to have a group meeting or two devoted to a consideration of objectives, it is recommended that a committee be established with the charge to draw up a taxonomy (organized listing) of objectives for consideration by the staff. The committee should acquaint itself with practices in setting objectives, preliminary to making its first report to the staff. While this committee is engaged in formulating objectives, other committees should be concentrating on other topics—such as materials of instruction, teaching techniques, organizational plans, to name only a few.

The Structure of the Reading Program

The staff must decide whether special classes in basal reading instruction will be set up. While some teachers believe that reading instruction can best be carried on in connection with other learning experiences, chiefly on an incidental basis, undoubtedly the great majority of schools provide for systematic reading instruction in scheduled periods for the development of basic skills. Systematic instruction in these skills does not preclude incidental instruction at various times throughout the school day. Nor does it take away the need of a strong literature program nor of the importance of teaching boys and girls to read in the content areas.

While it is true that some children learn to read well without any systematic instruction, acquiring all needed skills through abundant and highly motivated reading, the vast majority of children need instructional assistance if they are to learn to read at their best. The regularly scheduled reading period will continue to be indispensable for most teachers and with most children if essential skills are to be developed.

In schools in which a period is set aside in the school program for systematic read-

ing instruction, usually a reading series is used, either as in the manner described under "Diagnostic Grouping" (see p. 388) or as indicated, with variations, in the guidebooks for the teacher accompanying the series. If the latter forms the basis for organization of the basic reading program, certain general cautions should be observed in the planning of the program. These cautions grow out of facts and principles developed earlier in this book. For example, reliance should not be placed on a single basal reader for the whole class; indeed, it should not be placed on an entire single series. It is fortunate that, increasingly, newer reading textbook series have, as their basic plan of organization, levels of reading which cut across grade designations. If a series is organized by grade levels, with arrangements for variations in needs of boys and girls, the reader should not be labeled according to grade level of difficulty, although the publisher's estimate of difficulty level may be indicated by some code device. All basal readers should be amply supplemented with general reading materials on many subjects and representing many levels of reading difficulty. In the primary grades every effort should be put forth to make the initial experiences with books pleasurable and rewarding. In the intermediate grades the teacher should also try to relate specific reading skills to the reading situations arising in the various curricular areas. The reading in basal readers should be accompanied by reading activities in other textbooks calling for similar skills, such as locating information, summarizing a paragraph, or using the dictionary. Basal readers should not be used for mere oral drill, in smaller or larger groups, in which everyone marks time while one pupil struggles through a passage. Pupils who are able to complete the material in the basal reader rapidly and without instructional assistance should be permitted to go on to more difficult materials.

Instructional Materials, Equipment, and Special Facilities

In the preceding paragraph and at various other places in this book (see, for instance, p. 47), we have referred to the most popular of all reading materials, the basal reader. When planning reading programs in which basal readers are to be used extensively, the teachers should be well acquainted with various reading series, of which many excellent ones are on the market. Study of textbooks, with the materials accompanying them, can well be the focus of concentration for one or more committees.

There is reason to believe that much of the criticism hurled by some critics against basal readers should be made of the misuse, rather than use, of the better series. On request the teacher will receive from the publishers free materials explaining a series and highlighting the points of special excellence claimed for them. Publishers will also send a list indicating their supplementary materials. The R. R. Bowker publication, revised annually, *El-hi Textbooks in Print*, lists not only textbooks but also teaching materials such as dictionaries, booklets, and maps.

Among the publishers of textbooks in reading are the following:

Allyn and Bacon, Inc.
American Book Company
The Bobbs-Merrill Company
Educators Publishing Service
Ginn and Company
Harcourt Brace Jovanovich
Harper & Row, Publishers
D. C. Heath and Company
Holt, Rinehart and Winston
Houghton Mifflin Company
Laidlaw Brothers
J. B. Lippincott Company
The Macmillan Company
Charles E. Merrill Books
Open Court Publishing Company
Pitman Publishing Company
Prentice-Hall
Science Research Associates
Scott, Foresman and Company
Silver Burdett Company

Guidebooks for the teacher are published with all extensively used reading series. At times these are published as separate paperbacks; at other times the suggestions to the teacher are given in a teacher's edition of the book, in which a part of the book is the same as the pupil's edition and another part is designed only for the teacher's use. Often, even in the part reproducing what is given in the pupil's edition, suggestions for the teacher are included in the margins of the pages and/or as notations written along with the lines of the text. The guidebooks can be of great help to the teacher if they are used, as most of them are intended to be used, as suggestive of possible procedures to be followed, not as prescriptive.

With many of the basal reader series there are also consumable books for boys and girls, often referred to as workbooks. Workbooks of various types, when not used as "busy work," can be of real service. The better series have a well-developed sequence of workbooks designed to be used in conjunction with the hardback books, the regular readers. Most of these are written to give the boys and girls practice after the material in the textbook has been read. An examination of any workbook accompanying a reader will reveal a variety of ways in which it provides practice for work on word recognition and other reading skills.

Some teachers prefer making material of the workbook type themselves, believing that it is better suited to the needs of the particular boys and girls than that given in the workbooks. Although this practice has merit, it is time-consuming and not really necessary today. It is true, however, that when workbook materials were sterile in content and poor in selection of objectives to be accomplished, it was not difficult to justify the large amount of time that some teachers, especially in the lower grades, spent in devising and duplicating materials to provide practice beyond that given in the reader on various reading skills.

In using workbooks that are not made to accompany any one series of readers, there is the danger of lack of unity in objectives and procedures between reader and workbook. If the authors of the textbook series have in mind one program for the development of word recognition and the writers of the workbook follow a different sequence and observe other criteria, the articulation when using these two types of materials is often poor. This difficulty is especially likely to exist if the teacher is under pressure to require every pupil to do every page in a workbook, regardless of the appropriateness of the material to the rest of the program and to the needs of the boys and girls. Nevertheless, judicious use of workbooks that are made independently of any one series of readers can be helpful if the workbooks are based on sound principles of teaching reading.

In addition to basal readers, guidebooks, and workbooks a flood of materials for reading instruction has appeared on the market, some of which accompanies reading series, but much of which is produced without any single series in mind. They include word cards and phrase cards, films and filmstrips, slides, tapes and videotapes, cassettes, charts, instructional kits (often with multimedia materials), programed materials, records and recordings, among other materials. Machines for use with or without some of these materials include filmstrip viewers, filmstrip projectors, cassette players, reading rate accelerators of various kinds, motion picture machines, equipment for producing and showing videotapes, and much other equipment.

It may be the responsibility of a committee to study the supplementary materials produced by companies publishing basal readers and/or those placed on the market by some other publishers. They might wish to write to any of the companies listed earlier in this chapter (see p. 413) as well as to some of the following:

Addison-Wesley Publishing Company
American Guidance Services
Cambridge University Press
The Economy Company
Educational Developmental Laboratories
Educator's Progress Service
Enrichment Teaching Materials
Fearon Publishers
Follett Publishing Company
Longmans, Green and Company
McCormich-Mathers Publishing Company
Reader's Digest Association
Simon and Schuster
Society for Visual Education
Stanford University Press

Another subject for study by a committee might advisedly be audiovisual aids for the reading program, with special attention, possibly, to films, filmstrips, and recordings. Chapters in many professional books on teaching methods are an excellent source of ideas for using audiovisual aids.

Committees may wish to study these

types of audiovisual aids as they pertain to the teaching of reading.

1. Films Search for films should be concentrated both on those available for use by the teacher of reading for his information and for those of value to the boys and girls in the reading program. Films for boys and girls in the area of reading can be classified as those that deal with the skills of reading and those that deal with books for children. Catalogues from the audiovisual divisions of some state departments of education constitute one source for films both for the teacher as well as for the boys and girls. A letter requesting information from many of the companies listed in this section as distributors of audiovisual aids will be honored by the recipients.

2. Recordings Various series of records are available on outstanding books. There is, for example, the well-known Enrichment Records series, which accompany some of the Landmark Books published by Random House, The National Council of Teachers of English produces a series of records of stories such as "The Elves and the Shoemaker," "Rumplestiltskin," "Aladdin and the Wonderful Lamp," "Rip Van Winkle," "Just So Stories," and "The House at Pooh Corner." Also on the market are *Folkways Records* (Folkways Records and Service Corporation), *My First Golden Record Library* (Golden Records), and various "libraries" of books, with records, distributed by *The Columbia Children's Book and Record Library* (Department CBR, 51 West 52d Street, New York, N. Y. 10019).

Of considerable popularity are the *Newbery Award Records*, distributed by Newbery Award Record, Inc. They include titles such as *The Wheel on the School* (Meindert DeJong), *Call It Courage* (Armstrong Sperry), *Amos Fortune, Free Man* (Eliza-beth Yates), *Invincible Louisa* (Cornelia Meigs). Miller-Brody Productions, Inc. (342 Madison Avenue, New York, N. Y. 10017) publishes the Newbery Award Library, which includes the books with accompanying records, cassettes, and filmstrips.

Records are also available on subjects indicated by these titles: "Choral Speaking for Intermediate Grades" (Educational Record Sales); "Let's Try Choral Reading" (Young America Films); "It's Your Library" (Vocational Guidance Films).

There are also recordings of stories told by famous storytellers. For example, obtainable from the American Library Association are albums of stories told by Ruth Sawyer and Gudrun Thorne-Thomsen. Recordings, too, have been made of poets reading their own work, as for example, two recordings available through Caedmon, "Robert Frost Reads His Poetry" and "Poems for Children" by Carl Sandburg.

Sound-filmstrip sets, in which filmstrips are synchronized with recordings, are produced by several companies. For example, *Crow Boy* by Taro Yashima, *Petunia* by Roger Duvoisin, *Little Tim and the Brave Sea Captain* by Edward Ardizonne, and *Three Billy Goats Gruff* adapted by Marcia Brown are available as sound-filmstrips through Weston Woods Studios.

3. Guides to Selection of Audiovisual Aids The National Information Center for Educational Media (University of Southern California, University Park, Los Angeles 90007) publishes these indexes periodically:

NICEM Index to Educational Audio Tapes
NICEM Index to Educational Records
NICEM Index to Educational Video Tapes
NICEM Index to 8 mm Cartridges
NICEM Index to Filmstrips

NICEM Index to Overhead Transparencies

NICEM Index to Producers and Distributors

NICEM Index to 16 mm Educational Films

A few of the many additional guides to the selection of audiovisual aids are:

Aids in Selection of Materials for Children and Young People (American Library Association)

An Annotated List of Recordings for the Language Arts (National Council of Teachers of English)

Audio-Visual Catalog (Materials for Learning, Inc.)

Audio-Visual Materials Handbook (Indiana University, Bloomington)

Choosing a Classroom Film (McGraw Hill Book Company)

CBS Audio-Visual Catalog (Children's Reading Service, Brooklyn, N. Y.)

Educational Filmstrip Catalog (Society for Visual Education)

Educational Tape Catalog (Magnetic Tape Duplicators)

Educational Television Guidebook, Phillip Lewis (McGraw Hill Book Company)

Educational Television Motion Pictures, Descriptive Catalog (National Education Television Film Service, Audiovisual Center, University of Indiana, Bloomington)

Educator's Guide to Free Films (Educators Progress Service)

Educator's Guide to Free Filmstrips (Educators Progress Service)

Educator's Guide to Free Slidefilms (Educators Progress Service)

Educator's Guide to Free Tapes and Recordings (Educators Progress Service)

Filmstrip Guide (The H. W. Wilson Company)

Guides to Newer Media, Margaret L. Rufswold and Carolyn Gauss (American Library Association)

Picture Book Parade Motion Pictures, Filmstrips, and Records (Weston Woods Studios)

SVE Film and Filmstrip Catalogs (Society for Visual Education)

Sources of Information on Educational Media, John A. Moldstad (U. S. Printing Office)

The Tape Recorder in the Elementary Classroom (Minnesota Mining and Manufacturing Company)

4. Producers and Distributors of Audiovisual Aids Audiovisual aids can be obtained not only from many state universities and state departments of education, but also from various other sources. Agencies such as steamship lines, manufacturing companies, and consuls are also good sources of free aids. Some book companies, too, are distributors of audiovisual materials, such as McGraw-Hill Book Company, Harcourt Brace Jovanovich, and Scott, Foresman and Company. Some of the other names of publishers and/or distributors include:

American Council on Education (One Dupont Circle, N. W., Washington, D. C. 20036)

American Library Association (50 East Huron Street, Chicago, Ill. 60611)

American Museum of Natural History (Central Park West at 79th Street, New York, N. Y. 10023)

Audiovisual Research (1317 Eighth Street South, Waseca, Minn. 56093)

BFA Educational Media (2111 Michigan Ave., Santa Monica, Cal. 90404)

Caedmon Records (505 Eighth Avenue, New York, N. Y. 10018)

Columbia Records, Educational Division (799 Seventh Avenue, New York, N. Y. 10019)

Coronet Films (Coronet Building, 65 East South Water Street, Chicago, Ill. 60601)

Educators Progress Service (Randolph, Wis. 53956)

Encyclopedia Britannica Films (1150 Wilmette Avenue, Wilmette, Ill. 60091)

Folkways Records and Service Corporation (165 West 46th Street, New York, N. Y. 10036)

Ginn and Company, (191 Spring Street, Lexington, Mass. 02175)

Keystone View Division/Mast Development Company (2212 West 12th Street, Davenport, Iowa 52803)

London Records, Inc. (539 West 25th Street, New York, N. Y. 10001)

McGraw-Hill, Inc., (1221 Avenue of the Americas, New York, N. Y. 10036)

Media Materials, Inc., (2936 Remington Ave., Baltimore, Md. 21211)

Magnetic Tape Duplicators (6766 Sunset Boulevard, Hollywood, Cal. 90028)

National Council of Teachers of English (1111 Kenyon Road, Urbana, Ill. 61801)

National Center for Audio Tapes (Bureau of A-V Instruction, Stadium Building, Boulder, Col. 80302)

Newbery Award Record, Inc. (342 Madison Avenue, New York, N. Y. 10017)

Society for Visual Education, Subsidiary of Graflex, Inc. (1345 Diversey Parkway, Chicago, Ill. 60614)

United States Government Printing Office (Superintendent of Documents, Washington, D. C. 20025)

University of California (Children's Theater Committee, Theater Arts Department, Los Angeles, Cal. 40524)

Visual Educational Consultants, (2066 Helene Street, Madison, Wis. 53704)

Weston Woods Studios (Weston, Conn. 06833)

H. W. Wilson Company (950 University Avenue, Bronx, N. Y. 10452)

It is, indeed, difficult for the classroom teacher to evaluate the great variety of materials for the teaching of reading that are on the market. Such evaluation, on a limited scope, might, indeed, be the work of more than one committee in planning a reading program for a school. Of help may be the following resolution, entitled "Buyer Be Wary" and adopted by the Delegates Assembly of the Tenth Annual Convention of the International Reading Association in May 1969:

A wide variety of services, devices, and training materials which purport to produce the improvement of reading skills is currently being offered to the general public. In some instances, the advertising accompanying these materials approaches sensationalism, exaggeration and even misrepresentation, when judged with regard to the limits of present professional knowledge.

To aid the prospective user of reading improvement devices and services, the International Reading Association offers the following cautions:

1. Statements of possible benefits from reading improvement services should be characterized by modesty and due caution for the limits of professional skills which do not encompass cure-all powers.
2. The possible causes of inadequate or poor reading skills are many. There is no single treatment or approach known which will effectively correct all possible causes of difficulty.
3. No ethical person who is a professional in the area of reading improvement can or should guarantee marked improvement of skills for all users of his services.
4. Distributors of reading devices or materials have an ethical obligation to submit their products to fair scientific trials before marketing, and to make the data of these evaluations available to all prospective purchasers.

Interpreting the Reading Program to Parents

In any school, regardless of whether a new reading program is being proposed, careful thought needs to be given to the role of the parent. In the first place, parents have a right to know what the school's objectives in reading are and why it is using the particular procedures it has adopted in reading instruction. The intelligence and good judgment of parents should be respected. Many parents who are interested in their children's schooling are perfectly able to understand the principles on which the school's policies are based when these are clearly and, in many instances, simply explained to them. The school should make clear that it regards the education of children as a team project in which the home

Fathers, too, can help children develop interest in reading. (Patricia Elliott Dallmann)

and the school have a common interest.

Moreover, the school very much needs the help of the home in teaching the child to read. Parents can do much in creating a home atmosphere favorable to the development of reading ability. They are often in a better position than teachers to discover children's interests and to perceive the emotional reactions that children have toward the reading situation. By surrounding the young child with good books adapted to his level of ability, by setting the example of silent reading, by reading aloud to him and talking with him about stories and pictures, and in general by making reading an enjoyable experience for him from the earliest years, parents can lay the foundation for later success in reading.

Most parents, however, do not have the needed training for developing specific reading skills. While they should be kept informed about the changing trends in reading instruction, they should normally leave the formal instruction to the classroom teacher. When children ask questions about words or ideas encountered in the reading, they should not hesitate to give needed help. Reading drills, except perhaps occasionally at the request of the teacher, have no place in the home. Reading "games," yes; attractive books for pleasurable reading, yes; but word drills and phonics (except in play) at home, no. The best contribution parents can make to the reading progress of their children is to provide them with a secure and happy home, an abundance of love and encouragement, a great variety of play, creative and constructive experiences, and almost unlimited opportunity for free reading in good books and magazines. Time to read, encouragement to read, and materials to read are necessary; pressure and a sense of urgency may be dangerous.

Concepts of Special Interest to Parents

Parents can be helped to understand a number of important concepts of modern reading instruction. One of these is that of readiness (see Chapter 5A, "Readiness for Reading," and Chapter 5B, "Developing Readiness for Reading"). We know that not all children are ready to begin learning to read at the same chronological age. Since most parents assume that first grade is the time for all children to learn to read, it becomes necessary to explain to them that children vary in their readiness for initial reading instruction. Delay in reading instruction is by no means evidence of backwardness. The important thing to remember is that the first experiences with reading should be happy, successful ones. If for any reason a child, with methods and materials suited to his level, is not ready to learn to read with satisfaction, he should be given the opportunity to develop the needed maturity before being expected to engage in reading activities.

A second concept that frequently needs to be explained to parents is the beginning reading program used in the school, regardless of whether the code approach, the meaning approach, or a combination of the two is used. Parents will want to be informed about the role of phonics in the instructional program. A great many parents believe that the chief weakness of modern reading instruction is the neglect of phonics. Such complaints have been heard for a long time. They were vigorous in the decade of the twenties, when the importance of silent reading began to be stressed in many quarters. Parents should be assured that phonics instruction is still given in school but that in many schools it relies less than formerly on mechanical and memorization

methods. In many of these schools it is given at strategic times and to pupils who need a given type of help. It occupies an important place in the basal readers and in the teachers' manuals. Parents should also be helped to realize that phonics is only one of several aids to the recognition of words and that the use of additional methods, involving context clues and structural analysis, can strengthen the pupils' ability to recognize new words. Many parents will be pleased to know that the schools are not standing still in their efforts to teach children the diverse skills of word recognition.

If reading programs involving a linguistic approach or any other new or innovative programs in reading are in operation or are being planned, they should be discussed with the parents. Moreover, they should recognize that most reading outside of school is silent and that some of the skills of silent reading differ in important aspects, from those of oral reading. Parents should be helped to realize that schools, therefore, stress silent reading throughout the grades, giving attention to oral reading as a significant separate skill or using it as an aid in the improvement of silent reading. Parents whose own recollections of school reading are associated with oral communication or sounding of words may be interested in the reasons for the new emphasis. Most of them will be pleased to note the increased use of purposeful oral reading and the decline of oral reading exercises which required the class to mark time while one pupil recited.

Methods of Communicating with Parents

The best of all the methods for promoting home-school cooperation is the person-to-person conference. The principal might have a conference with one or both parents of every child entering school for the first time. In the course of the conference he could try to discover the viewpoints of the parents and their assessments of their children's needs and capacities, with the knowledge that he has much to learn from parents. At the same time he might explain to the parents the plan of reading instruction followed in the school and the major consideration that led to the adoption of the program. If he is able to show that the plan is getting good results, the great majority of parents will be satisfied with it.

In some schools certain days are set aside each year for teacher-parent conferences. On these days all teachers meet individually with parents of pupils in their classes. In these conferences teachers report the progress that the children are making in school and answer parents' questions about the instructional procedures employed. While the method is time-consuming, it recognizes the important fact that parents are most intimately concerned with the progress of their children and hence should be both consulted and informed.

At times it may be profitable to have the child present, as a contributing member, at a conference with the teacher and parent(s).

Additional suggestions for the teacher that may serve to make home-school conferences effective are:

1. Emphasize the fact that the home and the school have in common the goal of providing a program that will help each child progress to the limit of his potential without interfering with other important objectives.
2. Discuss with parents the relationship between a secure emotional atmosphere

in the home and the learning-to-read process, by means such as these: emphasizing the importance of developing or maintaining the learner's self-esteem; giving him the assurance of his being loved; helping him develop good work habits.

3. Suggest to parents various tangible ways in which they can help, such as: being supportive of sound programs of the school at voting booths; setting a good example for boys and girls in their own reading habits; taking time to listen to questions and comments of the boys and girls; providing the boys and girls with educational experiences that enhance their background of understanding such as field trips to a zoo, museum, an airport or even to more common places such as supermarkets, drug stores, libraries.

Some school systems publish attractively illustrated leaflets addressed to parents, setting forth in some of them the rationale of the reading program in the schools. Parents in many communities are invited, even urged, to visit the schools and to observe the reading program in action.

Another valuable device for involving parents in the work of the school is the occasional chatty newsletter, written by the teacher especially for the parents of his pupils. The first such newsletter can include the names of the children; some information about the teacher himself; references to the principal, clerk, nurse, custodians, and their duties; notes of appreciation for things parents have done for the school; and announcements of PTA meetings. Succeeding newsletters can report plans for various class activities; invite parents to visit the class; request materials for baking, construction, nature study, and the like; and, particularly, explain the educational significance and purpose of the activities.

Meetings of the Parent Teacher Association can serve as a valuable adjunct to the reading program. Discussion of topics such as these could serve a useful purpose: ways in which parents can help boys and girls become better readers; the importance of helping a child to develop or maintain his self-esteem and how to do it; the need for help from parents beyond the initial stage of reading instruction. Speakers such as the reading specialist, the librarian, the doctor, or a committee of teachers and parents might be in charge of a program. Materials, such as book lists, suggestions for purchasing books for boys and girls, information about TV programs, recent acquisitions of the library, might be distributed at the meetings. Reading games might be displayed and, possibly, the parents might be given the opportunity to play some of the games so as to enable them better to help children with them. The old-time practice of having the teacher demonstrate some phases of the teaching of reading by giving a demonstration lesson in which boys and girls take part could be followed. Films, filmstrips, and other audiovisual equipment might be used to inform parents about the teaching of reading. The PTA might sponsor book fairs, organize study clubs among parents, and help with the organization and maintenance of teacher-aide programs.

The International Reading Association has recently begun publishing, three times a year, a newsletter entitled "News for Parents" for use by local council members of that association. In the September 1980 issue is printed the booklist that follows.

Booklist—Publications for Parents

The following booklist was compiled by Gloria Smith, librarian at International Reading Association Headquarters. The publications listed here are guides for parents in helping their children become readers.

1. *Children's Reading in the Home* by May Hill Arbuthnot, Scott, Foresman.

2. *Reading Begins at Home* by Dorothy Butler and Marie Clay, Heinemann.

3. *Books and the Teenage Reader: A Guide for Teachers, Librarians and Parents* (2nd revised edition) by G. Robert Carlsen, Harper and Row.

4. *Books for You: A Booklist for Senior High Students*, Kenneth Donelson, ed., National Council of Teachers of English.

5. *A Parent's Guide to Children's Reading* (4th edition) by Nancy Larrick, Doubleday.

6. *Su nino y la lectura: Como usted puede ayudar*, Houghton Mifflin.

7. *Children and Books* (5th edition) by Zena Sutherland and May Hill Arbuthnot, Scott, Foresman.

8. *Preparing Your Child for Reading* by Miles Tinker, McGraw-Hill.

9. IRA series of ten micromonographs for parents. Single copies of each are available from the International Reading Association at a prepaid cost of US $.35 for IRA individual members and US $.50 for others.

10. *Parents and Reading*, Carl Smith ed., IRA. Available at a prepaid cost of US $3.50 for IRA individual members and US $5.00 for others.

11. *Helping Children Read: Ideas for Parents, Teachers, and Librarians*, Susan Glazer and Carol Brown, eds., New Jersey Reading Association. Available for US $6.00 + $.50 postage. Contact: Anne Ferrara, 202 Morningside Drive, Trenton, New Jersey 08618. Make checks payable to New Jersey Reading Association.

Reading and the Disadvantaged Home

So far we have given suggestions for home-school cooperation that will be of value when the home in question is not a disadvantaged one. To be sure, some of these suggestions—such as those pertaining to the need for development or maintenance of a child's self-esteem, the importance of interest by the parent in the child's reading activities—hold true regardless of the type of home in which the child lives. However, there are homes in which parents cannot read with fluency, where there are no, or practically no, worthwhile books for boys and girls, where there is no place for privacy for home reading or study, where there is little interest in the child's progress at school. While the teacher cannot be expected to be able to make a major impact on changing such situations—though it is remarkable what an impact an adult, such as a teacher, has made in some instances— the school must be cognizant of the problems that the child faces in his home. To whatever extent it is possible under the circumstances, the school should try to make up, at least in part, for deficiencies in the home environment. For example, if there are no good books in the home, special concern can be shown that the child signs out books from the library; if there is no one in the home to whom the child can read, the teacher can provide extra time for oral reading at school; if there is no one in the home who encourages his growth in reading, the teacher can make it a point to be especially complimentary to the child when situations warrant such encouragement.

We must not make the false assumption that parents of nondeprived homes necessarily have a greater interest in their children's progress at school. In fact, when approached tactfully and with understanding, parents of deprived homes often are as interested in the progress of their children as any of more fortunate circumstances. Furthermore, there are frequently conditions in the culturally and economically fortunate home that operate against the learning situation that make the children deprived. In

these homes parents often are inclined (1) to pressure their children unduly for accomplishment in reading, (2) to divert time that could be spent on reading by allowing the child to engage in an undue number of out-of-the-home activities, (3) to be absent from the home so much of the time that the child is lacking in parental guidance.

Reading and the Bi-Lingual Home

We must not make the error of assuming that the home in which a language other than English is the chief means of communication is necessarily the culturally deprived home. Some of the homes in which English is the second language are among the most cultured homes. However, it is true that, with the great extent of poverty among some such groups, frequently they are what we might, for lack of a better term, call disadvantaged. To be sure, knowledge by the child of a second language spoken in his home can be a decided asset to him in many respects. As has been said, the school frequently acts as if a second language is a shortcoming for a young child, only later in high school to try zealously to teach the child a second language. But, nevertheless, when matters of initial reading instruction are considered, the boy or girl from a home where English is not a commonly-used language, may need special attention in learning to read. It is, however, not the province of this book to outline a course of action for dealing with such situations. Suffice it here to point out that the teacher needs to be aware of resulting problems in learning to read and, if time permits, read some of the literature dealing with them. The reader is referred to some of the books listed at the end of Chapter 13.

Evaluation of the Reading Program

Appraisal of a schoolwide reading program is a difficult task, made especially puzzling by the fact that in spite of much research in the area of the teaching of reading, to very few major points, if any, has an unqualified solution been found. As one surveys, for example, the accounts of approaches to reading instruction and the investigations in that area, one looks in vain for a convincing answer. Enthusiasts of specific methods of procedure in teaching reading make contradictory claims. Interpreters of the same research often present different conclusions. The teacher as well as the parent may well ask: "What is the truth about the teaching of reading?"

In spite of lack of final answers to the question and in spite of the fact that any evaluative process necessarily involves many value judgments on matters for which research has thus far not been clearcut, all schools, whether venturing on a new program of reading instruction or continuing with one established earlier, should have as a priority concern the evaluation of the program. Though evaluation should be continuous, at intervals a rather comprehensive appraisal should be made either by the staff alone or with the help of one or more outside consultants expert in making evaluations and making recommendations on the basis of their findings. The evaluation should include more than a study of how well the boys and girls are reading, as described earlier (see Chapter 12), though that should certainly be an important phase of it. All factors that influence the success of the reading program should be considered.

Means of Evaluation

Just as there is no one known method of teaching reading that is accepted as *the* method, so there is no perfect device for determining what is the best currently used approach. However, there are various ways of helping the teacher with this question in addition to those already described. The thoughtful reading of reports on experimental setups and of research on innovative programs can be of aid in determining which approaches to the teaching of reading should be followed. Study of the literature on the teaching of reading—as found in books on methods of teaching, in periodicals, and in other publications—can form a background against which to make appraisals. In this book, chapter after chapter, there are suggested, directly or indirectly, those theories and practices for teaching reading that the authors consider valid.

Engaging in what used to be commonly called action research can also be of value to the teacher who desires to follow a program in the teaching of reading that will bring the best possible results. In other words, the teacher can try out in his own classroom some of the methods and techniques that seem to him to be of promise.

Finally, even after the teacher has attempted to the best of his ability to evaluate various approaches to teaching reading, he will still find that his appraisal is lacking in objectivity. But he cannot wait idly for a better day to come when evaluation techniques will give him more specific directions. The teacher in the classroom cannot postpone teaching reading until research has discovered without a doubt the most successful procedures. As day after day he attempts to do his work as effectively as he can, he must ever make use of the means of evaluation at his disposal, imperfect though they are. If he follows this suggestion, he will not be without a guide.

Related Issues

Our discussion of the evaluation of reading programs would hardly be complete without attention to two terms that are increasingly being used when referring to the appraisal of the success with which elementary school subjects, including reading, are being taught. They are *accountability* and *national assessment.*

Accountability

Accountability is not a new concept even though the term has not, until fairly recently, been used often in professional writing. Good teachers have always considered themselves accountable for their teaching, and poor teachers have been held accountable whether they have liked it or not. Teachers are accountable to the boys and girls they teach, to the parents of those children, to the school administration, and to the public that supports the schools. All evaluation of teachers—whether by boys and girls, parents, school administrators, or the general public—has always been an indication of accountability. School administrators and supervisors have exercised their responsibility for evaluation of teachers by means such as classroom visitation, examination of the academic achievements of boys and girls, consideration of reports about teachers, and conferences with them. Through formal and informal evaluative means they have made decisions on retention, salary increments, and promotions.

The public, too, has never been slow to express its opinion of teachers. It is only right and proper that teachers should be judged by the society which engages them to teach. Of late the voices raised in protest over what schools are doing are being heard increasingly. Nor is such increased criticism necessarily undesirable. It can bespeak more interest of the public in its schools—a plea for which schools have long made. That the evaluation has become less passive in nature we realize as we note the favorable reaction of the public to books highly critical of the schools and as we think of the fact that suit was filed by an eighteen-year-old graduate of the San Francisco Unified School District against the school district and the state department of education because of alleged failure to teach him to read up to his capacity.[1]

Undoubtedly the teaching profession needs to be reminded from time to time that it is accountable. Thereby, benefit can be derived from an insistence on accountability. However, there are also dangers involved in the concept of accountability as it is advocated by some of its chief proponents. An underlying difficulty stems from the fact that many advocates of accountability, as the term is now used, are seemingly unaware of the problems involved in obtaining a fair indication of the quality of a teacher's performance. Frequently they place their confidence in pre- and post-tests given the boys and girls near the beginning and toward the end of the school year. Specialists in the area of tests and measurements have long warned us that no test or combination of tests gives a perfect index of the achievement of the learner. Thus, through too much faith in test results, an erroneous impression of the performance of a boy or girl can be obtained. Some of the

[1]Gary Saretzky, "The Strangely Significant Case of Peter Doe," *Phi Delta Kappan,* vol. LIV, no. 9 (May 1973), pp. 589–592.

other factors that complicate and hinder the search for adequate means of holding teachers accountable are:

1. No perfect means of determining a child's potential—his learning capacity—have been devised. It is generally agreed that intelligence tests, as a rule, are the best indicators that we have. However, they are so far from reliable and valid instruments for measuring mental ability that great caution must be observed before a teacher is considered lacking because, according to test data, a child has not made progress commensurate with his ability.

2. The teacher cannot be given sole credit for the progress or lack of it made by a child. Home conditions may be favorable or unfavorable to learning. On the one hand, if all progress a child makes, let us say in reading, is attributed to the teaching, the teacher can be overrated; on the other hand, if all lack of progress is blamed on the teacher, the teacher can be sorely underrated. What complicates the appraisal is that during some periods of time home conditions can be a positive influence toward learning and at other times in the same home the environment may be devastating to intellectual development. Examples of other factors beyond the control of the teacher are: the opportunity the child has to read outside of school, the incentive for reading that he may get as he finds books in the public library that serve as reason for further exploration of the field of a newly acquired interest, the effect that a friend who enjoys reading may have on a pupil.

3. Psychologists who have specialized in the study of how learning takes place emphasize the point that learning often does not progress at an even rate, but that frequently it seemingly goes by spurts. A child may reach a plateau in his learning and remain on it, through no fault of his teacher, for much or all of a school year. Or, again, without credit to the teacher, he may be having a spurt in learning. Any system of accountability, to be fair, must take cognizance of knowledge such as this available from the field of the psychology of learning.

4. Care needs to be taken that more than academic achievement is taken into consideration as teachers are being held accountable. A teacher's influence on the whole child is of greater importance than his skill in teaching reading. Because of the difficulty of measuring even fairly accurately the effect a teacher may have on the total growing personality of the child, great caution needs to be exercised when putting into practice the concept of accountability.

5. One of the grave dangers of misuses of accountability is that some teachers may consider it advantageous to their rating to teach so that their pupils will make high scores on tests. Since no combination of tests can measure adequately all the variables we consider important for child growth and development, there is imminent danger that some of the more intangible but highly important results of teaching will not be emphasized.

6. If teachers are to be held increasingly accountable for their product, they must be provided with teaching situations in which excellent results can reasonably be expected. Overcrowded classrooms; poorly equipped libraries; lack of adequate supervision; little, if any, attention to in-service education of

teachers—all these can seriously affect the results a teacher can produce.

National Assessment of Educational Progress (NAEP)

National Assessment of Educational Progress, ever since its beginning in 1964, has been a much discussed and at times bitterly opposed issue. It was originally funded by the Carnegie Corporation, but now it receives its budget from the U.S. Office of Education. Dale Foreman,[2] formerly assistant director of research and analysis for the NAEP, states the purpose of the venture in these words:

> . . . to make available baseline censuslike data on the educational attainment of young Americans relative to certain evidence and periodically to obtain evidence concerning progress in meeting these objectives.

Reading is among the ten subject areas included in the project. After the objectives for reading had been drawn up, exercises were devised for testing the attainment of these objectives. The reading tests were given to individuals from four age groups, namely persons nine years of age, thirteen years, seventeen years, and to young adults varying in age between twenty-six and thirty-three. Test results were secured from about 29,500 in the nine-year-old category. They were tabulated to show the percentage of that population which could perform stated reading tasks. The intention is to make assessments every five years so that comparisons can be shown between the results obtained from successive assessments.

The opposition to NAEP from professional teacher organizations and individuals has stemmed from the fact that it is strongly suspected by some of involving more than a measurement of the level of achievement on a national scale. It has been feared by them that it may lead to a national curriculum and ultimately to an evaluation of the teacher, based on how well his students perform on national tests. In regard to some of these points John C. Mellon,[3] who chaired the NCTE Committee to Study the National Assessment of Educational Progress, states:

> In the early years, some educators feared that National Assessment would sooner or later become a nationwide achievement test and might lead to the establishment of a national curriculum including the mandatory measurement of accountability. But these fears have proven groundless. In fact, NAEP was designed specifically to measure the state of knowledge of various academic subjects without the need for administering batteries of achievement tests to the student population at large.

Regardless of what method of evaluation or assessment is used by local, state, or national groups, the dedicated teacher will continue to view reading in a broad setting. He will not make the mistake of assuming that the sole task of the teacher of reading is to develop proficiency in reading. Since both our experience and our observation lead us to a strong belief that reading makes a difference in how people think, feel, and act, we hold firmly to the conviction that schools must be deeply concerned about the total impact of the reading program on the child as a person and on his outlook on life. Therein lies the great continuing challenge in the teaching of reading.

---

[2]Dale J. Foreman, "National Assessment of Elementary Reading," *The Reading Teacher,* vol. 26, no. 3 (December 1972), p. 293.

[3]John C. Mellon, *National Assessment and the Teaching of English* (Urbana, Ill.: National Council of Teachers of English, 1975), p. 1.

For Further Study

Burg, Leslie A; Maurice Kaufman; Blanche Kerngold; and Albert Kovner, *The Complete Reading Supervisor* (Columbus, Ohio: Charles E. Merrill, 1978).

Burns, Paul C., and Betty D. Roe, *Teaching School*, 2d ed. (New York: Macmillan, 1979), Ch. 12, "Organization of Instruction: Administrative."

Carlson, Thorsten R., ed., *Administrators and Reading* (New York: Harcourt Brace Jovanovich, 1972).

Fay, Leo, *Organization and Administration of School Reading Programs* (Newark, Del.: International Reading Association, 1971).

Glazer, Susan Mandel, *How Can I Help My Child Build Positive Attitudes Toward Reading?* Micromonograph (Newark, Del.: International Reading Association, 1970).

Heilman, Arthur W., *Principles and Practices of Teaching Reading*, 4th ed. (Columbus, Ohio: Charles E. Merrill, 1977), Ch. 9, "Organizing the Classroom for Instruction."

Hittleman, Daniel R., *Developmental Reading: A Psycholinguistic Perspective* (Chicago: Rand McNally College Publishing Company, 1978), Ch. 1, "Reading Programs in Today's Society."

Lapp, Diane, *Use of Behavioral Objectives in Education* (Newark, Del.: International Reading Association, 1972).

Morrison, Coleman, and Mary C. Austin, *The Torchlighters Revisited* (Newark, Del.: International Reading Association, 1977).

Otto, Wayne, and Lawrence Erickson, *Inservice Education to Improve Reading Instruction* (Newark, Del.: International Reading Association, 1973).

Reading in Today's Elementary Schools, 2d ed. (Skokie, Ill.: Rand McNally, 1980), Ch. 10, "Classroom Management and Organization."

Bush, Clifford L., and Mildred H. Huebner, *Strategies for Reading in the Elementary*

Ransom, Grayce A., ed., *Evaluation of Teacher Education Programs in Reading* (Newark, Del.: International Reading Association, 1973).

———, *Preparing to Teach Reading* (Boston: Little, Brown, 1978), Ch. 4, "Curricular Approaches to Reading," and Ch. 5, "Organization of the School and Classroom."

Smith, Carl B., ed., *Parents and Reading* (Newark, Del.: International Reading Association, 1971).

Smith, Richard J.; Wayne Otto; and Lee Hansen, *The School Reading Program: A Handbook for Teachers, Supervisors, and Specialists* (Boston: Houghton Mifflin, 1978), Ch. 10, "Inservice Education: Guidelines and Examples."

Stieglits, Ezra L., and Robert T. Rude, *Methods and Materials in Teaching Reading: Competency Based Approach*, 2d ed. (Providence, R.I.: Rhode Island College, 1975).

Strain, Lucille B., *Accountability in Reading Instruction* (Columbus, Ohio: Charles E. Merrill, 1976).

Winebrenner, Rosemary, *How Can I Get My Teenager to Read.* Micromonograph (Newark, Del.: International Reading Association, 1971).

Zintz, Miles V., *The Reading Process: The Teacher and the Learner*, 3rd ed., (Dubuque, Iowa: Wm. C. Brown, 1980), Ch. 22, "Teaching Reading in Proper Perspective."

Questions and Comments for Thought and Discussion

1. Why is it important that no new schoolwide program in reading be planned that does not have the support of many teachers?
2. Too often there is very little communication between the elementary school, junior high school, and senior high school in terms of the reading needs of the pupils and programs that need to be developed. How could this communication and subsequent action be facilitated?

3. To most readers of this book there are undoubtedly available for examination many different types of supplementary materials for reading—materials other than the basal readers. Examination and evaluation of a variety of them are recommended as helpful activities.

4. You may wish to read more about the highly controversial project, *National Assessment of Educational Progress*, so that you will be more familiar with its advantages and/or limitations.

5. To what extent do you think a teacher of reading should be held accountable for his work? What dangers do you note in ways in which the concept of teacher accountability might be applied to school practices? Have you any suggestions as to how teachers should be held accountable for their work?

6. You may be interested in reading the article by Jacob Landers, "Accountability and Progress of Nomenclature: Old Ideas in New Bottles," in the April 1973 issue of *Phi Delta Kappan.* You may wish to discuss your reactions with your classmates.

7. If you have the opportunity to talk with a staff member of a school system in which a new reading program has been or is being planned, you may wish to get information on points such as the following: (a) the general procedure followed in planning the program; (b) means used for evaluating the program; (c) cautions to be observed when planning or putting into effect a new reading program.

8. If you had in your classroom in the lower elementary school a child who came from a home where the parents are illiterate, what are some of the strategies you might be able to use to help counteract the deficiencies in the child's background, in terms of the learning-to-read process?

9. Read again the last paragraph of this chapter, on page 426. What could you as a teacher do to help meet the continuing challenge in teaching reading?

Appendix A

Books on the Teaching of Reading: A General Bibliography

This bibliography contains some of the many recently published books that deal with the teaching of reading in the elementary school. The reader is also referred to the bibliographies at the end of many of the chapters. Professional magazines, such as *The Reading Teacher* and *Language Arts*, are good sources for titles of recent books.

Alexander, J. Estill, ed., *Teaching Reading* (Boston: Little, Brown and Company, 1979).

Aukerman, Robert C., *Approaches to Beginning Reading* (New York: John Wiley & Sons, Inc., 1971).

Aukerman, Robert C., and Louise R. Aukerman, *How Do I Teach Reading?* (New York: John Wiley & Sons, Inc., 1981).

Beery, Althea; Thomas C. Barrett; and William R. Powell, *Elementary Reading Instruction: Selected Materials,* 2d ed. (Boston: Allyn and Bacon, Inc., 1974).

Bond, Guy L.; Miles A. Tinker; and Barbara Wasson, *Reading Difficulties: Their Diagnosis and Correction,* 4th ed. (Englewood Cliffs, N.J.: Prentice-Hall, Inc., 1979).

Bracken, Dorothy Kendall, and Eve Malmquist, eds., *Improving Reading Ability around the World.* Proceedings of the IRA World Congress on Reading, Sydney, Australia, 1970 (Newark, Del.: International Reading Association, 1971).

Burg, Leslie A.; Maurice Kaufman; Blanche Korngold; and Albert Kovner, *The Complete Reading Supervisor* (Columbus, Ohio: Charles E. Merrill Publishing Company, 1978).

Burns, Paul C., and Betty D. Roe, *Teaching Reading in Today's Elementary Schools,* 2d ed. (Skokie, Ill.: Rand McNally & Company, 1980).

Bush, Clifford L., and Mildred H. Huebner, *Strategies for Reading in the Elementary*

School, 2d ed. (New York: The Macmillan Company, 1979).

Calfee, Robert, and Priscilla Drum, *Teaching Reading in Compensatory Classes* (Newark, Del.: International Reading Association, 1979).

Carillo, Lawrence W., *Teaching Reading: A Handbook*, 2d ed. (New York: St. Martin's Press, Inc. 1976).

Carlson, Thorsten R., ed., *Administrators and Reading* (New York: Harcourt Brace Jovanovich, Inc, 1972).

Cheek, Martha Collins, and Earl H. Cheek, Jr., *Diagnostic-Prescriptive Reading Instruction* (Dubuque, Iowa: Wm. C. Brown Company Publishers, 1980).

Ching, Doris C., *Reading and the Bilingual Child* (Newark, Del.: International Reading Association, 1976).

Criscuolo, Nicholas, *Activities for Reading Enrichment* (Dansville, N.Y.: The Instructor Publishing Company, 1975).

DeChant, Emerald V., and Henry P. Smith, *Psychology in Teaching Reading*, 2d ed. (Englewood Cliffs, N.J.: Prentice-Hall, Inc., 1977).

Douglass, Malcolm P., ed., *Reading in Education: A Broader View* (Columbus, Ohio: Charles E. Merrill Publishing Company, 1973).

Downing, John, and D. V. Thakray, *Reading Readiness* (Newark: Del.: International Reading Association, 1971).

Durkin, Dolores, *Teaching Them to Read*, 3d ed. (Boston: Allyn and Bacon, Inc., 1978).

———, *Teaching Young Children to Read*, 2d ed. (Boston: Allyn and Bacon, Inc., 1976).

Farr, Roger, and Nancy Roser, *Teaching a Child to Read* (New York: Harcourt Brace Jovanovich, Inc., 1979).

Fay, Leo, *Organization and Administration of School Reading Programs* (Newark, Del.: International Reading Association, 1971).

Figurel, J. Allen, ed., *Reading Goals for the Disadvantaged* (Newark, Del.: International Reading Association, 1970).

Forgan, Harry W., and Charles T. Mangrum, *Teaching Content Area Reading Skills* (Columbus, Ohio: Charles E. Merrill Publishing Company, 1976).

Friedman, Myles I., and Michael Rowls, *Teaching Reading and Thinking Skills* (New York: Longman, Inc., 1980).

Fry, Edward, *Reading Instruction for Classroom and Clinic* (New York: McGraw-Hill, Inc., 1972).

Gans, Roma, *Guiding Children's Reading through Experiences*, 2d ed. (New York: Teachers College Press, 1979).

Goodman, Kenneth S; E. Brooks Smith; and Robert Meredith, *Language and Thinking in the Elementary School* (New York: Holt, Rinehart and Winston, 1970).

Goodman, Yetta M., and Carolyn Burke, *Reading Strategies: Focus on Comprehension* (New York: Holt, Rinehart and Winston, 1980).

Grant, Carl A., *Multicultural Education: Commitments, Issues, and Applications* (Washington, D.C.; Association for Supervision and Curriculum Development, 1977).

Hall, Maryanne, *Language-Experience Approach for the Culturally Disadvantaged* (Newark, Del.: International Reading Association, 1972).

———, *Teaching Reading as a Language Experience*, 2d ed. (Columbus, Ohio: Charles E. Merrill Publishing Company, 1976).

Hall, Maryanne; Jerilyn K. Ribovich; and Christopher J. Ramig, *Reading and the Elementary School Child*, 2d ed. (New York: Van Nostrand Reinhold Company, 1979).

Harris, Albert J., and Edward R. Sipay, *How to Increase Reading Ability*, 6th ed. (New York: David McKay Company, Inc., 1975).

Harris, Larry A., and Carl B. Smith, *Reading Instruction: Diagnostic Teaching in the Classroom*, 3d ed. (New York: Holt, Rinehart and Winston, 1980).

Heilman, Arthur W., *Phonics in Proper Perspective*, 3d ed. (Columbus, Ohio: Charles E. Merrill Publishing Company, 1976).

Heilman, Arthur W.; Timothy R. Blair; and William H. Rupley, *Principles and Practices of Teaching Reading*, 5th ed. (Columbus, Ohio: Charles E. Merrill Publishing Company, 1981).

Hillerich, Robert L., *Reading Fundamentals for Preschool and Primary Children* (Columbus,

Ohio: Charles E. Merrill Publishing Company, 1977).

Hittleman, Daniel R., *Developmental Reading, a Psycholinguistic Perspective* (Chicago: Rand McNally College Publishing Company, 1978).

Horn, Thomas D., ed., *Reading for the Disadvantaged: Problems of Linguistically Different Learners* (New York: Harcourt Brace Jovanovich, Inc. 1970).

Howards, Melvin, *Reading Diagnosis and Instruction: An Integrated Approach* (Reston, Va.: Reston Publishing Company, 1980).

Johns, Jerry L., *Literacy for Diverse Learners: Promoting Reading Growth at All Levels* (Newark, Del.: International Reading Association, 1974).

Jongsma, Eugene, *The Cloze Procedure as a Teaching Technique* (Newark, Del.: International Reading Association, 1971).

Karlin, Robert, *Teaching Elementary Reading: Principles and Strategies*, 3d ed. (New York: Harcourt Brace Jovanovich, Inc., 1980).

Kennedy, Eddie C., *Methods in Teaching Developmental Reading*, 2d ed. (Itasca, Ill.: F.E. Peacock Publishers, Inc., 1981).

Labuda, Michael, *Creative Reading for Gifted Learners: A Design for Excellence* (Newark, Del.: International Reading Association, 1974).

Lamb, Pose, *Linguistics in Proper Perspective* (Columbus, Ohio: Charles E. Merrill Publishing Company, 1977).

Lamb, Pose, and Richard Arnold, eds., *Reading: Foundations and Instructional Strategies*, 2d ed. (Belmont, Cal.: Wadsworth Publishing Company, Inc., 1980).

Lapp, Diane, and James Flood, *Teaching Reading to Every Child* (New York: The Macmillan Company, 1978).

Mason, George, and Jay Blanchard, *Computer Applications in Reading* (Newark, Del.: International Reading Association, 1979).

Mazurkiewicz, Albert J., *Teaching about Phonics* (New York: St. Martin's Press, Inc., 1976).

Morrison, Coleman, and Mary C. Austin, *The Torch Lighters Revisited* (Newark, Del.: International Reading Association, 1977).

Musgrave, G. Ray, *Individualized Instruction: Teaching Strategies Focusing on the Learner* (Boston: Allyn and Bacon, Inc., 1975).

National Society for the Study of Education, *Innovations and Change in Reading Instruction.* The Sixty-seventh Yearbook of the National Society for the Study of Education, Part II, edited by Helen M. Robinson (Chicago: University of Chicago Press, 1968).

O'Brien, Carmen, *Teaching the Language-Different Child to Read* (Columbus, Ohio: Charles E. Merrill Publishing Company, 1973).

Olson, Joanne P., and Martha H. Dillner, *Learning to Teach Reading in the Elementary School: Utilizing a Competency-Based Instructional System* (New York: The Macmillan Company, 1976).

Otto, Wayne, and Lawrence Erickson, *Inservice Education to Improve Reading Instruction* (Newark, Del.: International Reading Association, 1973).

Pearson, P. David, and Dale D. Johnson, *Teaching Reading Comprehension* (New York: Holt, Rinehart and Winston, 1978).

Ransom, Grayce A., *Preparing to Teach Reading* (Boston: Little, Brown and Company, 1978).

Robinson, H. Alan, *Teaching Reading and Study Strategies: The Content Areas* (Boston: Allyn and Bacon, Inc., 1975).

Roe, Betty D.; Barbara D. Stoodt; and Paul C. Burns, *Reading Instruction in the Secondary School* (Chicago: Rand McNally College Publishing Company, 1978).

Russell, David H., and Etta E. Karp (rev. by Anne Marie Mueser), *Reading Aids through the Grades* (New York: Teachers College Press, Columbia University, 1975).

Savage, John F., ed., *Linguistics for Teachers: Selected Readings* (Chicago: Science Research Associates, Inc., 1973).

Schell, Leo M., *Fundamentals of Decoding for Teachers* (Skokie, Ill.: Rand McNally & Company, 1975).

Schubert, Delwyn G., and Theodore L. Torgerson, *Improving the Reading Process*, 4th ed. (Dubuque, Iowa: William C. Brown Company Publishers, 1976).

Shafer, Robert, ed., *Applied Linguistics and Reading* (Newark, Del.: International Reading Association, 1979).

Singer, Harry, and Robert B. Ruddell, eds., *Theoretical Models and Processes of Reading*, 2d ed. (Newark, Del.: International Reading Association, 1976).

Smith, Carl. B., ed., *Parents and Reading* (Newark, Del.: International Reading Association, 1971).

Smith, Frank, *Comprehension and Learning: A Conceptual Framework for Teachers* (New York: Holt, Rinehart and Winston, 1975).

Smith, Richard J., and Thomas C. Barrett, *Teaching Reading in the Middle Grades* (Menlo Park, Ca.: Addison-Wesley Publishing Company, 1974).

Smith, Richard J., and Dale D. Johnson, *Teaching Children to Read*, 2d ed. (Menlo Park, Ca.: Addison-Wesley Publishing Company, 1980).

Smith, Richard J.; Wayne Otto; and Lee Hansen, *The School Reading Program: A Handbook for Teachers, Supervisors, and Specialists* (Boston: Houghton Mifflin Company, 1978).

Southgate, Vera, et al., *Literacy at All Levels* Proceedings of the Eighth Annual Study Conference of the United Kingdom Reading Association, Manchester, 1971 (London: Word Lock Educational, 1972).

Spache, Evelyn B., *Reading Activities for Child Improvement* (Boston: Allyn and Bacon, Inc., 1973).

Spache, George D., *Diagnosing and Correcting Reading Disability* (Boston: Allyn and Bacon, Inc., 1976).

Spache, George D., and Evelyn B. Spache, *Reading in the Elementary School*, 4th ed. (Boston: Allyn and Bacon, Inc., 1977).

Staiger, Ralph C., *Roads to Reading*. A UNESCO publication (Newark, Del.: International Reading Association, distributor of English edition, 1979).

Stauffer, Russell G., *Directing the Reading Thinking Process* (New York: Harper & Row, Publishers, 1975).

Stieglits, Ezra L., and Robert T. Rude, *Methods and Materials in Teaching Reading: Competency Based Approach*, 2d ed. (Providence, R.I.: Rhode Island College, 1975).

Strain, Lucille, *Accountability in Reading Instruction* (Columbus, Ohio: Charles E. Merrill Publishing Company, 1976).

Thonis, Eleanor Wall, *Literacy for America's Spanish-speaking Children* (Newark, Del.: International Reading Association, 1976).

Tierney, Robert, and Diane Lapp, *National Assessment of Educational Progress in Reading* (Newark, Del.: International Reading Association, 1979).

Tinker, Miles A., and Constance M. McCullough, *Teaching Elementary Reading*, 4th ed. (Englewood Cliffs, N.J.: Prentice-Hall, Inc., 1975).

Trinker, Charles L., ed., *Teaching for Better Use of Libraries* (Hamden, Conn.: The Shoe String Press, 1970).

Veatch, Jeanette, *Reading in the Elementary School*, 2d ed. (New York: John Wiley & Sons, Inc., 1978).

Walcutt, Charles Child; Joan Lamport; and Glenn McCracken, *Teaching Reading: A Phonic/Linguistic Approach to Developmental Reading* (New York: The Macmillan Company, 1974).

West, Gail *Teaching Reading Skills in Content Areas* (Orlando, Fla.: The Sandpiper Press, 1974).

Wilson, Robert M., and Linda Gambrell, *Programmed Comprehension for Teachers* (Columbus, Ohio: Charles E. Merrill Publishing Company, 1976).

Witty, Paul A., ed. *Reading for the Gifted and Creative Student* (Newark, Del.: International Reading Association, 1972).

Zintz, Miles V., *Corrective Reading*, 2d ed. (Dubuque, Iowa: William C. Brown Company Publishers, 1981).

————, *The Reading Process: The Teacher and the Learner*, 3d ed. (Dubuque, Iowa: William C. Brown Company Publishers, 1980).

Informal Word Analysis Survey

Permission to reproduce this test
and all its related parts
is granted by the authors
Roger L. Rouch and Shirley Birr

Please list the authors' names
on duplicated copies

DESCRIPTION OF TEST ITEMS

Test 1: Auditory Discrimination

If a child cannot hear likenesses and differences in spoken sounds, he will obviously have difficulty in programs of reading instruction emphasizing phonics in decoding. Consequently, this is the first skill tested. Three double columns of words are provided. The ability to hear likenesses and differences in the initial, medial, and ending positions is tested.

Test 2: Visual Discrimination

Test two checks the child's ability to see likenesses and differences in written forms. At this point it is not necessary for the child to name the individual letters or words but only to pick from a group the key letter or group of letters. The ability to perform adequately in this task is directly related to the ability to learn to decode words.

Test 3: Knowledge of Capital Letters

The ability to identify and name the letters of the alphabet is one predictor of reading success. This is the first actual decoding skill tested.

Test 4: Consonant Letter Names and Sounds

Test four assesses ability in two areas. The child is to name each lower-case letter and also give a word which begins with the sound represented by the letter. Do not ask for the isolated sound represented by the letter unless the child cannot think of a word.

This test is used to assess sound representations and not spelling patterns. The child may, for example, give the word "cake" as a word beginning with the sound represented by the letter "k." Answers such as these are correct.

433

Test 5: Blends

The child is to give words which begin with the blends shown. Do not ask for the isolated sounds represented by the blends unless the child cannot think of a word.

Test 6: Consonant Digraphs

The child is to give words which begin with the consonant digraphs shown. Do not ask for the isolated sounds represented by the digraphs unless the child cannot think of a word.

Test 7: Vowel Letter Names

In test seven the child is to name the individual letters. In addition, the name *vowel*, which describes these words, is to be identified.

Test 8: Predictable Vowel Spelling Patterns

Test eight consists of seven columns of nonsense words; each column represents a certain vowel principle for purposes of pronunciation. The child is to pronounce the nonsense words in each column. The actual rule involved need not be stated.

Nonsense words are used to assure that the child understands the principles of pronunciation involved and is not simply reading some words which are known by sight.

The following vowel spelling patterns are represented in columns *a* through *g:*

Columns

a. Single vowels in closed syllables often represent short sounds.
b. In one-syllable words or in the final syllable of polysyllabic words which end with a VCV pattern, quite often, if the final vowel is an "e," the first vowel represents a long sound and the "e" is silent. An example of this occurring can be seen and heard in the words "made" and "refine."

c. The vowel is controlled by the letter "r" which follows it.
d. Vowel digraphs are combinations of vowels representing one sound. In words containing the vowel-digraph patterns "ee," "oa," "ai," and "ay" usually the first vowel represents a long sound and the second vowel is silent.
e. When an "a" is followed by the letters "l," "ll," "u," or "w," it usually does not represent either a long or short sound but rather the vowel sound heard in the word "Paul."
f. The vowel combinations in these words are called diphthongs or vowel blends. Two blended vowel sounds are pronounced.
g. Vowels in open and accented syllables frequently represent a long vowel sound.

Test 9: Division of Compound Words

The same rationale for using nonsense words as stated in test eight also applies to tests nine, ten, eleven, twelve and thirteen.

In test nine the child is to read each compound word. It is not necessary for the child to identify the two separate words if the compound word is read correctly.

Test 10: Identifying Inflectional Endings

The child is to read each nonsense word. If the word is read correctly, it is not necessary for each individual ending to be identified separately.

Test 11: Identifying Prefixes and Suffixes

In test 11 the child is asked to read each nonsense word. If the word is read correctly, it is not necessary for each individual prefix and suffix to be identified separately.

Test 12: Knowledge of Principles of Syllabication

The child is to make with a pencil, on the teacher copy of the test, the correct syllable division for each nonsense word in test twelve. The actual rule involved need not be verbalized by the child.

The syllabication rules for dividing the nonsense words follow:

rolex: v/cv

sabnet: vc/cv

hamfle: ending "le" and the preceding consonant as one syllable

defrontment: prefixes and suffixes as separate syllables

polampan: complex word: v/cv and vc/cv principles for syllabication both contained within the word

Test 13: Knowledge of Silent Letters

The child is to pronounce each nonsense word. If the initial consonant is sounded, the child needs to understand that a "g" before an "n'," a "w" before an "r," and a "k" before an "n," if at the beginning of a word, remain silent as the word is pronounced.

DIRECTIONS FOR ADMINISTERING THE INFORMAL WORD ANALYSIS SURVEY

A. *General Instructions*

All responses are recorded on the teacher copy.

The child reads from the child copy. The teacher reads the specific directions for each subtest as indicated on the teacher copy and records the responses of the child on the teacher copy. The only deviation from this procedure is in tests 2 (visual discrimination) and 12 (knowledge of principles of syllabication) which are marked by the child on the teacher copy. Marking procedures are as follows:

1. Circle any item in a test which the child does not know. Example: letter name "r" unknown:
2. Show by writing in the substitution the child makes. Example: Child says "d" for "p." Mark it "pd."

Tests 1, 2, and 12 do not appear on the child copy. Test 1 is auditory and the child is given no visual clues. Tests 2 and 12 should be marked by the child on the teacher copy.

Because the Informal World Analysis Survey covers a broad range of word-attack skills, teachers of the primary grades should use discretion as to how much of the diagnostic tool to administer to a particular child. It is not necessary to complete the entire test battery.

B. *Directions for Each Test*

1. Auditory Discrimination
    Stand behind the child. Read each column of words, first column *a,* then *b,* and then *c.* Call one pair of words at a time. Enunciate clearly but do not pro-

long pronunciation of a word. Ask the child: "Are these words the same or different?" If the child gives an incorrect response, upon completion of that particular column, repeat that pair and mark his responses accordingly.

2. Visual Discrimination
    This test is marked by the child on the teacher copy. The format of the teacher copy (test 2 in large print) is a reminder that the child works on this sheet. Say to the child: "Look at the first letter or word in the row. Then look across the row and circle a letter or word that looks just like it." (It may be necessary to use a piece of tagboard as a marker under each row.)

3. Knowledge of Capital Letters (Use window card if necessary.)
    The child is asked to name the capital letters. A $3'' \times 3''$ window card should be used to isolate each letter when a particular child is distracted by surrounding letters or has other visual problems.

4. Consonant Letter Names and Sounds (Use window card if necessary.)
    This subtest covers two skills. The child is told to name the lower-case letter and then to give a word beginning with the sound represented by the letter. Space is provided to record the child's answer. The child may instead give the sound represented by each letter if his reading instruction has been of that nature.

    The teacher should instruct the child to give words which represent both the hard and soft sounds of "c" and "g."

    Because this is an auditory test, not a spelling test, when a child responds with a word in which the sound representation is correctly indicated, it must be accepted. For example, the sound representation for "c" being "k" makes "kite" a correct answer.

5. Blends (Use window card if necessary.)
The child names a word beginning with each blend or, as a second choice, gives the sound represented by each blend.

6. Consonant Digraphs (Use window card if necessary.)
The child names a word beginning with each digraph or, as a second choice, gives the sound represented by each digraph.

7. Vowel Letter Names (Use window card if necessary.)
The child is asked to name each letter. He is then asked to categorize the letters by giving the word "vowel." The teacher indicates this answer (or inability to answer) on the space provided.

8. Predictable Vowel Spelling Patterns (Use mask.)
The seven common concepts represented in this test are the short vowel generalization (column *a*); the long vowel generalizations (columns *b*, *d*, and *g*); the controlled vowel generalizations (columns *c* and *e*); and the diphthong generalization (column *f*).

The child is asked to read down each column; column *a*, then *b*, then *c*, etc. Types of errors are recorded on the teacher's copy. A mask should cover all columns not yet read by the child.

9. Division of Compound Words
The child is asked to read each word to determine his skill in recognizing compound words.

10. Identifying Inflectional Endings
The child is asked to read each word to determine his skill in recognizing word endings.

11. Identifying Prefixes and Suffixes
The child is asked to read each word to determine his skill in recognizing prefixes and suffixes.

12. Knowledge of Principles of Syllabication
Using the teacher's copy, the child divides the words into syllables with a pencil to determine his skill with the four basic syllabication concepts.

13. Knowledge of Silent Letters
The child pronounces the three words to determine his skill mastery of the common silent letter spelling patterns.

Child's Name _____

Date _____

INFORMAL WORD ANALYSIS SURVEY:
Teacher Copy

Instructions: Pupil records his responses
to Items 2 and 12 on this
copy. Pupil refers to pupil
copy for other items. Teacher
marks pupil responses on
"Teacher Copy." Transfer errors to Informal Word Analysis Survey Individual Record
Sheet or Class Profile. Indicate "satisfactory" only if *no*
errors are made on a subtest.

1. Auditory Discrimination

Stand behind child. Ask the following question and record incorrect responses. "Are
these words the same or different?" Call
one pair at a time:

a. initial   b. medial

sun - sun   land - lend
hide - ride   gave - gave
pail - bail   pill - pal
find - find   fin - fun
come - some   walk - walk

c. final

pal - pan
coat - coat
kin - kit
yard - yard
name - nail

2. Visual Discrimination

Child records on this copy.
"Look at the first letter or word in the row.
Then look across the row and circle a letter
or word that looks just like it."

v	n	u	m	v
h	t	l	h	f
b	g	p	q	b
vin	vin	min	win	sin
ment	lent	ment	bent	tent
smiw	sim	swim	smiw	swin

3. Knowledge of Capital Letters

Ask the child to read the following capital
letters:

X	R	P	Y	K	U
O	S	M	J	T	H
V	G	C	E	L	W
D	B	Z	Q	A	F
I	N				

4. Consonant Letter Names and Sounds

Ask the child to point to each letter, saying
its name and giving a word that begins
with the sound represented by each letter:

f_____	q_____	z_____
b_____	n_____	w_____
l_____	*c_____	*g_____
v_____	h_____	t_____
j_____	d_____	m_____
s_____	k_____	y_____
p_____	r_____	

*Ask the child to give words representing
both the hard and soft sounds of "g" and
"c."

5. Blends

Ask the child to point to each blend giving
a word that begins with the sound represented by each blend:

bl_____   cl_____   fl_____
tr_____   sc_____   spr_____
br_____   gr_____   str_____
spl_____

6. Consonant Digraphs

Ask the child to point to each consonant digraph giving a word that begins with the sound represented by each digraph:

ch_____   ph_____   sh_____
th_____   wh_____

7. Vowel Letter Names

Ask the child to point to each letter giving its name:

o   e   u   a   i

Ask the child if he knows what special name these letters have. _____

8. Predictable Vowel Spelling Patterns

Ask the child to read each column of words. Cover all columns not being read.

(a)	(b)	(c)	(d)
em	teme	ter	teeb
bos	bose	bor	boam
fip	fipe	fir	waik
af	wafe	war	cay
nuk	nuke	nur	

(e)	(f)	(g)
naut	lew	te
gaw	moip	bo
vall	noy	hi
al	tue	wa
		nu

9. Division of Compound Words

Ask the child to read these nonsense words:

boycamp   foxwalk   housecone
treebat   rugflop

10. Identifying Inflectional Endings

Ask the child to read these nonsense words:

doys   jating   nowed
tayly   bomes

11. Identifying Prefixes and Suffixes

Ask the child to read these nonsense words:

inday   excome   refat   nitful

12. Knowledge of Principles of Syllabication

Child records on this copy.
Ask the child to divide the following nonsense words into syllables:

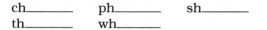

rolex   hamfle   polampan
sabnet   defrontment

13. Knowledge of Silent Letters

Ask the child to pronounce the following nonsense words:

wrip   gonx   knip

Child's Name _____

Date _____

INFORMAL WORD ANALYSIS SURVEY:
Pupil Copy

3. Knowledge of Capital Letters

X	R	P	Y	K	U	O	S	M
J	T	H	V	G	C	E	L	W
D	B	Z	Q	A	F	I	N	

4. Consonant Letter Names and Sounds

f	q	z	b	n
w	l	c	g	v
h	t	j	d	m
s	k	y	p	r

5. Blends

bl	cl	fl	br	gr
tr	sc	spr	str	spl

6. Consonant Digraphs

ch   ph   sh   th   wh

7. Vowel Letter Names

o   e   u   a   i

8. Predictable Vowel Spelling Patterns

em	teme	ter	teeb	naut	lew	te
bos	bose	bor	boam	gaw	moip	bo
fip	fipe	fir	waik	vall	noy	hi
af	wafe	war	cay	al	tue	wa
nuk	nuke	nur				nu

9. Division of Compound Words

boycamp   foxwalk   housecone

treebat   rugflop

10. Identifying Inflectional Endings

doys   jating   nowed

tayly   bomes

11. Identifying Prefixes and Suffixes

inday   excome   refat   nitful

12. Knowledge of Silent Letters

wrip   gnox   knip

A. *Individual Record Sheet*

The basic information needed for working with a child can be recorded on the individual record sheet. The data in the upper right-hand corner of the sheet are obtained from an Informal Reading Inventory.

Specific errors made are recorded for subtests one through thirteen. A subtest is not checked as satisfactory unless no errors were made. The teacher can then begin with the child by starting at the top of the record sheet and working with the first weakness found.

Items are only checked as satisfactory when the child has mastered that particular area. A word of caution: teachers too often expose children to needed skills and move on before the skill is learned. Exposure does not assure learning. Be certain the child fully understands the concept and shows proficiency through use before a new concept is introduced.

The sequence of skills as tested and recorded represents a typical sequence of skill development that children encounter as they learn to read.

B. *Class Profile*

Each child's Individual Record Sheet findings can be recorded on the Class Record Sheet. With this information, the teacher can quickly assemble groups of children who have the same skill needs and set up flexible skill groups composed only of those children needing a particular skill. Once the skill is mastered, the group is disbanded and the children are moved into new group settings.

Child's Name _____

INFORMAL WORD ANALYSIS SURVEY
INDIVIDUAL RECORD SHEET

IRI:
Instructional Level _____
Independent Level _____
Frustration Level _____

Area Tested	Errors	Satisfactory
1. Auditory Discrimination		
a. initial		
b. medial		
c. ending		
2. Visual Discrimination		
3. Capital Letters		
4. Consonants		
a. letter names		
b. letter sounds		
c. soft *c* & *g*		
5. Consonant Blends		
6. Consonant Digraphs		
7. Vowels		
a. names		
b. name "vowel"		
8. Predictable Vowel Spelling Patterns		
a. closed vowels		
b. silent *e*		
c. controlled *r*		
d. digraphs		
e. controlled *l, u, w, ll*		
f. diphthongs		
g. open vowels		
9. Compound Words		
10. Inflectional Endings		
11. Affixes		
a. prefixes		
b. suffixes		
12. Syllabication		
a. v/cv		
b. vc/cv		
c. cle		
d. pre/root/suf		
e. complex word		
13. Silent Letters		

INFORMAL WORD ANALYSIS SURVEY CLASS PROFILE

Class Record Sheet

NAME	Auditory Discrimination	Visual Discrimination	Capital Letters	Letter Names	Letter Sounds	Soft "c" and "g"	Consonant Blends	Consonant Digraphs	Vowel Names	Closed Vowels	Silent "e"	Controlled "r"	Vowel Digraphs	Controlled "l","w","u","r" + "ll"	Vowel Diphthongs	Open Vowels	Compound Words	Inflectional Endings	Prefixes	Suffixes	v/cv	vc/cv	c/"le"	pre/root/suf	complex word	silent letters

Consonants — Letter Names, Letter Sounds, Soft "c" and "g", Consonant Blends, Consonant Digraphs

Vowels — Vowel Names, Closed Vowels, Silent "e", Controlled "r", Vowel Digraphs, Controlled "l","w","u","r" + "ll", Vowel Diphthongs, Open Vowels

Structural Analysis — Compound Words, Inflectional Endings, Prefixes, Suffixes

Syllables — v/cv, vc/cv, c/"le", pre/root/suf, complex word, silent letters

Addresses of Publishing and Distributing Companies

In this appendix are given the names and addresses of many companies publishing and/or distributing books and/or other materials dealing with reading in the elementary school. Since names of some companies change and some go out of business and since the addresses of some change during the course of years, the reader may wish to consult reference books giving desired bibliographical information found in many libraries. One such source is *Books in Print,* published annually, of which the 1978–79 edition is the chief source of information given in the listing that follows.

Abelard-Schuman, Ltd. (10 East 53d Street, New York, NY 10022).

Abingdon Press (201 Eighth Avenue, South, Nashville, TN 37202).

Addison-Wesley Publishing Company, Inc. (Jacob Way, Reading, MA 01867).

Allyn & Bacon, Inc. (470 Atlantic Avenue, Boston, MA 02210).

American Book Company (A division of Litton Educational Publishing, 135 West 50th Street, New York, NY 10020).

American Council on Education (One Dupont Circle, Washington, DC 20036).

American Educational Research Association (1230 Seventeenth Street, N.W., Washington, DC 20036).

American Guidance Service, Inc. (Publishers' Building, Circle Pines, MN 55014).

American Heritage Publishing Company, Inc. (Ten Rockefeller Plaza, New York, NY 10020).

American Library Association (50 East Huron Street, Chicago IL 60611).

Association for Childhood Education International (3615 Wisconsin Avenue, N.W., Washington, DC 20016).

Atheneum Publishers (122 East 42d Street, New York, NY 10017).

Avon Books, (959 Eighth Avenue, New York, NY 10019).

BFA Educational Media (2211 Michigan Avenue, Santa Monica, CA 90404).

Bantam Books, Inc. (666 Fifth Avenue, New York, NY 10019).

Barnes & Noble, Inc. (Division of Harper & Row, Publishers, Inc., 10 East 53d Street, New York, NY 10022).

Behavioral Research Laboratories (Sullivan Language Schools, Box 577, Palo Alto, CA 94302).

Benefic Press (Division of Beckley-Cardy Company, 10300 West Roosevelt Road, Westchester, IL 60153).

Bobbs-Merrill Company, Inc. (A Thomas Audel Company, 4300 West 62d Street, Indianapolis, IN 46206).

Bowker, R.R., Company (A Xerox Publishing Company, 1180 Avenue of the Americas, New York, NY 10036).

Bowmar/Noble Publishers, Inc. (4563 Colorado Boulevard, Los Angeles, CA 90039).

Bro-Dart Foundation (Box 3488, Williamsport, PA 17701).

Brown, William C., Company Publishers (2460 Kerper Boulevard, Dubuque, IA 52001).

Burgess Publishing Company (7108 Ohms Lane, Minneapolis, MN 55435).

Center for Applied Linguistics (1611 North Kent Street, Arlington, VA 22209).

Century House, Inc. (Old Irelandville, Watkins Glen, NY 14891).

Child Study Press (c/o Child Study Association of America, 50 Madison Avenue, New York, NY 10010).

Children's Book Council, Inc. (67 Irving Place, New York, NY 10003).

Children's Press, Inc. (1224 West Van Buren Street, Chicago, IL 60607).

Compton, F.E., Company (Division of Encyclopedia Britannica, Inc., 425 North Michigan Avenue, Chicago, IL 60611).

Consulting Psychologists Press, Inc. (577 College Avenue, Palo Alto, CA 94306).

Cooperative Test Division (Educational Testing Service, Princeton, NJ 08540).

Coward, McCann & Geoghegan, Inc. (200 Madison Avenue, New York, NY 10016).

Criterion Books, Inc. (c/o Harper & Row Publishers, 10 East 53d Street, New York, NY 10022).

Crowell, Thomas Y., Company (Distributed by: Harper & Row, Publishers, Scranton, PA 18512).

Doubleday & Company, Inc. (501 Franklin Avenue, Garden City, NY 11530).

Dover Publications, Inc. (180 Varick Street, New York, NY 10014).

Dryden Press, Inc. (Division of Holt, Rinehart and Winston, 901 North Elm Street, Hinsdale, IL 60521).

Dutton, E.P. (2 Park Avenue, New York, NY 10016).

Economy Company (1901 North Walnut, P.O. Box 25308, Oklahoma City, OK 73125).

Education Center for Children's Books (Regenstein Library, University of Chicago, Chicago, IL 60637).

Educational Resources Information Center (ERIC) (U.S. Department of Health, Education and Welfare, Washington, DC 20201).

Educational Services, Inc. (350 Grove Street, Somerville, NJ 08876).

Educational Solutions, Inc. (80 Fifth Avenue, New York, NY 10011).

Educational Testing Service (Princeton, NJ 08540).

Educators Progress Services, Inc. (214 Center Street, Randolph, WI 53956).

Encyclopedia Britannica Educational Corporation (Affiliate of Encyclopedia Britannica, Inc., 425 North Michigan Avenue, Chicago, IL 60611).

Expression Company (P.O. Box 153, Londonderry, NH 03053).

Farrar, Straus, & Giroux, Inc. (19 Union Square, West, New York, NY 10003).

Fearon-Pitman Publishers, Inc. (6 Davis Drive, Belmont, CA 94002).

Fideler Company (31 Ottawa Avenue, N.W., Grand Rapids, MI 49503).

Follett Publishing Company (Division of Follett Corporation, 1010 West Washington Boulevard, Chicago, IL 60607).

Friendship Press (475 Riverside Drive, Room 772, New York, NY 10027).

Garrard Publishing Company (107 Cherry Street, New Canaan, CT 06840).

Ginn and Company (A Xerox Publishing Company, 191 Spring Street, Lexington, MA 02173).

Goodyear Publishing Company (1640 Fifth Street, Santa Monica, CA 90401).

Graflex, Inc., Singer Company (3750 Monroe Avenue, Rochester, NY 14603).

Grolier, Inc. (Sherman Turnpike, Danbury, CT 06816).

Grossett & Dunlap, Inc. (160 Park Avenue, South, New York, NY 10010).

Grune & Stratton, Inc. (111 Fifth Avenue, 12th Floor, New York, NY 10003).

Hale, E.M., and Company (128 West River Street, Chippewa Falls, WI 54729).

Hammond, Inc. (515 Valley Street, Maplewood, NJ 07040).

Harcourt Brace Jovanovich, Inc. (757 Third Avenue, New York, NY 10017).

Harlow Publishing Corporation (P.O. Box 1008, Norman, OK 73069).

Harper & Row, Publishers, Inc. (10 East 53d Street, New York, NY 10022).

Harvey House, Publishers (20 Waterside Plaza, New York, NY 10010).

Hastings House Publishers, Inc. (10 East 40th Street, New York, NY 10016).

Hayes School Publishing Company, Inc. (321 Pennwood Avenue, Wilkinsburg, PA 15221).

Heath, D.C., & Company (College Department, 125 Spring Street, Lexington, MA 02173).

Highlights for Children, Inc. (803 Church Street, Honesdale, PA 18431).

Holiday House, Inc. (18 East 53d Street, New York, NY 10022).

Holt, Rinehart and Winston, Inc. (383 Madison Avenue, New York, NY 10017).

Horn Book, Inc. (Park Square Building, 30 St. James Avenue, Boston, MA 02116).

Houghton Mifflin Company (2 Park Street, Boston, MA 02107).

Indiana University Press (10th and Morton Street, Bloomington, IN 47401).

Instructor Publishing Company, The (Dansville, NY 14437).

International Reading Association (800 Barksdale Road, Newark, DE 19711).

Judy Publishing Company (Box 5270, Main P.O., Chicago, IL 60680).

Kent State University Press (Kent, OH 44242).

Kenworthy Educational Service, Inc. (P.O. Box 3031, Buffalo, NY 14205).

Knopf, Alfred A., Inc. (Subsidiary of Random House, Inc., 201 East 50th Street, New York, NY 10022).

Laidlaw Brothers (Division of Doubleday and Company, Inc., Thatcher and Madison, River Forest, IL 60305).

Learning Research Associates (1501 Broadway, New York, NY 10036).

Lippincott, J.B., Company (East Washington Square, Philadelphia, PA 19105).

Little, Brown and Company (34 Beacon Street, Boston, MA 02114).

Liveright Publishing Corporation (Subsidiary of W.W. Norton Company, Inc., 500 Fifth Avenue, New York, NY 10036).

McCormick-Mathers Publishing Company (Division of Litton Educational Publishing, 135 West 50th Street, New York, NY 10020).

McGraw-Hill (1221 Avenue of the Americas, New York, NY 10020).

McKay, David, Company (750 Third Avenue, New York, NY 10017).

Macmillan Publishing Company, Inc. (866 Third Avenue, New York, NY 10022).

Markham Publishing Company (A Rand McNally College Publishing Company, P.O. Box 7600, Chicago, IL 60680).

Melmont Publishers, Inc. (Division of Children's Press, 1224 West Van Buren Street, Chicago, IL 60607).

Merrill, Charles E., Publishing Company (Division of Bell and Howell Company, 1300 Alum Creek Drive, Columbus, OH 43216).

Messner, Julian (A Simon and Schuster Division of Gulf and Western Corporation, 1230 Avenue of the Americas, New York, NY 10020).

Morrow, William, and Company, Inc. (105 Madison Avenue, New York, NY 10016).

National Council of Teachers of English (1111 Kenyon Road, Urbana, IL 61801).

National Education Association (1201 Sixteenth Street, N.W., Washington, DC 20036).

Nelson, Thomas, Inc. (30 East 42d Street, New York, NY 10017).

New York Public Library (Fifth Avenue and 42d Street, New York, NY 10018).

Odyssey Press (Distributor: Bobbs-Merrill Company, Inc., 4300 West 62d Street, Indianapolis, IN 46268).

Ohio State University Press (Hitchcock Hall, Room 316, 2070 Neil Avenue, Columbus, OH 43210).

Open Court Publishing Company (P.O. Box 599, LaSalle, IL 61301).

Owen, F.A., Publishing Company (*now* The Instructor Publishing Company, Dansville, NY 14437).

Oxford University Press, Inc. (200 Madison Avenue, New York, NY 10016).

Parents Magazine Press (52 Vanderbilt Avenue, New York, NY 10017).

Parnassus Press (4080 Halleck Street, Emeryville, CA 94608).

Pergamon Press, Inc. (Maxwell House, Fairview Park, Elmsford, NY 10523).

Personnel Press, Inc. (Division of Ginn and Company, 191 Spring Street, Lexington, MA 02173).

Plays, Inc. (8 Arlington Street, Boston, MA 02116).

Prentice-Hall, Inc. (301 Sylvan Avenue, Englewood Cliffs, NJ 07632).

Psychological Corporation (304 East 45th Street, New York, NY 10017).

Public School Publishing Company (Test division of Bobbs-Merrill Publishing Company, 4300 West 62d Street, Indianapolis, IN 46206).

Putnam's, G.P., Sons (200 Madison Avenue, New York, NY 10016).

Rand McNally & Company (P.O. Box 7600, Chicago, IL 60680).

Random House, Inc. (201 East 50th Street, New York, NY 10022).

Reader's Digest Association (Educational Division, Pleasantville, NY 10570).

Ronald Press Company (Division of John Wiley & Sons, Inc., 605 Third Avenue, New York, NY 10016).

Schocken Books, Inc. (200 Madison Avenue, New York, NY 10016).

Scholastic Book Services (Division of Scholastic Magazines, 50 West 44th Street, New York, NY 10036).

Science Research Associates (Subsidiary of IBM College Divison, 1540 Page Mill Road, Palo Alto, CA 94304).

Scott, Foresman and Company (1900 East Lake, Glenview, IL 60025).

Scribner's, Charles, Sons (597 Fifth Avenue, New York, NY 10017).

Silver Burdett Company (Division of General Learning Company, 250 James Street, Morristown, NY 07960).

Spencer International Press, Inc. (Subsidiary of Grolier, Inc., 575 Lexington Avenue, New York, NY 10022).

Stanford University Press (Stanford, CA 94305).

Steck-Vaughn Company (Box 2028, Austin TX 78767).

Sterling Publishing Company, Inc. (2 Park Avenue, New York, NY 10016).

Teachers College Press (Columbia University, 1234 Amsterdam Avenue, New York, NY 10027).

Tennessee Book Company (Box 367 Nashville, TN 37202).

Thomas, Charles C., Publishers (301–327 East Lawrence Avenue, Springfield, IL 62717).

United States Government Printing Office (Division of Public Documents, Washington, DC 20402).

University of Arizona Press (P.O. Box 3398, Tucson, AZ 85722).

University of California Press (2223 Fulton Street, Berkeley, CA 94720).

University of Chicago Press (5801 Ellis Avenue, Chicago, IL 60637).

University of Iowa Press (Graphic Services Building, Iowa City, IA 52242).

University of Minnesota Press (2037 University Avenue, S.E., Minneapolis, MN 55455).

University of Washington Press (Seattle, WA 98105).

Van Nostrand Reinhold Company (Division of Litton Educational Publishing, Inc., 135 West 50th Street, New York, NY 10020).

Viking Press, Inc. (625 Madison Avenue, New York, NY 10022).

Wadsworth Publishing Company, Inc. (10 Davis Drive, Belmont, CA 94022).

Wahr, George, Publishing Company (304½) South State Street, Ann Arbor, MI 48108).

Walck, Henry Z., Inc. (Division of David McKay

Company, Inc., Promotion Department, 750 Third Avenue, New York, NY 10017).

Warne, Frederick, and Company, Inc. (101 Fifth Avenue, New York, NY 10003).

Watts, Franklin, Inc. (Subsidiary of Grolier, Inc., 730 Fifth Avenue, New York, NY 10019).

Wayne State University Press (5959 Woodward Avenue, Detroit, MI 48202).

Webster (Division of McGraw-Hill Book Company, 1221 Avenue of the Americas, New York, NY 10020).

Western Reserve Press, Inc. (P.O. Box 675, Ashtabula, OH 44004).

Westminster Press (Room 905, Witherspoon Building, Philadelphia, PA 19107).

Whitman, Albert, and Company (560 West Lake Street, Chicago, IL 60606).

Wiley, John, & Sons, Inc. (605 Third Avenue; New York, NY 10016).

Williams & Wilkins Company (428 East Preston Street, Baltimore, MD 21202).

Wilson, H.W., Company (950 University Avenue, Bronx, NY 10452).

World Book-Childcraft International, Inc. (510 Merchandise Mart Plaza, Chicago, IL 60654).

Index